Continuity & Transformation: The Promise of Confluence

Proceedings of the Seventh National Conference of the
Association of College and Research Libraries
Pittsburgh, Pennsylvania
March 29–April 1, 1995

Edited by

Richard AmRhein
University of Las Vegas, Nevada
Las Vegas, Nevada

Association of College and Research Libraries
A Division of the American Library Association
Chicago, 1995

ASSOCIATION OF
COLLEGE
& RESEARCH
LIBRARIES
A DIVISION OF THE
AMERICAN LIBRARY ASSOCIATION

Published by the Association of College and Research Libraries
A Division of the American Library Association
50 East Huron Street
Chicago, IL 60611
1-800-545-2433

ISBN 0-8389-7786-3

Printed on recycled paper.

Printed in the United States of America.

CONTENTS

Theme Paper

Contributed Papers

Knowledge Workers and Their Organizations

March 29 - April 1, 1995, Pittsburgh, Pennsylvania

Technology and the Service-Centered Library

March 29 - April 1, 1995, Pittsburgh, Pennsylvania

Multiculturalism and Internationalism

Society, Economics, and Politics

Panel Sessions

Knowledge Workers and Their Organizations

Technology and the Service-Centered Library

Multiculturalism and Internationalism

Society, Economics, and Politics

INTRODUCTION

Pittsburgh served as the site for the seventh National Conference of the Association of College and Research Libraries, which took place 29 March through 1 April, 1995. Pittsburgh's location at the junction of the Monongahela and Allegheny rivers where they join to form the Ohio River suggested the conference theme—Continuity and Transformation: the Promise of Confluence. Academic librarians address the confluence of maintaining traditional library services and collections while grappling with the many challenges of changing user needs, the increasing volume of information, adopting and adapting new information technologies, and living with the realities of static or declining budgets. How do we define and maintain appropriate continuities while transforming our libraries into dynamic institutions prepared for the beginning of the 21st century?

To better address this complex theme, the Conference Planning Committee established four conference tracks:
- knowledge workers and their organizations
- technology and the service-centered library
- multiculturalism and internationalism
- society, economics and politics

A keynote speaker, conference papers, and panels address each track.

These proceedings—perhaps the last ACRL national conference proceedings to be published in print form—represent as complete a record of the conference as possible. Literally hundreds of people are responsible for making the 7th national conference happen. A myriad of authors and presenters created the 54 papers and 31 panels selected from 118 manuscript submissions and 98 panel proposals. More than 120 individuals participated in reviewing the paper and panel proposals. Several dozen of these serve as session moderators. The National Conference Planning Committee with its supporting structure of seven subcommittees involved dozens of dedicated ACRL members. We acknowledge all of these contributors in these proceedings.

I personally wish to thank several individuals for their special contributions. I thank Marge Hohenberger of California State University San Marcos Library Services for her quiet perseverence and dedication in coordinating the necessary office support for this venture. I thank colleague Sara Watstein, chair of the Panel Sessions Subcommittee, for her efforts and good humor in ensuring that the panel selection procedures were synchronized with manuscript selection activities. I thank Rick AmRhein for using his mastery of computing applications and good judgement to provide database information, to administer the conference listserve, and to edit these proceedings. And I thank Mary Ellen Davis and other assisting ACRL office staff for providing the necessary underpinnings to produce the proceedings.

May the reader find this work worthwhile!

Marion T. Reid, Chair
Contributed Papers Subcommittee

Reviewers of Contributed Papers

Mary Beth Allen
Ellen Altman
Susan Anthes
Stephen Atkins
Martha J. Bailey
Barry Baker
Betsy Baker
Donald A. Barclay
Lizabeth Bishoff
Caroline Blumenthal
Karin Borei
Jennie Boyarski
Jeanne M.K. Boydston
William S. Brockman
Charlotte B. Brown
Sharon Bullard
Charles Bunge
Dwight Burlingame
Janice Burrows
John T. Butler
Susan Cady
Jennifer Cargill
Tina E. Chrzastowski
Pat Cline
James Comes
Katherine Dahl
Indra M. David
Alma Dawson
Jose Diaz
Connie Dowell
Paul Dumont
Barbara Ammerman Durniak
Dennis East
Tami Echavarria
Margaret Fast
Janice Fennell
Robert Follet
Barbara Ford
Stuart Frazer
Beverlee French
Jeffrey N. Gatten
Mary W. George

Kristin H. Gerhard
Paul M. Gherman
William Gosling
Suzanne Gyaszly
Gary Handman
Barbara Henigman
Peter Hernon
W. Lee Hisle
Irene Hoadley
Stanley P. Hodge
Bonnie Horenstein
Samuel T. Huang
Willis Hubbard
Frances F. Jacobson
Cecily Johns
William G. Jones
Helen B. Josephine
Martin Kesselman
Susan Kroll
Kathleen Kurosman
Mary Larsgaard
Angela S.W. Lee
Mengxiong Liu
Ziming Liu
Thomas A. Lucas
Beverly P. Lynch
Mary Jo Lynch
Nancy Magnuson
Frances J. Maloy
Leslie Manning
Deanna Marcum
Charles Martell
Eleanor Mathews
Joan McConkey
Ray E. Metz
Tamara Miller
Craig Mulder
Robert F. Nardini
Dennis Norlin
Fred Olive
Cathleen C. Palmini
Maggie Parhamovich

Coleen Parmer
Maureen Pastine
Lois M. Pausch
Sara Penhale
Ruth J. Person
Shelley E. Phipps
Roger L. Presley
Patricia Promis
Mary L. Reichel
Marion Reid
Maxine Reneker
Donald E. Riggs
Peter J. Roberts
Ellen Robertson
Lynn Robinson
Carolyn L. Robison
Jordan Scepanski
Jasper Schad
Karen A. Schmidt
Rebecca Schreiner-Robles
Charles A. Schwartz
Charles A. Seavey
Judith Jamison Senkevitch
Charles R. Smith
Helen H. Spalding
Gloriana St. Clair
Kristina Starkus
Virginia Steel
Carla Stoffle
Michael V. Sullivan
Brett Sutton
Ellen D. Sutton
Charles T. Townley
David B. Walch
E. Paige Weston
Karen A. Williams
Susan G. Williamson
Barbara Wittkopf
Elaine Yontz
Mickey Zemon

Program Moderators

Susan Anthes
Stephen Atkins
Betsy Baker
Anne Beaubien
Michael Blake
Caroline Blumenthal
Patricia Breivik
Susan Cady
Tyrone Cannon
Shirley Cody
Indra David
Alma Dawson
Sandy Dolnick
Evan Farber
Laura Farwell
Barbara Ford
Bernard Fradkin
Jeff Gatten
Mary George

Paul Gherman
Bill Gosling
Vicki Gregory
Jennifer Hanlin
Peter Hernon
Lee Hisle
Samuel Huang
Cecily Johns
Amy Kautzman
Caroline M. Kent
Tom Kirk
Deborah Leather
Ron Lieberman
Beverly Lynch
Steve MacKinzie
Frances Maloy
Ray Metz
Anne Nolan
Maureen Pastine

Sara Penhale
Roger Presley
Mary Reichel
Don Riggs
Peter Roberts
Ilene Rockman
Jasper Schad
Mary Jane Scherdin
Charles Schwartz
Howard Simmons
Helen Spalding
Ed Tallent
Philip Tompkins
John Tyson
Susan Williamson
Barbara Wittkopf
Elaine Yontz
Mickey Zemon

National Conference Executive Committee

Joanne R. Euster
Chair

Charles Lowry
Local Arrangements Chair

Patricia Wand
Theme Speakers Chair

Thomas M. Peischl
Poster Sessions Chair

Cathy Henderson
Preconferences Chair

Marion Reid
Contributed Papers Chair

Sarah B. Watstein
Panel Sessions Chair

Linda Crismond
Joe Weed
Exhibits Advisory
Co-Chairs

Althea Jenkins
Member

Mary Ellen Davis
Conference Manager

Sandy Donnelly
Exhibits Manager

Acknowledgement

ACRL would like to extend its gratitude to Chadwyck-Healy, Inc. whose generous support contributed to the publication of these conference proceedings.

Theme Paper*

* ACRL wishes to thank Professor Saskia Sassen
  who generously provided her paper for publication
  in this proceedings.

The Global City:
Place, Production and the New Centrality [1]

Saskia Sassen

The central argument underlying this presentation is that the study of the global economy should incorporate a focus on the variety of ways in which global processes materialize in specific places and institutions. This means that the knowledge base about the global economy, as it is constituted for instance in research and college libraries, should include a broad range of materials not typically thought of as addressing "the" global economy. I will illustrate this argument through a discussion of a particular type of city which has emerged as a site for the implantation of global processes.

The combination of spatial dispersal and global integration has contributed to a strategic role for major cities in the current phase of the world economy. Beyond their sometimes long history as centers for world trade and banking, these cities now function as command points in the organization of the world economy; as key locations and marketplaces for the leading industries of this period, finance and specialized services for firms; and as sites for the production of innovations in those industries.

These cities have come to concentrate such vast resources and the leading industries have exercised such massive influence on the economic and social order of these cities that it raises the possibility of a new type of urbanization, of a new city. I call it the global city. Leading examples in the 1980's, are New York City, London and Tokyo. A limited number of cities emerge as transnational locations for investment, for firms, for the production of services and financial instruments, for various international markets.

A key dynamic explaining the place of major cities in the world economy is that they concentrate the infrastructure and the servicing that produce a capability for global control. The latter is essential if geographic dispersal of economic activity — whether factories, offices or financial markets — is to take place under continued concentration of ownership and profit appropriation. This capability for global control cannot simply be subsumed under the structural aspects of the globalization of economic activity. It needs to be produced. It is insufficient to posit, or take for granted, the awesome power of large corporations.

[1] The author thanks the Russell Sage Foundation for general support while a Visiting Scholar there in 1992-3, and Ms. Vivian Kaufman for her invaluable assistance in preparing this paper.

Saskia Sassen is Professor of Urban Planning, Columbia University, New York, New York.

3

By focusing on the production of this capability, we add a neglected dimension to the familiar issue of the power of large corporations. The emphasis shifts to the <u>practice</u> of global control: the work of producing and reproducing the organization and management of a global production system and a global marketplace for finance, both under conditions of economic concentration. Power is essential in the organization of the world economy, but so is production —including the production of those inputs that constitute the capability for global control and the infrastructure of jobs involved in this production. This allows us to focus on cities and on the urban social order associated with these activities.

Much analysis and general commentary on the global economy and the new growth sectors does not incorporate these multiple dimensions. Elsewhere I have argued that what we could think of as the dominant narrative or mainstream account of economic globalization is a **narrative of eviction** (Sassen 1993). Key concepts in the dominant account — globalization, information economy, and telematics — all suggest that place no longer matters and that the only type of worker that matters is the highly educated professional. This account privileges the capability for global transmission over the concentrations of built infrastructure that make transmission possible; information outputs over the workers producing those outputs, from specialists to secretaries; and the new transnational corporate culture over the multiplicity of cultural environments, including reterritorialized immigrant cultures, within which many of the "other" jobs of the global information economy take place. In brief, the dominant narrative concerns itself with the upper circuits of capital, not the lower ones, and with the global capacities of major economic actors, not the infrastructure of facilities and jobs underlying those capacities. This narrow focus has the effect of evicting from the account the <u>place</u>-boundedness of significant components of the global information economy.

One of the central concerns in my work has been to look at cities as production sites for the leading service industries of our time, and hence to recover the infrastructure of activities, firms and jobs, that is necessary to run the advanced corporate economy. Most of this chapter focuses on this particular aspect and on its spatial correlates.

1. GLOBAL COMMAND CENTERS

Much attention has gone to the territorial dispersal of economic activity at the national and world scale made possible by the massive development of telematics. Less attention has gone to the fact that this dispersal creates a need for expanded central control and management if the dispersal is to occur under conditions of continued economic concentration.

The domestic and international dispersal of loci of growth and the internationalization of finance bring to the fore questions concerning the incorporation of such growth into the profit-generating processes that contribute to economic concentration. That is to say, while in principle the territorial decentralization of economic activity could have been accompanied by a corresponding decentralization in ownership and hence in the appropriation of profits, there has been little movement in that direction. Though large firms have increased their subcontracting to smaller firms and many national firms in the newly industrializing countries have grown rapidly, this form of growth is ultimately part of a chain in which a limited number of corporations continue to control the end product and to reap the profits associated with selling on the world market. Even industrial homeworkers in remote rural areas are now part of that chain.

This is not only evident with firms, it is also evident with places. Thus, the internationalization and expansion of finance has brought growth to a large number of smaller financial markets, a growth which has fed the expansion of the global industry. But top level control and management of the industry has become concentrated in a few leading financial centers, especially New York, London and Tokyo. These account for a disproportionate share of all financial transactions and one that has grown rapidly since the early 1980's.

The fundamental dynamic posited here is that the more globalized the economy becomes the higher the agglomeration of central functions in global cities. The extremely high densities evident in the downtown districts of these cities are the spatial expression of this logic. The widely accepted notion that agglomeration has become obsolete when global telecommunication advances should allow for maximum dispersal, is only partly correct. It is, I argue, precisely because of the territorial dispersal facilitated by telecommunication advances that agglomeration of centralizing activities has expanded immensely. This is not a mere continuation of old patterns of agglomeration but, one could posit, a new logic for agglomeration. A key question is when will telecommunication advances be applied to these centralizing functions.

Information technologies make possible the geographic dispersal <u>and</u> simultaneous integration of many activities. But the distinct conditions under which such facilities are available have promoted centralization of the most advanced users in the most advanced telecommunications centers. Even though a few newer urban centers have built advanced telecommunications facilities, entry costs are increasingly high, and there is a tendency for telecommunications to be developed in conjunction with major users, which are typically firms with large national and global markets (Castells, 1989). Indeed there is a close relationship between the growth of international markets for finance and trade, the tendency for major firms to concentrate in major cities and the development of telecommunications infrastructures in such cities. Firms with global markets or global production processes require advanced telecommunications facilities. And the acceleration of the financial markets and their internationalization make access to advanced telecommunications facilities essential. The main demand for telecommunication services comes from information intensive industries which, in turn, tend to locate in major cities which have such facilities.

Centralized control and management over a geographically dispersed array of plants, offices, and service outlets does not come about inevitably as part of a "world system." It requires the development of a vast range of highly specialized services and of top level management and control functions. These constitute the components for "global control capability" (Sassen 1988). With the potential for global control capability, certain cities are becoming nodal points in a vast communications and market system. Advances in electronics and telecommunication have transformed geographically distant cities into centers for global communication and long-distance management.

In short, spatial dispersion of production and the reorganization of the financial industry have created new forms of centralization for the management and regulation of a global network of production sites and financial markets. Spatial dispersion of production, in some cases internationally, has stimulated growth of centralized service nodes for its management and regulation and telecommunications advances have facilitated both dispersal and centralized servicing.

2. THE INTERSECTION OF GLOBALIZATION AND THE SHIFT TO SERVICES

To understand the new or sharply expanded role of the global city in the world economy since the early 1980s, we need to focus on the intersection of two major processes. The first is the sharp growth in the globalization of economic activity; this has raised the scale and the complexity of transactions, thereby feeding the growth of top-level multinational headquarter functions and the growth of advanced corporate services.

It is important to note that even though globalization raises the scale and complexity of these operations, the latter are also evident at smaller geographic scales and lower orders of complexity, as is the case with firms that operate regionally. Thus while regionally oriented firms need not negotiate the complexities of international borders and the regulations of different countries, they are still faced with a regionally dispersed network of operations that requires centralized control and servicing.

The second process we need to consider is the growing **service intensity** in the organization of all industries. This has contributed to a massive growth in the demand for services by firms in all industries, from mining and manufacturing to finance and consumer services.[2] Cities are key sites for the production of services for firms. Hence the increase in service intensity in the organization of all industries has had a significant growth effect on cities in the 1980s. Again, we nee to recognize that this growth in services for firms is evident in cities at different levels of a nation's urban system. Some of these cities cater to regional or subnational markets; others cater to national markets and yet others cater to global markets. In this context, globalization becomes a question of scale and added complexity.

The key process from the perspective of the urban economy is the growing demand for services by firms in all industries and the fact that cities are preferred production sites for such services, whether at the global, national, or regional level. As a result we see in cities the formation of a new **urban economic core** of banking and service activities that comes to replace the older typically manufacturing oriented core.[3]

In the case of cities that are major international business centers, the scale, power, and profit levels of this new core suggest that we are seeing the formation of a new urban economy. This is so in at least two regards. First, even though these cities have long been centers for business and finance, since the late 1970s there have been dramatic changes in the structure of the business and financial sectors, as well as sharp increases in the overall magnitude of these sectors and their weight in the urban economy. Second, the ascendance of the new finance and services complex, particularly international finance, engenders what may be regarded as a new economic regime, that is, although this sector may account for only a fraction of the economy of a city, it imposes itself on that larger economy. Most notably, the possibility for superprofits in finance has the effect of devalorizing manufacturing insofar as the latter cannot generate the superprofits typical in much financial activity.

This is not to say that everything in the economy of these cities has changed. On the contrary, they still show a great deal of continuity and many similarities with cities that are not global nodes. Rather, the implantation of global processes and

---

[2] The expansion of producer services is a central feature of current growth in developed countries. In country after country we see a decline or slowdown in manufacturing alongside sharp growth in producer services. Elsewhere I have posited that the fundamental reason for this growth lies in the increased service intensity in the organization of all industries (Sassen 1991:166-168). Whether in manufacturing or in warehousing, firms use more legal, financial, advertising, consulting, and accounting services. These services can be seen as part of the supply capacity of an economy because they facilitate adjustments to changing economic circumstances; they are part of a broader intermediary space of economic activity. **Producer services** cover financial, legal, and general management matters, innovation, development, design, administration, personnel, production technology, maintenance, transport, communications, wholesale distribution, advertising, cleaning services for firms, security, and storage. Central components of the producer services category are a range of industries with mixed business and consumer markets. They are insurance, banking, financial services, real estate, legal services, accounting, and professional associations.

[3] Though disproportionately concentrated in the largest cities, producer services are actually growing at faster rates at the national level in most developed economies. The crucial process feeding the growth of producer services is the increasing use of service inputs by firms in all industries. Households have also raised their consumption of services, either directly (e.g., the growing use of accountants for preparation of tax returns), or indirectly via the reorganization of consumer industries (e.g., buying flowers or dinner from franchises or chains rather self-standing and privately owned "mom-and-pop" shops). Services directly bought by consumers tend to be located wherever population is concentrated. In that regard they are far less concentrated than producer services, especially those catering to top firms. The demand for specialized services by households, from accounting to architects, may be a key factor contributing to the growth of these services at the national level.

markets has meant that the internationalized sector of the economy has expanded sharply and has imposed a new valorization dynamic — that is, a new set of criteria for valuing or pricing various economic activites and outcomes. This has had devastating effects on large sectors of the urban economy. High prices and profit levels in the internationalized sector and its ancillary activities, such as top-of-the-line restaurants and hotels, have made it increasingly difficult for other sectors to compete for space and investments. Many of these other sectors have experienced considerable downgrading and/or displacement, as, for example, neighborhood shops tailored to local needs are replaced by upscale boutiques and restaurants catering to new high income urban elites.

Though at a different order of magnitude, these trends also became evident during the late 1980s in a number of major cities in the developing world that have become integrated into various world markets: Sao Paulo, Buenos Aires, Bangkok, Taipei, and Mexico City are only a few examples. Also here the new urban core was fed by the deregulation of financial markets, ascendance of finance and specialized services, and integration into the world markets. The opening of stock markets to foreign investors and the privatization of what were once public sector firms have been crucial institutional arenas for this articulation. Given the vast size of some of these cities, the impact of this new core on the broader city is not always as evident as in central London or Frankfurt, but the transformation is still very real.

It is important to recognize that manufacturing remains a crucial sector in all these economies, even when it may have ceased to be a dominant sector in major cities. Indeed, several scholars have argued that the producer services sector could not exist without manufacturing (Cohen and Zysman 1987; Markusen and Gwiasda 1993). In this context it has been argued, for example, that the weakening of the manufacturing sector in the broader New York region is a threat to the city's status as a leading financial and producer services center (Markusen and Gwiasda, 1993). A key proposition for these and other authors is that producer services are dependent on a strong manufacturing sector in order to grow. There is considerable debate around this issue (Noyelle and Dutka, 1988; Drennan, 1991; Sassen 1991). Drennan (1991), a leading analyst of the producer services sector in New York City, argues that a strong finance and producer services sector is possible in New York notwithstanding decline in its industrial base and that these sectors are so strongly integrated into the world markets that articulation with the larger region becomes secondary.

Sassen (1991), in a variant on both positions, argues that manufacturing indeed feeds the growth of the producer services sector, but that it does so whether located in the area in question, somewhere else in the country or overseas. Even though manufacturing — and mining and agriculture, for that matter —feeds growth in the demand for producer services, their actual location is of secondary importance in the case of global level service firms: thus whether manufacturing plants are located offshore or within a country may be quite irrelevant as long as it is part of a multinational corporation likely to buy the services from those top-level firms. Second, the territorial dispersal of plants, especially if international, actually raises the demand for producer services. This is yet another meaning, or consequence, of globalization: the growth of producer service firms headquartered in New York or London or Paris can be fed by manufacturing located anywhere in the world as long as it is part of a multinational corporate network. Third, a good part of the producer services sector is fed by financial and business transactions that either have nothing to do with manufacturing, as is the case in many of the global financial markets, or for which manufacturing is incidental, as in much merger and acquisition activity, which is centered on buying and selling firms rather than the buying of manufacturing firms as such.

Some of the figures on New York and London, two cities that experienced heavy losses in manufacturing and sharp gains in producer services, illustrate this point. New York lost 34 percent of its manufacturing jobs from 1969 to 1989 in a national economy that overall lost only 2 percent of such jobs, and there actually was manufacturing growth in many areas. The British economy lost 32 percent of its manufacturing jobs from 1971 to 1989, and the London region lost 47 percent of such jobs (Fainstein, et al 1993; Buck, Drennan and Newton, 1992). Yet both cities had sharp growth in producer services and raised their shares of such jobs in total city employment. Further, it is also worth noting the different conditions in each city's larger region: London's region had a 2 percent decline compared to a 22 percent job growth rate in the larger New York region. This divergence points to the fact that the finance and producer services complex in each city rests on a growth dynamic that is somewhat independent of the broader regional economy — a sharp change from the past, when a city was presumed to be deeply articulated with its hinterland.

3. PRODUCTION SITES AND MARKET-PLACES FOR GLOBAL CAPITAL.

Going beyond the domain of the existing literature on cities, I posit that global cities are a specific type of production site and I examine their central command functions as a production process. They are sites for a) the production of specialized services needed by complex organizations, including prominently top level management, control and servicing operations necessary for running a spatially dispersed network of factories, offices and service outlets under conditions of continued economic concentration; and b) the production of financial innovations and the making of markets, both central to the internationalization and expansion of the financial industry. There are two distinct activities here, one concerns the production of advanced services and the other the financial industry.

A key dynamic running through these various activities and organizing the analysis of the place of global cities in the world economy is the capability for global control. The latter is essential if

geographic dispersal of economic activity — whether factories, offices or financial markets — is to take place under continued concentration of ownership and profit appropriation. This capability for global control cannot simply be subsumed under the structural aspects of the globalization of economic activity. It needs to be produced. It is insufficient to posit, or take for granted, the awesome power of large corporations. Governments also face an increasingly complex environment where highly sophisticated machineries of centralized management and control are necessary. This is probably one reason why society has borne much of the cost of developing capabilities for controlling vast territories (a whole subject in itself).

By focusing on the production of this capability, I am seeking to displace the focus of attention from the familiar issue of the power of large corporations over governments and economies; or the issue of supracorporate concentration of power through interlocking directorates or organizations such as the IMF. I want to focus on an aspect that has received less attention, what could be referred to as the <u>practice</u> of global control: the work of producing and reproducing the organization and management of a global production system and a global marketplace for finance, both under conditions of economic concentration. My focus is not on power, but on production: the production of those inputs that constitute the capability for global control capability and the infrastructure of jobs involved in this production. This allows me to focus on cities and on the urban social order associated with these activities.

According to standard conceptions about information industries, the rapid growth and disproportionate concentration of producer services in central cities should not have happened. Because they are thoroughly embedded in the most advanced information technologies, producer services could be expected to have locational options that bypass the high costs and congestion typical of major cities. But cities offer agglomeration economies and highly innovative environments.

The growing complexity, diversity, and specialization of the services required has contributed to the economic viability of a free-standing specialized service sector.

The production process in these services benefits from proximity to other specialized services. This is especially the case in the leading and most innovative sectors of these industries. Complexity and innovation often require multiple highly specialized inputs from several industries. The production of a financial instrument, for example, requires inputs from accounting, advertising, legal expertise, economic consulting, public relations, designers, and printers. The particular characteristics of production of these services, especially those involved in complex and innovative operations, explain their pronounced concentration in major cities. The commonly heard explanation that high level professionals require face-to-face interactions, needs to be refined in several ways. Producer services, unlike other types of services, are not necessarily dependent on spatial proximity to the consumers, i.e. firms, served. Rather, economies occur in such specialized firms when they locate close to others that produce key inputs or whose proximity makes possible joint production of certain service offerings. The accounting firm can service its clients at a distance, but the nature of its service depends on proximity to specialists, lawyers, programmers. Moreover, concentration arises out of the needs and expectations of the people likely to be employed in these new high-skill jobs who tend to be attracted to the amenities and lifestyles that large urban centers can offer. Frequently, what is thought of as face-to-face communication is actually a production process that requires multiple simultaneous inputs and feedbacks. At the current stage of technical development, immediate and simultaneous access

to the pertinent experts is still the most effective way, especially when dealing with a highly complex product. The concentration of the most advanced telecommunications and computer network facilities in major cities is a key factor in what I refer to as the production process of these industries.[4]

Further, time replaces weight in these sectors as a force for agglomeration. In the past, the pressure of the weight of inputs from iron ore to unprocessed agricultural products, was a major constraint pushing toward agglomeration in sites where the heaviest inputs were located. Today, the acceleration of economic transactions and the premium put on time, have created new forces for agglomeration. This is increasingly not the case in routine operations. But where time is of the essence, as it is today in many of the leading sectors of these industries, the benefits of agglomeration are still extremely high — to the point where it is not simply a cost advantage, but an indispensable arrangement.

We see a general trend toward high concentration of finance and certain producer services in the downtowns of major international financial centers around the world: from Toronto and Sydney to Frankfurt and Zurich, we are seeing growing specialization in financial districts everywhere. It is worth noting that this trend is also evident in the multipolar urban system of the United States: against all odds, New York City has kept its place at the top in terms of concentration in banking and finance.

There is a strong suggestion in all of this that the agglomeration of producer services in major cities actually constitutes a production complex. This producer services complex is intimately connected to the world of corporate headquarters; they are often thought of as forming a joint

---

[4] The telecommunications infrastructure also contributes to concentration of leading sectors in major cities. Long-distance communications systems increasingly use fiber optic wires. These have several advantages over traditional copper wire: large carrying capacity, high speed, more security, and higher signal strength. Fiber systems tend to connect major communications hubs because they are not easily spliced and hence not desirable for connecting multiple lateral sites. Fiber systems tend to be installed along existing rights of way, whether rail, water or highways (Moss 1986). The growing use of fiber optic systems thus tends to strengthen the major existing telecommunication concentrations and therefore the existing hierarchies.

headquarterscorporate services complex. But in my reading, we need to distinguish the two. Although it is true that headquarters still tend to be disproportionately concentrated in cities, over the last two decades many have moved out. Headquarters can indeed locate outside cities, but they need a producer services complex somewhere in order to buy or contract for the needed specialized services and financing. Further, headquarters of firms with very high overseas activity or in highly innovative and complex lines of business tend to locate in major cities. In brief, firms in more routinized lines of activity, with predominantly regional or national markets, appear to be increasingly free to move or install their headquarters outside cities. Firms in highly competitive and innovative lines of activity and/or with a strong world market orientation appear to benefit from being located at the center of major international business centers, no matter how high the costs.

Both types of firms, however, need a corporate services complex to be located somewhere. Where this complex is located is probably increasingly unimportant from the perspective of many, though not all, headquarters. From the perspective of producer services firms, such a specialized complex is most likely to be in a city rather than, for example, a suburban office park. The latter will be the site for producer services firms but not for a services complex. And only such a complex is capable of handling the most advanced and complicated corporate demands.

Elsewhere (Sassen 1994), a somewhat detailed empirical examination of several cities served to explore different aspects of this trend towards spatial concentration in leading sectors of finance and the producer services. Here there is space only for a few observations. The case of Miami, for instance, allows us to see, almost in laboratory-like fashion, how a new international corporate sector can become implanted in a site. It allows us to understand something about the dynamic of globalization in the current period and how it is embedded in place. Miami has emerged as a significant regional site for global city functions though it lacks a long history as an international banking and business center as is typical for such global cities as New York or London.

The case of Toronto, a city whose financial district was built up only in recent years, allows us to see to what extent the pressure towards physical concentration is embedded in an economic dynamic rather than simply being the consequence of having inherited a built infrastructure from the past, as one could think was the case in older centers such as London or New York.[5] But the case also shows that it is particularly certain industries which are subject to the pressure towards spatial concentration, notably finance and its sister industries (Gad 1991).

The case of Sydney illuminates the interaction of a vast, continental economic scale and pressures towards spatial concentration. Rather than strengthening the multipolarity of the Australian urban system, the developments of the 1980s — increased internationalization of the Australian economy, sharp increases in foreign investment, a strong shift towards finance, real estate and producer services— contributed to a greater concentration of major economic activities and actors in Sydney. This included a loss of share of such activities and actors by Melbourne, long the center

---

[5] In his study of the financial district in Manhattan, Longcore found that the use of advanced information and telecommunication technologies has a strong impact on the spatial organization of the district because of the added spatial requirements of "intelligent" buildings. (See also Moss, 1991). A ring of new office buildings meeting these requirements was built over the last decade immediately around the old Wall Street core, where the narrow streets and lots made this difficult; furthermore, renovating old buildings in the Wall Street core is extremely expensive and often not possible. The occupants of the new buildings in the district were mostly corporate headquarters and the financial services industry. These firms tend to be extremely intensive users of telematics and availability of the most advanced forms typically is a major factor in their real estate and locational decisions. They need complete redundancy of telecommunications systems, high carrying capacity, often their own private branch exchange, etc. With this often goes a need for large spaces. For instance, the technical installations backing a firm's trading floor is likely to require additional space the size of the trading floor itself.

of commercial activity and wealth in Australia (Daly and Stimson, 1992).

Finally, the case of the leading financial centers in the world today is of continued interest since one might have expected that the growing number of financial centers now integrated into the global markets would have reduced the extent of concentration of financial activity in the top centers.[6] One would further expect this given the immense increases in the global volume of transactions. Yet the levels of concentration remain unchanged in the face of massive transformations in the financial industry and in the technological infrastructure this industry depends on.[7]

For example, international bank lending grew from US$1.89 trillion in 1980 to US$6.24 trillion in 1991 — a fivefold increase in a mere ten years. These three cities accounted for 42 percent of all such international lending in 1980 and for 41 percent in 1991 according to data from the Bank of International Settlements, the leading institution worldwide in charge of overseeing banking activity. There were compositional changes: Japan's share rose from 6.2 percent to 15.1 percent and the UK's fell from 26.2 percent to 16.3 percent; the U.S. share remained constant. All increased in absolute terms. Beyond these three, Switzerland, France, Germany, and Luxembourg bring the total share of the top centers to 64 percent in 1991, which is just about the same share these countries had in 1980. One city, Chicago dominates the world's trading in futures, accounting for 60 percent of worldwide contracts in options and futures in 1991.

THE SPACE ECONOMY OF THE CENTER

Today there is no longer a simple straightforward relation between centrality and such geographic entites as the downtown, or the central business district. In the past, and up to quite recently in fact, the center was synonymous with the downtown or the CBD. Today, the spatial correlate of the center can assume several geographic forms. It can be the CBD, as it still is largely in New York City, or it can extend into a metropolitan area in the form of a grid of nodes of intense business activity, as we see in Frankfurt (Keil and Ronneberg, 1993).

Elsewhere (1991) I have argued that we are also seeing the formation of a transterritorial "center" constituted via digital highways and intense economic transactions; there I argued that New York, London and Tokyo could be seen as constituting such a transterritorial terrain of centrality with regard to a specific complex of industries and activities. And at the limit we may see terrains of centrality that are disembodied, that lack any territorial correlate, that are, that is, in the electronically generated space we call cyberspace. Certain components of the financial industry, particularly the foreign currency markets, can be seen as operating partly in cyberspace.[8]

---

[6] Furthermore, this unchanged level of concentration has happened at a time when financial services are more mobile than ever before: globalization, deregulation (an essential ingredient for globalization), and **securitization** have been the key to this mobility — in the context of massive advances in telecommunications and electronic networks. One result is growing competition among centers for hypermobile financial activity. In my view there has been an overemphasis on competition in general and in specialized accounts on this subject. As I have argued elsewhere (Sassen, 1991: chapter 7), there is also a functional division of labor among various major financial centers. In that sense we can think of a transnational system with multiple locations.

[7] Much of the discussion around the formation of a single European market and financial system has raised the possibility, and even the need if it is to be competitive, of centralizing financial functions and capital in a limited number of cities rather than maintaining the current structure in which each country has a financial center.

[8] This also tells us something about cyberspace—often read as a purely technological event and in that sense a space of innocence. The cyberspaces of finance are spaces where profits are produced and power is thereby constituted. Insofar as these technologies strengthen the profit-making capability of finance and make possible the hyper-mobility of finance capital, they also contribute to the often devastating impacts of the ascendance of finance on other industries, on particular sectors of the population, and on whole economies. Cyberspace, like any other space can be inscribed in a multiplicity of ways. some benevolent or enlightening; others, not (see Sassen 1993a).

What is the urban form that accommodates this new economic core of activities? Three distinct patterns are emerging in major cities and their regions in the developed countries. First, in the 1980s there was a growing density of workplaces in the traditional urban center associated with growth in leading sectors and ancillary industries. This type of growth also took place in some of the most dynamic cities in developing countries, such as Bangkok, Taipei, Sao Paulo, Mexico City and, toward the end of the decade, Buenos Aires. Second, alongside this central city growth, came the formation of dense nodes of commercial development and business activity in a broader urban region, a pattern not evident in developing countries. These nodes assume different forms: suburban office complexes, **edge cities,** and **exopoles.** Though in peripheral areas, these nodes are completely connected to central locations via state of the art electronic means. Thus far, these forms are only rarely evident in developing countries, where vast urban sprawl with a seemingly endless metropolitanization of the region around cities has been the norm. In developed countries, the revitalized urban center and the new regional nodes together constitute the spatial base for cities at the top of transnational hierarchies. Third is the growing intensity in the local-ness or marginality of areas and sectors that operate outside that world-market oriented subsystem, and this includes an increase in poverty and disadvantage. This same general dynamic operates in cities with very diverse economic, political, social, and cultural arrangements.

A few questions spring to mind. one question here is whether the type of spatial organization characterized by dense strategic nodes spread over the broader region does or does not constitute a new form of organizing the territory of the "center," rather than, as in the more conventional view, an instance of suburbanization or geographic dispersal. Insofar as these various nodes are articulated through cyberroutes or digital highways they represent the new geographic correlate of the most advanced type of "center." The places that fall outside this new grid of digital highways are peripheralized; one question here is whether it is so to a much higher degree than in earlier periods, when the suburban or noncentral economic terrain was integrated into the center because it was primarily geared <u>to</u> the center.

Another question is whether this new terrain of centrality is differentiated? Basically, is the old central city, still the largest and densest of all the nodes, the most strategic and powerful node? Does it have a sort of gravitational power over the region that makes the new grid of nodes and digital highways cohere as a complex spatial agglomeration? From a larger transnational perspective these are vastly expanded central regions. This reconstitution of the center is different from agglomeration patterns still prevalent in most cities that have not seen a massive expansion in their role as sites for global city functions and the new regime of accumulation thereby entailed. We are seeing a reorganization of space-time dimensions in the urban economy.

It is under these conditions that the traditional perimeter of the city, a kind of periphery, unfolds its full industrial and structural growth potential. Commercial and office space development lead to a distinct form of decentralized reconcentration of economic activity on the urban periphery. This geographic shift has much to do with the locational decisions of transnational and national firms that make the urban peripheries the growth centers of the most dynamic industries. It is distinctly not the same as largely residential suburbanization or metropolitanization.

We may be seeing a difference in the pattern of global city formation in parts of the United States and in parts of Western Europe (Sassen 1994; Keil and Ronneberger 1993). In the United States, major cities such as New York and Chicago have large centers that have been rebuilt many times, given the brutal neglect suffered by much urban infrastructure and the imposed obsolescence so characteristic of U.S. cities. This neglect and accelerated obsolescence produce vast spaces for rebuilding the center according to the requirements of whatever regime of urban accumulation or pattern of spatial organization of the urban economy prevails at a given time.

In Europe, urban centers are far more protected and they rarely contain significant stretches of abandoned space; the expansion of workplaces and the need for intelligent buildings necessarily will have to take place partly outside the old centers. One of the most extreme cases is the complex of La Defense, the massive, state of the art office complex developed right outside Paris to avoid harming the built environment inside the city. This is an explicit instance of government policy and planning aimed at addressing the growing demand for central office space of prime quality. Yet another variant of this expansion of the "center" onto hitherto peripheral land can be seen in London's Docklands. Similar projects for recentralizing peripheral areas were launched in several major cities in Europe, North America, and Japan during the 1980s.

CONCLUSION: CONCENTRATION AND THE REDEFINITION OF THE CENTER

The notion of a global economy has become deeply entrenched in political and media circles all over the world. Yet its dominant images — the instantaneous transmission of money around the globe, the information economy, the neutralization of distance through **telematics** — are partial and hence profoundly inadequate representations of what globalization and the rise of an information economy actually entail for cities. Missing from this type of model are the actual material processes, activities, and infrastructures that are central to the implementation of globalization. Overlooking the spatial dimension of economic globalization and overemphasizing the information dimensions have served to distort the role played by major cities in the current phase of economic globalization.

The issues discussed in this chapter provide insights into the dynamics of contemporary globalization processes as they materialize in specific places. We can think of cities as command

centers and as production sites for the leading service industries of our time. This allows us to recover the infrastructure of activities, of firms and jobs, that is necessary to run the advanced corporate economy. Globalization generates a demand for types of production needed for the management, control, and servicing of worldwide networks of factories, offices and markets. These new types of production range from the development of telecommunications to that of specialized services for firms. These types of production have their own locational patterns; they tend toward high levels of agglomeration. The continuing concentration of the most advanced communications facilities in major cities further contributes to agglomeration of industries and firms that are intensive users of such facilities.

A focus on the production of specialized services for firms, or producer services, illuminates the question of place, and particularly the kind of place represented by cities, in processes of economic globalization. Specialized services are usually understood in terms of outputs rather than the production process involved. Their characteristics of production allow us to understand the locational concentration of leading sectors in urban centers in the face of the globalization of much economic activity, massive increases in the volume of international transactions, and revolutionary changes in technology that neutralize distance.

Concentration, then, remains a critical dimension particularly in the leading sectors such as financial services. There are however a multiplicity of spatial correlates for this concentration and in this sense we see emerging a new geography of the center. This new geography can consist of a transterritorial space connecting major cities worldwide through specific markets and transactions. Or it can involve a metropolitan grid of nodes connected through advanced telematics. We are also seeing the emergence of a space of centrality that assumes the form of cyberspace. All these new forms are redefinitions of the center; they point to a new centrality.

These new empirical trends and new theoretical developments have made cities prominent once again in most of the social sciences. Cities have reemerged not only as objects of study, but also as strategic sites for the theorization of a broad array of social, economic, and political processes central to the current era.

REFERENCES

Daly, M.T. and R.. Stimson. "Sydney: Australia's Gateway and Financial Capital" Chap.18. in E.. Blakely and T.J. Stimpson (eds.) *New Cities of the Pacific Rim* Institute for Urban & Regional Development, University of California, Berkeley. 1992.

Gad, Gunter. "Toronto's Financial District." *Canadian Urban Landscapes-l.* 1991, pp.203-207.

Keil, Roger and Klaus Rommeberger. "The City Turned Inside Out: Spatial Strategies and Local Politics". in Hitz, Hansruedi, et. al. (eds.) *Financial Metropoles in Restructuring: Zurich and Frankfurt En Route to Postfordism.* 1993.

Longcore, T.R. *Information Technology and World City Restructuring: The Case of New York City's Financial District.* (Unpublished thesis, Department of Geography, University of Delaware). 1993.

Markusen, A. and V. Gwiasda. "Multipolarity and the Layering of Functions in the World Cities: New York City's Struggle to Stay on Top" Presented in Tokyo at the Conference "New York, Tokyo & Paris" October 1991. Revised for Publication, 1993. Forthcoming, *International Journal of Urban and Regional Research.*

Cohen, Stephen S. and John Zysman. *Manufacturing Matters: The Myth of the Post-Industrial Economy.* New York: Basic Books. 1987.

Moss, M. "Telecommunications and the Future of Cities." *Land Development Studies,* 3: 33-44.

_____"New Fibers of Urban Economic Development. *Portfolio: A Ouarterly Review of Trade and Transportation.* 4, 1: 11-18.

Sassen, Saskia *The Global City: New York. London. Tokyo.* Princeton University Press, 1991.

_____"Analytic Borderlands: Race, Gender and Nationality in the New City." Forthcoming in A.King (ed.) *Re-presenting the City: Ethnicity, Capital and Culture in the 21st Century.* London: Macmillan. 1993.

_____(Co-curator) "Trade Routes." Catalogue, Exhibition at The New Museum of Contemporary Art, New York City. 1993a.

_____*Cities in a World Economy.* Thousand Oaks, California: Pine Forge/ Sage Press. 1994.

Contributed Papers

Knowledge Workers and
Their Organizations

Five Societal Revolutions in the Age of Information

Steven J. Bell

ABSTRACT

Change at institutions of higher education has historically been propelled by external influences. Five revolutions in particular symbolize the sweeping change occurring in American society. Each means profound change for college and universities, and in turn, the library services provided to these institutions. These revolutions are: 1) demographic revolution; 2) socio-cultural revolution; 3) economic revolution; 4) technological revolution; and 5) higher education revolution. This paper will describe and give examples of these revolutionary developments, and discuss how colleges and universities will be challenged to adapt to each. Participants in the planning process must be alert to societal "revolutions," and be proactive in reshaping the library.

Left to their own design academic institutions change little. Modern universities bear strong structural resemblance to their medieval ancestors. The uniquely American higher education institution, according to academic historian Laurence Vesey, has shown significant substantive change, but only minor structural change.[1] Failure to adapt is frequently linked to faculty aversion to altering programs, but the university's own inertia makes change difficult, especially in response to societal revolutions. Historically, change at American colleges and universities is the result of pressure from external influences. Whether societal, governmental or media based, these outside forces shaped the institution into what we know it to be today.

Strategic planning is relatively new to higher education. When George Keller wrote his landmark book *Academic Strategy* in 1983, only a few institutions had formal strategic planning processes.[2] Now, as many one-third of all colleges and universities perform strategic planning. A critical stage in the strategic planning process is environmental scanning. The institutional antennae must identify external influences and shifting societal forces as they form. Done properly, scanning allows institutions to prepare for and adapt to change. Failure to do so is the hallmark of organizations in crisis.

Steven J. Bell is Head of Circulation and Business Reference Librarian at the Lippincott Library of the Wharton School, University of Pennsylvania, Philadelphia, Pennsylvania.

A new series of societal revolutions have profound consequences for higher education institutions and their libraries. They are extraordinary and manifold, and stand to alter the structure of higher education. Five revolutions in particular symbolize the sweeping change occurring in American society. These shock waves are:

- demographic revolution
- socio-cultural revolution
- economic revolution
- technological revolution
- higher education revolution

Academic librarians can shape their organizations for the future by acknowledging and understanding how powerful external forces will change who they serve and what they do.

DEMOGRAPHIC REVOLUTION

The traditional student body is a homogeneous composition of white males in the 18-24 year old bracket. Owing to profound demographic shifts this traditional student is a vanishing breed on campus. Consider the "birth dearth." A dramatic decline in birth rates means the number of 18-22 year olds will shrink from 9 million in 1980 to 6.3 million in 1996. Between 1980 and 1990, the number of 18-24 years olds declined 11 percent.[3] Members of this age cohort should increase temporarily when the children of the baby-boom generation reach college age, but the long term outlook is that fewer young people will be available to attend colleges and universities. Competition for the best students already grows intense. Libraries are among campus services expected to serve as "show pieces" to help attract those students.

To replace students lost to declining birth rates, higher education closely follows trends in immigration. An influx of immigrants from Asia, Latin America, and Central America has created the greatest wave of immigration since the peak of 1907 to 1914. It is anticipated that 880,000 legal immigrants will enter this country each year in the 1990s, up from 500,000 per year in the previous

decade.[4] Academic librarians need to learn more about these new populations, and reassess techniques to attract and serve immigrants. Unfortunately, we receive little formal education about Asian and Latino cultures. This makes it difficult to evaluate our effectiveness in serving the needs of non-traditional students from other cultures.

While birth rates decline, the number of people over 65 increases rapidly. Between 2008 and 2009, 3.5 million people will pass age 62. That is 63 percent more than in 1990.[5] As the elderly become a much larger portion of the population, higher education will be compelled to seek the elderly as students. To succeed in serving the elderly, colleges and universities must reconsider the curriculum, and faculty their teaching methods. Do the elderly want to study microeconomics? Will large lecture halls be effective with older students? What types of courses and teaching environment would entice the elderly to enroll?

As their numbers increase on campus and the geriatric boom continues, academic librarians need to rethink services for the elderly. They differ greatly from traditional students. Meeting their information needs will require new skills and techniques. Given the impending geriatric boom, the profession needs more applied research, training and interaction to best serve the future wave of elderly students. For example, many senior citizens are unaccustomed to computers, and may be adverse to using them for database searching. Bibliographic instructors and reference librarians need research on special learning techniques that can help the elderly adapt to the "electronic library."

SOCIO-CULTURAL REVOLUTION

More alarming is the socio-cultural revolution in which the deterioration of social capital destroys the fabric of our society. The primary source of social capital, the nuclear family, is in collapse. Married couples with children accounted for 40 percent of all households in 1970 but has dropped to 25 percent in 1992, while the number of single parent households rose from 13 to 30 percent in the same period.[6] Social ills such as drug abuse, violence, illegitimacy, crime and high dropout rates increase as the transmission of values declines. Academic librarians must consider contributions they can make to the debate on how colleges and universities can encourage college enrollment among disenfranchised youths.

Compounding this challenge is the process of societal bifurcation. American society is polarizing into two camps of "haves" and "haves-nots." The middle class is shrinking while the number of rich and poor grows rapidly. This year, the Census Bureau reported that America's poverty level reached its highest level in ten years.[7] As a society, America includes the world's largest underclass, the world's highest crime and illiteracy rates. The poorest Americans are not, as often thought, the elderly, but single mothers.

This is a moral challenge for higher education. Institutions must decide who to enroll. Should the underprepared underclass be forgotten, or will remedial teaching be a permanent function of higher education? In the library, how will disenfranchised, poverty-stricken youths be equipped to work with OPACs and sophisticated databases? The socio-cultural changes that divide society can also divide higher education. Institutions which attract high caliber students bear less of the burden of coping with society's underprivileged class. Community colleges and lower tier schools, the potential "have-nots" of higher education, are the educators of minorities, immigrants and other underprepared students. Librarians must adapt to these parallel bifurcation processes. They can develop creative remedial library education programs that reflect the remedial learning programs their parent institutions offer.

ECONOMIC REVOLUTION

The third shock wave, the economic revolution, has shaken America's position as the world's dominant financial power. An enormous government debt, deficit stricken state and local governments, waves of factory closings, costly social programs, periodic recessions and crisis in our banking and financial markets combine to weaken America's economic viability. The consequences of our economic weakness impacts more directly on higher education than any other revolution.

Most colleges and universities were built when America was the world's richest country. The federal government pumped wealth into higher education for facilities and research. Now the trough of federal funding is depleted. Higher education costs spiral out of control, while American family income remains stagnant. Facing a future of declining economic support, colleges and universities will be making hard financial choices which are sure to impact on academic libraries. For example, Yale University, in order to maintain faculty salaries, allowed $1.5 billion in deferred maintenance to accumulate. Now, with many buildings in disrepair it is difficult to have the attractive, competitive campus needed to compete with peer institutions.

Once in a cycle of financial decline, only radical restructuring may save the institution. Bennington College made national news by eliminating 20 faculty members in response to decreased enrollments and a $1 million budget deficit. The academic restructuring included the elimination of programs, and the virtual end of tenure for new employees.[8] How will library directors find the money needed to buy the technology for the library of the future when they face drastic cuts in basic budget areas such as staff and collection development? In an era of economic revolution directors must understand how economic trends impact on higher education, and how it relates to changes their institutions will make to increase competitiveness and quality.

TECHNOLOGY REVOLUTION

Despite its economic ills, America remains a world leader in the fields of computer hardware, software and telecommunication technology. These technologies may serve to both help regain our economic strength and restore some stability in our culture. Their impact on all levels of education will be profound. Higher education, in particular, can use technology to further its reach, reduce expenses and improve pedagogical methods.

CD-ROMs, information networks and telecommunications will make it possible to spread instruction beyond campus, just as books revolutionized education through wider transmission of instructors' lectures. Instruction can be improved through the integration of better instructional media. Multimedia technology, for example, is a powerful teaching tool for incorporating video, audio, or slides into an instructor's presentation. Colleges and universities will be integrating more electronic technology, such as sophisticated video display monitors, into the classroom. Technological change is promising but costly.

That is why higher education must look to technologies that are widely available and affordable, and reinvent the educational process to incorporate these technologies. Distance learning via the Internet is an example of this trend. At the University of Pennsylvania, a faculty member in the Classics Department teaches a course on the Internet. Anyone with Internet access may enroll at a cost of $800, and will receive college credit. Students rendezvous for group discussions, and assignments are exchanged on the Internet. Other institutions are exploring similar distance learning via wireless telecommunication technologies such as satellite networks.

Few departments within higher education are more aggressive in seeking out and integrating new technology than academic libraries. It is critical to improving the institution's access to information in all formats. Technology allows libraries to stabilize expenses by increasing productivity. The challenge is that technology raises user expectations. Patrons believe everything is found in some computer databank, and they expect access to it through the library. Faculty and students may even grow irate when reference librarians suggest print resources, or cannot provide access to obscure databanks.

Library leaders will increasingly be challenged to acquire the latest information technologies to satisfy user demands. This will be most difficult for libraries supporting those educational institutions which serve the poorest and most underprepared students. In a parallel to sociocultural changes, technology can also create a dual class system of "haves" and "have-nots." Libraries affiliated with more successful institutions must still battle for their share of technological resources, but it is not clear how libraries in financially strapped institutions will achieve parity. Certainly, librarians at all levels must search for affordable technology, and lobby governments to keep information publicly accessible.

Technology is also changing the nature of information ownership. The danger is that information in its varying electronic forms will increasingly become the property of technology barons. We are the sole owners of our print collections, but may only access electronic databanks. Owners of proprietary sources of electronic information can potentially create barriers to access or deny it all together. Technology offers hope, but also much uncertainty, which means great risk for higher education and academic libraries.

HIGHER EDUCATION REVOLUTION

As expected, societal revolutions, acting as external influences, contribute to a new transformation of higher education. Individual institutions, in order to compete for students, attract top faculty or simply maintain economic equilibrium, are experimenting with curriculums and teaching methods as never before. Long standing academic traditions, from core curriculums to tenure, are being questioned. In the search for competitive advantage, colleges and universities are exploring change in all areas.

Today, the majority of students are females over age 25. One in six students is now non-white. College is traditionally a four year "rite of passage." Tomorrow's students attend part-time or enroll at a two-year school. Many work at full-time jobs. They are more likely to drop out then drop back into college. Certainly, the "new majority" students, as they are called by Robert Zemsky of the University of Pennsylvania's Institute for Research on Higher Education, are likely to have a longer college career, and be more diverse in ethnic and cultural background.[9]

To meet the scheduling needs of new majority students, some higher education institutions have begun significant structural change. Longer hours, weekend classes and multiple satellite campuses are more commonplace. New majority students, when choosing a college or university, make proximity and accessibility a priority. Most work and many have families so classes must be near to home or work, and offer night programming. Competition for students has forced many institutions to open networks of satellite campuses to attract the new majority student.

In the higher education revolution, the library administrator's challenge is to defend the library's value and contributions to the organization. As restructuring transforms higher education, libraries are not immune to change. When administrators and faculty begin to perceive information networks as offering complete information access throughout campus, academic libraries may be considered targets for significant downsizing. Savvy library directors must position the library as a competitive advantage for their institution, and be able to communicate to their superiors how the library adds to organizational competitiveness.

RECOMMENDATIONS & CONCLUSION

Faced with these societal shock waves, how will a standard college or university survive? What is the correct response to such dramatic challenges to the foundations of who is taught, what is taught and how it is taught? Crises such as these are what initially drove many institutions to perform strategic planning. Taking cues from strategic planning performed at corporations, institutions of higher education acknowledged they had to stop giving society what they wanted, and begin giving what society needed.

College presidents and faculty must work together to help the institution survive and maintain its competitiveness as it responds to societal change.

Librarians must act to assist the parent organization in this task. Opportunities for involvement in the institution's strategic planning process may be available for higher level library administrators. Other librarians can develop micro-level strategic planning to determine the direction in which the library should focus its energy and resources. Here are some other recommendations for ways in which librarians at all levels can become knowledgeable about societal trends and the institution's competitive position:

- Develop an enhanced awareness of your own institution's demographic profile, including student characteristics by age, sex, race, national or international origin, full and part-time status and other indicators of your student population. Information from your campus planning, admissions or institutional research office can indicate how the student body has changed over time, and what changes are projected.

- Gather information about the academic status and skills of your institution's student body. How many require remedial courses, and in what subject areas? The admissions office may be the best source of information about levels of student preparedness.

- Seek out information about non-traditional and "new majority" students. What special programs, if any, is your institution offering to enhance the educational opportunities and experience for these students? More importantly, does your institution regard these students as an essential part of its target market?

- Increase staff knowledge of trends in higher education, and societal trends that impact on higher education. Invite planning or institutional research officers to your staff meeting to give a presentation on these trends and your institution's strategic plan for maintaining or improving its competitive position. Make *The Chronicle of Higher Education* a "must read" for library staff.

- Learn about your institution's strategic planning program, and determine how it impacts on the library - and how the library can impact on the plan. That is, identify ways the library might enhance the institution's market advantage over its competitors. For example, is the library's configuration of information systems on par with or superior to those of competitor institutions? Identify, if not already known, those institutions that compete with your own for students.

According to Butler and Davis, one of the most important benefits of strategic planning is the opportunity to do environmental scanning. Environmental scanning highlights emerging trends and issues, and serves to identify opportunities, competitors and potential partners.[10] The listed examples of environmental scanning are techniques librarians may use to become more alert to societal trends and shock waves, which contributes to the development of a proactive stance in reshaping the library to adapt to radical external change.

NOTES

1. Laurence Vesey, "Stability and experiment in the American Undergraduate Curriculum," in Carl Kaysen, ed., *Content and Context: Essays on College Education* (New York:McGraw-Hill, 1973).

2. George Keller, *Academic strategy: the management revolution in American higher education* (Baltimore:John Hopkins University Press, 1983).

3. William Dunn, "Hanging Out With American Youth," *American Demographics* 14 (February 1992):24-33.

4. Judith Waldrop, "New Projections Show Faster Growth, More Diversity," *American Demographics* 15 (February 1993):9-10.

5. Judith Waldrop, "You'll Know It's the 21st Century When...," *American Demographics* 12 (December 1990):22-27.

6. Steve W. Rawlings, "Households and Families," in *Population Profile of the United States 1993 (Special Studies P23-185)* (Washington, D.C.:Bureau of the Census, 1993), 17.

7. R. A. Zaldivar, "Poverty rate rises despite growth in economy," *Philadelphia Inquirer* (October 7, 1994):A1.

8. Denise K. Magner, "Bennington Dismisses 20 Professors and Announces a Major Reorganization of Its Academic Structure," *The Chronicle of Higher Education* 60 (June 29, 1994):A16

9. Institute for Research on Higher Education, "Landscape: the Changing Faces of the American College Campus," *Change* 25 (September-October 1993):57-60.

10. Meredith Butler and Hiram Davis, "Strategic Planning as a Catalyst for Change in the 1990s," *College and Research Libraries* 53 (September, 1992):398.

Information Technology and Intraorganizational Power:

A Study of Libraries in Liberal Arts Colleges

Gregory A. Crawford

ABSTRACT

This research examines the effects that the adoption and control of electronic information technology has had on the power wielded by academic libraries within liberal arts colleges as indicated by changes in the structure and bases of power of the library within the college. Based upon theories espoused in the organizational structure and power literatures, a model of organizational power within liberal arts colleges is developed, tested, and modified. Major features of the model include subunit power variables, environmental variables, technology indexes, structural variables, and bases of power variables. Analyses include simple path coefficients and analysis of variance tests.

Results indicated overall support for the model of intraorganizational power, but several variables were dropped in constructing a modified model. Automation was shown to have significant effects on the bases of power variables which, in turn, were shown to have significant effects on the power variables. Several of the environmental variables were shown to affect the bases of power variables significantly, contrary to the hypothesized relationships. In addition, both the automation indexes and several environmental variables directly affected the power variables, contrary to the hypotheses. As a result, a modified model of causality is proposed.

INTRODUCTION

Communication and information technologies have greatly affected organizations, causing the reorganization of their structures and changing their inputs and outputs. Internal and external procedures have developed to cope with these effects, often altering the organization's power dynamics. This research seeks to understand the role that electronic information technologies have played in reshaping the distribution of power within organizations. The current research examines automation and changes in organizational struc-

Gregory A. Crawford is Head of Public Services at Heindel Library, Pennsylvania State University - Harrisburg, Middletown, Pennsylvania.

ture and power in a particular subunit, the library, within a specific class of organizations, the liberal arts college.

This research is grounded in organizational structure literature and the strategic contingencies theory of intraorganizational power. Structural theory states, in brief, that an organization's structure is a function of its technology. Power rests within this structure. Within the strategic contingencies theory of intraorganizational power, power is considered a dependent variable. A strategic contingency is defined as "a requirement of the activities of one subunit which is affected by the activities of another subunit."[1] Information is one such strategic contingency. As developed by Hickson et al., the strategic contingencies theory states that the control of contingencies needed by other subunits within the organization increases the power of the controlling subunit. The more necessary these contingencies are for the work of other subunits, the more power accrues to the controlling subunit. The strategic contingencies theory relates the power of a subunit to its ability to control strategic contingencies as predicated on its ability to cope with uncertainty (i.e., the provision of services or resources to an organization), its substitutability (i.e., the ability of other subunits to take over functions performed by another subunit), and its centrality to the organization (i.e., how the subunit fits within the mission of the organization).[2] Power is usually measured by the allocation of resources, both monetary and personnel, to a subunit or by measures of the perception of power held by a subunit.[3]

The model of intraorganizational power presented and tested in this research seeks to integrate structural theories of power and the strategic contingencies model with concepts drawn from the literature of the effects of technology on organizations. Figure 1 presents the integrative model. The dependent variables are three aspects of subunit power; the independent variables include environmental variables, technology indexes, and the bases of power.

For this research, technology is the major independent variable due to its importance in determining overall organizational structure.[4] The model also posits that time is an important variable in its own right. The study is longitudinal so that the effects of technology may appear both within the bases of power and within the power measures themselves.

In brief, the model (see Figure 1) states that as technology within the subunit changes over time, the bases of power react to these changes in technology. As a result, the manifestations of power as revealed by the power variables also change. Thus, the integrated model can be thought of as a path model: as technology changes, the bases of power change; and as the bases of power change, the manifested and perceived power of the subunit changes.

HYPOTHESES

One overarching research question guides this research: How does the control of information technologies affect power structures within organizations? In particular, the research question can be made more focused by asking: How does the control of library-related information technologies affect the library's role in the power structures of liberal arts colleges? Such a question gives rise to several hypotheses:

(H1) As the number of information technologies within a subunit of an organization change, the bases of power of the subunit within the organization change.

(H2) As the bases of power within a subunit of an organization change, its power within the organization changes.

(H3) As the environmental variables change, they do not significantly affect the bases of power variables.

(H4) Changes in the amount of automation and changes in the organizational environment do not directly affect the power of the subunit.

Time

1. Time 1   **2. Time 2**

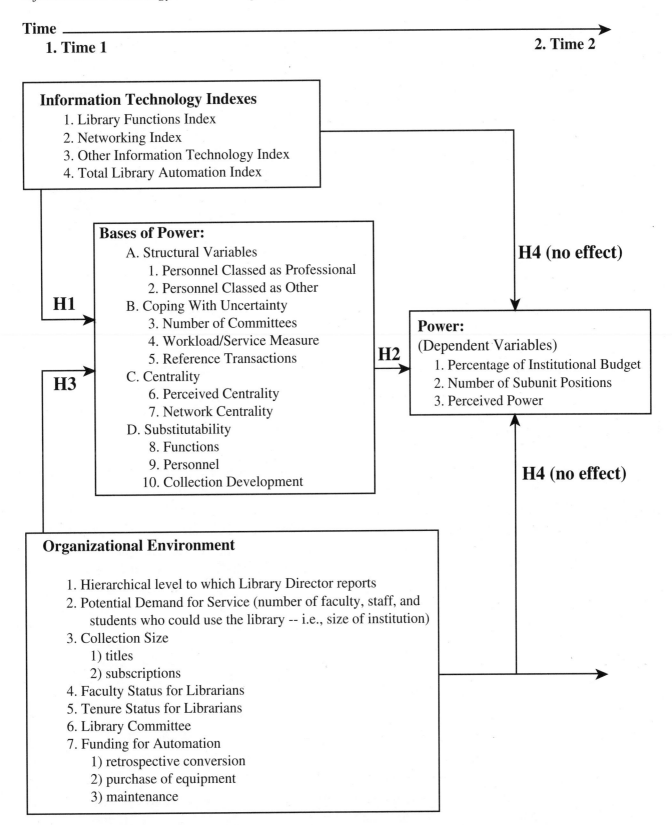

Figure 1: Integrated Model of Intraorganizational Power with Hypotheses

March 29 - April 1, 1995, Pittsburgh, Pennsylvania

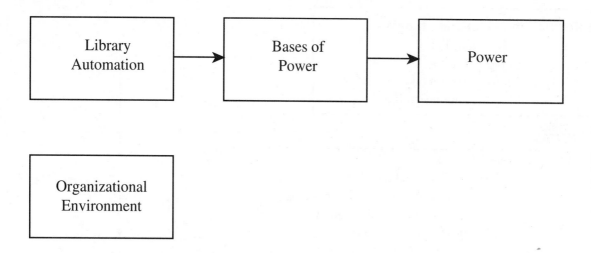

Figure 2: Hypothesized Causal Relationships Between Variables in Models

The overall null hypothesis states that as the number of information technologies within an organizational subunit changes, no other changes occur other than those resulting from chance.

Figure 1 presents the integrated model of intraorganizational power with the relevant research hypotheses noted. Figure 2 represents the hypothesized causal relationships between the variables in the model.

METHODOLOGY

The time frame for this research was the decade of the 1980s. Due to the limitations of available data, the two points in time were the academic years 1981-82 (Time 1) and 1989-90 (Time 2). Most variables were measured as changes occurring over this time span. This time frame coincided with a great expansion in the automation of many functions within the library. Online catalogs and circulation systems became common, CD-ROMs began to be used extensively, internal networking

capabilities increased as lower priced microcomputers were introduced into academic institutions, and external networks such as Bitnet and Internet became more readily accessible. This time frame, as a result, should provide adequate opportunity for changes in the bases of power to be manifested in the various power dependent variables.

The population frame for this study consisted of all those colleges classified as Liberal Arts Colleges I or Liberal Arts Colleges II by the Carnegie Foundation for the Advancement of Teaching (1987), a possible total of 572 colleges.[5] Only those colleges which completed both the 1982 HEGIS (Higher Education General Information Survey) and the 1990 IPEDS (Integrated Post-secondary Educational Data System) surveys and which were not part of a multi-library group were included in the study. The final total population for the study was 487 academic libraries. The study group includes 129 colleges classified as Liberal Arts I and 358 as Liberal Arts II. Of the 487 colleges, 24 are public in control and 463 are private.

Due to the nature of this research, several sources of data were used. The sources of data included archival data and two mailed questionnaires.

Archival sources

Variables calculated from the HEGIS and IPEDS data include: change in subunit budget as percent of institutional general and educational budget, change in number of subunit positions, change in potential demand for service (size), change in collection size (title and subscription counts), change in classification of personnel (professional and other), and change in workload or service of the subunit (circulation and reference transactions).

Mailed questionnaires

Two mailed questionnaires were developed for this research. The first mailed questionnaire sought data for the following variables: amount of library automation, perceived change in power, perceived change in centrality, and perceived change in substitutability of functions and personnel. Seven point Likert scales were used for perceived change in power, perceived change in centrality, and perceived change in substitutability (three measures). A coin flip decided whether each question stressed an increase or a decrease in the variable under consideration. A list of technologies was also presented and respondents indicated when each technology was made available in their libraries.

After pretesting, the survey was mailed to all 487 colleges. Eight weeks after the initial survey was mailed, a second follow-up survey packet was mailed to those libraries which had not yet responded. Responses were received from a total of 428 institutions (87.9% return). Of those from which responses were received, five colleges had closed, two reported that they did not consider themselves liberal arts colleges, three reported a lack of time to complete the survey, one was returned with no answers or explanation, and one was returned with the explanation that the survey could not be completed because the library had no automation during the particular times studied. Thus, the total usable return to the first survey was 416 (85.4%).

The responses to the first mailed questionnaire were dichotomized into those having the most and those having the least total library automation based on z-scores above 1.6 (i.e., those libraries haveing 10 or more functions automated) and below -1.6 (i.e., those libraries with no automation). This group was then narrowed to only those that agreed to provide additional information by checking that answer on the first questionnaire. Each of these remaining 38 libraries were sent a second questionnaire requesting the following information: level of institutional administration to which the library director reported, faculty status of librarians, tenure status of librarians, presence of faculty library committee, number of committees on which subunit staff are members, committee memberships (for network centrality analysis), and funding sources for library automation (retrospective conversion, automation machinery purchases, and maintenance). Of the 38 schools sent the second survey, 33 (87%) returned the form, although only 31 (82%) forms were usuable.

METHODS OF ANALYSIS

The main methods of analysis were analysis of variance measures for group differences and multiple regressions to determine simple path coefficients. For all statistical analyses, the level of significance was set at $a=.05$.

Path coefficients (Beta) were calculated by regressing each dependent variable upon all the available independent variables representing change between the two time periods. These path coefficients represent simple paths for the relationships between two variables.[6]

Library Functions Index
Automated Acquisitions
Automated Serials
Automated Cataloging
Automated Circulation
Online Public Access Catalog

Networking Index
Network Utility Membership (OCLC, RLIN, WLN, etc.)
Network-based Interlibrary Loan
Local Area Network Within Library
Node on Campus Network
Local/Regional Consortia, Networks

Other Technology Index
Telefacsimile
Public Computing Workstations
CD-ROM Indexes
Reference Database Searching
Librarian/Staff Workstations

Figure 3: Technology Indices

DESCRIPTIVE STATISTICS OF VARIABLES IN THE MODEL
Technology Indexes

The technology indexes were developed recursively from existing measures and various data sources for library automation. Four technology indexes were developed reflecting different types and levels of library automation: library functions, networking, and office technology/equipment, and total library automation. These four indexes attempted to determine if the technologies themselves were different in importance and/or impact upon the library. Figure 3 presents the functions included in the technology indices.

Of the 416 libraries completing the automation survey, the mean number of library functions automated during the time period 1982 to 1990 was 1.3 (SD=1.5), with 185 (44.5%) acquiring none and only 17 (4.1%) acquiring all 5.

The mean number of networking applications reported was 1.1 (SD=1.1). Of the 416 responses, 162 (38.9%) reported having none of the five functions, while only 2 (.5%) had all 5.

The other automation category had a mean of 2.7 (SD=1.5). Only 45 libraries (10.8%) reported having none, while 101 (24.3%) had 4 and 43 (10.3%) had all 5.

Finally, the total library automation index, which was composed of all three of the other indexes, had a mean of 5.1 (SD=2.9). A total of 33 libraries (7.9%) reported having none of the total of 15 separate items in the three indexes. Only 15 (3.1%) had 11 or more.

Bases of Power Variables

Two structural variables were measured: change in the number of staff classified as professional and change in the number of staff classified as other (i.e., not professional). The mean change in professional staff was 23% (SD=.68, N=487). The mean percentage change of staff classified as other was 34.2% (SD=1.3, N=457).

Three coping with uncertainty variables were included in the study: change in the number of college committees on which librarians served, change in the workload/service of the library as a whole, and change in the workload/service of the reference department.

Data for the change in the number of college committees on which librarians served variable comes only from the 23 (74.2%) institutions completing this question on the second survey. The mean change was 54.1% (SD=115.82), with 5 (21.7%) reporting a decline in the number of committees on which librarians serve, 9 (39.1%) reporting no change, and 9 (39.1%) reporting an increase.

Change in circulation per staff member served as an overall measure of library workload/service. The mean change in this variable was 578.1% (SD=129.2, N=480). This large increase is due to a very few outliers and, as a result, is highly misleading. If only the two greatest outliers are removed, the mean change in circulation is -16.7% (SD=.8, N=478). Over 75% of the 480 libraries for which there is available data showed a decline in the mean number of circulations per staff member.

The second workload/service variable, change in the number reference transactions, had a mean change of 160.6% (SD=8.4, N=444). As with the change in circulation variable, this mean is misleading due to several outliers. Over 50% of the institutions showed a decline in the number of reference transactions. When the 13 cases which show a ten-fold or greater increase were removed, the mean became 40% (SD=1.5, N=431).

Centrality was measured using two separate variables: perceived centrality and network centrality. Perceived centrality was measured on a 7-point scale, with 1 indicating a loss of centrality by the library and 7 indicating an increase in the centrality of the library on campus as the result of changes in the amount of library automation. Out of the total of 416 responses, 375 (90%) answered this question, giving a mean of 3.7 (SD=1.5). Thirty-three libraries (8.8%) reported a 1 or a 2 indicating a perception of strong loss of centrality

on campus. On the other hand, 109 (29.1%) reported a 6 or a 7 indicating a perception of a strong increase of centrality on campus as the result of an increase in library automation.

Only four schools provided sufficient data for use in analyzing network centrality. Change in network centrality was measured using standardized scores for the centrality of the library at each institution obtained by using UCINET IV software. Mean percentage change in the standardized network centrality of the libraries was -51.8% (SD=93.4, N=4).

Substitutability was measured using three perceptual variables: substitutability of functions, substitutability of personnel, and substitutability of collection development responsibilities.

The question on substitutability of functions asked for perceptions of the ability of other campus units to provide services similar to those traditionally supplied by the library. Two hundred responses (52.4%) indicated a strong disagreement (a 1 or 2) to the statement that other campus units became increasingly able to provide services similar to those provided by the library, while 52 (13.6%) indicated a strong agreement with the statement (6 or 7). The mean score on functional substitutability was 3.0 (SD=1.9, N=382).

The substitutability of personnel was measured on a 7-point scale using the statement, "It became more difficult to hire professional library staff with skills in automation during the period 1982 to 1990." The mean of this substitutability measure was 3.4 (SD=1.7, N=378). Of the reporting schools 128 (33.8%) indicated a strong disagreement with this statement (1 or 2 on the scale) and 40 (13.2%) strongly agreed with it (6 or 7).

The final substitutability measure involved the collection development responsibilities of librarians and faculty. The question asked if librarians, in comparison to faculty, lost responsibility for the selection of library materials during the time period of the study. Of the 390 responses (94%) to this question, 261 (66.9%) disagreed strongly (1 or 2) and only 18 (4.7%) agreed strongly. The mean response was 2.3 (SD=1.5).

Environmental variables

Environmental variables included change in the hierarchical level to which the library director reported, change in the potential demand for service, change in collection size (two measures), change in faculty status for librarians, change in tenure status for librarians, change in the presence of a faculty library committee, and funding for automation.

Change in the hierarchical level to which the library director reported was measured by counting how many levels the library director was below the president of the institution. Only one director reported a change in reporting level indicating that he reported to a lower level in 1989-90 than in 1982-83. Thus, virtually no change was evident in this variable over time.

Change in potential demand for library services was measured using the change in the number of students attending the institution. During the eight years covered by this research, these colleges witnessed a mean increase of 28.7% (SD=.8, N=476) in their student body. Almost 30% (142) saw a decrease in size while, in contrast, 7% (33) more than doubled.

Change in the collection size was measured two ways: change in the number of titles in the collection and change in the number of periodicals to which the library subscribed. The mean change in the number of titles was 30.7% (SD=2.1, N=405). Twenty-two percent (89) reported a decline in the number of titles in their collections while slightly more than 3% (13) reported at least a doubling of their collection size. There was one major outlier that reported an increase of over 4000%. When this outlier was removed, the mean increase in the number of titles was 20.5% (SD=.5, N=404). The mean change in the number of periodical subscriptions was 159.4% (SD=16.6, N=463). This large figure partially resulted from six major outliers who reported increases in excess of 1000%. When these outliers were removed, the mean increase in periodical subscriptions reduces to 23.3% (SD=.7, N=457).

Faculty status for librarians showed only slight variation over time among the 31 colleges answering this question on the second survey. Two colleges (6.5%) lost faculty status during the time of the study and two (6.5%) gained it, with a total of 18 schools indicating that librarians were considered to be faculty during each time period.

Change in the tenure status for librarians mirrors the results for faculty status. Among the 31 schools answering this question on the second survey, two (6.5%) gained and two (6.5%) lost tenure status, although the number of schools at which librarians were eligible for tenure was only 8 for both the 1981-82 and 1989-90 academic years.

Most colleges included in the second survey reported the existence of a faculty library committee. For the 1981-82 school year, 25 (83.3%) had such a committee and for the 1989-90 school year 23 (76.7%) reported one. Change over time shows that 4 schools (13.3%) lost a faculty library committee while 2 (6.7%) gained one.

Funding for automation came from two major sources for the second survey group: internal budget allocations and grants. Three aspects of funding for automation were examined: funding for retrospective conversion, funding for automation itself, and funding for maintenance of equipment. Grants for retrospective conversion were received by 13 schools (50% of those answering this question), although six of these also used their operating budgets in addition to their grants. Seven schools used only grants for retrospective conversion. Purchasing the equipment itself came for both grants and operating budgets. Nine schools (34.6%) report using only the operating budgets for such purchases; 6 (23.1%) report using only grants; and 11 (42.3%) report using both sources of funds. Maintenance of automation equipment was overwhelmingly paid for our of operating budgets, with only two schools (8%) reporting the receipt of grants for such purposes.

Power

Three measures of power served as the dependent variables in the model: change in the percentage of the institutional budget allocated to the library, percentage change in the number of subunit positions, and perceived power.

Budget data was complete for 482 of the institutions studied for both the 1981-82 and the 1989-90 academic years and showed a mean of -14% (SD=.4), representing a substantial decrease in the percentage of the budget devoted to the library of these institutions. Overall, 76.8% of the libraries witnessed a reduction in their support over the time period.

Using data from 482 libraries, analyses showed that there was an increase of 22.5% (SD=.6) in the total number of positions, excluding student employees, in these libraries. Seventy-two percent of the libraries saw an increase in the number of employees, while only 28% suffered a decrease.

The third measure of power was perceptual. The statement, "The power of the library at this college increased over the period 1982 to 1990 as a result of library automation," was used to ascertain perceptions of library power. Of those libraries completing the first survey, 378 (91%) answered this question with the mean score being 5.2 (SD=1.6), providing support for a perception of increased power as a result of library automation. Specifically, 31 (8.2%) strongly disagreed (answering a 1 or 2) while 172 (45.5%) strongly agreed (6 or 7).

TESTS OF HYPOTHESES

In keeping with the norms of path analysis, Beta coefficients derived from multiple analyses are presented in the following analyses.

Hypothesis 1

According to hypothesis 1, as the amount of technology within a subunit of an organization changes, the bases of power of the subunit within the organization change. Analyses were performed using each technology index separately and with the separate indexes added together to form an index of total library automation.

Analyses for only three of the ten separate bases of power variables yielded statistically significant Beta coefficients when regressed onto the total automation index: personnel classed as professional (0.11, p<.05), perceived centrality (0.23, p<.000), and substitutability of functions (0.12, p<.05).

Two bases of power had significant results for the library functions index: perceived centrality (0.17, p<.001) and substitutability of functions (0.13, p<.01).

Two analyses resulted in significant Beta coefficients when the bases of power variables were regressed onto the networking index: personnel classed as other (0.10, p<.05) and perceived centrality (0.11, p<.05).

Regressions of each base of power variable onto the other automation index for the total group resulted in three significant Beta coefficients: personnel classed as other (0.11, p<.05), perceived centrality (0.19, p<.001), and substitutability of functions (0.10, p<.05).

As these analyses show, hypothesis 1 received limited support.

Hypothesis 2

Hypothesis 2 states that as the bases of power of a subunit of an organization change, its power within the organization changes. In this research power was measured using three variables: change in the percentage of the institutional budget allocated to the subunit, percentage change in the number of subunit positions, and perceived power.

Structural Variables

Regressing each of the power variables onto the change in the personnel classed as <u>Coping with Uncertainty</u>

Regressing the three power variables onto the change in the number of committees on which librarians served and the workload/service variables resulted in no significant Beta coefficients.

The regression of the power variables onto the reference transactions variable resulted in one significant Beta: percentage change in the number of subunit positions (0.33, p<.000).

Centrality

Of the three power variables, only perceived power resulted in significant Beta coefficient when regressed onto the perceived centrality variable (0.77, p<.000).

Only four libraries provided sufficient data to perform network analyses. When the three power variables were regressed onto the change in network centrality variable, no significant Beta coefficients resulted.

Substitutability

Only one power variable, perceived power, resulted in a significant Beta (0.24, p<.000) when regressed onto substitutability of functions.

Only perceived power displayed a significant Beta coefficient (0.20, p<.001) when the power variables are regressed onto the substitutability of personnel variable.

Regression of the power variables onto the collection development variable yielded no significant results.

The second hypothesis examined power as a function of changes in the bases of power. Only partial support for this hypothesis was discovered in the analyses, although each power variable was represented by at least one significant result.

Hypothesis 3

Hypothesis 3 states, as the environmental variables change, they do not significantly affect the bases of power variables.

Environmental Variables

Since only one library of the 31 completing the second survey reported change in the hierarchical level to which the library director reported, no further analyses were undertaken.

Change in the potential demand for service was measured as the change in the number of students attending the college, since students represent the largest single group of potential library users on liberal arts college campuses. When the bases of power variables are regressed onto the change in the number of students, three significant Beta coefficients result: change in the percentage of personnel classed as professional (0.09, p<.05), change in the percentage of personnel classed as other (0.10, p<.05), and change in reference transactions (0.18, p<.001).

Collection size was measured using two variables: change in the number of titles and change in the number of subscriptions. When the bases of power variables were regressed onto the percentage change in number of titles in library variable, three significant Betas resulted: percentage change in reference transactions (0.80, p<.000), collection development (0.13, p<.05), and change in the number of committees on which librarians served (0.63, p<.01).

The second measure of change in collection size was change in the number of subscriptions. Three significant Beta coefficients were determined when the bases of power variables were regressed onto the change in the number of subscriptions variable: change in the percentage of personnel classed as professional (0.14, p<.01), change in the percentage of personnel classed as other (0.13, p<.01), and change in the number of committees on which librarians serve (0.59, p<.01).

Analysis of variance tests were used to determine differences between those institutions at which librarians gained faculty status, lost faculty status, or remained the same. Oneway ANOVA tests resulted in three significant results: change in the number of professional librarians (F=6.06, p<.01), change in the number of committees on which librarians served (F=18.68, p<.000), and change in the collection responsibility of librarians (F=8.87, p<.01). Post-hoc Scheffe' tests showed that for both change in the number of professional librarians and change in the number of committees on which librarians served the group which gained faculty status differed significantly from both the group which lost faculty status and the group which remained the same. For the change in the collection responsibility of librarians variable, the post-hoc Scheffe' tests showed that the group which gained faculty status differed significantly from the group which remained the same. All these results, however, must be viewed with caution due to the small number of libraries included in the group which gained faculty status and the group which lost faculty status.

Only one significant result was obtained for oneway analysis of variance tests using change in the presence of a faculty library committee as the independent variable: change in the number of staff classified as other (F=4.02, p<.05). A post-hoc Scheffe' test revealed that the group which gained a library committee differed significantly from the group which lost a library committee. Once again, the number of cases in each group is so small that doubt may be cast on the results.

No significant differences were found for any of the bases of power variables by type of funding for automation (those that used grants exclusively, those that used their operating budgets exclusively, and those that used a combination of grants and operating budgets).

The results of the analyses reject hypothesis 3. Therefore, environmental variables must be included in any model of intraorganizational power within libraries.

Hypothesis 4

Hypothesis 4 states, changes in the amount of automation and changes in the organizational environment do not directly affect the power of the subunit.

Technology Indexes

Two significant Beta coefficients resulted when the power variables were regressed directly onto the total library automation index: percentage change in the number of subunit positions (0.11, p<.05) and perceived power (0.28, p<.000).

Only the regression of perceived power onto the library functions index resulted in a significant Beta coefficient (0.23, p<.000). When the power variables were regressed directly onto the networking automation index, two significant Beta coefficients resulted: percentage change in the number of subunit positions (0.15, p<.01) and perceived power (0.16, p<.01). Only the regression of perceived power onto the other automation index yielded a significant Beta coefficient (0.19, p<.001).

Environmental Variables

Regression analyses show no significant results for the following environmental variables: change in the hierarchical level to which the library director reported, change in faculty status for librarians, change in tenure status for librarians, and change in the presence of a faculty library committee.

The percentage change in number of subunit positions is the only power variable that resulted in significant Beta coefficients when regressed onto the change in number of students (0.27, p<.000) and the change in number of titles (0.37, p<.000).

When the three power variables were regressed onto the change in number of subscriptions, the resulting Beta coefficients for all the power variables were significant: the coefficient for change in percentage of institutional budget was 0.39 (p<.000), for change in number of subunit positions 0.31 (p<.000), and for perceived power -0.15 (p<.01).

No significant differences for any of the three measures of power resulted from ANOVA tests for faculty status, tenure status, presence of a library committee, funding for retrospective conversion, or funding for automation equipment.

Two ANOVAs for the bases of power variables resulted in significant results, both for maintenance funding: change in budget allocated to the subunit (F=16.43, p<.000) and change in the number of staff in the subunit (F=12.31, p<.001). Post-hoc Scheffe' tests showed that for both variables, the group which used both grants and operating budget differed significantly from those that used grants exclusively and those that used their operating budget exclusively. These results are

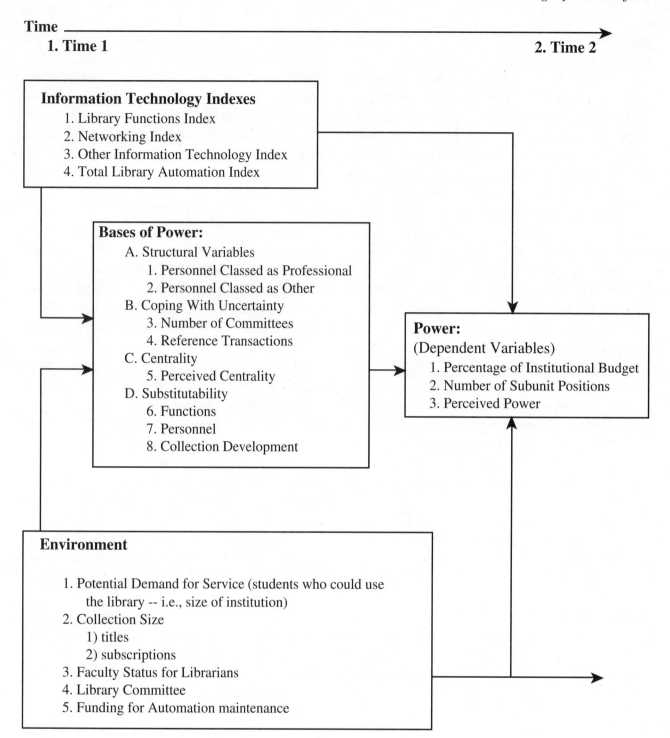

Time ──►
   1. Time 1   **2. Time 2**

Information Technology Indexes
    1. Library Functions Index
    2. Networking Index
    3. Other Information Technology Index
    4. Total Library Automation Index

Bases of Power:
    A. Structural Variables
        1. Personnel Classed as Professional
        2. Personnel Classed as Other
    B. Coping With Uncertainty
        3. Number of Committees
        4. Reference Transactions
    C. Centrality
        5. Perceived Centrality
    D. Substitutability
        6. Functions
        7. Personnel
        8. Collection Development

Power:
(Dependent Variables)
    1. Percentage of Institutional Budget
    2. Number of Subunit Positions
    3. Perceived Power

Environment

    1. Potential Demand for Service (students who could use
       the library -- i.e., size of institution)
    2. Collection Size
       1) titles
       2) subscriptions
    3. Faculty Status for Librarians
    4. Library Committee
    5. Funding for Automation maintenance

Each variable measures change from Time 1 to Time 2

Figure 4: Modified Integrated Model of Intraorganizational Power

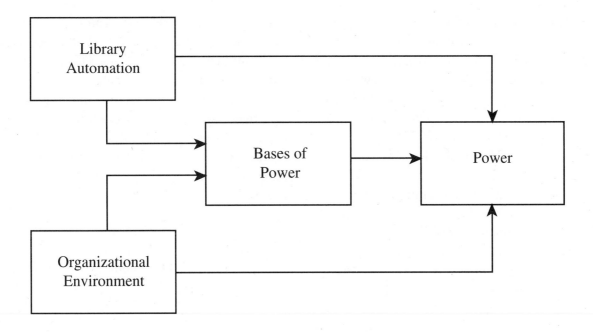

Figure 5: Modified Integrated Model of Intraorganizational Power Causality Diagram

highly suspect, however, since the group which used grants exclusively and the group which used both grants and operating budgets both consisted of only one library each.

These results show that Hypothesis 4 must be rejected. When regressed onto the automation indexes and the environmental variables, each power variable had at least one significant Beta coefficient showing that both the automation indexes and the environmental variables had direct effects on subunt power.

MODIFIED INTEGRATED MODEL OF INTRAORGANIZATIONAL POWER

Using the preceding results, a modified integrated model of intraorganizational power was developed (Figure 4). All variables whose analyses yielded at least one significant result either as an independent variable or as a dependent variable are included. (See Appendix 1 for a summary of the significant results) Thus, the model includes all four of the technology variables, eight of the

bases of power variables with at least one present from each individual base of power, and 6 environmental variables. A total of 6 variables were dropped from the original model.

In addition the lines of causality have also been redrawn as is shown in Figure 5. The new model posits that changes in both automation and the environment affect changes in the bases of power. In addition, automation, the environment, and the bases of power all directly affect the actual and perceived power of an organizational subunit. This new causality structure mirrors that identified by Welburn in his study of the allocation of collection development funds in academic libraries.[7]

CONCLUSION

The driving question behind this research was, how has library automation affected the academic library and its position on college campuses. To understand the processes of change set in motion by automation, the present study developed and tested a model of intraorganizational power based largely upon the strategic contingencies theory of intraorganizational power which states that intraorganizational power can be viewed as a function of a subunit's ability to cope with uncertainty, its centrality to the organization, and the substitutability of its functions and personnel within the organization. The model also added organizational structural and environmental variables to provide an integrated model of intraorganizational power and used three separate measures of power to increase the explanatory power of the model by measuring different aspects of power.

The main idea expressed in the model was that as automation within a library changed, the bases of power of that library also changed. Such changes in the bases of power would then cause changes in the power of the library on campus. The model also expressed the idea that the environmental variables would not have significant effects on the power variables and that library automation itself would have no direct influence on power.

The study provided mixed results. Automation was shown to affect specific bases of power variables, but several of the environmental variables were also shown to have significant relationships with the bases of power variables. Several of the bases of power variables did not show significant relationships with the power variables themselves and had to be dropped from the model. In addition, the analyses revealed significant relationships between automation and power and between the environment and power. Thus, the model was revised to take these relationships into account.

The significance of this study lies in its use of power as a variable worthy of study within librarianship. Welburn, in his study of the relationship between power and resource allocation for collection development in four academic libraries, states, "One of the major conclusions of this study was the importance of power as a paradigm for organizational research on libraries."[8]

The present study extends research to the power of the library on campus and adds the concept of automation as a change agent. This research also expands the use of the strategic contingencies theory of power more deeply into the study of libraries as subunits within organizations, providing an alternative perspective for understanding organizations which contrasts with the classical bureaucratic paradigm so heavily used to study libraries in the past.

NOTES

1. D. J. Hickson, C. R. Hinings, C. A. Lee, R. E. Schneck, and J. M. Pennings, "A strategic contingencies' theory of intraorganizational power," *Administrative Science Quarterly*, 16 (1971): 216-229.

2. Hickson et al.; R. Lachman, "Power from what? A reexamination of its relationships with structural conditions," *Administrative Science Quarterly*, 34 (1989): 231-251; G. R. Salancik and J. Pfeffer, "Who gets power -- and how they hold on to it: A strategic-contingency model of power," *Organizational Dynamics*, 5 (1977): 3-21.

3. J. D. Hackman, "Power and centrality in the allocation of resources in colleges and universities," *Administrative Science Quarterly*, 30 (1985): 61-77; J. Pfeffer, "Power and resource allocation in organizations," in B. M. Staw and G. R. Salancik (Eds.), *New Directions in Organizational Behavior* (pp. 235-265) (Chicago: St. Clair Press, 1977); J. Pfeffer, "Understanding power in organizations," *California Management Review*, 34 (2) (1992): 29-50; J. Pfeffer, and W. L. Moore, "Power and university budgeting: A replication and extension," *Administrative Science Quarterly*, 25 (1980): 637-653; and J. Pfeffer, and G. R. Salancik, "Organizational decision making as a political process: The case of a university budget," *Administrative Science Quarterly*, 19 (1974): 135-151.

4. C. C. Caufield, "An integrative research review of the relationship between technology and structure: A meta-analytic synthesis" (Doctoral dissertation, University of Iowa), *Dissertation Abstracts International*, 51 (1989): 553A; J. Pfeffer, *Power in organizations* (Cambridge, MA: Ballinger, 1981); J. Pfeffer, and H. Leblebici, "Information technol-

ogy and organizational structure," *Pacific Sociological Review*, 20 (1977): 241-261; and J. Woodward, *Industrial Organization: Theory and Practice* (New York: Oxford University Press, 1965).

5. Carnegie Foundation for the Advancement of Teaching, *A Classification of Institutions of Higher Education* (Princeton, NJ: Carnegie Foundation for the Advancement of Teaching, 1987).

6. E. J. Pedhazur, *Multiple Regression in Behavioral Research: Explanation and Prediction* (2nd ed.) (Fort Worth: Holt, Rinehart and Winston, 1982).

7. W. C. Welburn, "The organizational context of budgeting for collection development in academic libraries: A study of power and resource allocation in three universities" (Doctoral dissertation, Indiana University), *Dissertation Abstracts International*, 52 (1991): 330A.

8. Ibid., p. 166.

APPENDIX

SIGNIFICANT RESULTS

Independent Automation Index	Dependent Base of Power	Standardized Beta Coefficient
Total Library Automation	Professional Personnel	$B = 0.11*$
	Perceived Centrality	$B = 0.23***$
	Substitutability of Functions	$B = 0.12*$
Library Functions	Perceived Centrality	$B = 0.17***$
	Substitutability of Functions	$B = 0.13**$
Networking	Other Personnel	$B = 0.10*$
	Perceived Centrality	$B = 0.11**$
Other Automation	Other Personnel	$B = 0.11*$
	Perceived Centrality	$B = 0.19***$
	Substitutability of Functions	$B = 0.10*$

$*p<.05, **p<.01, ***p<.001$

Independent	Dependent	Standardized
Base of Power	**Power Variable**	**Beta Coefficient**
Professional Personnel	Budget	$B = 0.33^{***}$
	Subunit Positions	$B = 0.34^{***}$
	Perceived Power	$B = 0.13^{*}$
Other Personnel	Subunit Positions	$B = 0.64^{***}$
Reference Transactions	Subunit Positions	$B = 0.33^{***}$
Perceived Centrality	Perceived Power	$B = 0.77^{***}$
Substitutability of Functions	Perceived Power	$B = 0.24^{***}$
Substitutability of Personnel	Perceived Power	$B = 0.20^{***}$

$^{*}p<.05$, $^{**}p<.01$, $^{***}p<.001$

Independent	Dependent	Standardized
Environmental Variables	**Bases of Power**	**Beta Coefficient**
Number of Students	Professional Personnel	$B = 0.09*$
	Other Personnel	$B = 0.10*$
	Reference Transactions	$B = 0.18***$
Collection: Titles	Reference Transactions	$B = 0.80***$
	Substitutability of Collection Development	$B = 0.13*$
	Number of Committees	$B = 0.63**$
Collection: Subscriptions	Professional Personnel	$B = 0.14***$
	Other Personnel	$B = 0.13**$
	Number of Committees	$B = 0.59***$
Faculty Status	Professional Personnel	$F = 6.06**$
	Number of Committees	$F = 18.68***$
	Substitutability of Collection Development	$F = 8.88***$
Library Committee	Other Personnel	$F = 4.02*$

$*p<.05, **p<.01, ***p<.001$

Independent	Dependent	Standardized
Automation Index	**Power**	**Beta Coefficient**
Total Library Automation	Subunit Positions	$B = 0.11*$
	Perceived Power	$B = 0.28***$
Library Functions	Perceived Power	$B = 0.23***$
Networking	Subunit Positions	$B = 0.15***$
	Perceived Power	$B = 0.16***$
Other Automation	Perceived Power	$B = 0.19***$
Environmental Variables	**Power**	
Number of Students	Subunit Positions	$B = 0.27***$
Collection: Titles	Subunit Positions	$B = 0.37***$
Collection: Subscriptions	Budget	$B = 0.39***$
	Subunit Positions	$B = 0.31***$
	Perceived Power	$B = -0.15***$
Funding: Maintenance	Budget	$F = 16.43***$
	Subunit Positions	$F = 12.31***$

$*p<.05, **p<.01, ***p<.001$

Undergraduate Perceptions of Library Service:

Use of Focus Groups and Surveys in Strategic Planning

Thomas K. Fry

ABSTRACT

An oft-overlooked but crucial element of strategic planning is the perception of, and desire for, library service as seen by our stakeholders. This paper examines the need for obtaining this valuable information. It outlines the process, including use of focus groups and surveys; methodology including survey development and administration, focus group question development and administration; result analysis, presentation of findings; samples of survey forms and summaries of data collected; trends identified in focus groups and surveys. The research project was supported by a grant from a university department. This grant paid for printing and advertising. In addition the university's Associated Students donated monetary incentives for focus group participants. These two funding strategems are outlined. Applicability to other academic library strategic planning efforts and future plans are summarized.

Strategic planning in university libraries usually involves numerous brainstorming sessions and retreats in which the library managers go through various exercises to develop a mission statement and set goals. It is less usual to gather information from stakeholders- the students, faculty, staff and community users of our collections, facilities and services and include this in the strategic planning. This paper describes a project conducted at UCLA in 1993 that set about collecting information from undergraduates through the use of focus groups and user surveys. Undergraduates' feelings, perceptions, needs and desires were sought as a crucial element of strategic planning. The major findings of the research will be presented along with methods used to obtain support and funding from other campus departments. The ramifications for strategic planning are outlined and a framework for adaptation by other libraries is presented.

Thomas K. Fry is Associate Director for Public Services, Penrose Library, University of Denver, Denver, Colorado.

PROCESS: FOCUS GROUPS

While taking a lot of time to organize and run, focus groups have the advantage over other forms of data gathering of allowing for interaction between participants and facilitators. We saw these groups as an important element of our data gathering. Our goal was to involve a broad range of students, all class years, all majors, all ages, off-campus and commuter. We wanted library users and non-users. No library employees were permitted in these focus groups. To attract subjects we used a mass market approach. With funding support from the Office of Instructional Development; (1) we purchased two quarter page ads in the campus paper, the *Daily Bruin*, announcing the focus groups; (2) we had large (20" x 30") posters made and posted in the eight campus residence halls as well as the undergraduate library, and the University Research Library; (3) we had small (8 1/2" x 11") posters printed and posted in fraternity and sorority houses, residence halls, the student union, campus general bulletin boards and campus libraries. (See figure 1)

After a week of advertising we recruited enough students for five focus groups. The demographics were representative of the total student population. Two students were first year, seven second year, six third year, eight fourth year, and three fifth year seniors. Twelve were humanities majors, nine social science majors, three science majors, and two undecided. Seven lived on campus, the rest either within walking distance or commuting. Thirteen ranged in age from 18-20, eight between 21-23 and five were over 24 years old. The focus group discussions were led by two professionals from the campus Center for Human Resources. We met with them prior to conducting the groups to develop a list of questions and to answer questions they had about library jargon, pre-existing conditions, etc.

Each group began with an introduction by the College Librarian or designee stating the purpose, introducing the facilitators, thanking the students in advance for their time, stressing the importance of this endeavor. The Librarian then left the room

so the students could talk freely, expressing both positive and negative comments without worry of offending the "sponsor."

Questions asked in the focus groups were open-ended but tailored to specific areas of concern:

1. For what purposes do you use the library?
2. When do you use the library?
3. How often do you use the library?
4. Which library services currently being provided are critical for your educational and research needs?
5. Which services are being provided effectively?
6. Which services need improvement? In what way?
7. How do you feel about the following services? Hours, Reserves, Old exams, Core collection, Reference assistance, Term paper assistance, Teaching library use, Computing lab, Study space, Group study rooms, Lounge areas, Current periodicals, Current newspapers, The ORION system, The Melvyl system, Checkout policies, Phone renewal.
8. Would you attend workshops that the library would offer on such topics as researching a term paper or advanced ORION/Melvyl searching?
9. What other topics for workshops would interest you, if any?
10. What additional services would you like the library to provide?

PROCESS: USER SURVEYS

We knew we could gather significant amounts of data fairly painlessly by developing a survey instrument. A questionnaire was prepared in consultation with College Library staff and the library administration. During the Spring 1993 quarter the survey was handed out and completed by 452 students from large lower division lecture classes. Four professors graciously allowed the survey to be administered in their Biology, History, Geography, and English lectures. Two adjunct lecturers handed out the surveys to 60 students in two upper

Join a Library Undergraduate Focus Group

♦ The College Library wants your ideas for improving services to undergraduates in Towell and in Powell when we return in 1995.

♦ Associated Students UCLA is proud to support The College Library by offering a $10 Bruin Gold Card for undergraduates participating in library focus groups.

♦ Maximum Commitment - 2 hours. Begins May 17th.

If you are a UCLA undergraduate and interested in earning your $10 Bruin Gold Card, call (310) 825-4134, Monday - Friday, 8am - 5pm for more details.

Space is limited — Call TODAY
That's 310-825-4134

$10 Bruin Gold Card
Limited to 120 participants

Figure 1

division Library Science classes (GSLIS 110). Six hundred and seven surveys were handed out in Towell, the undergraduate library.

The questionnaire was broad based and covered attitudinal as well as historical areas. (See appendix) Demographic information was sought as well as information on their past library use habits such as which other campus libraries they use, and how often they use the library. There was overlap between the survey and focus groups in many areas such as reason for using the library, frequency of use, preference for various user education delivery vehicles. We asked for good-satisfactory-poor ratings of our service, lending policies, book collections, study facilities, staff, and hours of operation. We asked them to tell us where they did most of their studying, how many books they thought they checked out. In the realm of user education we asked them to check off on a list the things they thought were helpful to them in assisting them to use libraries. The list included the following:

> Library guide
> Library tours
> Library staff
> Library handouts
> High school course
> Library component of English 3
>   (basic composition class)
> GSLIS 110 (library school class)
> Public library staff
> Other college or high school library staff
> ORION demonstrations
> Fellow students

We asked if they felt that further instruction in library use would be helpful and if so to pick from a list that included tours, pamphlets, workshops, term paper clinics, signs, individual appointments with librarians. And lastly, since we were in the midst of a third or fourth round of serious budget cuts, we asked for their guidance in suggesting what we could stop doing in order to save money.

FINDINGS: FOCUS GROUPS

The focus group discussions reinforced some of our self-perceptions and revealed some new concerns. When asked why they use the library, 14 of the 26 participants said to do research, 12 to study, 11 for reserves (Table 1). Critical services identified in the focus groups had reserve in first place with 50% of the participants (Table 2); this was followed by 15% thinking the core collection and computer catalogs were critical and 10% thinking copiers and reference librarians were critical for their research and education needs. Furthermore, six additional areas emerged as common ground in each group.

1. Need to advertise service. Most students were unaware of the variety of services available in the library, such as computing lab and phone renewal. They suggested that we develop a comprehensive guide or "bible" (which, of course, we have, but they didn't realize that, in itself revealing!)

2. Desire to have reserve service automated. Students complained that it took too much time to fill out cards for every reserve item they wanted to check out. They'd like reserve checkout to be like regular checkout (Reserve use has actually increased over the last year and so have user frustrations with the slow process).

3. Appreciation for quality of assistance. The students felt that the librarians were friendly and helpful and available for their needs. Some wanted librarians available more hours- currently College Library is open 87 hours/week with reference service offered 62 hours/week. Generally the staff as a whole received positive comments.

4. Library education. Generally speaking the students were not interested in workshops on how to use the library. (Table 3) They felt they didn't have the time or interest and preferred to have access to a librarian when they needed an answer to a specific question. The library component of English 3, the required basic

Table 1: Why do you use the library?

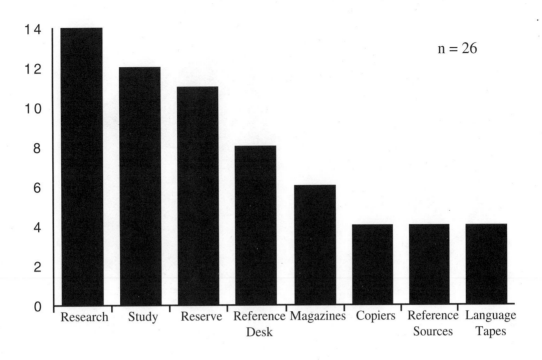

Table 2: Which services are critical for educational and research needs

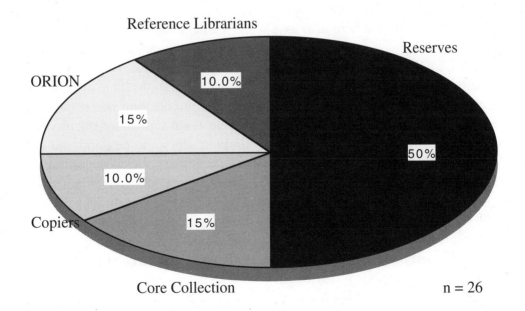

Table 3: Would you attend workshops on library use?

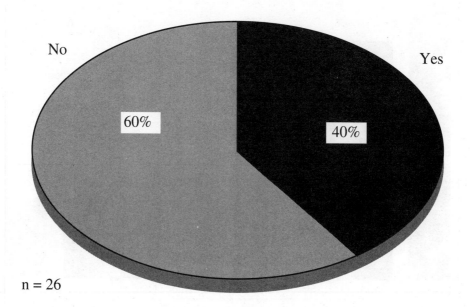

No

Yes

60%

40%

n = 26

composition class, received mixed reviews with some praising it and some feeling it was not useful. The idea of a published comprehensive guide was mentioned here also as a useful alternative.

5. ORION and MELVYL. Three themes were evident regarding ORION and MELVYL, the online catalogs. (1) The students thought these systems had a lot more in them than they knew how to get. (2) They found them hard to use — "user hostile"— and were confused as to why each system had different commands. (3) They didn't understand the differences between ORION and MELVYL and when to use one or the other,

6. Checkout policies. Almost all of the participants wanted longer loan periods—four weeks vs. two — on our regular collection books.

FINDINGS: USER SURVEYS

Analysis of the 1119 surveys returned reveal some interesting information about library users.

Taking the mode response for each question produces the following profile:

College Library users are between 18-21 years old, walk to campus, work 16 hours/week, use the library once a week. The main reason for using the library is to study their own material, followed closely by checking out class reserve material. (Table 4) On a good-satisfactory-poor scale, they find our service to be good, our collection numbers, lending policies and study facilities to be satisfactory; hours convenient; and staff helpful. Two-thirds felt that they knew something about libraries before coming to UCLA. (Table 5) When asked what was most useful to them when further assistance was needed they favored asking the library staff over other means such as tours or GSLIS 110. (Table 6) Slightly more than half felt that further guidance in using libraries would be useful. When presented with a list of options for this guidance such as tours, workshops, handouts, signs, and a self-help video, the undergraduates

Table 4: Why do you use the library?

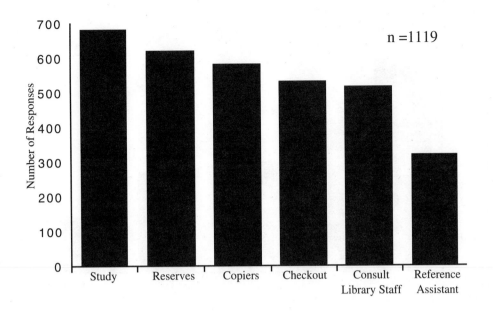

Table 5: Prior Knowledge of How to Use a Library

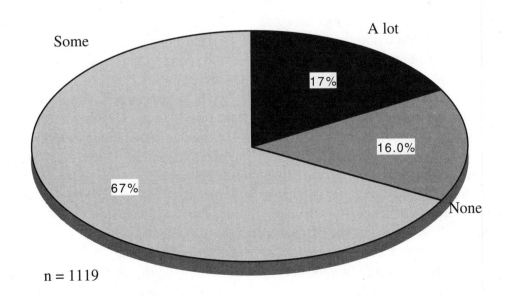

Table 6: What is helpful in assisting you to use libraries?

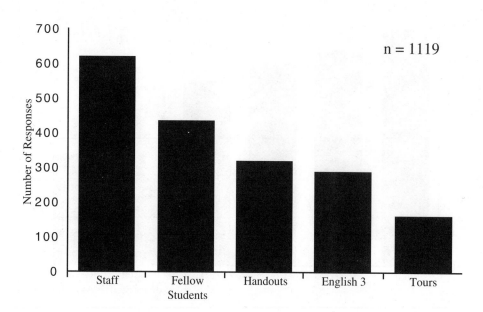

n = 1119

felt handouts would be most helpful followed closely by more signs. (Table 7) Workshops, a self-paced skills booklet, and tours were thought to be least helpful in learning more about using the library. When asked to provide guidance to us regarding areas that could be cut if needed due to shrinking budgets, the students felt that exhibits and travel guides could be stopped; they did not want to see reference service or reserves eliminated.

There are two elements in this user survey process that beg for further description and explanation. The first is the opportunity to establish or strengthen ties with complementary organizations on your campus. The second is the chance to strengthen ties with another large and important student service operation- your campus student center or bookstore.

1. Organizational ties.

I consulted with and asked for assistance from two separate important campus organizations. The

Office of Instructional Development, among its many charges, provides grants to faculty for research that improves teaching. They provided budgetary support to pay for advertisements in the campus papers, print posters, flyers, the actual survey form; in this case a total cost of just under $1,000.

The other campus organization that played a big role was the Center for Human Resources. Two human resource counselors acted as the focus group facilitators. Their skill in interviewing, neutral orientation (at least they weren't from the library), and professional manner greatly aided the focus group discussion.

2. Student Center.

Knowing that it would be difficult if not impossible to get students to give up two hours of their time to come to a focus group unless an incentive were offered, I contacted the Executive Director of the Associated Students of UCLA to see if they would be interested in this project. I was

Table 7: Further Guidance in Library Use

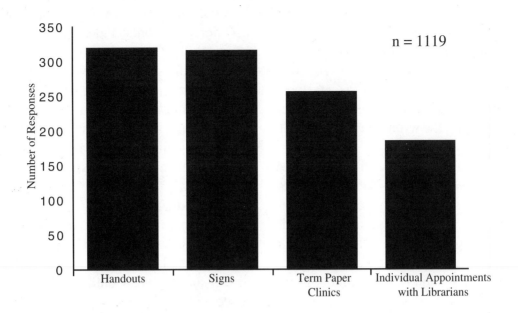

hoping for a free ice cream cone or leftover Bear Wear t-shirt to offer participants. Not only were they interested but they were extraordinarily generous in their support. They involved one of their staff graphic designers in the layout of our poster and ad, they also helped with the survey form and perhaps most importantly they provided a $10 Bruin gold card- the campus debit card good for purchase of food, supplies, clothes, electronics- to every focus group participant. This added up to a $300 commitment.

While all of the organizations involved in this participated altruistically it became evident to me during the process that this information could be very valuable to them as well as the library. The OID people would get a profile of undergraduates and what they liked to use in the library. This could help them with future research or support decisions. The CHR staff gained experience in working with students rather than staff and this could be an area they could develop further. The

ASUCLA folks got a good idea of how the library study facilities were used and since study space is at such a premium at UCLA they take a large role in the provision of study space by keeping their eating areas open long hours. In fact they provided the only 24 hour study facility on campus at the time of this research.

It would be quite easy to modify focus groups and survey questions to gather information to help sponsors. This would further cooperation which is going to be more essential in the future. For example we could easily ask if students wanted food and drink while studying. Since the answer would probably be yes and we see the number one use of our facility as "study own material" then our student centers could offer late night study space, sell food and coffee, recover their costs, make a profit and relieve the campus of having to fund the library to stay open late or all night.

What are the implications for strategic planning? This depends on your general philosophy. If your organization is a customer service operation you tailor your operations to meet customers' needs. To succeed, a business has to provide what customers want. Of course university libraries aren't businesses. We provide a service and serve as a resource to students and faculty. We won't have to file Chapter 11 if we don't meet our customers' needs, but we will waste our scarce resources perhaps on the wrong services and collections.

Some clear examples emerged from the UCLA research which could have us re-orient our efforts. For example our students don't appreciate the classes we teach in how to do research but they do appreciate one on one reference help; there was a fairly high interest in term paper clinics, a service we did not offer; they don't care about our travel guides but they do want and use our reserve collection. In the context of strategic planning this information can translate into a goal. For example, with overwhelming user feedback that BI is not important to them but one-on-one reference is, we can write a goal that says something like "Maximize reference service delivery by providing assistance all hours the library is open. Redirect librarians from existing instructional efforts to strengthening the library's publications program." Regarding the lack of interest in travel guides we can develop a goal that says "Continue to meet the required reading needs of students by enhancing the reserve acquisitions budget. Reallocate existing funds where needed."

Strategic planning without benefit of stakeholder perceptions and needs will not accomplish all it sets out to do. Not only will the information gathered from focus groups and surveys help in goal setting, but it will help library management communicate concrete needs to university administrators. It will also help library management get "buy-in" from library staff as they set about ac-complishing the goals set in strategic planning. I intend to replicate the UCLA survey at DU and am in negotiation with three other academic libraries in Colorado to conduct identical focus groups and user surveys. Comparison across a broad range of library settings should provide an interesting opportunity to gather a large profile of the library expectations our students have. The focus group questions and survey forms presented here can be used in any university library as it embarks on a strategic planning exercise.

Acknowledgements

As mentioned in the text of this paper, support for the project was provided by a number of UCLA departments. I would like to acknowledge Karen Savlov and Marsha Coutin of Human Resources for conducting focus groups and preparing reports and transcripts. Dr. Larry Loeher, Director of the Office of Instructional Development, willingly provided budgetary support for questionnaire and flyer printing and for ads in the campus newspaper, *The Daily Bruin*. Margaret Snow of ASUCLA generously provided Bruin Gold Cards for focus group participants and helped design the posters, flyers and *Bruin* ads.

Ellen Watanabe of the Library's Graphic Arts Service did a tremendous job in designing the questionnaire. Student Assistant Kristy Mateer not only helped administer the questionnaire in classes but she also handed it out to students entering both libraries. Lou MacDonald developed the dBase program used in data analysis. And last but definitely not least, College Library Administrative Assistant Lista Ammirati scheduled all focus groups, coordinated production of flyers and questionnaires, input data from the questionnaires and prepared reports seemingly without trouble and almost instantly.

UNDERGRADUATE QUESTIONAIRE

On Library Use

We are gathering Information on how undergraduates use our library and what they like and don't like about our service, collection, hours, etc.

We want to be sure that we are providing the kind of library that meets your needs now and will be useful to you in the future. Please take a few minutes to answer this questionaire. Thank you for your comments

---

Personal Information

1. ❏ Freshman ❏ Sophomore ❏ Junior ❏ Senior
2. Age: ❏ Under 18 ❏ 18-21 ❏ 22-25 ❏ 26-30 ❏ 31+
3. Ethnic Background (optional)
   ❏ African-American ❏ Asian-American ❏ Caucasian
   ❏ Hispanic/Latino ❏ Native American ❏ Other _____
4. What is your major field of study?
   ❏ Humanities ❏ Social Sciences ❏ Sciences
5. Do you live in the dorms? _____ ❏ Yes ❏ No
6. If not, do you live within walking distance to UCLA? ❏ Yes ❏ No
7. Do you work while attending UCLA? ❏ Yes ❏ No
   If yes, how many hours/week? _____
8. Do you have a personal computer? ❏ Yes ❏ No
   If yes, do you use e-mail? ❏ Yes ❏ No
   Do you have an ORION account? ❏ Yes ❏ No

---

9. How often do you use the College Library?
   ❏ Have never used ❏ Once a quarter ❏ Twice a month ❏ Twice a week
   ❏ Once a year ❏ Once a month ❏ Once a week ❏ More often
10. When do you use the College Library? *(Check more than one if applicable)*
   ❏ First half of quarter ❏ At finals ❏ Throughout quarter
   ❏ Second half of quarter ❏ Between quarters ❏ NA
11. Why do you use the College Library? *(Check more than one if applicable)*
   ❏ To consult library materials ❏ To use computers to type papers
   ❏ To borrow library material ❏ For information and library assistance from library staff
   ❏ To make photocopies ❏ To check out reserve items
   ❏ To study own material ❏ Other _____
12. Put a **single** checkmark by beside the UCLA libraries and services you have used , and **two** checkmarks beside those you use regularly:

Towell Library Building
(central campus)
❏❏ Book Collection
❏❏ Reference Service
❏❏ Reserve Service
❏❏ Audio Listening
❏❏ Humanities Computing Lab
❏❏ Study Space
❏❏ Current Periodicals

University Research Library
(north campus)
❏❏ Circulation Desk and Book Collection
❏❏ Reference Service
❏❏ Periodicals Room
❏❏ Graduate Reserve Service
❏❏ Catalog Information Service
❏❏ Public Affairs Service
❏❏ Special Collections
❏❏ East Asian Library
❏❏ Microform Reading Service

Other Campus Libraries & Services

❑❑ Arts	❑❑ Geology/Geophysics	❑❑ Law
❑❑ Biomedical	❑❑ Graduate School of Management	❑❑ Map
❑❑ Chemistry	❑❑ Instructional Media Lab (Powell)	❑❑ Music
❑❑ Engineering/Math Sciences	❑❑ Language Lab (Powell)	❑❑ Physics

13. In using the College Library, how would you rate our

Service?　　　　　❑ Good　❑ Satisfactory　❑ Poor
　　　　　　　　　　　Comment _____

Lending Policies?　❑ Good　❑ Satisfactory　❑ Poor
　　　　　　　　　　　Comment _____

Book Collections?　❑ Good　❑ Satisfactory　❑ Poor
　　　　　　　　　　　Comment _____

Study Facilities?　❑ Good　❑ Satisfactory　❑ Poor
　　　　　　　　　　　Comment _____

Staff?　　　　　　❑ Instructive　❑ Helpful　❑ Too busy
　　　　　　　　　　　Comment _____

Hours?　　　　　　❑ Convenient　❑ Inconvenient

User Expectations for Quality Library Services Identified Through Application of the SERVQUAL Scale in an Academic Library

Danuta A. Nitecki

ABSTRACT

The SERVQUAL is an instrument which measures service quality, defined as the gap between the customer's expectations of excellent service and perceptions of actual service received. It is the basis for a questionnaire mailed to 564 users of ILL, reference, and reserve services in one research library. Initial findings, based on responses from 351 (63.6%) returned questionnaires, address the following questions: What is essential to users for delivery of excellent library services? What is most important to users in their evaluation of the quality of library services? How do expectations for quality services among library users compare to such expectations of customers in other service industries? Implications for management and for future research conclude the paper.

Academic libraries are service organizations. Increased demands for their accountability has fostered new interest in ways to measure library effectiveness. Traditionally, the quality of an academic, especially research, library has been described in terms of its collection, and most frequently measured in terms of the size of a library's holdings of published materials. Although theoretical arguments for user-based evaluation of libraries as information systems have been posed, few measurement tools have been developed for managers to gather accountability data based on userbased criteria for measuring quality of library services. Library user studies frequently focus on identifying information seeking behavior or on proclaimed user satisfaction. What have not been found in the library and information science literature are widely accepted user-based criteria for the measurement of library service quality and analytical tools to apply such criteria to the evaluation

Danuta A. Nitecki is Associate Director for Public Services at the University of Maryland at College Park Libraries, College Park, Maryland.

of a specific library's services. As managerial attitudes, including those developing in higher education, are shifting toward incorporating the customer perspective in planning and evaluating services, there is an increasing need to develop such tools for demonstrating library accountability. The purpose of this paper is to describe some of the initial findings from dissertation research underway to study the applicability in the library setting of an instrument developed to measure service quality from the customer's perspective.

Within the business literature, most of the attempts to identify and measure quality have emerged from analysis of products. Yet, the results of this research do not apply well to understanding service quality. Among the key reasons cited for this lack of transfer are three characteristics of services: intangibility, heterogeneity, and inseparability. Because services are intangible, are performances rather than objects, they seldom have precisely set specifications for uniform quality, and thus cannot be measured and verified as products. Because services are labor intensive, their performance frequently differ from provider to provider, customer to customer, and day to day; service personnel behavior is difficult to assure and thus service performance is heterogeneous and difficult to measure. Finally, because the production and consumption of most services are inseparable, service quality is not created on an assembly line and delivered intact to the customer, but rather quality occurs during the service delivery, the interaction between customer and the contact service provider.

A review of the business literature on service quality identified a body of writings from which three themes emerge:

- Service quality is more difficult for the consumer to evaluate than goods quality.
- Service quality perceptions result from a comparison of consumer expectations with actual service performance.
- Quality evaluations are not made solely on the outcome of a service; they also involve evaluations for the process of service delivery.[1]

In addition, the current business emphasis on improving and maintaining high quality of services, as defined by customers, will likely influence management practices throughout this decade, if not longer. The study in progress turns to findings in the business, and specifically marketing, literature, for potential guidance on evaluating service quality for application in a library setting.

The work of Parasuraman, Zeithaml, and Berry offer a particularly intriguing approach to measure service quality. They define service quality to be perceived by the customers, and to be "the extent of discrepancy between customers' expectations or desires and their perceptions."[2] They have developed a comprehensive measurement instrument, known as SERVQUAL, to measure perceived service quality, which is instrumental in the empirical confirmation of their conceptual model, the Gaps Model of Service Quality.

The model summarizes insights obtained from extensive interviews with executives and focus groups of consumers in four service categories reflecting a cross section of service industries (retail banking, credit card, securities brokerage, and product repair and maintenance).[3] The foundations of the Gaps Model are a set of four gaps which are the major contributors to the service-quality gap customers may perceive: Gap 1, the discrepancy between customers' expectations and managements' perceptions of these expectations; Gap 2, the discrepancy between managements' perceptions of customers' expectations and service-quality specifications; Gap 3, the discrepancy between service-quality specifications and actual service delivery; and Gap 4, the discrepancy between actual service delivery and what is communicated to customers about it.[4]

Parasuraman, Zeithaml, and Berry conceptualize service quality as a 5-dimensional construct, consisting of tangibles, reliability, responsiveness, assurance, and empathy. These are defined as follows:

Tangibles: Physical facilities, equipment, and appearance of personnel;

Reliability: Ability to perform the promised service dependably and accurately;

Responsiveness: Willingness to help customers and provide prompt service;

Assurance: Knowledge and courtesy of employees and their abiliity to inspire trust and confidence;

Empathy: Caring, individualized attention the firm provides its customers.[5]

Through several iterations, based on a series of studies, the authors identified 22 items to measure these five dimensions, universally across service industries. In its final form, the SERVQUAL consists of 22 pairs of statements, used once to measure the responding customer's expectations for excellent service in the service industry, and again to measure the respondent's perceptions of level of service of a particular service organization. Service quality is measured as a calculation of the difference in scores between corresponding items (perceptions minus expectations). In addition, the SERVQUAL questionnaire includes a section requesting participants to rank the importance of each of the five dimensions in evaluating a company's quality of service.[6]

The SERVQUAL instrument is designed to be broadly applicable to service industries, though the authors encourage replication to test the validity of their claim. Added data, specific to a particular service or specific to a providing service firm, can be added, though for comparative analysis the authors suggest segmented data gathering and analysis. The SERVQUAL has been used by researchers in replication studies in other service industries than those used by the developing authors (such as hospitals, leisure exercise facilities, and car rental agencies).[7]

A study was designed to validate the applicability of the SERVQUAL to evaluate the quality of library services in an academic library, and data were gathered in spring 1994. This paper, in addition to the brief description of the theoretical basis

for the instrument, will describe the study's modifications of the instrument for use in a library setting, the initial findings concerning what library users identified as their expectations for quality in the three services selected for study, and the rankings of importance among library users as compared to customers in other service industries.

No evidence has been found that the SERVQUAL has been used in an academic library setting prior to this study. Recently, a dissertation completed at the University of Toronto and a published article report the findings of a study of the quality of ILL services in Canadian public libraries which uses the SERVQUAL.[8] An investigation of the applicability of the SERVQUAL among special libraries is the focus of research funded by the Special Library Association.[9] The instrument offers a potential framework for identifying user-based criteria for evaluating library service quality, and a mechanism for evaluating it. If applicable, the instrument can be used by library managers to monitor, over time, the impact on users, of efforts to improve library services, and by library administrators to compare the quality of different library services. The SERVQUAL also is a potential tool for developing service quality benchmarks among comparable libraries. Although tools exist to measure user satisfaction with library services, no instruments have been identified which focus on measuring library service quality from the user's perspective. The successful applicability, among diverse service industries, of the SERVQUAL as a diagnostic tool for evaluating service quality by consumers attracts exploration of its usefulness to libraries. The research in progress undertakes such an exploration within an academic research library setting, using interlibrary loan, general reference and reserve services as a cross section of library services.

The focus of this paper is limited to an identification of user expectations for service quality of these three selected library services derived from initial analysis of data gathered for the validation study underway. Specifically, the following questions will be addressed:

1) What is essential to users for delivery of excellent library services? To what extent are these expectations different among users of different library services?

2) What is most important to users in their evaluation of the quality of library services? and

3) How do expectations for quality services among library users compare to such expectations of customers in other service industries?

METHODOLOGY

Most decisions made about this study's design were motivated by the primary purpose to validate a preexisting instrument for application in an academic library setting. A modified and expanded version of the SERVQUAL instrument was mailed to randomly selected samples of users of three library services offered during the spring 1994 semester at the main library of the University of Maryland at College Park (UMCP) campus.

The Setting

The UMCP Libraries is a research facility on the flagship campus of the state's system of higher education and serves a local population of over 35,000 students and faculty. McKeldin Library, the main library on campus and setting for the study, houses over half of the two million cataloged titles contained in the UMCP Libraries collections, a wide range of user services, as well as a mix of recently renovated facilities and space for study. Six separate and full service branch libraries on campus offer collections and services which emphasize architecture, art, chemistry, engineering and physical sciences, music, and undergraduate studies. During the academic year, the McKeldin Library is open every day except for major national holidays and weekends during academic breaks, totaling approximately 90 hours per week. The Library is visited by over half a million people annually.

Three user services offered in McKeldin Library were selected for the study. These are 1) interlibrary loan services, 2) general reference services offered at the main information service site, and 3) reserve services offered through the Graduate Reserves unit. These three services were selected for several reasons. They are basic services commonly offered in American academic libraries. They differ along key service categories, as classified by marketing researchers, offering a cross section of library services. In addition, each entails contact with library staff during the service transaction, facilitating identification of users for selection to participate in this study. Even though they are not an exhaustive representation of all library services offered in academic libraries, these three services were selected as a diverse setting for testing the applicability of the SERVQUAL instrument in academic libraries.

In McKeldin Library, general reference assistance is offered to anyone by reference librarians from an enclosed area behind the main information desk where student and paraprofessional staff offer general information assistance. During the spring 1994 semester, 2570 general reference queries were addressed from this McKeldin Library site.

The Interlibrary Loan (ILL) service offered to eligible UMCP researchers provides access to copies of books or articles not available on campus. The Libraries absorb costs to obtain materials not held within its collections unless the charges from the supplier exceed $15, in which case the user is billed full costs. During fiscal year 1994, 12,831 ILL requests were initiated by UMCP users, of which 9,958 (78%) were successfully filled.

The Graduate Reserves facility houses materials identified as recommended reading for upper-division undergraduate and graduate level courses, as well as photocopier machines, and seating for users at tables and individual carrels. Access to the reserve materials is limited to eligible library borrowers and is provided by paraprofessional and student staff. During the fiscal year 1994, 12,106 loan transactions from the Graduate Reserve collection occurred .

The Instrument

The questionnaire is organized into five sections. A separate version was prepared with minor word changes to focus on each of the three library services studied. In the first section, respondents are asked to rate on a 7-point scale, the degree to which they expect each service item described in 22 statements, to be essential for delivery of the excellent library service in question. They are also asked to identify and rate any additional expectations not addressed by the 22 statements. The same items are again posed in the third section of the questionnaire, in 22 statements about the particular service offered at the McKeldin Library and respondents are asked to rate the extent to which they perceive that each factor applies to the UMCP library service experienced. The discrepancy, at an item or dimension level, between user perceptions of service delivered and user expectations for excellent service is the basis for measuring service quality as defined by the SERVQUAL designers. In the second section, respondents are asked to allocate 100 points to five possible criteria of quality services, as a way to rate the importance users attribute to each service dimension in their evaluation of the service's quality. These three sections closely replicate the SERVQUAL instrument developed in other service industries.

The fourth section seeks information to describe the users' extent of experience with the service evaluated, their overall rating of its quality, their recollection of problems with it and their intentions to recommend it to a friend. The fifth and final section of the instrument asks several demographic questions including age, gender, and nature of academic activities.

A self-addressed stamped envelop and a cover letter identifying the purpose of the study, assuring confidentiality, and encouraging quick response, accompanied the mailed questionnaire. Note was made in the coverletter that completing the questionnaire should take approximately 15 minutes, an estimate derived from observing a couple of people who were asked to proof and complete the questionnaire. A teabag was also included with second mailings to non-respondents with a suggestion that in the time it took to brew and enjoy a cup of tea, the questionnaire could be answered.

Samples

Creating a sample frame was a unique process for each of the three services. Existing forms for ILL requests, completed between January 1 and March 15 were used to identify 237 unique ILL users from which a sample was randomly selected. Addresses for each was identified through the current online circulation patron file. No user records are kept routinely for reserve or reference service transactions. A form for manually processed reserve loans used during times when the automated system is unavailable was used for all reserve requests at the Graduate Reserve Desk between the same first three months of the year. Using this approach, 221 unique users of graduate reserve services were identified and a sample was randomly selected from the corresponding set of forms. This familiar form captured the user's name and social security number from which a current address was identified later in the online circulation patron file for those names selected for the study's sample.

Identifying users of the reference services posed the greatest challenge. The other two services both are offered only to eligible UMCP library borrowers and thus current mailing information is recorded in the automated circulation patron file. In contrast, general reference services are available to anyone using the library on-site, regardless of affiliation with the university. Typically no identification is ever requested from users of this service. For the purpose of this study, however, reference librarians were asked to have users complete a simple identification form prior to stating their general reference service query. It was clear that this procedure was not consistently followed; reference librarians complained that it was diffi-

Table 1: Returns by service group

Service group	# delivered*	# returned	% returned
ILL	n = 184	140	76.1%
Reference	n = 184	97	52.7%
Reserve	n = 184	114	62.0%
Total	n = 552	351	63.6%

* In each group, 188 questionnaires were originally mailed and 4 were returned as undelivered.

cult to have people complete the form during busy times. With repeated urging to have forms completed during the spring semester, a sample frame of 201 users was established and a randomly drawn sample used.

Because the primary purpose of the study was to validate an instrument, the sample size was determined by the number of variables tested; a minimum of 75 respondents for each service group was sought to perform the expected statistical analyses. A 40% response rate was projected and thus a sample of 188 users per service group was drawn. A total of 564 questionnaires were mailed April 8; one reminder with a second copy of the appropriate questionnaire was mailed to non-respondents on May 2. In each service group, four undelivered letters were returned. A total of 552 questionnaires were successfully delivered to eligible users.

FINDINGS

A total of 351 usable questionnaires were received by July 24, reflecting an overall response rate of 63.6%. The returns by service are summarized in Table 1.

Responses were coded, entered and analyzed using a software version of the Statistical Package for the Social Sciences (SPSSPC). For the data reported here, simple frequency counts and mean scores were calculated.

The findings reported here are based on a respectable response rate from a randomly drawn sample of users in one academic library setting. The samples were not randomly selected to reflect all academic libraries, nor even all users in the UMCP library setting. Therefore these findings should be viewed as exploratory of the research questions posed and not conclusive for academic library users in general.

The demographic data collected on the respondents are summarized in Table 2 and reflect a few patterns about the users of the three services selected for study.

ILL users are typically male graduate students using the service for their research; nearly half (47%) have used it six or more times at McKeldin Library, but most (62%) had not used ILL elsewhere. Approximately a fifth of the responding ILL users have experienced a service problem during the past year, two-thirds of which were satisfied with its resolution. Reference users are typically female undergraduates, using the service in support of course work, most having used the service five times or less and most (89%) had used reference services elsewhere than in McKeldin Library. Nearly a third (31%) experienced a problem with the service, with 61% not being satisfied with its resolution. Reserve users are typically female graduate students using the service in support of course work. Most (58%) have used it six or more times, a slight majority experienced reserve services elsewhere than in McKeldin. Nearly half (48%) have experienced a service problem, with 70% not satisfied with its resolution. Although nearly a third of all users participating in the study noted that they had experienced a service problem within the past year, and even though over half of these were not satisfied that the prob-

Table 2: Demographic and behavior characteristics of respondents

Characteristic	ILL	Reference	Reserve	Total
Gender (E6)				
(n =)	(139)	(96)	(111)	(346)
% female	48%	52%	60%	53%
% male	52%	48%	40%	47%
Campus status (E4)				
(n =)	(140)	(97)	(112)	(349)
% undergrads	9%	55%	4%	20%
% grad student	66%	33%	84%	62%
% faculty	16%	2%	3%	8%
% other	10%	10%	10%	9%
Activity supported (E3)				
(n =)	(139)	(97)	(110)	(346)
% course work	7%	45%	66%	37%
% research	68%	22%	12%	37%
% teaching	1%	0%	1%	1%
%other or mix	24%	33%	21%	26%
Times Service Used (E1)				
(n =)	(139)	(97)	(110)	(346)
% first time user	14%	19%	11%	14%
% used 2 -5 times	40%	46%	31%	39%
% used 6 -10 times	20%	21%	26%	22%
% used 11 or more times	27%	14%	32%	25%
Used Elsewhere (E2)				
(n =)	(139)	(97)	(110)	(346)
% yes	38%	89%	57%	58%
% no	62%	11%	43%	42%
Experienced Problems (D2)				
(n =)	(138)	(93)	(109)	(340)
% yes	22%	31%	45%	32%
% no	78%	69%	55%	68%
Satisfied with problem resolution (D4)				
(n =)	(30)	(33)	(47)	(110)
% yes	67%	39%	30%	43%
% no	33%	61%	70%	57%
Valued information (D5)				
(n=)	(124)	(91)	(97)	(312)
% yes	98%	89%	91%	92%
% no	2%	11%	9%	7%
Recommend service (D6)				
(n =)	(129)	(89)	(92)	(310)
% yes	98%	94%	89%	95%
% no	2%	6%	11%	5%

**Table 3: Mean score ratings of essential dimensions
expected for excellent library services.**

Dimension	ILL	Reference	Reserve	Total
Tangibles	3.799	4.596	3.809	4.024
Reliability	6.566	6.451	6.619	6.552
Responsiveness	6.310	6.356	6.399	6.351
Assurance	6.193	6.339	6.269	6.259
Empathy	6.180	6.268	6.149	6.195

(scale 1 = "not at all essential" 7 = "absolutely essential")

lem was resolved, most users rated the service quality fairly high. The vast majority of users of all three services found the information received as a result of the transaction to be valuable, and they'd recommend the service to a friend. The study is not designed to evaluate the specific services offered in the McKeldin Library, although user comments were shared with service providers.

Question 1: What is essential to users for delivery of excellent library services? To what extent are these expectations different among users of different library services?

Mean scores were calculated for responses to the items grouped by the five SERVQUAL dimensions to address the first question posed in this study. The results, as defined by service group, are summarized in Table 3.

Regardless of service, the pattern is the same for how essential each dimension is rated to be in users' expectations for excellent service quality. Consistently, reliability ranks highest, followed in descending order, by responsiveness, assurance, empathy, and tangibles. The mean score for the tangibles dimension in each service group is considerably lower than the average score for any other dimension; the tangible dimension score averages 4.0, while the score for any other dimension averages above 6.1.

Examining the expected essentialness rating of the individual 22 items contributing to the calculated SERVQUAL dimension ratings, a few interesting patterns emerge (see Table 4). The

average scores for all the items contributing to the four highest ranked dimensions — reliability, responsiveness, assurance and empathy — are above 6.0 (when scores are rounded) across all services. Regardless of service, the mean rating of item 12, "employees in excellent libraries' [service] units will always be willing to help users," was highest, averaging 6.75 on the 7-point scale anchored with 7 equal to "absolutely essential." This item contributes to the SERVQUAL responsiveness dimension, which appears second in importance among library users. It is, however, the only item rated over 6.7 among those in this dimension, while in the more highly ranked reliability dimension, three items (numbers 5, 6, and 8) rated 6.7 or more (when scores are rounded) among ILL and reserve service users. These three items, stated below, are also the highest rated items among reference users:

A5: When excellent libraries' [service] units promise to do something by a certain time, they will do so;

A6: When a user has a problem, excellent libraries' [service] units will show a sincere interest in solving it;

A8: Excellent libraries will provide . . . services right the first time.

Not surprisingly, the average scores for each item contributing to the tangibles dimension, regardless of service, is below 4.8. The first item, " excellent libraries' [service] units will have mod-

**Table 4: Mean score ratings of essential items
expected for excellent library services.**

Item	ILL	Reference	Reserve	Total
Tangibles:				
A1	3.612	4.292	3.568	3.786
A2	3.640	4.670	4.054	4.060
A3	3.857	4.784	3.770	4.086
A4	4.114	4.608	3.813	4.155
Reliability:				
A5	6.688	6.505	6.737	6.653
A6	6.707	6.792	6.746	6.729
A7	6.443	6.172	6.513	6.391
A8	6.676	6.567	6.717	6.659
A9	6.277	6.278	6.333	6.296
Responsiveness:				
A10	5.954	6.165	6.209	6.094
A 11	6.543	6.495	6.625	6.556
A12	6.721	6.814	6.723	6.748
A13	6.043	5.948	6.080	6.029
Assurance:				
A14	6.257	6.186	6.044	6.169
Al5	6.022	6.137	6.120	6.086
A16	6.205	6.443	6.225	6.278
A17	6.252	6.557	6.634	6.460
Empathy:				
A18	6.201	6.258	6.009	6.156
Al9	6.144	6.278	6.301	6.232
A20	6.115	6.330	6.027	6.147
A21	6.286	6.278	6.342	6.302
A22	6.095	6.196	6.036	6.104

ern-looking equipment," was rated lowest among users of each service, ranging from 3.6 among reserve and ILL users and 4.3 among reference users. The remaining three items contributing to this SERVQUAL dimension, noted below, are all rated between 3.6 and 4.8, with the slightly higher scores appearing among reference service users. This suggests that library users do not have high expectations for these items in the delivery of excellent services:

A2: The physical facilities at excellent libraries' [service] units will be visually appealing.

A3: Employees at excellent libraries' [service] units will be neat-appearing.

A4: Materials associated with the . . . services (such as pamphlets or statements) will be visually appealing in an excellent library.

**Table 5: Expectations for excellent services
beyond factors cited in the questionnaire?**

Question	ILL	Reference	Reserve	Total
A23 (n =)	(124)	(94)	(102)	(346)
% yes	20%	23%	24%	22%
% no	80%	79%	76%	78%
B8 (n =)	(108)	(88)	(93)	(289)
% yes	13%	20%	26%	19%
% no	87%	80%	79%	81%

As part of the study's examination of the instrument's face validity, users of the services studied were asked twice to confirm whether or not the SERVQUAL dimensions and statements adequately reflect expected service quality factors in a library setting. Question A23 appears at the end of the first section and asks respondents, "do you have any other expectations for excellent . . . services not asked thus far on this questionnaire?" This is followed by a structured opportunity to identify additional expectations and rank their importance in evaluating the quality of service. Later in the questionnaire, question B8, similarly asks "is there anything else not included in these five factors which you find important in evaluating the quality of . . . services?" Table 5 summaries the replies to these two questions.

The clear majority of those responding to both questions, indicated that there were no expectations beyond those identified in the questionnaire, adding support to the face validity of the instrument. Yet, since about a fifth of the respondents did note additional factors, a brief summary of what was indicated may be of interest in our exploration of what factors users expect of quality library services. Table 6 highlights specific expectations noted in response to these two questions, by service.

Qualitative responses to these questions reinforce the importance of some of the SERVQUAL dimensions incorporated in the questionnaire, such as reliability of information services, responsiveness of staff, empathetic attitude and behavior among service providers, and even elements of tangibles in study facilities and computerized equipment. These user added factors also suggest some specific service features which most operations could easily incorporate and thus perhaps respond to meeting customer expectations.

Question 2: What is most important to users in their evaluation of the quality of library services?

The second section of the questionnaire used in this study sought users' ranking of the importance of the five SERVQUAL dimensions in their evaluation of the quality of library services. The five dimensions were descriptively stated (B1 through B5) and respondents were asked to allocate a total of 100 points among them according to how important each is to the respondent. In addition, a question (B6) asked respondents to identify which one dimension from the five is most important to them. The results, by service group, are summarized in Table 7.

The pattern seen earlier when the SERVQUAL dimension expectation scores were calculated from the ratings of the 22 items is almost identical in the responses to these questions. With one exception, reliability ranks most important, followed by re-

Table 6: User expectations for excellent library services identified in addition to factors cited in the SERVQUAL instrument. (Questions A23 & B8)

by ILL users:
- expertise in locating materials requested; closer relations to librarians who have subject expertise
- better feedback when ILL request fails; at least every ten day status reports
- extended hours, at least once per week
- clear copy of citation with document
- more flexibility with loan period, especially when items arrive a few days before they are due back
- post expected turnaround/arrival date at time of request submission
- speed — prompt response and delivery
- notification by phone and/or e-mail
- request tracking information for pickup, returns, receipts, availability, and renewal
- high visibility of service within library
- electronic submission of requests, with internet access or via OPAC
- ask what language is needed at time of request submission

by reference users:
- printers with computers
- technology and modern equipment
- cleanliness
- quiet setting
- electronic files and various reference materials
- guides and instructions on using resources
- sympathetic and friendly attitude among staff
- well trained staff
- courteous staff
- staff who anticipate user needs
- access to updated information
- easily found items
- books on shelves if noted to be there

by reserve users:
- comfortable and adequate numbers of chairs and tables
- material to be there when needed
- helpful staff
- trained staff to locate items
- accurate, complete and timely processing of items to be placed in reserve collection

sponsiveness, assurance, empathy, and tangibles. The exception is seen in the responses by users of the reference service to the question asking to identify the single most important service feature. The percentage of reference users was nearly evenly split between rating responsiveness (37%) and reliability (32%) as most important. Their allocation of 100 points reflects a relative importance where these two dimensions are again closely ranked first and second with reliability averaging a 25.8 point allocation and responsiveness averaging a 24.6 point allocation. Reference users also deviate from the pattern set by the users of the other two library services in the importance given to the empathy dimension. Less than 4% of both ILL and reserve users identified this dimension to be most important, while 10% of the reference users prioritized this dimension over the others. Similarly, only 3% of the responding ILL users rated the assurance dimension as most important while 13% and 18% of the reserve and reference users, respectively, identified this dimension as most important.

Question 3: How do expectations for quality services among library users compare to expectations of customers in other service industries?

The SERVQUAL scale designers, Zeithaml, Parasuraman, and Berry, conclude from their studies that, regardless of service industry, customers universally rank reliability as the most important factor in their evaluation of the quality of service, and that tangibles rank least important.[10] Table 8 compares the results reported by these researchers from their studies across several service industries using responses from 1936 customers, and the responses by library users from the present study. This table summarizes the percentage of the 100 points allocated to each dimension by the respondents.

The combined library services data correspond very closely to the pattern found by Parasuraman, Zeithaml and Berry in their research across multiple service industries. This similarity suggests

Table 7: Importance of SERVQUAL dimensions in three library services

	Dimension Percentage of respondents indicating dimension is most important	Relative importance of dimension when users allocate 100 points
ILL users:	(n = 138)	(n = 140)
Tangibles	1%	8.543
Reliability	72%	38.779
Responsiveness	18%	23.257
Assurance	3%	16.600
Empathy	3%	12.721
Reference users:	(n = 92)	(n = 95)
Tangibles	1%	10.453
Reliability	32%	25.821
Responsiveness	37%	24.621
Assurance	18%	21.853
Empathy	10%	17.621
Reserve users:	(n = 109)	(n = 101)
Tangibles	1%	8.865
Reliability	62%	34.9 55
Responsiveness	21%	24.225
Assurance	13%	19.315
Empathy	1%	12.865
All users:		
Tangibles	1%	9.171
Reliability	58%	33.994
Responsiveness	24%	23.942
Assurance	10%	18.913
Empathy	4%	14.113

Table 8: Comparison of percent allocation of 100 points to five SERVQUAL dimensions cross multiple service industries

Dimension	Multi-service industries	ILL	Reference	Reserve	All library
	(n = 1936)	(n=140)	(n = 95)	(n =111)	(n=346)
Tangibles	11%	9%	10%	9%	9%
Reliability	32%	39%	26%	35%	34%
Responsiveness	22%	23%	25%	24%	24%
Assurance	19%	17%	22%	19%	19%
Empathy	16%	13%	18%	13%	14%

the claim by these researchers that the five SERVQUAL dimensions offer a core set of criteria important to customers in evaluating the quality of services, regardless of the service. It further suggests that people may have similar expectations when using library services than they do when they are customers of other services. The deviation from the pattern found among this study's users of reference services, where reliability and assurance receive a slightly different proportion of importance than found in evaluation of these dimensions among users of other services, invites further exploration about expectations for reference services.

Hebert's study of Canadian public library users of ILL services utilized the SERVQUAL scale. The mean score for expectations among these users is 5.65.[11] The present study's means score for expectations among the ILL users is 5.86. In both cases, expectations are fairly high. Hebert warns that these might be unrealistic expectations, distinguishing between ideal and adequate expectations. She suggests that the positive image surrounding the public library and the lack of ILL experience of most public library users might contribute to creating higher expectations for services. Academic library users were not novices to ILL in the present study, with 87% being repeat users of the service. Given a high level of expectation among these experienced users, there may be a positive effect of satisfactory experience on levels of expectation, an area for further exploration. The rankings of relative importance of service quality dimensions in the Hebert study of ILL users confirmed the findings from other U.S. studies[12]; the present study again reflects similar rankings.

SUMMARY AND FUTURE STUDY

The initial findings from data gathered in one academic library encourages further exploration of the applicability of the SERVQUAL instrument to measure customer evaluation of the quality of library services. These initial summaries of the data suggest that library users of ILL, reference and reserve services share core expectations with customers across service industries. They expect relatively high performance on dimensions of reliability, responsiveness, assurance and empathy in excellent library services. They have lower expectations for tangibles such as the appearances of facilities, staff and promotional materials. There is little difference in the ranking of these expectations among users of the three library services selected for study here, though slight variations found among users of reference services invite further examination.

Determining user expectations is only the first step in diagnosing the quality of library services. The SERVQUAL instrument offers a method to measure customer perceptions of service quality and has been validated for application in a number of service industries. The validation of the instrument for use in an academic library setting is yet to be completed and is the focus of the remainder of the study reported here in part. If applicable, the instrument could offer library managers a tool by which not only to evaluate user satisfaction, but also to identify specific areas where the quality gaps exist between what the users ideally expect and what they actually perceive to receive from library services. It could offer us a method by which to monitor progress in improving local services over time or by which to benchmark the quality of operations among a group of libraries offering similar services. Beyond the use of this instrument, the Gap Model of Service offers librarians a new approach to conceive of the value of their activities; it offers quantifiable methods by which to evaluate service quality based on customer-based criteria and by which managers can focus on the various organizational barriers needed to be overcome to improve their service quality. If the SERVQUAL instrument proves not to be fully applicable to the academic library setting, it still can offer managers an excellent starting point by which to begin measuring user expectations and to start thinking about service delivery from a customer's perspective.

NOTES

1. A. Parasuraman, V. A. Zeithaml, and L. L. Berry. "A conceptual model of service quality and its implications for future research." *Journal of Marketing,* 49 (4), (Fall, 1985), p. 42.

2. V. A. Zeithaml, A. Parasuraman, and L. L. Berry. *Delivering quality service: Balancing customer perceptions and expectations.* New York, The Free Press, 1990, p. 19.

3. Parasuraman et al. (1985).

4. Zeithaml et al (1990), p. 49.

5. A. Parasuraman, V. A. Zeithaml, and L. L. Berry. "SERVQUAL: A Multiple-item scale for measuring customer perceptions of service quality." *Journal of Retailing.* 64(1), (Spring 1988), 23.

6. A. Parasuraman, L. L. Berry, and V. A. Zeithaml. "Refinement and reassessment of the SERVQUAL scale." *Journal of Retailing* 67 (4), (Winter 1991), 420-450.

7. See, for example: E. Babakus and G. W. Boller. "An empirical assessment of the SERVQUAL scale." *Journal of Business Research.* 24 (1992) 253-268; J. M. Carman. "Consumer perceptions of service quality: an assessment of the SERVQUAL dimensions." *Journal of Retailing.* 66 (Spring, 1990) 33-35; J. L. Crompton and K. J. Mackay. "Users' perceptions of the relative importance of service quality dimensions in selected public recreation programs." *Leisure Sciences.* 11 (1989), 367-75; D. W. Finn and C. W. Lamb. "An evaluation of the SERVQUAL scales in a retailing setting." A*dvances in Consumer Research.* 18 (1991), 483-490; A. M. Ford. *A test of the generalizability of the SERVQUAL scale for assessing consumer expectations of service quality.* PhD Dissertation. University of Georgia, 1990; C. S. Hartshorn. *Service quality as perceived by public, private and voluntary sector managers of the leisure fitness industry.* PhD Dissertation. Indiana University, 1990; D. E. Headley. *Percived service quality: its measurement and relationship to consumer behavior in a medical care setting.* PhD Dissertation. Oklahoma State University, 1989; L. L. Johnson, M. J. Dotson, B. J. and Dunlap. "Service quality determinants and effectiveness in the real estate brokerage industry." *The Journal of Real Estate Research. 3* (1988), *21-36;* R. A. Kilkenny. At *your service: public sector service quality in monopolistic versus competitive envirnoments.* PhD Dissertation. University of Colorado at Denver, 1992; T. M. Steffen. *Determinants of service quality in health care organizations (nursing homes).* PhD Dissertation. University of Wisconsin — Milwaukee, 1992; A. Walsh. *Customer perception of quality of service and response to the complaint-handling process of a rental car company.* PhD Dissertation. Texas Woman's University, 1992; C. Webster. "Can consumers be segmented on the basis of their service quality expectations?" *The Journal of Services Marketing.* 3 (1989), 35-53; A. G. Woodside, L. L. Frey. and R. T. Daly. "Linking service quality, customer satisfaction, and behavioral intention." *Journal of Health Care Marketing.* 9 (December, 1989), 5-17.

8. Francoise Hebert. *The Quality of Interlibrary Borrowing Services in Large Urban Public Libraries in Canada.* PhD dissertation. University of Toronto, 1993; and Francoise Hebert. Service quality: An unobtrusive investigation of interlibrary loan in large public libraries in Canada. *LISR* 16 (1994), 3-21.

9. Marilyn Domas White, Eileen Abels, and Danuta Nitecki. *Measuring the value of information service in special libraries.* Special Libraries Association 85th Annual Conference, Atlanta, Georgia, June 13, 1994 (unpublished presentation); and Marilyn Domas White et al. Measuring Customer Satisfaction and Quality of Service in Special Libraries. Final Report to the Special Library Association, September 1, 1994.

10. Zeithaml, et al (1990), p. 28.

11. Hebert (1994), p. 13-14.

12. Hebert (1994), p. 16 .

TQM Training Leads to QC Circle Approach to Problem Solving

Jeanette N. McQuitty

ABSTRACT

The *Total Quality Management Assessment Inventory* by Sashkin and Kiser was administered to the Northeastern (Oklahoma) State University Library's User Services faculty and staff in the summer of 1993. Results revealed strengths and weaknesses and indicated a need for training. Training in TQM techniques for problem solving and process/product improvement led to implementation of a QC (quality control) circle approach to problem solving. Tools and techniques for using process control to reduce or eliminate causes of problems and a seven-step problem-solving model are discussed in this paper.

A student asks why the library is not open on Saturday and says having to wait until Sunday limits his weekend study. A very tall student points out that the one CD-ROM work station with Science Citation Index is "hidden" under the stairs. An agitated customer says that some of the microfilm reader-printers are always broken, and some users monopolize the machines that are working for long periods of time. Also, he complains that there isn't anyone on 2nd floor to help him, and if by chance someone is there, it would only be a work-study student and they don't know anything. Another student spends two hours on Thursday attempting to get one good copy for a research project with no luck and is still waiting for someone to help her get those copies made on Friday.

How does an academic library team operating in a university Total Quality Management (TQM) environment address the needs of its customers and the symptoms of problems that are registered by their complaints? According to industry research reported by Sinha in his article, "Winning Back Angry Customers,"

- An average customer who has a complaint tells nine or ten people about it; on the other hand, customers who have complaints resolved satisfactorily tell only five other people.
- A customer must have twelve positive experiences to overcome one negative experience.
- Most companies spend 95% of service time redressing problems and only 5% trying to figure out what went wrong to make the customer angry in the first place.[1]

Jeanette N. McQuitty is Director, User Services, John Vaughan Library, Northeastern State University, Tahlequah, Oklahoma.

Scholtes and Hacquebord in their "Guidelines for Quality," mirror the 14 points associated with TQM. The first two stress that the purpose of quality is for the customer:

- Quality begins with delighting the customers.
- The quality organization must learn how to listen to customers and help customers identify and articulate their needs.[2]

CONDUCTING A TQM MANAGEMENT ASSESSMENT INVENTORY

Before embarking on a program of improvement an organization must first assess "how well the unit works, in terms of the principles and practices of TQM." Marshall Sashkin and Kenneth J. Kaiser, who developed the *Total Quality Management Assessment Inventory*, tell us that an "important principle of TQM is that we must collect numerical, quantified information" to help us understand current conditions and problems and to decide how to improve things.[3]

The *TQM Assessment Inventory* has three parts: the first asks about the extent to which the various "tools" and techniques commonly associated with TQM are used in the organization and the extent to which training in their use is provided. The ten items on the inventory ask such questions as, "In this organization, to what extent do people...develop Pareto charts?" or "...participate in quality circles or quality action teams?" Five responses are possible ranging from "To little or no extent" to "To a very great extent."[4]

The second part examines the degree to which concern about quality for the customer is designed into management operations with fifteen items, such as, "In this organization...we constantly track customer satisfaction with our products or services" or "...those who do the production or service work are also responsible for assessing the quality of their finished work."[5]

The third part measures culture elements, "the values and beliefs people share and the practices that grow out of them." These are the type of questions addressed in the 24 inventory items: "In

this organization...people typically have the authority to make decisions and take actions in regard to their work responsibilities without higher level approval" or "...decisions must always be cleared and approved by higher levels prior to any action." Responses to the second and third parts range from "Does not apply" to "Applies completely."[6]

The *TQM Assessment Inventory* was administered to User Services personnel at Northeastern (Oklahoma) State University's Library/Learning Resources Center during the summer of 1993 before any in-depth TQM training had taken place. Employees, however, were familiar with the major TQM concepts and strategies.

The *TQM Assessment Inventory* provides a carbonless print-through form on which the individual circles a response so that numerical scores underneath are also circled. When the top form is removed, the numbers that appear are added to yield scores for each of the scales. Appropriate sets of scales are then added to obtain scores for the three parts of the inventory.

Almost all of the items in the use of "TQM Quality Tools and Techniques" part of the inventory received scores of 1 or 2, "to little or no extent" or "to a slight extent." The "Customer Quality" organizational scores mostly fell into the 6-8 score range, "some attention but little activity." Only one, "Quality work processes," fell into the 9-11 score range, "Moderate attention, some specific actions." "TQM Culture" organizational scores were the highest, either generally recognized or strong and stable. Two weak culture elements were "rewards for results" and "ownership."

Individual as well as average organizational scores were figured from the scoring form. All participants were able to plot their own personal scores in each of the three parts of the inventory and were able to compare them with the organization averages in another triangle. Individual and organizational scores were plotted on a scale to give a visual profile of TQM culture element scores.

PROVIDING TRAINING IN CUSTOMER SERVICE AND STAFF PRODUCTIVITY

It was obvious from the assessment inventory scores that little was known about using the TQM tools and techniques and that in the perception of the employees, not enough was being done to foster improved quality of service to customers. Although the organization's culture elements were generally in good shape, it was evident that without a feeling of ownership, the staff would not feel empowered to continue to improve the quality of customer satisfaction and their own productivity.

Repeatedly Scholtes and Hacquebord's guidelines for quality stress the importance of staff training and the collection of data to solve problems:

- In a quality organization, everyone must know his or her job.
- The quality organization uses data and a scientific approach to plan work, solve problems, make decisions, and pursue improvements.
- The culture of the quality organization supports and nourishes the improvement efforts of every group and individual in the company.[7]

Therefore, the staff decided that the next step involved training in the use of TQM tools and techniques as well as a new approach to problem solving.

All training was done by the university's College of Business and Industry faculty. The first training session, an overview of some of the most common, simple to use techniques for data collection and problem solving was presented by Dr. Steve Archer, assistant professor of technology at Northeastern State University. Subsequent training in TQM philosophy and techniques was presented in half-day workshops on four consecutive Mondays by Gene Roberts, a quality consultant who is also an assistant professor of technology at the university. An approach to problem solving and meeting customer needs was presented in a workshop by Dr. P. K. Ebert, associate professor of computer and information science. Training sessions provided some simple ways to approach problem solving in addition to the more complex data collection and analysis techniques.

Quality in an organization occurs when assignable causes of process variation or service variation can be identified and reduced or eliminated.[8] Quality is assurance that every time you order a hamburger and French fries from a McDonald's, they will have the same taste, crispness, texture and freshness. Quality occurs in a library when you can be assured that the book you are looking for is always where it should be, when the microform reader-printer makes readable copies every time you use it, and when the service at the reference desk is helpful, friendly, and accurate no matter who is staffing it. The problem TQM addresses is finding the causes of variation through process control and taking corrective action to reduce or eliminate variation.

TQM uses statistical process control (SPC), defined as "all those methods that use statistical principles and techniques for the control of quality. SPC is used in quality productivity improvement to monitor the way a process behaves and to make the process behave the way you want it to through timely feedback of information."[9]

Sashkin and Kiser tell us that "the tools and techniques are the least important aspect of TQM," an opinion held by Dr. Joseph M. Juran, a world-renowned quality expert. However, Sashkin and Kiser advise that "in order to apply TQM, people must effectively use at least two or three of the basic tools."[10]

FORMING QUALITY CONTROL CIRCLES FOR PROBLEM SOLVING

Another major tenet of TQM relates to teamwork:

Teamwork in a quality organization must be based on commitment to the customers and to constant improvement.[11]

Yoshida, describes the QC (Quality Control) circle as "essentially a movement toward changing the work environment from one in which employees work exactly as directed by managers to one in which employees who know the process best use their brains, abilities and ideas to improve the process." Members of the QC circle select problems that each member faces daily and that can be solved relatively easily. Gradually they move to more complex problems that are more demanding and require sophisticated problem-solving techniques. It is of the utmost importance that the problem can be solved and that the circle produce concrete results. When one problem is solved, the group moves on to a new problem while managing the implementation of earlier solutions.[12]

Before the User Services staff divided into QC circles, a general discussion was held on a symptom which is frequently observed among the library's users—"people in a hurry." The objective—"Reduce the amount of time spent because of human or machine error." A fishbone diagram was constructed to reflect the problems associated with the symptom. Before the next meeting, the causes over which the staff had no control were marked out of the fishbone and all customer suggestions, complaints or problems encountered during the week were noted.

The unreliability of the library's photocopying/ microprinting services surfaced as a major problem. A User Services QC circle was formed to address the problem of reducing human and machine failure on the library's copiers.

The basic TQM problem-solving tools can be as simple as gathering data on a checklist posted next to a microprinter (Figure 1). Once data is collected, factors can be sorted out and related to one another on the Ishikawa fishbone diagram which provides cause and effect analysis. The fishbone can be used as a guide for discussion, for brainstorming, for collecting or classifying data, and it can be used for any problem. Cause factors may include material, machine, measurement, man/woman, method and environment.[13] Possible

"fixes" that will lead to a reduction or elimination of the problem are also diagrammed. The "copier" QC circle gathered data on the microprinter checklist, classified it and transferred it to the fishbone diagram (Figure 2).

The Pareto diagram can be used to prioritize problems. It provides a method by which causes of a problem can be arranged by their relative importance. The basic idea of the Pareto is to visually point out and separate the "vital few" from the "trivial many." This separation allows the corrective action team to concentrate on "fixing" the "high drivers" for effective quality improvement. Eliminating one or two primary causes results in dramatic quality improvement with the least amount of effort.[14] The Pareto diagram in Figure 3 arranges the causes of copying failure by frequency (Figure 3).

The Seven-Step Problem-Solving Model, introduced by Dr. Ebert, provided a system to be used by the QC circles. The seven steps are:

• Recognize the Symptoms
• Define the Problem
• Brainstorm Possible Causes
• Analyze the Data
• Brainstorm Possible Solutions
• Reach Consensus
• Write Action Plan

The results of the work done by the QC circle on copiers using the problem solving model are shown in Figures 4-9.

TQM ASSESSMENT INVENTORY AFTER A YEAR OF TRAINING AND QC CIRCLES

The same Sashkin and Kiser *TQM Assessment Inventory* was administered in the summer of 1994, a year after the first one was taken by the User Services staff. The use of TQM "tools and techniques" showed an increase of 6.7 points; "customer quality" increased 1.5 points and "culture elements" 1.6 points.

The stronger the values and beliefs held in common by members of an organization or team,

```
PLEASE NOTE ANY PROBLEMS WITH THE MICROCOPIERS BY RECORDING THE DATE
ON THE APPROPRIATE LINE (ex. Lens sticks .. 3-1, 3-15, 3-18, 3-18)
```

Light intensity (condenser lens) doesn't match lens size . . .	
Bad film quality	
Auto load won't pull the film . .	
Door won't stay shut	4-10, 4-23, 5-3
Spring pops up when tray comes out	
Lens sticks	
Fast-forward/Rewind don't work . .	4-18, 4-27
Coin box rejects dimes	4-3, 4-6, 4-12, 4-18, 4-21, 4-27
Pos/Neg setting wrong	
Gray streaks on copies	
White streaks on copies	
Glass plates won't close	
Won't focus	
Fuse is out	
Bulb is out	
Out of paper	4-5, 4-12, 4-21, 4-26, 4-30, 5-1, 5-6, 5-15
Out of toner	4-10, 4-23, 5-10
Paper jam	
not enough paper	
black lever not on top of paper	
pulled in more than one sheet	
paper guide not in place (A/B)	
Operator error	
film loaded incorrectly . . .	4-3, 4-6, 4-8, 4-10, 4-15, 4-21, 4-28, 5-3, 5-10
improper focusing	4-23
carriage not aligned properly	
glass plates not closed . . .	4-17
masking prevented complete copy	4-13, 5-8
used coin other than dime . .	4-9, 4-13, 4-21, 4-27, 5-1
other_____	
other_____	
Other *complaints-long lines*	4-1, 4-3, 4-5, 4-8, 4-13, 4-15, 4-20, 4-23
Other " "	4-28, 4-30, 5-3, 5-4, 5-6
Other *complaints-no assistance*	4-9, 4-12, 4-17, 5-3
Other_____	
Other_____	
Other_____	
Required service call	4-12, 4-19, 4-29, 5-10

4/94

Figure 1: Simple TQM Tool: Gathering Data on a Checklist

Copying Failure

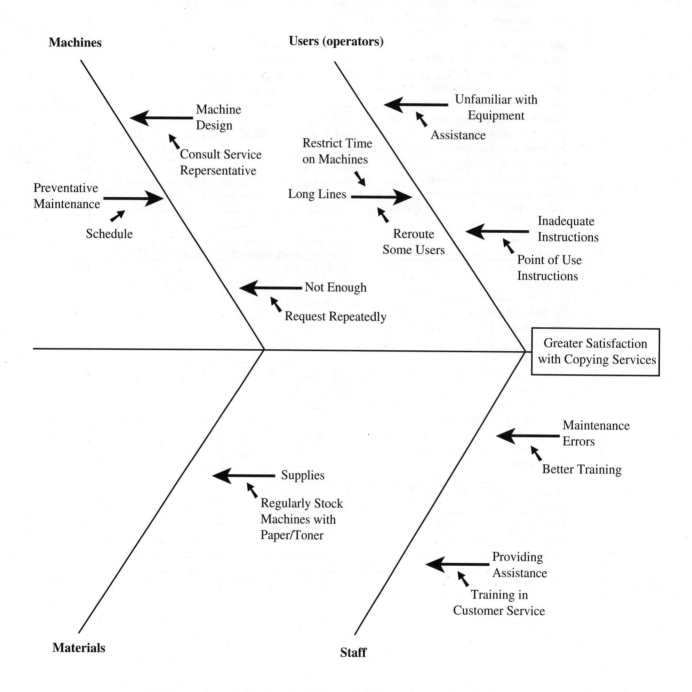

Figure 2: Ishikawa Fishbone (Cause and Effect Diagram)

Causes of Copying Failure

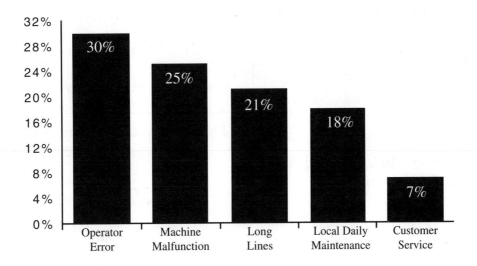

Figure 3: Pareto Diagram

the more influence they have over most people's actions. Culture elements such as rewards for results, fairness and ownership are perceived by a significant number of the library's User Services employees to be low, as they were in the first inventory.

However, the year of training in the use of TQM "tools and techniques" appears to have made a difference in the way staff look for causes of problems and find ways to reduce or eliminate them. They now have a problem solving model to follow, and the QC circle teamwork approach allows those employees who are closest to the problems the opportunity to find solutions and to implement improvements. A sense of "ownership" of their work comes from having authority over what they do.

Knowing the tools of TQM is not enough. The ultimate reason for TQM is a concern for what customers want and need. Building quality for the customer in services is the single most central concept behind TQM. With the tools and techniques now at the disposal of the staff, they can address the needs of their customers and the symptoms of problems that are registered by their complaints.

ACKNOWLEDGMENTS
The John Vaughan Library's Instructional Services Department assisted with illustrative material and provided the hard copy and the computer disk copy. Special thanks to Tracye Rowland.

SYMPTOMS

- Long lines at copy machines (both photo and micro)
- Customer complaints (both photo and micro)
- Frequent breakdowns (both photo and micro)
- Length of downtime (both photo and micro)
- Reluctance of customers to use microforms
- Reluctance of customers to use the older models (micro)
- Missing bypass keys (micro)
- Numerous refunds (both photo and micro)
- Reluctance of customers to share/take turns
- Bad copy quality (both photo and micro)

**Figure 4: Seven-Step Problem Solving Model
"Recognize the Symptoms"**

PROBLEMS

(A) Machine failure

(B) Operator error

(C) Poor quality of service

(D) Number of machines

**Figure 5: Seven-Step Problem Solving Model
"Define the Problem"**

POSSIBLE CAUSES

(A)
- Old machines
- Improper or inadequate preventive maintenance
- Machine design (including coin-ops)
- Inadequate copier supplies from auxiliary services.

(B)
- Users unfamiliar with equipment
- Inadequate instructions (point of use)

(C)
- Not enough assistance

(D)
- Too few machines

**Figure 6: Seven-Step Problem Solving Model
"Brainstorm Possible Causes"**

DATA TO GATHER

(A)
- Log service calls, noting what problems occur, and what was fixed.
- Chart failures over time.

(B)
- Log types and frequency of operator errors. Case study/direct observation: note problems encountered by a novice user.

(C)
- Log service calls, noting response time.

(D)
- Observe length of lines, frequency of lines.

**Figure 7: Seven-Step Problem Solving Model
"Analyze the Data"**

POSSIBLE SOLUTIONS

- Compile complaints and forward to Auxiliary Services.
- Improve signage and point-of-use instructions.
- Route Genealogy patrons to micro printer in Special Collections.
- Use micro printer in SPC when lines form on 2nd.
- Give Genealogy one of the old machines/ suggest they purchase their own.
- Modify opening or closing routine to include stocking machines/printers with paper, ink, toner and checking operational status.

Figure 8: Seven-Step Problem Solving Model "Brainstorm Possible Solutions"

PLAN OF ACTION

(A) Take action based on analysis of Minolta service logs.
(B) Develop a preventive service schedule.
(C) Set standard for the quality of copies placed on reserve.
(D) Transfer an older microform reader- printer to Genealogy.
(E) Recommend the purchase of a new reader-printer.
(F) Post point-of-use instructions.

Figure 9: Seven-Step Problem Solving Mo del "Writ e Acti on Plan"

NOTES

1. Madhav N. Sinha, "Winning Back Angry Customers," *Quality Progress* 26 (November, 1993): 53-54.
2. Peter R. Scholtes and Heero Hacquebord, "Beginning the Quality Transformation, Part I," *Quality Progress* 21 (July, 1988): 28.
3. Marshall Sashkin and Kenneth J. Kiser, *Total Quality Management Assessment Inventory* (Seabrook, Maryland: Docochon Press, 1992), 1.
4. Marshall Sashkin, *Total Quality Management Assessment Inventory Trainer Guide* (Seabrook, Maryland: Docochon Press, 1992), 10-11.
5. Ibid., 12-13.
6. Ibid., 14-15.
7. Scholtes and Hacquebord, "Beginning the Quality Transformation," 29.
8. Gene Roberts, *How to Use the Tools of Quality for Process/Product Improvement* (Broken Arrow, Oklahoma: Quality Consulting Service, n.d.), 17.
9. Roberts, *How to Use the Tools of Quality*, 28-29.
10. Sashkin and Kiser, *Total Quality Management Assessment Inventory*, 9.
11. Scholtes and Hacquebord, "Beginning the Quality Transformation," 29.
12. Kosaku Yoshida, "The Joy of Work: Optimizing Service Quality through Education and Training," *Quality Progress* 26 (November, 1993):31.
13. Roberts, *How to Use the Tools of Quality*, 51-52.
14. Roberts, *How to Use the Tools of Quality*, 83.

Five Steps to Redefining Workload:
An Academic Library Case Study in Progress

Eileen Wakiji and Kelly Janousek

ABSTRACT

California State University, Long Beach librarians are seeking out survival strategies for the 1990s. They are searching for methods to logically redefine librarian workload. The Library's Professional Development Committee, charged with finding solutions to workload problems, planned out a five-step pilot project. Planning and holding a retreat is step one. In step two, the Committee gathers data. Step three involves dividing the librarians into teams which have a specific focus-area assignment. In step four, the teams come to a consensus on their "favored" recommendation. In the final step, the librarians initiate the favored plan for one year.

During the 1980s, the California State University, Long Beach (CSULB) Library's evolution included the consolidation of three separate reference areas into one and the movement of all technical services librarians into public services. The management of access services, special collections and technical services departments was shifted to non-librarian personnel. Severe budget cuts and unreplenished librarian positions in the 1990s forced the librarians to look for innovative ways to redefine their workload again. The Professional Development Committee, as the guide, created a five-step plan to help locate answers to workload. How the five-steps evolved will be described in this paper.

BACKGROUND

CSULB is the second largest campus in the 23 California State University system with a student body of 26,277 and a faculty of 4,156 (Fall 1994). The University Library has a collection of approximately 1,060,000 volumes, 1.5 million microfiche, 36,837 media items and 5,861 periodicals.

Unique to the situation at CSULB is the organizational structure of the Library. Over the past ten years, the Library organization has gone through changes with the current Library Director (Britton 1988). The Library Faculty structure, today, is based on instructional faculty models. Up until 1993, librarians were divided into four subject

Eileen Wakiji is a Senior Assistant Librarian and Kelly Janousek is an Associate Librarian at California State University, Long Beach, California.

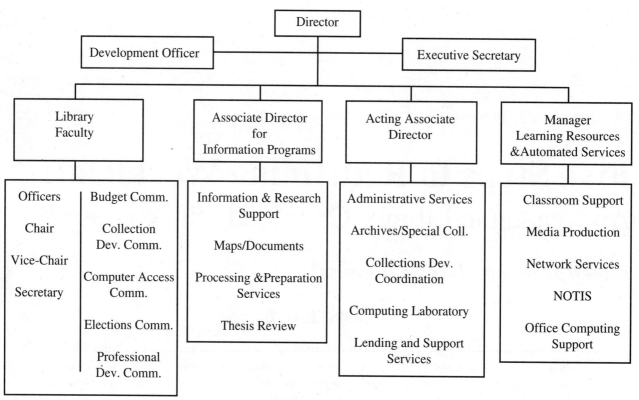

Figure 1

groups: Humanities, Business, Social and Behavioral Sciences and Science, each led by a group chair (Whitson 1987). This changed in 1993 with the librarian attrition rate. When numbers decreased dramatically, the librarians decided to forgo the groups. It was felt that there were not enough librarians to divide into four groups and we would try to make decisions as one group, the Library Faculty. This faculty utilizes a faculty senate prototype as its governance. Policies and procedures are developed through five governing committees Budget, Collection Development, Computerized Access, Elections, and Professional Development. These three member committees are accountable to the Library Faculty senate. The Library organization is seen in figure 1.

Our workload problem developed in trying to meet traditional expectations with snowballing technology. Librarians had been questioning how to survive continual budget cuts and lost profes-

sional positions just to meet these demands. This questioning started the process towards redefining workload.

PLAN

Redefining workload actually commenced because of various proposals to rewrite our governance document, the University Library Faculty Constitution. During one of our discussions, the Library Director inquired if it would be advantageous to go off campus to discuss workload issues. The Library Faculty agreed that it would be desirable and the importance of advance planning for such an effort was articulated. To give structure to the planning, the Library Faculty charged the Professional Development Committee with the organization of the "retreat" (VanGundy 1992, 97-119). This committee first created a survey to determine what issues were to be accomplished and when the librarians were available for the retreat. The survey results showed a preference to commence laying the foundation for team building and relearning how to work with each other in a downsized environment. The retreat was held with an outside moderator who piloted us through team building exercises. After completing the Team Work and Team Roles Inventory (Mumma 1992) each librarian discovered where they fit in the work cycle. This created an awareness as to how the group dynamics were working or not working. It showed why some committees could get work done and why others could not. The team preferences seemed to be playing a part in our work production, or lack thereof. It was one explanation for the feelings of frustration felt by some librarians in not being able to get things accomplished.

Nine months later in May 1994, the Professional Development Committee made arrangements for another retreat. Prior to the retreat, the committee conducted a librarian workload retreat survey and the results gleaned answers to questions such as—What is workload? What are our problems with workload? What can't you get done and what do you not want to do? The committee once more relied on an outside facilitator and an off campus locality. The facilitator guided the librarians through exercises to reinforce team work and to look at our role within the library.

In retrospect, the follow-up to the first retreat was riddled with delays. It forced us to relearn team work and team building in our second retreat when we actually may have been ready to start specific workload issue discussions.

STEPS

Since one of the wrap-up comments of the second retreat requested an expeditious follow-up, the Professional Development Committee's involvement continued. The committee brainstormed about follow-up and what needed to be done. They decided that the librarians could work in teams because of their retreat experiences. They discussed reviewing the literature for

workload and downsizing ideas, setting up potential workload arrangements, and proposed that teams present "radical" ideas to test for one year. In trying to come up with the process, the five-step plan evolved. This plan seemed workable and looked like the "quickest" approach to our burdensome workload problem. The reference desk is staffed with four librarians for the major portion of the day, thus it is next to impossible to get all librarians together. By breaking into smaller teams of 6 instead of the full faculty, it was then possible for the librarians to meet.

The first step had been accomplished with the retreats. The second step had the Professional Development Committee locating in-house materials that had been developed over the years concerning workload divisions. This step also included looking at articles recently published on redefining reference models and other issues that affect our daily environment. The third step divided the librarians into teams to work on a program area assignment. The fourth step involved the teams creating recommendations as answers to the workload program areas of collection development, reference and instruction. This step included the selection of a workable recommendation for each program area. The final step proposed the testing for one year of the selected recommendations.

Because of the governance process, the Professional Development Committee had to present their five-step plan before the Library Faculty to confirm its merits. The Library Faculty did agree that the areas to start discussions on were Collection Development, Instruction and Reference. The librarians' viewpoint was that these areas were their responsibilities and they should be the ones making the decisions. The Library Faculty granted the committee the authority to continue with their planning efforts.

Since the first step had been completed, the Professional Development Committee gathered pertinent documents to help in the decision-making process. Items for the decision making process included: "Competencies Needed By Librar-

---

COMPETENCIES NEEDED BY LIBRARIANS

Reference Skills:
Knowledge of core collection (see separate list called Standard Base of Knowledge Sources) and of specialized sources in assigned subject areas
Ability to work well with patrons, making them feel comfortable in the Library, and helping them to determine their needs (reference interview)
Ability to determine when to refer patrons to colleagues or to sources outside the library

Teaching Skills:
Ability to develop (in coordination with teaching faculty) and present library instruction at level appropriate to the audience
Ability to produce handouts (for class use or general library use) and media type aids to enhance instruction

Searching Skills:
Understanding of all electronic systems in reference area: OCLC, INNOVACQ, COAST, CD-ROMs, etc.
Ability to advise patrons about use of CD-ROMs, self-service searching, mediated searching
Ability to do mediated searching in assigned subject areas

Collection development skills:
Ability to evaluate collection and select book and non-book materials (in consultation with teaching faculty) in assigned subject areas
Ability to analyze needs for changing curriculum and work with vendors to refine approval plans

Service skills:
Willingness to do one's share of library and university committee work
Involvement in professional organizations (library or subject-oriented groups)

Research skills:
Ability to engage in research and scholarly activities that would be of benefit to the library, the university or the library profession
Willingness to share new insights and skills with colleagues

General skills:
Ability to communicate effectively both orally and in writing
Ability to analyze problems, to organize information and to produce results in a timely manner
Knowledge of library procedures and policies
Willingness to keep current on developments in library world through workshops, training, reading of professional journals, etc.
Ability to work cooperatively with library administration, faculty and staff to promote what is best for the library

(Library Faculty Meeting, March 16, 1992)

Figure 2

ians," an internal document listing expectations of each faculty member of the Library (figure 2); an internal study called the Librarian Staffing document developed in 1991 to establish the number of librarian positions needed; the Librarian Workload Retreat Survey Results, previously mentioned, a document surveying the Library Faculty on workload expectations; and a list of concerns over program areas that the Library Director had expressed. The Professional Development Committee also included appropriate articles (when found) for team discussions. While reviewing some of these documents, it became evident to the committee that in three years our situation had changed dramatically. In 1991, the subject groups had documented and attempted to obtain more librar-

CSULB Has 52%
Fewer Librarians Today
Than It Had Ten Years Ago

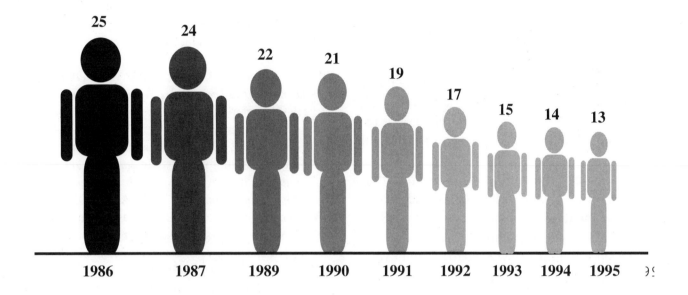

Figure 3

ian positions. In 1994, the librarians were meeting because some of the original librarian positions had gone unfilled and were likely to remain that way (figure 3). Hence, the teams were creatively trying to redefine what could be done with fewer librarians.

The third step served to begin the work by using the skills learned at the retreats. The committee provided each librarian with brief instructions and a timetable, as well as, the team assignments. The Professional Development Committee divided the Library Faculty into three teams with a convener whose function was to make sure the teams met. The committee could have established team formation by voluntary sign ups but the decision was made to assign Library Faculty alphabetically to specific teams. When looking at each teams' makeup it became apparent that an

optimum balance had been struck according to our Team Work and Team Roles Inventory (Mumma 1992) survey. A program area was not delegated to a specific team but by luck of the draw. This use of chance seemed to be the most innovative way to delegate these issues without any preconceptions.

Currently, the teams have convened and are working on their recommendations. Team ideas have been reported once at a Library Faculty meeting.

SUMMARY

The five-step plan has been completed up to this point. In the months to follow the librarians will be completing the fourth and fifth steps of the plan. Each team will be defining and explaining the components of their program area, what constitutes the program area as it is today, and what should be done and or not done in the future of that program area. The teams have to decide how its program is impacted by the various academic disciplines, external campus and community environment and resources available. Another concern will be how much should librarians be alike and how much should they differ in these program areas. Each team will make recommendations of how their area should work. These will include potential resolutions to the workload issues according to our current situation. The Library Faculty will then convene and determine the favored recommendation from each team. The group will then test pilot the program areas' recommendations for one year to see if they are viable options.

This case study could seem premature without the final results but we felt other libraries may be struggling with some of these same issues. Since our review of the literature regarding workload produced very little, we wanted to add our experiences to the profession.

FUTURE

Nothing is etched in stone and with the dynamics of the information dichotomy this may only work for one year before workload issues again change.

REFERENCES

Britton, H. H., 1987. "Interactions: a library faculty matrix organization and a public policy and administration program." *The Reference Librarian* 20: 187-20.

Mumma, F. S. 1992. *What makes your team tick? Team-Work & Team-Roles.* King of Prussia, Pa: The HRD Quarterly; managed by Organization Design and Development, Inc.

VanGundy, A. B. 1992. "Conducting and facilitating problem-solving retreats." In *Idea power: Techniques & resources to unleash the creativity in your organization.* New York: AMACOM.

Whitson, H. 1987. "CSU Librarians chapter spring workshop: Who's in charge—or what's going on here? CSU library governance/structure." *California State University Librarians Chapter Newsletter*, 1987, no. 3:1-4, 11-13.

Toppling Hire-archies:
Support Staff and the Restructured Library

Kathlin L. Ray

ABSTRACT

Whether by design or default, libraries have become increasingly dependent on paraprofessionals and support staff. Driven by technological change and budget reductions librarians must now rely on staff to manage complex and highly skilled activities in an ever-changing work environment. Libraries' urgent demands require staff members who feel enlivened rather than threatened by challenge and constant change. Transforming libraries into flatter, more team-oriented organizations requires staff who will thrive in and help build these new structures. This paper critiques typical hiring practices and recommends that librarians rethink the way they recruit and hire library staff.

Today's academic libraries are struggling to become more flexible, adaptive and innovative organizations. In response to diminishing budgets, new technologies and ever-increasing user demands, libraries are flattening hierarchies, streamlining workflows and empowering staff. But amidst the noise and confusion of reconstruction, one important area has been overlooked: the recruitment and hiring of support staff. In light of libraries' escalating dependence on staff this is a surprising oversight.

Library managers recognize the importance of examining a wide spectrum of abilities and attitudes when hiring librarians. With support staff, however, we too often revert to an outdated scientific management style and focus on technical

skills. When a staff position opens up we tend to overlook the big picture—the job within the context of the library's new culture—and zero in on specific tasks and duties. A staff job advertisement ordinarily lists requirements such as clerical-level computer skills and previous library experience. State Civil Service requirements, our institution's employee classification systems, union rules, and, yes, even the application forms themselves collude in an effort to keep us in a rigid, narrow, task-oriented state. (A classic case of administrative codependency.)

But, if **we** focus solely on tasks and procedures when hiring, we may find ourselves with staff who do the same; task-specific employees who actually prefer routine, repetitive jobs, who have few

---

Kathlin L. Ray is Head, Circulation/Reference Librarian, University of the Pacific, Stockton, California.

aspirations for personal growth or increased responsibility.[1] Yet, the type of person today's library needs to attract does not want a dead-end, task-oriented job. And because we rarely mention the elements that appeal to these kind of workers - the opportunities for growth, innovation and participation - they rarely apply.

Few libraries actively promote their dynamic new cultures at the support staff level. Yet, the health and vibrancy of the restructured library depends on the full participation of **all** its employees, not just its librarians and administrators. The dismantling of our old hierarchal structures has been accompanied by a transformation in organizational values.[2] Rather than expecting obedience and strict production quotas from lower level employees, many organizations now desire autonomous workers who value individual achievement yet also recognize the need to work with others toward a common vision and mission. This ideology is what David Limerick and Bert Cunnington call "collaborative individualism".[3] Libraries need staff (and librarians) who are "multifaceted and ambidextrous", staff able to work with and across other functions and units.[4] If we want to attract *this* type of person to our library, we need to examine and rethink our current methods of recruiting and hiring.

JOB DESIGN

It begins with job design. Before filling a vacancy, most of us reexamine the job and the way it functions within the library. But we usually concentrate on tasks and functions, technical issues or reporting structures and seldom look beyond the departmental niche of the position. We don't ask a very important question: does this position provide meaningful work for an intelligent, responsible person - particularly if we ask for a college education in the job requirements? Will it provide opportunities to grow, to exercise judgement, to develop interpersonal skills?

If libraries want innovative and responsible employees, staff jobs must be designed with these factors in mind. Staff positions should promote the use of critical thinking skills and push employees to look beyond departmental boundaries. Enlarged, more complex jobs are an integral part of a healthy restructured library. Research shows that the "judicious expansion" of certain jobs contributes to higher productivity, lower absenteeism and increased job satisfaction.[5] Moreover, limiting employees to routine and repetitive tasks discourages initiative and tends to produce apathetic and uncommitted employees.[6] Menial tasks, therefore, should be automated or contracted out, performed by student assistants or even dropped altogether. Motivated, committed and productive staff are energized by jobs that provide challenge and responsibility.

A "restructured" job description can no longer simply describe specific duties and narrow responsibilities. It needs to include a description of the library's "culture" or social system, its informal groups, the position's possible interactions with others. Potential employees will then begin to understand that the commitment expected of them extends beyond certain tasks. In actuality, they are "being asked to become a member of a culture, to commit a larger part of [themselves] than is usually requested."[7]

DETERMINING HIRING CRITERIA

After examining the job and preparing a job description, librarians often continue to rely on scientific management principles when developing hiring criteria. We **say** we desire diversity and that we value the cross-pollination of disparate ideas and viewpoints yet we sabotage our own efforts to gain these benefits by compartmentalizing and circumscribing staff positions. We say we want staff who are self-starters, team players, people committed to the library's mission—but when it comes down to the final hiring decision we too often value established skills over aptitudes. Yet, the personal attributes of a successful "restructured" worker are more crucial to a productive workforce than any technical competencies or library-specific skills. We can train people to search OCLC. We can teach them computer applications and library esoterica.[8] But it is very difficult to teach "innovation", "flexibility" or "holistic thinking" to staff who were hired to follow rigid rules and instructed not stray from procedure.

Now, there are a few "hard" skills and other external qualifications that may be essential for a new staff member to have: basic keyboard skills, for example. Supervisory experience or the ability to deal calmly and effectively with the public may be essential qualifications; but not knowledge of specific library utilities or software packages or even library experience.

A preference for hiring people with a library background can actually work against the library's best interests. The fresh perspective offered by bright, enthusiastic neophytes more than compensates for their lack of library know-how. They lend new insight and energy to a library's procedures and services. Of course, the knowledge and experience of seasoned library workers can be a terrific boon - if they embrace the values and understand the demands of the library's evolving culture. Some have trouble making this adjustment and use their past experience as a shield against new ideas: "I've worked in libraries for 20 years and we've never done it this way!" Hiring staff based on "restructured" criteria will help us choose people who will thrive in a more fluid organizational environment.

RECRUITING

After determining the hiring criteria, libraries put an ad together which customarily lists three things: the required technical competencies, the hours, and the wage. It's very straightforward— this is the job, these are the hours, this is the pay. There's only one problem: what's the attraction? Or more specifically, is this sort of job ad likely to attract the kind of person needed by today's library? There's no mention of growth opportunities or challenge. Not a clue that the position might actually provide fulfilling or meaningful work. No hint that the library is an integral part of the university's educational mission or that libraries play a vital role in an expanding global electronic information network. Instead, our job ads perpetuate the stereotypical view that library work is primarily clerical in nature.

If libraries want to recruit people who value stimulating and challenging jobs they need to emphasize the rewards of working in the library. Fortunately, many self-motivated, committed workers place a high value on psychological rewards and are not primarily motivated by money.[9] This is not an excuse to underpay library staff; it simply means that even a library that can't pay top dollar should be able to attract workers who seek responsibility and growth. By basing recruiting efforts on the non-monetary rewards of the job, libraries will be more likely to attract people with the attributes we've just described. (And who knows better than librarians the importance of non-monetary rewards.)

REVIEWING APPLICATIONS

Librarians' subliminal dependence on old scientific management theory is also evident in the way we evaluate job applications. When sorting through a pile of forms, the standard procedure is to rate applicants according to their education levels, job experience and past accomplishments. We set aside applications from people with service backgrounds, favoring those with clerical or technical experience. Continuing in this logical, methodical manner, we finally choose a handful of candidates—most of whom would be highly successful in a 1960's library. But we're now in the 1990's and we need to identify employees who will become productive members of a still-evolving organization.

Admittedly, it's just about impossible to deduce someone's aptitudes or personal characteristics from an application form. But this doesn't mean we have to resort to a mechanistic or checklist approach. Take an applicant's job history, for instance. A careful and thoughtful look at past experience can provide us with valuable clues to an applicant's strengths and gauge their suitability to our organizational environment.

When reviewing an applicant's employment history the most important consideration is whether the skills acquired in previous jobs will transfer to a library setting. I'd be willing to bet that most librarians assume that a technical or clerical background is superior to a service background. For example, who would you say has more transferable skills, a clerk or a waitress? Most of us would vote for the clerk but if hiring criteria are grounded in the requisites of the restructured library, it is the waitress who actually has more of the skills we're looking for. A *good* (note that qualifier) waitress (or waiter) possesses well-developed social skills and a strong customer service orientation. She has to prioritize, manage a myriad of rapidly changing demands and work effectively with other constituencies such as hostesses, buspeople, and cooks. These skills - thinking in terms of the customer, juggling priorities, and building effective work relationships -are vital to the restructured library.

As for the clerk or technician: computer and filing skills may be transferable but are they all that important? Most library computer systems and filing rules are fairly easy to learn. What other transferable skills would this type of worker possess? It is unlikely that a clerk would have had many decision-making responsibilities. A technician is not usually conditioned to collaborate with others or think in terms of the customer. Sometimes a clerical or technical background can produce workers who are too detail-oriented and unable (or unwilling) to see the larger purpose of their task. If they are accustomed to working in a non-interactive environment they may have weak social skills and have difficulty working in a team structure. By carefully and imaginatively analyzing an applicant's past job experience we will be more successful in selecting a group of candidates with the strengths and attributes we desire.

INTERVIEWING

After working through the applicant pool, a handful of candidates are invited to interview for the position. Most managers know the basics of interviewing: put the candidate at ease, ask open-ended questions, have the candidate do most of the talking.[10] In a typical staff-level interview we tend to ask questions about the candidates' experience, skills and training. However, hiring a person who will be successful in a restructured library involves determining predispositions and attitudes. The interview provides a library manager with an opportunity to learn more about these factors.

If we are trying to assess candidates' attitudes, capacities and abilities we need to ask a different kind of question. For example, we usually ask about computer skills but do we also ask about a candidate's ability to work across functions? Do we ask the candidate how she makes decisions? Do we attempt to ascertain his effectiveness in a continually changing work environment or her ability to adapt to new technology? Do we ask candidates to explain how they tackle work-related problems?

Although the primary purpose of the interview is to assess the suitability of a candidate, we might also use the interview to educate him or her. If we explain our library's culture and lay out expectations and responsibilities, potential employees can decide if they will be comfortable in our organization's environment. The candidate who is fully aware of both the challenges and rewards of working in our restructured library can make a better employment decision.

CONCLUSION

In conclusion, I freely admit that this revisionist view of the recruitment and hiring of support staff is not without its problems. There are significant obstacles to overcome before libraries can implement these suggestions. Civil Service requirements and union rules are two rather obvious and formidable stumbling blocks. Less formidable but still frustrating is the lack of input many libraries have in staff employment issues. Without the freedom to write their own job ads, for example, these libraries have little control over the content.

Finally, a fully "restructured" organization is still more dream than reality for most college and university libraries. Although the trend toward flatter, more participative structures continues to grow, it's not happening overnight. Not only are bureaucratic structures by nature slow to change but not every library manager embraces this vision of a more autonomous, empowered staff. A library manager interested in change might simply examine established hiring procedures and begin asking questions. It is only by our willingness to rethink and reevaluate current assumptions and practices that we begin to lay the groundwork for change.

NOTES

1. Harold M. F. Rush, *Job Design for Motivation* (New York: The Conference Board, 1971), 28-29; Chris Argyris, *Integrating the Individual and the Organization* (New Brunswick, N.J.: Transaction Publishers, 1990), 301-304.
2. See, for example, Rosabeth Moss Kanter, *When Giants Learn to Dance* (New York: Simon and Schuster, 1989) and David Limerick and Bert Cunnington, *Managing the New Organization* (San Francisco, Jossey-Bass, 1993).
3. Limerick and Cunnington, *Managing the New Organization*, 112-3.
4. Kanter, *When Giants Learn to Dance*, 364.
5. Argyris, *Integrating the Individual and the Organization*, 228-240; Jack A. Siggins, "Job Satisfaction and Performance,"*Library Trends* 41 (Fall 1992): 311.
6. Argyris, *Integrating the Individual and the Organization*, 54-56, 80-81.
7. Ibid., 238.
8. Leigh Estabrook, Lisa Mason, Sara Suelflow, "Managing The Work of Support Staff," *Library Trends* 41 (Fall 1992): 236.
9. Argyris, *Integrating the Individual and the Organization*, 63, 250.
10. For help with both generalities and specifics see, Richard Rubin, *Hiring Library Employees: A How-To-Do-It Manual,* (New York: Neal Schuman, 1993) and Robert Half, *Robert Half on Hiring,* (New York: Crown Publishers, 1985).

Comparable Rewards:
Librarian Career Paths

Maralyn H. Schad

ABSTRACT

Over twenty years ago, ALA adopted a statement of policy supporting comparable rewards for librarians in both administrative and service positions. In so doing, ALA supported the concept that librarians need not seek administrative positions in order to advance in their careers; they should be eligible for advancement within their various areas of professional specialization. This paper reviews the limited literature on comparable rewards and concludes that this concept has not been broadly implemented in academic libraries. One possible cause is in the way academic librarians tend to view success—advancement through the administrative hierarchy. This attitude contrasts sharply with that of academic faculty from more collegially structured teaching departments. Success, in that environment, is viewed more in terms of research and teaching, and administrative work tends to be seen as an onerous responsibility, at best. The implications of this difference are explored. Finally, this issue takes on additional significance in light of trends toward organizational change and management styles that emphasize empowerment.

Awhile back I was working in the library of a small school that trained young people to be fashion merchandisers and designers. One day in a "heart-to-heart" talk with one of our students, we reached the part of the conversation in which I stated that no, I had never wanted to be a fashion designer; she looked at me with total disbelief. From her young perspective, fashion designing was so obviously glamorous and desirable that the only reason all were not trying to become designers was that they were realistic enough to know that they did not have the talent.

I am reminded of this conversation whenever I talk with colleagues or look at the literature on "advancement in librarianship." Librarians seem to assume that advancing in one's career means accepting administrative responsibilities. Consider Leslie M. Kong and R.A.H. Goodfellow's glum conclusion.

The organizational structure of academic libraries adheres closely to the traditional bureaucratic pyramidal model.... Those not interested in management positions but wishing to advance within the organization have limited career opportunities.[1]

Maralyn H. Schad is the Education/Communication Librarian at Ablah Library, Wichita State University, Wichita, Kansas.

Why does our profession tend to recognize and reward only one career path, i.e., administrative advancement? Is this tendency related to the professional inferiority complex that is frequently attributed to librarians? Why should comparable rewards for nonadministrative expertise be developed? What difference does it make anyway? This issue is the focus of this paper.

When I began exploring this issue, I was surprised to discover that the American Library Association had supposedly resolved this issue over twenty years ago when it directed the Office for Library Personnel Resources to develop a statement in support of "comparable rewards." That statement appeared as Paragraph 19 of *Library Education and Personnel Utilization*. It was worded in part:

> Highly qualified persons with specialist responsibilities in some aspects of librarianship—archives, bibliography, reference, for example—should be eligible for advanced status and financial rewards without being forced to abandon for administrative responsibilities their areas of major competence.[2]

Two-track personnel plans have been discussed as early as 1962, when Robert Vosper wrote,

> We must have scholarly librarians of genuine intellectual stature, librarians whose intellectual curiosity and search for learning do not end with the first job or the second academic degree. Thus we need, within libraries, a classification and pay plan that will give at least two ladders for staff to climb, each of the same height.[3]

Vosper's analysis associates the problem with changes that took place in the 1940s. At that time, many libraries functioned in "completely unpatterned, whimsical, and autocratic" ways. In order to correct the situation, we began to establish procedures relating library tasks to "planned, published, and just pay...."[4] We borrowed from civil service and business, areas that had developed more sophisticated procedures at the time. This borrowing, however, has brought with it certain limitations, i.e., structures that primarily reward administrative skills and qualifications, and, according to Vosper, we have seldom attracted or bred scholar librarians.

In 1978, Weber and Kass added survey results to this limited literature.[5] Their survey was sent to 111 academic institutions and it asked such questions as how is Paragraph 19 applied in your system? to what degree has it been applied? do you believe it should be modified?. Twenty-nine per cent responded to the survey. After discounting an unspecified number of college libraries whose staffs were too small to distinguish clearly between administrative and service responsibilities, the authors suggested that the remaining respondents claimed to be whole-heartedly in support of the policy. Several, however, went on to say that they do find it necessary **to add some special increment in order to attract administrators** — "an increment which may be as high as $2000."[6] Obviously, this raises questions about the understanding of the policy or the wholeheartedness of the support.

In giving this brief background, I have discussed the Vosper article, the ALA policy statement, and the Weber and Kass article **not** because they represent the highlights of the literature, but because they seem to **be** the literature. Despite diligent research, appropriate, focused subject headings still have not been found. What has been located has been found by accident. It seems we have not even agreed upon a way of talking about the subject. The rest of this paper will focus on why this issue should be addressed.

MANAGEMENT IMAGE PROBLEM

There is a body of literature generated by a segment of the women's movement that is devoted to exploring why women are not as frequently found in management positions as are men. This literature suggests that the "problem" is in the individual's "poor" self-concept. Consider, for example, Matina Horner's work[7] with women's motivational conflict between desire for and fear of success (i.e., that success will lead to negative consequences). Such motivational conflict in women **who seek managerial advancement** is certainly a real problem (or such conflict in men as well, as subsequent research suggests), but the popularity of such literature and the subsequent development of such catch phrases as "fear of success" have caused us to see "fear" where it may not exist. "Fear of success" is not the only reason for preferring career paths other than administration. To the extent that we fail to understand this, we remain nonresponsive to the motivations of many of our colleagues. Managerial advancement has become trendy and glamorous. In an area like librarianship, which seems to be obsessed with its "image," the image of managerial advancement is particularly seductive.

A 1985 study of academic librarians and MLS students intending to become academic librarians (Swisher, et al.[8]) provides a good example of the subtle effects of this attitude toward managerial advancement. The researchers measured the group's "motivation to manage" using the Miner Sentence Completion Scale, an instrument of demonstrated effectiveness in predicting upward movement in highly structured organizations. They confirmed that, overall, this group was less motivated toward management than groups in the for-profit sector the researchers had studied previously. However, they were surprised to discover no gender differential—"...it seems that both men and women select librarianship as a career because a large majority do not want to be managers."[9] The authors take this as a problem, but not as an organizational problem. They see it as a personal problem of self-concept—"The self-concept among most male and female library school students appears to preclude a perceived aptitude for managing."[10]

In elaborating on their results, the researchers characterize the librarian group's low "motivation to manage" as a "narrow view". The phrase implies that these librarians possess "broader" capabilities; the authors **assume** that librarians are unaware of their capabilities simply because they are not seeking administrative positions. In other words, the researchers suppose that all librarians would want to move in that direction if they believed they had the aptitude. They did not consider the idea that one may fully perceive one's own managerial potential yet choose to realize other potentials.

I am not criticizing the importance of Horner's work or the Swisher study. Their studies extend the ongoing work of the women's movement to understand and root out sexism. This body of literature focuses on fulfilling that function for one very real group of people—women who seek administrative advancement. My criticism is aimed merely at the assumption that that group is all of us.

IMPLICATIONS

This issue is important to the future of academic librarianship for several reasons. Among them, the question of who is attracted to the field is influenced by what types of organizational patterns are associated with the work. Studies show that the majority of academic librarians have some form of faculty status.[11] The collegial organizational structures that are typically associated with faculty status are different from managerial, hierarchical structures, and they attract people with different goals and attitudes. To the extent that it is positive for librarianship to attract academically oriented individuals, we need to be responsive to those differences.

To illustrate this attitudinal difference, try to imagine the words below being addressed to librarians, instead of academic historians. The author attempts to present a balanced view of administrators while describing "History as a Way of Life":

An administrator who has to make the hard decisions regarding academic policy is in an unenviable situation. . . . He has to negotiate, arbitrate, cajole, placate, and, when all else fails, decree. **Very few of those who sneer at the school bureaucrats** could endure the strain. The truth is, **though academics are reluctant to admit it,** . . . administrative talent is more rare and at least as important as scholarly aptitude. . . . **To some scholars it may sound like heresy**, but good administrators earn the high salaries they receive.[12] (Emphasis added.)

The writer clearly understands the prejudices of the audience he is addressing; it is important that we understand those prejudices as well—not that we should shift and blindly accept academic prejudices against bureaucratic administrators. We should, however, be sophisticated enough in our understanding of human motivation to realize that there are human beings with valuable skills for our profession who view administrative work in such a light.

Perhaps even more important than who is attracted to the profession of librarianship, is the question of what work is most valued in the workplace. Although administrative skills are important to our organizations, so are teaching and communication skills, intellectual abilities, creativity—all of those aspects of professional performance that tempted many of us to enter librarianship in the first place. If we are to move beyond our professional inferiority complex, we must affirm as worthy of reward the skills and activities that are unique to our profession.

CURRENT SITUATION

ALA's comparable reward policy was set down over twenty years ago. Has the situation changed in the intervening years? The 1991 ARL SPEC Kit on Organization Charts[13] refers to "few significant changes" in organizational structures, although it does point out that there are more committee structures, which in other fields have signaled a movement to "flatter, more participative structures." A brief look at salaries offered for new positions in the *Chronicle of Higher Education* (comparing March/April 1980 with March/April 1990) revealed that the average salary differential between reference positions without and with administrative duties has remained approximately the same. Administrative duties boost salaries by about 22% It also remains the case that there are

few senior librarian positions advertised without administrative duties.

Because the evidence suggests that most academic librarians have not entered the profession in order to become administrators, should we not be focusing more intensely on the question of structuring our organizations in order to nurture professional level performance and creativity, rather than psychologizing librarians. Obviously, an organization as complex as a university library cannot function effectively if it is structured as loosely and collegially as a small, teaching department. That does not mean, however, that the only option is a bureaucratic, rigid hierarchy. Our organizational structures must combine the efficiency of the hierarchy with the professional nurturance of the collegial structure. There must be space and encouragement within creative organizational structures of academic libraries for both the sophisticated library administrator, who thrives on the challenge of making the organization work well and the student-oriented scholar librarian, who is essentially an educator finding meaning in the bringing together of students with ideas.

SUMMARY

What does it means to have a **successful** career as a librarian? Does the profession reward only one career track—the administrative career track? Although ALA answered that in the negative over twenty years ago, most of us work in settings where alternative career tracks are not being fully implemented. An appropriate agenda to correct this situation would begin with studies that explore the current state of affairs in order to document that this perception is correct.

Also, we need to explore the library functions that are potentially professional, and what it means to perform these functions at a professional level. Before we can sensibly argue for comparable rewards for nonadministrative expertise, we must be able to clearly specify what is meant by such expertise and performance.

Finally, we must evolve better organizational structures and reward systems that nurture and develop professional forms of nonadministrative expertise. This includes learning how executive authority and professional authority can function effectively and productively within the same organizations.

The current social and economic climate underscores the importance of this agenda. Budgets are tight; reorganizational projects are rampant. There is a frequent and clear demand to streamline our organizations. A clear understanding of the types of changes that are beneficial to the development of the profession **as a profession** could be crucial to the future of academic libraries as we move away from the historical warehousing function.

NOTES

1. Leslie M. Kong and R.A.H. Goodfellow, "Charting a Career Path in the Information Professions," *College and Research Libraries* 49(3):207-216, May 1988.
2. American Library Association: Office for Library Personnel Resources Advisory Committee, *Library Education and Personnel Utilization*, rev. ed. (Chicago: ALA, 1976).
3. Robert Vosper, "Needed: An Open End Career Policy," *ALA Bulletin* 56 (October 1962): 835.
4. *Ibid.* 833.
5. David C. Weber and Tina Kass, "Comparable Rewards: The Case for Equal Compensation for Nonadministrative Expertise," *Library Journal* 103 (April 15, 1978): 824-827.
6. *Ibid.*
7. See, e.g., Matina S. Horner, "Fail: Bright Women," *Psychology Today* 3 (November 1969): 36-38, 62; and Horner, "Toward an Understanding of Achievement Related Conflicts in Women," *Journal of Social Issues* 28 (Issue #2, 1972); 157-175.
8. Robert Swisher, Rosemary Ruhig DuMont, and Calvin Boyer, "The Motivation to Manage: A Study of academic Librarians and Library Science Students," *Library Trends* 34 (Fall 1985): 219-234.
9. *Ibid.* 230.
10. *Ibid.* 231.
11. See, for example, John N. DePew, "The ACRL Standards for Faculty Status: Panacea or Placebo?" *College & Research Libraries* 44 (Nov. 1983): 407-413; Anthony G. Tassin, "Faculty Status for Librarians: Progress and Perplex," *LLA Bulletin* 47 (Fall 1984): 83-86; Marjorie A. Benedict, Jacquelyn A. Gavaryk, and Harlan C. Selvin, "Status of Academic Librarians in New York State," *College & Research Libraries* 44 (Jan. 1983): 12-19; Fred E. Hill and Robert Hauptman, "A New Perspective on Faculty Status," *College & Research Libraries* 47 (Mar. 1986): 156-159; or *Academic Status for Librarians in ARL Libraries*, SPEC Kit #182 (1992).
12. Theodore S. Hamerow, *Reflections on History and Historians* (Madison, WI: University of Wisconsin Press, 1987): 135.
13. *Organization Charts in ARL Libraries*, SPEC Kit #170 (Washington, D.C.: Systems and Procedures Exchange Center, Office of Management Services, Association of Research Libraries): January 1991.

Merging Federal Documents with General Reference:

A Transformation in Usage and in Librarian Stature

Barbara B. Alexander and Sharon K. Naylor

ABSTRACT

This case study demonstrates how a subject-divided library mainstreamed federal documents into the general reference department, achieving higher visibility and increasing use of the documents collection. The catalyst for the move came when both unit supervisors retired and administration decided to move the documents collection to the library's main floor. The focus of the general reference division shifted from general information to in-depth reference, more fully utilizing the skills of each member. Combining the disparate collections continues to be a work in progress, but both staff and administration view it as a success.

Addressing the information explosion in a time of tight budgets and financial constraints compels library administrators to examine the use patterns of collections and the productivity of service points. Federal documents provide an excellent opportunity for both of these, as well as suggest a number of philosophic questions. Why should federal documents be treated as a unique collection? Would they be used more if they could be "mainstreamed?" Why stop to consider "if" document collections should be included in online catalogs? While there may be compelling reasons

to combine documents service points with those of other departments, attempts to do so have not always met with success. Illinois State University's Milner Library merged its federal documents collection with general reference in 1992, and although it remains a "work in progress," the results have been favorable.

Milner Library is a subject divided library with four subject floors and a general reference collection and service desk located on the main floor. When the new library building opened in 1976, the federal documents collection was located on Floor

Barbara B. Alexander is Head of General Reference and Documents and Sharon K. Naylor is a General Reference and Documents Librarian at Illinois State University, Normal, Illinois.

5 with the science and technology collections. In the intervening years, library administration began to feel the documents collection received relatively little use, yet took a great deal of space and staff time. The catalyst for change came when both the veteran Documents Librarian and the Library Technical Assistant retired within a few weeks of each other. The time seemed right to reevaluate the collection and look at alternative solutions.

In order to gather as much information as possible, Administration invited Susan Bekiares, Head of the Documents Library at the University of Illinois at Urbana-Champaign, to serve as consultant. After viewing the physical layout and visiting with the library administration and with documents staff, Susan responded with a twelve page report recommending the documents collection be merged with the General Reference Division located on the main floor, floor two. At the same time, an ad hoc library committee addressed space, reference, and personnel issues. Both the Bekiares and internal studies concluded a shift in location would be the best course of action.

Several major issues emerged from the studies. Concern that the government documents collection was being underutilized provided impetus for the studies. One possible factor contributing to the low use was the location of the collection on a floor which received less traffic than most of the other floors. Another may have been a general perception that there was one "documents librarian" and she was the only one qualified to answer documents questions. Staff on other floors perceived the collection as segregated and somewhat unapproachable. The general reference librarians on the main floor thought of the federal documents collection only as a resource for statistics questions requiring census materials. Other patrons who knew they were looking for the Congressional Record or the CFR might find their way to fifth floor, but documents were not viewed as a basic reference source. Few documents were cataloged, and there was no concerted effort to teach patrons about the Superintendent of Docu-

ments (SuDocs) classification system. The depository librarian viewed the collection as "archival" rather than a "working collection," despite the fact that Milner Library is an active undergraduate library, and the University of Illinois holds a well preserved, 95% selective depository 45 minutes away.

At the same time, library administration expressed concern that the reference librarians on the main floor could be better utilized. Although the majority of public access terminals in the building were located on the main floor and staff routinely handled numerous ready reference questions and one-on-one bibliographic sessions, the librarians were expected to refer difficult reference questions to the subject floors. The majority of the bound popular periodicals were located on the main floor along with many of the paper copiers and microfilm reader/printers, and professional librarians spent a disproportionate amount of time servicing the machines. Administration preferred to use students to address those tasks, and to assign more professional responsibilities to the main floor faculty.

As in most libraries, space was a concern. Floor five was out of growth space, and over a period of time the science faculty expressed concern about the amount of material sent to remote storage. Moving the documents from floor five would relieve the situation on that floor, but where could they go? The main floor seemed the logical choice but several issues required attention first. A large amount of space on floor two was dedicated to a divided card catalog that was no longer being maintained. Floor two supported a collection of bound periodicals selected primarily because of their inclusion in Readers' Guide to Periodical Literature, a source that had for all practical purposes been supplanted by electronic access to the Wilson indexes and by InfoTrac. Locating a small collection of bound periodicals on the main floor no longer made sense since all others were located on the subject floors.

Coincidentally, the head of the general reference unit retired. The problems other libraries encountered in combining two departments would not be present with a new division head having no allegiance to one department or another. Hiring a newcomer also presented the opportunity to bring in a person with a background in both reference and documents.

The documents move was based on philosophic considerations aimed at improving service and more effectively using staff, and was not a measure designed to "downsize" or save money. Administration and library staff did not perceive the move as a cost-cutting measure, nor were any positions cut. Floor five maintained three tenure track positions. The documents processing staff remained intact, and General Reference retained its status quo, eventually converting two year-to-year contracted professionals to tenure track and boosting the single support position by adding the two documents positions.

The decision to move the documents collection came after careful consideration and planning, and the administration realized that undertaking such a major shift should involve library personnel at all levels. The first step was the search for a head of the newly created General Reference and Documents (GRD) Division. Bound volumes of the general reference periodical collection were shifted from floor two to the subject floors, and the library's card catalog was moved from floor two to floor three where it was still accessible but no longer updated and/or promoted.

Once the newly hired Head of General Reference and Documents (GRD) came on board, an organizational chart was drawn up, taking into consideration the training and backgrounds of the staff members. Documents collection development was assigned to the GRD librarian who maintained the documents collection during the interim between department heads. Because the new head of GRD had experience in documents processing, she assumed leadership in this area, assuming supervision for the daily workflow of the two documents support staff. The documents processing unit was physically relocated to the Acquisition Division, a moved based on 1) putting like functions together and 2) space available. Administratively both staff reported to the Head of Acquisitions since they spent approximately half their time in processing working with federal documents. The other half of their time was devoted to desk responsibilities, meetings and work in the collection itself.

Once personnel were in place, they faced the major challenge of physically moving the documents collection. Milner selects approximately 48% of depository materials. While both the administration and the documents staff felt a total reevaluation and major weed of the collection were in order, time constraints were also a factor. Accordingly, the decision was made to go forward with the move and address collection development and retention issues later.

The first step was securing additional shelving and developing a new arrangement for the main floor. Rather than a gradual move, which could be confusing for both patrons and staff, administration decided to involve all library staff in a one day undertaking. Two GRD staff members lead the planning; one measured shelves, plotted call number locations, and made signs designating the new locations; the other scheduled two-hour shifts with various teams working on either floor two or five. The move began at 8:00 a.m. on a Friday morning and finished at 4:10 p.m., five minutes ahead of schedule. Though much work was left to be done, the move was an effort in which the whole staff participated. Several administrators took on double shifts, and faculty and staff worked side by side, becoming acquainted with personnel from other departments. While details of the workflow may not have gone exactly as anticipated, everyone was flexible and maintained a good sense of humor.

Although the physical move of the collection seemed to absorb most of the time and attention initially, and certainly provided the most "noticeable" change, the task of training the GRD staff was just beginning, presentcollection was perceived as being a unique and frequently idiosyncratic collection that could be quite difficult to manage. Even though several of the GRD staff had some experience in working with government documents, they did not yet view themselves as competent to provide the level of service they felt the patrons deserved. The influx of CD-ROMs and allusions to internet and gopher access contributed to the professional anxiety.

In order to introduce the collection and its reference tools, the Head of GRD assigned various sources to different GRD librarians who then presented one hour training sessions to all interested library staff. A few of the sources included were GPO SilverPlatter, Census CD-ROMs, ASI/CIS, and the Serial Set. Since all Milner librarians rotate staffing at GRD Desk on weekends, these workshops were well attended. During that first semester, the Head of GRD also offered orientation sessions each Friday for librarians working weekends.

GRD librarians felt concern about the level of service they were able to provide at the reference desk. Initially, individuals at the desk referred many questions to the two staff members who had the most documents experience. However, the Division Head encouraged staff to tackle even difficult questions and follow through as far as possible. A conscious attempt was made to staff the desk in a way that allowed one person to spend time on in-depth questions. This represented a change from the previous model in which most of the patron service was considered "quick" or "ready reference." A great deal of training turned out to be one-on-one as individuals observed each other handling different types of questions. The librarian concentrating on documents collection development compiled documents handouts and training information into a "GRD Documents Notebook," a ready source of information relied on by those working at the desk.

Staff were also encouraged to attend workshops and national, regional, state and local meetings. Networking with other documents staffs was encouraged, particularly through field trips to the regional depository at the Illinois State Library, Springfield, and to the depository at Illinois

Wesleyan University, located in the adjacent city of Bloomington. Various staff members subscribed to different listservs and routed pertinent messages throughout the department. Two of the documents-related listservs monitored were GOVDOC-L and IGI-L (Illinois Government Issues).

Milner has now operated a combined general reference and documents department for almost two years, and the move appears to be a success. Although circulation statistics were not kept prior to moving federal documents to the main floor, longtime staff in that unit estimate an increase from a half dozen documents per month before the move to more than an average of 70 per month. The ability of the GRD staff to refer patrons to general collections or to documents has increased the effectiveness of reference, both from the point of view of the library and the user.

While there are various factors involved in the success of the move, one of the most important was strong administrative support. Once the decision was made to merge the two departments, administration involved the staff in decision making and allowed them time to plan the move. The University Librarian put up shelves with student workers; the Associate University Librarian for Public Services shelved documents. The shift itself was not seen or approached as a cost-cutting measure designed to exact more work from fewer people. Instead, administration, as well as floors five and two, viewed the move as a win/win situation. Floor five gained a faculty person who could devote his full time to the science collection. Floor two librarians were relieved of mundane, often boring, tasks and offered the opportunity to provide more in-depth reference. Two of the GRD librarians were recently moved into tenure track positions and the department is in a stronger position than it was before the move.

The willingness of the general reference librarians to adapt to change and to work toward making the merger a success continues to be a major factor. Although not all librarians initially embraced the move with the same degree of enthusiasm, once the final decision was made, all were willing to pull together. The librarian who initially expressed the most concern became one of the team planning the one-day move and put every effort into seeing that it went smoothly. Working together at the desk and helping each other when difficult questions arose was also a factor in reducing the stress, or even panic, one can feel when presented with a difficult question in an unfamiliar collection. Milner was fortunate that two of the librarians had considerable experience in documents, and two of the others had been involved in limited documents reference. Without this experience, the transition might have been considerably more difficult.

Another consideration is that Milner merged two collections, not two departments. No personnel actually changed departments. GRD was given a new collection at the same time it acquired a new department head. While certainly a major change, this situation is far different than merging two areas with different personnel. The personnel in the department had worked well together before the move, and they continued to do so after the move. Combining two sets of personalities might have created problems.

In some ways, the merging of the two departments seems to be a project far from completion. While staff takes pride in what has been accomplished, all of them are very aware of new challenges and are committed to further developing the services provided. The library profession as a whole has been faced with dramatic change in the last few years, but at Milner Library, the general reference area has been presented with a proportionately higher degree than other units. For instance, only two years after a major move, GRD received the challenge of incorporating eight full text Infotrac workstations onto the floor and of cooperatively developing procedures to address 24 hour access for the first time. Both of these resulted from the work and cooperation of an Illinois State University Student Regent and the University President looking for other options with funding previously used for athletics. The

President considers 24 hour access and full text databases high priorities, as do library staff. As a result, GRD is changing and shifting again, although on a smaller scale, but certainly with as much impact.

The increase in electronic access to government documents has been a challenge for everyone involved in documents. In order to address this growing area, work assignments have been realigned. The librarian originally assigned documents collection development will work along with two GRD librarians, the documents processing clerk and a liaison from the library's Systems Division, to address access to and management of electronic resources. Three other GRD librarians work together managing the traditional aspects of the collection, addressing paper versus microform formats, space needs and collection development.

Training needs are continuous. Trying to keep current with both general reference and federal documents looms as a daunting task for most of the staff. They point out that it is no longer possible to master each tool—being able to know where to start and relying on each other for support and assistance have become more and more important.

Staffing patterns remain a concern because of the aforementioned original purpose of the desk, to provide ready reference and directional questions. Letting go of a policy long in place has proven to be somewhat difficult, combined with the fact that informational questions, both walk-ins and telephone contacts, are directed to the GRD Desk. While GRD staff realize many libraries currently face the issue of balancing quick with in-depth questions, the length of time involved in documents reference may exacerbate the problem. To meet this challenge, staff have discussed the possibility of setting up appointments and of establishing electronic reference, and have considered establishing a librarian "on call" system. The whole issue of levels of service has been studied and discussed extensively and cannot be resolved at this point except to say that it is a challenge.

One issue that has surfaced is the placement of the technical services unit. The physical move to the Acquisitions Department has not been entirely successful. The processing staff feels isolated from the rest of GRD and from the collection with which they work, and the GRD staff housed on the main floor feel they would benefit from the knowledge of the processing staff if they were more readily available. Since the processing staff also are assigned to the reference desk, they would like the exposure to the collection that only close proximity provides. The processing staff are responsible to two department heads and their different management styles. This situation requires cooperation between the supervisors, but it still remains a bit awkward. Unfortunately, space considerations are a major factor in the location of the unit, so no easy solution is available.

Another question that arises involves hiring new librarians. There has traditionally been a high turnover in general reference as librarians receive excellent training in the unit and then move on, whether in-house or elsewhere. One librarian has been brought in since the move. The turnover rate may well slow down now that there are three tenure track positions in addition to the department head, but when hiring new persons, the question arises how much, if any, emphasis needs to placed on documents experience. Again, this is a question that cannot be resolved quickly, and decisions may have to be made on a case-by-case basis.

As GRD staff move into the role of advocates for documents, they have begun to promote the need for a fully cataloged collection. With the division head's prior experience in this area and with administration's on-going support for the promotion and integration of the collection, this should soon be a reality.

Whither the Reference Desk?
A History of the Future

Inga H. Barnello

ABSTRACT

This paper reviews benchmarks in the development of reference service in search of a perspective with which to confront the profound changes afoot in reference librarianship today in the face of virtual access. Reference service, as it developed in academic libraries, is examined in terms of its interconnectedness to educational movements, the interpersonal dimensions between librarian and patron, and technological innovation. The current and alternative models for reference service being considered are placed in historical context and a future of reference service is contemplated.

Imagine, if you will, a present without a past. What if we wake up one morning and we decide to invent libraries? How would we structure the facility? What discussions would we have? What would be the agreed upon guiding principles, policies, and procedures?

Does it not seem as though we are starting from scratch? In some ways libraries and librarianship are in the process of being reinvented. We are having discussions about function and structure in light of the construction of a virtual community. We are questioning our role vis a vis instruction, support staff, and technological innovation. We are rethinking reference in the context of shrinking financial resources, greater demand for service, increased access, and new formats and protocols.

But what of rethinking reference in the context of history? We do have a past. What is it that our past holds for us? Can it predict our future? How can it guide us?

This paper is not about how to make reference less stressful, nor is it about how to redesign it. It is not about change or managing change. It is about perspective—putting change in perspective. A question like "where are we going from here?" cannot be addressed effectively without taking a look back at how we progressed to this point. History may provide that deep, cleansing breath we need to discuss how we are to most effectively interact with our patrons as reference librarians in the future.

The historian in me believes that the historical perspective is a valuable one to those that are

Inga H. Barnello is the Social Sciences Reference Librarian at the Le Moyne College Library, Syracuse, New York.

looking ahead. I assume that the historical process is more than a series of events senselessly succeeding one another in time. There is some meaningful theme lying within history to be discovered that can enable us to forecast the future development of society. I agree with Toynbee that history conforms to regular and recurrent cycles of change. Although his sweeping overview of history is criticized as inaccurate by narrower specialists, it is thought by his proponents to be the only way to see rhythms and patterns.[1]

So I take the long view and enter this foray knowing that 1) I am leaving a lot out, and 2) there is no value-free history. My observations are limited by what I know and by what I believe to be important.

ORIGINS OF REFERENCE SERVICE

How naive it was of me to think that I could construct a time line of the history of reference. How does one draw an oblique blur? The history of reference service is part event and part attitudinal change. It is part the history of the growth of a profession and part the history of education. Like anything else reference service developed interconnectedly with the forces from within and from without.

Rothstein has written that "the beginnings of reference service are lost in antiquity."[2] Actually we have him, along with James Rettig and Charles Bunge, to thank for keeping track of it all for us.

The beginnings of reference are both tentative and contentious. Reference was not initially a part of librarianship. It began in the public libraries as a response to patron needs for assistance in interpreting the catalog. The accepted benchmark of the origin of reference service, Samuel Green's 1876 article, "Personal Relations between Librarians and Readers," speaks to the need to guide users in their use of the non-fiction collection. His idea of personal relations was "a hearty reception by a sympathizing friend." His article is a hesitant call to librarians to bolster patrons' ability to select from among the non-fiction titles. He recognized

that even once the catalogs were more complete much assistance would still be needed by the patrons of "popular libraries."[3]

The development of reference moved more slowly in academic libraries. It was not until Melvil Dewey advocated the "modern library idea" at Columbia in 1885 that academic libraries joined in the chorus. It was not until World War I that reference became a regular service in academic libraries.[4] Rothstein describes the development of reference service in academic libraries as a "cause." He describes how librarians contended for their place with faculty who scoffed at the notion that even they, as teachers, were experts in a subject. Certainly librarians were not to be called on for scholarship.[5]

TRANSFORMATION OF HIGHER EDUCATION

Once textbook-based education gave way to learning-by-inquiry, the idea of research evolved and libraries were utilized in a totally new way. This was a time of great change in higher education, in publishing, and in librarianship. Libraries grew in size, in hours of service, and in this fledgling reference interaction.

Another major movement that effected the advancement of reference service was the adult education movement of the 1920s. In response, readers advisory was developed to assist adult learners to select a reading list. Although separate from the reference service, this was a highly interactive service involving an interview and the development of a bibliography customized to the patron's interest and ability. Librarians followed up with patrons and updated them on new titles.

So these two developments in education fostered the development of reference service. It was born of client needs and fed by the changes from without. There was contention for this niche of guiding young scholars. The history of reference service relative to the educational changes that have occurred is one of initiative as librarians have responded to client needs and filled niches.

INTERPERSONAL DIMENSION

As the collection of non-fiction titles of Samuel Green's day grew to include reference books as we define them today and access tools like bibliographies and periodical indices, patrons needed help in this complex environment. Librarianship responded by defining and developing reference service. The goal of reference service remained staunchly "conservative," as academic librarians guided students to use library resources entirely on their own.

The reference desk seems anachronistic today in a history of reference that shows us to be increasingly interactive. The way we have interacted with patrons has gone from the cautious approach of Mr. Green of pointing the way, to the "sage on the stage" of the height of the bibliographic instruction movement, to the appointment-based service of Brandeis and Johns Hopkins. Since Green's first allusion to the "personal relations," through the last three decades of research on reference, reference librarianship has elevated this interaction to something that is difficult to qualify as solely a technical skill or artistic ability. Although we have a good deal of advice from the research, we have no agreed upon way of conducting ourselves as reference librarians. The closest we come is the RASD guidelines first developed in 1976, one hundred years after Green's article.

In the long run we have become more sensitive to the psychological and sociological aspects of reference work. Calls for counseling models and appointment-based service with information desks that are surfacing today began in the 1960s. We have also become increasingly interested in the last 25 years in the reference interview. Through this body of research, we learned that 1) patrons cannot distinguish from among the employees in a library who work at other service desks, 2) that we are effective only 55% of the time, and 3) that we infrequently conduct these interviews. But we do not seem to know what to do with this information.

The history of reference service relative to the relationship between librarians and patrons is one resembling a game of hide and seek. It appears that librarians have been seeking patrons ever since the stacks opened. Librarians in Green's day began to accompany them to the catalog and into the stacks. Today we have captive audiences in the classroom. We seek "teaching moments" in the reference area. Yet amidst all this seeking, we have insisted on hiding behind the reference desk. We want to help, but mostly on our terms. The desk has stood as a bulwark through decades of change.

TECHNOLOGICAL INNOVATION

The history of reference service that makes the biggest impact is that relative to technological innovation. From the invention of electric lighting, the telephone, the telex, computers and photocopiers to the advent of telefacsimile machines, optical storage, and fiber optic cable, librarians have transformed reference service, and thereby their profession, from desk attendant to information technology consultant.

With each technology we have been granted the ability to extend service and we have done so. We extended hours once we could see into the night. We served patrons remotely with telephones. We obtained material from afar and more and more quickly. Yet all along, these innovations make more demands on us. They have imposed the burden of instruction. And today they stand as challenges to the definition of our profession. The virtual community of our future will witness a wholly different function and structure of librarianship. The future development of librarianship will be played out in an environment of economic uncertainty and contentious advocacy.

LOOKING BACK, LOOKING AHEAD

The pattern of the history of reference service has been a rhythmic movement of librarians toward patrons. Librarians have done more, from farther away, each time technology has made it possible and when new educational models were introduced. Reference service in its first one hundred years has evolved from a tentative, distant activity (from an interpersonal standpoint) to a collaborative interaction that teaches and counsels. Reference service has been transformed as education is transformed. It has sped up and reached out with technological innovation.

Looking back, librarians came out of the metamorphosis in higher education at the turn of the century triumphantly. It was our best moment. We did well thirty years later in the adult education movement. In the 1960s librarians began to tackle the construction of a national database and network with the formation and applications of OCLC.

Now thirty years hence we have another wave of change and it is a big one. Fiber optic cable networks are connecting homes, libraries, schools, campuses, corporations, and the government. Instruction is entering another phase of metamorphosis. Lewis Perelman, author of *School's Out*, describes "hyperlearning" as a new degree of connectedness of people and machine in learning through case-based reasoning and simulation. It is replacing the lecture-research model. Teamwork and virtualizing will replace the individualized, hierarchical classroom, according to Perelman.[6]

What emerges from this glance backward is the realization that we have been at this juncture before. Along with this realization is the comfort in knowing that librarians have come out of these periods of change well-positioned. Once again we will be in a contentious position at a time of profound change. My confidence is tempered by the economic uncertainty and the speed with which change is occurring. But with this high speed life of ours comes an awareness, among those we serve, and among ourselves, that sweeping change is upon us. People are generally cognizant that information technology is changing rapidly. The mainstream press is full of the information superhighway and such. We do, after all, have a name for our era as we experience it. The people of the 15th century did not call their time the Renaissance. Eighteenth century citizens did not say "hey look, we're living in the Industrial Revolution." The awareness of the information age is something for librarians to bank on. There is something uniquely positive in store for informa-

tion providers in an age of information technology, if we take the user's point of view in reforming reference service. Our customers are continually forming and reforming what they want from us. I do not know that we are listening. We still find ourselves tentative about how to be reference librarians.

I am optimistic about our profession's future in terms of people needing us. With the growing complexity of information technology comes loud cries for help. Knowledge seekers will want a search partner. While poking around in campus networks and cyberspace, they will need help along the way either with a Gopher site, with a remote search of the online catalog, or with a Dialog or Nexis search. All will wish they had a knowledgeable person at their side.

The 1976 reference guidelines stipulate under "environment" that "service points be as near as possible to the main focal point of activity." The 1990 document, under "access," calls for libraries "to support state-of-the-art communications methods for access to information resources for users whether within or outside its building." [7]

For the most part inquirers will not look for us at the reference desk in the next century. They will find us at the opposite end of their keyboards. I see a future of interactive workstations staffed by librarians, scheduled as needed, at locations that suit librarians. Our service front is widening again. We must retain in-person reference service as dictated by the needs of our patrons, but expand it by following our patrons online. We already see electronic reference via email. We will integrate it into our opacs. We will have what I will call conference searching where patrons will call us into their online searches when they need assistance.

Barbara Ford, in contemplating life without a reference desk at this conference nine years ago, suggested "if reference desks were closed, librarians might be astonished at either how little people missed the service or how terribly frustrated patrons would be in trying to use the library."[8] She was right. We have two kinds of patrons, those that want our help and those who do not. Among those who want our help (and the forces are growing), there are those that will come into the library for it and those that will want remote access to us.

In what promises to be a time of profound change and complexity, patrons deserve the continuity of having a librarian in the role as research guide. An algorithm of artificial intelligence just will not make the grade. Hypertext guides and "intelligent agents" will serve a limited band of our electronic community with a limited range of effectiveness. There will be no effective reference service without the human factor. We have more work to do on reforming the interpersonal dimension of reference service.

The last prediction that I will make is that there will be a liberalizing of the reference service philosophy. Librarians will do more for patrons. We have done this before when we responded to the needs of adult learners with reader's advisory. I think we can do this at the same time that we enhance the interpersonal dimension electronically. The complexity of electronic information will make academic library patrons more dependent on librarians for their highly skilled searching techniques. I do not think we can teach them everything in the reference interview. I harbor some doubt that we can teach them it in one class. We will be doing more and more searching for them. I do not predict as big a paradigm shift towards unilaterally and routinely doing all searching for patrons as Terry Ann Mood does,[9] but I see in my daily work that I am constructing more search strategies for students.

It makes sense that librarianship be in the throws of change at a time like the one we are living in. If it were not, we would be in an even more difficult position than we find ourselves already. The debates that are raging over "finding versus teaching" are an important part of the visioning process. We must question everything we do if we are to remain viable. We have to know our clientele, give them what they need, and fill that niche like we have done so many times before.

We should welcome the contention and enter the debate.

We seek comfort in the past in the form of nostalgic tribute. In this tumultuous present of ours, we can take some solace in knowing that the past indicates that we are on the right track.

NOTES

1. William H. McNeill, "Some Basic Assumptions of Toynbee's *A Study of History*," in *The Intent of Toynbee's History*, ed. E.T Gargan, (Chicago: Loyola University Press, 1961), 27-46.

2. Samuel Rothstein, *The Development of Reference Service Through Academic Traditions, Public Library Practice and Special Librarianship*. (Chicago: Assn. of College and Research Libraries, 1955), ACRL Monographs, no. 14.

3. Samuel S. Green, "Personal Relations Between Librarians and Readers," *American Library Journal* 1 (October 1876): 74-81.

4. James Rettig, "Reference and Information Services," in *World Encyclopedia of Library and Information Services*. Third edition. ed. Robert Wedgeworth, (Chicago: American Library Association, 1993), 703-708.

5. Samuel Rothstein, "An Unfinished History: A Developmental Analysis of Reference Services in American Academic Libraries," *Reference Librarian* 25/26 (1989): 365-409.

6. Lewis J. Perelman, *School's Out: Hyperlearning, the New Technology, and the End of Education*. (New York: William Morrow, 1992).

7. The 1976 document, "A Commitment to Information Services: Developmental Guidelines," appears in B. Vavrek, "Bless You Samuel Green!" *Library Journal* 101 (1976): 971-974. The Standards and Guidelines Committee of RASD revised them as "Information Services for Information Consumers: Guidelines for Providers," RQ 30 (1990): 262-265.

8. Barbara J. Ford, "Reference Beyond (and Without) the Reference Desk," *College and Research Libraries* 47 (September 1986): 491-494.

9. Terry Ann Mood, "Of Sundials and Digital Watches: A Further Step Toward the New Paradigm of Reference," *RSR: Reference Services Review* 22, no. 3 (1994): 24-32, 95.

Integrating Library Computer Skills into a Credit Course at Trident Technical College

Rosetta P. Martin

ABSTRACT

In 1992-1993 Trident College Learning Resources Center and Counseling/Career Development Services integrated a library computer skills program into the College Skills 103 bridge course. As commercial software vendors saturate the library market with electronic information retrieval databases, this flood of information is proving to be too much to cover in the traditional one-hour bibliographic instruction (BI) session. This position paper examines the why, how, and what should be done to develop a shift from the traditional one-hour BI session to additional teaching hours in a credit course. The paper focuses on steps used to integrate and implement a library computer skills teaching component into a credit course, followed by evaluations to determine its effectiveness. A beginning approach to "quality management" of teaching library skills, this model can be adapted or modified for use by other two year or community colleges.

INTRODUCTION
Definition of the Need to Implement

The announcement in July 1993 of the Charleston Navy Base and Naval Shipyard closing over a three year time frame(1996) will probably have an impact on increase enrollment of adult students. Students will probably return to school to update job skills or change careers for the technical job market. Enrollment during the Fall Semester of 1993 is expected to rise above 10,000 students with the greatest diversity of backgrounds.

Trident Technical College (TTC) is a comprehensive, public,two-year institution in Charleston, South Carolina The college provides quality education in Berkeley, Charleston, and Dorchester counties, known as the Trident area. The college offers diverse technical, professional, and college transfer programs, as well as developmental education and support services necessary for students to succeed. There are three campuses -Main Campus in North Charleston, Palmer Campus in downtown Charleston and Berkeley Campus in Moncks

Rosetta P. Martin is a Reference Librarian and Coordinator of Bibliographic Instruction at the Learning Resources Center, Trident Technical College, Charleston, South Carolina.

Corner. More than 400 faculty and staff work at the three campus locations. Enrollment at the three campuses peaked in 1992 at more than 8000 students.

A serious concern among Trident's librarians at present is how to address the increased demand for "one-on-one" instruction in the use of electronic databases at the reference desk. The ever increasing number of online databases, lack of standardization among database interfaces, now the increasing availability of information resources world-wide via the internet, limited library budgets, limited staff, increased enrollment are some of the factors contributing to the library instructional challenges. Integrating library computer skills as a component of a "credit" course seems to be the best approach to the "information over load" challenge. The current challenges of teaching how to search electronic information databases effectively are of broad concern to all librarians: two-year colleges, four-year colleges, universities, etc.

Problems that Justify Reasons to Implement

The best justification for any innovation is that it attempts to solve problems. There are three specific problems that create the need to teach library computer search skills in a credit course at Trident: (1) proliferation of electronic information databases and its impact on the one-hour library orientation. (2) students demand for "librarian-to student,one-to-one" instructions on how to use the automated systems and (3) increased student enrollment.

1. Proliferation of Electronic Information Databases and the One- Hour Library Orientation Session

Brief examination of library literature indicates that the above problems are not unique to Trident Learning Resources Centers, but shared by other libraries. Although all library information databases present problems, one specific problem is the lack of standardization of search commands by software vendors. Blumenthal calls this specific problem that instruction librarians encounter "technostress". " A challenge that already occurs when doing instruction for CD-ROMs., and that will only get worse as more databases are added is the differing software syndrome. When teaching a class in which several databases are used, it is difficult to demonstrate one database using one software, then switch to another database and another database, perhaps even making a third or fourth switch, all while explaining the intricacies of each database and its search commands."[1] This is a specific problem that is here to stay and will not go away. Electronic information databases are powerful. The old way of providing the one-hour library orientation tour is proving to be ineffective because of this specific problem.

Added to the above problem, Cooper states that "one hour bibliographic instruction session...may be perceived by students as irrelevant to their specific needs.... Students are too often passive recipients of instruction, retaining little of what is presented in the orientation."[2] The fifty-minute lecture may have little impact on students overall library research skills. One problem is students lack of motivation to master these skills. A major stimulus is generally unavailable to instruction librarians; the power of the grade. Although teaching faculty have the capability to grade students, most have neither the inclination nor the knowledge of how to evaluate students library skills with a grade.... Librarians play a relatively minor role in development of information-seeking skills.[3]

Mellon and Pagles noted, "As instruction librarians, we have all looked out upon a sea of uncomprehending or disinterested faces as we held up a book, showed slides, described the organization of information, and tried to whip up interest with our knowledge and enthusiasm. But we know it doesn't work!". Patterson and Howell also described the problem: "The major and constant source of dissatisfaction and frustration...is observable apathy and resulting boredom by many students."[4]

Table 1

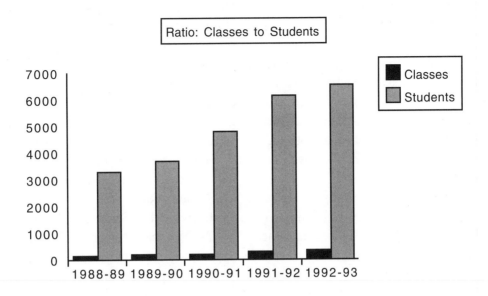

	Classes	**Students**
1988-89	171	3306
1989-90	191	3680
1990-91	215	4812
1991-92	282	6171
1992-93	346	6531

2. Students Demand For "Librarian-To-Student-One-On-One" Instruction

Demand for "one-on-one" assistance on how to use library computers is just about impossible in the automated library. Students come to the library without any idea of what they will do once they get there. "These technical machines tend to provide students with more complete up-to-date information.... But each new machine also seems to generate additional time for student instruction."[5] Students continue to pressure librarians at Trident to teach then "one-on-one" to meet their different individual educational needs. It is now time that students and faculty realize that learning how to use library automated systems is a structured learning process. Demand for the "one-on-one show me how quick fix" only creates continuous repetitive demands for ongoing frustrations. "Computerized technology requires critical thinking applications in order to selectively process the overwhelming deluge of information that come forth. As software changes, and hopefully continues to improve, even more selective applications will be necessary to sift and choose appropriate information."[6]

3. Increased Student Enrollment at Trident.

Another major reason for implementing a library computer skills component at Trident is based on the ratio bibliographic instruction (BI) classes to students. BI classes and student enrolled in theses classes have increased by 50% in five years. The professional staff has increased by one full-time and one part-time librarian within in five years. Currently, five full-time and two part-time librarians try to teach over 350 BI classes to an approximate total of over 6000 students. Table 1 shows a vivid picture of the ratio of BI classes to students.

According to Becker "if the BI program is well-done and effective, word-of-mouth and publicity can soon create a demand for instruction beyond the scope of the reference department's capacities. We cannot demand staffing increases commensurate with increases in activity we are experiencing and which we have a large part created ourselves....[7] This is "catch 22" for instruction librarians. However, it seems that both faculty and students realize a need to know how to use the automated systems. The faculty is very cooperative and supportive of the BI program at Trident. A large number of faculty schedule two one-hour BI sessions to be sure students learn the basics of computer research. Others bring classes to the library to work in a student--teacher-librarians interactive environment.

Librarians often express concerns about presenting one-hour class after class to students over and over, day after day feeling guilty that coverage of materials needed is deficient. Librarians also express the feeling of a lingering after thought "did I cover everything , what did I forget". In addition to working the reference desk, serving on college committees, participating in collection development and other wide variety of duties, do librarians set themselves up for "burn-out"? Librarians are no different than classroom teachers, they also suffer the same feelings. However added to stress and burn-out of librarians Becker states that instruction librarians' contact with students is limited to dealing with an unpleasant aspect of students' lives: a library research assignment. There is never an opportunity to know the individual student as a whole person with likes and dislikes, hopes, fears, successes and failures.[8] A structured library computer skills program provides the opportunity for librarians to teach in a friendly non-threatening environment.

INTEGRATION AND IMPLEMENTATION
College Skills 103 and the Library Computer Skills Component

College skills 103 is a college orientation 3 credit course taught by professional counselors in the Counseling/Career Development Services Department. The purpose of the course is to help students build classroom success skills, learn to make decisions, and identify personal goals. The course includes selected topics such as career planning, problem solving, study skills, library research, reasoning, critical thinking, and other group activities that facilitate student success. Teaching students how to effectively use information databases in the library also involves reasoning, critical thinking, and problem solving.

Trident began conversion from the Quarter System to the Semester System during the 1992-1993 school year. This seemed the most opportune time to begin teaching library computer skills in depth because of the additional weeks "expanded time span" within the Semester. Integrating library skills as a component of College Skills 103 began June 1992 and continued through both the Fall and Spring Semesters.

The Process Used To Integrate The Library Component Included Eight Steps:

First, the Dean of Learning Resources Center and Dean, Center for Student Success met to approve the project.

Second, the deans assigned the task of working out the details necessary to integrate library skills into the College Skills 103 course to the director of advising.

Third, the reference librarian prepared a library skills curriculum proposal outlining purpose, justification, basic objectives, terminal objectives, performance objectives, and teaching activities. The proposal was submitted and accepted by the director of advising.

Fourth, the director of advising carefully merged four one-hour consecutive class sessions of library skills into each College Skills 103 section offered.

Fifth, the reference librarian prepared a schedule inserting rotating dates for each librarian to teach four consecutive one-hour classes in each section of College Skill 103.

Sixth, the librarians prepared four one-hour class lesson plans. The plans include:

a) computer "hands-on exercises" for students to complete out- of-class

b) one- hour class lecture,

c) two-hour class sessions demonstrating how to use library computers: OPAC, NEWSBANK, PROQUEST and microfilm/fiche reader printers.

d) one-hour class session for questions, review and test.

Seventh, students had to complete hands-on exercise assignments using all the computers in the library in order to pass the course.

Eighth, librarians graded exercises and gave a test. Students received 50% of the grade for the completed exercises and 50% for the final test. (It is the responsibility of the teaching counselor to give the final grade for the course. The library skills grade counts only one-third of the grade for the course.)

SUMMARY OF THE PROGRAM AND RESULTS

Weaknesses and Strengths

By any measure, the program was a success; however, every program has a number of obvious weaknesses and strengths. Both weaknesses and strengths are included here to provide a fuller picture of the evaluation results.

Weaknesses:

1. There were not enough computer terminals in Trident's libraries to support a course of this magnitude. Students complained bitterly about having to wait in line to use computer terminals to complete th hands- on exercise assignments.

2. Because each library (Palmer, Berkeley, Main, libraries) has its own specific arrangement, the skill of locating materials in one library is not always transferable to another library. This skill needs further study and revision.

3. Computer search skills CHANGE ABRUPTLY every time software systems are updated or enhanced. The computer hands-on exercise assignments had to be altered twice during implementation. Students were very upset and frustrated when this happened.

4. Students have to unlearn old library skills and relearn basic new ones. It is the "never knowing", unlearning and relearning library skills that create mass confusion and frustration. Basic computer terminology was difficult to understand for adult students returning to school after many years absence.

Strengths:

1. The course provides students an opportunity to concentrate and learn and really learn how to use the library. Major concentration is on how to do research, not on finding content materials for a class assignment.

2. Students MUST USE THE COMPUTERS in order to complete the exercise assignments. Hands-on experience is a repetitive transferable skill. Repetitive use of computers strengthens search strategy skills long-term.

3. The five page hands-on exercise packet is not as threatening as a detailed library skills workbook. Assigned topics to search were relevant to career changes and employment (very relevant to Navy Yard workers). The idea of getting a grade for the test and completion of the exercises was the MOTIVATOR for learning how to search electronic databases.

4. Older adult students and students returning to school after many years absence had an opportunity to vent frustrations, fears, and anxiety using computers prior to using them for required courses.

5. Developmental study students who are not quite ready to take required courses have and opportunity to develop library research skills.

6. One of the greatest strengths of this program during implementation was the cooperation

Table 2: Number of Students Enrolled and Classes Scheduled

Campus	Summer		Fall		Spring		Totals	
	Classes	Students	Class	Students	Classes	Students	Classes	Students
Main	3	54	7	153	6	125	16	332
Palmer	1	18	2	50	1	24	4	92
Berkeley	1	8	1	18	1	12	3	38
Totals	5	80	10	221	8	161	23	462

Four librarians taught two classes each during the Fall Semester

Number of students enrolled : 462   Number of students completed the component: 326

Passed: 274   Incomplete: 37   Failed: 15

Average final grade: 91.4   Average test scores: 93.8

and support from the dean, director of advising, teaching counselors from the Counseling / Career Development Services.

Student Evaluation

During implementation, librarians became particularly sensitive to students attitudes and perceptions that, when shared, formed the "climate" within which the program developed. This evaluation report covers random sampling during the fall semester and complete evaluation of each class during the spring semester. The following information is based only on the number of students that returned the completed evaluation forms. The following results are based on a 59% response rate from the 324 students.

CONCLUSIONS AND FUTURE IMPLICATIONS

1. The one-hour orientation session is on longer effective because the automated library.
2. Library computer hands-on exercises provide students with an opportunity to become familiar with basic searching and develop self-confidence without the pressures of "writing a term paper or special assignment".
3. The brief 5 page hands-on exercises help students understand WHAT TO DO and HOW TO DO IT when they sit at the computer terminals.
4. Repetitive practice in retrieving information from electronic databases is necessary for reinforcing long-term retention of computer

Table 3

Number of Students that Completed Evaluation Form: 191

	Excellent	Good	Average	Poor
1) How would you rate the library computer skills component?				
	39% (75)	46% (88)	15% (28)	
3) How would you rate the teaching ability of the librari				
	21% (41)	56% (107	23% (44)	

	YES	NO	Did Not Respond
2) After Completion of the COMPONENT could you use the library without assistance ?			
	84% (160)	16% (31)	
7) Because of on-going changes in computer technology and continuous updating of information retreival systems, do you think LIBRARY COMPUTER SKILLS should be offered as a CREDIT COURSE in the future?			
	63% (121)	16% (31)	21% (39)

TOTAL HIGHEST PERCENTAGES OF ANSWERS:

4) What DID YOU LIKE most about the course?

Using computers	Course helpful	Aware of library changes
57% (109)	46% (87)	30% (57)

5) Name what you DID NOT LIKE about the course ?

Waiting to use Computer	Not enough Computers	Class time short
60% (114)	27% (53)	44% (83)

6) What improvement would you suggest for the future?
   a) to learn more about COASTNET. [9]
   b) course should be required to all first-year students prior to required courses such as English 101 and English 102.
   c) divide the class into smaller groups.Computer demonstrations should not be given in the library. "I could not see".

QUESTIONS 1,3,2,7 were designed to find out the effectiveness of the teaching/learning process and students' attitudes toward the idea of a library skills CREDIT COURSE.

QUESTIONS 4,5,6 were designed to solicit feedback about PROBLEMS,likes, dislikes and suggestions for improvements.

March 29 - April 1, 1995, Pittsburgh, Pennsylvania

research skills. Although many of the exercises address skills particular to Trident libraries,(e.g. OPAC and other computerized databases), the next time students use library technology systems, elsewhere, it will be a bit easier and the one after that easier and the one after that almost effortless.

5. Library technology is powerful. Electronic information systems are very expensive. The major purpose for purchasing these systems is for students to use. It is not cost effective if students are not taught how to effectively use them.

6. Future trends indicate that multimedia technology, digitized audiovisual technology, hypermedia and other electronic computerized learning tools will revolutionize how the one-hour- BI session is taught in the future.

7. Future trends also indicate there will be a need to teach library computer skills for "credit" in curriculum or special courses. Other disciplines have had to yield to the ELECTRONIC MONSTERS (science, math, English and WORDPERFECT, medicine, etc) as part of the teaching environment.

8. Participation in classroom activities affords librarians an opportunity to function as educator and contribute directly to students' academic experiences.

9. TQM: implementation of this library component examines WHAT SHOULD BE DONE TO DEVELOP A PARADIGM SHIFT from the traditional one-hour bibliographic instruction to structured teaching in a credit course here at Trident.

10. This program can be modified or adapted for use at any two-year college library. [10] (lesson plans, etc., may be obtained by request)

A Few Recommended (non-measurable) Guidelines

1. Expect academic politics. According to Miller, "planning for changes requires objectivity and presupposes a willingness to recognize...limitations." He further states that "planning may also entail staff conflict and dissatisfaction; every current activity has an advocate with passionate reasons why things must continue to be done as they always have been done." [11]

2. Begin by selecting an introductory course, bridge course or developmental studies course.

3. Strive for cooperation between librarians and participating faculty. This links the "grade and grading" process to the library component.

4. Select electronic databases as instructional medium only if they are applicable to the type of instruction to be offered by the selected course.

5. Choose, if possible, software databases, hardware, equipment or other technology used elsewhere in your local area (e.g. public library, local college consortiums, etc.,). Databases that are familiar to other professional librarians, can assist in the "teaching- learning-RETENTION-process.

6. Plan and survey, databases, hardware (computers, multimedia, etc), etc. to be sure there are reasonable numbers to accommodate the number of students to be enrolled in the component (ideally there will never be enough computers, because of budget constraints, each library is different).

NOTES

1. Carol Blumenthal, Mary Jo Howard, and William R. Kinyon, "The Impact of CD-ROM Technology on a Bibliographic Instruction Program," *College & Research Libraries* 54 (Jan. 1993):15.

2. John E. Cooper, "Using CAI to teach Library Skills," *College & Research Libraries News* 54 (Feb. 1993):75.

3. Karen A. Becker, "The Characteristics of Bibliographic Instruction in Relation to the Causes and Symptoms of Burnout," *RQ* (Spring 1993):349.

4. Ibid., 350.

5. William Miller, "What's Wrong with Reference: Coping with Success and Failures at the Reference Desk,"*American Libraries* 15 (May 1984): 306.

6. Blumenthal, Howard, and Kinyon, "Impact of CD-ROM," 15

7. Becker, "Characteristics of Bibliographic Instruction," 352.

8. Ibid., 348

9. **COASTNET** is the online computer local area network of library holdings in the Charleston area academic, medical and public libraries searchable on OPAC. **COASTNET** also includes selected periodical indexes. Students may search a topic for both books and periodicals on **COASTNET**.

10. A model of this program (to be modified or adapted for use) is available by request. The program includes the proposal, hands-on exercises, lesson plan, test and evaluation form.

11. Miller, "What's Wrong," 321.

Are Faculty Attitudes Towards Information Literacy Affected by Their Use of Electronic Databases?
A Survey

Fran Nowakowski and Elizabeth Frick

ABSTRACT

Students face an increasingly complex system of scholarly information transfer. It is the faculty that controls the university curriculum design in virtually all disciplines. The researchers hypothesized that faculty attitudes towards information literacy, their disciplincary inclinations, their own background and experience with information, are variables that affect the transmission of information literacy skills to students. Therefore, the researchers conducted a survey of faculty members in all disciplines at Dalhousie University, in Nova Scotia, Canada. Faculty members responded to nearly 60 demographic, attitudinal and experiential questions. These questions explored instructor's expectations of students library knowledge, attitudes towards librarians roles, priorities regarding teaching and information literacy and the instructor's use of the library. The basic results reveal a great deal of faculty support for student information literacy. The paper reviews the development of the survey and examines the results including correlations between attitudes and such factors as disciplines and actual library experience. Strategies for using the results to redesign an existing library instruction program will also be examined.

BACKGROUND

Students, both graduate and undergraduate, face an increasingly complex system of scholarly information transfer. Since information plays a pivotal rôle in society, it is imperative that educa- tion include a component which stresses methods of information access and critical thinking skills. In an information-based economy, intelligent in- formation-seeking behaviour is a necessary pre- cursor to intelligent information use.

Fran Nowakowski is a Reference Librarian at Killam Library and Elizabeth Frick is a Professor in the School of Library & Information Studies at Dalhousie University, Halifax, Nova Scotia, Canada.

A large sector of the information system is now available only through electronic means such as online public access catalogues, CD-ROM databases, and electronic journals. The complexity and multi-form nature of this information system has reached a level that makes it difficult to countenance graduating students without providing them with the skills of information literacy — the ability to find the materials they need, to apply critical thinking in their searches, and to keep themselves abreast of new developments in their chosen field.

In most universities and colleges it is the teaching faculty who control the design of the university curriculum in all disciplines. Thus the importance given to teaching the skills of information access and critical thinking is determined by the faculty. It is, therefore, hypothesized that the attitudes of faculty toward information literacy as well as their disciplinary focus and their own experience with information, are variables that affect the transmission of information literacy skills to students.

The objective of the authors is to provide useful data for designing more effective programs of bibliographic instruction — programs that, rather than being an interruption to disciplinary learning, would be acknowledged as an essential part of disciplinary concerns. There are a number of factors that might affect the shape and success of any one instruction program: curriculum design, nature of the student body, human and financial resources, library mandate, intellectual culture are among these. The authors chose to examine faculty attitudes as being one critical factor in determining the effective delivery of information literacy skills in a university setting.

It was determined that a survey would be the most effective way to obtain evidence of faculty attitudes. A survey would also allow us to obtain demographic details, and previous and current research experience — both of which might affect attitudes.

PREVIOUS LITERATURE

A literature search indicated that while there have been surveys to determine librarians' attitudes to instruction programs, only four surveys have been conducted examining faculty attitudes. Joy Thomas examined the faculty California State University, Long Beach about their preferred types of library instruction.[1] This study does not relate these preferences to disciplinary or other variables. The author recently updated this study in 1994.[2] Larry Hardesty developed a scale to measure attitudes of classroom instructors toward the role of the academic library in undergraduate education.[3] He found correlations between these attitudes and variables in the instructor populations. While his findings and instrument formed the basis for our work, Hardesty was not able to gather comparative data involving the faculty at professional schools and liberal arts schools, to do comparisons between attitudes in graduate and undergraduate education, or to gather data relating to the instructors' own use of the library. J. Edmund Maynard tested a small specialized (204 military college faculty) group.[4] Most recently Anita Cannon surveyed faculty in a Canadian academic setting.[5] Her population was the social sciences and humanities faculty. Her questions dealt particularly with instruction modes and perceived student abilities. She asked few demographic questions, only determining faculty, department and subject specialty/field. She surveyed all 565 faculty members and received a 41% response rate.

There has been a consistent strain in the literature emphasizing the critical importance of faculty attitudes toward the role of libraries in higher education. For instance, Patricia Breivik, in her book *Information Literacy: Revolution in the Library* states, "Academic leaders should understand why the realities of the information explosion require a change in faculty attitudes toward what constitutes a 'good' library."[6] Earlier she makes a pointed plea for a change in faculty attitudes to what she terms "library-based learning:"

To graduate independent learners, academic leaders will need to encourage faculty to move beyond the old approach to become facilitators of learning, assisting students to make use of the wide range of materials available in and through campus libraries. But many faculty will not become facilitators until they learn a new approach to their own research process . . . . . The challenge is for institutions to ensure an integrated approach that offers incentives . . . through faculty-development programs for faculty to become more active facilitators of learning.[7]

SURVEY PROCEDURE

The survey was conducted at Dalhousie University, Halifax, Nova Scotia. Dalhousie is an institution with about 12,000 students, both graduate and undergraduate. It includes the traditional undergraduate faculties in the Arts, Social Sciences and Sciences as well as graduate professional schools in Medicine, Law and Management.

A draft of the questionnaire was completed by a small test group and the results prompted numerous changes in the wording of the statements. A final version of the survey was sent to all 665 faculty at the University in the Spring of 1991. 439 replies were received, a return rate of 66%, considered excellent for further analysis. The raw data was encoded using SPSS with the aid of the Survey Centre at Gorsebrook Research Institute. A brief report of this phase of the research appeared in the Spring of 1993.[8]

The questionnaire was based on that of Hardesty[9] with adaptations and additions for local needs. It consisted of nearly 56 questions roughly divided into three catagories: nine preliminary "demographic" questions dealt with department, rank, age, gender and teaching load. Thirty-six offered "attitude" statements with 7-point scales of response ranging from "I strongly agree with this statement" to "I strongly disagree with this statement"; finally, 12 questions dealt with the faculty member's own use of the library facilities or the "experience" of the survey population. The attitude statements explored the instructors' expectations of student library knowledge, attitudes towards librarians roles, views of who should teach information skills, priorities (e.g. library use instruction versus teaching disciplinary content, or how significant the acquisition of life-long learning skills is to students), and view of library use assignments.

Initial examination of the raw data provided some interesting results. (See Figure 1) 97.6% of faculty responding agreed that undergraduate students should know how to do library research, and in fact an overwhelming 99.5% of those faculty responding agreed that it will be essential to students in later life that they be able to find information efficiently. 72.2% of those responding also agreed that they did not have enough time to teach both basic course material and library research skills. Only 62.3% of those responding presently design assignments which require library use for their undergraduate students.

Librarians will be encouraged to learn that not only do 90.9% of the responding faculty agree that librarians and faculty are partners in the educational process but that 91.2% agreed that a requirement of the Baccalaureate degree should be that students know how to do library research.

There is obviously great faculty support for the librarian's view that information literacy is an essential skill that all students should have. But it is clear both from the survey and actual experience that there are other obstacles which are preventing the incorporation of these skills into the curriculum.

RECENCY OF ELECTRONIC DATABASE USE AND INSTRUCTION

The fact that faculty controls university curriculum, argues that understanding faculty will be one critical factor for instructional design. Such understanding will play a substantial rôle in the success of any instructional effort.

Our survey was designed to obtain a variety of information from faculty - information that would provide a foundation for better understanding them.

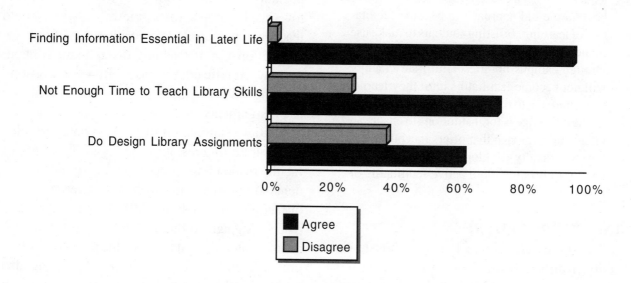

Figure 1: Comparison of Three Questions

We are particularly interested in the material resulting from the cross tabulations between the categories of demographics, attitudes and experience.

The first cross tabulations to be looked at, are those showing high significance. A critical point to examine are which aspects of demography or experience might have significant correlations with faculty attitudes towards instruction. We are examining, for instance, the results of comparing questions of discipline, age, rank, etc. (demographic) with the questions of how long, how much instruction (attitude). Also we are comparing questions on the importance of instruction to students (attitude) with the graduate study experience of the faculty member (experience). What impact does a faculty member's experience in the library, and the recency of that experience, have on his/her perception of instruction and instructional objectives? Focusing on a particular variable to find the significant factors is an example of one such examination.

For this paper we chose to examine the hypothesis that an intimate, recent knowledge of library resources increases understanding of the com-

plexity of library research, and underscores the need for more extensive bibliographic instruction.

For example, is there a useful (significant) correlation between those who reported recent us of electronic databases and those who thought their students needed more than one session to learn necessary library skills? And is there a difference in perception about the time needed to teach the skills to graduate students versus undergraduate students based on the recency of the faculty member's experience with electronic databases?

The following two statements were examined: *"I have made use of one of the electronic databases (online or CD-ROM) at the library in the last . . ",*

- 58.1% had not used such databases for a month or more.
- 23.7% had used an electronic database within the past month, but not within the past week.
- 18.28% had used one within the past week.

"It should take more than one class for students to learn the skills needed to do library research for my courses,"

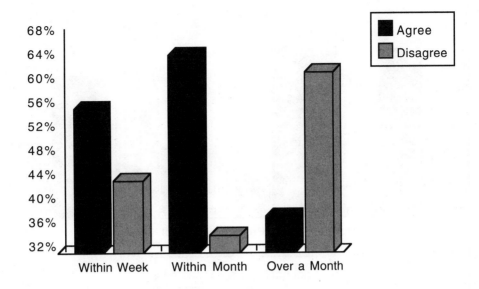

**Figure 2: More Than One Class to Teach Library Skills to Grads //
Recency of Database Usage by Faculty**

The <u>undergraduate</u> section of that question received 396 responses.
- 43.2% strongly agreed, agreed or slightly agreed.
- 43.7% strongly disagreed, disagreed or slightly disagreed.
- 13.1% responded "not applicable".

The <u>graduate</u> student section had almost the same balance among the 338 who answered.
- 41.1% agreed.
- 43.8% disagreed.
- 15.1% reported "not applicable".

Undergraduate

Of those faculty who had NOT used electronic databases for more than a month, most (61.7%) did not agree that their undergraduates needed more than one library instruction class. Only 38.3% felt it would take more than one class. Whereas, of those faculty members who HAD used a database within the last month, 70.6% felt that it should take their undergraduates more than one class session to learn these skills. Only 29.4% thought it should not take undergraduates more than one class.

Graduate

A similar statistical pattern emerges regarding perceptions of graduate student needs when correlated with recent use of electronic databases in the library. The percentage who felt that it should take their graduate students more than one session was only slightly less than it was for undergraduates. (See Figure 2)

It appears clear that the more professors use electronic databases, the more they feel students need time to learn them. And this perception holds for both graduate and undergraduate level students.

Experience and attitudes

Other "experience/attitude" questions also showed significant correlations. One, similar to the question analyzed above, asked how often faculty used the library when conducting their research. This showed a high correlation when matched with a statement regarding the design of assignments requiring library use. The more frequently a faculty member used the library while conducting research, the more likely they were to

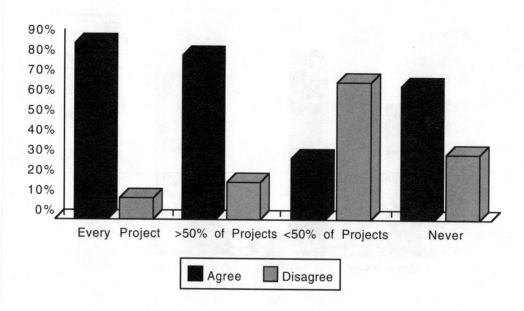

**Figure 3: Design Assignments for Grads Requiring Library Use //
Personal Library Use for Research**

design assignments for their students requiring use of the library. (See Figure 3)

A significant statistical relationship is shown between faculty's view of the amount of instruction needed for their graduate students, and the question about whether they themselves learned their library research skills as undergraduates from their professors. A significant relationship is shown between faculty's view of the amount of instruction needed for both graduate and undergraduates, and the question of whether they learned their library skills as undergraduates from librarians.

Certainly this is a correlation (perceived amount of time to be allotted for instruction and who taught library research skills to whom) that we will want to examine closely.

FINDINGS

Initial analysis supports the view that recent/ frequent use of library resources (electronic and print) by faculty will convince them that students need extensive opportunities to learn the skills involved in their use. These findings indicate perhaps that familiarity with library research is

one good way to convince faculty of the need for more training in library research skills.

How might information literacy and instructional programs respond practically to this information? At least two possible ways occur:
*   Aim information literacy programs particularly at the disciplines/departments where faculty members with searching skills are prevalent.
*   Offer free training and opportunities to faculty to learn and practice electronic teaching in their research areas.

The first response builds on the existent strengths in the faculty. It gives librarians a place to start and allows them to build success from a strong base. Instruction librarians have long recognized the relative ease of preaching to the converted. Bibliographic instruction that builds on an audience of faculty convinced of the possibilities and complexity of information access in an electronic age, has a much better chance of taking firm hold in the curriculum.

The second response explores new areas of possible success. It also begins to deal with the problem of change which the technology has made even more critical. As Hardesty says,

Changes in curriculum can take away much of the significance of an individual's life work . . . . [K.P.] Cross [*Accent on Learning*, San Francisco: Jossey-Bass, 1976] suggested that traditional disciplines now may be facing problems similar to those met by the classical curriculum around the turn of the century . . . .[10]

Involving faculty in the increasing changes of the technology, makes them stakeholders in the education of their students to the demands imposed by those changes.

CONCLUSIONS AND NEED FOR FUTURE RESEARCH AND ANALYSIS

Obviously, this is only one small focus of analysis in a wider spectrum that might be examined in this and similar research. Hardesty, in his thorough and scholarly examinations of the research literature in this area, has opened out many avenues. Particularly, his observations on faculty culture are ones which shed a good deal of light on some of the present findings.[11] They present us with fertile ground for further research.

This project intends to look at more of the experiential factors that intersect with attitudes. It will also examine as many of the cross tabulations between demographic factors and attitudes as seem significant. The study will aim not only at the analysis of the data collected, but will seek to find ways to make the findings applicable to academic libraries and their educational function.

The authors gratefully acknowledge the support provided by the Faculty of Graduate Studies (Research Development Fund) and the Associate Vice-President (Research) at Dalhousie University.

NOTES

1. Joy Thomas, "The University Faculty and Library Instruction," *RQ* 23 (Summer 1984):431-436.
2. Joy Thomas, "Faculty Attitudes and Habits Concerning Library Instruction: How much has changed since 1982?" *Research Strategies* 12 (Fall 1994): 209-223.
3. Larry Hardesty, *The Development of a Set of Scales to Measure the Attitudes of Classroom Instructors Toward the Undergraduate Educational Role of the Academic Library* (Ph.D. diss., Indiana University, 1982).
4. J. Edmund Maynard, "A Case Study of Faculty Attitudes Toward Library Instruction: The Citadel Experience," *RSR: Reference Services Review* 18 (Summer 1990):67-76.
5. Anita Cannon, "Faculty Survey on Library Research Instruction," *RQ* 33 (Summer 1994): 524-541.
6. Patricia Breivik, *Information Literacy: Revolution in the Library* (New York, NY: American Council on Education, 1989), 177.
7. Ibid., 36-37.
8. Fran Nowakowski, "Faculty Support Information Literacy," *C&RL News* 54 (March 1993):124.
9. Larry Hardesty, *Faculty and the Library: The Undergraduate Experience* (New York, NY: Ablex, 1991) and Hardesty, "The Development of a Set of Scales."
10. Hardesty, *Faculty and the Library*, 108.
11. Ibid., particularly Chapters 7 and 8, "Faculty Culture: A Historical Perspective" and "Contemporary Faculty Culture."

BIBLIOGRAPHY

Breivik, Patricia. *Information Literacy: Revolution in the Library*. (New York, N.Y.: American Council on Education, 1989).

Cannon, Anita. "Faculty Survey on Library Research Instruction." *RQ* 33 (Summer 1994): 524-541

Hardesty, Larry. *The Development of a Set of Scales to Measure the Attitudes of Classroom Instructors Toward the Undergraduate Educational Role of the Academic Library*. Ph.D. diss., Indiana University, 1982.

_____. "The Influence of Selected Variables on Attitudes of Classroom Instructors Toward the Undergraduate Educational Role of the Academic Library." in *Academic Libraries: Myths and Realities: Proceedings of the Third National Conference of the Association of College and Research Libraries.* pp. 365-377 (Chicago: Association of College and Research Libraries, 1984)

_____. *Faculty and the Library: The Undergraduate Experience.* (Norwood, NJ: Ablex, 1991)

Haws, Rae; Lorna Peterson and Diana Shonrock. "Survey of Faculty Attitudes Towards a Basic Library Skills Course." *College & Research Libraries News* 50 (March 1989): 201-203.

Maynard, J. Edmund. "A Case Study of Faculty Attitudes Toward Library Instruction: The Citadel Experience." *RSR: Reference Services Review* 18 (Summer 1990): 67-76.

Nowakowski, Fran. "Faculty Support Information Literacy." *C&RL News* 54 (March 1993):124.

Thomas, Joy. "Faculty Attitudes and Habits Concerning Library Instruction: How much has changed since 1982?" *Research Strategies* 12 (Fall 1994): 209-223.

Thomas, Joy. "The University Faculty and Library Instruction." *RQ* 2(Summer 1984): 431-436.

Listening to Our Users:
Should Traditional Librarians Become Extinct?

Nancy Pippen Eckerman

ABSTRACT

Some experts are urging academic medical librarians to divest themselves of traditional roles and skills or become extinct. Literature on the library research skills of scientists and clinicians or physicians tells us that these library users need the services of a traditional librarian more than his colleagues in the humanities. Further, studies indicate that physicians and scientists are satisfied with the information provided by librarians. All librarians should study the skills which are really needed to best serve their clients.

Erwin H. Ackerknecht, M.D. introduces his classic book *A Short History of Medicine* with the observation "for many members of the medical profession have at all times displayed a queer mixture of unreasonable conservatism and no more reasonable addiction to the latest novelties."[1] I would like for us as librarians to substitute library profession into the quote. Does not "unreasonable conservatism" fit the popular image of librarians? Over there we see the librarians grimly charging out books, filing catalog cards and refusing to consider exceptions to any rule.

As librarians, don't just a few of us feel "the no more reasonable addiction to the latest novelties" portion of the quote applies to the headlong jump we're making or being forced to make, onto the information super highway?

"Librarian" may not be part of our job title. We scramble to rid ourselves of our identity as librarians in order to disappear into the administrative suites. We remove ourselves from the scholarly work of research by choice or fiscal necessity, assigning public contact work to paraprofessionals. We then wonder why administrators and faculty don't see the need for more librarians or why we are not respected as colleagues by the teaching faculty.

Many librarians are all still recovering from Nicholson Baker's attack on librarians and automated card catalogs in the *New Yorker's* article, "Discard".[2] This lengthy eulogy to the card catalog labeled the scrapping of card catalogs "one of the odder features of this national paroxysm of shortsightedness and anti-intellectualism". Mr.

Nancy Pippen Eckerman is the Special Collections Librarian at Ruth Lilly Medical Library, Indiana University School of Medicine, Indianapolis, Indiana.

Baker accuses librarians of destroying their most important and irreplaceable contribution to scholarship, our knowledge of books within the intricate web of literary and historical context.

As the Special Collections Librarian and History of Medicine Librarian in an academic health sciences library, I sometimes feel about as up to date as one of the dinosaurs in Jurassic Park. I am the *libraria litteratarum,* librarian of letters, not the *medicala informatica,* medical informatics specialist.[3] (I tried to use the "Latin" found in Robert M. Braude's article. However, Dr. Braude, Assistant Dean for Information Resources at the Samuel J. Wood Library/C.V. Starr Biomedical Information Center, Cornell University Medical College, did not take the time to verify his made up Latin terms. I have corrected and feminized what I could and left the other terms as he made them up.) Old medical books are a dusty nuisance and contradict the sleek image of modernity that most health science information specialists want to project to other medical professionals.

As I was thinking of ways for the *libraria litteratarum* to coexist with the *medicala informatica* I noticed something which the articles on the future of medical librarians don't mention. The physicians whom I assist with history of medicine research topics, were grateful for the traditional services I provide to them. In fact, they were more than grateful. They need the talents of a traditional librarian with a knowledge of the organization of the entire spectrum of knowledge.

Contrasting the research techniques of physicians and historians, the non-medical users of the history of medicine collection, I thought, might be a useful method to discover why physicians relied on the traditional skills of the librarian more than the historian.

My first impression was that the difference in attitude displayed by the physicians and historians when they approached a history of medicine research topic was due to the physician being accustomed to the crisp immediate answers provided by electronic citation bases and other electronic data.

Physicians, I believed, were technology dependent.

Historians, on the other hand, never able to luxuriate in the latest computer technology, still possessed the stamina and ingenuity to fight their way into and out of a jungle of primary sources. Photocopying is still the greatest technological change in historical research since the printing press. Incidentally, photocopying also ranks very high in the list of "library services" most used by scientists.

My look into the research patterns of historians and physicians revealed technology was not the reason why physicians and historians approached the history of medicine librarian with different expectations.

Differences in the expectations displayed by physicians and historians appear to result from differing levels of information literacy, information literacy of traditional print sources.

Information literacy is defined as: "The ability to effectively access and evaluate information for a given need." Shirley Behrens' recent article on information literacy amplifies this definition to include an integrated set of skills and knowledge developed through the acquisition of attitudes. These attitudes include persistence, attention to detail, and caution in accepting the printed word and single sources. Information literacy is time and labor intensive and need-driven. It is a problem-solving activity.[4]

By the above definition of information literacy, historians are intrinsically information literate, at least in their own field. The historian's work is to read, condense, collect, assimilate, transform and synthesize materials conveying historical information.[5] Expertise on a given historical topic implies knowledge of the original source materials and writings of experts in that field. By their very nature, historians are critical of sources and theories. Only the novice historian, or historian expanding his area of expertise, would rely on the librarian to give direction to their research.

Historians and other humanities scholars usually approach the history of medicine librarian only for access to previously identified materials. Historians generally make few demands besides requesting physical access to items in the special collection. No librarian needs to tell historians: the importance of attention to detail; that citations must be verified; to cross check sources; and research is time consuming.

By contrast, physicians emerge from medical schools malnourished on the principles of critical reading and weak in English 101 research skills. By the above definition of information literacy, they are not literate.

Looking for confirmation of my evaluation of the level of information literacy in the medical profession, I found this statement. "Available evidence indicates that medical information is more likely to be unsubstantiated than not, and the more positive the claim, the lower the probability that the claim is valid." [6] The author of that statement, Peter G. Goldschmidt proposes a new field of medical writing called information synthesis. The suggested technique for this process is as follows:

1. Define your topic narrowly and the audience for which it is intended.
2. Systematically search for all information relevant to that topic.
3. Assess the validity of the information with reference to the chosen audience.
4. Present the valid finding in a form useful to the intended audience.

He continues. "When searching literature never under estimate the task and remember that a good job involves effort beyond the obvious." Goldschmidt also warns to resist two common tendencies. One is to think all published information is valid and the other is to assume all information is equally valid.[7] Dr. Goldschmidt reinvents the concept of information literacy for the medical profession.

The editor of the *New England Journal of Medicine* moans medical students don't read medical journals, at least not his. Dr. Kassirer, the editor, then outlines how to skim journals for "items of interest".[8] However, authors of other studies claim that recent medical school graduates rely more on journal material to answer clinical questions than their predecessors did.[9]

Many physicians have no patience with false drops in computer searches of databases. However, statistics provided by our LAN (local area network) show few of our users enter sophisticated search strategies. Most users of our Medline system, the electronic version of the *Index Medicus*, do not appear to make the best use of it.

Personal experience also indicates once our users find relevant articles for their research, they can't extract bibliographic citations from the printout for a journal article. Almost hourly the general reference desk receives calls from secretaries trying to complete citations. Some academic medical libraries insist libraries verify bibliographies in faculty articles.

Are there any signs that medical educators see the need to make our future physicians more information literate?

Rumbles caused by "unreasonable conservatism" resound when medical school curricula are restructured by problem based learning. This method, we are told, will produce physicians who can be life-long learners and hopefully, information literate.

Medical educators concur that medical students need to devote more time to critical thinking and problem solving, and less time to memorizaion, while in medical school.[10]

Physicians are seeking ways to have their information filtered and evaluated before consuming it. They are finding ways to benefit from someone else's ability to read critically. [11] This might be done by seeking out state-of-the-science reviews or what's called "latest update" articles.

More often, the process of information filtering directly involves the physician with another person. This person is often a colleague or specialist in the area in which the physician needs information. The history of medicine librarian serves this function when physicians research historical topics. I listen to the researcher and help them define their informational needs.

A more formalized alliance of physicians and librarians has also been tried. Clinical medical librarians are part of a clinical team and research questions raised by health care professionals during rounds. The articles the clinical medical librarian supplied physicians generally pleased them.[12]

Even scientists, who make little use of the library, if it is too far from their offices, believe that librarians should be the professionals to make sense out of the myriad of forms in which information is now distributed. [13]

With so many studies showing a high level of satisfaction with the skills of the traditional-albeit-technology knowledgeable librarian, why do librarians fear the human touch is no longer needed? [14] Perhaps they are listening to experts who have never been a traditional librarian or experts who believe technology can overcome information illiteracy.

This paper is not an unreasoned cry for the good-old-days. But the words of Richard Selzer, a medical writer, thrill a *libraria litteratarum*, such as myself. "The machine does not exist that can take the place of the divining physician."[15] Lucretia McClure adapted his words for librarians. "The machine does not exist that can take the place of the thinking librarian."[16]

Many of us agree the traditional divinations of a librarian surpass the featureless printouts of many electronic citation bases and online catalogs which are instantly available and often unintelligible to the information illiterate. Yet, academic librarians' resumes are evaluated by the presence of increasingly responsible administrative duties, not by demonstrated ability in meeting the needs of users, and to be colleagues in the business of research.

I never suspected how much physicians need the traditional library service until I did the literature search for this paper. Surely I am not the only librarian who meets the needs of her users by affirming the partnership of the academic librarian in the business of scholarship?

Let me close with another quote from Ackerknecht. He is commenting about what happens when the medical profession forgets its history. "They live thus, with the misconception that every good thought and useful technique was invented only yesterday and that the most important problems are very close to final solution."[17]

Information illiteracy is not conquered by computer literacy alone. Librarians should train themselves to know the difference.

NOTES

1. Erwin H. Ackerknecht, *A Short History of Medicine* (Baltimore: Johns Hopkins Univ. Pr., 1982), xx.
2. Nicholson Baker "Discard" *New Yorker* 70 (April 4, 1994), 64-70+.
3. Robert M. Braude "Impact of Information Technology on the Role of Health Sciences Librarians" *Bulletin of the Medical Library Association* 81 (October 1993), p. 411.
4. Shirley J. Behrens "A Conceptual Analysis and Historical Overview of Information Literacy" *College and Research Libraries* 55 (July 1994): 312.
5. Donald Owen Case "The Collection and Use of Information by Some American Historians: a Study of Motives and Methods" *Library Quarterly* 61, no.1 (1991): 63.
6. Peter G. Goldschmidt "Information Synthesis: A Practical Guide" *HSR: Health Services Research* 21 (June 1986, pt. I): 224.
7. Ibid., 217.
8. Jerome P Kassirer "Learning Medicine: Too Many Books, Too Few Journals" *New England Journal of Medicine* 326 (May 21, 1992): 1427.
9. Larry D. Gruppen "Physician Information Seeking: Improving Relevance through Research: *Bulletin of the Medical Library Association* 78 (April 1990): 168.
10. Clive R. Taylor "Occasional Notes-Great Expectations-the Reading Habits of Year II Medical Students" *New England Journal of Medicine* 326 (May 21, 1992): 1439.
11. Alice B. Kuller, Charles B. Wessel, David S. Ginn,

and Thomas P. Martin "Quality Filtering of the Clinical Literature by Librarians and Physicians: *Bulletin of the Medical Library Association* 81 (January 1993).

12. Jean M. Demas and Logan T. Ludwig " Clinical Medical Librarian: the Last Unicorn" *Bulletin of the Medical Library Association* 79 (January, 1991).

13. Suzanne Grefsheim, Jon Franklin, and Diana Cunningham "Biotechnology Awareness Study, Part 1: Where Scientists Get Their Information" *Bulletin of the Medical Library Association* 79 (January 1991): 43.

14. For some examples not cited separately, see Joan G. Marshall "The Impact of the Hospital Library on Clinical Decision Making: the Rochester Study" *Bulletin of the Medical Library Association* 80 (April 1992); David N. King "The Contribution of Hospital Library Information Services to Clinical Care: A Study in Eight Hospitals" *Bulletin of the Medical Library Association* 75 (October 1987).; and Steven H. Woolf and Dennis A. Benson "The Medical Information Needs of Internists and Pediatricians at an Academic Medical Center" *Bulletin of the Medical Library Association* 77 (October 1989);

15. Richard Selzer *Letters to a Young Doctor* (New York: Simon and Schuster, 1982), 17.

16. Lucretia McClure "Remembering Our History: the Roots of Knowledge" *Bulletin of the Medical Library Association* 78 (January 1990), 67.

17. Ackerknecht, *A Short History,* xvi.

Changing a Library Services Faculty Model:

The Major & Minor (M&M) Approach

Jay Schafer and Camila A. Alire

ABSTRACT

Fiscal limitations, human resources concerns, and inadequate services forced the Auraria Library to create a unique library faculty model to alleviate the problems adversely affecting its services to the campus. A description of the previous model is included along with a discussion about the need for change. The M&M Model was designed to provide the best fit between the Library (and the services it must provide) and its library faculty. The model focuses on library faculty working in specific "major and minor" areas. The process for changing models and the results of the change are included.

A relatively young institution, Auraria Library was established in 1976 as part of the new Auraria campus in downtown Denver, which serves as home to the Community College of Denver, Metropolitan State College of Denver, and the University of Colorado at Denver. Formed by merging the existing libraries from the three schools, Auraria Library serves approximately 2,000 faculty and 35,000 students (23,000 FTE). In addition, the Library receives about ten percent of its use from local residents. This diverse user group requires the Library to support curricula varying from community college to graduate and professional programs, and to serve the research needs of the faculty.

To provide 87.5 hours of service each week, the Library depends on a staff of twenty-six Library faculty/administrative staff and sixty paraprofessional staff working under the Colorado state classified personnel system. The collection consists of approximately 740,000 volumes, including government publications and a relatively large microforms collection. The Library learning materials budget was $1.4 million in 1993/94.

Jay Schafer is Coordinator of Collection Development Services and Camila A. Alire is Dean at Auraria Library, University of Colorado at Denver, Denver, Colorado.

AURARIA LIBRARY'S PREVIOUS ORGANIZATIONAL STRUCTURE

The basic responsibilities of collection development, instruction, and reference activities can be structured either functionally or by subject discipline. Between 1981 and 1988, the Auraria Library evolved into a subject discipline organization in which Library faculty assumed responsibility for the link between the Library and the clients in particular subject areas. These liaisons performed the intellectual functions of the Library in relation to its clients.

The Library Faculty Liaison (LFL) Model, in effect, creates a branch librarian for each discipline without the added expense and duplication of a branch facility. It creates the personal interactions that take place in a branch without the physical reality. Faculty and students within a subject area have one individual to contact for all library and information services. The liaison librarian may not be able to provide all services but is responsible for funneling the request to the appropriate person or location. This coupled with the fact that the liaison is aware of all aspects of service in a given subject area, creates a system which in its perfect execution could not be more effective.[1]

A managerial structure was established to develop skills relating to reference, instruction, and collection development and to integrate the individual programs of the various disciplines into a comprehensive plan. Middle management "Coordinator" positions were established to coordinate the discipline-oriented plans of the liaison librarians with professional expertise in collection development, instruction, and reference. The coordinators also became responsible for the non-subject related aspects of user services such as Interlibrary Loan and Computer Assisted Research.

This model brought about an organizational structure (Figure I) consisting of two divisions: Collection and Automation Services Division (CASD) and the Instruction and Research Services Division (IRSD). CASD, consisting of the intellectual and technical activities relating to col-

lection access, was managed by an Assistant Director and Coordinators of Acquisitions, Bibliographic and Circulation Services. IRSD was managed by an Assistant Director and Coordinators of Collection Development, Bibliographic Instruction, and Reference Services.

IDENTIFIED NEED FOR CHANGE

When a new administrator assumed responsibility for the Instruction and Research Services Division, three issues became very apparent. The first was that the library faculty in IRSD were very frustrated, dissatisfied and unhappy. When IRSD faculty had the opportunity to express their concerns individually, what surfaced universally was the feeling of being burned out and a concern for providing less than quality service. In trying to be all things to all people, the IRSD liaison librarians felt that they were spread so thin that quality service to the campus community was being compromised.

There were conditions which justified these concerns. Auraria Library was not funded to adequately support the LFL Model. 1990 IPEDS - Integrated Postsecondary Education Data Systems data (Figure II) demonstrated that the Library was ranked the *lowest* among all Colorado university and four-year college libraries in:

- Materials expenditure per student FTE;
- Total operating expenditures per student FTE; and,
- Library staff (professional and paraprofessional) per 1,000 students.[2]

The second issue was the evaluation process. The LFL Model called for each IRSD library faculty member to be evaluated by multiple supervisors, one from each of the three coordinating units. Annual planning prioritized efforts in each area, but what resulted on a yearly basis was librarians maintaining heavy reference desk and bibliographic instruction schedules and, inevitably, scurrying at the last minute to spend out the materials budgets allocated in their three to eight

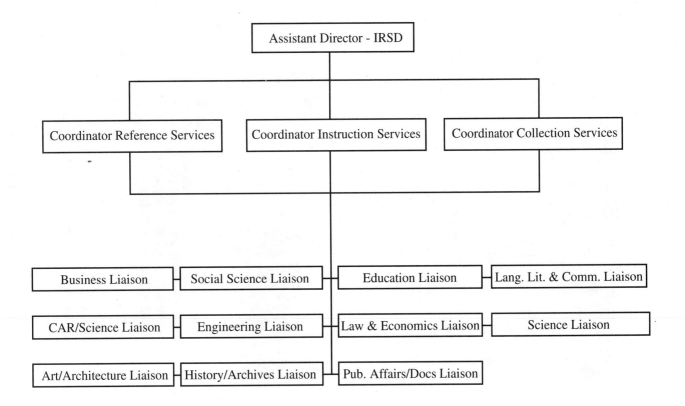

Figure I: Library Organization
Instruction and Reference Services Division (IRSD)
Library Faculty Liaison Model

subject disciplines. It became very apparent that there was a definite need to rethink the LFL Model and create a model that was more conducive to the Auraria environment and limited fiscal realities.

The third issue was a deep tension simmering between the three coordinating units within IRSD — Reference, Bibliographic Instruction, and Collection Development. The Coordinators from these three units were under pressure to provide appropriate services to the campus both by positioning their individual areas and by trying to balance this importance with the overall success of the Library.

PROCESS FOR CHANGE

At the same time the need to create a new model for IRSD liaison librarians was identified,

the Library was completing a strategic planning process. This process resulted in the Library developing a new mission statement and five strategic goals to accomplish that mission. These strategic goals, in rank order, were:

- Collection development;
- Database clean-up;
- Organizational self-esteem;
- Improved communications; and,
- Information access.

Once these strategic goals were developed, a proposed model for a complete library reorganization was considered. Briefly, the new model disposed of divisions (CASD and IRSD) and combined all coordinating units under one area called

Figure II.   1990 IPEDS Comparisons of Colorado Public Higher Education (Source: Colorado State Library, Library Research Service)

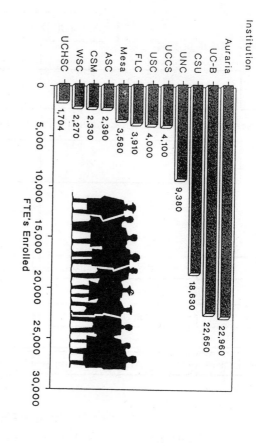

Full-Time Equivalent Enrollments Served
By Auraria Library & Other Public
Four-Year Institutions, 1990

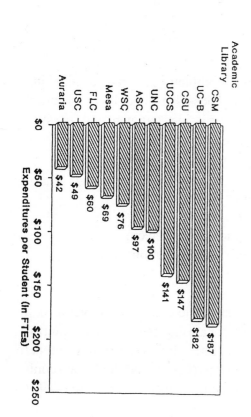

Librarians & Total Staff per 1,000
Students for Auraria Library & Other
Public Four-Year Institutions, 1990

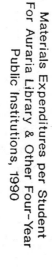

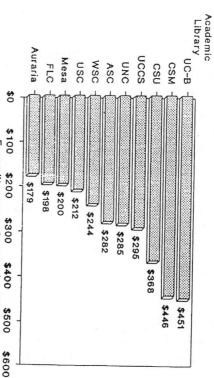

Total Operating Expenditures per Student
For Auraria Library & Other Four-Year
Public Institutions, 1990

Materials Expenditures per Student
For Auraria Library & Other Four-Year
Public Institutions, 1990

"Library Services."[3] It also established a new and creative way to deal with the staffing issue of only 1.13 librarians for every 1,000 students.

The result of this effort was the Major and Minor Model or the M&M Model (Figure III). Each librarian could "major" in one of the coordinating areas — reference, collection development (bibliography), library instruction, or cataloging. They could then "minor" in one of three areas — reference, instruction, or program management (supervision of a unit such as government publications, architecture branch library, or original cataloging). In designing the model, it was decided that there would be no part-time bibliographers, thus no minor in collection development. This would remove the conflict between demanding reference/instruction schedules and the collection development responsibility.

Prior to the new model, the average number of hours on the reference desk was eight per week. Some librarians wanted to increase this number, while others were admittedly burned out with reference service. With the M&M Model, the average number of hours would be closer to 14 hours. Those librarians wanting to major in reference would now be able to concentrate on more hours at the desk, and librarians burned out would be able to concentrate on an area other than reference. In addition, the reference librarians would have time to work on much needed reference projects which had been delayed because of the lack of staffing.

In order to continue staffing the reference desk the same number of hours with fewer librarians, the role of library paraprofessionals in reference was re-examined. The reorganization would allow the Library to empower reference paraprofessionals to work the reference desk more hours than ever before. These paraprofessionals were seasoned reference desk personnel, probably even more so than some of the junior librarians immediately out of library school. With a combination of reference librarians and seasoned reference paraprofessionals, the reference desk would be staffed by individuals who chose to work in that coordinating area.

The bibliographic instruction program at Auraria Library was billed as the largest academic BI program in Colorado and was a well-respected program on campus. However, there were concerns about the program which included:

- Its labor intensive nature;
- Continued program growth with no increase in staffing;
- A concentration on mainstream instruction at the expense of subject level instruction; and,
- The lack of a systematic student evaluation process assessing program effectiveness.

A Library Instruction Advisory Committee designed a new model for library instruction which included a menu of options for teaching faculty and students from which to choose. This allowed those librarians who majored in instruction to concentrated on subject level instruction for upper-division and graduate-level courses.

LIBRARY FACULTY INPUT AND REASSIGNMENT

Once the M&M Model concept was developed, it was presented to faculty librarians for response. The only requested modification was the option of minoring in collection development. After careful consideration, it was decided to retain the philosophy of the original plan and disallow a minor in CD. Librarians were then asked to submit their request for major and minor areas with a rationale. Obviously there were concerns that librarians would request the same major/minor areas. Also, there was a requirement to have certain levels of staffing at the reference desk, teaching instruction courses, and functioning as bibliographers. The pleasant surprise was that based on all requests, each librarian was placed in the desired major and minor area and the staffing needs in all three service areas were met.

Jay Schafer and Camila A. Alire

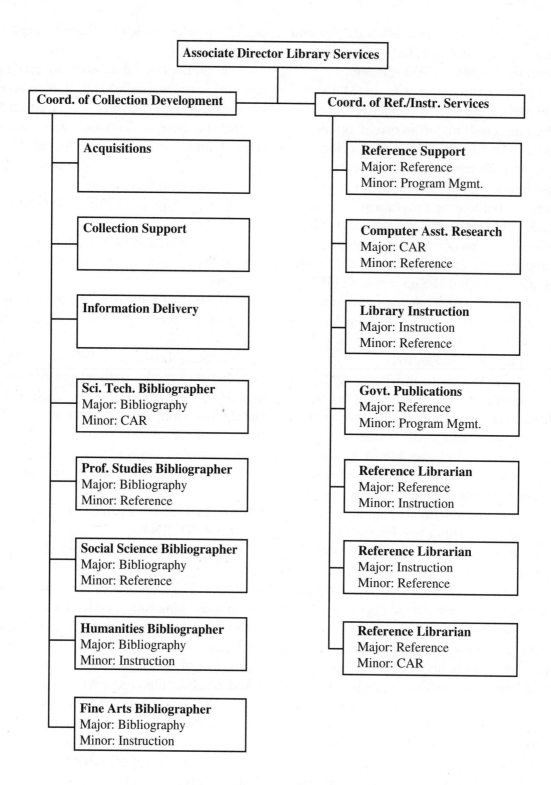

**Figure III: Library Re-Organization
Major/Minor (M&M) Model
(2 of 5 Coordinating Units)**

The Model was implemented on October 1, 1991, after notifying all teaching faculty of the changes as they related to their subject-area bibliographers.

THREE-YEARS LATER

After three years of experience with the M&M Model, there has not been one complaint from library faculty about the organizational model. One reason is that each person now has only one primary supervisor. As a result, the evaluation process has been simplified while still allowing for input by the "minor" supervisor. Also, the Coordinators are more satisfied with their greater ability to plan and complete specific projects and goals.

Under the M&M Model, significant programmatic goals have been achieved. In Reference, a weeding project has been completed; the paraprofessionals have been successful in offering quality service; and, a CD ROM network has been installed. Library instruction has implemented a mainstream program which is

less labor intensive using the *Library Handbook*, PAC demonstrations, Library Use Guides, and Point of Use instruction sheets. The collection development effort has been vastly enhanced with greater attention to selection; a collection management effort that has included weeding the entire collection for the first time ever; and, improved communication with classroom faculty, including a program of subject area reviews.

Internally, the M&M Model has provided Auraria Library with a mechanism to cope with the extremely limited human and financial resources. This internal success is characterized by a marked increase in the retention rate of library faculty.

However, the most significant indications that this reorganization has been successful are from the campus users themselves. The Library Dean, often the recipient of comments by students, faculty and other academic administrators, has noted a marked change in attitude toward the Library over the past three years - from open hostility to an appreciation for what the Library accomplishes with acknowledged limited resources.

NOTES

1. Peggy Johnson, "Matrix Management: An Organizational Alternative for Libraries,"*The Journal of Academic Librarianship* 16 (September, 1990): 223-229.
2. Julie J. Boucher, *Statistics and Input-Output Measures for Colorado Academic Libraries* (Colorado State Library: Denver, 1991): 31-66.
3. Irene B. Hoadley and John Corbin, "Up the Beanstalk: An Evolutionary Organizational Structure for Libraries," *American Libraries* 21 (July/August, 1990): 677.

BIBLIOGRAPHY

Julie J. Boucher, *Statistics and Input-Output Measures for Colorado Academic Libraries* (Colorado State Library: Denver, 1991).

Irene B. Hoadley and John Corbin, "Up the Beanstalk: An Evolutionary Organizational Structure for Libraries,"*American Libraries* 21 (July/August, 1990): 676-678.

Peggy Johnson, "Matrix Management: An Organizational Alternative for Libraries," *The Journal of Academic Librarianship* 16 (September, 1990): 223-229.

Beverly P. Lynch, *The Academic Library in Transistion* (New York: Neal-Schuman, 1989).

Job Satisfaction of Four Year College and University Library Employees in Pennsylvania:

Work-Related Characteristics[1]

Douglas L. Cook

ABSTRACT

This study looks at the work-related variables which impact the job satisfaction of Pennsylvania academic library employees. It was hypothesized that the amount of discretion maintained over daily work tasks, the amount of variety in the job, the amount of immediate feedback received relating to job performance, the level of autonomy experienced, and the amount of significance placed by the employee on his/her job would be statistically related to the reported level of job satisfaction. The data indicates only discretion is not related. It is important for library administrators to realize that factors under their control — variables relating to the actual library work environment — influence the job satisfaction of their employees.

The effectiveness of organizations has been measured from many different perspectives. One recent theory of measuring organizational effectiveness, as outlined by Michael Keeley, is based on the concept of social justice.[2] According to this theory an organization holds an implied social contract with its participants. An organization exists to effect the most good for its stakeholders. Keeley goes on to explain that organizations ought to be judged effective if they provide positive benefits to their customers and employees. It follows that organizations which are not meeting the needs of their stakeholders or which are actually causing harm to them could be labelled as ineffective.

Applying this organizational theory to the library, an effective library would be one which provides for the general well-being of those involved in the library — employees and patrons. One methodology for measuring the well-being of

Douglas L. Cook is Media Librarian/Assistant Professor at Ezra Lehman Library, Shippensburg University, Shippensburg, Pennsylvania.

these stakeholders (and therefore the library's effectiveness as an organization) is to measure their levels of satisfaction. This study describes an attempt to gauge the effectiveness of Pennsylvania academic libraries by measuring the job satisfaction of employees.

Although job satisfaction has been a subject of social science research for many years, it has only been since the 1970's that library researchers in the United States have focused their efforts on the measurement of this variable.[3] Since that time more than 20 studies have been published relating in some way to the job satisfaction of library personnel.

The majority of these studies have focused on the relationship of personal characteristics, such as age and income, to job satisfaction. The current study attempts to look beyond demographics by asking, "What is the relationship of job satisfaction to variables concerning the actual work done by Pennsylvania academic library employees?"

One typical recent study of job satisfaction which looks primarily at personal characteristics is that of Parmer and East[4]. They studied the relationships of library department, length of time employed, whether or not the library employee works with patrons, job classification, full-time job status, job commitment, gender, educational level, library size and supervisory status to the overall job satisfaction of 434 library support staff in 12 Ohio academic libraries. Other than the variable pertaining to working with patrons, these variables fall into the category of personal characteristics. Parmer and East's study [5] and other similar studies have neglected the actual tasks undertaken by library employees.

Of these studies of job satisfaction in libraries, only two include any attempt to discover a relationship between the daily tasks performed in the library and job satisfaction. Estabrook, Bird and Gilmore[6] looked at the actual work environment when they studied the relationship of job discretion and job satisfaction in a sample of 402 library personnel. These researchers discovered that those library employees who felt that they had a lot of

control over their daily tasks also reported higher levels of job satisfaction. Also, in their 1987 replication study of their original 1983 research, Lynch and Verdin[7] looked beyond worker demographics to the actual tasks performed by employees. To begin to do this, they looked at the amount of variety extant in the tasks performed by library personnel. These researchers found that there was a statistically significant relationship between job variety and job satisfaction. They found that library personnel with more routine jobs were less satisfied than those with more variety in their daily tasks.

Other than the two studies just mentioned, researchers have focused almost entirely on variables related to personal characteristics. As Lynch and Verdin[8] point out, there is a need for researchers to look at variables related to the work context of libraries. This current study is an attempt to begin to rectify the lack of information available concerning the specific work-related components of academic libraries which in some way contribute to the overall job satisfaction of the library employee.

This study duplicated the two aforementioned studies by looking at the relationship of job satisfaction to job discretion and to job variety in academic libraries. Further an attempt was made to flesh out this area of research by including other variables which are related to the actual work environment of other organizations. These variables include job feedback, job autonomy and task significance. These variables have been included in studies of employees other than those in libraries and have been found to be significantly related to job satisfaction. For example, Pearson,[9] in a study of 76 rail workers found that employees given appropriate job related feedback were more likely to be satisfied with their jobs. Liou, Sylvia and Brunk,[10] in a 1990 national sample of U.S. citizens over 18 found that workers who felt that they had a greater amount of autonomy also reported a higher level of job satisfaction. Finally, Butler,[11] in a study of 404 social workers found that those employees who felt strongly that the job they were doing was worthwhile were also more likely to report higher levels of job satisfaction.

This study focuses on five variables and their relationship to the job satisfaction of Pennsylvania academic library employees. The null hypothesis was used in analyzing these variables. The factors studied can be summarized as follows: **discretion** — the amount of control maintained over daily work tasks; **variety** — the amount of daily variety in the job; **feedback** — the amount of immediate feedback received relating to job performance; **autonomy** — the amount of time spent without direct supervision by a superior; and **significance** — the amount of importance placed by the employee on his/her job.

METHODOLOGY

This current study of Pennsylvania academic library personnel was undertaken in the spring of 1994. These work-related variables reported here are only a part of the complete study which explored other variables also related to job satisfaction. Packets containing surveys and letters of explanation were sent to directors of the 112 academic libraries which support four-year degree programs and are listed in the *1993 Directory of Pennsylvania Libraries*.[12] Each packet contained from one to sixteen surveys depending on the number of employees at each institution. The letter to the library director explained the study and asked him/her to distribute half of the surveys to support staff and half to librarians. This stratified procedure was chosen to ensure that personnel from the two major segments of the library workforce were equally represented. Directors were also asked to distribute surveys according to an alphabetized roster of library employees. This procedure ensured randomness within each library. Of the 112 institutions sent survey packets, 79 were represented in the final results. This portrays 71% of the institutions polled. Of the 449 surveys which were sent out, 281 were returned. This represents a participants' response rate of 63%.

The survey instrument was pilot tested at the library of a medium-sized Pennsylvania academic library not included in the final population.[13] The instrument was made up of 45 questions. Each participant was asked to respond on a five point Likert-type scale. For most questions the number 1 indicated "never" and the number 5 indicated "constantly". When measures were based on two questions, responses were added together to create a scale with the number 2 as the lowest possible score and the number 10 as the highest. (Some responses needed reverse coding.) Each of the following was measured with one item — feedback and autonomy. Discretion, variety, and significance were each measured with 2 items. (See Appendix) The survey also measured participants' personal characteristics, work-related personal characteristics, as well as their attitudes about their work-related environment. Only characteristics related to work itself will be reported here.

Job satisfaction was measured by a four question scale based on that used by Hage and Aiken.[14] This scale is simple to administer and easy for respondents to understand. Participants were asked to respond to each question by circling a number on a seven point scale. Total dissatisfaction was represented by circling the number 1 and complete satisfaction was indicated by circling the number 7. In the final analysis the four scores were totaled to obtain a final score. Possible scores could range from a low overall satisfaction score of 4 to a high of 28 points.

Hage and Aiken's[15] scale measures four important elements of job satisfaction: (1) it allows the respondent to compare his/her job with similar positions; (2) it allows the respondent to measure progress which he/she has made toward individual work goals; (3) it allows the respondent to compare the current job situation with expectations which were created at the time of hiring; (4) and it allows the respondent to measure the progress which he/she has made toward career goals. (See Appendix)

Lynch and Verdin[16, 17] also used the current adaptation of this scale to measure job satisfaction of library personnel. Their reported reliability, measured by Cronbach's alpha, was .8 for their 1983 use and .86 for their 1987 use of this scale. The Cronbach's alpha for the current use of the scale is .87.

The surveys were completely anonymous. However participants were asked to send back a postcard indicating that they had completed and mailed their survey. (These postcards became the basis for the institutional response rate.)

Data from the 281 surveys returned were coded and run on the Statistical Package for the Social Sciences (SPSS). Oneway ANOVAs were used to test hypotheses. The Pearson Correlation procedure was used to further study the relationships of each variable with overall job satisfaction.

RESULTS

The average job satisfaction score for this sample of library employees was a moderately high 21 points on a possible scale from 4 points to 28 points. The personal characteristics of this sample of library employees can be summarized as follows. The average library employee was 40 to 49 years old, Caucasian, married or living with a partner, and had a family income of $40,001 to $50,000 per year. Of the participants, 52% were librarians, 20% were paraprofessionals, and 28% were support staff. Of the group, 53% were supervisors. Public Services was represented by 54% of the group and Technical Services was represented by 46%. The average employee had held his/her current job for 6 to 10 years and had been a library employee for 11 to 15 years.

On the average these workers felt that they were always allowed autonomy in their daily work. These participants felt that they had a moderately high amount of daily variety (7 points on a scale which ranged from a possible of 2 to 10 points) in their jobs. Participants felt strongly, on the average, that their jobs were significant (8 points on a scale which ranged from 2 to 10 points). However, participants felt that they had only a moderate (6

points on a scale which ranged from 2 to 10 points) amount of discretion over their daily tasks. Also, on the average, participants reported that they received necessary job related feedback from their immediate supervisors only half the time.

As can be observed in Table One, of the five null hypotheses under consideration, there was enough evidence to reject four of them at the .05 level. For these variables, the alternate hypotheses that there were differences in the means created by variable subgroupings of job satisfaction were supported. Only discretion — the amount of control participants felt that they had over their daily tasks — did not show a statistical relationship with job satisfaction. Variety, feedback, autonomy, and significance were statistically related to job satisfaction when tested with the SPSS Oneway ANOVA.

In order to further clarify the relationships between these four statistically significant variables and job satisfaction, Pearson's Correlations were run. Each variable which showed a significant difference in means with the ANOVA procedure, also showed a statistically significant linear relationship with job satisfaction at the .05 level with the Pearson's procedure, as can be seen in Table Two.

These relationships can be expressed as follows. Library personnel who felt that their jobs provided them with a great deal of variety were more likely to report a high level of job satisfaction. Those participants who received feedback from their supervisors on a regular basis were also more likely to be satisfied with their jobs. Those participants who felt that they were trusted enough to be left alone to do their jobs were more likely to be satisfied with their jobs. And, participants who felt that their jobs were significant also were satisfied with their jobs.

DISCUSSION

Work related variables seem to be related to job satisfaction, since four of the five statistical analyses in this study showed significant relationships below the .05 level. Following is a compari-

TABLE 1: RELATIONSHIP OF JOB SATISFACTION TO VARIABLES - ANOVAS
(job satisfaction - possible range 4=low to 28=high)

HYPOTHESIS	n	MEAN	F RATIO	p
discretion	275	20.66	1.67	.11*
(range: low=2 to high=10)				
2	2	14.50		
3	3	13.67		
4	28	20.07		
5	90	20.66		
6	70	20.06		
7	50	22.10		
8	21	21.91		
9	9	19.67		
10	2	21.50		
variety				
(range: low=2 to high=10)	274	20.66	6.40	.00
2	1	6.00		
3	3	9.67		
4	9	15.00		
5	15	18.47		
6	41	20.39		
7	57	20.00		
8	77	20.84		
9	53	22.83		
10	18	23.56		
feedback	272	20.61	7.84	.00
never	20	17.35		
occasionally	77	18.70		
about half the time	27	19.89		
most of the time	125	22.05		
constantly	23	22.87		
autonomy	274	20.68	2.90	.04
never	0			
occasionally	2	11.00		
about half the time	2	15.50		
most of the time	58	20.28		
constantly	212	20.93		
significance	273	20.73	37.58	.00
(range: low=2 to high=10)				
4	3	12.67		
5	12	11.25		
6	33	14.76		
7	29	19.07		
8	120	21.53		
9	32	23.38		
10	44	25.30		

*not statistically significant at the .05 level

TABLE 2: RELATIONSHIP OF JOB SATISFACTION
TO VARIABLES - CORRELATIONS

	r	n	p
autonomy	.14	274	.03
feedback	.32	272	.00
variety	.36	274	.00
significance	.66	273	.00

son of each of these four analyses to other similar findings in the literature. Also, suggestions for practice are tendered.

The current study discovered a significant relationship between job variety and job satisfaction. Lynch and Verdin[18] found a similar relationship when they studied 292 library personnel. These studies show that the higher the variety extant in a job, the more likely the library employee will be to report high job satisfaction.

The very nature of much of what goes on in the library workplace is routine. Unfortunately library administrators have little control over the content of the daily tasks which need to be undertaken in a library. However, it may be possible to influence job satisfaction by redistributing these routine tasks. If routine tasks could be interspersed with more interesting ones, it is possible that levels of job satisfaction could be raised in libraries.

Appropriate feedback from an immediate supervisor regarding job performance was a variable which the current study found to be significant. Those library employees who received feedback about their jobs were more likely to be satisfied with them. Pearson,[19] in a recent longitudinal study of 76 railroad maintenance workers, found that those employees who received regular job-related feedback were also more likely to display high levels of job satisfaction.

Evidence based on one library-related study is obviously not enough to allow anything more than an indication that receiving job related feedback is important to the job satisfaction of library employees. However, since the respondents in this study felt that they received proper job feedback only half the time, it could be conjectured that this may be a current problem in academic libraries. Although many academic libraries have in place an annual job review, possibly more in-depth or more immediate performance-related information needs to be provided to the employee. Informal feedback, such as daily encouragement, could also be helpful.

Autonomy — defined here as the amount of time spent without direct supervision by a supervisor — was found to be significantly related to job satisfaction in this sample of library employees. Those employees who reported having a high level of autonomy on the job were more likely to also report a high level of job satisfaction. Liou, Sylvia and Brunk[20] reported similar findings based on a national sample study of U.S. citizens over the age of 18.

Library workers need to feel that they are trusted by their supervisors. Library supervisors should allow employees opportunity to complete tasks without immediate direct supervision.

And as can be seen in Table Two, the current study found task significance — the overall importance one places upon his/her job — to be the variable most strongly related to job satisfaction. Butler,[21] reported a similar strong relationship in a study of 404 professional social workers .

It is important to feel that one's job matters. Often lost in the daily shuffle of working in a library is any realization about how meaningful one's job really is to colleagues, patrons and to the academic institution. It is important for library administrators and supervisors to help employees understand the significance of their daily tasks. Employees could be assisted to understand that their jobs are important by being involved in a staff development workshop promoting this fact.

Of the five variables reported in this study, only job discretion was found to have had no statistical relationship with job satisfaction. A recent study by Estabrook, Bird and Gilmore[22] disagreed. This disagreement points up an area which needs further research and study.

This study shows that the arrangement of the daily work environment does impact the overall job satisfaction of the library employee. Library administrators cannot afford to blame low job satisfaction on employees' personal characteristics. Nor should library policies and regulations be instituted or changed without considering their ultimate impact on employee satisfaction. Often library directors, department heads and supervisors have not had the benefit of human resources management training. It would behoove these administrators to attend seminars, workshops or classes in management techniques. Shaping the daily work environment does have an impact on job satisfaction.

Variety, feedback, autonomy and significance have been found to be statistically related to job satisfaction in this sample of academic library employees. Library administrators can take advantage of this information by using these job characteristics to create a positive work environment.

CONCLUSION

Effective libraries ought to meet the needs of those involved in the organization. Judging by the overall job satisfaction of these employees responding to this survey, Pennsylvania libraries are effective organizations in the sense that these organizations evoke a moderately high level of job satisfaction in the employees polled.

It is important for library administrators and supervisors to realize that factors under their control — variables relating to the actual library work environment — impact job satisfaction. The way in which one's work is structured does have an impact on one's job satisfaction.

It should be noted that the area of the "library work context" needs further study. A number of library-related studies have been done regarding personal characteristics, but fewer have been done looking at the actual library work context and its relationship to job satisfaction. This should be rectified.

This study shows that there is a relationship between an academic library employee's job satisfaction and variables related to his/her work context. Workers who reported higher levels of variety, feedback, autonomy, and task significance reported higher levels of job satisfaction.

NOTES

1. This study was funded almost entirely by a Shippensburg University Faculty Professional Development Grant and by the Ezra Lehman Library.
2. Keeley, Michael. A Social-Contract Theory of Organizations. Notre Dame: Notre Dame Press, 1988.
3. Donna K. Fitch, "Job Satisfaction Among Library Support Staff in Alabama Academic Libraries," *College and Research Libraries* 51 (July 1990): 313-20.
4. Colleen Parmer and Dennis East, "Job Satisfaction Among Support Staff in Twelve Ohio Academic Libraries, *College and Research Libraries* 54 (January 1993): 43-57.
5. Ibid.

6. Leigh Estabrook, Chloe Bird and Frederick L. Gilmore, "Job Satisfaction: Does Automation Make a Difference?" *Journal of Library Administration* 13, no. 1/2 (1990): 175-94.

7. Beverly P. Lynch and Jo Ann Verdin, "Job Satisfaction in Libraries: A Replication," *Library Quarterly* 57 (April 1987): 190-202.

8. Ibid.

9. C.A.L. Pearson, "An Assessment of Extrinsic Feedback on Participation, Role Perceptions, Motivation, and Job Satisfaction in a Self-Managed System for Monitoring Group Achievement," *Human Relations* 44 (May 1991): 517-37.

10. Kuo-Tsai Liou, Ronald D. Sylvia and Gregory Brunk, "Non-Work Factors and Job Satisfaction Revisited," *Human Relations* 43 (January 1990): 77-86.

11. Beverly B. Butler, "Job Satisfaction: Management's Continuing Challenge," *Social Work* 35 (March 1990): 112-7.

12. Library Development, Commonwealth Libraries, *Directory of Pennsylvania Libraries* (Harrisburg, PA: Pennsylvania Department of Education, 1993).

13. The survey instrument was pilot tested with the help of my colleagues at Ezra Lehman Library. Special thanks to them for their valuable comments.

14. Jerald Hage and Michael Aiken, "Program Change and Organizational Properties: A Comparative Analysis," *The American Journal of Sociology* 72 (March 1967): 503-19.

15. Ibid.

16. Beverly P. Lynch and Jo Ann Verdin, "Job Satisfaction in Libraries: Relationships of the Work Itself, Age, Sex, Occupational Group, Tenure, Supervisory Level, Career Commitment, and Library Department," *Library Quarterly* 53 (October 1983): 434-47.

17. Lynch and Verdin, "Job Satisfaction in Libraries: A Replication".

18. Ibid.

19. Pearson, "An Assessment of Extrinsic Feedback".

20. Liou, Sylvia and Brunk, "Non-Work Factors and Job Satisfaction Revisited".

21. Butler, "Job Satisfaction".

22. Estabrook, Bird and Gilmore, "Job Satisfaction".

APPENDIX

SURVEY QUESTIONS USED TO GATHER DATA

DISCRETION
   a. In your job, how often do you follow a routine way of doing your work?
   b. In your job, how often do you create procedures for new tasks?

VARIETY
   a. How often does your work provide you with the chance to do a variety of duties?
   b. How often does your work provide you the chance to do something new?

FEEDBACK
   Does your immediate supervisor give you some indication as to how well you are performing your job?

AUTONOMY
   How often does your supervisor leave you on your own to do your own work?

SIGNIFICANCE
   a. How often do you feel that your job allows you to do something worthwhile?
   b. How often do you feel that your job gives you a feeling of accomplishment?

JOB SATISFACTION
   a. How satisfied are you with your present job when you compare it to similar positions in other departments or other libraries?
   b. How satisfied are you with the progress you are making toward the goals that you have set for yourself in your present position?
   c. How satisfied are you with your present job when you consider the expectations you had when you took the job?
   d. How satisfied are you with your present job in light of your career expectations?

The Levels of Decisions and Involvement in Decision-Making:
Effectiveness and Job Satisfaction in Academic Library Technical Services

Lynn Silipigni Connaway

ABSTRACT

The widespread availability of cataloging networks, library budget reductions, technological innovations in libraries, and cataloging educational concerns have influenced the library profession during the past decade. In order to make knowledgeable decisions concerning technical services operations and budgets, it is necessary to identify the tasks performed and the decisions made by technical services managers and catalogers.

Twenty-nine technical services managers and catalogers from seven academic libraries participated in this study. Non-parametric tests were computed to test for associations between the demographics of the technical services managers and catalogers and the amount of participation in decision-making; the levels of decisions; the quality of the bibliographic record, production volume, and job satisfaction. Tests were also computed for associations between amount of participation in decision-making and the level of decisions and quality of the bibliographic record, production volume, and job satisfaction. Descriptives and frequencies were also calculated for each variable.

The MLS and the level in the organizational hierarchy are positively associated with the amount of participation in decision-making, level of decisions, production volume, and job satisfaction. There is also a negative association between level in the organizational hierarchy and descriptive cataloging errors.

The widespread availability of cataloging networks, the concept of outsourcing cataloging, library budget reductions, and technological innovations in libraries have influenced the library profession during the past decade. Before making decisions concerning technical services opera-

Lynn Silipigni Connaway is an Assistant Professor in the School of Library and Informational Science, University of Missouri - Columbia.

tions and budgets, it is necessary to identify the tasks performed and the decisions made by technical services managers and catalogers. Non-parametric tests were computed to identify associations between the demographics of twenty-nine academic library technical services managers and catalogers and the amount of participation in decision-making; the levels of decisions; the quality of the bibliographic record, production volume, and job satisfaction.

There have been a number of issues facing those who organize and control bibliographic records in academic libraries. The widespread availability of cataloging networks, the concept of outsourcing cataloging, library budget reductions, and technological innovations in libraries have influenced the library profession during the past decade. These issue have also spurred the discussion of the deprofessionalization of cataloging.[1] There is an assumption that a majority of academic library materials are cataloged on networks, enabling library assistants or clerks to adequately perform copy cataloging and diminishing the need for professional catalogers.[2]

The extent of technical services managers' and catalogers' involvement in decision-making in academic libraries and the tasks they perform are unknown. A study conducted by Charles McClure[3] suggests that technical services librarians are less likely to be involved in decision-making than administrators and public service librarians. Herbert White[4] proposes that cataloging decisions are too important to be left exclusively to the discretion of catalogers, yet catalogers should be involved and consulted in all major organizational decisions. Besides the need to determine the involvement of academic library technical services managers and catalogers in decision-making, there is a need to investigate the variables that affect involvement in decision-making and the effects of this involvement. This study attempts: 1) to identify and analyze the levels of decisions made by technical services managers and catalogers in academic libraries; 2) to investigate the variables that affect involvement in deci-

sion-making; and 3) to examine the effects of this involvement.

METHODOLOGY

The case study method was chosen for this study since the behaviors of the technical services managers and catalogers were not manipulated by the researcher and the study is centered on contemporary events. Multiple cases were selected with the assumption that the sites were similar, allowing the methodology to be replicated.

The criteria for selection of the study sites were: 1) the institutions that the academic libraries serve must offer at least a four-year liberal arts degree and must be public institutions of higher education; 2) student enrollment at these institutions must be between 10,000 and 15,000; 3) the academic libraries must have centralized cataloging; 4) the technical services managers and catalogers at the academic libraries must have documentation of their original cataloging records; and 5) participation in OCLC or another bibliographic utility that requires the use of machine readable cataloging format (MARC).

There are sixty-two public institutions of higher education in the United States with a student enrollment of 10,000 to 15,000 that were considered for this study.[5] Of these, thirty-three academic library technical services departments met all of the selection criteria of the study and would consider participating in the study.

Of the thirty-three academic libraries, the largest geographic clusters occurred in the Southeastern and Midwestern United States. Two academic libraries in the Southeast and five academic libraries in the Midwest agreed to participate in the research. Five technical services managers and twenty-four catalogers, totaling twenty-nine technical services managers and catalogers participated in the research.

Technical services managers are persons who hold the positions of chair, head, assistant director, or director of catalog or technical services departments. Catalogers are paraprofessionals or professionals who hold positions in technical services and cataloging departments. They also spend at least 50% of their work time cataloging (by their perception), including original cataloging and the supervision of copy cataloging, the development of cataloging and classification policies and procedures, the assignment of subject headings and classification numbers, and the description of materials in a designated format for the purpose of retrieval. They may or may not hold an MLS degree.

The researcher visited each of the seven academic libraries and spent between one and three days at each site. The researcher conducted each of the site visits according to the same scheduled plan. The purposes of the site visits were: 1) to introduce and explain the study to the participants; 2) to explain the tasks and task logs to the participants; 3) to meet with the individual technical services managers and catalogers and to create a rapport and trust between them and the researcher; 4) to observe the work flow patterns and department procedures; 5) to review procedure and policy manuals; and 6) to administer the amount of participation scale and the Job Descriptive Index.

The independent variables include those variables that might affect the technical services managers' and catalogers' participation in decision-making; the intervening variables include the technical services managers' and catalogers' amount of participation in decision-making and the levels of decisions they make; and the dependent variables include the quality of the bibliographic record and the efficiency and job satisfaction of the technical services managers and catalogers. See **Table 1** for the hypothesized decision-making model in technical services.

The independent variables include: **age, gender, formal education, cataloging coursework, whether the subjects had planned to be catalogers in library school, the number of years cataloging experience, length of service at the academic institution, percent of time spent cataloging, level in the organizational hierarchy, the amount of continuing education received** (in the past two years), and **the amount of cataloging training** (on the job in the past two years).

Intervening variables are variables that come between dependent and independent variables. The **amount of participation** in decision-making and the **levels of decisions** made by technical services managers and catalogers are hypothesized to intervene between certain characteristics of the technical services managers and catalogers and the quality of the bibliographic record and the efficiency and job satisfaction of the technical services managers and catalogers.

The **amount of participation** in decision-making is measured by a scale based on ten questions. The amount of participation scale is included in the Appendix.

The **levels of decisions** are measured by task logs completed by the technical services managers and catalogers on a daily basis. The logs were mailed to the researcher on a weekly basis for a four-week period. If questions or discrepancies emanated from the logs, the technical services managers and catalogers were contacted by telephone by the researcher for explanations. The task log is included in the Appendix.

The decisions are categorized as 1) **restricted discretion**, 2) **moderate discretion**, and 3) **extensive discretion** level decisions. The definitions of the three levels of decisions have been developed by consulting the public administration and library and information science literature.[6] The **restricted discretion level** of decision-making limits the discretion in decision-making to routine details, since policies and rules dictate the decisions made and little reliance is placed upon judgement. The **moderate discretion level** of decision-making allows for some discretion to adjust to local conditions and special situations; however, policies and rules dictate most of the important decisions of the job. The **extensive discretion level** of decision-making gives individuals a broad range of discretion in decision-making, allowing flexibility to adjust to local and special situations and relying upon the judgement and competence

TABLE 1: Hypothesized Decision-Making Model in Technical Services

Variables Affecting Cataloger Participation in Decision-Making	Participation in Decision-Making	Effects of Participation
INDEPENDENT VARIABLES	**INTERVENING VARIABLES**	**DEPENDENT VARIABLES**
Catalogers and Technical Service Managers 1. Age 2. Gender 3. Formal education 4. Cataloging coursework 5. Plan to be cataloger 6. Number of years cataloging experience 7. Length of service at academic institution 8. Percent of time spent cataloging 9. Level in organizational hierarchy 10. Hours of continuing education (last 2 years) 11. Cataloging training (on the job in past 2 years)	**Amount of Participation in Decision-Making**	**Effectiveness** 1. Quality of bibliographic record 2. Production volume of technical services managers and catalogers

	Level of Decision
	(Melcher 1976; Kovacs 1983; 1990)
	1. RESTRICTED DISCRETION
	   a. Searching and editing OCLC
	   b. Descriptive cataloging
	   c. Copy cataloging
	   d. MARC format
	   e. Creating item records
	   f. Catalog maintenance
	   g. Processing
	   h. Acquisitions
		Job Satisfaction

	2. MODERATE DISCRETION
	   a. Classification number
	   b. Subject headings
	   c. Authority files/records and cross references
	   d. Preservation decisions
	   e. Training others
	   f. Procedure formulation	

	3. EXTENSIVE DISCRETION
	   a. Work assignment
	   b. Work flow
	   c. Develop and set policies
	   d. Personnel issues	

of the decision-maker.[7] For the description of specific tasks by decision level, see **Table 1**.

The dependent variables are **effectiveness** and **job satisfaction**. **Effectiveness** consists of two components: the **quality of the bibliographic record** and the **production volume** of the technical services managers and catalogers.

The technical services managers and catalogers were asked to submit to the researcher documentation of their original cataloging records for a four-week period. A maximum of twenty-five original bibliographic records were evaluated for errors for the study regardless of the number of records completed during the four-week period. The records were evaluated by the quality standards developed by the Library of Congress and the Georgia State University Library.[8] Examples of errors are: 1) incorrect MARC tags, qualifiers and delimiters; 2) incorrect or missing fixed field tags; 3) subject headings or subdivisions that are not prescribed by the Library of Congress or Sears; 4) incorrect choice of entry; 5) incorrect form of entry; 6) omissions of descriptive elements that are expected to be present in level two cataloging; 7) misspellings in author, title, series, notes, and added entry fields; and 8) incorrect descriptive data as outlined in *Anglo-American Cataloging Rules*, second edition or in *LC Rule Interpretations*. For the purposes of this study, each error carries an equal weight since all of the listed errors affect the retrieval of information.

The technical services managers and catalogers participating in this study were asked to record the number of original cataloging records they completed during a four-week period. This number is defined as **production volume**.

Job satisfaction is measured by the Job Descriptive Index (JDI). The JDI is a seventy-two item paper and pencil test that measures job satisfaction in the areas of pay, supervision, work, promotion, co-workers, and the job in general and is included in the Appendix.

FINDINGS

There is an emerging profile of the characteristics of the twenty-nine technical services managers and catalogers. They are middle-aged, females (twenty-four are females), more than half of whom have earned an MLS. All five of the technical services managers are females. Of the seventeen who possess an MLS, nine did not plan to be catalogers and eight did plan to be catalogers in library school. The majority who participated in the study have taken at least one cataloging course, regardless of the MLS. The median is two cataloging courses. The catalogers are experienced (14.21 mean years of cataloging experience) and more than half have been employed at the academic institution for at least seven years. They documented that they receive more on-the-job training than continuing education through work shops, seminars, or conferences. They reported 19.93 mean hours of continuing education in the past two years and a median of twelve hours, compared to 149.48 mean hours of on-the-job training in the past two years and a median of fifty hours.

The majority perceive they have a lot of say in decision-making. More than half believe they have some or a lot of say in the quality or accuracy of the work done in the department. All believe they have some or a lot of say in the work they get done in a day. They also believe they have some or a lot of say in developing both department policies and procedures. They do not believe they have much say in developing library policies or handling complaints or grievances from the staff. They believe they have some or a lot of say in their work assignments and in departmental decisions, but not in library-wide decisions.

The greatest number of decisions made by the technical services managers and catalogers are restricted discretion level decisions, followed by moderate discretion level decisions, and extensive level decisions in this order. A median of 26.75 hours and a mean of 30.48 hours were spent in the library, but not assigned to a decision level, i.e., reading mail, visiting, breaks, etc.

Searching and editing OCLC, a **restricted discretion level decision**, constituted the greatest percent of time spent on a task, with a mean of 14.5%. Descriptive cataloging, also a **restricted discretion level decision**, followed with a mean of 11.46%. The mean percent of total hours spent in performing administrative duties, an **extensive discretion level decision**, is 9.58. The mean percent of total hours spent problem solving, a **moderate discretion level decision**, is 8.77.

The **production volume** was calculated by the total number of original bibliographic records created in a four-week period, although a maximum of twenty-five records were evaluated for quality. The greatest number of original bibliographic records created in a four-week period is thirty-one. The mean number of original bibliographic records created is 10.28 and the median is five original bibliographic records. The twenty-nine technical services managers and catalogers created 286 bibliographic records in a four-week period. Seven created no original bibliographic records in a four-week period.

This may seem low, but the quality is very high. The maximum number of total errors per record is five. The greatest number of errors per record is MARC errors, followed by errors in descriptive cataloging, and notes. The majority of the notes errors are errors in the order the notes are listed. There are minimal errors per record in both access points and subject headings. There are no errors in the creation of classification numbers. When evaluating the records, the item or copy of the chief source of information was not available to the researcher. It was therefore impossible to evaluate the intellectual content of the bibliographic record, i.e., classification numbers and subject headings, and only possible to evaluate whether the classification numbers and subject headings were authorized and constructed correctly.

In proportion to total errors, notes errors have the greatest mean and median, followed by MARC and descriptive cataloging errors. The more hours of on-the-job training, the less notes errors. This could indicate that the order and content of notes is dictated by policy and learned on the job. The mean errors per record is 1.22.

The greatest number of significant associations is between the independent variable, MLS, and the intervening and dependent variables. If one has an MLS, the amount of participation in decision-making increases. If one possesses an MLS, the percent of restricted level decisions decreases and the percent of extensive discretion level decisions increases. If the cataloger possesses an MLS, more original bibliographic records were created during the four-week period. If a cataloger possesses an MLS, more satisfaction was expressed with the opportunities for advancement, with supervision, and with coworkers. Since the MLS is considered the professional degree to work as a librarian, it would be unlikely that one would have a great number of opportunities for advancement without the MLS.

During the individual interviews, twenty-two of the study participants stated they planned their day and decided what work to do in a day. Seven, all support staff, decide what work to do in a day within limits, i.e., they have designated times to work on the OCLC and online catalog terminals. All of the technical services and cataloging departments have regularly scheduled department or section meetings. Department policies and procedures are often developed during these meetings.

CONCLUSIONS

The findings from this study suggest that catalogers do perform the more routine cataloging tasks, but that they also perform tasks within the higher decision levels. The technical services managers and catalogers who participated in this study are involved in a broad range of tasks, dispersed within the three decision levels. They spend much of their time problem solving and answering questions. They are responsible for following the rules and standards for cataloging, as well as for interpreting and applying the rules and standards. They are also responsible for developing policies for cataloging. Most of the technical services managers and catalogers who participated in this study have administrative responsibilities, i.e., personnel, budget, work flow, policy and procedure development, in addition to their cataloging duties.

This study has identified the types of decision made and the tasks performed by technical services managers and catalogers in academic libraries. It has helped to alleviate the void in the library and information science literature concerning the nature of decision-making of technical services managers and catalogers.

Further research should combine the time spent on each task identified in this research with the costs for performing these tasks, the costs of telecommunications and bibliographic utilities, the costs of processing materials, and the costs of processing supplies. This information would aid in management decisions made in technical services departments, including decisions made in regard to the outsourcing of cataloging.

NOTES

1. Ruth Hafter, *Academic Librarians and Cataloging Networks: Visibility, Quality Control, and Professional Status* (New York: Greenwood, 1986); Harold Borko, "Getting Started in Library Expert Systems Research," *Information Processing & Management* 23:81-87 (1987); Roy Davies, "Outlines of the Emerging Paradigm in Cataloguing," *Information Processing & Management* 23:89-98 (1987); Patricia F. Stenstrom, "Current Management Literature for Technical Services," *Illinois Libraries* 69:96-103 (Feb. 1987); Don Thompson, "AI - Tailormade for Librarians," *Canadian Library Journal* 45:73-75 (Apr. 1988); *The Future is Now: The Changing Face of Technical Services.* Proceedings of the OCLC Symposium, ALA Midwinter Conference, Feb. 4, 1994. Dublin, Ohio: OCLC Online Computer Library Center, 1994.

2. Hafter, *Academic Librarians and Cataloging Networks*; *The Future is Now*, Proceedings of the OCLC Symposium.

3. Charles Robert McClure, *Information for Academic Library Decision Making: The Case for Organizational Information Management* (Westport, Conn.: Greenwood Press, 1980).

4. Herbert S. White, "Catalogers - Yesterday, Today, Tomorrow," *Library Journal* 112:48-49 (Apr. 1, 1987).

5. Susan G. Broyles, *1989-90 Directory of Postsecondary Institutions*, Vol.1, 4-year and 2-year (Washington, D.C.: National Center for Education Statistics, 1990).

6. Arlyn J. Melcher, *Structure and Process of Organizations: A Systems Approach* (Englewood Cliffs, NJ: Prentice-Hall, 1976); Beatrice Kovacs, "Decision-Making in Collection Development: Medical School Libraries," Ph.D. diss., Columbia Univ., 1983; Beatrice Kovacs, *The Decision-Making Process for Library Collections: Case Studies in Four Types of Libraries* (New York: Greenwood Press 1990).

7. Melcher, *Structure and Process of Organizations*.

8. Richard Reeb, "A Quantitative Method for Evaluating the Quality of Cataloging," *Cataloging & Classification Quarterly* 5:21-26 (Winter 1984); "NCCP Quality Review Procedures," (Library of Congress, 1987, Photocopy); "National Coordinated Cataloging Program, Review of Bibliographic Records," (Library of Congress, Subject Cataloging Division, 1990, Photocopy).

APPENDIX

Name _____

Date _____

Participation Scale

How much say do you have in theses areas?	(1) None	(2) A little	(3) Some	(4) A Lot
1. Which staff join your department				
2. Who should be fired				
3. Who gets promoted				
4. Who should do what job in your department				
5. The quality or accuracy of the work done in your department				
6. What work you get done in a day				
7. Developing methods and procedures — the way work is done				
8. Developing policies within the department that affect the procedures of your department				
9. Developing policies outside the department (library-wide)				
10. Handling complaints or grievances from staff				

Name of person completing the log —————————————————————————

TASKS TIME LOG FOR THE DAY OF _____

Each block represents **15 minutes**. Please put an "X" in each 15 minute block next to the task done in the block of time. If 45 minutes were spent searching for copy on OCLC, put and "X" in 3 blocks next to "Searching and Editing OCLC." Each time during the day that you search for copy, add to this 45 minute block by addin an "X" in the relevant number of 15 minute blocks.

TASKS	15 MINUTE TIME BLOCKS										
Searching & Editing OCLC											
Descriptive Cataloging											
Copy Cataloging											
Authority Files/Records and Cross References											
Creating Item Records											
Creating Call Numbers											
Assigning Subject Headings											
Recataloging											
Catalog Maintenance											
Retrospective Conversion											
Problem-solving											
Training Others											
Procedure Formulation											
Attending Meetings											
Administration											
Preservation Decisions											
Collection Development											
Acquisitions											
Processing											
Other Activities											

Were there any activities you **could not** find a place on the log to record? If so, please **list the activity and the estimated time spent on this activity.**

March 29 - April 1, 1995, Pittsburgh, Pennsylvania

JOB DESCRIPTION INDEX

In the blank beside each word or phrase below, write Y for Yes, N for No, or ? if you cannot decide.

Work on the Present Job	**Supervision**
_____ Fascinating	_____ Asks my advice
_____ Routine	_____ Hard to please
_____ Satisfying	_____ Impolite
_____ Boring	_____ Praises good work
_____ Good	_____ Tactful
_____ Creative	_____ Influential
_____ Respected	_____ Up-to-date
_____ Uncomfortable	_____ Doesn't supervise enough
_____ Pleasant	_____ Has favorites
_____ Useful	_____ Tells me where I stand
_____ Tiring	_____ Annoying
_____ Healthful	_____ Stubborn
_____ Challenging	_____ Knows job well
_____ Too much to do	_____ Bad
_____ Frustrating	_____ Intelligent
_____ Simple	_____ Poor planner
_____ Repetitive	_____ Around when needed
_____ Gives sense of accomplishment	_____ Lazy

Present Pay

_____ Income Adequate for normal expenses

_____ Fair

_____ Barely live on income

_____ Income provides luxuries

_____ Insecure

_____ Less than I deserve

_____ Well paid

_____ Underpaid

Opportunities for Promotion

_____ Good opportunities for promotion

_____ Opportunities somewhat limited

_____ Promotion on ability

_____ Dead-end job

_____ Good chance for promotion

_____ Unfair promotion policy

_____ Infrequent promotions

_____ Regular promotions

_____ Fairly good chance for promotion

Co-Workers (People)

_____ Stimulating

_____ Boring

_____ Slow

_____ Helpful

_____ Stupid

_____ Responsible

_____ Fast

_____ Intelligent

_____ Easy to make enemies

_____ Talk too much

_____ Smart

_____ Lazy

_____ Unpleasant

_____ Gossipy

_____ Active

_____ Narrow Interests

_____ Loyal

_____ Stubborn

Job in General

_____ Pleasant

_____ Bad

_____ Ideal

_____ Waste of time

_____ Good

_____ Undesirable

_____ Worthwhile

_____ Worse than most

_____ Acceptable

_____ Superior

_____ Better than most

_____ Disagreeable

_____ Makes me content

_____ Inadequate

_____ Excellent

_____ Rotten

_____ Enjoyable

_____ Poor

Preparing Entrepreneurial Leaders for Tomorrow's Academic and Research Libraries

Meredith A. Butler, Thomas Galvin, and Suzanne Orlando

ABSTRACT

In discussions about the qualities and characteristics needed by information professionals for tomorrow's information society, academic library administrators are asking library schools to produce more visionary, entrepreneurial leaders; individuals who will be innovative, creative, risk taking and open to change. Are entrepreneurs born or can they be made? Are there inherent qualities unique to entrepreneurs, or can entrepreneurial qualities be developed in individuals through education and experience? These and other questions about entrepreneurship are being explored in a team-taught graduate course on library management at the University at Albany using an active learning model. Instructors discuss the learning objectives of the assignment they developed to engage students in the topic, the expected and unexpected results, and what they learned in the process. A student in the course also provides her perspective on her learning experience.

Frequent articles in our professional literature of the past decade address the complex and worrisome issues related to the demise of schools of library and information science and the future of education for librarianship. Many of these articles provide thoughtful analyses of the rapidly evolving information society, and present a daunting picture of the challenges and opportunities facing tomorrow's information professionals. Equally thoughtful are their analyses of the weaknesses of current models of library education and their proposals for curricular reform, revision of the accreditation process, changes in faculty qualifications and in student preparation and recruitment.

No group has been more critical of the perceived shortcomings of the schools than have library managers. Warren J. Haas' assessment of the failure of library schools to prepare their gradu-

Meredith A. Butler is Dean and Director of Libraries, Thomas Galvin is a Professor in the School of Information Science and Policy and is Director of the Information Science Ph.D. program, and Suzanne Orlando received her MLS from the School of Information Science and Policy at the University at Albany, SUNY, Albany, New York.

ates for higher level managerial responsibilities led to several Council on Library Resources' long term projects including the administrative intern and UCLA Senior Fellows programs. Toward the end of his tenure as CLR President, discussing the need to prepare a new generation of library leaders, Haas ruefully concluded that "the great majority of library schools seem unlikely to develop the capabilities and vitality that a hard-pressed profession desperately needs."[1]

Some recurring specific criticisms of library administration or management courses are that they have:

- failed to recognize that management is an applied, rather than a theoretical discipline;
- failed to prepare students realistically for the harsh realities of the contemporary managerial environment;
- failed to develop in students a recognition that the central tasks of management are problem analysis and problem solving, which are almost always situational rather than generic;
- failed to instill in students a recognition and acceptance of the responsibility of the library manager to create, not merely to consume, revenues;
- failed to relate library management to the discipline of general management.

As early as 1949, Kenneth Shaffer, then Dean of the School of Library and Information Science at Simmons College, responded to these criticisms and tried to reform the teaching of library management by substituting the case study method, with its emphasis on problem-solving, for traditional textbook and lecture teaching of library management. While both case studies and simulation teaching of library management, the latter pioneered by Martha Jane Zachert at Florida State University, are helpful in addressing some of the critics' concerns, they have not proven to be universal remedies for the ills of library management education.[2] Too many new graduates are unable to view operational problems and choices in libraries

from an holistic, managerial perspective. They often have difficulty coping with real problems that do not lend themselves to pat "right or wrong" textbook solutions and are ill-prepared to assume leadership roles in their organizations.

Perhaps the difficulty lies not in the curricula, but in the fact that the management skills that librarians need today are those that reside not in the cognitive, but in the affective domain. The limitations of classroom learning in developing such behavioral characteristics as creativity, vision, risk-taking, and a zest for rapid technological and organizational change are well known. Summarizing a 1981 Council on Library Resources sponsored educator-practitioner symposium, Thomas Galvin suggested that what employers found lacking in new graduates was less the absence of specific skills and knowledge and more the failure to exhibit positive attitudes and behaviors.[3] Kathleen Heim, writing a decade later, agreed, but asserted that the fault lay not with what or how library schools teach, but with the profession's inability to produce "an applicant pool of bright, inquiring, risk-taking students."[4]

John Kotter and Rosebeth Moss Kanter are among many contemporary critics who contrast management with leadership, and who assert strongly that what organizations need is less of the former and more of the latter.[5] Library educators, library administrators and librarians agree. They also agree that leadership qualities such as openness to change, innovation, creativity, and risk taking are personal characteristics essential to the success of tomorrow's information professionals and library leaders.[6] Frederick Kilgour, in his 1992 article on entrepreneurial leadership, celebrated these qualities in the library leaders of the past and described the entrepreneurial opportunities for librarianship in the foreseeable future. He defined entrepreneurship as "innovation tinged with risk" and saw the entrepreneur as a successful innovator, "someone who can take something that runs and make it work."[7] Kilgour believes these are the leaders we need for the future.

Kilgour inspires us to think about librarianship and librarians in new ways. No longer need our view be limited by the traditional definition of the entrepreneur as a person who organizes, operates, and assumes the financial risks of a business or commercial venture. Rather, we should adopt a broader definition of an entrepreneur as someone who challenges the status quo, who sees a new and imaginative way to provide a service or satisfy a need, and takes the risk to implement the idea. Everyone can see the obvious, but it is the entrepreneur who sees the unexpected. An entrepreneur is a person who looks at the same reality that others look at, but where they see only problems, the entrepreneur also sees opportunities. To paraphrase John F. Kennedy, the manager asks 'why', but the entrepreneur asks 'why not'? The cry in libraries, as in all types of enterprises today, is for schools to produce more visionary, entrepreneurial leaders, but the question remains, how do we do it?

CAN ENTREPRENEURSHIP BE TAUGHT?

Can entrepreneurship be taught? Do entrepreneurs have to be born or can they be made? Is there something inherent in the individual make-up and personal qualities of entrepreneurs that makes them unique, or can these qualities be developed in individuals through education and experience? To find answers to these and other questions, the authors introduced the topic of entrepreneurship in their team-taught graduate course in the Management of Information Agencies at the University at Albany in the Spring of 1994. In the remainder of this paper, the instructors will discuss why they pursued the topic of entrepreneurship in a course on library management, the learning objectives of the assignment they developed to engage students in the topic, the expected and unexpected results of the experiment, and what they learned in the process. A student in the course also provides her perspective on the significance of the experiment.

EXPERIENCE WITH STUDENTS IN LIBRARY MANAGEMENT CLASS

In the Fall 1993 semester, Meredith Butler, Dean and Director of Libraries at the University at Albany, State University of New York, and Thomas Galvin, Professor in the School of Information Science and Policy, team-taught the School's beginning level graduate course on the management of information agencies for the first time. The course relied heavily on the case study method both to convey the content of library management and to improve and increase students' problem analysis and problem-solving abilities. During the semester's class discussions, the instructors were troubled by the predominance of dichotomous thinking and the conventional "wisdom" that students demonstrated in problem-solving sessions. Usually convinced that their only option was to chose between alternatives A or B, students often failed to see that there were many more options to consider. In addition, they were sometimes resistant to the idea that a solution to a complex problem might be crafted from several alternatives, some of which could at first glance appear to be competing or mutually exclusive. Moreover, many students expressed a reluctance to embrace solutions that they judged too entrepreneurial or too risky.

The instructors began asking themselves what prior experiences and influences led very bright and articulate students to such conventional thinking and risk avoidance? They hypothesized that students were seldom asked to find creative solutions to complex problems, that they seldom had the opportunity to see connections between creativity and risk taking, and that they could not relate entrepreneurial thinking to library decision-making. Most often in traditional library school courses, students are asked to review the relevant literature on a topic or issue, and use it to support their own analysis and conclusions. When asked to solve complex, situational management problems involving money, people and politics, this standard approach proved too limiting. Case method, although of significant value in management courses, tends to present managerial problem-solving as a choice between two mutually exclusive alternatives. After considering the weaknesses of these traditional approaches, the instructors decided to restructure the content of the course to emphasize and illustrate the entrepreneurial dimension of problem-solving, and the need for creativity, risk taking, and collaboration in library management. Their hope was that students would learn that the best way to solve problems in the real world may be to combine the best elements of opposing solutions, or to seek options that are not obvious and sometimes counter intuitive. In short, they hoped that students would learn to think like an entrepreneur.

CAN ONE LEARN TO BE ENTREPRENEURIAL?

Believing that the most meaningful learning is self-acquired knowledge, the instructors decided to teach about entrepreneurship in library management by involving the students actively in their own learning. In the Spring 1994 semester, they made the topic of entrepreneurship a central component of the course. Lectures, readings from management literature, and problem case study analysis were combined with a short paper on entrepreneurship due about one third of the way through the course. The culmination of the entrepreneurship assignment was a guest lecture by a librarian whose professional accomplishments exemplified the very qualities of creativity, entrepreneurial thinking and risk taking that students had been investigating through their research.

Building on their assigned reading for the course and a summary outline on creating the entrepreneurial environment from Rosabeth Moss Kantor's The Change Masters, students were asked in their papers to identify and describe an entrepreneurial event, activity, experience, or person in the management of libraries or information agencies. Further, they were asked to define the characteristics that made what they chose entrepreneurial, and to relate those characteristics to the Kantor

outline. Finally, and perhaps most important, students were asked what they learned from doing the assignment that they didn't know before they started to think about entrepreneurship, and to list their recommendations for fostering and encouraging entrepreneurship in the library profession. Students were encouraged to use any approach or combination of approaches to pursue their assignment including: sources from the professional literature, information from personal interviews of library professionals, or personal experience.

From the beginning, perhaps half of the students were uncomfortable to varying degrees with this assignment. It was unlike other assignments they had been asked to do and they weren't sure how to approach it. Many students wanted to pursue the familiar "term paper" route of going to the library and reading the literature to give them more background and help them know what to think about entrepreneurship. But library literature proved to be nearly barren on the topic. The business literature, although extensive on entrepreneurship, focussed on the more traditional concept of an entrepreneur as someone who starts a new business or turns a stagnant business around. These modes of entrepreneurship were hard to relate to the management of not-for-profits.

The instructors quickly explained that what was wanted was not a traditional research paper. The assignment, they pointed out, had to be approached in a different way, and required more than rote summaries of the literature on the topic. They challenged students to think creatively and innovatively about their own past or present work and/or professional educational experiences. As students pursued their own ideas, their anxieties lessened and they began to prepare for the guest lecturer.

The instructors were fortunate in persuading Peggy Barber, Associate Executive Director of the American Library Association, to accept the guest lecturer assignment. Although the lecture itself had to be cancelled on the penultimate day because the lecturer was stranded in transit by a snow storm, students had the benefit of an extensive portfolio of ideas and news stories about innovative librarianship that she had prepared. A number of students also were able to attend Ms. Barber's public lecture on entrepreneurship on the following day.

WHAT STUDENTS LEARNED?

Perhaps the strongest evidence for the value of this learning experiment comes from the students who participated in it. Instructors were encouraged by comments such as these:

"Half way through this assignment, I almost gave up, deciding that it was an impossible task. I kept trying to figure out how to think entrepreneurially and began to own my ideas. Trusting myself enough to get past my initial reluctance as I developed my own entrepreneurial plan has been a real eye-opener for me. I now believe I could put my plan into action with proper research and support."

"Before taking this course and working on this assignment, I had never used the words "entrepreneurial" and "librarian" in the same thought, and to do so has proven to be enlightening. I really liked being able to dream my dreams." "This paper has been a true learning experience. It has taught me to act on ideas that I have and to develop them into something that could make change happen."

"I have learned that the entrepreneurial process is political. It is not enough to have a good idea, you have to sell it to others."

"The entrepreneurial experience I described is based on true events. Unfortunately, the actual process never went past page one. The experience of retelling this idea made me realize its entrepreneurial value. With my initial look at this assignment, I saw dollar signs. I always thought of entrepreneurs not just as innovators, but as big money makers. The idea of entrepreneurship is much more interesting and appealing now that I have a clearer understanding of it. I also came to realize more fully what is meant by taking risks. As I presented my idea, I realized that each step is a new risk. It is not just the success or failure of the end product that is a risk, but each stage in getting

there can be a frightening uncertainty. Knowing who to approach to gain support for an idea and when is a delicate business, requiring keen judgment and always alternative plans."

"We need to realize our potential as information entrepreneurs and learn how to creatively raise the funds we require. The first step, I believe, is a change of attitude from one which tells us that we can only do so much, to one that reminds us there is so much we can do."

STUDENT ADVICE ON FOSTERING ENTREPRENEURS IN LIBRARIES

Among students' suggestions were these:

"Managers should ask questions and listen. Ask people to look at previously attempted solutions and build on the good ideas. Work with people to offer solutions instead of presenting problems. Help people by encouraging them to persevere."

"Library managers need to foster open communication and to encourage and support staff. They need to empower staff to translate their ideas into workable plans."

"To encourage entrepreneurship in our profession, librarians need to find more free time for creative thinking."

"These days, you can't say "library" without saying "underfunded." This is a real obstacle when trying to innovate. So many ideas are rejected in their infancy due to financial constraints. Perhaps greater cooperation among librarians and economists trained in the economics of non-profit agencies would be beneficial. Forming alliances with local businesses is another excellent way to cultivate new ideas while raising community awareness and library visibility.

"Librarians need to hear more about entrepreneurship. We need to encourage entrepreneurial librarians to write about their experiences in a regular column in the professional journals."

"I would like to see a conference devoted to fostering entrepreneurial activities and creativity."

ENTREPRENEURIAL LIBRARIANSHIP

In challenging the conventional wisdom about entrepreneurship and libraries, these students began to learn to think unconventionally. They learned the importance of being open to new ideas, of garnering support from colleagues and administrators by selling those ideas, and of focusing on solutions rather than on problems. They learned that risk taking is a step by step process for which one can develop personal tolerance. They also learned that entrepreneurship can be found in libraries and can be applied to library decision-making.

WHAT THE INSTRUCTORS LEARNED

Perhaps the most important outcome of the course resulted from the positive consequences of the practitioner-educator team approach. It was the practitioner member of the teaching team who insisted that course content must be more relevant to today's management needs. Both instructors agreed that the worst sin in professional education is not bad teaching--which the best students will overcome; but teaching that is irrelevant to the realities of current practice. A major challenge for educators in a professional school is to keep their image of practice up to date, to conform to a changing reality of practice. By emphasizing innovation and entrepreneurship, the instructors themselves learned to think in new ways and helped students apply their skills to problem-solving in today's management environment. A second lesson the instructors learned from this experiment was that students, even those actively involved in their own learning, must be carefully prepared and encouraged to think in new ways, and that learning must be reinforced and the skills continuously exercised. Instructors saw the evidence of students' learning to think in new ways, but it remains to be seen to what degree such changes can be nurtured and developed. The instructors believe these results have implications for curricular change in library professional education and illustrate the need for new assumptions about what can be taught and what students can learn when they are engaged in their own learning process.

The instructors are repeating this experiment twice during the 1994-95 academic year and gathering pre and post-test data from students to measure any attitudinal changes among them toward entrepreneurial concepts such as risk taking, innovation, and dealing effectively with ambiguity.

WHY IS ALL THIS IMPORTANT?

Today's library leaders and managers know that transformational leaders are required for our libraries. We cannot wait for these leaders to just show up, we have to create them. Library operations are too complex and interdependent for such leadership to reside only at the top. Leadership, creativity, risk taking, and a tolerance for ambiguity must permeate the organization. We aren't just hiring people to run our operations, we are hiring new professionals to cope creatively with organizations in the throes of transformative change. These professionals must quickly grasp users' needs and develop effective and responsive services. They need to be skilled at communicating complex information to others and inspiring others to work collaboratively with fewer resources than they had even five years ago. Library schools are preparing the new generation of library leaders and managers and their education is too important to be left solely to library educators. Practitioners can and should take an active part in influencing both what is taught and how it is taught. The goal should not be to produce graduates who can step into our libraries and catalog our books or answer our reference questions with little training. Rather we should work in active partnership, librarians and library educators, to foster the qualities of mind, attitude and character we need in tomorrow's leaders. And having educated them to think creatively and develop greater tolerance for ambiguity and taking risks, we then need to provide them with work environments where those qualities are celebrated and reinforced. Only in this way will we be successful in creating the new research and learning environments of the new century and the librarians who will lead them.

NOTES

1. Council on Library Resources, *Thirty-Second Annual Report, 1988.* Washington, 1988, p. 18.

2. For a description of Shaffer's work, see Thomas J. Galvin, *The Case Method in Library Education and In-Service Training.* Metuchen, N.J., Scarecrow Press, 1973. See also Martha Jane K. Zachert, Simulation Teaching of Library Administration. New York: Bowker, 1974.

3. Thomas J. Galvin, "The Results as Seen By a Library Educator," in Robert M. Hayes, ed., *Universities, Information Technology, and Academic Libraries: The Next Twenty Years.* Academic Libraries Frontier Conference, UCLA Lake Arrowhead Conference Center, 134-17 December 1981, pp. 251-252.

4. Kathleen M. Heim, "Not With a Bang But a Whimper: the Erosion of Support for Library and Information Science Education," Background paper for Kellogg Foundation Sponsored Symposium, November 13-15, 1991, p. 12.

5. John P. Kotter, *A Force for Change: How Leadership Differs from Management.* New York: Free Press, 1990; Rosabeth Moss Kanter, *The Change Masters: Innovation and Entrepreneurship in the American Corporation.* Simon & Schuster, 1983.

6. See for example: Joanne R. Euster, "Creativity and Innovation," *Journal of Library Administration,* 10 (1989): 27-38.

7. Frederick G. Kilgour, "Entrepreneurial Leadership," *Library Trends,* 40, no.3 (Winter 1992): 157.

Permanent White Water:
Navigating Change with the Aid of Humor

Karen S. Seibert

ABSTRACT

President Clinton's difficulties aside, "permanent white water" is a borrowed metaphor meant to convey the drama and uncertainty of academic library staff shooting the rapids of continuous change. Navigating a course with tradition and transformation as coordinates will challenge our skills and test our resolve. In this session, we will look at humor as an all-purpose tool to ease the pain of growth and change. Only recently taken seriously by psychologists, sociologists, and management consultants, humor is now seen as a complex phenomenon that has a multiplicity of uses. We will briefly examine its effect on general social relations and personal health, its power as an antidote to stress and conflict, and its potential as a facilitator in team building, learning, and creative thinking. The session will conclude with a few words of advice on creating opportunities for healthy humor in the library. Your insights and suggestions will also be solicited.

INTRODUCTION

Exhilarated by the danger, stimulated by the challenge, and, hopefully, redeemed by the shared relief of laughter, academic librarians are pushing off into the "permanent white water"[1] of unrelenting change. The aim, as the conference organizers put it, is to turn the promise of confluence into reality, to steer a course that allows for continuity of traditional services and collections, while undertaking transformations as participants in the building of the new information infrastructure.

The litany of driving forces is familiar: inadequate budgetary support, external pressures on academe, changing user needs, and emerging information technologies that bring new costs and new opportunities. Peter Vaill suggests that what we are in:

is first and foremost a revolution of the total situation. It is not just new kinds of problems and opportunities that we are facing, but whole new contexts within which these problems and opportunities reside (1989, 2-3).

Permanent white water or a revolution of the total situation, the impact on individuals and their

---

Karen S. Siebert is a Doctoral Student in the Graduate School of Library and Information Science at the University of Texas at Austin.

libraries will be substantial, given the stressful and often painful nature of growth and change.

In other venues at this conference, speakers will be talking about strategies to manage that change. Vision and leadership, continuous improvement and total quality management, diversity and demographic shifts, flattening hierarchies and re-engineering—all will be discussed in the hallways, if not in the meeting rooms. Since we are academic librarians, there will be the inevitable abundance of acronyms, arcane to the outsider, but comforting to the initiated. It is of easing the pain of transition, humanizing change, and bringing comfort through strategies of a humorous kind that I want to talk today.

THE CASE FOR HUMOR

> *The realization that there may be more to joking than just joking may surprise some practitioners.*[2]
>
> *Karen L. Vinton*

Researchers find humor a difficult phenomenon to investigate. Part of the reason is that it can be seen as stimulus, as response, or as disposition, not too amazing for an emotion that is estimated to occur ten or more times often than all the rest of our emotional behaviors put together (Chapman and Foot 1976). Because it is such an individual and pervasive affair, figuring out its causes is especially challenging for theorists (Duncan, Smeltzer, and Leap 1990, 258-9). Some take the view that we react with humor at the incongruity when our expectations are suddenly shifted to a different path. Others try to understand humor as one aspect of a general emotional process that involves physiological arousal that we then interpret cognitively. Another group of theorists focuses on the notion that humor is really about establishing or sharing feelings of superiority to others.

Not researchers, but experts of a kind nonetheless, the general public knows that humor is whatever makes one laugh, or grin, or grimace, saying "Oh, no" with rolling eyes. *Psychology Today* conducted a humor survey of 14,500 readers and found, among other things, that in a random sample of respondents only 1 percent ended an average day without someone laughing at their humor (Hassett and Houlihan 1979, 68). Such a basic human emotion should not be ignored because it takes place at the office.

Any number of authors agree, and tantalized by the mystery of humor, try to find the perfect epigram to describe its possibilities:

- "a diagnostic tool" (Kahn 1989, 46)
- "a lightning rod" (Cheatwood 1983, 332)
- "good medicine" (Cousins 1979, 40)
- "the sharpest arrow in the manager's quiver" (Barsoux 1991, 66)
- "an intervention strategy" (Buhler 1991, 23)
- "a mini-aerobic workout" (Feigelson 1989, 8)
- "a social lubricant" (Morreall 1991, 371)

These characterizations hint at humor's complexity. Let us delve more deeply into its major functions.

AN ALL-PURPOSE TOOL

> *It is always wise to think of work group humor as more than idle behavior.*[3]
>
> *W. Jack Duncan and J. Philip Feisal*

Perhaps because of the Protestant Work Ethic, humor has, until recently, been viewed as a distraction or obstacle. Our culture has treated humor and work as "mutually exclusive activities" (Duncan, Smeltzer, and Leap 1990, 255), fostering "a work climate in which emotional expression, especially enjoyment or playfulness, are deemphasized" (Dandridge 1986, 159) or censured. The general shift in society from manual work to information handling represents a switch from mind-numbing routine to thought-provoking unique problems. One result is that today's workers "want a sense of involvement and shared meaning" (McDonald and Gandz 1992, 66). Humor undergirds both, smoothing our social interactions, helping us tolerate our own and each others mistakes and failures, and letting us get on with the job (Morreall 1991, 371).

Our physical capacity to do that job is enhanced by humor as well. Research indicates that:

> hearty laughter causes huffing and puffing similar to that resulting from exercise. It speeds up the heart rate, raises blood pressure, accelerates breathing and increases oxygen consumption. A robust laugh gives the muscles of the face, shoulders, diaphragm and abdomen a vigorous workout, and with sidesplitting laughter, even the leg and arm muscles get involved. . . As laughter subsides, a brief period of relaxation occurs . . . It results in a calming effect (Slovenko 1988, x).

Self-taught icon of perseverance, Norman Cousins puts it succinctly: "It has always seemed to me that hearty laughter is a good way to jog internally without having to go outdoors" (1979, 84).

Academic librarians today need that release since we are living fast-paced, complicated lives. Stress comes from many quarters: trying to do more with less; keeping old skills in tact, while developing new forms of expertise; finding time to prepare for tomorrow's inevitable meetings; adjusting to organizational restructuring; and on and on. Our perspective shrinks with the inevitable result being a narrowing of personal focus to the here and now; we see many trees and few forests.

Laughter and joking let us step back and regain some of the control lost when stress holds sway (Morreall 1991). Individuals with a high humor quotient have been found to cope better, for example, dealing with stress in a more direct problem-solving way and putting a healthy distance between their emotions and the causal event (Martin and others 1993, 95). Lessons can be learned from the corporate world, too, which responds to stress with humor consultants (Lasden 1985), laugh lounges with continuous comedy reruns (Buhler

1991), and humor workshops for managers (Duncan and Feisal 1989).

Stress is a socially acceptable modern miasma. It is something we can talk about openly. Less amenable to general discussion are conflict, aggression, and anger, but they exist in our libraries these days and need to be dealt with. Not everyone will embrace change at the same rate or with the same degree of equanimity. Feelings and attitudes about "total quality," for example, will vary. Some staff will see exciting opportunities in working more closely with patrons to assess and meet their needs; others will resent what seems like an attack on the way service was provided in the past. Humor can be used to defuse resulting personality clashes (McClane and Singer 1991, 69), to resolve or diffuse other forms of conflict (Cheatwood 1983, 332; Morreall 1991, 371), and to allow constructive expressions of hostility (Kahn 1989, 52). Humor used in these ways can unbottle emotions that are corrosive to the spirit and to collaborative work relationships.

Given the social nature of our work lives, these uses of humor as healer and mediator will continue, but there is much more to be gained by acknowledging the potent force humor can be in group dynamics, learning situations, and innovative problem-solving.

A LANGUAGE OF INSIGHT AND POWER

> *Humor is felt to facilitate an array of behaviors that positively impact organizational change processes.*[4]
> *William E. McClane and Daniel D. Singer*

Team building is *au courant*. Many experts are putting their oars in that particular part of the permanent white water (Bolman and Deal 1992a, 1992b; Hackman 1990; Parker 1990; Quinn 1988; Vaill 1989). The best of them, in my view, delve into the dynamics that encourage commitment and healthy group identity.

Humor can serve many functions in a team environment. Let me outline a few. It can help people bond (Buhler 1991), celebrate trust, and express values (Duncan and Feisal 1989). It can act as a control mechanism, letting the group deal with unacceptable behavior or performance (Dwyer 1991) by delivering serious messages in a face-saving ambiguous way (Kahn 1989). Humor also "deflates, unmasks, and frees us from unreal, pretentious, and imprisoning beliefs or perceptions" (Siporin 1984, 460), another way of saying it can help the group to reframe and come to new perspectives on what is possible. It can puncture hubris (Kets de Vries 1990) and over- involvement in the trivial (Barsoux 1991, 68). A bridging mechanism with other groups, a good dose of laughter can also nonplus legitimate opponents in negotiations and give your team the advantage (Barsoux 1991, 66). In decision-making, humor can help relieve impasses and overcome resistance to change (McClane and Singer 1991, 70). Cohesion and commitment, cooperation and collaboration—all can be enhanced by expressions of mutual caring through shared laughter.

In the training environment, humor is recommended as a powerful communications strategy, workable with staff or patrons. One expert paraphrases a familiar old saw: "Laugh and the whole class learns with you" (Kokalis 1991, 13). Joel Goodman of the HUMOR Project explains how the process works to maximize retention: humor commands the learner's attention, dispels anxiety and fear, and then encourages involvement and momentum (1983, 4).

Training is, of course, not the only kind of learning that goes on in an organization. Humor can assist with the socialization of new staff or team members (Vinton 1989, 162) and the introduction of new information (Dwyer 1991, 3). Peter Senge of *The Fifth Discipline* fame talks about teams and the "defensive routines that thwart learning also [holding] great potential for fostering learning, if we can only learn how to unlock the energy they contain" (1990, 237). He might well consider humor as a skeleton key to good effect.

Many of the functions of humor already discussed apply to problem-solving. Norman Stevens reminds us that "apprehension, hostility, and tension are not conducive to creative thinking and innovation" (1988, 145). Instead, an environment of trust, tolerance, and encouragement, aided by kind laughter and a supportive smile, brings forth mental flexibility, divergent thinking, and risk-taking (Morreall 1991). Humor also serves to "loosen people's psychological grips on the status quo of their organizations . . ." (Kahn 1989, 61) and open them to change. It takes a powerful bead on the howitzers that threaten blue sky thinking, and, because we feel safe, untethers our imaginations and lets whimsy bring unexpected insights.

Most humor in the workplace, and perhaps the best, is unrehearsed, arising out of shared experiences, shared values, and a shared willingness to disengage, if just for a moment, from the demands of the day. But it is also true that we can make a conscious effort to generate opportunities for the healing power of laughter in our daily work lives.

A PRIMER OF PRACTICAL APPLICATIONS

> *I say it's time to take humor out of the closet. Change the work place motto from Grim and Bear It to Grin and Share It.*[5]
> *Sheila Feigelson*

With that thought in mind, I would like to end with a change of pace and some accumulated words of advice. Perhaps, in the question and answer period, you can help add to the list.

- For starters, bring your whole self to work.
- Listen to the humor (or its absence) around you and hear what it tells you about your environment.
- Share your awareness and approval of humor's benefits.
- Take fun seriously...
- But relax. A sense of humor is what is important, not your ability to tell a joke.
- Remember you are human; learn to laugh at yourself.

- Cherish the gadfly. Don't send her to the principal's office in your mind.
- Question formality.
- Create ceremony; don't stand on it.
- Learn the downsides of humor; take a position **for** human dignity and respect.
- Recognize limits: too much humor may be as bad as too little.
- Avoid the putdown and the sarcastic comeback.
- Remember: gallows humor is not necessarily an attack on your leadership.
- Share the humor spotlight: monopolies are illegal.
- Keep a humor log and use it to refresh yourself and others.
- Take the time to thank co-workers who have just the right humorous touch in easing your team's work life.
- Hire the serious, not the solemn; and most of all,
- ENJOY!

NOTES

1. Peter Vaill in *Managing as a Performing Art* (San Francisco: Jossey-Bass, 1989, p. xiv) uses the metaphor of "permanent white water" to convey the drama and uncertainty of managers' shooting rapids that never quite end. Gone are the still waters and temporary disruptions of the past; instead, chaos is a given.
2. Vinton, Karen L. 1989. Humor in the workplace: It is more than telling jokes. *Small Group Behavior* 20 (May): 165.
3. Duncan, W. Jack, and J. Philip Feisal. 1989. No laughing matter: Patterns of humor in the workplace. *Organizational Dynamics* 17 (Spring): 29.
4. McClane, William E., and Daniel D. Singer. 1991. The effective use of humor in organizational development. *Organization Development Journal* 9 (Spring): 68.
5. Feigelson, Sheila. 1989. Take humor out of the closet: Mixing mirth and management. *Supervision* 50 (November): 6.

REFERENCES

Barsoux, Jean-Louis. 1991. Is business a laughing matter? *Director* 44 (June): 65-68.

Bolman, Lee G., and Terrence E. Deal. 1992a. *Reframing organizations: Artistry, Choice and Leadership.* San Francisco: Jossey-Bass.

_____. 1992b. What makes a team work? *Organizational Dynamics* 21 (Autumn): 34-44.

Buhler, Patricia. 1991. Wanted: Humor in the workplace. *Supervision* 52 (July): 21-23.

Chapman, Antony J., and Hugh C. Foot. 1976. *Humour and laughter: Theory, research, and applications.* London: John Wiley & Sons.

Cheatwood, Derral. 1983. Sociability and the sociology of humor. *Sociology and Social Research* 67 (April): 324-38.

Cousins, Norman. 1979. *Anatomy of an illness as perceived by the patient: Reflections on healing and regeneration.* With an Introduction by René Dubos. New York: W. W. Norton.

Dandridge, Thomas C. 1986. Ceremony as an integration of work and play. *Organization Studies* 7 (2): 159-70.

Duncan, W. Jack, and J. Philip Feisal. 1989. No laughing matter: Patterns of humor in the workplace. *Organizational Dynamics* 17 (Spring): 18-30.

Duncan, W. Jack, Larry R. Smeltzer, and Terry L. Leap. 1990. Humor and work: Applications of joking behavior to management. *Journal of Management* 16 (June): 255-78.

Dwyer, Tom. 1991. Humor, power, and change in organizations. *Human Relations* 44 (January): 1-19.

Feigelson, Sheila. 1989. Take humor out of the closet: Mixing mirth and management. *Supervision* 50 (November): 6-8.

Goodman, Joel. 1983. How to get more smileage out of your life: Making sense of humor, then serving it. In *Handbook of humor research*, ed. by Paul E. McGhee and Jeffrey H. Goldstein, 1-21. New York: Springer-Verlag.

Hackman, J. Richard, ed. 1990. *Groups that work (and those that don't): Creating conditions for effective teamwork.* San Francisco: Jossey-Bass.

Hassett, James, and John Houlihan. 1979. A report on PT's humor survey: Different jokes for different folks. *Psychology Today* 12 (January): 64-71.

Kahn, William A. 1989. Toward a sense of organizational humor: Implications for organizational diagnosis and change. *Journal of Applied Behavioral Science* 25 (1): 45-63.

Kets de Vries, Manfred F. R. 1990. The organizational fool: Balancing a leader's hubris. *Human Relations* 43 (8): 751-70.

Kokalis, Jerry, Jr. 1991. Humor-based training. *Training & Development* 45 (September): 13-14.

Lasden, Martin. 1985. Laughter gives you an edge. *Computer Decisions* 17 (April 23): 70-144 passim.

McClane, William E., and Daniel D. Singer. 1991. The effective use of humor in organizational development. *Organization Development Journal* 9 (Spring): 67-72.

MacDonald, Paul, and Jeffrey Gandz. 1992. Getting value from shared values. *Organizational Dynamics* 20 (Winter): 64-77.

Martin, Rod A., Nicholas A. Kuiper, L. Joan Olinger, and Kathryn A. Dance. 1993. Humor, coping with stress, self-concept, and psychological well-being. *Humor* 6 (1): 89-104.

Morreall, John. 1991. Humor and work. *Humor* 4 (3/4): 359-73.

Parker, Glenn M. 1990. *Team Players and teamwork.* San Francisco: Jossey-Bass.

Quinn, Robert E. 1988. *Beyond rational management: Masteringthe paradoxes and competing demands of high performance.* San Francisco: Jossey-Bass.

Senge, Peter M. 1990. *The fifth discipline: The art and practice of the learning organization.* New York: Doubleday.

Siporin, Max. 1984. Have you heard the one about social work humor? *Social Casework* 65 (October): 459-64.

Slovenko, Ralph. 1988. Foreword. In *The anatomy of humor: Biopsychosocial and therapeutic perspectives,* by Robin A. Haig, vii-xiv. Springfield: Charles C. Thomas.

Stevens, Norman D. 1988. Humor and creativity. *College & Research Libraries News* 49 (March): 145-6.

Vaill, Peter B. 1989. *Managing as a performing art: New ideas for a world of chaotic change.* San Francisco: Jossey-Bass.

Vinton, Karen S. 1989. Humor in the workplace: It is more than telling jokes. *Small Group Behavior* 20 (May): 151-66.

Library Anxiety Among College Students:

An Exploratory Study

Terrence F. Mech and Charles I. Brooks

ABSTRACT

Using qualitative methods Constance Mellon developed a theory of library anxiety. The present study, using quantitative methods, examined and compared library anxiety with the general psychological trait of anxiety among an availability sample of 153 college students. The results indicated no differences among students on trait anxiety, but clear differences on library anxiety. Library anxiety—the situation of being uneasy about the search process and using the library— appears to be different than the psychological trait of being anxious. Freshmen reported significantly higher levels of library anxiety, lower assessments of their library skills, and less confidence in their ability to use a college library than seniors. Correlations between library anxiety and selected variables are presented. Gender and frequency of library use do not appear to be factors in students' library anxiety.

After two years of qualitative research among 6,000 students, Constance Mellon put forth a grounded theory of library anxiety.[1] In Mellon's research many students described their initial responses to library research in terms of fear or anxiety. These feelings of anxiety came from four sources: (1) the relative size of the library; (2) a lack of knowledge about where things were located; (3) how to begin, and (4) what to do. According to Mellon's theory, students generally feel that their library skills are inadequate while the skills of other students are adequate. Students believe this inadequacy is shameful, should be hidden from others, and that the asking of questions would reveal their inadequacy. This fear of the library is attributed to a lack of understanding of libraries and how to use them.

In addition, students experience difficulties with the research process. Based on qualitative research, Kuhlthau indicates that anxiety, confu-

Terrence F. Mech is Vice President for Information and Instructional Technologies and Director of the Library and Charles I. Brooks is Professor of Psychology at King's College, Wilkes-Barre, Pennsylvania.

sion, and uncertainty are feelings students commonly experience during the search process, particularly in the early stages of the complex dynamic process.[2]

For the vast majority of college students, using a college library is an adjustment from using their high school or local public library. For many college students their high school library and research experiences were superficial. Essentially, many students lack any significant library experience. Consequently, when students get to college they feel a lack of knowledge about where things are, how to begin, or what to do.[3] Students must overcome their initial anxieties and fears of the library and the search process before they can take advantage of the library's resources.

Anxiety potentially inhibits individuals from learning or making the most of the opportunities before them. The most effective treatment for various anxieties is to acknowledge their existence and legitimacy and then provide positive experiences to counteract them.[4] The sensitivity of faculty to various recognized forms of situational anxieties—test, math, and computer to name a few—encountered in the teaching and learning process enables faculty to be better teachers. For faculty familiar with the library and the research process it is easy to take that personal knowledge, gained over many years, for granted and to assume that others have it too. To the extent that the present and subsequent studies can elucidate the anxieties associated with students' initial use of libraries and the search process, this information can be conveyed to classroom teachers to facilitate the teaching and learning process.

THE STUDY

The purpose of this exploratory study was to build upon the qualitative research on library anxiety. Using quantitative methods the authors sought to further document and describe the nature of library anxiety and to determine the extent to which library anxiety is a separate condition from the general psychological trait of anxiety. By examining how library anxiety is distributed among college students the researchers sought to develop a better understanding of library anxiety over time. The relationships of library anxiety with students' assessments of their library skills and their confidence in using a library were examined in the process.

The setting for this study was a private comprehensive college with a full-time equivalent enrollment of 1,926 students. In April, 1994, questionnaires were distributed to selected faculty who agreed to hand them out in their classes. Usable responses were received from 153 students (77 women, 75 men), most of whom were full-time students (148). The researchers designed the selection process to provide a good cross-section of students by year in school. Although the cell counts for freshmen and senior students were less than desired, they were large enough to be statistically valid.

THE INSTRUMENTS

The forty item State-Trait Inventory measures both transitory (state) and generalized (trait) anxiety.[5] State anxiety is defined as a conscious perception of anxiety that varies in intensity, fluctuates over time, and is influenced by situations. Trait anxiety is defined as a relatively stable characteristic of people reflecting their proneness to experience anxiety across all situations.

Test-retest reliability for the trait anxiety scale is good (.73 to .86); coefficients for the state anxiety scale are expectedly lower (.16 to .54), reflecting the influence of situational factors on this scale. Considerable evidence supports the construct validity of the State-Trait Anxiety Inventory. The test correlates well with other measures of anxiety such as the Taylor Manifest Anxiety Scale.[6] There is strong additional support for the construct validity of the test and the usefulness of the state-trait distinction.[7]

The situational anxiety scale of the inventory was presented to students within a specific context. Students were given the following description of a library-related assignment and asked to answer the first twenty items of the instrument in the context of that assignment:

> Your professor has announced that a twenty page typed paper is due at the end of the semester. The paper, references, and footnotes are to be prepared in the proper format. You are to select a topic and trace its evolution over time. A review of the literature will be required to identify the formation of the topic and the supporting research studies relevant to the topic. In addition to the historical review of the literature, your professor is interested in your ability to identify and evaluate recent research findings or theoretical developments which bear upon the topic. Your analysis must include the current evaluation of the topic by scholars and the general public. Your paper will be evaluated on your ability to structure and succinctly present your work. Your appropriate use of references and footnotes should demonstrate your knowledge of the literature and the range of information available to you.

Thus, inventory questions like, "I feel tense," or "I feel calm," were answered by the students in the situational context of the library assignment. In addition to the State-Trait Inventory students completed eight questions designed to measure their confidence in using a library. The first four questions in the scale were taken directly from Jacobson's Library Anxiety Scale.[8] Others were adapted from Jacobson's computer-related anxiety scales. Using a four point Likert scale (strongly agree to strongly disagree), students were asked to answer the following questions:

- I feel I know what I'm doing when I use a library.
- Libraries are intimidating places.
- I enjoy using libraries.
- When I walk into a library I feel unsure of myself.
- I feel comfortable asking librarians for assistance.
- Having to use computers in the library makes me feel uneasy.
- I feel confident in my ability to use the library's automated catalog.
- I feel confident in my ability to use the library's compact disc databases.

Students were also asked a number of demographic questions (gender, age, year in school, and major) as well as, "How often do you go to the library?" and "How would you rate your library skills?" Although this exploratory study did not control for the influence of potentially confounding variables, the results are enlightening nevertheless.

RESULTS

The SPSS statistical package was used to analyze the data with a .05 level of statistical significance. The transitory state of being uneasy about using a library was found to be a different condition from the general psychological trait of anxiety. A paired T-test revealed significant differences between library anxiety and trait anxiety (t [152] = 9.60). This result indicates that library anxiety, as measured by the instrument, is a separate condition from the trait of general anxiety.

Five items (anxiety, library anxiety, library skills, library confidence, and frequency of library use) were compared across classes by one-way analyses of variance, with post-hoc comparisons using Newman-Keuls (see Table 1). The general trait of anxiety was equally distributed among classes and did not vary significantly by class. However, library anxiety was not randomly distributed among students and varied significantly by class. Freshmen and sophomores reported significantly higher amounts of library anxiety than seniors.

Not surprisingly freshmen reported significantly lower self assessments of their library skills than did the students in the other three classes (see Table 1). Freshmen also reported significantly less confidence in their ability to use a library than juniors and seniors. It should also be noted that sophomores reported significantly less confidence

TABLE 1: Analysis of Variance

VARIABLE	Freshman (n=20)		Sophomore (n=50)		Junior (n=52)		Senior (n=28)	
	M	SD	M	SD	M	SD	M	SD
ANXIETY	46.4	7.4	42.9	8.1	43.1	7.8	40.9	7.9
LIBRARY ANXIETY	54.8	10.7[a]	51.3	10.6[a]	50.2	9.9	45.3	12.2[b]
LIBRARY SKILLS	3.4	.9[b]	3.9	.6[a]	3.8	.7[a]	3.9	.6[a]
CONFIDENCE	21.5	5.7[b]	23.1	3.4[d]	24.1	3.8[a]	25.5	3.1[ac]
GO TO LIBRARY	4.2	5.7	4.0	1.1	4.0	1.2	3.8	1.3

[ab]   Refers to comparisons within a row where the mean scores of group [a] are significantly (p<.05) higher than the mean scores of group [b].

[cd]   Refers to comparisons within a row where the mean scores of group [c] are significantly (p<.05) higher than the mean scores of group [d].

in their ability to use a library than seniors. This difference suggests that the development of students' confidence in their ability to use a library is the most rapid during their freshmen and sophomore years, but continues to develop through their senior year.

It is interesting to note that there were no significant differences in how often students go to the library. What is not known is how students use the library. Freshmen and seniors may frequent the library equally, but are there progressive differences in what they are doing in the library?

Although Jacobson found male high school seniors had significantly higher levels of library anxiety than female high school seniors,[9] there were no significant differences in the levels of anxiety, library anxiety, library skills, library confidence, or how often they went to the library between the men and women students in the present study.

Table 2 presents the individual questions which make up the library confidence scale and reveals the differences between freshmen and seniors' confidence in their abilities to use a library. The differences are most clearly seen in the results of the first two questions. Over a third of the freshmen found libraries to be intimidating places and felt unsure of themselves while there. This is a notable difference compared with the less than four percent of the seniors who were intimidated and unsure of themselves in libraries.

Although 70 percent of the freshmen were comfortable asking a librarian for assistance, there does not seem to be as much growth in that area as

TABLE 2: Library Confidence

ITEM	Freshman (n=20) %	Senior (n=28) %	All (n=153) %
Libraries are intimidating places			
Agree	35	3.5	17.7
Disagree	65	96.4	81.7
Missing			.7
Feel unsure of myself in the library			
Agree	35	3.6	13.7
Disagree	65	96.5	85.0
Missing			1.3
Enjoy using the library			
Agree	55	82.1	61.5
Disagree	40	17.9	37.2
Missing	5		1.3
Feel comfortable asking librarian for assistance			
Agree	70	89.3	71.9
Disagree	30	10.7	27.5
Missing			.7
Confident using automated catalog			
Agree	70	92.9	84.9
Disagree	30	7.2	13.8
Missing			1.3
Confident using CD-ROM databases			
Agree	35	78.5	59.4
Disagree	65	21.4	39.9
Missing			.7

the results of the top two statements suggest. Only 82 percent of the seniors were comfortable asking librarians for assistance. Freshmen (79%) and seniors (93%) were more confident in their abilities to use the online catalog than they were to use CD-ROM databases. Only 35 percent of the freshmen and 78.5 percent of the seniors were confident of their abilities to use the CD-ROM databases.

Given the exploratory nature of this study a look at some correlations may be insightful. It should be noted that correlations do not imply causality, but rather they indicate that, for whatever reason a correlation or relationship of some type exists between two variables. Perhaps, the nature of these relationship can be clarified in subsequent studies.

There were significant but low negative correlations between students' levels of library anxiety and their assessment of their library skills (r = -.22), their confidence in their ability to use a library (r = -.37), and their year in school (r = -.24). Entering students have high levels of library anxiety and low assessments of their library skills and their confidence in their ability to use a library. However, as students progress in their education they develop their information skills (r = .18) and confidence in their abilities to use a library (r = .29). As a result, their level of library anxiety declines. There was a moderate correlation between students' assessment of their library skills and their confidence in their ability to use a library (r = .57). There was no significant correlation between how often students go to the library and library anxiety.

DISCUSSION

The use of the State-Trait Inventory in this study appears to be a fruitful way to measure library anxiety. Creating the assignment scenario was effective in assessing anxiety as it relates specifically to the library and in showing that library anxiety is different from a general tendency to be anxious. That is, the students we measured did not differ in their tendency to be anxious individuals in general. The differences in library anxiety suggests that it was the library and the related assignment, per se, which were responsible for students' anxiety.

Library anxiety does not keep students from going to the library. More than likely, the anxiety expresses itself in the kind of activities students engage in while in the library. The results show that library anxiety and lack of confidence in their ability to use a library are problems for students early in their college careers. These factors manifest themselves in a perceived lack of skill and competence when it comes to using the library for a traditional assignment. Library anxiety and the accompanying devaluating perceptions attenuate significantly as students progress to their senior year.

The results from this exploratory research show that there is a clear need for early intervention strategies to reduce students' library anxiety, particularly among freshmen and sophomores. This intervention should consist of an honest introduction to the realities of the dynamic multi-stage search process, and reassuring students that the confusion and uneasiness they feel are part of a familiar process experienced by all students, and not unique to a given individual. This anxiety reduction strategy, along with skill development, should increase students' confidence in their abilities to use a library and its resources, and enable students to be more effective users of information resources.

The authors believe that additional research is needed to document fully the nature of library anxiety. Important questions are unanswered about library anxiety's potential relationship to students' adjustment to college, retention, and academic success. Are students who are unable to reduce their library anxiety more likely to leave school or do poorly?. To what extent is library anxiety a manifestation of students' levels of personal development or maturation (ability to tolerate ambiguities[10]) or of academic deficiencies? Research indicates that students' assessments of their academic competence increase during their four years of college.[11] Is the reduction in library anxiety the result of students learning to meet or circumvent curricular and faculty expectations or of librarians' instructional efforts? Is it possible to obtain reductions in library anxiety without students developing sophisticated information skills?

Would the pattern found in this study be the same for students at other colleges and universities? If so, what are the implications for how information skills are taught? To be effective the results of these future studies need to be published and widely disseminated in the teaching and research literature of several disciplines.

NOTES

1. Constance Mellon, "Library Anxiety: A Grounded Theory and Its Development," *College & Research Libraries* 47(March 1986):160-165.
2. Carol Kuhlthau, "Developing a Model of the Library Search Process: Cognitive and Effective Aspects," *RQ* 28(Winter 1988):232-242.
3. Mellon, "Library Anxiety."
4. Ibid., p.162.
5. Charles Speilberger, Rogelio Gorsuch and Robert Lushene, *State-Trait Anxiety Inventory Manual* (Palo Alto, CA: Consulting Psychologist Press, 1970).
6. Janet Taylor, "A Personality Scale of Manifest Anxiety," *Journal of Abnormal and Social Psychology* 48(April 1953):285-290.
7. Ralph Dreger and Edward Katkin, reviews of the State-Trait Anxiety Inventory. In Oscar Buros (Ed.), *The Eight Mental Measurements Yearbook.* (Highland Park, NJ: Gryphon Press, 1978), 1094-1096.
8. Frances F. Jacobson, "Gender Differences in Attitudes Toward Using Computers in Libraries: An Exploratory Study," *Library and Information Science Research* 13(July-Sept 1991):267-279.
9. Ibid., p.273.
10. William Perry, *Forms of Intellectual and Ethical Development in the College Years: A scheme* (New York: Holt, Rinehart and Winston, 1970).
11. Ernest T. Pascarella and Patrick T. Terenzini, *How College Affects Students: Findings and Insights from Twenty Years of Research.* (San Francisco: Jossey-Bass, 1991), p. 173.

Customer Input into Library Decision Making

Joyce A. Meldrem, Carolyn V. Johnson, and Connie J. Ury

ABSTRACT

Decisions about library instruction and services must be made with the customer's needs in mind if we are to meet the challenges of the ever-increasing information volume and cost in academic libraries today. This is not to say that libraries have ignored the needs of their users in the past. Indeed, one of the pillars of librarianship has always been service to our patrons. However, the quality and quantity of our service has traditionally been evaluated or determined by librarians rather than library users. Decisions made in the 1990s must be made objectively, driven by user needs as perceived by our internal and external customers. Librarians can utilize tools of total quality management such as focus groups, customer satisfaction surveys, interviews, and instructional assessment instruments to provide decision making teams with vital customer input. The presenters of this paper highlight total quality management customer feedback tools and demonstrate how these tools are used to enhance and guide decision making at Owens Library, Northwest Missouri State University.

> *It is likely that part of librarians' reluctance to use survey data for future planning derives from the traditionally bureaucratic organization of libraries.* [1]

INTRODUCTION

Until recently, most academic libraries operated under a hierarchical structure. Planning for library programs, services and procedures originated from the top down. Management by self-directed work teams and an increasing focus on customer satisfaction have brought many changes to library planning and decision making.

Owens Library, a medium-sized, state-funded academic library serving approximately 5,600 students at Northwest Missouri State University, reorganized from a bureaucratic to a team management structure in Summer 1990. The teams were empowered to envision projects, examine policies, recommend and implement actions. Rec-

Joyce A. Meldrem is Distribution Team Leader, Carolyn V. Johnson is Information Focus Team Leader, and Connie J. Ury is Coordinator of the Library Use Instruction Study Group at Owens Library, Northwest Missouri State University, Maryville, Missouri.

ommendations requiring University budget increases or policy changes were referred to the management team. One of the prime benefits of the team structure was the ownership of programs which flourished among the staff as they offered input, evaluated results and made decisions. We moved from an environment in which administrators made decisions in isolation to cooperative agreement by the people who did the work. The focus and mission of our teams gradually shifted from an environment of "we've always done it this way" to a collective attitude about the importance of involving staff and patrons in decision making.

Owens Library has five teams comprised of library faculty and staff:

- Coordination of Resources - collection development
- Distribution - circulation, reserve, interlibrary loan, periodicals, and audiovisuals
- Information Focus - reference and library use instruction
- Technical Services - acquisitions and cataloging
- Management - comprised of the library director, elected library faculty team leaders, the assistant to the library director, and an elected library staff member

Because of our team structure and growing participation from team members, we found that we moved beyond our reluctance to use customer input for decision making to actively seeking their opinions and definitions of quality. Teams help to diminish the attitude that says, ìI just do what Iím told, no matter how archaic or inefficient it seems.î Decisions are reached by the group as a whole and no one person is held responsible for an idea that flops. Likewise, successes belong to the team as a whole and help employees feel that they have a stake in the success of a project.

We discovered communication is improved in a team environment when everyone is given an equal opportunity to express their viewpoint. Since decisions are reached in the presence of all those

affected, information is accurately disseminated. Trust, openness and honesty have developed as the communication structure becomes inclusively horizontal. Because employees are helping to make the decisions directly related to their work, they feel a responsibility for and pride in those decisions. Finally, creativity and self-fulfillment are possibilities for members of teams. We have a vehicle for input of ideas and the chance to provide services that we once just dreamed about. Once team members felt free to provide input, we saw the need to provide that same freedom to our customers.

REFERENCE APPLICATIONS

With the advent of team management, the Information Focus Team, responsible for reference and library use instruction, began to offer services we thought our patrons would be interested in receiving. At the same time, we wanted to collect data from our customers that would help determine if we were offering services they wanted and if we could improve the results of those services.

We implemented a term paper consultation program after an extensive literature search regarding why and how to offer tiered reference service. Our goal was to provide in-depth, personalized research assistance that would enable students to be more self-sufficient in search strategy and information retrieval. An opinionnaire was designed as part of a pilot project to determine if we met our goal and if the customer felt the service was helpful.

We asked the students to evaluate the service based on the kind of help they perceived they needed. We told the students we would make a decision, based upon their input, about offering the service permanently. We offered 118 consultations in a six week period during Spring 1992. Out of 71 responses, 61 felt the service was very helpful, eight felt it was helpful but not as much as they expected, one felt the service was not much help, and one did not respond.

Because of this very positive customer response to our pilot project and an opinionnaire return rate of 60.2%, we decided to offer this service on a regular basis. As our customers answered strategically open-ended questions, they identified added benefits of the service that we had not envisioned. We found that the service lessened their frustration with technology, increased their awareness of our professional expertise, helped them narrow their research focus, and decreased their search time. It was possible for us to staff this service without increasing human resources or decreasing other services because team management gave us a forum for envisioning flexible work loads and recruiting personnel to participate.

LIBRARY USE INSTRUCTION APPLICATIONS

The Information Focus Team also collected assessment data to guide our instructional decision and planning processes. Interested team members formed the Library Use Instruction Study Group in Fall 1991. We moved from offering minimal instruction upon request to proactively marketing services we believed would enhance the students' abilities to map and execute search strategies. One of the sites targeted for instruction was the second level English composition course required for all freshmen where a research paper component allows us to provide instruction at a point of need.

Thomas Shaughnessy suggests that total quality management will have a more profound impact upon academia than zero based budgeting or management by objective because it not only emphasizes staff empowerment, but also focuses on the customer. 2 We followed this model as we solicited feedback through focus groups and personal interviews with English composition faculty and classes, as well as library personnel. The English composition component of our tiered instructional plan was launched as a "trial run" in Fall 1991 with a small number of sections. The English instructors involved were asked to provide suggestions in one-on-one interviews with the Coordinator of the Library Use Instruction Study Group. Library personnel who did not staff the program provided peer evaluation.

Suggestions regarding the instruction were solicited in Spring 1992. Thirteen of twenty three English professors responded to a written survey (56.5% return rate). A focus group strategy was also employed with 50% of the English faculty members attending. Library instructors for the program met for a group interview to assess the program. The results of these assessments were analyzed and used to implement instructional improvements in the Spring 1993 including:

- Scheduling classes throughout the semester rather than limiting instruction to six weeks;
- Adding an extra class period of hands-on instructional time;
- Expanding demonstrations of electronic indexes to include subject specific databases in addition to general databases.

English instructors were also surveyed in Spring 1993 and offered suggestions for improvements. Nine of twenty-one instructors responded (42.9% return rate). A group interview of the eight library employees offering instruction also generated feedback. Enhancements generated from this input for Spring 1994 included:

- Building accountability into worksheet assignments;
- Generating lists of possible subjects to reduce the number of repeated topics and simultaneous requests for the same materials;
- Providing optional hands-on instructional time;
- Encouraging English faculty to personalize instruction for their classes;
- Reducing from eight to three the number of library staff who provide instruction;
- Releasing library instructors from Reference Desk duty during the heaviest period of

Information collected	Decision made
The students weren't sure who to ask for help if they needed it. (There had been a major rearrangement of personnel and office space prior to the Fall 1992 semester.)	We provided the students with a staff schedule so they would know who was available to help during their shift.
The students felt they needed extra help during busy hours.	Beginning with the next semester, we decided to double staff one hour each afternoon and two hours each evening.
A number of students suggested that we cover the Reference Desk (located near the Circulation Desk) for more hours because they were being asked Reference questions.	We extended the hours ninety minutes each day and posted a sign telling patrons when the librarian would be available to help them.

Figure 1

instructional scheduling. Reference shifts were staffed by librarians not providing instruction. Both groups were able to focus on a primary work assignment, rather than fragmenting their efforts among various service points.

During Spring 1994, students were asked to provide short answer assessments at the conclusion of sessions. These front-line customer comments are currently under analysis and will be used to facilitate the instruction in Spring 1995.

CIRCULATION APPLICATIONS

Numerous decisions are made on a continual basis at the Circulation/Reserve Desk, a service point coordinated by our Distribution Team. Many student employees, our internal customers, are the primary front line service providers for this area. As Elizabeth J. Wood states in Strategic Market-

ing for Libraries, "The staff's experience and unique perspective will make their perceptions with respect to . . . key issues valuable.[3]

In November 1992, we asked students who worked at the Circulation/Reserve Desk:

- What do you like about your job?
- What do you dislike about your job?
- If you could change anything about your job, what would it be and how would you do it?

We knew student employees had concerns about their work, but we were unsure of the nature of the problems. Therefore, we asked very general questions to solicit ideas for possible improvements. The first two questions yielded typical responses. However, the third question gave us grist for the mill. (See Figure 1)

We shared the responses with our student employees along with the impact of their input on decisions made by the Distribution and Information Focus Teams. These solutions were obvious once the problems were pointed out, but we needed input from our internal customers to help us make better decisions and provide the information they needed to successfully complete their job.

In Spring 1993, we made changes in Circulation procedures to address problems identified by customers who were receiving overdue notices when they were positive they had returned their books. We examined our circulation processes for the possibility of human error. Student employees were checking out and checking in materials in two different modes on one computer and desensitizing and sensitizing materials on a single piece of equipment which required them to remember to switch back and forth. To correct this problem, we created separate stations for checkout and checkin reducing the possibility for human error. We asked the student employees to evaluate the new procedures and they responded that it "helped avoid a lot of confusion."

CONCLUSION

Team management has helped change our work environment so that we are more flexible and open to customer input. Before team management, we wore blinders, only able to trust our own problem-solving ability. With the implementation of team management, our vision moved beyond ourselves to encompass our internal and external customer populations. Through the use of surveys, focus groups, individual interviews and assessment data, we have determined some of our customers' requirements. The decisions cited in this paper were made by each team in response to data and opinions collected. Crist suggests "...there is an emerging imperative for libraries of all types to build in an ability to clearly show responsiveness to 'customers' in decision making.î 4 Through our team orientation, we have increased our ability to respond to customer needs.

NOTES

1. Doris J. Schlichter and J. Michael Pemberton, "The Emperor's New Clothes? Problems of the User Survey as a Planning Tool in Academic Libraries," *College & Research Libraries* 53 (May 1992), p. 260.
2. Thomas W. Shaughnessy, "Benchmarking, Total Quality Management, and Libraries," *Library Administration & Management* 7 (Winter 1993), p. 7.
3. Elizabeth J. Wood, *Strategic Marketing for Libraries* (Westport, CT: Greenwood Press, Inc., 1988), p. 25.
4. Margo Crist, Peggy Daub, and Barbara MacAdam, "User Studies: Reality Check and Future Perfect," *Wilson Library Bulletin* (February 1994), p. 38.

Perceptions of Transformational vs. Transactional Leadership in University Libraries

Rosie L. Albritton

ABSTRACT

Transformational leaders are described as capable of motivating subordinates to do more than they ever expected to do. Transactional leadership is described as a social exchange in which the leader gives something and gets something in return. This study tested the transformational vs. transactional model to determine whether perceptions of these two styles of leadership were present in a sample of medium-sized university libraries. The results suggest that the perceptions of leadership behavior are associated with perceptions of satisfaction, effectiveness and extra effort of subordinates. Transformational leadership was also perceived as having more effect on selected outcomes than transactional leadership.

INTRODUCTION

Transformational leaders are needed in academic libraries to help encourage librarians and other staff to move toward individual renewal and organizational revitalization. As technological and societal changes continue to affect librarianship, higher education, and the nature of library services in academic libraries, there will be a corresponding need for leaders with vision and energy to foster the development of new paradigms for libraries. In order to develop leadership potential in future library administrators and to promote the success of incumbents, it is necessary to determine leadership effectiveness and its relationship to organizational outcomes in academic libraries. Very little research has been done on the study of leadership in the field of library and information science.

Transformational leadership, as defined by Burns[1] and Bass[2], represents an important addition to previous conceptualizations of leadership. The purpose of this study was to determine whether perceptions of transformational leadership, as defined by the Bass Multifactor Leadership Questionnaire (MLQ)[3], were present in medium-sized university libraries.

Rosie L. Albritton is an Assistant Professor in the Library and Information Science Program, Wayne State University, Detroit, Michigan.

In 1985, Bernard Bass[4] proposed a **new model** of leadership, based on the work of James M. Burns[5], in which he described leaders as **transformational or transactional**. Bass theorized that there is a certain kind of leader who is capable of inspiring subordinates to heights they never intended to achieve. He referred to these leaders as transformational. The transactional leader, on the other hand, is rooted in two-way influence: a social exchange in which the leader gives something and gets something in return. In his book, *Leadership and Performance Beyond Expectations*, Bass[6] stated that the transactional leader recognizes what subordinates want to derive from their work and provides appropriate rewards for expected performance, that is, responds to subordinates' immediate self-interest (p.11)[7]. He described the transformational leaders as: a) motivating subordinates to do more than they ever expected to do by raising their level of awareness and consciousness about the importance and value of reaching designated outcomes; b) encouraging subordinates to transcend their own self-interest for the sake of the organization; and c) altering subordinates' need levels on Maslow's hierarchy or expanding their portfolio on needs and wants (p. 20)[8]. For Bass, "the transactional leader works within the organizational culture as it exists; the transformational leader changes the organizational culture (p.24)."[9]

Burns[10] had identified these two types in the field of political leadership, and Bass applied the concepts to organizational management. He identified four factors of transformational leadership (**charisma, inspiration, individualized consideration, and intellectual stimulation**), two factors of transactional leadership (**contingent reward and management by exception**) and one factor of non-leadership (**laissez-faire**), and defined as follows:

Transformational Leadership Factors:

Idealized Influence (Charisma) - Leader has a vision and a sense of mission. Gains respect, trust, and confidence. Acquires a strong individual identification from followers.

Inspirational - Leader gives pep talks, increases optimism and enthusiasm, and communicates his or her vision with fluency and confidence.

Intellectual Stimulation - Leader actively encourages a new look at old methods, fosters creativity, and stresses the use of intelligence. Provokes rethinking and reexamination of assumptions and contexts on which previous assessments of possibilities, capabilities, strategies, and goals were based.

Individualized Consideration - Leader gives personal attention to all members, making each individual feel valued and each individual's contribution important. Coaches, advises, and provides feedback in ways easiest for each group member to accept, understand, and to use for personal development.

Transactional Leadership Factors:

Contingent Reward - Contracts exchange of rewards for effort and agreed upon levels of performance. Gives individual a clear understanding of what is expected of them.

Management-by-Exception - Intervenes only if standards are not met or if something goes wrong.

Laissez-Faire (Non-Leadership Factor):

Indicates the absence of leadership, the avoidance of intervention, or both. There are generally neither transactions nor agreements with followers. Decisions are often delayed; feedback, rewards, and involvement are absent; and there is not an attempt to motivate the followers or to recognize and satisfy their needs. Leader is uninvolved, withdraws when needed, reluctant to take a responsible stand; believes the best leadership is the least leadership.[11]

The instrument developed by Bass (1985) to quantitatively assess the constructs of his model is the **Multifactor Leadership Questionnaire (MLQ)**. The **MLQ** has been found to be reliable and valid as the result of exhaustive research since the early 1980's and is now published by Consulting Psychologist Press, Palo Alto, California.[12]

Statement of Problem

The theoretical constructs presented by Bass and his colleagues,[13] provide a model of organizational leadership which seeks to explain differences in outstanding and ordinary leadership. These earlier research findings indicate that transformational and transactional leadership both appear to be related to organizational outcomes such as effectiveness, satisfaction and extra-effort of subordinates. However, transformational factors seem to have incremental effects on these outcomes, above and beyond that of transactional factors, thus suggesting that differences in transactional and transformational leadership may also differentiate outstanding and ordinary leaders.

The transformational leadership model seems to have research potential for studying academic library management by providing the following: 1) a systematic approach for exploring leadership behavior as a means of enhancing the overall administration and management of libraries and for exploring leadership as a means of enhancing the overall administration and management of libraries, and 2) a conceptual link for further explanation and development of approaches to the study of organizational effectiveness. It does not appear that the transformational model has been tested in libraries.

Exactly how and to what degree a leader effects the organization has been the subject of some research and much speculation. Even though the problem is yet to be resolved, because of the importance of leadership as a key element in the understanding of the functioning of the organization, additions to the body of knowledge of leadership theory contributed by research should be of value to both those who administer libraries and to those who educate future library administrators.

Purpose of Study

The general over-all purpose of this research was to increase the base of knowledge that concerns the development of leaders and leadership processes in university libraries. It was presumed that the outcomes of this study could ultimately influence how library administrators and mangers facilitate and promote the improvement of library organizational effectiveness. Toward that end, this study tested the transformational vs. transactional model to determine whether perceptions of transformational leadership were present in the sample from medium-sized university libraries, and if these perceptions were related to leadership outcomes. Transformational leadership was tested for any incremental effect in satisfaction, effectiveness, and extra effort of subordinates beyond that of transactional leadership. The study also examined the influence of selected demographics of the respondents on their perceptions of leadership behavior and effectiveness outcomes.

Research Questions and Hypotheses

The research questions addressed in this study were:

1. Will the transformational vs. transactional leadership model of organizational leadership appear in a sample of university libraries in configurations similar to those found in studies of other formal organizations?

2. Will perceptions of transformational leadership be more highly correlated than transactional leadership, with perceptions of subordinates' extra-effort, satisfaction with leader and perceived leadership effectiveness?

Based on the cited research of the Bass transformational leadership model and the research questions stated above, the following hypotheses were derived and tested:

Hypothesis 1

The transformational vs. transactional model of leadership, as measured by the MLQ, will appear in a sample of university libraries in configurations similar to those found in studies of other formal organizations as follows: Four transformational factors - (Charisma, Inspiration, Intellectual Stimulation, and Individual Consideration); and, two transactional factors - (Contingent Reward and Management-by-Exception).

Hypothesis 2

Transformational leadership factors as perceived by the library sample, will be more highly correlated than transactional leadership factors with the three "outcome" measures of the MLQ: extra-effort of subordinates, satisfaction with leader, and leadership effectiveness.

METHODOLOGY

The research was designed as a correlational (ex post facto) field study, and the data were collected within the existing organizations by using survey research methodology. In correlational research, the intent is to determine the degree to which various measures are related to one another. Survey research involves asking a random sample to respond to a set of questions.

Survey Instrument

The instrument used to assess perceptions of transformational and transactional leadership behavior was the **Multifactor Leadership Questionnaire - 5R (MLQ)**;[14] published by Consulting Psychologists Press, Palo Alto, CA. The questionnaire contains 80 items, 70 of which require a **rating-scale response.** A five-point **ratio-based rating scale** for rating the frequency of observed leader behaviors is used for both the leader and the follower forms of the questionnaire. The five response choices ranged from "frequently, if not always" to "not at all."

Sample

Subjects

The subjects were university library directors, members of their administrative/management teams, and other library staff randomly selected

from medium-sized U.S. academic libraries holding membership in the Association of College and Research Libraries (ACRL), and the Association of Research Libraries (ARL). The choice of medium-sized university library settings was the result of a preferential choice of the researcher, primarily due to extensive experience and educational background in these libraries as an administrator, management intern, and research investigator. The **ACRL University Library Statistics: 1987-88,**[15] and the **ARL Statistics: 1989-90,**[16] were used to develop a list of 104 medium-sized U. S. university libraries meeting the following criteria: total staff size of 80 to 300; and a full-time appointed library director. Medium-sized libraries were identified by combining Rank Order Tables for Staff Size from the ARL and the ACRL Statistics, and selecting those libraries from the bottom 50% of the ARL list and the top 50% of the ACRL table.

Sample Size and Data Collection

In terms of sample size for generating results from the application of correlational statistical procedures, i. e., descriptive correlations, multiple regressions, and factor analyses, the number of respondents (cases) available for this study were considered acceptable. From pilot data and the literature review on the MLQ and the transformational leadership model, the range of correlations (r), multiple correlations (R), and coefficients of determination (Rsq) were estimated.

Letters and consent forms inviting participation in the study were sent to 90 library directors by applying proportional stratified random sampling to the sampling frame of 104 medium-sized libraries. Ninety letters of invitation were mailed in order to obtain as close to 30 directors as possible (the sample size determined by power analysis calculations). Pilot study data collected prior to the study indicated a volunteer acceptance rate of approximately 35%

Twenty-three directors agreed to have their libraries participate. From each of the 23 lists of library staff, 6 were randomly selected to evaluate leadership behavior and organizational effectiveness. The questionnaires were mailed along with a cover letter to the 23 directors and 138 library staff reporting to them (a total of 161 potential cases). Of the 161 questionnaires distributed, 146 (91%) were returned. The 23 libraries in the sample provided responses from 146 individuals, well within the acceptable sample size range established by power analysis, for the quantitative data analysis needed for testing the hypotheses addressed in this study. Since library directors were volunteers, there is a potential for bias in that part of the sample; furthermore, the possibility of reluctance to answer questions on the part of the subordinates about one's superior might have inhibited certain portions of the potential subordinate sample from participation.

Analysis of Data

Multiple regression models were used to determine the incremental contribution of transformational leadership above that of transactional leadership, to predict extra effort, satisfaction, and effectiveness in university library settings. Selected "background" or "status" variables (type of respondent-self or rater; respondents' institutional support-private or state funded; respondents' library governance style-faculty status or other; respondents' library type-research or college) were added to the analyses as control variables. Descriptive statistics were calculated for questionnaire items and demographic data from the instrument. Factor analysis and principal components analysis were applied to the MLQ to confirm the presence of the leadership model. The data were entered into a SPSS-X mainframe computer statistical analysis program to determine associations between variables, i.e., correlations, multiple regressions, means tables, and ANOVA.

RESULTS

Both hypotheses concerning the perceptions of transformational and transactional leadership by library directors and their staff in medium-sized university libraries were supported by studying this sample.

Hypothesis 1:

The university library sample tested in this study displayed perceptions of transformational and transactional leadership behaviors that are similar to the Bass model and other previous research. In testing hypothesis 1, the factor analysis of the MLQ were compared with other factor analyses of the MLQ in order to discover whether similar factors could be accounted for in the library sample.

Transformational and transactional leadership characteristics were confirmed and measured by six factors: idealized influence (charisma), inspiration, individualized consideration, and intellectual stimulation representing perceptions of transformational behaviors; and contingent reward and management of exception, representing perceptions of transactional behaviors.

Hypothesis 2:

Transformational leadership behaviors were perceived as having more effect on leadership outcomes, than transactional leadership, by the respondents from the sample of university libraries tested with the Bass MLQ: satisfaction with the leader, effectiveness of the leader, and extra effort of followers. Hypothesis 2 was tested by computing correlations between the leadership factors and the outcome measures, and then applying hierarchical multiple regression analyses to the variables representing transformational and transactional leadership, satisfaction with leader, effectiveness of leader, and extra-effort of followers. Independent variables were the transformational and transactional leadership variables; the dependent variables were the three "outcome" scales of extra-effort, satisfaction, and effectiveness, and two control variables -position of the respondent and support of institution.

The correlations of the transformational factors with the outcome measures were strong (.634 to .869, p>.01), while the transactional factors are much lower. Contingent reward was .502 to .576, p<.01, and management by exception was only .023 to -.137, p<.01.

The results of the regression analysis of the MLQ leadership factors on the outcome measures indicate that transformational leadership behavior, as measured by the MLQ, was perceived by the library sample as having more effect on the three outcome measures than transactional leadership behavior. The transformational factors and significant incremental effects (from 28.7% to 43.2% more variance) on the predictability of extra-effort, satisfaction, and effectiveness) above the effect of transactional factors. These findings suggest that perceptions of transformational leadership were associated with higher levels of performance by followers (extra-effort), satisfaction with leader (satisfaction), and leadership effectiveness (effectiveness) in the university library sample.

CONCLUSIONS

In general, the overall results of this study suggest that perceptions of leadership behavior (both transactional and transformational), by this sample, are associated with perceptions of satisfaction with the leader, effectiveness of the leader and amount of extra effort by followers. As expected, "transformational" leadership was perceived by the library sample as augmenting, or having more effect on leadership outcomes and dimensions of organizational effectiveness, than "transactional" leadership. While these findings agree with the conclusions of the research of Bass and his associates (Bass;[18,19,20] Bass & Avolio;[21] Hater & Bass;[22] Seltzer & Bass;[23] Waldman, Bass, & Yammarino[24]), they have further substantiated that the model may have meaning and applicability to settings other than industrial and military settings investigated by earlier studies, and particularly to the academic library.

Based on the results of this study, the following conclusions may be drawn:

1. The university library sample tested in this study displayed perceptions of transformational and transactional leadership behaviors that are similar to the Bass[25] model and other previous research on transformational and transactional leadership.

2. Transformational leadership behaviors are perceived as having more effect on leadership outcomes, than transactional leadership, by the respondents from the sample of university libraries tested with the Bass MLQ: satisfaction with the leader, effectiveness of the leader, and extra effort of followers.

3. The background, status, and other demographic characteristics of the respondents had a strong influence on the perceived effect of transformational and transactional leadership behaviors on leadership outcomes. The background characteristics found to have influence in this study were: leader vs. follower; affiliation with privately or state supported institution; faculty status or other governance structure for librarians at the university; and affiliation with a research or college-level library. Group differences were significant for all four control variables in most cases.

This study of transformational leadership and leadership effectiveness is clearly only a beginning of further research on these models in libraries, in general, and in university libraries, in particular. Recommendations and suggestions for further research:

1. Research should be conducted to further test, affirm, or expand the theoretical framework of transformational leadership in academic libraries with larger samples.

2. Research should be conducted to examine possible gender differences in leadership behavior among library administrators.

3. This study could be replicated by studying different types of libraries and information centers.

4. The design of longitudinal studies should be encouraged to determine transformational leadership and effectiveness changes in libraries in general, and particularly university libraries, over time.

5. Case studies and other forms of in-depth qualitative data collection and research methodolo-

gies should be conducted in libraries to determine similarities and differences in perceptions of transformational leadership and effectiveness and develop profiles from perspectives other than quantitative data and analyses.

The conclusions of this study are limited to the population of university libraries who participated in the study and also limited by the use of perceptual self-report instruments rather than direct measures. Despite these limitations, the results of the study do suggest some implications for the practice of library administration and management, library education, and library human resource development. This study provides some evidence that certain factors of the transformational/transactional leadership model can indeed be used to enhance performance:

1. The factor of charisma appears to be powerful in predicting satisfaction and effectiveness. This scale reflects the expression of enthusiasm, optimism, and confidence. Library leaders can be trained to develop these qualities and can be evaluated on their success in these areas.

2. The personal attention measured by the individualized consideration factor and intellectual stimulation measured by that scale can also be taught as elements of leadership to library administrators. Since these concepts are important to the satisfaction and effectiveness of followers, individualized consideration and intellectual stimulation should be expected of library managers, and encouraged by library administration. The actual scales of the Bass MLQ may be suitable for evaluating the extent to which library managers and administrators employ transformational leadership skills and behaviors.

3. In terms of transactional leadership, library administrators and leaders should be aware that rewards and contingent reinforcement may be transformational as well as transactional. They should be trained in using rewards to develop enhanced performance rather that using rewards which they control for only meeting the status quo or ordinary expectations. Academic libraries are labor intensive organizations whose most important resource is its staff.

Efforts to develop transformational leadership require that we do more than just increase specific skills. As this study and other related research indicates, transformational leadership is not a mysterious process, but a measurable construct, whereby the perceptions of identifiable behaviors such as the articulation of transcendent goals, demonstration of strong self-confidence and confidence in others, setting a personal example for followers, showing high expectations for followers' performance, and the ability to communicate one's faith in one's goals. Therefore, what is needed is training and education that promotes self-understanding, awareness and appreciation of the range of potential leadership behaviors used by effective transformational and transactional leaders.

The study also suggests guidelines to library educators who seek to improve the preparation of students for managerial and administrative library positions. Better understanding of theoretical foundations of leadership and management should improve the education given to new and potential leaders. This should also be of great importance for continuing professional development after library school.

The theoretical framework of this study focuses on the effective leadership and management of libraries. The results of this study do not necessarily mean that university libraries have the same kind of leadership as industrial or corporate organizations, nor that one kind of leadership is better or worse than another. The study was designed to investigate one specific model of leadership, but leadership may indeed consist of more than transformational and transactional factors, and did not attempt to find one definitive strategy of leadership or of organizational effectiveness that could be universally applied to all university libraries, or other types of libraries in general. The model investigated was theoretical and represented a conceptual framework that attempted to describe relationships between organizational constructs which were operationalized as leadership factors, leadership outcomes, and effectiveness measures. However, since the study was guided by theory and tested under real conditions, the research should be helpful in bridging the gap between practice and theory. The patterns revealed by this study that appear to be similar to other research simply suggests that libraries and other formal organizations are similar in their patterns of perceptions of leadership behaviors and descriptions of effectiveness and outcomes. The findings of this research will help to increase awareness of the need to continue to investigate perceived leadership behaviors and their influence on perceptions of organizational and leadership effectiveness.

Acknowledgments

This paper is based on the *1994 ALISE Doctoral Dissertation Competition Award* dissertation: "Transformational vs. Transactional Leadership in University Libraries: A Test of the Model and Its Relationship to Perceived Library Organizational Effectiveness," May 1993, Graduate School of Library and Information Science, University of Illinois, Urbana-Champaign. The author wishes to express appreciation and thanks to her Dissertation Advisor, Bryce Allen, and other members of her committee, Linda Smith and Terry Weech.

This research was funded in part by the following awards:

- The *1992 ACRL/ISI Doctoral Dissertation Fellowship*, Spring 1992.
- A *Doctoral Dissertation Research Grant* from the Graduate College, University of Illinois, Urbana-Champaign, 1991-92
- A *Reece Award Research Grant from the Graduate School of Library and Information Science*, University of Illinois, Urbana-Champaign, 1990-91. (Supported Pilot Study)

NOTES

1. James M. Burns, *Leadership* (New York: Harper & Row, 1978).
2. Bernard Bass, *Leadership and Performance Beyond Expectations* (New York: Free Press, 1985).
3. Bernard Bass and Bruce Avolio, *Manual for the Multifactor Leadership Questionnaire* (Palo Alto, CA.: Consulting Psychologists Press, 1990).
4. Bass, *Leadership and Performance*, 1985.
5. Burns, *Leadership*, 1978.
6. Bass, *Leadership and Performance*, 17.
7. Ibid., 17.
8. Ibid., 20.
9. Ibid., 24.
10. Burns, *Leadership*, 1978.
11. Bass, and Avolio, *Manual for the MLQ*, 1990.
12. Ibid., 19-20.
13. Bernard Bass and Bruce Avolio, "The Implications of Transactional and Transformational Leadership for Individual, Team and Organizational Development," in *Research in Organizational Change and Development* (Greenwich, Conn: JAI Press, 1990), 231-272.
14. Bass and Avolio, *Manual for the MLQ*, 1990.
15. Association of College & Research Libraries, *ACRL University Library Statistics: 1987-88* (Chicago: ALA, 1989).
16. Association of Research Libraries, *ARL Statistics: 1989-90* (Washington, D.C.: ARL, 1990).
17. Marija Norusis, *SPSS-X Introductory Statistics Student Guide* (Chicago: SPSS, Inc., 1990).
18. Bass, *Leadership and Performance*, 1985.
19. Bernard Bass, "Leadership: Good, better, best," *Organizational Dynamics* 13 (1985): 26-41.
20. Bernard Bass, "From transactional to transformational leadership: Learning to share the vision" *Organizational Dynamics* 18 (1990): 19-36.
21. Bass and Avolio, "The Implications of transactional," 1990.
22. James Hater and Bernard Bass, "Superiors' evaluations and subordinates' perceptions of transformational and transactional leadership" *Journal of Applied Psychology* 73 (1988): 695-702.

23. Jerome Seltzer and Bernard Bass, "Transformational leadership: Beyond initiation and consideration" *Journal of Management* 16 (1990): 693-703.

24. Edward Waldman, Bernard Bass, and Frank Yammarino, "Adding to contingency reward behavior: The augmenting effect of charismatic leadership" *Group and Organizational Studies* 15 (1990): 381-394.

25. Bass, *Leadership and Performance*, 1985.

How Do You Flatten an AUL?
Making the Transition from a Hierarchical Organization

Connie Kearns McCarthy

ABSTRACT

The paper examines the conceptual shift of the role of the Associate or Assistant University Librarian from a position previously defined by line supervisory managerial responsibilities to that of a leadership partnership with the Library Director. It looks at models from academic libraries that have moved to "flatten" organizations in the context of changing environmental needs and the application of principles of continuous improvement. The new leadership role for the AUL is discussed in the context of a progressive career path.

The organizational culture today strives to "flatten" the hierarchical structure and to empower the staff at the operational and mid-management level. Organizations, be they corporate or academic, are evolving into less hierarchical structures. I say less hierarchical because I don't see academic libraries as non-hierarchical yet (maybe not achievable?), for the library still operates within a very hierarchical university setting.

Any information or communication business today is experiencing rapid technological changes propelling them to change how they do business. Add to that a generous dose of Continuous Improvement or Total Quality Management and the basic structure begins to take on different dimensions.

In addition, the challenge becomes: do more with less; offer services in new areas with fewer resources. Rosabeth Moss Kanter characterizes this process as "an elephant learning to dance," an organization trying to become more agile by collapsing several layers of management hierarchy, the "ultimate corporate balancing act."[1]

What is the particular role for the senior manager, the Assistant or Associate University Library, (AUL), in the academic library organization, where the role was previously defined in a hierarchical or supervisory structure? I will exam-

---

Connie Kearns McCarthy is Associate University Librarian at Perkins Library, Duke University, Durham, North Carolina.

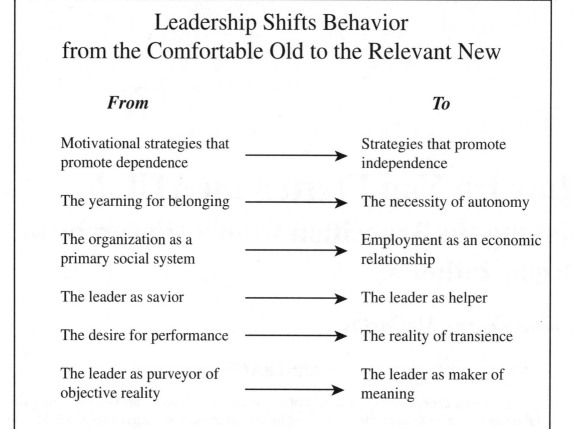

Leadership Shifts Behavior
from the Comfortable Old to the Relevant New

From	*To*
Motivational strategies that promote dependence	Strategies that promote independence
The yearning for belonging	The necessity of autonomy
The organization as a primary social system	Employment as an economic relationship
The leader as savior	The leader as helper
The desire for performance	The reality of transience
The leader as purveyor of objective reality	The leader as maker of meaning

Noer, David M. *Healing the Wounds: Overcoming the Trauma of Layoffs and Revitalizing Downsized Organizations* (San Francisco: Jossey-Bass, 1993) 192. Used with permission.

Figure 1.

ine some current options or models, try to outline some strategies for AULs making the transition , and make some observations on the issue of a progressive career path. And of course, as you might guess, I do have a personal bias. I do believe that there is a role for an AUL in today's changing academic library, and that it is an important one.

What then are the major changes in the role? The major conceptual change that I will focus on is strengthening the AUL leadership role in the library. It means moving away from the idea that to be a senior administrator is to be a supervisor—to have quantities of people "reporting" to the administrator requiring direct line responsibilities. Instead, the focus shifts to providing strategies for independence within the organization. It suggests moving away from the dependency structure promoted by the reporting structure traditional for an AUL position and facilitating the

move to staff empowerment. David Noer in the title *Healing the Wounds: Overcoming the Trauma of Layoffs and Revitalizing Downsized Organizations* describes the shift as a move from the "comfortable old to the relevant new." For him, "Being a leader within the new paradigm requires taking unselfish responsibility for helping others wallow through continuing disequilibrium."[2] His shift asks the leader to move from applying motivational strategies that promote dependence to strategies that promote independence, from viewing the organization as primarily a social system to viewing the organization as an economic relationship, and the leader as savior and purveyor of objective reality to the leader as helper and a maker of meaning.(See Figure 1)

The AUL as a "maker of meaning" seems to me to be a appropriate characterization. Several leadership skills are implied here. The leader, or

AUL, shares and interprets the vision of the library; she makes sense out of the changes moving from the old reality to the new. Facilitation skills, communication skills, and the ability to envision different approaches and different strategies are all needed. Peter Senge, the proponent of the "learning organization," characterizes the shift in the role of the leader as a shift from setting the vision to working with the staff to build a shared vision; from making key decisions and creating structures to control local actions to enabling good decisions to be made throughout the organization through the design of learning processes; and a shift from political mediation of conflict to supporting a dialogue and integration of diverse views.[3]

The horizontal dimension becomes much more important than the vertical dimension in the new environment. The perspective of the AUL becomes broader than the responsibilities of a "division". A broad organizational view is important as well as the ability to help others in the organization acquire a broader perspective. As we are aware, the perspective needs to include inter-institutional, national and international developments as we move forward on any library front. This may be a particular role for the AUL.

What are some of the models that incorporate a different role for the AUL? I will talk about three models: Here today, gone tomorrow; Partners of the Firm; and Auxiliary Services. All of the models move the AUL out of direct "line" positions, into staff positions.

Here today, gone tomorrow: This is a model that needs to be seriously considered. While it can be painful for an organization and certainly for an individual, there are serious questions that need to be asked: How much management is needed at the top? How do we add value to top management? How do we meet the increasing service demands with steady state personnel budgets?

Partners of the Firm: This model depends on the size and the complexity of the practice. A small town practice may not need any partners. A larger firm dealing with many and varied clients may need several partners. Let me dwell on this model for a moment for the "partner" concept is a model we have followed at my institution.

First, a bit of background on how we have restructured the library. We have grouped service clusters together into Quality Circles, composed of home teams with home team leaders. The senior policy making body of the library is a Leadership Circle, composed of a representative from each of the Quality Circles, the University Librarian, Director of Library Development, Director of Library Personnel, Assistant Vice-Provost for Academic Computing, Deputy University Librarian, Associate University Librarian, and Assistant University Librarian. (See Figure 2)

We have described the administrative role of the AULs and the University Librarian as a "leadership partnership," responsible for ensuring that the entire library moves together toward a shared mission and vision. The University Librarian position for a large and complex system places multiple demands on the Librarian's time on and off campus. Therefore, he is not able to work directly with all parts of the system and provide leadership for all system-wide activities. The AULs help with the leadership role; they support, guide, and coordinate the work of an empowered staff and quality circles. They encourage initiative and risk-taking for the long term. In providing information and expertise at the "big picture" level, they improve the linkages, particularly in terms of communication, of the quality circles with each other and with the administration. In addition, each of the AULs has a particular system-wide and external responsibility. The Deputy University Librarian is responsible for the coordination of our Continuous Improvement effort and management of the operating budget; the Associate University Librarian is responsible for collections and access; the Assistant University Librarian is responsible for coordination of user feedback and library services to researchers.

In practice, each of the AULs and the director works directly with a particular Quality Circle on an annual rotating basis, participating as a full

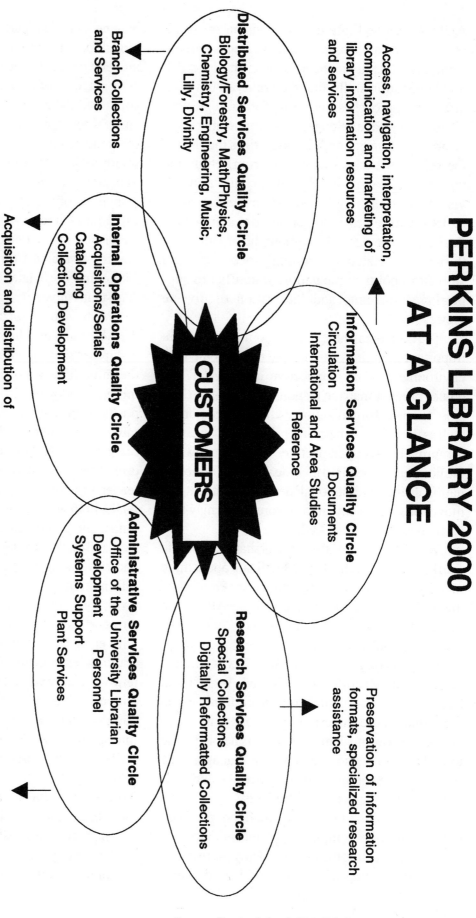

PERKINS LIBRARY 2000 AT A GLANCE

Access, navigation, interpretation, communication and marketing of library information resources and services

Distributed Services Quality Circle
Biology/Forestry, Math/Physics, Chemistry, Engineering, Music, Lilly, Divinity

Branch Collections and Services

Information Services Quality Circle
Circulation
Documents
International and Area Studies
Reference

CUSTOMERS

Internal Operations Quality Circle
Acquisitions/Serials
Cataloging
Collection Development

Acquisition and distribution of commercial information products & services, records creation and maintenance

Administrative Services Quality Circle
Office of the University Librarian
Development   Personnel
Systems Support
Plant Services

Research Services Quality Circle
Special Collections
Digitally Reformatted Collections

Preservation of information formats, specialized research assistance

Provides vision, strategic planning, personnel financial management, and library systems support to lead the Perkins Library System

Figure 2

member in Quality Circle meetings, helping to provide information and expertise at the "big picture" level. The intent is to strengthen the ties of the Quality Circles with the administration and to assist the Quality Circles in making better informed decisions affecting the system as a whole.

Auxiliary Services: In this model, the AULs move to provide essential support services for the organization: Budgeting, Personnel, Staff Development and Training, Grants management, Development.   While these are essential support services for the organization, and skills that need to be in a director's portfolio, I have concerns about the career implications of an AUL being in a service position for a long period of time without a strong link and broader involvement with staff in the organization.

What strategies might I offer other AULs in making the transition? Plan ahead. It is important for the organization to think through and be clear on the future role of an AUL in the organization. We focused on the empowerment of teams and team leaders and found we needed better clarity on the administrative role. As a result, it was confusing to the staff. On the other hand, it was very easy for the team leaders and the AULs to drop the hierarchical "reporting" roles. What I think we all did not realize, was that there was a stronger information and resource relationship that was severed.   From my perspective I lost a regular flow of information for what was going on in the organization. From the perspective of some team leaders, they missed the regular assistance of an AUL as an institutional resource. For other team leaders, who felt "empowered to the max," they did not want the administration to know all that they were doing!

It becomes just as important for senior administrators to build on their skill set as it is for the staff in a learning organization. Rosabeth Moss Kanter says that the corporate ladder is losing rungs and stability.   Climbing the corporate ladder is replaced by the willingness to keep learning, the ability to collaborate and become connected with new teams in various ways, as well as a belief in self rather than in the power of a position alone.

How do the evolving roles for an AUL provide a training ground for future library directors? To gain a perspective, I examined ads for library directors for the last year in a professional journal. This was by no means an exhaustive search, but it gave me a flavor of the movement to the role of library director as library leader. I was surprised to still find a substantial number of ads describing the role as administrative (planning, managing, budgeting).   Requirements were experience in administration and supervision. Granted that that experience is valuable, ads that focused on leadership generally did not contain the administrative and supervisory words. I would like to quote from a couple of ads that support the idea that the conceptual evolution of the AUL role away from a hierarchical, supervisory role fits in with a progressive career path. "The Director must have the vision and skills necessary to provide creative, progressive leadership and strategic direction for the achievement of programs and services that respond to rapid change. MUST HAVE excellent problem solving and group dynamic skills, demonstrated ability to lead and manage change. It is critically important for the Director to be able to provide leadership and vision, demonstrated ability to articulate a clear vision for the future role of libraries in the rapidly developing information age."

Today's academic library environment presents us with numerous challenges and opportunities to redefine our work and the role we as individuals play in the library of the future. I leave you with another analogy in thinking about the changes in the role of senior managers. Think of being in permanent white water. There is a sense of rapid movement, energy, a changing turbulent environment. We are navigators and yet must confess, not always with a lot of control. New leadership skills, knowledge and experience are needed. And above all-it is an exhilarating ride!

NOTES

1. Rosabeth Moss Kanter, *When Giants Learn to Dance* (New York: Simon & Schuster, 1989), 31.
2. David Noer, *Healing the Wounds: Overcoming the Trauma of Layoffs and Revitalizing Downsized Organizations* (San Francisco: Jossey-Bass, 1993), 129.
3. Peter M. Senge, "Transforming the Practice of Management," *Human Resource Development Quarterly* 4 (Spring 1993): 9.

Acquisitions in Transition:
On the Road to the Electronic Library

William J. Kara

ABSTRACT

Although print publications still dominate library acquisitions, there is a steadily increasing number of titles in various electronic formats. Technical Services traditionally has had the skills to process items efficiently for the collection. Acquisitions and Serials Units need to accept new responsibilities for processing electronic items as well. This cannot be done without training, planning, or discussing the many issues involved. To meet the challenges of the future, technical services needs to be involved and must fully participate in the evolution of the electronic library. This paper describes two projects at Mann Library which have involved developing new skills and procedures in the Acquisitions Unit.

INTRODUCTION

During the last decade the electronic library has moved from the hypothetical to the tangible. Although most libraries and their acquisitions budgets still concentrate on print media, electronic information is becoming increasingly essential to any collection. This is not news. What should be news is discussions among technical services librarians about their role in these changes.

The Albert R. Mann Library, at Cornell University, has been a leader in utilizing new technologies. Access is provided to an ever-increasing number of electronic resources, including bibliographic, numeric, and full-text files. Mann Library's Gateway provides a single point of access to these many files, and although it is the most visible and widely used of our electronic library initiatives, it is only one of many.

These initiatives are part of what the director, Jan Olsen, refers to as "pushing the frontier." The phrase "pushing the frontier" also relates to the commitment she and many others in Mann Library have made to meet the challenges and opportunities afforded by new technology. This involves not only seeing what can be done with existing technology, but also how technology can be further developed to enhance the Library's collection and services. It is through active participation that librarians can maintain an important role in the development of information services. Not being

William J. Kara is Acquisitions Librarian at Albert R. Mann Library, Cornell University, Ithaca, New York.

merely content with the present, but seeking to extend or push the frontier, to help define and shape the future, rather than merely reacting to the changes it brings.

During the last decade and even now, there are suggestions that libraries have failed to take the lead, and are possibly forfeiting their traditional information service roles. Even in libraries that have not let this happen, many of the new, innovative services have been public services initiatives without significant technical services involvement. This is particularly true of many acquisitions operations.[1]

For technical services, discussions about technology and electronic communication have primarily concentrated on two very important areas. The first is the online public catalog. The creation, maintenance, and enhancement of this catalog is an essential component of any electronic library. The second is how technology can assist in processing. For acquisitions, this involves the automating of many procedures, including not only the online processing of orders, payments, receipts, and claims, but the more recent advances in EDI (Electronic Data Interchange). These efforts have demanded considerable time, planning, and coordination.

In addition to automating these processing activities, however, the electronic library provides many new challenges for technical services staff. Technical services skills include the ability to acquire, process, and organize items for the collection. These same skills can and should be applied to all materials regardless of format.

Acquisitions units, including those responsible for monographs, serials, or both, should not shy away from new processing initiatives. As managers, acquisitions librarians need to rethink existing procedures and policies and be flexible and creative. It is essential to work closely with staff throughout the library, including the administration, and become involved. It is important to learn the vocabulary and develop the computer skills in order for acquisitions librarians and staff to be active participants in the changes that will affect all our work.

Electronically-accessible information is not only here to stay, it is growing in importance. Whether that information comes in a physical form (floppies, magnetic tapes, or CD-ROMs) or only in an electronic form (for example, Internet-accessible files or electronic journals) should not matter. Acquisitions units acquire and process items for the library. This processing has not been static during the last decade and cannot remain unchanged in the evolution to the electronic library.

At Mann Library access is now provided to over 1000 titles in various electronic media, whether physically located in the library, or remotely accessible. In a collection of 650,000 volumes this is still a relatively small percentage of actual titles. These numbers, however, are misleading. That print collection was built over a period of a century, while the electronic collection is only a few years old. In fiscal year 1993/94 over 15% of our 1.2 million dollar materials budget was spent on electronic resources or access to electronic files. These files include the most heavily used indexes, abstracts, and statistical sets in our collection.

These approximately 1000 titles are only a beginning, and more are selected for the collection each month. In response, the Acquisitions Unit has developed new procedures and workflows. This requires a willingness to learn and become involved in order to be part of the future and not become a relic of the past.

Certain elements in processing remain the same regardless of whether the material is print or electronic. An item is acquired which includes the initial order and payment. Bibliographic and holdings records are created for those items. When the items are received they are prepared for cataloging, or if already cataloged (as with an ongoing serial), processed for the collection.

To this very basic list, electronic media add new twists. For example, is it necessary to have a legal contract which governs how and by whom that resource can be used? How is the item acquired, for example through FTP via the Internet? Do files on floppy diskettes need to be backed up as part of Technical Services processing?

Some items are mainstreamed or integrated into existing procedures more easily than others. Titles in a physical medium, such as a floppy diskette or CD-ROM, follow a somewhat different processing stream, but one with many similarities to print titles. These have been more easily incorporated into existing procedural models.

NEW ACQUISITIONS RESPONSIBILITIES

Not all titles, however, are easily integrated into our existing procedures. The following two examples from Mann Library illustrate the role of acquisitions in the emerging electronic library.

Example 1: Numeric Files

The first project involves processing datasets received from the USDA's Economic Research Service (ERS) and National Agricultural Statistics Service (NASS). Mann Library, in cooperation with ERS and NASS, agreed to provide Internet access to numeric files produced by the USDA. The agencies provide the data, and the Library agreed to organize the files on a locally-maintained gopher. There are approximately 150 different datasets, and approximately 6 updates are received each month.[2]

These files are now processed routinely in the Acquisitions Unit. Datasets, both new titles and updates, are received on floppy diskettes. The files are transferred from a DOS-operating environment to a UNIX gopher server via FTP. For all titles, a cataloger determined the directory and subdirectory structure on the gopher. The ERS files are divided into 11 directories or subject categories (for example, crops, livestock, or trade). This predetermined gopher directory is used by the serials staff during the uploading or processing of files. The online catalog holdings are then updated to include a record of the new data received.

The following is an outline of the procedure for a newly acquired ERS title, the Unit responsible for the activity is indicated in brackets:

1. Acquire the files (on floppy diskettes) <Acquisitions>
2. Create the basic bibliographic and holdings records in the local online catalog <Acquisitions>
3. Determine the organizational structure of the gopher and create the directories and subdirectories <Cataloging>
4. Complete the bibliographic record <Cataloging>
5. Upload the files to the gopher <Acquisitions>

These ERS files, although received on floppy diskettes, need additional, fairly unique steps. The procedure requires some UNIX skills and experience with the structure and history of these approximately 150 titles. Fortunately these are somewhat related files, rather than 150 files created by 150 producers, each potentially requiring unique handling.

These procedures were not developed without planning, training, and a great deal of cooperation. An important factor that helped make it successful was our existing processing skills. Attention to many details is important in technical services work. For example, there are many complexities in print serials, such as marking, recording holdings, and binding differences. A variety of procedures have been put into place to handle the sometimes unique needs of many print titles. In a similar fashion, electronic serials present new variations on older processing models.

The ERS files and many other electronic resources are handled or "mainstreamed" in the Acquisitions Unit, but many of the definitions have expanded with new responsibilities. Acquisition can be through an electronic mail subscription or retrieval through FTP. After the issues or updates are "acquired," receiving and check-in involves the uploading or transferring of files. These more than subtle differences require a broader, more inclusive interpretation of acquisitions and technical services responsibilities.

Example 2: Electronic Journals

The second example, which is moving from research project to implementation phase during late 1994 or early 1995, is electronic journals. Mann Library's electronic journal system, which utilizes World Wide Web technology, will provide access to selected electronic journals archived locally and those residing at remote locations.[3] What began as a research and development initiative, is now ready to move into the implementation phase. It is a time for the process to move from someone hired specifically for his programming skills to staff hired for their processing skills. The practical considerations of receiving and processing issues of these journals are being explored.

Individual issues and backsets of the journals need to be retrieved via telnet or FTP. Once retrieved they are marked up using HTML (HyperText Markup Language) for easier retrieval and access. This involves logically dividing the issue into discrete sections by assigning HTML codes or field identifiers, which indicate the author and title of individual articles. After completing this processing in Acquisitions, these issues are uploaded to the electronic journal system.

Mann Library never set out to organize and mark-up (with HTML codes) the countless electronic journals and newsletters already available. National standards or guidelines, preferably applied by the producer, are necessary. As a research library, however, it is essential for Mann Library to acquire and archive the core literature in our subject areas now, even in the absence of nationally recognized standards.

Although the Library's collection is still dominated and will remain dominated by print publications for the forseeable future, there has been a steady increase in the acquisition of electronic resources. Important electronically available information is of immediate use to researchers and needs to be archived for the future. For the Acquisitions Unit, it is not a choice whether to undertake new processing responsibilities or not. Instead, it is just as important for the acquisitions staff to assert their role in acquiring and receiving electronic files as it has been for processing physical volumes.

PREPARING FOR CHANGE

The same technology that brings these new responsibilities also enables change. Integrated online systems permit faster serials and monographs processing. For example, claiming is only one of many activities which is much more efficient in the online environment. The serials staff no longer need to type claims on three-part forms, but can generate claims and other correspondence directly from our online order/payment/receipt records. This time savings in serials receipt and maintenance is significant, but admittedly only after the investment of considerable time to convert to online serials processing. These and other benefits of automation can speed many acquisitions activities.

In the Acquisitions Unit, procedures could evolve with automation. Not only are the same tasks done very differently, entire workflows have been reevaluated. For example, at Mann Library over a quarter of all monographs are "fast"cataloged in the Acquisitions Unit. During fastcataloging full LC cataloging copy is accepted with few changes and LC CIP is upgraded. The Acquisitions staff can complete the cataloging and processing for these titles on receipt. This significantly diminishes the need for additional handling, and enables staff in Technical Services to work on innovative projects.

The Library has also developed a Technical Services Workstation, which provides online access to numerous reference tools, simultaneous sessions with other bibliographic databases and software packages, and macros for more efficient execution of routine commands. All have helped streamline many procedures.

In using this technology, staff have developed new skills and confidence in using their computers. Staff are involved and have come to expect involvement. For example, in developing the Technical Services Workstation, staff who would be using it were consulted at each stage. The leadership of the Library and the Technical Services Division have not only encouraged this participation, but expect it. The interest and support of staff at all levels for these changes has been strong.

This environment does not come into being without effort. Staff need adequate hardware and software support, and there needs to be time. Skills are built over time, changes are incorporated over time, and staff acceptance and trust in the process develop over time. It is important that goals and expectations be perceived to be reasonable and equitable. A well-articulated vision helps set the tone, while a supportive, collaborative effort by the staff allows the Library to realize these goals.

CONCLUSION

For the Acquisitions Unit at Mann Library, the processing of datasets and electronic journals is only a beginning. There will be many more changes during the next few years. Some have questioned whether it is the role of technical services to process electronic files. If these activities remain or become the sole responsibility of computer technicians or other staff, the acquisitions and cataloging units will become increasingly and severely cut off from the emerging electronic library. At Mann Library the decision was made to involve all units in the discussions and planning for the electronic library. It was in the individual units, such as acquisitions and cataloging, that specialized skills, such as processing and subject cataloging, already existed. It would have been counterproductive to build a new structure just to handle resources in different formats.

Without actively participating and preparing for change, technical services librarians will unnecessarily and regretably limit their role in the profession. The electronic library presents many opportunities and challenges. These can be daunting times, yet are also exciting times for libraries.

Technical services and acquisitions have important contributions to make. Flexibility, adaptability, and a willingness to become involved will help ensure our role as technical services professionals in this future.

NOTES

1. For more information on the issues and challenges facing technical services, see, for example, Peter S. Graham, "Electronic Information and Research Library Technical Services," *College & Research Libraries* 51:3 (May 1990): 241-250 and Gillian M. McCombs, "The Internet and Technical Services," *Library Resources and Technical Services* 38:2 (April 1994): 169-177. For additional information specifically on the evolving nature of acquisitions, see, for example, Ross Atkinson, "The Acquisitions Librarian as Change Agent in the Transition to the Electronic Library," *Library Resources and Technical Services* 36:1 (January 1992): 7-20 and Meta Nissley, "Rave New World : Librarians and Electronic Acquisitions," *Library Acquisitions : Practice & Theory* 17:2 (1993): 165-173.

2. Access instructions to the "U.S. Department of Agriculture's Economics and Statistics on the Internet":

   Gopher (recommended access method):
   Host=usda.mannlib.cornell.edu
   Port Number=70

   Telnet:
   Host=usda.mannlib.cornell.edu
   User ID= usda <lower case>

   FTP:
   Host=usda.mannlib.cornell.edu
   User ID= anonymous
   Password= <your e-mail address / optional>(after logging in, change the directory with the following command: cd usda)

3. For more information on changes in Mann Library Technical Services and on the electronic journals project, see: Janet McCue, "Technical Services and the Electronic Library : Defining our Roles and Divining the Partnership," *Library Hi Tech* 12:3 (1994): 63-70. This article includes a sidebar by Dongming Zhang: "Providing Access to Electronic Journals" on p.68.

Incremental Re-engineering:
Changes in the Roles of Technical Services Librarians

Joan Giesecke and Katherine L. Walter

ABSTRACT

The role of technical services librarians is being questioned as libraries downsize their operations. Technical services librarians can take a proactive approach to redefining their roles rather than waiting for change to be forced upon them. At one ARL library, technical services librarians initiated discussions with the administration to redefine their roles, increase their involvement in library decision-making, and improve their own career development opportunities. This paper will describe the process used at one library and how this model can be applied in other settings.

The role of the technical services librarian, particularly the cataloger, has been slowly changing as libraries automate their operations, downsize technical services departments, and place an increased emphasis on direct patron service. Support staff in technical services now handle most of the day-to-day routine activities from the ordering of books and serials to copy cataloging, database maintenance, and authority control work. As support staff assume many of the duties once carried out by professionals, professional librarians are concentrating on original cataloging of items when copy cataloging can not be found, problem-solving, and staff training.[1] Furthermore some technical services librarians are participat-ing in traditional public service activities including serving at the reference desk, and providing support for bibliographic instruction and collection development.[2]

Within this context is the question of how individual technical services librarians can advance in their careers and survive in an era of downsizing. These are the practical questions that need to be addressed even as the organization addresses the larger questions of how to reorganize in an era of decreasing resources.

In order to address questions of this nature, Lee Bolman and Terrence Deal, in their book *Reframing Organizations*, argue that managers in complex organizations need to view change from

Joan Giesecke is Associate Dean for Collections and Services and Katherine L. Walter is Chair of the Serials Department at Love Library, University of Nebraska-Lincoln.

four perspectives or frames: structurally, politically, symbolically, and from a human resources viewpoint. Structurally managers review policy and procedures, organizational structure, formal roles and relationships, and reporting lines. From a political viewpoint, managers examine power structures, competition for scarce resources, review negotiating strategies, and seek coalitions. The symbolic frame emphasizes rituals, myths, symbols, and the meaning of work. Finally the human resources view emphasizes the interdependence between employees and the organization, improving the organization's ability to motivate people, and seeking a better fit between individual and organizational goals.[3]

All these aspects of an organization are affected when change is introduced into the organization. Structurally change alters roles and responsibilities. Formal procedures are disrupted and policies need to be revised. Politically change generates conflict. Issues need to be brought to appropriate arenas to be negotiated and resolved or issues will remain as disruptive elements in the organization. From a symbolic viewpoint change creates a sense of loss. Rituals change and people seek ways to soothe their pain. From a human resources frame, change disrupts interpersonal interactions and the informal structure of the organization. People may feel powerless or incompetent as they face needing to develop new skills, new relationships, and new ways to be involved in the organization.

Change becomes very personal when it impacts individual's career potential. Stress increases. To address individual career concerns organizations need to take a human relations viewpoint and examine the impact changes are having on individuals and the possible impact of future changes. Involving individuals in those discussions is crucial to developing a humane approach to downsizing and change.

The issue then is how to design a process that will result in the definition of the role of the technical services librarian in an era of change. In this paper changes in one technical services unit of

an ARL (Associate of Research Libraries) institution will be examined. An analysis of the process used to make changes will be presented as a model to other institutions exploring similar questions.

THE UNIVERSITY LIBRARIES, UNIVERSITY OF NEBRASKA-LINCOLN

Issues relating to the role of Technical Services librarians at the University of Nebraska-Lincoln (UNL) began to surface early in 1993. In part, these questions arose because of changes that occurred in the role of the Public Services librarians at UNL. Public Services librarians had conducted an analysis of their activities in 1991/92. As a result of the analysis, four Program Groups were formed to coordinate the activities of Public Services librarians. The groups serve as decision-making bodies within Public Services and make recommendations that affect the Libraries as a whole. These four groups are Electronic Resources Program Group (ERPG), Access Program Group (APG), Library Instruction Program Group (LIPG), and (a previously existing committee) Collection Development Committee (CDC). It was the perception of the Technical Services librarians that these program groups were discussing issues of primary importance to the future of the University Libraries. With the exception of Collection Development Committee, no program groups had Technical Services librarians as members.

Concurrently, the Library Administration announced that six to nine positions would be reallocated from Technical to Public Services in 1992/93. This announcement was not a surprise. Public service points were being stretched considerably as usage of the University Libraries' Innovative Interfaces, Inc. online integrated library system, called Innovative Research Information System or IRIS, increased. In just four years, circulation had increased 44.5 percent, reference questions were up 35.9 percent, and borrowing in Interlibrary Loan had increased by about 20 percent. Simultaneously, reduced buying power for materials due to inflation had decreased the number of new items received in Technical Services. Having fewer new materials meant that Technical Services had been able to tackle long-standing backlogs and clean-up projects to fill the void; however, the Library Administration felt that this was rapidly becoming a luxury that the Libraries could no longer afford.

With the announcement of the staffing reallocations and the perception that many of the recommendations regarding the future of the University Libraries were coming out of Public Services, the Technical Services librarians began to feel that the value of their role was being glossed over. It seemed to the Technical Services librarians that they had skills with the potential to enrich the Libraries which had not yet been tapped.

In March 1993, the Technical Services librarians discussed their current roles, and what the future of professional catalogers might be. Among the roles identified were: serving as resource people for peers and support staff on questions relating to language, subject, theoretical aspects of cataloging, and for related analytical work; problem solving; writing documentation; training staff; performing original cataloging; serving on library committees; answering questions from other libraries (particularly in the state of Nebraska); participating in policy discussions; and providing quality control.

The librarians discussed the concept that in the future, all cataloging would be done from a few major centers. The group felt that in the foreseeable future, the odds of developing such centers are slim. It was felt that national standards are not standard enough to eliminate the need for local practices. For example, for titles that may be treated as either monographs or serials, the treatment may need to vary with the emphases of the collections. Access points or headings may vary by collection or user needs. Or, bibliographic records may not be available in a timely manner from a central source. An example of this might be government documents. GPO cataloging records are usually available on tape within six months

after pieces arrive, but for high use items this may not be acceptable.

While support staff know local practice and can verify if a heading (for example) is valid, they are not trained to interpret rules or to catch if a better heading should be used. The national rules are not hard and fast, but require judgement in knowing when to apply them. Professional catalogers understand how to apply the cataloging rules and are aware of trends in cataloging. They create and influence the development of databases on the online catalog, are involved in providing access to electronic databases, and understand how information is packaged. These skills were felt to be too important to be overlooked.

Following this discussion, the librarians agreed to develop a proposal for what role they wanted as Technical Services librarians at UNL, and to address where they saw the field going. Various points were considered in developing their position. Besides addressing some of the skills mentioned above, the Technical Services librarians felt that they needed career options and opportunities. Individually, they developed ideas of the major elements, tasks, or assignments they would like to see as part of their responsibilities. Not surprisingly, there was a great deal of variety in the assignments they identified. The continuum ranged from one person who want to spend 80% of her time cataloging to those who wanted other options. Possible activities or job components included everything from cataloging (the norm) to collection development, computer systems, distance learning, and public relations. In all twenty-eight general areas of interest were identified. The one area that all agreed upon was "involvement in decision-making."

It was agreed that the proposal should advance a number of models that could be available to librarians for advancing career options. These included internships (one year commitment, 20 hours per week); staff exchanges; and staff sharing (working up to 5 hours per week in another department) proposed either by the librarian or by departments.

Several actions were taken as a result of the discussions. First, Technical Services librarians participated in a time study to identify where their time was being spent and to consider what time might be available for other activities. They also discussed where decisions are made within the organization and who makes them.

With this background information, the Technical Services librarians felt prepared to make some recommendations to the University Libraries' Administration. A small task force of three librarians prepared a first draft of a report entitled "Technical Services Librarians Position Paper". The draft was distributed to all Technical Services librarians and was discussed. Minor changes were completed and the finished paper was sent to the Dean of Libraries.

Among roles envisioned is one with enhanced involvement in technological advancements on campus through creation of catalogs and databases. Another role is to explore providing specialized expertise to other institutions in the state or region. For example, UNL Technical Services librarians are already actively involved in presenting workshops on cataloging for NEBASE, Nebraska's OCLC affiliate network. There is a need for consulting services in the area of authority work, and for contract services in certain areas of strength (e.g. music cataloging, preservation planning, and grantwriting.)

The paper suggests too that Technical Services librarians with language and subject expertise might be good candidates for assisting Public Services in collection development and liaison activities. The position paper concludes "Technical Services librarians possess a range of aptitudes, interests, and experience that are vital to the success of the Libraries."

As the discussions developed over this period, the Associate Dean for Collections and Technical Services raised some of the issues in various meetings with the Library Administration. As a result, some changes occurred concurrently with the development of the position paper. One of the changes was that a librarian who does not have management responsibilities was added to the Administrative Group--a management team consisting of the Dean of Libraries, the two associate deans, and one department chair--on a three month rotation.

The Dean of Libraries met with the Technical Services librarians in May 1994, and indicated his support for the ideas presented in the position paper. The support of the Library Administration helped to set the scene for several changes relating to the Technical Services librarians' roles. One change that has occurred is that Program Groups now have a member-at-large position. Technical Services librarians are encouraged to apply for these positions and decisions regarding membership on the Program Groups are made by the joint department chairs (Public and Technical Services.)

Another change is that Technical Services librarians are now involved in cataloging titles for the University's Gopher. Depending upon whether holdings are archived at UNL, the cataloging is in either MARC or non-MARC. This has enabled Technical Services staff to learn more about the Gopher and to make recommendations to Collection Development Committee concerning treatment of various databases on the system.

The University Libraries has had a management internship program for about six years. Partly in response to the Technical Services librarians' request for additional career opportunities, other internships are being considered. A Resource Sharing internship in Interlibrary Loan was developed and Technical Services librarians were encouraged to apply.

Having increased opportunities does not mean that librarians have always been able to take advantage of them. UNL currently is involved in several grant projects requiring a time commitment on the part of staff. Projects include cataloging a special collection of Emily Dickinson materials, the Nebraska Newspaper Project, and the Kellogg Rural Economic Development Archive contract with the Heartland Center. Priorities of the institution may take precedence over the desires of individuals.

ANALYSIS OF THE PROCESS

Bolman and Deal provide a framework for analyzing the context and events surrounding the discussions of the Technical Services librarians. From a structural viewpoint, the librarians reviewed roles, policies and procedures in light of the changes in the field. They identified key areas of expertise and showed how those skills are still valid. They confirmed the role of the technical services librarian within the context of the library situation. No major changes in structure were proposed by the group. This is not surprising since the outcome of the discussions tended to confirm established practice rather than change it.

Politically the process involved a variety of negotiating opportunities. While the librarians were discussing their place in the libraries, the Associate Dean was working with Public Services to develop ways to expand the involvement of the Technical Services librarians in decision making options. By coincidence a vacancy came open on one of the Program Groups giving the Associate Dean an opening for suggesting that the groups evaluate their membership. Current members of the group who had now served for two years on the Program Groups were willing to consider changes. The groups were willing to add a general member-at-large slot that would be open to any librarian. This way, both Public and Technical Services librarians could volunteer for membership on the committees.

At the same time as the Associate Dean was working with Public Services to find ways to include the Technical Services librarians, the administration was looking at ways to expand management training opportunities for the librarians. The Dean decided to add a faculty member to the administrative group on a three month rotating basis so that non-management librarians would have an opportunities to learn how this administrative group functions. The Dean chose a Technical Services librarian as the first appointee, knowing that these librarians had expressed an interest in learning more about management. Had the Technical Services librarians not raise the issue ini-

tially, it is quite likely that the Dean would have chosen a Public Services librarian for this new opportunity since the Public Services librarians were seen as more interested in the activities of the organization.

By looking for appropriate arenas in which to discuss the issues, and taking advantage of changes as they occurred rather than waiting for a final report before beginning to make changes, the librarians and the administration were able to implement changes during the planning process.

From a human resources viewpoint, the process was very successful. The librarians achieved their major objectives with a minimum amount of stress. They were able to express their views, discuss different approaches, and redefine how they could participate in the institution. They no longer felt powerless, unable to affect their own futures. They had established a measure of control over their own careers and created opportunities for all the librarians to participate more fully in the library decision making processes.

Symbolically the librarians found they could influence library management. They confronted the myth that all decisions were made in Public Services and created avenues of their own for influencing the organization. They presented their views to the Dean in a logical manner and were able to influence how the Dean of Libraries viewed their activities. By confronting organizational myths and perceptions they found that they had as much influence as they wanted in the organization.

CONCLUSIONS

Change in organizations can be very stressful. Bolman and Deal point out that managers need to think multidimensionally if they are to be cognizant of the many elements that are part of the change process. Their framework helps provide managers with a guide for how to look at complex operations. For the Technical Services librarians, a multi-part approach to their question proved to be very successful. Rather than limiting their actions to one process, discussion of the issues and creation of a set of recommendations to the administration, the librarians were able to implement changes even as they planned the types of changes they wanted to see. By seeing that they had personal control of their careers they were able to create opportunities so that they could gain the skills they needed while increasing their participation in the organization. They took advantage of opportunities as they arose, working incrementally to impact the organization while fulfilling their own needs.

This framework can be helpful to other institutions in planning and evaluating change. By looking at the process from a variety of perspectives, managers are more likely to recognize multiple opportunities for advancing an agenda while keeping watch for problems and concerns that may arise during the change process. Often managers concentrate on one or two aspects of an organization, missing subtle parts of the process.

By thinking more broadly about the process, options for change, and the meaning of the process, managers are more likely to succeed in their activities. At UNL by looking at the broader question of career development for Technical Services librarians, and not stopping with the narrower question of how Technical Services librarians could be involved in the Public Services decision making activities, the Librarians were able to create a wider role for themselves in the library while designing strategies to advance their own careers.

NOTES

1. Lizbeth Bishoff, "Who Says We Don't Need Catalogers?," *American Libraries*, September, 1987, 694-96.
2. Patricia A. Eskoz, "Catalog Librarians and Public Services -A Changing Role," *Library Resources and Technical Services* 35(1989):76-86.
3. Lee Bolman and Terrence Deal, *Reframing Organizations* (San Francisco: Jossey-Bass, 1991).

Contributed Papers

Technology and the
Service-Centered Library

Multimedia in the Research Library:
Collections and Services

Zsuzsa Koltay

ABSTRACT

Multimedia, the combination of text, sound, graphics, animation and video, is rapidly becoming the buzzword in everything from scientific visualization and training to adult entertainment and education. Although it has many facets that are outside the scope of the research library, it has enough applications and implications to make it worthy of our attention. This paper, based on the model developed at the Albert R. Mann Library of Cornell University, will focus on the major collection development and service issues presented by multimedia. First, I will define multimedia and identify the major challenges of this medium for the collection developer and the service provider. Then, after a brief introduction to Cornell's Mann Library, I will present the systematic approach taken there to meet these challenges.

Definitions of multimedia in the literature differ greatly, partly due to the fact that the word is often being used interchangeably, now for a kind of technology, now for specific and sometimes diverse applications of this technology. Lois Lunin offers the following general definition for multimedia as a technology:

"multimedia is a specifically designed way of combining sound, still and motion images, graphics and animation, and data and text together with the interactive capabilities of a computer. ... Neither a market nor an application, multimedia is a series of technologies and an often complex subject matter which work together." [1]

Lunin also makes the point that it is only the design and the interactivity that differentiate multimedia from the audiovisual technology. Multimedia as an application has a quite different and more limited meaning. Multimedia applications are similar to books in that they come with a specific title, more importantly, they present a certain intellectual content in a familiar format (for example factual information on mammals organized around the principles of an encyclopedia); but they do so with the help of multimedia technology (they can, for example, not only describe but also electronically reproduce an elephant's vocalization, or they can show in visu-

Zsuzsa Koltay is the Numeric Files and Multimedia Librarian at Albert R. Mann Library, Cornell University in Ithaca, New York.

ally concrete terms how apes care for their babies). This, in effect, constitutes a prepackaged, interactive bundling of different media to bring the intellectual contents to life by providing illustrations to the text. Multimedia technology can be used in yet another way, in the form of multimedia tools for the visualization of data. Scholars and scientists use such tools to help make vast amounts of numeric data visually and aurally palpable. (Interactive three-dimensional fly-throughs of the Grand Canyon, for example, would belong to this category.) These tools are not only creating a new way for perceiving data, they are also defining a new model of scientific communication with important consequences for the research library.

The emergence of multimedia presents a number of difficulties for the collection development activities of today's research library. Which aspects of multimedia should we consider adopting? How can we fit them into the existing model of selection and collection, or, alternatively, how will the latter have to change in response to the new conditions spawned by multimedia? What kinds of skills and expertise will be needed to make informed decisions about not merely the intellectual content and the quality of presentation, but also about emerging standards and hardware/software requirements? The state of the multimedia industry itself is also a cause for concern. It is a fast-changing scene, where the biggest market share seems to be represented by entertainment packages such as games and adult material, as well as by packages targeted towards the home market and K-12. Despite the proliferation of multimedia products, there is relatively little that could be considered to be within the scope of the research library. Still another issue is how the new patterns of scientific communication made possible by multimedia tools can be supported by the modern library.

Once multimedia resources are acquired they have to be supported by a whole array of services. Access and delivery mechanisms have to be worked out such as the cataloging of titles, making sure hardware and software requirements are fully met

and that access can keep up with the level of expected demand. Staff training is also essential both for providing instructional and user support and for integrating these resources into the rest of the library's services.

Cornell University's Albert A. Mann Library has worked on systematically addressing both the collection development and the service aspects of collecting multimedia. Mann Library is the second largest library collection on the Cornell campus. It serves primarily the College of Agriculture and Life Sciences, the College of Human Ecology, the Division of Biological Sciences, and the Division of Nutritional Sciences. Consequently it collects mainly in the areas of agriculture, life sciences, and social and behavioral sciences. For the last decade Mann Library has been a leader in adapting and mainstreaming information technology to create a strong amalgam of electronic and print resources supported by an active program of diverse user services. Mann's electronic library, the Gateway, provides campus-wide access to hundreds of bibliographic, numeric, and full-text databases, and it is being very heavily used. For years we have been very active in acquiring and providing access to CD-ROMs housing numeric and spatial databases. We have also recently started offering geographic information systems to be used in conjunction with our data. Another unique aspect of the library is its full-service microcomputer center that provides access to the Gateway and the Internet and offers dozens of general and subject-specific application software packages for use.

Since Mann has been successfully collecting and servicing a vast array of electronic resources for years, it has already established a workable collection development model to respond to the additional challenges of the digital world. We call this system the genre model, because instead of dividing up selection responsibilities by subject, we identified genres such as full-text, numeric and bibliographic files, application software, and, the newest one: multimedia. Each genre has a specialist who not only fulfills the role of selector but also serves as an advocate for the genre. This model accomplishes a number of different things. First of all, the various types of electronic information have their own specific requirements for both a technical and a service infrastructure. The genre specialist can become an expert on these issues and he or she can help facilitate the process from beginning to end. Another benefit of this system is that similar kinds of data will get evaluated by the same selector regardless of its format and delivery mechanism, meaning that numeric file decisions are made by one and the same person for CD-ROM, diskette, tape, on-line, and Internet resources. Selection decisions that pose new questions about infrastructure and support get routed through the Electronic Resources Council. This body is made up of the heads of the main functional areas of the library including collection development, public and technical services, the Information Technology Section, and the Gateway coordinator.

Multimedia is the newest collection development genre at Mann Library. The first step was for the genre specialist to formulate a collection development policy statement for multimedia. The completion of this project was a relatively complex and time-consuming task that involved research, consultations and discussions, as well as the employment of a systematic, analytical approach. One of the hardest aspects of developing this statement was how to define multimedia as a genre. This definition had to be constructed in such a way as to minimize the overlap between multimedia and other genres such as full-text, numeric data and application software. The definition currently in use is as follows: multimedia as a collection development category is defined as a combination of three or more of the following attributes: text, sound, graphics, animation, and video. The role of the multimedia selector is defined as specializing in assessing the value of the presentation of the multimedia products available on the commercial market or on the Internet. In terms of the various definitions at the beginning of this paper, the multimedia genre specialist covers only the area of multimedia applications. Scientific visualization and modeling multimedia tools are monitored by the numeric files specialist.

Although it is practical to treat multimedia as a separate category at this time due to special access and infrastructure concerns, it is important to treat different multimedia applications in accordance with the intellectual category to which they belong. For example, the functional and intellectual contents of a given multimedia title determine its funding sources. We have identified two major categories of multimedia applications that fall within the scope of an academic library: computer-assisted instruction and training, and full-text reference resources. Scope guidelines are articulated on the basis and in consideration of the given intellectual contents. Multimedia reference resources, for example, should not be judged too differently from their print counterparts. Multimedia resources include more features that must be taken into consideration, but fundamentally the decision process about selection is analogous to that employed for print resources.

The multimedia collection of Mann Library is still relatively small. Titles are fully cataloged and can be found in the on-line catalog. The disks are located in a CD-ROM storage cabinet by call number and can be used on standalone machines. We regard this arrangement as a very modest beginning, the first step towards our goal of a large collection of research titles eventually accessible through the client-server version of the Gateway. The foundations have been laid, and the real work begins only now.

NOTES

1. Lois F. Lunin, *Multimedia in the Information Industry* (Philadelphia: The National Federation of Abstracting and Information Services, 1992), 6.

Texts, Images, Sounds, & Movies:
Using a World Wide Web Server for Instruction

Jill H. Powell

ABSTRACT

Teaching network–based information retrieval skills has traditionally focused on finding text–based sources, such as searching bibliographic databases and retrieving documents. However, many researchers also require a variety of data structures, including images, animations, simulations, and matrices. Using the World Wide Web, librarians can teach students to find these data structures on the Internet. This paper presents concepts of teaching information retrieval skills on the Internet, illustrated with interactive handouts residing on a library Web server. It discusses how to find texts, images, sounds, and movies on such topics as remote sensing, art, history, and space exploration. It also shows how to locate the necessary public–domain software to view the multimedia discussed.

INTRODUCTION

Teaching network–based information skills to students has given library instruction an exciting new dimension. Text sources such as listserv discussion groups, newsletters, journals, online bibliographic databases, and text-based servers have been popular to teach, as were the powerful search and retrieval tools Veronica, WAIS, FTP, and Archie. However, with the popularity of the World Wide Web (WWW or Web), network searching is not limited to text only. Web browsers, such as Mosaic, MacWeb, Cello, and Mosaic Netscape, bring many Internet tools (including Gopher, WAIS, WWW, FTP, Telnet, Usenet News, and Archie) together under one application to enable one to take advantage of the features of each tool without having to learn each application. One can download color images from the Smithsonian Institution, NASA, and museums as well as sounds, animations and movies from other servers. This is welcomed by academic research-ers, particularly in the scientific community, who require a wide variety of data structures, including images, palettes, animation sequences, computer simulations, matrices, and data.[1] Web browsers allow for the organization, integration, and view-ing of the complex data structures many scholars need. Using hypermedia–based WWW, students can retrieve a variety of data formats from the

Jill Powell is the Associate Engineering Librarian for Reference/Instruction at Cornell University in Ithaca, New York.

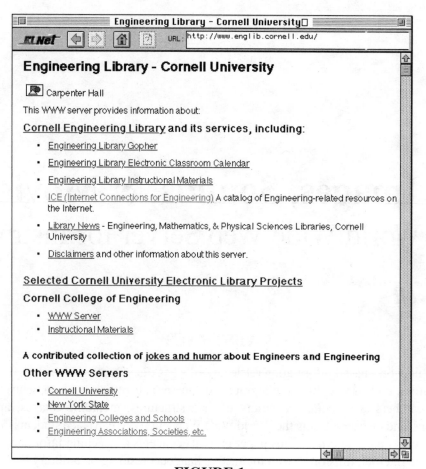

FIGURE 1

Internet for traditional and multimedia class assignments for many fields.

This paper will focus on teaching librarians to teach students information retrieval skills using a complex reference tool, the Internet. It will show how a library Web server can be used to help this process by serving instruction handouts in HTML (hypertext markup language) format. Concepts used and resources retrieved for engineering and other classes will be presented, including such topics as government documents, cancer research, remote sensing, art, history, physics, the space shuttle, and satellite and imaging radar photographs. Also included is information on how to locate the necessary public-domain software.

SERVING INSTRUCTION HANDOUTS ON THE WEB

Our Engineering Library Web server (http://www.englib.cornell.edu, Figure 1) contains infor-

mation about the library and its policies, newsletters, library projects, and ICE (Internet Connections for Engineering, our catalog of Engineering-related resources on the Internet). It also includes instructional materials, created by librarians for information retrieval classes and by faculty for College of Engineering courses. Since Fall 1994, my colleagues and I have been converting instruction handouts into HTML so they can be accessed via Web browsers on our Web server (see Figure 2). These handouts contain the class outline, practice questions, and live links to selective resources on the Internet. Students learn how to use the Web by viewing this handout on the Web, and following the exercises. Students can access these handouts 24 hours a day, and whenever we update them they will always see the latest version. It is also an excellent way to share teaching materials with other colleagues. For articles on how libraries use the Internet and library Web servers, see references 2 and 5.

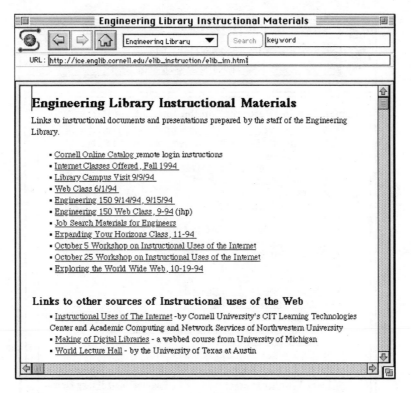

FIGURE 2

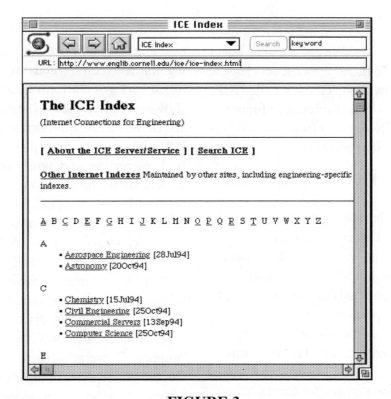

FIGURE 3

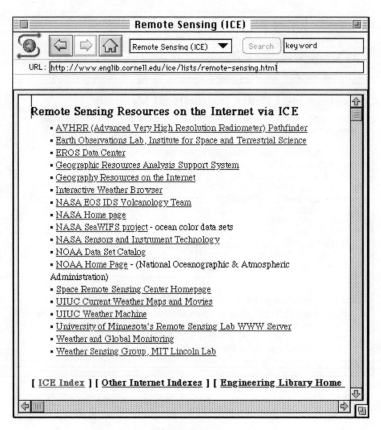

FIGURE 4

Many of the handouts listed in Figure 2 are for introductory Web classes. We also create subject bibliographies in HTML for upper-level classes, and put these in our own subject index, called ICE, on our Web server. ICE is displayed in Figure 3. See Figure 4 for a bibliography (with hyperlinks) created for a remote sensing class.

THE COMPLEXITY OF TEACHING THE INTERNET

The Internet has been compared to the city of Venice.[3] Venice is not exactly a user-friendly city. It is easy to get lost; the water buses don't necessarily arrive on time, but it is a truly captivating place. Everywhere one finds fascinating items to keep one occupied. The Internet is also chaotic but engrossing like Venice. The scope of information available is mind-boggling, and Internet instructors frequently lack the time to search, compile, and organize appropriate sites for their students. Some librarians dislike the changes brought by the Internet – for an article about this, see reference 4.

However, the complexity can be reduced by teaching three ways to search the internet: browsing, index searching, and direct addressing (entering in URLs or Uniform Resource Locators). By showing students how to search these three ways, and finding a few appropriate Internet indexes and URL sites, an Internet explorer is well-equipped to find interesting and wide-ranging sources in a variety of formats: texts, images, sounds, and movies. Each format will be discussed, along with examples of scholarly resources which can be used in class assignments. Specific Internet sites mentioned will be followed by their appropriate URL addresses in parenthesis for easy reference, although many can be found through subject indexes on the Internet discussed below. Gopher users should enter only the characters after the "gopher://" prefix when connecting to another Gopher; Web users should include the entire URL address. The slashes following the addresses refer to directory paths.

THREE WAYS TO SEARCH THE INTERNET: BROWSING, INDEX SEARCHING, AND DIRECT ADDRESSING

One browses the Internet like browsing for books in the stacks. After starting a Web client, a home page appears with underlined phrases of texts called hyperlinks. Clicking on these underlined phrases leads to one screen or more of related text, which can lead to another screen and another. If you're lucky, you'll find the information you're looking for. Browsing is one way of exploring the Internet, but it isn't very precise, which is why one should also teach index searching.

Index searching involves using the various Internet indexes that are available. Some are arranged by subject, like the EINet Galaxy, World Wide Virtual Library, Whole Internet Catalog, Yanoff's Special Internet Connections, Yahoo (Stanford's directory), and others. Each has its own subject strengths, and many users develop a favorite. The can be accessed and compared at http://mosaic.mcom.com/home/internet-directory.html.

Other indexes specialize in keyword and boolean searching, such as Search the Galaxy, WebCrawler, the Lycos Home Page, the Query Interface (also known as Harvest system), and the World Wide Web Worm. They are described at http://mosaic.mcom.com/home/internet-search.html and can be accessed from that site. A more complete list of indexes (including Gopher indexes) can be found at W3 Search Engines at

http://cui_www.unige.ch/ meta-index.html, but there are no descriptions here. I recommend trying a few of these indexes out until you find one or two which covers your subject area well, and which would be best suited to show to a class. Showing all these indexes would be obviously overwhelming. For this paper I have chosen to highlight the subject index World Wide Virtual Library (http://info.cern.ch/hypertext/DataSources/bySubject/Overview.html) and keyword index Searching the Galaxy (http://galaxy.einet.net/search.html).

Lastly, direct addressing is also important to learning how to search the Web. Everyone will need to know how to enter a URL so they can find the Web sites you are recommending. Students will need to know what an address is and what it looks like so they can navigate and not get lost in cyberspace.

Mosaic and other Web browsers have grown more popular due to some limitations of Gopher. Up until a year ago, Gopher Jewels (http://galaxy.einet.net/GJ/index.html or gopher://cwis.usc.edu) was one of the most popular Internet subject indexes where one could find texts, images, sounds, and movies. It is still excellent and accessible via Search the Galaxy. However its indexing is limited to Gopher sites only. It cannot index Web servers, for while Web browsers can access Gopher sites, Gopher cannot access Web sites. Gopher lacks a standard network locator like the uniform resource locator used in the WWW, plus it does not use SGML (Standard Generalized Markup Language, ISO 8879), a standard approved by the ISO for the descriptive markup and presentation of texts, graphics, and any other data form. Also, in Gopher, each menu item may be only one line of up to 70 characters and must be either a branch to further items or an end point.[5] Because of these restrictions, menu items may not be descriptive enough to help a user decide what to open, and there is no formatted text that would make the page easier to read. These restrictions don't exist in the World Wide Web, so hyperlinks can be embellished with explantory information in bold, underlined, and italicized text (see Figure 5). For further details on how to use Mosaic, see references 5 through 9.

While Gopher has been preferred by some on low–end computers, new Web browsers are being developed all the time to work on more platforms. MacWeb is currently the leanest, and operates on 700K RAM. It is available from ftp://ftp.einet.net/einet. NCSA Mosaic needs 1100K RAM and is available from ftp://ftp.ncsa.uiuc.edu/Mosaic.

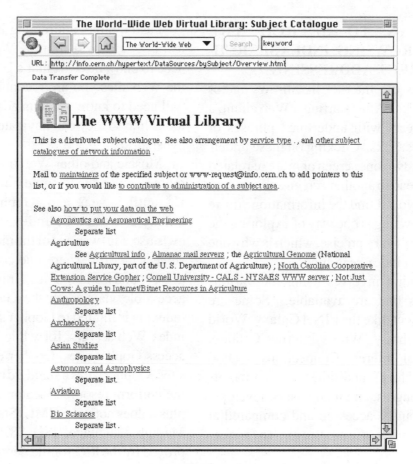

FIGURE 5

Mosaic Netscape requires 2 MB RAM and is available from ftp://ftp.mcom.com/pub/netscape. Netscape requires a 68020 processor or better (Mac II series and later models) and System 7.

INTERNET SUBJECT AND KEYWORD INDEXES

One subject index I demonstrate in classes is the WWW Virtual Library, one of many subject indexes available. It is particularly strong in engineering resources. To access the WWW Virtual Library, one needs a Web browser, such as MacWeb, Mosaic, or Netscape mentioned above.

After opening the Mosaic program, for example, under the Navigate menu is the Internet Resources MetaIndex, which allows one to access many useful Internet indexes, including the WWW Virtual Library (http://info.cern.ch/hypertext/DataSources/bySubject/Overview.html). See Figure 5. MacWeb and Netscape have similar ways of accessing internet indexes.

In addition to subject indexes, the WWW has searchable keyword indexes. One is called "Searching the Galaxy" at http://galaxy.einet.net/search.html. It allows one to search the WWW, Gopher Jewels, Gopherspace, Hytelnet Services, Directory of Scholarly E-Conferences, Subject-Oriented Internet Resource Guides, and much more. This and many other Internet indexes are updated continually by computer indexing programs monitoring the Internet. See Figure 6.

TEXTS, IMAGES, SOUNDS, AND MOVIES

Examples of Internet resources retrieved from the WWW Virtual Library and Search the Galaxy using Web browsers will be discussed below.

Texts

Text and bibliographic information is available via listserv discussion groups, Usenet News, and locally mounted databases (such as the Wilson

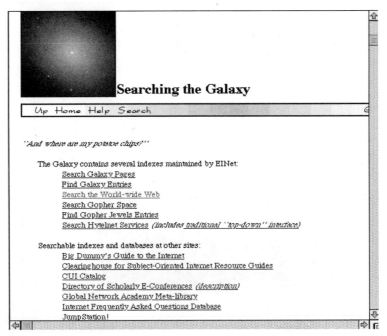

FIGURE 6

indexes, Dialog databases, etc.). Internet sites are rich with text and statistical documents from the U.S. Government, such as White House speeches, legislative acts, the U.S. Budget, and Supreme Court decisions.

One can browse for government information via Gopher Jewels under Federal Agencies and Related Gopher. However I recommend using a Web browser which provides a more visually interesting presentation. Figure 7 shows the Web server for the White House, located at http://www.whitehouse.gov. The White House Web page began in October 1994. One can go on a tour of the White House, view electronic publications

of press releases and major documents, such as the U.S. Constitution, Declaration of Independence, North American Free Trade Agreement, and Health Security Act. Via the Executive Branch button, the White House Web has pointers to other branches of government, including the House, Senate, Library of Congress, federal agencies, the President's Cabinet, and FedWorld's subject index to government information servers. In the future hopefully more pointers will be added,

including commercial ones, such as gopher://wiretap.spies.com, where many famous inaugural and other political speeches can be found under U.S. Speeches and Addresses.

The Smithsonian Institution Web Page (http://www.si.edu) leads to several museum Web servers and projects, including an ftp archive at ftp://photo1.si. edu. It is a wonderful source for images, which are arranged in these categories: air-space, art, new photo-uploads, people-places, science-nature, and technology-history. To best utilize this resource, one needs to download their searchable catalog, since the image names are not descriptive enough to be found via Search the Galaxy. The searchable catalog is in hypercard and DOS formats (ftp://photo1.si.edu/images/catalogs). Examples include some 27 images from the Clinton inauguration and views of many Washington, D.C. monuments. These pictures will be of interest to students in government and history. Images of artifacts from the National Air & Space Museum as well as astronauts working on recent space shuttle missions are popular with engineering and science students. The Space Shuttle Photograph

FIGURE 7

Repository, a collection of photographs taken by astronauts, and the Center for Earth and Planetary Studies, a site for images from planetary missions is also accessible from the Smithsonian Home Page.

The above–mentioned documents can be demonstrated to students in many fields, including government, business, economics, and history classes. A chemical engineering class was recently studying how the drug taxol can be used to treat cancer and wanted library instruction. By performing a search on taxol at Search the Galaxy, I was able to find a significant document detailing the drug's history, clinical trials, and side effects published by the National Cancer Institute. The Search Gopher Space option at Search the Galaxy produced results while Search the Web didn't, so don't overlook all the information still available through Gopher servers. In addition to the Web browser, I taught the use of bibliographic indexes (Engineering Index and Science Citation Index) as well, available electronically at our institution.

Images

Images can be found in many disciplines, and more and more Web sites administrators are adding images to enhance their Web pages. I have started using images on my HTML instruction handouts. Images are highly clustered under the subjects art, museums, aviation, geography, space, and meteorology/weather in the WWW Virtual Library. In preparing for classes, one may have to hunt across several indexes to find useful information.

By double-clicking on the hyperlinks from the WWW Virtual Library, one can download these images effortlessly, without having to know special Internet addresses. One does need a few viewing applications, which will be discussed later. Art history students will be intrigued by the

Annular Solar Eclipse, May 10, 1994

"Full Disk images of the sun taken in H-alpha light received 94/05/10 from Holloman AFB, New Mexico. The images are 512 wide by 480 high, 8 bits per pixel in GIF format and are approximately 100 to 150 kbytes in size. The images were taken with the Solar Optical Observing Network (SOON) telescope operated by the US Air Force."- http://www.sel.bldrdoc.gov/images/eclipse.html

FIGURE 8

many images available from the Art Gallery page at http://www.comlab.ox.ac.uk/archive/other/museums.html, which provides access to WebLouvre, St. Petersburg Picture Gallery, and many more. One can browse for paintings by artists at gopher://unix5.nysed.gov/11/K-12 Resources/Arts & Humanities/Gallery. The Dallas Museum of Art (gopher://gopher.unt.edu/11/dfw/dma) contains a catalog of thumbnail pictures of its artifacts, making selections easier. Current weather satellite images and movies can be found at http://clunix.cl.msu.edu/weather. My favorite spot for historical weather images of Hurricanes Beryl, Emily, Hugo, and Kevin can be found at gopher://groucho.unidata.ucar.edu/11/Images/archive.

One particular FTP site (ftp://gboro.rowan.edu/pub/Coasters) contains roller coaster images, statistical information, animations, and movies. This site was not found via a subject heading, but with a Gopher search on "roller and coasters." Two students required to produce a multimedia project on a technical subject for the course, Engineering in Context at Cornell, utilized the resources at this site for a presentation on the design and physics of roller coasters. With over 180 images, this site is rich with different types of roller coasters, com-

plete with definitions of terminology used by roller coaster designers. The students captured these images and uploaded them into the presentation software PowerPoint for their final project.

For astronomers, pictures of the May 10, 1994 solar eclipse can be found at the Space Environment Laboratory, WWW site http://www.sel.bldrdoc.gov/ images/eclipse.html (Figure 8). One can also find these images through the WWW Virtual Library/Astronomy/Space. These images were generated by the Space Environment Laboratory in New Mexico and were available immediately after the eclipse. Remote sensing scientists are interested in Space Imaging Radar of earth taken from space shuttle missions, which are available from the NASA WWW site http://www.jpl.nasa.gov/sircxsar.html. Another interesting NASA collection is the Sample Ocean Color Images and Data Sets Derived from the Nimbus-7 Coastal Zone Color Scanner. The WWW home page for all NASA information is http://hypatia.gsfc.nasa.gov /NASA_homepage. html. This address provides hyperlinks to home pages at 10 NASA centers, NASA Gophers (which have images of planets), and a subject index to NASA technical information.

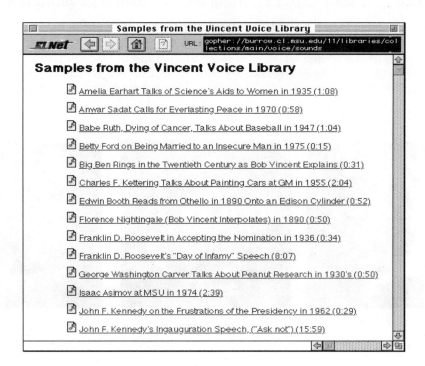

FIGURE 9

Sounds

Sounds are an intriguing Internet resource. Whale, bird, and other animal sounds, movie themes such as Jurassic Park and Mission Impossible, classical music, famous one-liners from movies and television, numerous sound effects (train whistle, thunder and lightning, etc.), and even tennis player John McEnroe venting frustration at a match are available at gopher://burrow.cl.msu.edu/11/libraries/collections/main/voice/sounds. The Vincent Voice Archive (see Figure 9) contains famous and unusual speeches (spoken not text). Winston Churchill, John F. Kennedy, Franklin D. Roosevelt, Amelia Earhart, and others are listed, some including speeches up to 15 minutes long (which will take up a lot of disk space). Sounds are very useful to include in oral multimedia presentations.

Movies and Animations

Movies are moving real images; animations are moving drawings. Some can be found via Gopher Jewels, but the majority are more readily available on World Wide Web servers and can be found under a variety of headings in the WWW Virtual Library. One can also do a keyword search on "movies" in an index, such as Searching the Galaxy. The Space Movie archive at http://www.univ-rennes1.fr/ASTRO/anim-e.html (or WWW Virtual Library/Astronomy/Space/Astronomical pictures in English) has animations and movies on meteorology, science fiction, and space. Sample movies include video clips of the Hubble Telescope repair, activity of the Sun, space walks by astronauts, aurora and hurricane activity, and the Earth rotating.

The Matlab Gallery (http://www.mathworks.com/gallery.html) includes examples of images, animations, and matrices used by computer scientists. Matlab is a popular engineering software program that integrates numerical analysis, matrix computation, signal processing, and graphics. An example of a matrix generated by Matlab is a Fast Fourier transform of a very large matrix solution. A frame from a vibrating L-shaped membrane movie, also generated by Matlab, is shown in Figure 10.

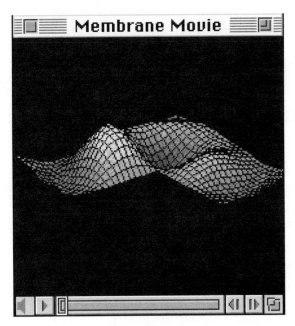

FIGURE 10

Engineers use 3-dimensional computer graphics for many applications, ranging from computer-aided design of mechanical parts to the fantasy world of film and television.

APPLICATION PROGRAMS FOR VIEWING IMAGES, SOUNDS, AND MOVIES

While text documents require only TurboGopher or a Web browser such as Mosaic to display, one must acquire a few viewer (also called helper) applications in order to view images, sound, and movies. Common extension names for these files are .gif and .jpeg for images, .mpeg for movies, and .au for sounds. The main applications needed to view the mentioned resources are JPEGView for images, QuickTime (an extension), Sparkle, and SimplePlayer for movies and animations, and SoundMachine for sounds. StuffIt Expander is necessary for decompressing the files once they have been downloaded. One can download all these helper applications from ftp://ftp.ncsa.uiuc.edu/Mosaic/Mac/Helpers or from the University of Minnesota Home Gopher (gopher://gopher.tc.umn.edu/Info about Gopher/Gopher Software Distribution/Macintosh-TurboGopher/

helper-applications). These helper-applications work for both Gopher and WWW users.

INTEGRATING THESE FORMATS INTO INSTRUCTION

While it is not feasible to show all these formats in one library instruction session, including at least one colorful non-textual resource can be an effective motivator. In a typical class, I demonstrate the online catalog, appropriate electronic bibliographic databases, and introduction to the Web. Students follow my exercises on the electronic handout, which is in HTML on our library Web server. There is little need to devote time instructing users how to FTP, Telnet, or Archie. Web browsers can retrieve information from these servers directly without asking the users to move to a different application for each one. By showing them images of the space shuttle, a solar eclipse, or a picture of art, and demonstrating how these resources can be found, I find that students ask more questions and seem more interested in library research than if I focus purely on bibliographic sources and textual documents. My goal is to stimulate their interest in researching Internet

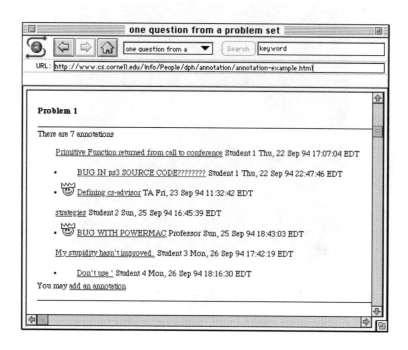

FIGURE 11

resources, and to raise their awareness level of the wide scope of information available. We see this happening in that students are contributing information themselves on Gopher and WWW servers for their departments, and hopefully they will do so for companies and government agencies as their careers develop.

Besides our regular instruction classes, we are encouraging faculty to serve their instructional materials on our Web server as well. Library staff provide FTP (file transfer protocol) and HTTP (hypertext transfer protocol) servers and HTML instruction for faculty so they can learn how to author their own HTML documents. We create a folder for their course, and they mount lecture notes, homework assignments, sample exams, tutorials, student papers, and shared annotations as a means of facilitating learning for their students. We have classes on chemical engineering, computer science, operations research, math, computer-aided design, and dynamics participating.

In some cases students are authoring information for the course modules themselves. A computer class is using shared annotations as a means for teaching problem-solving (see Figure 11). The system distinguishes between authors and users, so everyone can see the problem, the "authoritative" annotations, and the student discussions.

As more faculty contribute instructional materials in HTML, we hope to create more and more hyperlinks to this information. Improvements to HTML, such as the proposed HTML+, promises such features as support for tabular information, mathematical text, and words that wrap around images.[9] Such improvements will probably be welcomed by our faculty and encourage more activity on our Web server.

How does one decide how much time in a class to devote to various Internet research skills? As I prepare to teach library/Internet research sessions, I like to keep in mind the following objectives listed by Irene F. Rockman, Kennedy Library,

California Polytechnic State University-San Luis Obispo from her article on teaching the Internet as a formal course option:

Objectives for a Formal Course on the Internet

1. To provide students with fundamental skills for searching remotedatabases (catalogs, indexes, full-text sources) through direct, front-end, or gateway connections.
2. To enable students to complete their individual research assignments, for this class and others, using Internet resources.
3. To assist students in gaining skill, confidence, and knowledge when searching bibliographic files and in using such techniques as keyword searching, boolean operators, truncation, and limited commands.
4. To acquaint students with computer-mediated conferences, electronic mail services, campus-wide information systems, directories of electronic journals, and sources of non-bibliographic information.
5. To help students evaluate the appropriateness of which tool to use.
6. To guide students in their evaluation and assessment of the useful of information found.
7. To share knowledge, insights, and experiences with each other.[10]

Keeping these objectives in mind, and using valuable Internet tools such as the WWW Virtual Library and Search the Galaxy to teach the concepts of Internet searching, an instructor has one last crucial hurdle: staying current. My best recommendation is to subscribe to the listserv discussion group Web4Lib, where librarians discuss the creation and management of library Web servers, and to the Net-Happenings list, where Gopher Jewels and WWW server additions are announced daily. Subscribe to Web4Lib by sending a message to listserv@library.berkeley.edu saying *subscribe Web4Lib your name.* To sub-scribe to Net-Happenings, send a message to majordomo@is.internic.net saying *subscribe net-happings your email address.* Then explore these resources and update your software applications on a regular basis.

CONCLUSION

Reference librarians are always seeking better ways of teaching library instruction. The Internet has given us an exciting information resource to tap, and unlike many traditional bibliographic indexes, most students find it exciting. Using handouts and hyperlinked bibliographies on a library Web server, librarians can teach classes that help students learn how to search the Internet effectively for their coursework. Using the World Wide Web, they can learn to search, view, organize and annotate many data structures, including texts, images, sounds, and movies from a variety of sites.

Acknowledgements

Figures 2-5, 8, and 10-11 were accessed from World Wide Web servers using the browser NCSA Mosaic. NCSA Mosaic was developed at the National Center for Supercomputing Applications at the University of Illinois, Urbana-Champaign. Marc Andreessen and Eric Bina were principal developers.

Figure 7 was accessed using Mosaic Netscape developed by Marc Andreessen of Mosaic Communications Corporation.

Figures 1, 6, and 9 were accessed using MacWeb, developed by John Hardin of Enterprise Network (EINet), Microelectronics and Computer Technology Corporation. Wayne Allen and Bruce Speyer of the same company created Searching the Galaxy.

Figure 10 is reproduced with the permission of Mathworks Inc. Cleve Moler is the author of Matlab.

Figure 11 shows the shared annotation system developed by Jim Davis from Xerox and Dan Huttenlocher from the Cornell University Computer Science Department.

NOTES

1. Marc Andreessen and Eric Bina, "NCSA Mosaic: A Global Hypermedia System," *Internet Research* 4 (Spring 1994): 13.

2. Gail P. Clement, "Library Without Walls," *Internet World* 5 (September 1994): 60-64.

3. GraceAnne Andreassi DeCandido, "The Internet as Venice," *Wilson Library Bulletin* 68 (May 1993): 8.

4. Crawford Killian, "Why Teachers Fear the Internet," *Internet World* 5 (November/December 1994): 86-87.

5. James Powell, "Adventures with World Wide Web: Creating a Hypertext Library Information System," *Database* 17 (February 1994): 66.

6. Andreessen, "NCSA Mosaic," 7-17.

7. James Powell, "Adventures with World Wide Web," 59-66.

8. Frank M. Baker, "Navigating the Network with NCSA Mosaic," *Educom Review*, 29 (January/February 1994): 46-51.

9. Richard W. Wiggins, "Examining Mosaic: A History and Review," *Internet World,* 5 (October 1994): 50.

10. Ilene F. Rockman, "Teaching About the Internet: The Format Course Option," *Reference Librarian* 39: 1993: 67.

Who is Gloria Stineman and Why Can't I Find Her on LUIS?

Sheila Delacroix and Claudine Arnold Jenda

ABSTRACT

Now that library catalogs have been held captive in little, plastic boxes for some time, and given names like LOLA, LUIS, and MUSE, are users as sophisticated as the systems? Visual, as well as statistical analysis of transaction logs is one good method to use in searching for an answer to this question. This paper will review what others have concluded from using this method and seek to compare Auburn University library users with previously studied groups. Are our patrons truly expert at maneuvering in the Online Public Access Catalog? Users rarely tell us face to face what we can find out by this form of electronic eavesdropping. Librarians must meet the challenge of using the valuable information found in transaction logs to better understand the users they serve and improve customer service.

In a paper presented at the National Online Meeting of 1989, Bruce Shuman looks into the future of online systems and fantasizes about a time when "systems don't just do what you tell them to. . . they do what you *want* them to." Shuman describes four possible stages of development for these systems and details some of the problems which might be encountered at each stage. For example, as we enter the stage of voice activated systems, we face problems brought on by different languages, accents, local idioms, and idiosyncratic pronunciations. In the end, Shuman conjures up a system which is accessed through "neurotransmission of requests from the searcher's mind directly into the system." The system "responds to thoughts, rather than words." [1] This is the system our users are looking for, and have been looking for since the introduction of automated information retrieval systems in libraries. Even in the landmark online catalog use studies of 1981 funded by the Council on Library Resources (CLR), users were telling us to head in this direction. Patrons who answered questionnaires and participated in focus groups, when asked what they would like to see in the future, told researchers: "I want [the catalog to show me] indexes of books so I can see whether I want the book." "The computer could read the introduction [of a book] to you." "I

Sheila Delacroix is Assistant Dean for Reference & Information Services and Claudine Arnold Jenda is Head of the Science & Technology Department at the Auburn University Libraries, Auburn University, Alabama.

would like the computer to talk to me." "I want to walk to a type of telephone booth, punch in my topic, and the machine gives me the actual book or whatever it was."[2]

What our users did not want then and do not want now is a system which is rigid, unforgiving, and cloaked in rituals which only the initiated can hope to master. Unfortunately, these are precisely the characteristics of the online catalog systems which patrons encounter in too many academic libraries, systems which coyly refuse to confirm or deny ownership of a title because you have typed in "T= **THE** MANAGER AS NEGOTIATOR," or won't give you a clue as to who Gloria is because you don't know the precise spelling of her last name. Even more unfortunate is the fact that many users approach our public catalogs, type in "A=ALAN GUTTMAN" or "FIND GLORIA STINEMAN," get a message saying there is nothing to match what they have entered, and walk away. They don't come to us and ask for assistance. They don't settle in and read the layers and layers of help screens. Paradoxically, they don't always walk away dissatisfied! After all, they asked a question and got an answer - that must be the end of the story. They do walk away, however, with their information needs unfulfilled, and librarians often are none the wiser.

PREVIOUS STUDIES

With the advent of online catalogs capable of capturing all of the data entered by every patron at every terminal, we began to have the ability to read the tracks of these brave pioneers on the new information frontier. The computer could log and save for us these patron/machine transactions. We could see where the patron had been and in many cases get a good idea as to the success or failure of the journey. In an exhaustive article on the history and development of transaction log analysis, Thomas Peters says that this ability to follow a trail through a logging or listing of transactions after the fact goes back about twenty-five years. He identifies one of the earliest of these types of studies in 1967.[3] The library literature is chock full of articles, chapters, and books describing research and discussing issues concerning transaction log analysis. Peters, Kurth, and Kaske annotate over 200 such works in a bibliography published in 1993.[4]

Transaction Log Analysis (TLA) is used as a tool for looking at the types of searching behaviors and levels of competence users exhibit, and also as a means to examine the mechanical aspects of systems. Even though the studies to this point have by no means followed a standard method or pattern, or even used a standard vocabulary, and even though their results are sometimes contradictory, most TLA researchers would probably agree on the following points.

First, online catalog users execute a substantial number of searches which result in the retrieval of no records (zero hits), or which result in the retrieval of overly large sets which are of little or no use to the searcher. Second, searching by subject, when that is defined as using a controlled vocabulary of terms, results in the highest number of unsatisfactory searches. Third, good spelling and keyboarding skills would go a long way toward raising the success rates of catalog users, as would a system with a spell-check package that could correct some of these mistakes. Fourth, the ability to conceptualize information needs and communicate them to the system is a tall order for most end users of library information retrieval systems. Fifth, some of the problems experienced by users of online systems are the result of system design, while some are attributable to a variety of other factors, such as lack of training, poor physical facilities, and/or user disposition. Finally, TLA is a great way to get to know your users better, to unobtrusively observe user searching behavior, and to determine how your system is being used. Other methods of evaluation, such as surveys, questionnaires, and focus groups fail to accurately decribe user/system interactions. Despite the limitations outlined by Martin Kurth,[5] TLA is well worth the time and effort to pursue.

PROBLEM STATEMENT

This paper is the result of a conversation about the untapped possibilities for our own edification and education lurking within the hidden world of transaction logs at our institution. The authors had both caught glimpses of transaction logs and transaction log studies over the years, but had never earnestly explored them. We wanted to see what was out there, but more important, see what could be learned from analyses of our own logs. It seemed logical to us, as it has to many before us, that these documents were rich veins of data waiting to be mined for clues as to how well we were doing the job of delivering information services to our clientele, and how we might go about improving the service. We believed with Brian Nielsen that "the log data [could be] invaluable to grounding librarians in concrete knowledge about the behavior of users."[6]

At Auburn University Libraries, computer enhancements to the library's systems come along at a fast clip. We like to believe that these advancements and the ready availability of reference assistance for users assure access to needed information, but there has been no comprehensive evaluation of how well users search the OPAC. As the library prepares for more computer enhancements to the OPAC, as well as the installation of more OPAC-accessible databases, this seems to be a good time to assess how well the users search the present catalog. We would also like to ascertain if users are ready for the additional sophisticated search capabilities that the next level of enhancements entail. Because the annual, voluntary survey of users conducted by the library reflects consistently highly favorable comments in almost all categories, our hopes and expectations are that library users find it easy to locate the information they need. But, as other studies have rightly pointed out,[7] surveys of this type only measure users' opinions of the service, and not necessarily how well they interacted with the system when searching.

SETTING

Auburn University, located in Auburn, Alabama is a comprehensive, public, land-grant university. The student population for 1993-94 consisted of 21,363 students, pursuing studies in 150 areas at the undergraduate level, and 226 areas at the graduate level. Auburn University Libraries is a member of the Association of Research Libraries (ARL). The main library is the Ralph Brown Draughon Library and there are branch libraries at the College of Veterinary Medicine and the School of Architecture. The collections include 2,058,000 physical volumes, 2,084,000 items in microformat, 1,402,158 government publications, and 50,733 architectural slides. The University Archives, which is a department within the Library, contains more than 900 archival collections, 4700 motion pictures, 7,188 oral history and recorded sound tapes, and approximately 160,000 photographs. Auburn University is a U.S. government documents depository library selecting about 98% of all depository items.

Auburn University Libraries' Online system, AUBIE (Auburn University Bibliographic and Information Exchange), is a NOTIS system and provides access to the following: LUIS, the online catalog; DHUM, a database consisting of H. W. Wilson's *Art Index*, *Humanities Index*, and *Readers' Guide to Periodical Literature*; DSOC, a database made up of Wilson's *Business Periodicals Index* and *Social Sciences Index*; DSCI, composed of Wilson's *Applied Science and Technology Index*, *Biological and Agricultural Index* and *General Science Index*; ERIC, the database produced by the Educational Resources Information Center; ABI/Inform, periodical references from the *Abstracts of Business Information* database, and CATS, a grouping of library catalogs from three other institutions of higher education in the state. Auburn has employed the NOTIS integrated library management system since 1983.

Patrons searching AUBIE may search by Keyword (by giving the command K=), Author (A=), Title (T=), Subject (S=), Call Number (C=), US Government Documents Number (CS=), Juvenile Books by Subject (SC=), and Other Call Number (CO=). This last category includes materials which are classified by format, e.g. theses, dissertations, microforms, and sound recordings. AUBIE is available within the main library on 48 public terminals. These terminals are arranged in banks of twelve in each of the main public service areas of the building. AUBIE is also accessible across the campus network, through dial-in ports and through telnet and other information gateways.

The Reference and Information Services Division of Auburn University Libraries, is made up of eight public service departments: Science and Technology, Social Sciences, Humanities and General Information, Microforms and Government Documents, Special Collections, University Archives, and two branch libraries, Architecture and Veterinary Medicine. The main library is divided by subject, with each major subject category occupying a different floor. A full service reference desk is maintained on each floor. The desks are staffed at all times that the library is open - 99 hours per week when school is in session. Of these 99 hours, desks are staffed by professional librarians approximately 65 hours per week. The public terminal banks are in plain sight of the reference desk on each floor, about ten steps across an open area.

METHODS & PROCEDURES

This process began with an examination of what we called the Summary Data logs. These data are captured at the end of each month and record overall figures such as count of search type by database, count of search type by terminal and database, count of search type by hour, time of day use patterns, daily count of search type by hour, and hit statistics for searches by database and type. In addition, this information is divided by where the search originated, i.e. at a public terminal, a staff terminal, a networked terminal, through a

dial-up port, or from a branch library. For the purposes of this study, only the 48 public access terminals in the main library have been targeted for consideration. The period of time studied was November 1, 1993 through October 30, 1994. In addition, for our purposes, a search is defined as the act of entering a command (A=, T=, etc.) plus a character string.

The total number of searches performed on these terminals during the period studied was 1,553,372. Table I shows that peak months for use of the system were October (178,229), November (182,237), February (197,938) and May (178,512). Least use of the system was made during quarter breaks in December (77,786), June (68,863), and September (56,575).

Since AUBIE offers more than just a catalog of our book and journal holdings, we were curious to see how searching is distributed over the available databases. LUIS, the library's catalog, came out by far the heaviest used unit of the system. Sixty-seven percent (67%) of all searches during this time were executed within the LUIS database. While this figure in itself may not seem alarming, it brings several questions to mind. Does this mean that users still think of the library mostly as the place you go to get books? Does this reflect a true picture of our users needs, i.e. can 70% of what patrons are searching for in a large academic library be supplied from monographs? Does this reflect confusion on the part of the user as to what database to search for what type of material? Or does it reflect a confusion with the mechanics of the system. Auburn's online catalog, when that was all it was, was called LUIS. As more databases were made available on the system, it was confusing to call the online catalog LUIS and also to call the whole system LUIS, when there was also ERIC, DHUM and others. In an attempt to clarify the situation, we called the entire system AUBIE (after the university mascot), and gave each database a distinct name. While this is surely a step in the right direction, many users, we suspect, are still a bit befuddled. Professors have been heard referring to LUIS in the old, generic sense so

TABLE I: Search Totals by Month

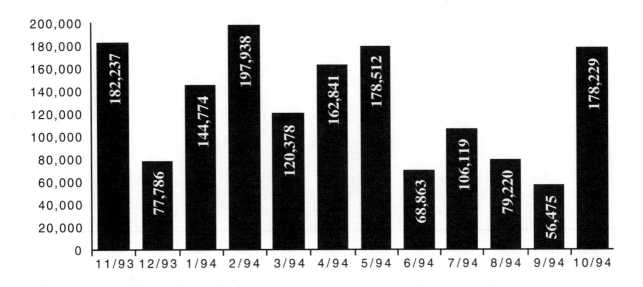

students come to the library and try to do what they are told, "Find three articles on LUIS."

Searches executed in the remaining, non-LUIS, databases revealed the following pattern (expressed as a percent of total searches): DSCI - 11.4%, DSOC - 8.9%, DHUM - 7.3%, ERIC - 4.7%. ABI/Inform was introduced on a limited bases in the middle of the period being studied and did not account for a significant amount of the total activity.

Of the total 1.5 million searches, 34.6% were keyword searches (K=), 27.1% were subject searches (S=), 22.9% were title searches (T=), and 14.9% were author searches (A=). The only other system commands which were used were children's subject (CS=) and call number (C=). However since the combined use of these commands was .5%, they were dropped from further consideration. Table II shows that this K-S-T-A pattern holds true for almost every month when the total database is viewed. However, if we compare LUIS to the periodical indexes two different patterns emerge. In LUIS overall, the pattern is T-S-K-A.

While in the non-LUIS databases, the pattern is K-S-T-A for DSOC and DHUM, and K-S-A-T for DSCI and ERIC. This gives reason for encouragement, since it seems to say that users are approaching the periodical indexes logically, starting their searches with a concept in these databases where it is unlikely that they would know a specific author or title.

LESS-THAN-DESIRABLE OUTCOMES

Much of the literature concerning transaction logs of library catalogs focuses on the "failed search." Every author has her or his definition of what constitutes a failed search. Zink uses the term "unsuccessful" and puts any transaction which retrieves no records in this category.[8] Peters[9] and Hunter[10] also define failure as zero hits. We confess to being uncomfortable with the use of the term failure, and have chosen instead to use the phrase "undesirable outcomes." We have defined this category, in a manner similar to Carol Hustuft, as any search which retrieves either no records or a set consisting of more than 251 records.[11] While

TABLE II: Us e of Commands by Percent and Month

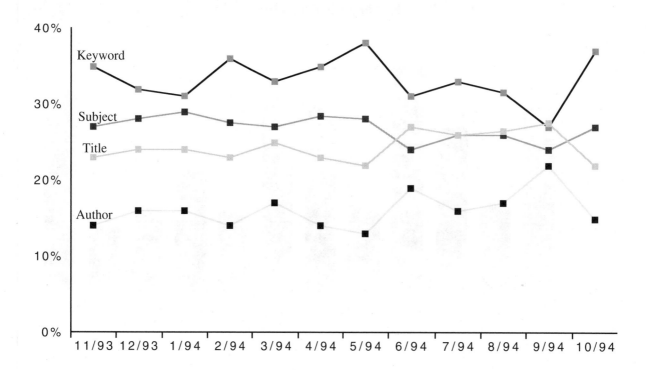

we, and previous authors, are aware that a patron may very well have his or her needs met by a transaction which falls into these categories, actually reading the logs tells you that this is rarely the case.

Of the 1.5 million searches performed during this time period, almost half - 47.9% - fell into the "undesirable outcome" category. This is similar to the rate reported by Hustuft, and is an outcome which we consider distressing. Table III shows the distribution of these by search command compared to total searches performed.

SAMPLE LOGS OF SEARCH SESSIONS

In order to move from the summary data to the line by line analysis of actual transactions, two terminals in each of the four main banks of public terminals were monitored every day from October 16, 1994 through October 29, 1994. October is one of the heaviest months for system use and we felt that a variety of users and search situations would be captured from machines in each major subject department. The results of this monitoring

filled 2,055 computer pages. Because these were public terminals that do not require a login to start a search, and because the data capture was done retrospectively, there is no means of determining which user performed what search, thus users' identities and privacy are preserved.

These printed records of search transactions were visually analyzed initially to distinguish and group search statements that belong to a particular users' transaction, i.e. to decide where one search session stopped and the next began. A search session is defined as the interaction of a single user with the system. This of course is the Achilles heel of transaction log analysis. Generally TLA does not allow for a definitive determination of when one person has completed a session and another has begun. In addition, TLA does not offer a means of judging the intent of the searchers, of finding out what is *really* needed. We cannot yet plug into those neurotransmitters that Shuman refers to. But after going over these tracks for a while, we can begin to read the signs, to walk in the shoes of our users, and plug into their thoughts

**TABLE III: Number of Undesirable Outcomes Compared
to Total Number of Searches in Each Category**

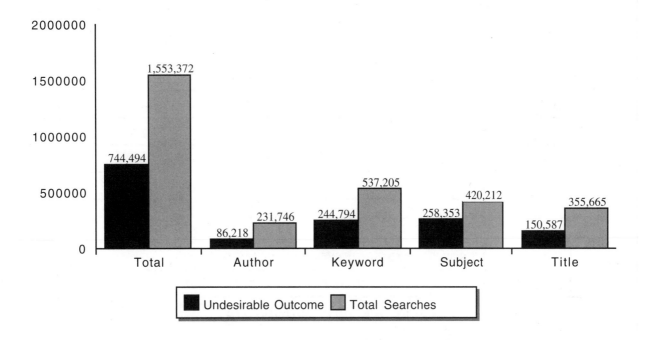

to an amazing degree. Of course sometimes they make it easy by simply typing their frustrations into the system in pointed and/or profane language.

To facilitate further analysis of the logs, a sample of search transactions were input into a database utilizing PFS First Choice Software. The resulting database could be sorted by department, database, command used, or any combination of these and other defined factors as needed. This set consisted of 144 search sessions, approximately 36 selected from each terminal bank. There was no magic in these particular numbers. It was simply decided that this was a manageable amount of data for this stage of the evaluation.

Looking at the 144 sample search sessions which had been input into the file, the question became how many of these would we judge to be successful and how many would be seen as unsuccessful. Here we are not judging individual searches, but rather trying to think like the user and decide whether or not she or he went away satisfied. These judgements, of course, are very subjective and the authors had to struggle to downplay what could be described as an expert user bias. There was ever present the temptation to say, "Well, sure, he got SOME useful records, but I could have shown him how to obtain much more useful/relevant/current data."

Using this perspective, the label of success is applied rather liberally to any session which was judged in the end to have provided the user with SOMETHING of use on the topic which he or she seemed to be exploring. A session was seen as successful if the user appeared to catch on to the workings of the system, even if several major errors had been made initially. An unsuccessful search was one which did not appear to provide any relevant data to the user. In order to make this determination, the majority of the sessions were re-keyed by the authors to examine results. Tables IVa and IVb give examples of successful and unsuccessful searches.

Of the 144 separate search sessions evaluated, 78 (54%) were judged to be successful, while 66 (46%) were seen as unsuccessful. It is interesting,

TABLE IVa: Examples of Successful Search Sessions

SESSION #	DATABASE	TRANSACTION	# HITS	# VIEWED
S 1	LUIS	K FORAGE SEED PRODUCTION	2	0
	DSCI	K FORAGE SEED PRODUCTION	4	2
	DSCI	K GRASS SEED PRODUCTION	17	5
	DSCI	K GRASS SEED	111	3
	DSCI	K FORAGE LEGUME SEED PRODUCTION	0	0
	DSCI	K FORAGE YIELD	247	11
	DSCI	K FORAGE SEED	20	1
	DSCI	K HERBAGE YIELD	70	8
	DSCI	T=AMERICAN JOURNAL OF ALTERNATIVE AGRICULTURE	0	0
	DSCI	T SOIL SCIENCE SOCIETY OF AMERICAN JOURNAL	0	0
	LUIS	T=SOIL SCIENCE SOCIETY OF AMERICA JOURNAL	1	1
	LUIS	T=AMERICAN JOURNAL OF ALTERNATIVE AGRICULTURE	1	1
	LUIS	T=ASPECTS OF APPLIED BIOLOGY	3	1
	LUIS	K FORAGE PHYSIOLOGY	0	0
	LUIS	K FORAGE CROP PHYSIOLOGY	0	0
	LUIS	T FORAGE CROP PHYSIOLOGY	0	0
	LUIS	T PHYSIOLOGY OF FORAGE CROPS	0	0
	LUIS	K PORAGE	0	0
	LUIS	K FORAGE CROPS	49	0
	LUIS	K FORAGE GRASS	30	1
	LUIS	T SOIL SCIENCE SOCIETY OF AMERICA JOURNAL	1	1
S 2	LUIS	K=GOETEXTILES	0	0
	DSCI	K=GEOTEXTILES	268	29
S 3	DSCI	K=SOYBEANS	3864	0
	DSCI	K =SOYBEANS AND GROWTH OR GROWTH HABIT	302	47
	DSCI	K =SOYBEANS AND WEED COMPETITION	48	6
	DSCI	K =SOYBEANS AND CROWN CROP CANOPY	27	1

TABLE IVb: Examples of Unsuccessful Search Sessions

SESSION #	DATABASE	TRANSACTION	# HITS	# VIEWED
S 1	LUIS	T=ASSASINS OF MEMORY	0	0
	LUIS	T= ASSASINS OF MEMORY	0	0
	LUIS	T=ASSASINS OF MEMORY	0	0
	LUIS	S=HOLOCOUST	0	0
	LUIS	S=DENIAL	10	0
S 2	LUIS	S=SUPREME COURT JUSTICES	0	0
	LUIS	S=JUSTICES	105	0
	LUIS	S=SUPREME COURT	4	0
	LUIS	COURT JUSTICES	0	0
	LUIS	S=COURT JUSTICES	0	0
	LUIS	T=CONSTITUTION	1807	2
S 3	DSOC	T= UNION AT RISK	0	0
	DSOC	T= UNION AT RISK	0	0
	DSOC	EXPLAIN TITLE		
	DHUM	T= UNION AT RISK	4	1
S 4	LUIS	S= PHYSICAL THERAPY	215	1
	LUIS	S=SPORTS PHYSICAL THERAPY	0	0
	LUIS	S=SPORTS PHYSICAL THRAPY	4	1
	LUIS	K=REHAB	23	1
	LUIS	K=PHYSICAL THERAPY, REHAB	0	0
	LUIS	K=PHYSICAL THERAPY REHAB	0	0
	LUIS	K=REHAB PHYSICAL THERAPY	0	0
	LUIS	PHYSICAL REHAB	0	0
	LUIS	PHYSICAL THERAPY	0	0
	LUIS	PHYSICAL THERAPY	0	0
	LUIS	S=REHAB PHYSICAL THERAPY	0	0
	ERIC	K=PHYSICAL THERAPY	244	2

TABLE V

Database	Transaction	# of Hits	Records Viewed
DSOC	K=Rules of Administration	0	0
DSOC	K=Adminstration	18961	0
DSOC	K=General Motors and Adminstration	40	2
DSOC	K=Salary and Government Regulations	0	0
DSOC	K=Government Regulations	1112	0
DSOC	K=General Motors and Government Regulations	0	0
DSOC	K=GM and Government Regulations	1	1

and not a little disturbing, that when success is judged on completely objective criteria, i.e. number of zero hits or number of hits over 251, the percentage of undesirable search outcomes approaches 50%. And when the criteria is subjective, as it is here in the assessment of individual search sessions, the result is the same, about half of all online catalog users are not interacting successfully with the system.

While it was often the case that several factors contributed to the unsatisfactory outcome, an attempt was made to assign a primary cause for each session which was judged to be unsuccessful. In 21 of the 66 unsuccessful sessions, this cause could be described as a problem of concept expression. Often these sessions would have produced viable results had they been rephrased or rearranged. Table V gives an example of this type of session.

Other causes for unsuccessful sessions included: 1) using terms that were too broad which retrieved unmanageable sets - 15 sessions; 2) choosing the wrong command for the type of information being searched, e.g. S=Journal of Metals - 12 sessions; 3) choosing an inappropriate database for the subject being searched - 7 sessions; 4) uncorrected spelling/keyboarding errors - 6 sessions; 5) choosing overly narrow terms - 3 sessions; 6) failure to type in any commands - 1 session.

CONCLUSIONS

Needless to say, the poor quality of searching that takes place on our OPAC is a point for concern. Even if you disagree with the high rates of failure detailed in the literature, or quarrel with definitions of successful sessions and unsuccessful sessions, reading transaction logs reveals that a great many of our patrons are in need of intervention in their search processes. Over and over we see entries that are obviously book or journal titles being searched in periodical databases, or entries that are repeated five, six, twelve times with the same word misspelled each time, or searches with all the right words in all the wrong configurations. So where do we go from here? Perhaps the first response is to try to fix everything all at once, but we know that is not possible. An old vaudeville joke goes, "How do you eat an elephant?" The answer comes back, "One bite at a time." Librarians are munching on this electronic elephant we call the OPAC, but maybe we should invite a few more folks to the feast.

TLA tells us we need better, more responsive systems that can correct simple mistakes (spelling, typing), shed archaic logic (ignore initial articles, take plurals into account, get past the necessity for Boolean operators), and provide feedback for searchers as they go along. As our once humble listing-of-what-we-have-in-this-building mushrooms into a mega-catalog-of-the-universe, systems must be designed which show the occasional user, the "permanent novice,"[12] how to swim through this ocean of data without drowning. Barbara Quint in a positive, hopeful column on the present and future of natural language searching says, "In the past two decades, search services [and online catalog systems] have tried to convince the world that it should learn the elaborate conventions and rituals of online search engines. The world has disagreed." [13] And so do we.

TLA also underscores the necessity for more user instruction of every variety, at every opportunity. It points to the need for a librarian at the elbow of many patrons. Adeane Bregman and Barbara Mento described a program of "Reference Roving" at Boston College which could prove to be an excellent step toward positioning a skilled intermediary between patron and machine on a continuous basis.[14]

Analysis of transaction logs tells us that our cataloging of materials is inadequate. Information buried in book chapters and essay collections needs to be liberated through the addition of monographic tables of contents which can be searched on the OPAC.

Finally, analyzing transaction logs reveals to us the necessity to analyze transaction logs. While users tell us politely and sincerely on survey after survey that we are wonderful and that they love the computers, the logs tell us what the user is too embarrassed or too confused or too uninformed to reveal. Librarians must engage systems personnel and library administrators in this quest for valid feedback. We must convince them that we need to have random logs run and evaluated periodically in order to do the job we are all here to do. We must convince them that this tool, already bought and paid for, is underutilized. By combining the efforts of system designers, system administrators, catalogers, reference librarians, bibliographic instruction librarians, and library administrators, perhaps in the future transaction logs will not reflect the frustration of the patron who tries repeatedly to interact with the system, gets nowhere and types "EAT MY SHORTS LUIS!" at the top of his lungs and walks away.

NOTES

1. Bruce A. Shuman, "Expert Systems and the Future of Interactive Searching" Paper presented at the National Online Meeting, New York, NY, May 9-11, 1989. ERIC ED 322 906.
2. Karen Markey, "Thus Spake the OPAC User" *Information Technology and Libraries* 2:4 (1983): 87-92.
3. Thomas A. Peters, "The History and Development of Transaction Log Analysis" *Library Hi Tech* 11:2 (1993): 41-66.
4. Thomas A. Peters, Neal K. Kaske, and Martin Kurth, "Transaction Log Analysis" Library Hi *Tech Bibliography* No.9 (1993) 151-183.
5. Martin Kurth, "The Limits and Limitations of Transaction Log Analysis" *Library Hi Tech* 11:2 (1993): 98-104.
6. Brian Nielsen, "What They Say They Do and What They Do: Assessing Online Catalog Use Instruction through Transaction Monitoring" *Information Technology and Libraries* 5 (March 1986): 28-34.
7. Thomas A. Peters, "When Smart People Fail: An Analysis of the Transaction Log of an Online Public Access Catalog" *The Journal of Academic Librarianship* 15 (November 1989): 267-273.
8. Steven D. Zink, "Monitoring User Search Success Through Transaction Log Analysis: The WolfPAC Example" *Reference Service Review* 19:1 (Spring 1991): 49-56.

9. Thomas A. Peters, "When Smart People Fail: An Analysis of the Transaction Log of an Online Public Access Catalog," p.270.

10. Rhonda N. Hunter, "Successes and Failures of Patrons Searching the Online Catalog at a Large Academic Library: A Transaction Log Analysis" *RQ* 30 (Spring 1991): 396.

11. Referenced in Thomas A. Peters, "The History and Development of Transaction Log Analysis," p. 49.

12. Christine L. Borgman, "Why Are Online Catalogs Hard to Use? Lessons from Information-Retrieval Studies" Journal of the American Society for Information Science 37:6(1986):387-400.

13. Barbara Quint, "Nature's Way" *Wilson Library Bulletin* 69 (March, 1994): 61+.

14. Adeane Bregman and Barbara Mento, "Reference Roving at Boston College" *C&RL News* 53:10 (November 1992): 634-636.

@*&!#@ This Computer and the Horse It Rode in On:
Patron Frustration and Failure at the OPAC

Jane Scott, Jeffrey A. Trimble, and L. Fleming Fallon

ABSTRACT

The purpose of this research was to investigate use of a second generation OPAC. Specifically, the study addressed how often and why patrons fail when using keywords and subjects in searching for monographs and serials. OSCAR, Slippery Rock University's OPAC using NOTIS LMS 5.1 and NOTIS MDAS 3.1, was analyzed regarding patron use. Macroanalysis of transaction logs for the local bibliographic database with integrated Wilson indexes included public access terminals, and all remote users. Failures were operationally defined as keyword or subject searches that produced no hits. Microanalysis of actual searches was also employed to clarify the nature of the failed searches. During two hours of the day throughout the study "snapshots" were made of searches, detailing patrons' search strategies. Failures were coded as to probable cause. During this study librarians altered the searching environment to note changes in patrons' success rate. Changes included loading LCSH authority records, changing OPAC screen displays, and changing the default boolean/positional operators for keyword searches. All of the three changes affected the interaction between the user and the system resulting in improved success rates for keyword searching. Two of the three interventions also improved the success rates for subject searching. Simple steps to modify the system and educate the user are suggested.

INTRODUCTION

Data from patrons using first generation OPACs revealed the need for improved keyword/subject capabilities. The expansive study by the Council on Library Resources, involving analysis of sixteen OPACs, concluded that topical subject searching was more often used than author/title known item searching. However, patrons indicated that topical subject searching often resulted in unfavorable experiences with not enough or too many retrievals.[1] Larson's more recent six year study of OPAC transaction logs revealed a consistent decline in the frequency of subject index use with a corresponding increase in the frequency of

Jane Scott is Associate Professor/Coordinator of Bibliographic Instruction and Jeffrey A. Trimble is Instructor, Head of the Catalog Department at Bailey Library, Slippery Rock University, Slippery Rock, Pennsylvania. L. Fleming Fallon is a physician at Jameson Hospital in New Castle, Pennsylvania.

title keyword searching.[2] The use of subjects as the basis for searching, according to Larson, is most likely to lead to frustration. He cited subject searching as "the access point most likely to fail." His earlier study on the same MELVYL system found that 48.5% of subject searches failed to retrieve any records.[3] Peters 1989 study reported overall failure rate to be 40.5%, with LCSH subject searches accounting for 52.0% of the failures.[4]

In response to the studies indicating keyword searching capabilities were needed, second generation OPACs were designed with keyword access. However, patron success rate is still unacceptably low and the librarians' mental model of the card catalog may be a significant factor. Peters states:

The information professional's mental model of the online catalog may be narrow, with major carryover from the mental model of the card catalog. We may assume incorrectly that there is a correct way to use the online catalog.[5]

Kranich and others found that of thirty-four OPAC users interviewed, only one person performed a keyword search. The authors hypothesized that the users were not aware of the keyword option and confused keyword and subject searching.[6] Ensor found that a high percentage (44.4%) of the most experienced LUIS searchers said they were "not aware of keyword searching."[7]

In a scan over the Internet in 1994, it appeared that the majority of libraries with second generation OPACs continue to promote author, title, and subject searching before keyword searching, to the detriment of the search process. Fifty-eight OPAC screens were viewed. Of these, 35 (60%) suggested subject searching before keyword searching. Thirteen presented the keyword option before the subject, but these options appeared in the middle or at the bottom of the menu. Only 10 (17%) promoted the keyword capability at the top of the menu screen.

Failure to promote keyword capabilities is an example of the librarians' present inability to make the much needed paradigm shift that Cochrane addressed a decade ago.[8] Carrying the mental model of the card catalog, we continue to market LCSH subject searching over the often more successful keyword approach.

Thorne and Whitlatch affirm the fact that users are better served by selecting keyword rather than subject headings as their first access strategy, and that keyword searching should be listed above subject searching on the screen. In this promotion of keyword searching, they realized a keyword success rate of 83.3% and a subject success rate of 50.7%. [9]

Hildreth stressed the need to improve the interaction between the user and the system.[10] Libraries have invested much money and time in making keyword searching a possibility, but many patrons do not even know it exists. Simple redesigns of the introductory screens can improve this interaction by simultaneously modifying the system and educating the user. In this study an attempt was made to analyze patron failure when using keyword and subject searching and to investigate ways to modify the system to improve the interaction and increase success rates for the user.

METHODOLOGY

Transaction logs for the Slippery Rock University OPAC using NOTIS LMS 5.1 and NOTIS MDAS 3.1 were analyzed for a sixteen month period from July 1993 through October 1994. During the study the OPAC, OSCAR, contained the library holdings as well as integrated Wilson indexes grouped into four databases. The "General" database contained the Education, Social Sciences, Humanities, Biography, and Essay and General Literature indexes. The "Science" database contained the General Science and Biological and Agricultural indexes. Reader's Guide with Abstracts and Business Index with Abstracts were loaded into their own separate databases. The NOTIS Library Management Software (LMS) provided several batch programs that reported various OPAC transactions and statistics.

For the macroanalysis the "OPAC Summary Activity Report" provided monthly statistics for items such as total searches attempted per database. These were also arranged by type of search (i.e., author, title, subject, keyword, etc.) and by terminal IDs. In addition, the report listed the number of "valid hits" and "no hits." Failures were operationally defined as searches that produced no hits and each significant search was treated as a discrete entity. The batch program reported every search that was attempted on the OPAC.

Monthly statistics of the summary report were analyzed and tabulated for subject and keyword searches across all databases. NOTIS' Library Management Software has a "true" keyword/boolean search engine that searches the entire bibliographic record. A T-test was used to analyze data and the level of significance was set at 0.05.

For the microanalysis the "OPAC Detailed Transaction Activity Report" captured the actual text of the searches attempted. The first "snapshot" was taken from 12:00 to 1:00 p.m. on a weekday in March 1994. This sample is shown in figure 1. The next "snapshot" was taken in November 1994 on a weekday from 1:00-2:00 p.m. Searches that resulted in zero hits were coded as to probable causes for failure. The categories of probable causes, consistent with those identified by Peters, were used to analyze failures and suggest system modifications.[11]

A baseline of patron success rates for keyword and subject searching for July through December 1993 was established. After this time three interventions were made. The analysis of patrons failed searches suggested several system modifications. The first intervention entailed tape loading the complete LCSH authority records in January 1994. As the failure rate for LCSH searches was high, it was predictable that the addition of authority records with cross references from incorrect subjects would lead patrons to correct subjects and appropriate monographs.

Custom colored key caps were also added to all library keyboards at this time. The intent of the keycaps was to increase the accuracy of maneuvering on the keyboard and thus decrease errors and lockups. Messages on the ten keycaps in-

cluded "Reposition Cursor", "Reset"," Enter", "=" (equal sign), "Index" (the "i" key), and "Review" (the "r" key). It was the subjective opinion of the librarians that these keycaps greatly decreased the incidence of jammed keyboards, although the OPAC reports did not address the incidence of lockups, and there is no measurable data regarding the effect of this change.

The second intervention was the promotion of keyword searching on the screens. In May 1994 all five introductory screens for the bibliographic database and journal indexes were redesigned. The keyword option was the first choice to be presented on the screen.

The last intervention occurred in September 1994 when the boolean/positional defaults were changed from "near" to "and." A "near" search found two adjacent words in any order, whereas, an "and" search was more expansive, finding the two words anywhere in the record.

PRESENTATION AND ANALYSIS OF DATA

Annual statistics for this period indicated that patrons searched by keyword more than twice as often (45.5%) as by subject (19.2%). The incidence of other types of searches was as follows: title 22.1%, author 12.3%, other .85%.

Patrons looking for the library's holdings by LCSH terms had a success rate of 53.2% at the beginning of the study. The recorded attempts for subject searching of monographs totaled 7,614. In January, when LCSH authority records with cross-references were loaded, patron success rates began to improve. From January through April success rates for subject searches increased significantly ($t=10.34$; $df=11912$; $p<0.0001$) to 63.2%, with recorded attempts totaling 12,428.

In March the first "snapshot" was analyzed to discern probable causes for the failed searches. Table 1 shows a list of all problem categories used in the study, in order as to their relative frequency. Many transactions had more than one problem. In these cases multiple error types were coded to the transaction.

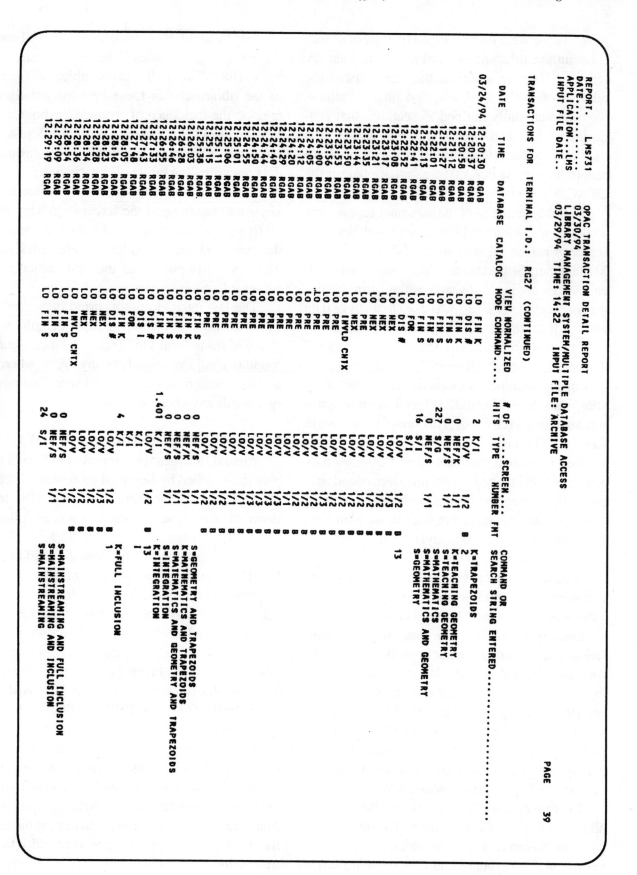

Figure 1: Snapshot of Patron Searches

TABLE 1: Probable Causes of User Problems with OSCAR
March 1994

Error Type	Frequency	%
Item was not in database	43	36.7
Confusion about rules specific to system	33	28.2
Wrong search type was used	24	20.5
Spelling error	12	10.2
Typographical error	2	1.7
Misunderstanding of the controlled vocabulary	1	.8
Person's first name entered before last	1	.8
Malicious entry	1	.8
Confusion with other OPAC commands	0	0
Confusion about structure of databases	0	0
Attempted boolean search where not possible	0	0
TOTAL	**117**	**99.7**

The most frequent cause of failure was attributed to the item not being in the database (36.7%). Confusion about rules specific to the system (28.2%) and use of the wrong search type (20.5%) were the next most frequent causes for problems. These two problem areas were closely analyzed with emphasis on possible solutions. Thirty-three transactions indicated confusion about NOTIS rules and twenty-four of these could have been alleviated if the default operator had been "and" rather than "near". For example, in figure 1, the search "k=teaching geometry" would have yielded 18 hits if the default operator were "and" ("teaching and geometry" rather than "teaching near geometry.")

The wrong search type was used twenty-four times and a keyword search of the same term would have resulted in success for twenty of these transactions. These observations directed the nature of the next two interventions.

The second intervention was implemented in May with a redesign of the introductory screens. Figure 2 shows the introductory screens for the library's collection and the "General" database for journal citations. When the keyword directions were prominently placed at the beginning of the screen, success rates for both keyword and subject searching improved in four of the five databases. The database that contained the library's holdings showed the most improvement in the keyword search success rate from 65.2% to 69.3% (t=6.71; df=33035; p<0.0001).

Surprisingly, this intervention to promote keyword searching had the greatest impact on the success of subject searching. Figure 3 shows that the largest improvement of the study occurred in the success of subject searching at this time. It is hypothesized that patrons used keywords to locate a few good records, then expanded their search by using newly learned "correct" subjects. The Library of Congress Subject Headings (LCSH) and Wilson subject descriptors appear on the screen of the brief view of the bibliographic record with a suggestion to "use s= <search>".

This technique, to begin with keywords and refine search strategies with learned subject headings, is taught in formal bibliographic instruction classes, as well as in one-to-one reference instruction. The frequency of subject searching remained about the same before (19.33%) and after (19.90%) this intervention. The use of keyword searching declined (45.79% to 41.03%) (t=35.10; df=579430;

```
                                                              SRU COLLECTION
                                                                  Introduction
-----------------------------------------------------------------------------------------
                       Slippery Rock University Online Catalog

OSCAR includes SR, the online catalog for materials in the Slippery Rock University library.

To search by:    Keyword          Type:    k=      Example:    k=    movies
                 Author                    a=                  a=    rita brown
                 Title                     t=                  t=    sound and the fury
                 LC Subject Heading        s=                  s=    motion picture
                 LC Call Numbers           cl=                 cl=   PS6003.E282
                 Dewey Call Numbers        cd=                 cd=   308
                 "Other" call numbers      co=                 co=   CD 0234


For more information on searching, type F and press <ENTER>
--------------------------------------------------------- + Page 1 of 3 ----------------------------------
                       Enter search command<F8>   FORward page



NEXT COMMAND:
```

```
                                                           Humanities, Social Scien
                                                                  Introduction
-----------------------------------------------------------------------------------------
                            Journal articles and research in
                      HUMANITIES, SOCIAL SCIENCES, EDUCATION,
                      BIOGRAPHY, ESSAY and GENERAL LITERATURE indexes

To search by:    Keyword          Type:    k=      Example:    k=    gun control
                 Author                    a=                  a=    morsink c
                 Title                     t=                  t=    whats happening in self
                 Subject                   s=                  s=    firearms--laws

Type cho and press <ENTER> to return to database selection menu.

Need more help?  Ask at the Reference Desk.


------------------------------------------------------------- Page 1 of 1 ------------------------------
                            Enter search command
                            NEWS

NEXT COMMAND:
```

Figure 2: OPAC Screens for SRU Collection and a Wilson Journal Index Database

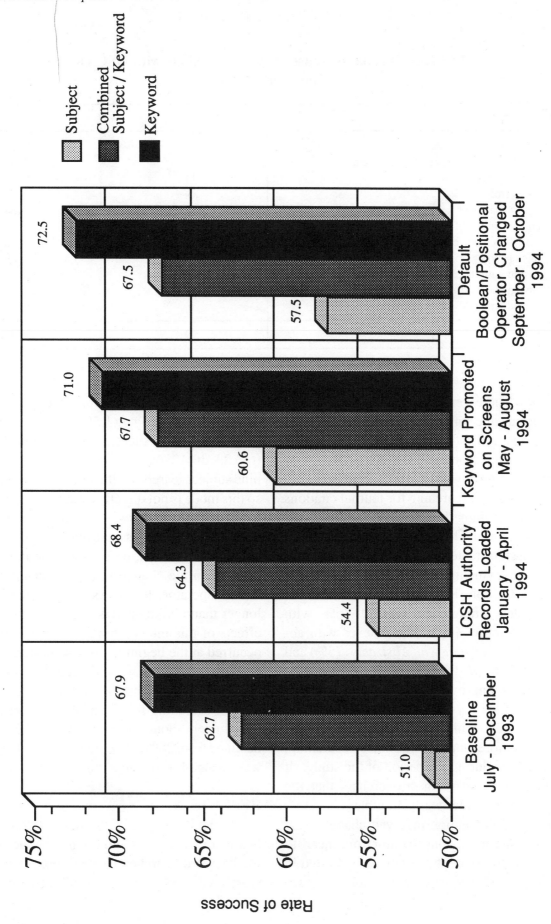

Figure 3: Success Rates of Keyword and Subject Searching

TABLE 2: Probable Causes of User Problems with OSCAR
November 1994

Error Type	Frequency	%
Item was not in database	26	44.07
Confusion about rules specific to system	5	8.47
Wrong search type was used	11	18.64
Spelling error	5	8.47
Typographical error	11	18.64
Misunderstanding of the controlled vocabulary	0	0
Person's first name entered before last	0	0
Malicious entry	1	1.69
Confusion with other OPAC commands	0	0
Confusion about structure of databases	0	0
Attempted boolean search where not possible	0	0
TOTAL	**59**	**100**

$p<0.0001$). There were 361,734 total searches (all types) during the ten months before the screen changes and 217,698 total searches in the six months after the changes.

When using keyword, patrons were generally more successful in searching for journal citations than when searching the database containing the library's holdings. This may be a result of patrons wanting current materials, more likely found in journal indexes mounted with our OPAC, than in the SRU collection. Keyword success rates in the journal indexes ranged between 69-76%, with notable differences in the two indexes with abstracts, *Reader's Guide with Abstracts* (75%) and *Business Index with Abstracts* (76%). Predictably, success rates improve with the addition of an abstract field for keyword searching.

User guides, which also described keyword searching before author/title/subject searching, were available during the period of the study. It was the perception of the researchers that the impact of these guides was negligible.

The last intervention involved changing the boolean/positional default operator from "near" to "and". This transparent intervention occurred in September 1994, and its effect was observed for only two months. Keyword success rates increased significantly by 1.5% ($t=2.51$; $df=27351$; $p<0.01$). Subject success rates dropped by 3.1% ($t=3.23$; $df=12766$; $p<0.01$). Patrons can not combine subject searches with any boolean operators, so this mode is not directly affected by the change in the default operator. It is suggested that this decrease in the success rate may have been due to incoming freshmen, unfamiliar with the system, rather than the change in the boolean/positional default operator. It is also suggested that a period longer than two months is needed to observe the effects of this intervention, especially since this occurred at the beginning of a semester.

The second "snapshot" occurred in November. Table 2 shows that the recorded failures for an hour of searching fell from 117 in March to 59. "Confusion about rules specific to the system" declined from 28% to 8% after the default operator was changed from "near" to "and".

RESULTS

At the beginning of the study it was evident that there was a substantially higher success rate for keyword searches (67.9%) than for subject searches (51.0%) ($t=19.36$; $df=21218$; $p<0.0001$)

(figure 3). As both success rates improved throughout the study this distinction continued, indicating patrons are generally more successful with keyword searches. This finding is limited by the researcher's definition of success (hits) and failure (no hits). Precision and too many hits are not addressed by this definition of success, nor did they appear to be of current concern, given the size of the SRU collection and the needs of the largely undergraduate population.

Two of the interventions significantly improved the success for both keyword and subject searching. The loading of Library of Congress Subject Headings authority records improved subject searching for monographs by 10%. The subject success rate for monographs only, at the end of the study, was 66.4%. This compares favorably to the LCSH success rates reported by Larson (51.5%),[12] Peters (48.0%)[13] and Thorne (50.7%).[14]

The greatest improvement in the success of both keyword and subject searching occurred when keyword searching was promoted on the OPAC screens. Keyword success at the end of the study, after the keyword option was placed prominently at the top of all five database menus, was 72.5%. The final combined subject/keyword success rate was 67.5%. This average was calculated by totaling all keyword and subject searches and then comparing them with all successful keyword and subject hits. Although studies are difficult to compare, do to the lack of uniformity in systems, this success rate is notable when contrasted with Peter's combined subject/keyword success rate of 54%.[15] The study by Thorne and Whitlatch would indicate a combined subject/keyword success rate of 61.9%.[16]

IMPLICATIONS

There are several implications from this study. First, the results reaffirm the importance of good authority control. The loading of LCSH authority records resulted in a marked improvement in subject searching. Second, keyword searching appears to be consistently be more successful than

subject searching, but there may be a symbiotic relationship between the two. Users might be encouraged to begin with keyword searching and refine their searches with the precision of learned (controlled) subject headings. Finally, OPAC screen designs can have substantial impact on the success of the search process. The mental model of the card catalog, however, should not drive the design of OPAC screens. Librarians need to explore creative OPAC screen designs to assist patrons in more fully exploiting online systems.

ACKNOWLEDGEMENT
The authors wish to thank Michael LeRoy for his assistance with the graphic design.

NOTES

1. Karen Markey, "Users and the Online Catalog: Subject Access Problems," in Joseph R. Matthews, ed., *Impact of Online Catalogs* (New York: Neal-Schuman, 1986).
2. Ray R. Larson, "The Decline of Subject Searching: Long Term Trends and Patterns of Index Use in an Online Catalog," *Journal of the American Society for Information Science* 42 (1991): 197-215.
3. Ray R. Larson, *Workload Characteristics and Computer System Utilization in Online Library Catalogs* (Ph.D. diss., University of California at Berkeley: University Micro-films, 1986).
4. Thomas A. Peters, *The Online Catalog: A Critical Examination of Public Use* (Jefferson, North Carolina: McFarland & Co., 1991).
5. Thomas Peters, "When Smart People Fail: An Analysis of the Transaction Log of an Online Public Access Catalog," *Journal of Academic Librarianship* (November 1989): 267-273.
6. N.C. Kranich, Christina M. Spelman, Deborah Hecht, and Gail Persky, "Evaluating the Online Catalog from a Public Services Perspective: A Case Study at the NYU Libraries," in Matthews, *Impact of Online Catalogs*: 89-117.
7. Pat Ensor, "User Characteristics of Keyword Searching Using an OPAC," *College & Research Libraries* 53 (1992): 72-80.
8. Pauline A. Cochrane, "Guest Editorial: A Paradigm Shift in Library Science," *Information Technology and Libraries* 2 (March 1983): 3-4.

9. Rosemary Thorne and Jo Bell Whitlatch, "Patron Online Catalog Success," *College & Research Libraries* 55 (1994): 479-97.

10. Charles Hildreth, "Beyond Boolean: Designing the Next Generation of Online Catalogs," *Library Trends* 35 (1987): 647-667.

11. Peters, "When Smart People Fail," 270.

12. Larson, "Workload Characteristics and Computer System Utilization in Online Catalogs," 1986.

13. Peters, "When Smart People Fail," 269.

14. Thorne, "Patron Online Catalog Success," 489.

15. Peters, "When Smart People Fail," 269.

16. Thorne, "Patron Online Catalog Success," 489.

A New Service From Libraries:
Electronic Publishing

Gail McMillan

ABSTRACT

Libraries are continuously improving traditional services but now they are also responding to stringent economic times by producing and distributing information electronically. Publishing electronic journals, distributing pre-publication abstracts, digitizing images, incorporating hyperlinks between and within documents and databases, and providing online access to local news are some of the innovative services academic libraries have begun to provide. This paper describes how one library addressed the challenges and took advantage of opportunities and readily available new technologies to meet the information needs of their future remote clients as well as their current local patrons.

Many challenges face libraries today and these challenges often provide us with the incentives to initiate innovative and sometimes experimental services. One of these effective new services available from Virginia Tech's University Libraries is the electronic production—as well as the distribution—of information. The rapidly growing number of personal computers and the increasing use of world-wide computer networks are radically influencing the range of available library services as well as the nature of academic publishing.

Faculty awareness of the growing pervasiveness of Internet connections among their colleagues on other campuses helped push many on my campus to consider publishing electronic jour-nals. An article in the April 1991 Virginia Tech faculty/staff newspaper served to alert many of us in the library to the early stages of what in hind-site has become an historical event. The article named two faculty members who were going to edit a new journal that would be published only on the Internet by an entity called the "Scholarly Communica-tions Project." Innocuous though the article may have seemed, library administrators, front-line librarians, and support staff needed no further prodding to begin planning how to provide access to this and future electronic journals. We shared a common belief that electronic journals would develop into a standard source of information to which libraries would provide access, along with, not instead of, materials in traditional formats. We

---

Gail McMillan is Director of the Scholarly Communications Project at Virginia Polytechnic Institute and State University, Blacksburg, Virginia

did not, however, anticipate that one journal published by the fledgling Scholarly Communications Project would grow so rapidly to include nine journals, three newspapers, collections of data and images, a listserv, and monographs in the form of theses and dissertations.

The Scholarly Communications Project was visualized by its founding director, Lon Savage, as an exploratory effort into new means of scholarly communications that could, among many things, reduce the costly distribution of print journals normally done through commercial publishers. Paul Gherman, then-University Librarian, felt strongly that the Project belonged in the library, that it would get librarians involved in new and expanding publishing efforts that should become an integral part of the library's mission. These benefits and other service considerations converged in an academic library to improve access to scholarly information through still-developing technology. In July 1991, the Scholarly Communications Project moved out of the broad-based Communication Network Systems unit (that is, away from hand fulls of computer experts and high powered equipment) into the University Libraries where locating and providing information and a strong service orientation has nurtured its development.

In four years, the Scholarly Communications Project has demonstrated that the libraries can perform very well as information providers through a variety of electronic publishing activities, such as:

1. Publishing a no-frills electronic-only journal that is e-mailed to subscribers as each article passes peer review (*JIAHR*)
2. Publishing full online versions of hard-copy journals (*Catalyst, JITE, JTE, JVME*)
3. Distributing abstracts through listservs (*Modal Analysis*)
4. Providing online images (still and full motion, color and black and white, with and without audio) from many sources including journal articles, experiments, and digitized special col-

lections (*JTE, JVME*, uniforms, N & W, *Spectrum, WDBJ-7*)
5. Providing access to raw research data and specialized databases (*JFE Databank, FDA Approve Drug Database*)
6. Publishing local and regional newspapers (*Roanoke Times* and *Virginian Pilot*)
7. Publishing university and library publications (*Spectrum* and *BiblioTech*)
8. Providing Internet access and word-searching of the archives of a listserv (*VPIEJ-L*)
9. Publishing theses and dissertations electronically
10. Providing electronic access to collections of library materials (*Electronic Reserve*)

As a library builds its collection of digital information through electronic publishing, it is in essence building a virtual branch library with many of the same elements and concerns of any branch. However, it can provide constant access, timely, and uninterrupted access to all of its holdings.

Another advantage of electronic publishing is the ability to reach a vastly expanded and diverse audience of readers—people who might otherwise never see the printed publication and never be exposed to the research and ideas documented in these specialized, scholarly journals. For example, the *Journal of Technology Education*, published in our remote corner of southwest Virginia for the relatively small field of teachers of technology (previously industrial arts) at the high school, college, and university levels, is regularly accessed online by people around the world. It had quite limited exposure when it was solely a quarterly, hard-copy publication relying on the postal system to deliver it into the hands of its 500 paid subscribers. However, since it has become an electronic journal, in 1993 its articles were accessed over 13,000 times and in 1994 over 29,000 times by Gopher alone.

The Scholarly Communications Project is also like a university press in that it publishes scholarly information that has been through full peer re-

About the Scholarly Communications Project

Electronic Journals

- **The Community Services CATALYST**
- **The Journal of Fluids Engineering DATABANK and related resources**
- **Journal of Industrial Teacher Education**
- **Journal of Mathematical Systems, Estimation, and Control**
- **Journal of Technology Education**
- **Journal of the International Academy of Hospitality Research**
- **Journal of Veterinary Medical Education**
- **Journal of Youth Services in Libraries**
- **Modal Analysis**

Project Collections

Digital Image Collection - from the Special Collections Department of University Libraries.
Virginia News Archive - Virginia newspapers, television broadcasts, news scripts.
Theses and Dissertations - VPI & SU Theses and Dissertations.

Other Publications

```
* FDA Approved Animal Drug Data Base      * The Virginia Tech Spectrum
* VPIEJ-L Discussion Archives             * Alternate versions of the Spectrum
* VPI & SU Theses and Dissertations       * BiblioTech
* University Libraries Electronic Reserve
```

   Copyright Statement
   Project articles, reports and software
   Usage Statistics for Scholar Web Server

Search:

When exploring this site, select Return to Scholar Home Page to return to the top level.

---

webmaster@scholar.lib.vt.edu

March 29 - April 1, 1995, Pittsburgh, Pennsylvania

view. It does not provide editorial assistance but it provides some guidance about online display and fully indexes all publications. The range of publishing services it provides includes: (1) offering editors a variety of electronic publication options, (2) offering readers and subscribers a range of electronic access options, (3) indexing and word-searchable databases, (4) hyperlinks within and between articles and publications, (5) timely access to online information, (6) constant online availability of all of its information and publications, and (7) statistical reports.

There are two principal reasons for not restricting these activities to a single electronic publishing routine. One is that electronic publishing is such a new and developing phenomenon that no one yet knows what will become the standard, or accepted, or expected means for electronically publishing scholarly works. Secondly, a small but stable staff with relatively few publications can handle a lot of varied tasks, but as our staff of 2 FTE remains constant but our publication list grows, we find ourselves relying more on automated conversion software and editor-defined access. What this means is that if an editor gives us her journal as text with HTML tags, we no longer offer to reformat files for direct Gopher access. Instead, we provide additional full-text access to such a journal with a character-based Web browser such as Lynx.

With Internet access, some interested staff, and the appropriate equipment, libraries can begin small by publishing electronic-only journals that have no frills. Encourage your editors not to delay publication until they have amassed a set number of articles or pages needed to meet a printer's requirements. Take this step away from paper publications that will lead to timely dissemination of scholarly research and demonstrate one of the true advantages of electronic publishing. We discourage our editors from restricting access and charging for subscriptions because in over four years none of our print-also electronic journals has lost any paid subscribers as a result of the publications also being freely available electronically.

Most editors of paper-based journals are still anxious to replicate printed journals because they believe that this familiarity will ease the transition from paper to screen for their current subscribers. Editors of new, electronic-only journals, however, do not have this tie to a subscriber base and are more alert to attracting subscribers by offering features that are unique to electronic journals.

When libraries begin electronically publishing existing, paper-based journals, they are generally not going to be able to retrospectively convert the entire set of back issues. The Scholarly Communications Project publishes eight journals that began as and continue to be simultaneously published in paper, and the older ones are available online only from the point at which the Project began publishing them electronically. A newer publication begun in 1989, however, the *Journal of Technology Education*, is available at any hour of any day from the first to the most current issue, because the editor required and saved all submissions on diskettes. When he read about electronic publishing opportunities available through the Scholarly Communications Project, he retrieved copies of all the diskettes as they had been prepared for the campus print shop so that they could be made available through the Internet. Important lessons have been learned from publishing each electronic journal and these we have compiled into "Guidelines for Editors of Electronic Journals." Many of these are very practical lessons that are shared with potential editors of new electronic journals. For example, each article should be separated into individual files so that readers can retrieve just the article(s) they want to read, not necessarily the entire journal. This also reduces the size of the files being accessed and, therefore, improves the time it takes to download and/or print the articles. A result of separating the components of a journal is that each part needs to include identifying information. With each article should display of the name of the journal, the issue number and/or date, and a copyright statement. Because electronic journals are not confined within covers where this information usually can be found, nor do the files of articles usually include displays of headers or footers, it takes a conscious effort to make this information a visible part of each article published electronically.

In addition to publishing full electronic journals, libraries can publish article abstracts and tables of contents. This is one way libraries can introduce a segment of their new clientele—both the journal's subscribers and its sponsors to some of the advantages of the Internet and to electronic publishing.

While libraries may be ready to publish electronic journals, many editorial and advisory boards are quite hesitant. They are afraid to "give too much away" to non-subscribers. "Too much" may include the abstracts as well as articles, so they may feel more comfortable limiting online access to the table of contents. However, most of our editors appreciate reaching a worldwide audience that will be exposed to its articles, and perhaps increase the paid subscriber list, as well as promote the goals of the sponsoring organization. As with traditional library services, our virtual branch must also be ready to meet the needs of a wide-ranging user community that includes editors and the readers of their journals as well as the virtual library's others patrons.

Some editors will bring new ideas that can help lead libraries to publishing information that might not otherwise be generally available. The editor of the *Journal of Fluids Engineering* suggested trying something unique—neither full text nor abstracts. The Project provides Internet access to the raw data upon which his authors' articles and research are based. This gives other researchers access to the same data to repeat the analysis or to use the data in other ways. In July 1994, the Project also began publishing *JFE*'s experiments in fluids engineering in the form of video clips. Project personnel digitized three short segments and scanned a still image for experimental online access. This editor also wants to create an interactive online discussion forum that validates each participant, another experiment in scholarly communications.

In addition to having ready access to faculty editors on our campuses, libraries usually also have a working relationship with academic publishers. These relationships may lead to opportunities for libraries and publishers to cooperatively publish electronic journals. We are cooperating with MIT Press to serve as an access point as well as an archival site for its first electronic journals, the *Chicago Journal of Theoretical Computer Science* and its *Journal of Functional and Logic Programming*. This means that regional subscribers may want to use the bookmark functions of their World Wide Web browsers to link to our server rather than the home server at MIT. We have also been queried by an Internet service provider notifying us that they wanted to link their users to our site. The only concern we had about this was if MIT Press expected us to monitor users to be sure they had paid their subscriptions. However, this is not our responsibility and MIT Press is allowing open and free access with readers operating on the honor system to pay for their subscriptions. Another service we will provide for the MIT Press is what we already do for all of our journal editors—report statistics about use per title from each type of access point (i.e., Gopher, World Wide Web, etc.).

The Scholarly Communications Project has discussed electronic publishing with representatives of scholarly societies and commercial publishers in the United States and Great Britain. For one publisher, the Proejct may electronically publish the peer-reviewed articles while the paper journal will contain only the article abstracts. Other journals will be printed in full on paper and the Project will publish abstracts as articles are accepted for publication or as the issue is ready for distribution as an advance notice of what subscribers can look for in the next issue. Whether these abstracts will merely be posted for impromptu retrieval and/or e-mailed to subscribers is yet to be determined but we have learned that listserv maintenance and e-mail distribution requires the active participation of the electronic journal's managing editor because resolving problems with individual e-mail address is very time consuming.

In addition to focussing on scholarly activities, libraries often provide access to information of local and regional interest. The goals of the Scholarly Communications Project call for promoting the advantages of electronic publishing for works of regional interest as well as to experiment with electronic access to scholarly information. Last fall (1994) we began experimenting with providing access to newspapers for the Blacksburg Electronic Village (BEV) as well as to improve library services. BEV is a cooperative venture with the town, the local telephone company, and the university, and among its many offerings it wanted to provide access to current issues of our regional newspaper, including the local section called the *New River Current*. The library's newspaper indexer as well as its Special Collections staff have other motives for having newspapers online, that is, to avoid current manual and labor-intensive clipping, filing, and indexing duties and potentially costly Internet access through pay-per-use services.

One of the most recent additions to the Project's list of publications is "Virginia News." Here we provide access to two daily newspapers, the *Virginian-Pilot & Ledger Star* and the *Roanoke Times & World News*. Discussions and negotiations with the parent company, Landmark Communications, began in February 1994, and by July, Project staff could dial into the newspaper's library to downloaded the daily files to the Project's server. These were marked with HTML tags and indexed before being available for public access. Today an automatic script calls the newspaper's computer in the pre-dawn hours, downloads the files, and inserts HTML tags for timely public access. Each newspaper gave us tapes of several years of back issues and we responded with quite timely availability and word indexing. The files, however, are so numerous that indexing must be batched for the weekends.

Providing access to newspapers also means working with a different client that has a stronger economic motivation than most scholarly societies that sponsor electronic journals. The newspapers' representative agreed to allow us same-day access to the most current issue of each newspaper, the archaic computer system in each newspaper's library can not yet compile the files that comprise the printed tabloid within the same day of publication. I am optimistic that a trial period, including monitoring paid subscriptions and the number of times an issue is accessed will provide preliminary evidence that electronic access will not lead to lost revenues and may increase readership among the electronic village's citizens.

As libraries experiment in each new area of electronic publication, distribution, and access, we should try not just to replicate print publications and traditional library services but to improve upon them. One way to improve information access is by linking various sources of similar information such as local and regional news. Last year two separate donations lead us to create the Virginia News link on our World Wide Web home page. In addition to the newspaper files, our local CBS-affiliated television station, WDBJ-7, offered my library their scripts, logs, and videos of news from 1950 to the present. Because of physical (not virtual) space limitations, the only way the library could accept the archive would be to convert the paper and video tapes to digital files for online storage and access. The Scholarly Communications Project agreed to digitize this tremendous source of regional and local information so that we could create a really fantastic amalgamation of news reports with hyperlinks and word-searchable files. This project is in an experimental phase—we entered a sample of the newscasters' scripts and digitized a small portion of the accompanying videos. One of the important lessons learned from this experiment is that the news clips need to be quite short or the time required to download the clip is exorbitant. It is also a good service to display the play time of the clip as well as its file size.

A service of the Scholarly Communications Project

University Libraries, Virginia Polytechnic Institute and State University

---

The Roanoke Times and
World-News

The Virginian-Pilot

WDBJ-7 Multimedia News Archive

Return to Scholar Home Page

---

webmaster@scholar.lib.vt.edu

This opportunity followed closely on another collaborative endeavor with the university's PhotoGraphic Services Unit and the library's Special Collections Department to improve access to fragile but extremely popular materials. Special Collections houses many thousands of photographs, glass slides, and negatives donated by the Norfolk and Western Railroad Corporation and others. To prepare a prototype digital collection for demonstrations, we collaborated to bring up on the World Wide Web a sample of these images. The prototype was designed to do several things. First, PhotoGraphic Services wanted to demonstrate some of the recent technology that could enable them to inexpensively produce, high-quality digital images—if they had the financial resources to buy the latest equipment. Second, Special Collections wanted to show how new technology could preserve the collections and at the same time give vastly improved access to them through the Internet. And, third, the Project welcomed the opportunity to incorporate digital images and hyperlinks (text to image, image to image) into its published information. At the Project, each high resolution image (sent by PhotoGraphic Services to Kodak for digitizing and production of a photoCD) was loaded into the Project's server and converted to an appropriate screen resolution suitable for computer displays and to fewer bytes to be transmitted across most networks at reasonable speeds.

At the same time that we began experimenting with image displays, we began taking advantage of other system and software capabilities. We drafted a form so that on- and off-campus viewers could do two things. They could request (and pay) for reproductions—from high-quality color slides and overheads for impressive presentations to less expensive black-and-white photocopies for classroom handouts. We also considered an online "comment" capability so that Tech alumni, for example, viewing our images locally or from anywhere in the world could send us messages identifying pictures that might be particularly useful for putting the images in the context of their experiences on campus and in town.

These are some of the ways to improve library resources and services and to enhance the use of the digital image databases, and to reduce the wear-and-tear on popular but fragile library materials. Another area where academic libraries can enhance their services through Internet access is by electronically publishing theses and dissertations. We are working with our Graduate School to determine the form of Internet access and the workflow. We also have a library task force that is determining how to reduce redundant data entry at each processing point. We have also created an experimental electronic library reserves collection that provides access by course number and instructor's name to course materials. Both the electronic reserve system and electronic theses and dissertations system use World Wide Web capabilities and Adobe Acrobat software to provide access to a wide variety of original file formats. Both Web browsers and the Acrobat Reader are free to those readers who have Internet access.

Libraries can also provide Internet access to internal documents and reports as a service to their staffs and well as their sister institutions. The Scholarly Communications Project has published the University Libraries' second report on policies regarding electronic journals, which is a complete revision of the 1991 document, as well as its semiannual publication, *BiblioTech*.

The Project's publications can be accessed with a World Wide Web browser at http://scholar.lib.vt.edu/ as well as with Gopher (URL:gopher://scholar.lib.vt.edu:70/) and FTP (URL:ftp://scholar.lib.vt.edu). The Scholarly Communications Project is committed to maintaining all issues of its publications online indefinitely. And, while the Project's staff has increased .5 FTE since its founding, its budget has been reduced but its activities, including but not limited to electronic publishing, have increased at least ten-fold.

University Libraries

Digital Image Collection

- 📁Browse by Subject
- 📁Browse by Collection
- 📁Browse by Icons
- ❓Search For Images and Related Materials Using VTLS
- ❓Search Image Collection Using WAIS
- 📄Submit Image Requests
- 📄Comments or Suggestions
- 📄*Copyright Statement*

 Return to Scholar Home Page

---

webmaster@scholar.lib.vt.edu

CONCLUSION

Libraries are not just buildings where information passively resides waiting to be discovered. Academic libraries are initiating innovative services such as producing and distributing information electronically. Publishing electronic journals, distributing pre-publication abstracts, storing and providing open access to digital images and raw data, and creating hypertext links between databases and among files are some of the effective new services academic libraries have successfully initiated. Taking advantage of new technology to provide innovative services is not, necessarily, to have found *The Way*. The library and the Scholarly Communications Project at Virginia Tech are experimenting as part of the (r)evolution—trying different approaches (systems, formats, platforms) and weeding out the ones that do not work as well as those that do. All of this and more has been accomplished without demanding more from the library's budget, by working with the ever-developing expertise of in-house library personnel, and by collaborating with our university community and others who have an interest in the academy and improved library services.

Mainstreaming Electronic Numeric Data Files:

The Impact on Technical Services

Marijo S. Wilson

ABSTRACT

The explosive growth of electronic information systems has yielded both the capability and the necessity of providing enhanced access to all forms of information, including non-bibliographic forms such as numeric data. The Albert R. Mann Library at Cornell University has actively pursued the development of user-friendly online systems for accessing numeric data. This paper describes the development of two of these systems, concentrating on the participation of Technical Services staff. While this activity falls within the scope of traditional Technical Services responsibilities of acquiring, describing and organizing information, the processing of electronic resources requires that new skills be developed.

Technical services librarians have long embraced automation as a means of expediting their work. That work can be rather simplistically summarized as the identification, acquisition, description and organization of information for easy access and retrieval. In the not too distant past information referred primarily to printed materials, e.g. books and journals. The explosive growth of electronic information systems has yielded both the capability and the necessity of providing enhanced access to all forms of information, including non-bibliographic forms such as numeric data. The Albert R. Mann Library at Cornell University has actively pursued the development of user-friendly online systems for the identification, description, retrieval and manipulation of numeric datasets. This paper describes the development of two of these systems, concentrating on the participation of Cataloging and other Technical Services staff and what was learned from the experience. Staff in all divisions of the library have been involved in these projects, progressing from an "Interactive Numeric Files Retrieval System" (INFeRS), designed and created in-house using relational database management software, to a Gopher server created to provide Internet access to

Marijo S. Wilson is an Associate Librarian, Cataloging Services at Albert R. Mann Library, Cornell University, Ithaca, New York.

data sets produced by the Economic Research Service and the National Agricultural Statistics Service of the United States Department of Agriculture.

The first project, dubbed INFeRS and begun in 1989, was an early attempt to evolve beyond Mann Library's previous experience with a data archives service. As described by Chiang et al.[1] the goal of INFeRS was to provide the end-user of statistical data with online, interactive access via their personal workstation and the campus network to selected datasets in the biological and agricultural sciences. The INFeRS interface would simplify the process of extracting subsets of data from large files, eliminating the need for user programming skills or an intermediary, such as a data archives technical consultant or librarian. This was accomplished by creating a windowed menuing system that led the user first through an explanation of the system, its use and resident data resources, followed by a series of menus and selection windows for the formulation of search criteria and selection of output format. The project relied on a relational database management software package, Informix, running on a minicomputer and a project team that included the computer files librarian, an interface design specialist, a programmer/systems analyst, a statistician and a cataloger. The cataloger was drafted from Technical Services to address data and database relationship questions, including inter- and intra- data file issues, the codification of data and the idea of exerting authority control over numeric files. In its final form two databases, the USDA County Crops Estimates and the National Resources Inventory, were successfully loaded on INFeRS and made available to the Cornell campus through the Mann Library Gateway information system which provides online access to electronic information resources. Users were able to customize their data output to suit their needs by defining their search strategy with specific variables (e.g. acreage planted and bushels of sweet corn produced in Tompkins and Erie County, New York in 1986). A subject index was compiled primarily to assist users who were unfamiliar with the subject content or variables of the two databases. The cataloger constructed this index by analyzing the codebooks for subject or concept keywords that appeared in field names or field descriptions. All relevant fields were listed under each keyword. References from alternate forms of keywords were provided and where possible the same terminology was used for both databases. Since catalogers are used to working with an existing indexing language (e.g. Library of Congress Subject Headings) rather than creating their own, the indexing of the numeric data files proved to be an interesting challenge and indicated an area worthy of more study. While INFeRS drew primarily on traditional cataloging skills, echoing Geraci and Langschied's[2] conclusion that "many traditional librarian skills are transferable ones in the data arena," it also highlighted the need, as noted by McCue[3], for Technical Services to "reengineer and retool." Exposure to database maanagement issues and interaction with an interface designer and programmer throughout the project reinforced Graham's[4] observation that "the role of technical services [in the electronic information explosion] is to become more technologically adept."

The final report on INFeRS was issued in 1991, coincidently the same year the Microcomputer Center at the University of Minnesota designed the Internet Gopher Protocol. This is a client-server protocol that facilitates world-wide access to Gopher and other information servers as well as providing the means for constructing a distributed information delivery system. Gopher has become extremely popular as a resource discovery tool, but Mann Library's interests lay in using it as a numeric data delivery system to replace the INFeRS model. Mann's first Gopher servers[5] were initiated by the Numeric Files Librarian of the Public Services Division and mounted on the Mann Library Gateway. The first Gopher application, "User Guides and Help", instructs users on the use of the Gateway resources, while the second Gopher provides access to selected New York State data from the 1990 Census of

Population and Housing. The third Gopher server grew out of common desire of Mann Library and the U.S. Department of Agriculture to provide Internet access to USDA's Economic Research Service (ERS) and National Agricultural Statistics Service (NASS) datafiles of domestic and international agricultural statistics. The resulting Gopher provides researchers around the world with desktop access to 160 datasets consisting mainly of statistical data (requiring the use of common spreadsheet software such as Lotus 1-2-3 or Excel), with a small complement of text files and software programs. The files are accessible through three Internet protocols, Gopher, Telnet and FTP, although Gopher access is recommended for its ease in downloading files. The USDA Economics and Statistics Gopher server is registered with the Mother of Gophers at the University of Minnesota to allow subject searching on menu items via Veronica. WAIS indexing also is provided for searching keywords in the README documents of all the ERS/NASS files.

With the aim of mainstreaming the processing of electronic numeric datafiles, staff from the Technical Services Division, in cooperation with the Numeric Files Librarian and the library's Information Technology Section, were involved in construction of the USDA Gopher. Technical Services activities were divided amongst the Government Information Librarian and the Serials Records Specialist in the Acquisitions Department and, in the Cataloging Department, the Catalog Librarian who had been involved in the INFeRS Project. Acquisitions staff are responsible for the traditional activities of receiving the datafiles in the form of 3.5" diskettes, check-in, and creation of an acquisitions record for the OPAC. Beyond this the Serials Records Specialist has developed the skills necessary to access the datafiles, upload the files to the Gopher server on Mann's minicomputer and remove superseded files. The Catalog Librarian analyses the README file and determines the content of each file. Using UNIX, the cataloger makes the directories and subdirectories to accomodate the datafiles, composes the menus for

the Gopher and updates the "What's New" file. Each datafile also is fully cataloged on the local NOTIS system and these records eventually will be uploaded to the RLIN database.

Since making the Gopher available to the general public in December 1993 it has received enthusiastic use (averaging 1012 logons per week through the first quarter of 1994) and the feedback from the USDA has been extremely positive.

The experience of mainstreaming the ERS/NASS datafiles has on the whole been a very positive one for Technical Services as well. While this activity falls within the scope of the traditional Technical Service responsibilities of acquiring, describing and organizing information, the process of making electronic resources accessible required that new skills be developed. These included use of UNIX programming commands, file transfer protocols, EMACS text editing, writing script shells, WAIS indexing, and basic knowledge of the Internet Gopher Protocol. It also required that staff learn new ways to look at information and how it is structured. Given the strong search capabilities provided by Veronica and WAIS it was not necessary to build an extensive subject index as was done for INFeRS. It was, however, necessary to closely examine how USDA was presenting the datafiles and how users (especially experienced users familiar with the files) would expect to find them. In essence the basic organization of the Gopher was dictated by the USDA's catalog of ERS/NASS electronic data products which uses eleven broad subject categories (e.g. crops, farm sector economics, food, etc.); the USDA Gopher's main menu utilizes the same categories. The USDA catalog was also useful in determining the commonly used title for some of the datasets since the README files and the diskettes were generally inconsistent. Organization of the directories and subdirectories beyond the main menu required close analysis of the README file for each dataset to determine any inherently useful way of organizing the menu display, especially in view of its serving as the basis for Veronica searches. Care was taken to

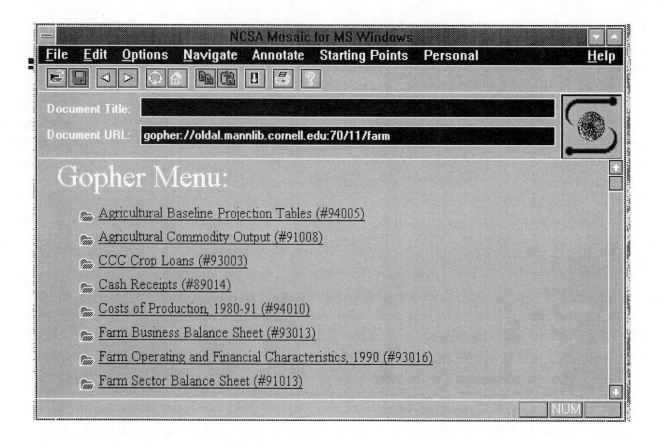

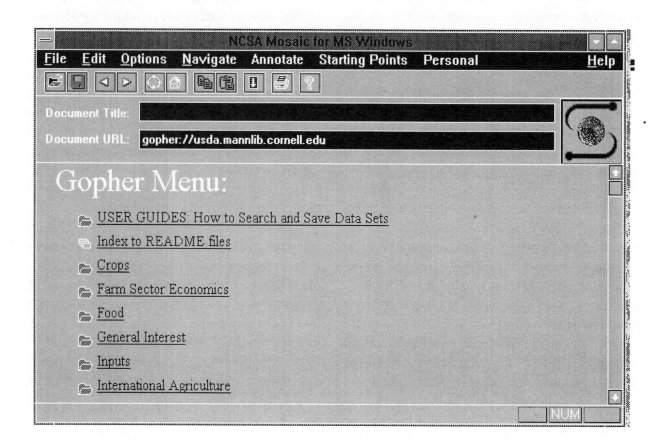

keep the Gopher's hierarchical menu structure as compact, uncluttered and direct as possible. The staff's technical education on how to provide access to electronic datafiles is by no means complete. Increasing staff involvement with systems like the USDA Gopher instills greater enthusiasm for exploring new ways of achieving improved information access for the end-user.

In addition to developing new technical skills, old skills had to be updated. A goal of mainstreaming electronic resources was to make them an integral part of the library's collection. This meant formulating bibliographic records for the datasets that would be accessible through the Cornell University Library OPAC and RLIN. Since the majority of the ERS/NASS titles are serial in nature, a Catalog Librarian responsible for serials cataloging was drafted to devise a template on which to base the bibliogreaphic record for each of the ERS/NASS datasets. This template includes a 956 field which is the local implementation (for OPAC display purposes) of the proposed USMARC 856 field for "Electronic Location and Access". The 856 field is intended to provide the information necessary to locate and access an electronic item, particularly Internet resources. Use of this field required a decision on how the library's electronic resources should appear in the OPAC and how their electronic location should be described for access by both local and remote users.

Much of the recent literature has shifted focus from how to simply find resources on the Internet to how to catalog its myriad electronic resources to facilitate that process. McCombs[6] encourages technical services librarians to explore the Internet and to frame new ways and means for supporting electronic resources. The two projects outlined here suggest a broader role for technical services staff in organizing and maintaining the information systems that comprise the Internet. As libraries begin mounting their own resources through Gopher and World Wide Web servers, catalogers should be ready to contribute their knowledge of organizational information structures to the design and creation of usable electronic resources.

NOTES

1. Katherine Chiang and others, "Beyond the Data Archive: The Creation of an Interactive Numeric File Retrieval System," *Library Hi Tech* 11, no. 3: 57-72 (1993).
2. Diane Geraci and Linda Langschied, "Mainstreaming Data: Challenges to Libraries," *Information Technology and Libraries* 11, no. 1:10-18 (1992).
3. Janet McCue, "Technical Services and the Electronic Library: Defining Our Roles and and Divining the Partnership," *Library Hi Tech* 12, no. 3: 63-70 (1994).
4. Peter S . Graham, "Electronic Information and Research Library Technical Services," *College & Research Libraries* 51, no. 3: 241-250 (1990).
5. Oya Rieger, "Organizing Information on the Internet: Sample Gopher Servers," in *NIT '93: 6th International Conference, New Information Technology: Proceedings, San Juan, Puerto Rico, Novenber 1988*, ed. Ching-chih Chen (West Newton, Mass.: MicroUse Information, 1993), p. 289-303.
6. Gillian M. McCombs, "The Internet and Technical Services: A Point Break Approach," *Library Resources & Technical Services* 38:169-177 (1994).

Gopher as a Reference Tool:
Organization and Use

Dena Hutto, Helen Sheehy, and Lynne Stuart

ABSTRACT

Gophers have made the expanding world of the Internet accessible and even convenient for librarians - but are they easy enough to explain at the reference desk? Are they reliable enough to be used as a standard resource? Do they answer real reference questions? Our answer is yes. Late-breaking news stories, statistics, and government policies are only a few of the full text, searchable electronic resources available through a computer and network connection. As librarians who work with general reference sources and government documents, we will present a case study of how we have integrated gopher as a reference tool into our library's services. Because gopher sites change rapidly, we organized our "electronic bookshelf" menu as a logical starting point for searching gophers. We introduced basic skills in staff training sessions and divided up subject areas for independent exploration. Through these experiences we've become proficient in using gophers to answer real reference questions. A sense of adventure is essential to using gophers effectively, and we find it easy to share our enthusiasm with students and faculty. Once our users have seen a librarian find the answer to their questions on a gopher, they are excited about connecting with the Internet on their own.

INTRODUCTION

At this point in the Internet's development, gopher client/servers offer the easiest and most universally accessible method of navigating the Internet. At a time when many are computing with less than state-of-the-art equipment, anyone who has the ability to Telnet to a public gopher client can tap into gopher resources. Gophers, with their transparent, menu-driven interface and a few easy-to-understand commands, enable computer novices to locate and use thousands of computer sites worldwide. Mark McCahill, a manager in the Computer Services Department at the University of Minnesota and developer of the first gopher client/server, has explained: "Gopher came out around when the techie elite of the Internet started realizing that there was no way to train everyone in the arcana of anonymous FTP, and the tools that

Dena Hutto is a Documents Librarian/Cataloger, Helen Sheehy is an International Documents Librarian, and Lynne Stuart a General Reference/Documents Librarian at Pattee Library, Pennsylvania State University, University Park, Pennsylvania.

```
┌─────────────────────────────────────────────────────────┐
│            The Electronic Bookshelf (this way to our Gopher)         │
│                                                                       │
│  >    1.   SEARCH all the gophers everywhere by keyword/              │
│            ************************************************           │
│       3.   Electronic Books and Texts/                               │
│       4.   Government, Politics, and Law Shelf/                       │
│       5.   Periodicals Shelf (Check SUBJECT SHELF for more journals)/ │
│       6.   Reference Shelf/                                           │
│       7.   Special Collections Shelf/                                 │
│       8.   Subject Shelf (Check PERIODICALS SHELF for more journals)/ │
│            ************************************************           │
│      10.   Penn State Information Shelf/                              │
│      11.   University Libraries Information Shelf/                    │
│      12.   INTERNAL USE ONLY/                                        │
│            ************************************************           │
│                                                                       │
│      Resources found in this gopher are directly based on other      │
│      collections like Gopher Jewels, Riceinfo, and NCSU as well       │
│      as original contributions from Penn State librarians.           │
└─────────────────────────────────────────────────────────┘
```

Figure 1: The Electronic Bookshelf

are easy for computer nerds to use aren't easy enough for everyone else."[1]

Since gopher was developed in 1991, an estimated 2,600 sites have sprung into existence.[2] Many academic institutions have established one gopher/client server, and many large universities have several. At Penn State University there is a parent university-wide gopher. Several colleges, including the University Libraries, have established their own gopher sites. The Libraries' gopher, the "Electronic Bookshelf," was created by a team of four librarians working with programmers in Library Computing Services. They began work in 1992 and by early Spring 1993, the Bookshelf, with initial links to major Internet resources, was a menu item on LIAS, our online catalogue and gateway system. (See figure 1)

In this paper, we will discuss how Penn State's documents section participates in the selection of gopher resources and how we have integrated gopher into our services as a reference tool. We will discuss how this new technology was introduced to the documents reference staff and how

we organized a government information directory on the Libraries' gopher to meet our reference needs. Lastly, we will share examples off how gopher has been used to answer questions at the documents reference desk.

CREATING A NEW REFERENCE TOOL

Identifying gopher resources for inclusion on the Electronic Bookshelf is an ongoing process that is considered an integral part of a librarians' collection development responsibilities. Subject specialists are expected to regularly survey Internet resources and recommend materials for inclusion on the gopher. To facilitate the development of gopher resources, the Gopher Team, working with the Libraries' collection development coordinator, has developed a "Selector Resources" directory. This directory includes files that provide guidelines for the selection of materials, a description of what should be included in a gopher file, and an explanation of the kind of information the Gopher Team needs in order to establish links to gopher resources. In addition, this shelf contains

Selector Resources

1. README first
2. Go To Any Gopher Anywhere (specify address) <?>
3. SEARCH Gopherspace by Keyword/

***** Penn State Libraries Selector Information *****
6. American Geophysical Union et al vs. Texaco, Inc./
7. Collection Development Specialists [19-Nov-1993]
8. Criteria for Evaluating Gopher Resources (PSU)
9. Gopher Activities for the Selector (PSU)
10. University Libraries Gopher Policy

***** Other Gopher Collections To Examine *****
13. Clearinghouse of Subject-Oriented Guides (U-Mich)/
14. Eurogopher Subject Tree/
15. Gopher Jewels (by subject)
16. Study Carrels from NCSU (by subject)/
17. Subject Information (Rice University)/
18. The LC Global Electronic Library (by subject)/

Figure 2: Selector Resources Shelf

links to major gopher holes such as Gopher Jewels, the Eurogopher Subject Tree, and the LC Global Electronic Library. (See figure 2)

After attending a library-wide orientation to gopher resources, the documents librarians began exploring the gopher and quickly realized its reference potential. We then began planning for integration of gopher resources into routine reference service.

Faculty and students who experimented with the Electronic Bookshelf responded positively to gopher for several reasons.

- **Ease of Use.** The arrangement of information in logical categories allowed users to browse and locate information. Finding and downloading all kinds of electronic documents was no longer an arduous task that required searching through documentation about remote logins and anonymous File Transfer Protocol (FTP).
- **Timely information**. Patrons were excited about the currency of the information that they found. Materials that were slow to appear in paper format were now quickly available.

- **Keyword searchability.** Patrons liked being able to search by keyword in individual documents or using the searching tools Veronica and Jughead to explore directories or files anywhere on the Internet, without learning complicated search protocols.
- **Remote Access.** Once they were introduced to basic gopher searching and had located useful files or directories with help from reference librarians, our patrons were able to search for and use these resources at their convenience from offices, homes, or student computer labs.

The demand for Internet resources has dramatically increased during the last year. Requests from faculty to introduce students to the Internet are also increasing. Gopher has allowed us to introduce the Internet to many more students and faculty than would be possible if we needed to teach the intricacies of Archie and FTP.

While there are many advantages to using the gopher, there are also disadvantages which must be acknowledged.

- **Response time.** Since our ability to connect to and retrieve material from the Internet is directly related to the amount of Internet traffic — and traffic is rapidly increasing[3] — it can be difficult to demonstrate and use the gopher. Demand on our own system is sometimes so heavy that users are shut out during peak times.
- **Gopher sites change rapidly.** Gopher resources can change or disappear without warning, leaving users and librarians frustrated. As gopher administrators at remote sites revise directory structures, links disappear. Sometimes entire documents disappear when gopher administrators decide that they are no longer valuable. This phenomenon has serious implications for the long term research needs of the academic community.
- **Quality of Information.** Despite the wealth of useful information on the Internet there is much of questionable value. This has implications for collection development and for teaching critical evaluation skills to students who often suffer from the "if it comes from a computer it must be accurate" syndrome.
- **Staff time.** Becoming familiar with the vast resources of the Internet requires a substantial investment of staff time. Library administrators must be supportive of this investment.

Despite these drawbacks, we believe that the advantages of using gopher outweigh the disadvantages. A revolution is taking place in the way governments disseminate information to the public. At the federal level, the Clinton administration has encouraged agencies to place more and more material on the Internet. In the past year, state and local governments have begun to add legislative and other materials to the Internet. International bodies such as the United Nations and NATO distribute press releases and other documents on the Internet. Foreign Governments, including Canada, France, and Israel, distribute much of their information via the Internet. Even commercial services such as Legi-slate and Congressional Quarterly are creating their own gophers. By the time our Electronic Bookshelf was available, it was clear that it would be a disservice to our library users if we did not incorporate Internet resources into our collections and reference services.

EDUCATING AND INVOLVING STAFF

The Penn State University Libraries is a depository for United States, Pennsylvania, Canada, and European Union government publications which are located in the Libraries' documents section. The collection includes documents of local governments, the United Nations and other international organizations, and foreign countries. The documents staff provides reference service for all of these collections as well as legal and political science materials. These materials are used by faculty and students who are looking for directory information, grants and research reports, census data, press releases, court decisions, and more. The collection in its paper, microfiche, microfilm, and electronic formats, supports this varied reference work but we are not always able to fulfill time-sensitive information needs.

At the documents reference desk, we wanted as many of our staff, from full-time librarians to part-timers who work primarily nights and weekends, to be able to use gopher as they would any other type of resource in our collection. In order to achieve this goal, everyone who worked at the reference desk needed to be able to connect to the gopher, use basic gopher searching tools, and demonstrate gopher use to students and faculty. They needed to be familiar with the kinds of information resources that can be found on gopher and to judge where this new tool fits into a given reference query. Lastly, they needed to know how to search gopherspace for a particular reference source.

We used two strategies to build our staff's comfort level with gopher resources and searching techniques. First, we held a training session on gopher basics for the entire staff. One librarian experienced in gopher use at the reference desk explained what gopher is, how it developed and is

```
               Government, Politics, and Law Shelf

     1.    Current Topics/
           *******************************************
     3.    International Organizations Information/
     4.    Foreign Country Information/
           *******************************************
     6.    US Information/
     7.    State and Local Information/
           *******************************************
     9.    Gateway Information (Other Government BBS and Databases)/
    10.    Legal Information/
    11.    Reference Information/
```

Figure 3: Government, Politics, and Law Shelf

developing, and its basic system features and commands. She demonstrated several specific databases and files that are used at our reference desk. The staff, which has learned many new technologies in the last few years, was quick to see gopher's advantages. Navigating the menu-driven gopher is much easier than using some other electronic resources in documents reference work.

Our second strategy was to involve the staff in hands-on gopher use. Staff needed practice in using the gopher, and librarians needed help in searching through gopherspace for possible reference materials. To help everyone get started, we compiled a list of government agencies and other subject areas covered by our collection. Each staff member chose two or three agencies or topics to explore and located gopher directories, documents, and databases that everyone working at the documents reference desk should know. As we located resources, we passed along gopher address information to our coordinator.

ORGANIZING THE GOVERNMENT, POLITICS, AND LAW GOPHER SHELF

Having compiled a lengthy list of resources, we needed a way of keeping track of what they were and where they were located. We decided to use the gopher itself by creating a "Government, Politics, and Law Shelf." On this shelf a single screen gives a quick and logical overview of the selected resources. (See figure 3)

Next, we made decisions about the organization of directories on the Government, Politics, and Law Shelf. The first question was whether we should think like documents librarians and arrange government information on the gopher in the same way that our traditional documents collection is organized — by the source of information, such as the government agency or international organization that had issued the material. The alternative was to break out of the documents mold and organize information by subject, as other areas of the library organize their collections.

After some discussion, we decided that the Government, Politics, and Law Shelf, like the documents collection, should be organized by source of information. As documents librarians we often approach a question by first determining what agency would be the most likely candidate to produce the needed information. Organizing the shelf by information source would help us integrate gopher resources into the basic search strategy we use in documents reference service. We created four directory names that correspond to parts of the documents collection: "U.S. Information," "State and Local Information," "International Organizations Information," and "Foreign Country Information." Because Penn State's law collection is served by the documents reference desk, we also included a directory called "Legal Information."

Our decision to use the organizational approach on the Government, Politics, and Law Shelf does not mean that we oppose a subject approach to government information whenever possible. Happily, in organizing gopher resources, we are able to have it both ways. Location is simply a matter of programming address information into one or more directories. For example, NASA Spacelink can be found on the Government, Politics, and Law Shelf under "U.S. Information" and on the Subject Shelf under "Astronomy and Astrophysics."

These primary information directories provide a logical framework for the Government, Politics, and Law Shelf, but they require us to go through several levels of gopher directories to find commonly-used sources. Just as our reference desk has its own "ready reference" collection, we wanted our gopher shelf to have directories set aside for the most used and frequently consulted information sources. This way, our favorite sources would always be one directory level away from the introductory screen.

We established three additional directories for materials that require quick access: "Reference Information," "Current Topics," and "Gateway Information." The Reference Information Shelf includes frequently consulted sources such as Congressional directory information and telephone "books" for government agencies. Current Topics contains government policy documents that have been in the news, such as Clinton's Health Care Reform proposal and the NAFTA Free Trade Agreement. The Gateway Information directory provides a shortcut to gopher sites and other online systems such as the National Technical Information Service's FedWorld and the Library of Congress's LC Marvel.

With all these decisions made, our next step was to meet with a representative of the Libraries' Gopher Team. (Since this time, because of the explosion of government information available on gophers, one member of the documents staff has been added to the gopher team and a second person will soon join.) This librarian assured us that programming the additions and changes would be a simple matter. Within two weeks the Government, Politics, and Law Shelf structure was in place on the Electronic Bookshelf. The entire organization process was completed in about six weeks, from mid October to November 1993. The ongoing process of expanding gopher resources has been a cooperative effort among librarians and staff members who routinely forward information on new gopher sites to our Gopher Team representative.

GOPHER REFERENCE IN ACTION

At this writing, the documents section has had eight months of experience in using gopher at our reference desk. Here are a few of the questions that we have answered:

- A faculty member from the College of Human Development had unsuccessfully searched for the address and phone number of a new staff member at the National Institutes of Health. We were able to locate an up-to-date directory entry for this person using the National Institutes of Health Gopher. She was amazed that we were able to find this information so quickly and pleased to learn that she could perform

```
                        NIH Gopher

        1.    Announcements [November 21, 1994]
        2.    About This and other Gophers at NIH/
        3.    Health and Clinical Information/
        4.    Grants and Research Information/
        5.    Molecular Biology Databases/
        6.    Library and Literature Sources/
        7.    NIH Campus Info/
        8.    NIH Computer and Network Information /
        9.    Weather and Area Information/
        10.   Gopher Tunnels (To Other Gopher and WAIS Sites)/
        11.   E-mail and Directory Services/
        12.   Search NIH Phone Book <?>
        13.   Search Menus at this Gopher Site by Keyword <?>
```

Figure 4: NIH Gopher

similar searches from her office computer. (See figure 4)

- Graduate students and faculty frequently ask questions about National Science Foundation grants. Who has received a given type of grant? What were the specifications in a particular grant application? It's difficult to acquire documents containing this information through the Depository Library Program, but try using the "Index to NSF Award Abstracts" on the gopher. A keyword search on "archaeology," for example, produces fifteen screens of successful grant abstracts in this area. Once our patrons have been shown how to find the Index, they are able to track grant proposals on their own. (See figure 5)

- While Penn State's documents collection is extensive, printed documents can never be current enough to satisfy all our patrons' needs. Within hours of the signing of the GATT Treaty in December 1993, we had requests for copies. We immediately found and loaded on our gopher the official thirty-page summary of

the GATT Treaty released by the Commerce Department and had its gopher location linked to our Government, Politics, and Law Shelf. Within a week the full text of GATT — all 2,000 pages — was available on the gopher. (See figure 6)

- Every semester, students from Penn State's required writing courses and speech classes come to the library seeking background material and statistics for short papers and speeches. Government agencies are beginning to release information circulars on the Internet using gopher. For example, "Bureau of Justice Statistics Documents," a directory one the Department of Justice Gopher, lists dozens of reports on high-interest topics such as capital punishment, rape, and mandatory sentencing. The documents are concise and give basic statistical information. We receive this series of documents in print through the Depository Library Program, but they are so popular that they are often checked out during the semester. The gopher serves as a reliable back-up for

Federal Grants and Funding Opportunities

*** FOR ADDITIONAL INFORMATION SEE INDIVIDUAL AGENCIES ***
****

3.   Commerce Business Daily (via CBD in Internet)/
4.   Catalog of Federal Domestic Assistance/
     ****
6.   Agriculture Dept: CRIS - Current Research Information System <?>
7.   EPA: Information about Grants, Contracts (RFPs), and Financing/
8.   Education Dept: ED Board -- Grants and Contract Bulletin Board/
9.   Education Dept: Library Services for Indian Tribes - LCSA IV/
10. Federal Information Exchange (FEDIX)/
11. GrantSource (SM) -- via University of North Carolina/
12. HUD: Partnerships Against Violence--Funding Sources/
13. NCJRS: Criminal Justice Funding Opportunities and Program Initiati../
14. NIEHS: Research Grants and Contracts/
15. NIH: Grants and Research Information/
16. NSF: Index to NSF Award Abstracts/
17. NSF: National Science Foundation Gopher/
18. National Technology Transfer Center (Business Gold) <TEL>

Figure 5: Federal Grants and Funding Shelf

December 15, 1993

MEMORANDUM FOR THE UNITED STATES TRADE REPRESENTATIVE

SUBJECT: Trade Agreements Resulting from the Uruguay Round of
                Multilateral Trade Negotiations

I have today sent the atteached letters to the Speaker of the U.S.
House of Representatives and the President of the Senate.

You are authorized and directed to publish this memorandum and
its attachments in the Federal Register.

Figure 6: Text of GATT Executive Summary and Transmittal Letter

```
┌─────────────────────────────────────────────────────────────────┐
│  DoJ Full-text Reports on U.S. Crime (NESE 1994, Via U. M. St. Louis) │
│                                                                   │
│   1.   *** Via the University of Missouri-St. Louis ***           │
│   2.   Program Description                                        │
│   3.   Crime in the Nation's Households, 1991                     │
│   4.   Patterns of Robbery & Burglary in Nine States, 1984-88     │
│   5.   Crime Victimization in City, Suburbaan & Rural Areas       │
│   6.   Elderly Victims, 1993                                      │
│   7.   Elderly Victims, 1992                                      │
│   8.   Murder in Large Urban Counties, 1988                       │
│   9.   Press Release: Violence Against Women                      │
│  10.   Women in Prison                                            │
│  11.   Female Victims of Violent Crimes                           │
│  12.   School Crime                                               │
│  13.   Census of State and Local Law Enforcement Agencies, 1992   │
│  14.   Prosecuting Criminal Enterprises: Federal Offenses and     │
│  15.   The Costs of Crime to Victims: Crime Data Brief            │
│  16.   Carjacking: National Crime Victimization Survey            │
│  17.   Telephone Contacts '94                                     │
│  18.   Crime and Neighborhoods                                    │
└─────────────────────────────────────────────────────────────────┘
```

Figure 7: Department of Justice Documents

those students who didn't get to the library first. (See figure 7)

THE FUTURE OF GOPHER REFERENCE

We began this discussion by stating that gopher is the easiest-to-use tool for navigating the Internet — but the Internet environment changes rapidly. Gopher is only one of many "navigation tools" that make it possible to use Internet resources for reference transactions. Will other navigation tools overtake gopher in popularity and ease of use? Already there is the World Wide Web (WWW). For the moment, gopher offers far more resources, and WWW requires more sophisticated computer software and hardware than we currently offer at most public workstations in the Penn State University libraries. However, as more students gain access to the Internet from remote sites and as the library upgrades equipment, it is likely that the WWW will become a standard reference desk tool. We already include connections to some WWW sites running the Lynx browser on our gopher menus. Penn State's Center for Academic Computing has developed a homepage, and plans are in place to begin development of a Libraries' homepage for the WWW. Both the Lynx browser and Mosaic will be used. The Lynx browser will be available where the equipment will support only text files. Mosaic, which supports sound, color, and images will be available to those with more sophisticated equipment, including many reference desks.

For now, we can only be sure that new generations of Internet navigation tools are coming, and that they will continue to simplify the problem of locating and using Internet resources. As new tools, arrive we will need to integrate these technologies into our reference service as well. While, gopher as a reference tool will become outdated sooner or later, electronic sources on the Internet will continue to play a role in our libraries. The approaches we used in integrating gopher into our reference services will continue to be of use as we learn to utilize future navigation tools.

NOTES

1. James Crawley, "Useful Gophers Proliferating Like Rabbits," *San Diego Union-Tribune*, (1 February 1994) Computer Link Section, p. 6.

2. Ibid.

3. David S. Jackson and Samuel Ratan, "The Battle for the Soul of the Internet," *Time* 144 (25 July 1994) p. 50-56.

The Impact of the Internet on the Scholarly Research Process in the Social Sciences and Humanities

Vivienne Monty and P. Warren-Wenk

ABSTRACT

The penetration of the Internet into the scholarly research process will introduce some fundamental changes into the way in which research is conducted and disseminated in the social sciences and humanities. More than simply grafting traditional research techniques into the electronic arena, Internet users can revise methodologies and chart practices appropriate for a new medium. In this paper, the authors deconstruct the traditional steps of the research process in the social sciences and humanities - from gathering data and conducting surveys to writing and publishing results - and propose ways in which the process must evolve in order to make better use of electronic forums. The authors report on faculty use of electronic journals, discussion groups, and other Internet tools, and share insights on the evolution of the research process and the changing cycle of scholarly communication.

INTRODUCTION

The Internet has gradually come to play a role of undeniable importance on the university campus, drawing converts from across the spectrum and, as it gains credibility, becoming a new symbol of proficiency in academic circles. Long an important tool for those in the computer and hard sciences, the Internet has the potential to change the way research is conducted in the social sciences and humanities. To what extent are scholars in these disciplines using the Internet as a research tool to supplement or replace traditional tools? Is the research process itself undergoing a fundamental and radical evolution as researchers gradually incorporate the Internet into the process of scholarly investigation?

Vivienne Monty is Senior Librarian and P. Warren-Wenk is an academic reference librarian in the social sciences and humanities at York University Libraries, Toronto, Canada.

Methodology: To gauge how scholars were using the Internet in their research, social scientists and humanists, who were known to be avid Internet users, were contacted. In spring 1994, a series of interviews were conducted with faculty at dozens of universities and institutes in Canada and the United States, using a list of pre-established questions to interview users by telephone, in person, and via e-mail. (These discussions invariably veered from the set questions into myriad issues regarding the Internet's role and potential). We gathered examples of specific uses and projects, contacted editors of e-journals and moderators of discussion groups, and posted inquiries to the memberships of two LIST-SERVs: P.O.R. (public opinion researchers), and METHODS (a group discussing research methodologies). We also engaged in a little 'virtual voyeurism' for the purposes of case study, subscribing to the e-journal PSYCHOLOQUY to see how scholarly communication takes place in that venue. From the data gathered, we distilled themes, issues, and questions for the future, and share with you a preliminary analysis of the impact of the Internet on the research process.

PATTERNS OF INTERNET USE BY SOCIAL SCIENTISTS AND HUMANISTS

E-mail was the only Internet function used, without exception, by all respondents. It has four uses as a research tool. First, it serves to generate links with other researchers and to identify information on products, papers, or potential collaborators.[1] Thus, e-mail acts as a nexus, joining people or information relating to the research activity. Second, e-mail facilitates trouble-shooting by allowing researchers to ask questions or seek help. Third, e-mail plays a crucial role in project administration, enabling remote teams to work in tandem on large projects. E-mail functions as an agent of democratization, providing a forum where explorers of all stripes share equal access to each other by virtue of their joint participation in the Internet world.

The next most frequently used function was **discussion groups**. These were used to monitor developments within an area or on a specific topic. Scholars working at smaller institutions, far from colleagues with similar interests, found discussion groups especially critical for exchanges. Those involved in multidisciplinary work cited them as a ready means of gathering information from adjunct fields. Discussion groups also perform an important role in preliminary scholarly criticism during the early stages of a research project, as investigators could test a new idea or do a larger than usual pilot run before venturing more deeply into a project. The practice of vetting a project in its early stages before a large audience in an informal setting adds an extra step to the research process, and constitutes a modification of the traditional cycle of scholarly investigation.

Of those respondents professing to use **e-journals** regularly, most employed them as a device to monitor developments in a field, much as they used discussion groups. However, discussion groups were considered to be a **new** forum for scholarly discussion, whereas e-journals supplemented, but did not replace, print journals. Several issues arise here. The primary contribution of e-journals to academic exchange is a temporal one - specifically, the amount of time required to bring a piece of work to its audience, and to receive feedback on that work, is considerably reduced. Stevan Harnad, editor of the peer-reviewed PSYCHOLOQUY, estimates that, in best case scenarios, only 4 weeks elapse between acceptance of an article and its publication, and feedback is immediate. This is a stark contrast to the print medium, where publication can require months or even years, and feedback comes several months later in the form of letters to the editor, articles of response, or conferences. E-journals act to significantly shorten the traditionally long cycle of scholarly communication.[2] Time is also a factor in subscription activity. The basic unit of time in subscribing to a print journal is one year. This compares unfavorably with the electronic medium, where subscription and unsubscription are instantaneous, and subscription practices permit quick response to changes in a scholar's interests.

The most serious drawback of electronic journals occurs in the area of credibility in the eyes of the academy. A relatively new phenomenon, e-journals do not rival their print siblings in terms of prestige or weight in the tenure and promotion process. Even though an e-journal can reach a far wider audience than a print journal, they are not yet mainstream, and few are systematically indexed in the traditional indexing and abstracting services. Because recognition is a key feature of academic work, articles that aren't cited or weighted as much as their print equivalents simply are not given full value in academe's reward system. What can the academic community do to change this? Namely, work to improve the quality of e-journals, ensure they are indexed in the appropriate venues, use and cite e-sources, expand network training programs for faculty, lobby promotion and tenure committees to broaden the categories of publication considered acceptable, and facilitate library and departmental access to e-archives.

Most respondents expressed delight with the capacity to connect to an ever-increasing number of library catalogs with a wide variety of subject strengths and archival collections. The ability to search bibliographic databases such as OCLC, unmediated, was considered a boon, as was desktop access to Census data and national catalogs. Clearly, the Internet plays a significant role in secondary research activities, although faculty don't yet expect new 'Net sources to displant the major indexes in their own fields.

Telnet, or its equivalent, underpins distance education programs, while travelling scholars appreciate logging in to their own workspaces from afar. Fewer respondents mentioned **file transfer**, **WWW (Mosaic)**, or **gopher**. Of those who did, humanists found it particularly integral to their work. Complex linguistic analysis, image manipulation, and ready access to manuscript facsimiles are just a few of the activities mentioned. Although **gopher** was cited as a user-friendly tool,

respondents seemed to use it randomly, and few knew of the best gopher sites for their subject areas. One hopes that the scholarly community will make better use of these tools as the second generation of gophers and similar devices evolves into organized forums for scholarly discussion, or true 'research units,' where the tools of the trade - working papers, discussion groups, syllabi, conferences, etc. - are all clearly laid out.

THE CHANGING RESEARCH PROCESS

Research can be defined as a process of systematic inquiry, using a methodology that is either qualitative, quantitative, or historical in nature. The traditional research process comprises four steps: project design, data collection or experimentation, data analysis, and the dissemination of results. How does the Internet change this process?

Research Design: As scholars avail themselves of advice from a much larger audience during the preliminary stages of research design, this step is augmented to allow some preliminary scholarly criticism to enter the equation early in the process. Data-gathering mechanisms can undergo a much larger pretest. Theoretically, larger pretests may produce more accurate test results which could, in turn, lead to better research.

Data Gathering: Traditional mechanisms for gathering data include surveys, case studies, standardized tests, attitude scales, oral histories, and interviews. Alternately, social scientists may use behavioral experimentation, observation, or simulation. Most, if not all, of these methods of collecting data are possible on the Internet, and some are already ubiquitous. (A recent one-month scan of USENET newsfeeds identified over 800 surveys, of which 360 were formal academic surveys.)[3] The Internet provides an ideal laboratory for multi-user simulation environments, which permit simulations of a sort not readily possible (gender swapping, role playing) in a pre-Internet world. The advent of multimedia/interactive technology involving a conjunction of video, sound, and data transmission on the Internet - already making inroads in distance education - will allow behavioral experimentation. The advantages of collecting data electronically include larger sample sizes, an inherently cross-cultural perpective, a possible assuaging of experimenter bias and of the Hawthorne effect (in which subjects react positively due to observation). Furthermore, primary data can be shared, allowing social scientists to conduct new research on previously collected data.

However, data-gathering on the Internet raises some concerns. In traditional sampling methods, the exact size of the sample and of the response rate is known. With electronic sampling, researchers may have no idea how many people received a questionnaire, especially among newsgroup users, so response rate cannot be calculated. Secondly, doing sampling on the 'Net can be likened to doing sampling via phone books in the early era of the telephone - the group is self-selected.[4] Thus, two core determinants of sampling reliability, size and randomness of sample, may be compromised.

Data Analysis: Social science data is typically tabulated from pre-coded questionnaires by means of a statistical package. However, the traditional tools of data analysis may not work with net-encoded data, and scholars may need to rework these tools or develop new ones. Too, the amount of data gathered on the 'Net may far exceed a researcher's expectations or experience and, as current Internet debates attest, analysis requires the allocation of additional time or resources.

Humanists have separate concerns. As research in the humanities is often historical in nature, the original text, manuscript, or image is of primary importance. Important too is the version of an e-text, especially to classicists for whom a translator or edition is crucial. At present, choice is often dictated by copyright or by mere availability in digital form. Finally, these scholars are usually beholden to a specific search engine, inextricably bound to the text itself, for textual analysis. However, SGML coding, which allows a separation between digitized text and search en-

gine, is rapidly becoming a standard and may ease some of these concerns.

Dissemination of results: Outcomes can be shared on the Internet in stages, from early drafts to finished products, rapidly and efficiently, significantly shortening the cycle of scholarly communication. However, publication in electronic form continues to be a nebulous area, as the system of academic rewards is firmly ensconced in the print culture. Issues of concern in the electronic dissemination of research include loss of authorial control over the text itself, and, as Clifford Lynch points out, a compromising of the accuracy and integrity of the written record.[5]

CHANGING PATTERNS

Scholars seem to be using the Internet as something of an **informal SDI service**, establishing their own 'profiles' by selecting discussion groups and journals, using 'tables of contents' databases, and setting pointers to specific sites. Some are revising their notions of ownership and no longer keep physical copies of secondary materials, opting instead for bookmarks at reliable host and mirror sites, and trusting the Internet as an archive.

But the greatest change effected by the 'Net is in the area of **communication** at all stages of a project. Researchers ask advice, find collaborators, administer projects, share work-in-progress, perform large pre-tests, publish results to wider audiences, and gain feedback in record time. This increased ability to communicate is coupled with lower apparent **costs** to the individual researcher, helping to palliate high subscription fees and dwindling support for conferences and travel. An electronic environment promotes **timeliness**, shortening the cycle of publication, dissemination of results, and response. Research activity benefits from a **specificity of discussion** in an environment where discussion groups are carefully organized by subject area and people share earlier drafts of technical reports. The **international** and **multidisciplinary** nature of the Internet encourages a multiplicity of viewpoints and broadens perspective. Research questions are mediated by **'group-think'** to a greater extent than before. **Accuracy** of results may increase, as postings distributed in the early stages of a project reach 2000 people instead of 20, and errors are more apt to be caught. Similarly, research **ethics** may improve in an environment open to large-scale scrutiny. Academic filters for proper conduct in research carry over to the BITNET world because of university and granting agency policies and requirements. And, just as the official world of scholarly criticism is sometimes shadowed by a personal one which finds its outlet in letters to the editor, ivory tower gossip, or even unsolicited input in a tenure file, so the Internet world has **'flaming'** and **'spamming.'** Questions about the incorporation of e-publishing into the **peer review** process abound, aggravated by serious concerns about the **authenticity of the public record**[6] in a world where hackers, or even inadvertent manipulation of text, can pose a threat.

CONCLUSION

As the Internet grows in importance, it is critical for us in the academic world to understand the nature of this new research environment and its evolving modes of academic exchange. Those using the Internet for research now are establishing basic premises for its use in the future. There are numerous implications for younger scholars, who will use the 'Net as a learning tool, a laboratory, and a means of publication. It will be interesting to see how the next generation of scholars initiates changes to the research process and to the reward system in order to gain recognition in the academy through this medium.

NOTES

1. Interview with Sam Lanfranco, Economics, York University, 1994.
2. Stevan Harnad. "Post-Gutenberg Galaxy: The Fourth Revolution in the Means of Production of Knowledge," *The Public-Access Computer Systems Review* 2 (1991)
3. Alex Black and Malcom Parks. Rationale for a

Survey on Ethical USENET Research. [electronic file, spring 1994]. Available via e-mail from al@debra.dgbt.gov.ca
4. Interview with Chuck Humphrey. Social scientist and data librarian, University of Alberta, 1994.
5. Clifford A. Lynch. "Rethinking the Integrity of the Scholarly Record in the Networked Information Age," *EDUCOM Review*, March-April (1994).
6. Ibid.

BIBLIOGRAPHY

Black, Alex and Malcom Parks. Rationale for the Survey on Ethical USENET Research. [electronic file]. Available via e-mail from al@debra.dgbt.gov.ca; INTERNET.

Fierheller, George. "A Fabric of Intelligence - How our Supercomputing Network is Weaving the Next Human Renaissance," *Canadian Journal of Library and Information Science / Revue canadienne des sciences d'information et de bibliothéconomie* 19 (1994): 31-38.

Harnad, Stevan. "Implementing Peer-Review on the Net: Scientific Quality Control in Scholarly Electronic Journals," in *Proceedings of the International Conference on Refereed Electronic Journals: Towards a Consortium for Networked Publications* (in press).

____. "Post-Gutenberg Galaxy: The Fourth Revolution in the Means of Production of Knowledge," *The Public-Access Computer Systems Review* 2 (1991): 39-53.

____. "Scholarly Skywriting and the Prepublication Continuum of Scientific Inquiry," *Psychological Science* 1 (1990): 342-344.

Hockey, Susan. "Developing Access to Electronic Texts in the Humanities," *Computers in Libraries* 13 (1993): 41-3.

Kessler, Jack. "Networked Information in France, 1993: The Internet's Future?" *Internet Research* 4 (1994): 18-30.

Lowry, Anita K. "Electronic Texts in the Humanities: A Selected Bibliography," *Information Technology and Libraries* 13 (1994): 43-9.

Lynch, Clifford A. "Rethinking the Integrity of the Scholarly Record in the Networked Information Age," *EDUCOM Review*, March-April (1994).

Macedonia, Michael R. and Donald P. Brutzman. "MBone Provides Audio and Video Across the Internet," *IEEE Computer*, April (1994): 30-6.

Neuman, Michael. "The Very Pulse of the Machine: Three Trends Toward Improvement in Electronic Versions of Humanities Texts," *Computers and the Humanities* 25 (1991): 363-75.

Okerson, Ann, ed. *Visions and Opportunities in Electronic Publishing: Proceedings of the Second Symposium.* Washington, DC: Association of Research Libraries, Office of Scientific and Academic Publishing, 1993.

Okerson, Ann, and Dru Mogge, eds. *Gateways, Gatekeepers, and Roles in the Information Omniverse: Proceedings from the Third Sympo-* *sium.* Washington, DC: Association of Research Libraries, Office of Scientific and Academic Publishing, 1994.

Price-Wilkin, John. "Text Files in RLG Academic Libraries: A Survey of Support and Activities," *Journal of Academic Librarianship* 17 (1991): 19-25.

Sever, Irene. "Electronic Information Retrieval as Culture Shock: An Anthropological Exploration," *RQ* 33 (1994): 336-41.

Warren-Wenk, P. "Moving Toward Internet Literacy on the University Campus," in *The Internet Library: Case Studies of Library Internet Management and Use.* Edited by Julie Still. Westport, CT: Mecklermedia, 1994, 127-165.

Luddites in Library Instruction:
Back to Basics

Karen A. Becker

ABSTRACT

Current economic, personnel, and technological developments in today's academic libraries demand that we critically re-examine bibliographic instruction philosophies and curriculums. These new transitional factors include techno-stress, complex AV and computerized teaching aids, shrinking staffs, the emphasis on educational theory with little training, and burnout among BI librarians. Challenges are exacerbated when developing a program which instructs 5,600 freshmen students annually. These factors, along with classroom teachers' demands for more practical sessions, have led to a "back-to-basics" underground movement among BI librarians.

In the 1990s, while bibliographic instruction has become an expected and accepted component of library public service work, it has also become more complex. There are many recent factors contributing to the need to rethink our BI philosophies and curriculums, especially regarding large-scale freshmen library instruction programs. The time is right for re-examination of some basic assumptions about BI in general. Eadie notes: "The 1960s and 1970s were a period of expansion and experimentation. Libraries and librarians sought new roles. New and special services were created. The 1980s and early 1990s are a time for reassessment, retrenchment, elimination of frills — such as, perhaps, user education."[1] While we may not be ready to jettison BI, it is still important to critically examine library instruction in terms of current economic, personnel, and technological developments in today's libraries.

TRANSITIONAL FACTORS

One BI transitional challenge we face today is techno-stress. Online catalogs have become commonplace in our libraries. Periodical index databases may also be loaded on the OPAC. Multiple CD-ROM products are commonly available. Public access to other systems, such as OCLC or online databases may be an option for patrons. Many libraries are facilitating access to the Internet, either through their own OPACs or with dedicated terminals. As instruction librarians, we have found ourselves attempting to instruct patrons in the use

---

Karen A. Becker is the Coordinator of Library Instruction at Northern Illinois University Libraries, DeKalb, Illinois.

of all of these new technologies as the systems have been made available in the reference department. Our lectures become a jumble of demonstrations (or even worse, overhead transparencies) of these computer services. The sessions can prove every bit as dull and boring as our previous habit of holding up a series of reference books and describing them.

A related form of techno-stress may also be the obligation we feel to incorporate all forms of audiovisual and computer technology into our BI curriculums. A slick, fancy program incorporating self-guided audio-tape tours, workbooks, videotape programs, slide/tape shows, or computer-aided instruction (sometimes even using hypertext or interactive CD) places incredible burdens on library staff to produce a high quality initial product, and more importantly, to keep the materials up to date as the library facilities, resources, and personnel change. Many librarians have spent hundreds of hours creating a video or computer program, only to have it become quickly outdated, or to have a newly hired BI librarian decide to develop an all new program.

A third factor challenging BI librarians today is the shrinking size of our professional and support staffs. At the Northern Illinois University Libraries general reference department, for example, we lost one professional position a few years ago, another this year, and with the demise of the Graduate School of Library Science, will be losing our semi-trained graduate assistants. Many libraries are facing similar staffing crises. In addition, high turnover in entry level reference positions (the staff who often provide the bulk of instruction) raises issues relating to the need for constant training of new staff members. Librarians can also become weary of change simply for changes sake, as each trendy teaching innovation is incorporated into the BI curriculum. Some level of stability becomes desirable.

A fairly recent factor increasing our instructional challenge is the current emphasis in the BI literature on concepts such as the science of knowledge, conceptual frameworks, educational theory,

problem solving, critical thinking, and abstract reasoning. However, with little or no formal training or background in educational theory, BI librarians have difficulty incorporating these high-level concepts into their BI curriculums. Based on their survey of BI librarians, Patterson & Howell concluded, "Professional education (for BI) remains uneven and haphazard, and few instruction librarians have had the necessary courses and practical experience in their formal education programs to prepare them even minimally for what is encountered on the job."[2] These untrained BI librarians must then train the remainder of the reference librarians in these complex teaching strategies, as well as motivate librarians who may not agree that this level of instruction is necessary or even desirable. Also, when these concepts are applied poorly, incorrectly, or half-heartedly by librarians, a poor quality of teaching takes place, and feelings of failure of frustration on the part of both students and librarians are sure to result. Feinberg and King address the use of educational theory and systematic methodology for teaching long-term library competency:

> While ... leading writers present forceful and thought-provoking ideas, the author of this article doubt the ideas are practical. What these writers exhort us to do, e.g., teach logic, abstract reasoning, the organization of literature in different disciplines, and critical evaluation of sources, are the things we seem to do least well. And those things we do best, such as teaching students library mechanics, helping them to achieve short term competencies, and developing confidence in using the library, are what the leaders disparage as having limited value.[3]

All of the factors listed above may be contributing to increased levels of burnout among instruction librarians. Characteristics of BI are strongly related to the causes and symptoms of burnout as detailed in the psychological and sociological burnout literature.[4] A 1987 survey of BI librarians also found burnout to be significant phenomena: 39.3 percent of respondents indicated that burnout was a problem for them.[5]

INVESTIGATING THE PROBLEM

At Northern Illinois University (NIU) Libraries, our library instruction is separated into three major programs: 1) Freshmen & General Orientation (orientation to library building and services, how to find books, how to find articles); 2) Library Automated Systems (OPAC, CD-ROM, Internet, organization of electronic information); and 3) Subject-Specific Instruction (organization of a specific field of knowledge, research strategies, specific print and electronic resources.) The freshmen and orientation programs are developed to meet the needs of a specific clientele. Instruction on automated systems and subject disciplines assumes a foundation of basic library skills covered by the freshmen or orientation BI sessions. As outlined above, new trends affecting the bibliographic instruction scenario (techno-stress, intensive production of computer or AV programs, shrinking staffs, burnout, and implementation of educational theory) can be greatly exacerbated when dealing with a large-scale, introductory freshmen instruction program.

At NIU Libraries, we certainly were experiencing these stressful BI related transitions, and most importantly, we were worried that because of them our instruction was becoming less effective. In 1991/1992 the general reference department taught over 5,600 Freshmen English students. Our freshmen library instruction program is tied into NIU's Freshmen English program. The basic Freshmen English program consists of a two semester series. The first semester (English 103) concentrates on basic writing skills and creative writing. The second semester (English 104) focuses on research skills, analytical writing, and the term paper. As part of the Freshmen English curriculum, instructors are required to bring their classes to the library for BI once each semester.

In 1990 the general reference librarians responsible for the Freshmen English library instruction program held a series of meetings to discuss these changing aspects of BI, our frustrations, and the need to re-think our freshmen BI philosophy. These lively discussions generated a consensus to adopt a "back-to-basics" philosophy. (Remember, students will have more sophisticated instruction opportunities available closer to the time of a specific need.) In order to concentrate on basics, the lectures were drastically cut to fifteen or twenty minutes each, and the rest of each session would be spent on some type of hands-on exercise. Regarding the shortened lecture, our librarians agreed with Engeldinger, when he noted, "At first glance, fifteen minutes may seem inadequate, but remember, we are not creating catalogers or preparing the students (nor should we be) for every possible eventuality. We are teaching a very simple research strategy."[6] But what would be covered in those brief lectures? We each came to the next meeting with a list of the the "ten essential items" to be taught to the Freshmen English students. Again, the consensus process generated some heated discussions. We actually ended up, with more than ten items. Topics which were eliminated included all automated sources except the online catalog; reference books; the steps of the research process; and exceptions to any library rules. Coverage of the Library of Congress Subject Headings and periodical indexes was pared back to the basics. Next, we split up the items between the English 103 and English 104 courses as appropriate.

The next step was to determine how the material would be taught. Our goal was to limit ourselves to the stated "essential items," and our motto was to "Keep it Simple; Keep it Practical; and Keep is Process-Oriented." Traditionally, NIU Libraries has shown a strong commitment to library instruction. An early NIU library orientation librarian, Verna Mellum Beardsley summed up her philosophy: "Instruction should be left until it can correlated with course work. But first-year and other new students can be introduced to the library in ways that will motivate future instruction." Her 1960s plan included a warm welcome, and orientation to people and services, an introduction to a few important reference sources and indexes, and the provision of future opportunities to learn more about the library through advanced instruction sessions.[7]

Regarding support materials, we wanted to keep our dependence on computer and audiovisual hardware or software to a minium. We wanted to choose a format which would permit quick and easy training of new library staff members. Printed materials should be basic and straightforward, and need minimal updating each semester. But, most importantly, the new curriculum should meet the needs and expectations of the Freshmen English instructors and students. Our English instructors agreed with Allen's finding at the University of Illinois. There the teachers demanded "... that instruction for their students more specifically address what they felt were the most complicated library processes: using the online catalog to find books on a subject, and using periodical indexes and abstracts to identify relevant articles ... They also requested that more time be spent with hands-on instruction in the library."[8] At NIU, we experimented with some different ideas, including term paper clinics and laboratory settings, to see if we could incorporate any ideas from these environments.[9] The year long discussion, experimentation, and review process yielded our final proposal.

THE SOLUTION

The English 103 session has become strictly an orientation, featuring an introduction to library facilities and services. It begins with a welcome and a description of the two session series We do a live demonstration of a title search on the online catalog using and LCD display panel and overhead projector. Next, we talk briefly about the existence and purpose of periodical indexes, and indicate that we will cover how to use indexes in depth at the second session. We distribute a list of basic Wilson indexes to carry the students through the current semester. Remember, though they will not be doing library research for this English 103 class. The lecture takes only ten to fifteen minutes.

While a fifteen minute lecture sounds unrealistic, remember, most of the instruction will be taking place during the tour.

Next we distribute a library exercise, which the students bring along to work on during a library building tour. It is amazing how this exercise focuses their attention during the tour - they hang on every word. We have six versions (to discourage cheating) of about twenty matching and multiple choice questions regarding facilities, collections, and services. The English instructor receives the answer key and collects the completed exercises later in the week. The students are able to complete all of the questions during the tour except one, which requires them to look up a title on the online catalog after the instruction session is over. The only problem we have experienced with the new format is with the computer equipment, for example, the LCD display panel not working or the OPAC being down. The session is simple, straightforward, and the students learn what we and the English instructors want them to learn.

The English 104 sessions have become a very basic introduction to library research. This was by far the more challenging session to develop. There was so much we wanted to cover, but again we had to severely limit ourselves to cover only the basics. During a short twenty minute lecture we cover a brief introduction to: the Library of Congress Subject Headings, including BT, NT, and RT; live demonstration of a subject search on the Online Catalog; a description of a typical periodical index; the difference between a magazine and a journal; and our periodicals holding list. The students also receive one of three (Social Sciences, Humanities, or Sciences) eight-page bibliographies/pathfinders appropriate to their topic. The librarian is encouraged to keep the lecture short to ensure the most time for one-on-one instruction in the reference area using real sources.

The class then adjourns down to the general reference area to work on a library research worksheet. For their own individual topic, the student must: select a few Library of Congress subject headings; find one book on the online catalog; find one journal article citation; and check our periodicals holdings list. Needless to say, it gets somewhat chaotic working with twenty-five students who suddenly find that they actually do have questions about the LCSH or choosing a periodical index. However, they seem to have minimal trouble using the online catalog or using the periodicals holdings list. The English instructor also pitches in and assists the students. This format has proven to provide some unexpected benefits. If a student's topic needs to be broadened, narrowed, or changed completely based on materials available in our collection, the instructor is right there to negotiate the topic and give an OK. Also, many of the English instructors are graduate students themselves, and some have commented that they learned new things about the LCSH or discovered previously unknown indexes during the hands-on sessions. Librarians and instructors also gain new respect for each other while working together as a team, helping and instructing the students. Unexpectedly, some of the English instructors have found the hands-on sessions so effective that they have their classes meet in the reference section later in the semester for additional library work time.

Again, for this session, we sometimes run into problems with equipment or telecommunications during the live demonstration of the Online Catalog. The only other problem we have found is conveying to the English department the importance of scheduling the BI session at an appropriate point in the students' research process; ideally after students have selected a fairly narrow topic, but before they have begun their library research. The librarians and the English instructors find the session to be a lot more fun than a lecture, and the students leave with a feeling of accomplishment: they have the beginnings of a working bibliography, they know their way around the reference department, they have interacted on a one-to-one basis with a librarian, and they have discovered that we are knowledgeable information specialists as well as pretty nice people.

THE CONCLUSIONS

The strengths of a "Back-to-Basics," hands-on approach for a large-scale freshmen program are:

- It is more enjoyable and less boring for librarians, English instructors, and students;
- An initial positive experience with the library and with librarians helps alleviate students' future library anxiety;
- English instructors see the sessions as directly meeting the need of their students and curriculum;
- Students are learning practical, immediately applicable library survival skills which address current needs for their first year of college;
- BI support materials (printed handouts) are simple, straightforward, and easy to update;
- Within a framework of the goals for each session, librarians are free to incorporate individual teaching styles;
- BI training for new library staff members is easy for the trainer and intuitive for the trainee;
- The program provides a solid foundation for any subject-specific or technology-specific library instruction students may receive in the future.

At NIU, we are very pleased with our classic, no frills library instruction program for freshmen. Our librarians agree whole-heartedly with Feinberg and King, who encourage librarians to do what they do best: "1) teach for short term research competence; 2) raise students' confidence in using the library so they will develop a positive attitude about libraries in general; and 3) demonstrate that librarians are information specialists who can direct users today and, by implication, tomorrow, toward the best approach to research a particular question."[10] Even though it has taken the challenges of unpleasant economic, personnel, and technological transitions to initiate these changes, we have achieved the positive result of meeting these goals in our Freshmen English library instruction program.

NOTES

1. Tom Eadie, "Immodest Proposals: User Instruction for Students Does not Work," *Library Journal* 115:43 (October 15, 1990).

2. Charles D. Patterson and Donna W. Howell, "Library User Education: Assessing the Attitudes of Those Who Teach," *RQ* 29:522 (Summer 1990).

3. Richard Feinberg and Christine King, "Short-Term Library Skill Competencies: Arguing for the Achievable," *College & Research Libraries* 49:25 (January 1988).

4. Karen A. Becker, "The Characteristics of Bibliographic Instruction in Relation to the Causes and Symptoms of Burnout," *RQ* 74:346 (Spring 1993).

5. Patterson, p. 521.

6. Eugene A. Engeldinger, "Teaching Only the Essentials - The Thirty Minute Stand," *RSR* 4:48 (1988).

7. Verna Melum Beardsley, "Library Instruction in Colleges and Universities in the Seventies: A Viewpoint," in *Educating the Library User*, ed. John Lubans (New York: Bowker, 1974), p.111-112.

8. Mary Beth Allen, "Focusing the One-Shot Lecture," *Research Strategies* 7:101 (Summer 1989).

9. Karen A. Becker, "Individual Library Research Clinics for College Freshmen," *Research Strategies* 11:202 (Fall 1993).

10. Feinberg, p.26.

The Concept of Equity:
Implications for Electronic Reference and Information Literacy

Gary B. Thompson and Billie Reinhart

ABSTRACT

Equity in educational technology provides a challenge for academic reference service and information literacy programs. Part I introduces the concept of equity and reviews the use of the term in professional educational and library literature. Part II discusses the implications of equity for reference service in this electronic information age. Part III discusses the concept of equity for academic librarians striving to provide a more inclusive and accessible instructional programs. Methods for assessing the equity of access, process and outcomes in reference and instruction are put forward. Finally areas for future research are suggested.

THE CONCEPT OF EDUCATIONAL EQUITY

The purpose of this paper is to discuss the means of assessing educational equity in the provision of academic reference service and library instruction in this technological and multicultural society.

The fifth edition of *The Encyclopedia of Educational Research* (1982) identifies the three common assumptions underlying most definitions of educational equity: (1) recognition of differing attributes of learners; (2) commitment to restructure the educational process; and (3) dedication to an outcome-based educational philosophy.[1] Recent discussions of equity have concentrated on the broader issues of access to education, an educational process based upon fair and just treatment recognizing differing backgrounds and learning styles, and an emphasis upon achievement of uniform objectives. Rosemary Sutton's 1991 article "Equity and Computers in the Schools: A Decade of Research" synthesizes research findings on educational equity related to (1) access to computers; (2) processes involved in computer-based learning; and (3) competence in computer skills.[2] The central question for educational and computer equity is this: Assuming that students start with differing experiences, abilities and ex-

Gary B. Thompson is Head of Information Services and Billie Reinhart is Coordinator of Information Literacy at Cleveland State University Library, Cleveland, Ohio.

Search Term	Education Index 1983-	ERIC 1983-	Library Lit. 1984-
Equity	457	3384	76
w/gender	55	341	4
w/race	8	110	0
w/Black+	11	195	0
w/pay	23	165	39
w/computers or technology	29	646	9
Equal access	49	1569	13
Equality	296	1206	60

FIGURE 1: Number of Items relating to Equity in FirstSearch 1983-October 1994

pectations, how can educators produce the best outcomes for the greatest number by expanding universal access to learning and enhancing the learning process.

For this paper, the authors did a content analysis of the educational and library professional literature from 1983 to October 1994 using FirstSearch. (See figure 1)

Library Literature, while obviously a smaller universe than ERIC or *Education Index*, had only 76 occurrences of the term "equity," 60 for "equality" and 13 for "equal access." Pay equity accounted for over 50% of the references to the term equity in *Library Literature* (compared to 5% in *Education Index*). Of the remaining 37 items discussing educational equity, few dealt directly with reference service, library instruction, or computer equity in libraries. More research is needed on the equity of education provided by today's highly automated academic libraries.

The current American Library Association's Policy Manual states that priority A is that "all individuals have equal access to libraries and information services."[3] The 1990 ALA/RASD standards document, "Information Services for Information Consumers: Guidelines for Provid-

ers." confirms that "the Library should make service areas for information services highly visible and readily accessible to all users."[4] In an article entitled "Ethical Issues in Reference Service" Susan Rathburn states: "Differences in the amount and quality of service rendered to clients... are examples of unethical treatment of the clientele."[5]

Ronald D. Doctor challenges librarians to provide equitable access to electronic information in the fullest meaning: "A simple right to access very likely will be insufficient to remedy the equity problems with which we are concerned. Access will be of little benefit to large portions of the population unless it is accompanied by equipment and training that allow effective use of that access. What we need then is a right to access in the broader sense of a right to benefit from access."[6] David Bender recently called upon librarians to "add value to information by lowering 'social barriers' to its access. These barriers include, on the part of the information consumer, a lack of technology skills to access the material, as well as a lack of awareness on what information resources are available."[7]

While most librarians concur with these eloquent statements about equal access to information, the question remains how can we put this overarching philosophy into practice. We need to develop assessment measures to weigh how well we are meeting the task of providing equitable service and then to use these instruments to move closer to our goal of "universal information access."

EQUITY IN REFERENCE

An ALA/RASD task force is assembling a group of field-tested instruments into a Reference Assessment Manual (to be published by Pierian Press in 1995) concerning such factors as the physical environment, adequacy of staffing and patron satisfaction. Below we outline some of the key issues to be addressed in developing similar instruments for assessing the equity of reference service and the equity of library instruction.

While the ALA Code of Ethics establishes the principle of "skillful, accurate, unbiased and courteous responses to all requests for assistance,"[8] it is difficult to carry this out in practice at a busy university reference center. Therefore, reference librarians must assess the equity of reference assistance in terms of access, process, and outcomes. Do all students have equal access to reference assistance in terms of location, hours, physical arrangement? If your Library cannot reach everyone, have you clearly defined the primary and secondary constituencies whom you serve? Other assessment factors of equal **access** concern service charges(e.g.. online searching), service restrictions (e.g., CD-ROM use, Internet use), and computer equity (e.g. number of workstations per student, access to information technology by students with disabilities).

The assessment of equity in the **reference process** involves such issues as queuing, time allotment per patron, restrictions on telephone inquiries versus in-person inquiries, status differentiation (students versus faculty versus general public), and adjustments of the amount of reference help in terms of the educational purpose of the inquiry. Do you have performance standards for reference librarians concerning fair and equitable service? Do you have a diversity of staff and services to accommodate patron preferences to learn from professionals or peers and from oral or written instructions? How does the reference staff deal with rising expectations of patrons for greater assistance and instantaneous access to information of any kind? Do you have special services for new patrons unfamiliar with OPAC or CD-ROM's?

In assessing **outcomes**, it is important to establish a methodology for gathering data from users of reference services. The most widely used methods are general and targeted user surveys and suggestion boxes. Valuable other methods are needs assessment, focus groups, and analyses of OPAC transaction logs and CD-ROM session meter logs. Do you use students to pretest menus and help screens for the electronic workstations? Do you know which kinds of students feel comfortable coming to the reference desk for help and which students return for help? What can you do differently to attract those students presently not being reached? Are juniors and seniors able to use the OPAC and CD-ROM's more independently than freshmen and sophomores? Are there certain kinds of students who do not have access to information technology?

EQUITY IN LIBRARY INSTRUCTION

Some educators believed that computers would be the great equalizers. However, Paul Resta states the dilemma: "It is clear that students who are already familiar and comfortable in using computers are able to take full advantage of these new information tools... students entering college who are unfamiliar with the use of these powerful new information tools will find it more and more difficult to compete.."[9] Equity can only be achieved when all students obtain the skills needed to access the vast technological information systems. This achievement may be accelerated by the design of user friendly systems containing easily understandable help and instruction screens. As instructors and reference librarians we find there are few if any systems available that all students are able to learn without librarian intervention.

Wheelock noted that "unequal distribution of favorable learning conditions virtually institutionalizes patterns of unequal achievement."[10] The difficulty arises in defining "favorable learning conditions" for all segments of the population within an institution. As in reference, assessment of equity in library instruction must include the equity of access, process and outcomes. In assessing **access** to instruction on the use of electronic information the following should be taken into consideration. What percentage of students are reached by the program? Are instruction sessions required or voluntary? (If voluntary there may be lack of interest rather than lack of need.) Are classes too large or too brief to give individual attention to students? What percentage of classes with information gathering assignments are reached? Are laboratories with tutors available for hands-on experience? Are help screens and computer tutorials available? Are workshops available for evening and weekend students?

There are three general assumptions about the role of equity in the **teaching process**: (1) differential treatment is given on the basis of individual qualifications; (2) all students are given the same treatment regardless of background; (3) groups of students are provided differential treatment as needed.[11] Should not students with lack of information gathering skills be given individual or special group instruction or mentoring? Is giving special instruction to students with unequal information skills equity? It has been argued that the increasing needs of various groups may be causing competition for funds and staff between them and the "regular" students?[12]

In addition to whom and when the instruction is given, other factors within the program should be considered: the qualifications of the staff to teach information technology, the demeanor of the instructors toward the students, teacher preparation time, and the student/ librarian-instructor ratio. Is there uniformity in the basic skills presentations? Are all learning styles addressed? Are

methods to overcome computer anxiety incorporated? In lab settings is one sex or race dominating the keyboard? Is collaborative work on assignments encouraged? Are teaching staff available for follow up consultations?

While Mathews and Winkle define equity as "equal access to computer literacy for each person,"[13] we feel that equity in information literacy requires the provision of the instruction necessary to ensure that all students achieve a set of goals by educational level and graduation. **Outcomes of instruction** are difficult to assess. Do students understand the research process? Are pretests and post-tests given? Are classroom instructors contacted to ascertain if the students used their information skills well in their assignments? Attitudes toward the technology may be as important as the specific skills acquired. They may necessitate a survey or a focus group to obtain an assessment.

FUTURE DIRECTIONS

1. Develop a checklist which librarians can use to assess the equity of reference service and library instruction.
2. Conduct research on specific issues relating to equity of service in reference and instruction in academic libraries, using concepts and theories from the literature on educational equity.
3. Conduct research on computer equity in academic libraries.
4. Develop action plans to ensure that all segments of the educational community have access and assistance in using information technology.
5. Convince library administrators of the importance of funding projects to advance educational equity.

There are many questions that remains to be answered concerning how educational equity should influence the future direction of academic libraries. For example: How are academic librarians going to provide library/information skills training through distance learning? How can we use the Internet to promote information literacy? Do students find computers more user-friendly than librarians? Can public and academic libraries work together to provide greater access? Do statewide networks eliminate or exacerbate inequities among their member institutions? How can we open up the world of information for all students at all levels?

NOTES

1. Harold E. Mitzel, ed. *Encyclopedia of Educational Research* 5th ed. (New York: Free Press, 1982), s.v. "Equity Issues in Education" by Patricia B. Campbell and Susan Klein.
2. Rosemary E. Sutton, "Equity and Computers in the Schools: A Decade of Research," *Review of Educational Research* 61 (Winter 1991): 475-503.
3. American Library Association, *ALA Handbook of Organization* 1992/93 (Chicago: American Library Association, 1992), 133.
4. "Information Services for Information Consumers: Guidelines for Providers," *RQ* (Winter 1990): 262-265.
5. Susan R. Rathburn, "Ethics Issues in Reference Service: Overview and Analysis," *North Carolina Libraries* 51 (Spring 1993): 12.
6. Ronald D. Doctor, "Information Technologies and Social Equity: Confronting the Revolution," *Journal of the ASIS* 42(3) (1991): 217.
7. Bender, David. "There are Dangers Lurking on the Information Highway," *Information Today* (June 1994): 15.
8. *ALA Handbook of Organizations 1992/93,* 148.
9. Paul Resta, "Organizing Education for Minorities: Enhancing Minority Access and use of the New Information Technologies in Higher Education," *Education & Computing* 8 (1992): 11
10. A. Wheelock, *Crossing the Tracks: How "Untracking" Can Save America's Schools.* (New York: New Press, 1992), 9.
11. Mitzel, *Encyclopedia*, 584..
12. Mitzel, *Encyclopedia*, 585.
13. Sutton, "Equity and Computers," 494.

The Past Is Prologue:

Designing Information Services for Historic Preservationists

Ada D. Jarred and Martha V. Henderson

ABSTRACT

Ten recommendations are offered for the design of information services to persons in the multidisciplinary field of historic preservation. Supporting rationale is detailed, based on a survey of the communication patterns and information needs of cultural resource managers, as well as on an extensive literature review.

INTRODUCTION

As the end of the twentieth century nears, academic librarians and historic preservationists are experiencing sweeping currents of change. Librarians are required to maintain quality service against overwhelming odds, adapt to and even capitalize on rapidly transforming technologies, cope effectively with the information explosion, stretch shrinking budgets, and motivate downsized groups of personnel to produce more. At the same time preservationists are challenged to ensure the quality of preservation, utilize and benefit from new technologies, navigate the flooding waters of information, and justify funds for preservation when costs are rising.

Establishment of the National Center for Preservation Technology and Training at Northwestern State University of Louisiana (Reclamation Projects Authorization and Adjustment Act of 1992, P.L. 102-575) created a new clientele for Watson Library, historic preservationists or cultural resource managers. The Center operates under the auspices of the National Park Service, a component of the Department of the Interior. A working definition for preservation technology states:

> Preservation technology refers broadly to any equipment, methods, and techniques that can be applied to the discovery; analysis; interpretation; restoration; conservation; protection; and management of cultural property, including prehistoric and historic sites, structures, objects, and landscapes.[1]

Ada D. Jarred is Director of Libraries and Martha V. Henderson is Coordinator of Library Automation at the Eugene P. Watson Memorial Library, Northwestern State University of Louisiana, Natchitoches, Louisiana.

The Concept Paper for the Center outlines three functional areas: research, training and education, and information management.[2] This paper addresses the last of the three functions.

As early as 1986 the Office of Technology Assessment recognized, "One of the most critical problems confronting historic preservation involves the storage, retrieval, and dissemination of technical and other information on prehistoric and historic sites, structures and landscapes."[3] In preparation for implementing information services to both Center personnel and its clientele, Northwestern's Watson Library faculty members surveyed the communication patterns and information needs of historic preservationists. Findings from the survey were reported earlier in *Advances in Knowledge Organization, Volume Four*[4]. Historic preservationists are interesting subjects of research; they vary widely in academic preparation, practical experience, and professional assignment. Some focus on a highly specialized area of a discipline such as paint analysis in materials technology, while others attend a wide interdisciplinary spectrum as museum management. The investigation revealed, however, a profile of the cultural resources manager: a male in his 40s with a master's degree, academic studies most likely in architecture, and a career as an independent contractor. These findings and others, as well as additional planning documents for the Center, led to ten recommendations for information services to this new national entity. The rationale for the proposals is delineated in this paper.

RECOMMENDATIONS
1. Increase both private and public access to online information.

Global Internet connectivity offers opportunities for collaboration and information sharing. However, difficult and highly complicated questions about financing, providing access, and coping with copyright issues and standards must be addressed. In response to widespread concerns, the National Institute for Standards and Technol-

ogy is presently conducting a series of working conferences on the Virtual Library to address major issues and questions of this nature. Significantly, despite the tremendous development of electronic resources and the increase in technological literacy, seventy percent of the historic preservationists responding to the Northwestern survey do not have access to online electronic databases. Peter Stott and Arlene Fleming, telecommunications and cultural resource management consultants, recently reported that no evidence exists of a State Historical Preservation Office with an Internet connection. A National Park Service Internet node, accessible through the agency's mail system, became operational in late June 1994, and can be accessed by state offices.[5]

Responses to the local survey indicated that electronic information resources are not used due to a lack of equipment (37 percent), deficit of skills/confidence (37 percent), and absence of funding (25 percent). Many respondents (38 percent) commented that they need information about what electronic resources are available and how to locate and access such information.

Successful implementation of this recommendation may be dependent on initially providing information to and educating preservationists about electronic resources. Workshops and/or seminars specifically designed for this clientele are valid activities to stimulate interest and to initiate projects providing access to online information.

2. Enable connections between databases developed by individual agencies.

A 1990 survey by the National Park Service indicated a commitment to automating basic inventory information. Large resource databases and smaller specialized ones continue to be developed. However, many databases are fragmented, often redundant, and especially difficult to identify and access by people outside a particular agency or its divisions. Also, the databases often do not provide the important relational information so critical to the field. For example, collections of historical sites data were developed separately from systems describing grant money. Documentation and user manuals are lacking. Formats are varied and little standardization of information occurs.[6]

Other serious attempts by private foundations, academic institutions, and government agencies have been made to provide access to databases. Management of the Getty Foundation's Conservation Information Network (CIN) is now under the Canadian Heritage Information Network (CHIN) which links over 400 institutions in all regions of Canada and in more than 22 countries. The Getty databases include: a Bibliographic Database from *Art and Archaeology Technical Abstracts*, materials and suppliers databases relevant to the practice of conservation, and the library catalog of the International Center for the Study of Preservation and Restoration of Cultural Property (ICROM). Also, academic communities are rapidly adding gophers on the Internet for access to various databases. VICTOR, University of Maryland system; CARL, Colorado Alliance of Research Libraries; and ArchNet, the University of Connecticut, are examples.

Information services for the Center can provide a medium for developing and locating existing information about databases, adding gophers and World Wide Web servers to the Internet, and adopting national standards for the production of such databases. Workshops and seminars, newsletters, training sessions, and information exchange services can assist in these endeavors.

3. Encourage development of standardized terminology and/or natural language searching techniques.

Historic preservation is a multidisciplinary field, and even though some resources have become more interdisciplinary in nature, many researchers often are poorly served by the classification and indexing schemes used by libraries. Donald O. Case, a faculty member in the Graduate School of Library and Information Science, University of California at Los Angeles, recommended

that the problem-oriented model of knowledge may be more serviceable when considering how new resources can be effectively developed. Guides to translate the terms of one specialization into words and examples familiar to another discipline could be compiled, for example. At the 1987 ASIS Annual Meeting, Bella Weinberg questioned the ability to reflect point of view or context through an index, and Helen Tibbo, a Ph.D. student at the University of Maryland in 1989, suggested that historical abstracts need to describe not only elements of time, geographic/political units, and topic but also names of individuals and social groups, descriptions of the author's thesis and arguments, and the primary sources used in the investigation. A graduate student in the Department of Computer & Information Science, Linköping University, Sweden, Lisbeth Björklund, at the 1994 conference of the International Society for Knowledge Organization, described a theoretical collaborative tool for use in ad-hoc construction of a dynamic thesaurus to support group knowledge building and information sharing.[7]

The *Art and Architecture Thesaurus* represents a major accomplishment in attempting to provide standardized or controlled terminology for some multidisciplinary fields. In addition, the proliferation of databases that use keyword and/or natural language searching will help address retrieval problems currently associated with some indexing and abstracting of documents. Increasing acceptance and use of the MARC-AMC format by archives and museums also provide positive effects on the use of keyword and/or subject headings search techniques in locating information critical to this field.

The information specialist can assist in the development of such tools and services for the field of historic preservation. Until such times as these inter- and/or multidisciplinary tools are available, the information specialist must provide additional reference services to assist clientele in dealing with various thesauri and index descriptors.

4. Provide current contents type information for appropriate publications.

A number of commercial vendors, private firms, academic libraries, and professional organizations now provide current awareness services. For example, the UnCover Company publishes table of contents index which includes many periodicals heavily used by preservationists and archaeologists. Services range from providing copies of specific journals' tables of contents to a detailed analysis of information available on an identified topic. The large number of periodicals available in the field of historic preservation make this service especially desirable. The *Avery Index to Architectural Periodicals* and the *Index to Historical Preservation Periodicals*, a publication of the National Trust Library Collection, University of Maryland, index most of the journals. The *Avery Index* is now available on CD-ROM, and the National Trust Library Collection index and online catalog will be accessible through the Internet in January 1995. However, a large number of regional and local publications are not indexed.

Numerous academic libraries have initiated current awareness services for selected faculty. Evaluations of these activities indicate extremely positive responses from faculty recipients.[8] A major issue, however, is the cost due to the labor intensive nature of these services. Current awareness activities are dependent on the development of an accurate profile of the patron and/or project. The interdisciplinary nature of the historic preservation field with its many highly specialized areas creates additional problems that will need to be addressed in developing such services. Nevertheless, a project to provide data about this type service could focus initially on those clientele directly served by the Center. Again, the survey respondents' indication of a need for information about what is available could be answered in this manner.

5. Increase information literacy.

Responses to the local survey provided some contradictory information about historic preserva-

tionists' tactics and skills in locating needed information. Eighty-three percent indicated that they use libraries/information centers on a regular basis, one to five times per month. The majority stated that they are self-reliant in seeking information, and only 12 percent rely on librarians or information specialists. Effectiveness in locating information was rated as excellent/skilled by 42 percent and satisfactory by 54 percent. On the other hand, personal books and personal or office files were ranked as most useful in locating information, and only a small percentage (11 percent) reported familiarity with electronic information sources. When asked to identify associations, journals, and indexes, respondents named only a few of the more recognized ones, such as the *Association for Preservation Technology Bulletin*, *National Trust for Historic Preservation Bulletin*, *Old House Journal*, *Architecture*, and *Traditional Building*. Many major ones, such as *Cultural Resource Management Bulletin*, *Technology & Conservation*, and *Progressive Architecture*, were not consistently named. Repeatedly, respondents indicated a need for information about what is available and how to locate and use finding aids. Most respondents also expressed an interest in but a lack of training in the use of electronic information resources.

Again, the interdisciplinary nature of the field creates a need for knowledge about wide-ranging subject areas which may or may not have been areas of formal educational studies. Seminars, workshops, newsletters, current awareness services, and other similar activities may be suitable in addressing this recommendation.

6. Expand and actively market document delivery services.

When personal and local library collections lack the materials needed by the preservationist, several options are available. Resources may be obtained through traditional interlibrary loan services (ILL), sometimes free of charge. However, an uncertain time lag is necessarily associated with obtaining materials in this fashion, a feature discouraging to many users. A newer alternative is a commercial document delivery service, a company which specializes in quickly providing copies of original material for profit. This solution is usually more timely and may be less expensive than ILL.

Referring to businesses such as CARL Systems, Inc. and Faxon Research Services, Ronald Leach and Judith Tribble of the Indiana State University Libraries asserted in 1993: "These services allow students, faculty, and campus administrators using computers in their local libraries or at their desks to electronically search databases containing tables of contents, and in some cases article abstracts, from <u>thousands</u> of journals. Furthermore, these services allow end users to obtain copies of articles the same day they are ordered."[9] On the other hand, Kathleen Kurosman and Barbara Ammerman Durniak of Vassar College, following a comparison of commercial document suppliers and ILL, concluded in 1994, "...In most cases the use of commercial document delivery suppliers did not appear to be a more effective or efficient means of obtaining access to articles not available at our library."[10]

Sixty-three percent of the preservationists surveyed in the Northwestern study reported using such services. Those in academic settings are more familiar with these document delivery companies, so it will be necessary to market the delivery services to cultural resource managers in the private sector. Another related concern for the National Center may be to verify that journals critical to the field are covered by the companies or to encourage their coverage if sparse or nonexistent.

7. Cultivate appreciation for the expertise of the information specialist.

In 1992, David Penniman, President of the Council on Library Resources, rhetorically asked, "What sets librarians apart from other professions in terms of its values? The librarian facilitates access to information by assuring preservation of recorded information, organizing information to enable retrieval, providing equal opportunity for access to information, and fostering a climate that promotes use."[11]

Innovative information systems have not replaced these professional values nor the need for the librarian—indeed, they may have intensified that need—but technology has altered our vocabulary. According to Susan K. Martin of Georgetown University, "Some advocate replacing the title 'librarian' with a more futuristic term such as 'information specialist.'"[12] Regardless of the term preferred the role is still vital: to locate information, to provide directions to information, to inventory information, and to evaluate information.

Julie Bichteler of the Graduate School of Library and Information Science, University of Texas, and Dederick Ward, Geology Librarian and Associate Professor of Library Administration, University of Illinois at Urbana, Champagne, found geoscientists highly appreciative of librarians: "Dependence of library users on librarians increases as geologists have less and less time for information seeking. Those in private companies indicate they often just describe a new project to the librarian and then return to their offices, waiting for reports, database searches, etc., to appear."[13] Although historic preservation is a much younger profession than geoscience, this finding suggests that the location and packaging of information for historic preservationists may raise <u>their</u> appreciation for the librarian. Developing contractual information services for them may do the same, for architects are engineers and businesspeople as well as artists.

Respect and appreciation are attitudes that must be earned, so it goes without saying that the information services provided to historic resource managers, as well as the workshops, publications, etc. used to promote them, must have the hallmark of quality.

8. Initiate cohort groups to foster usage of Internet, electronic bulletin boards, and e-mail.

Stott and Fleming identified twelve gophers, eight world-wide web servers, seventeen listservs, five usenet newsgroups, four full-text databases, and ten indexes and databases relating to preservation that were available on the Internet in May 1994.[14] Clearly, pertinent electronic information is becoming available for this field. In discussing the gathering and use of information by American historians, Case suggested: "...Electronic mail and computer bulletin boards might be exploited to facilitate the exchange of information among historians, archivists, and librarians about the location and use of source materials. The formation of 'invisible colleges' could in this way be encouraged, and librarians and archivists could more easily become part of them."[15]

This strategy also could be employed with historic conservationists. The survey of preservationists cited earlier determined that 35 percent of respondents were familiar with e-mail; 24 percent used the Internet; and 19 percent were experienced with electronic bulletin boards. These numbers indicate a basic group of interested users on which to cultivate and expand the use of electronic networking for the purpose of sharing and distributing preservation information.

Use of peer groups is an effective way of reaching professionals. The National Center certainly can influence preservationists through professional organizations, such as the American Institute of Architects and the Association for Preservation Technology, and through the literature of the field. Offering workshops on electronic networking also should be beneficial.

9. Develop contractual information services focusing on the unique needs of various entities within the field.

The National Translations Center, Document Delivery, of the Library of Congress supplies unpublished translations from other languages into English in subject areas of the medical, natural, physical, and social sciences. This fee-based governmental service could serve as a model for the National Center to offer other information services that meet the needs of historic preservationists.

As reported earlier, some cultural resource managers do not have access to computers. Others lack skills/confidence for online searching; 24 percent professed a lack of time for such activity. These preservationists could find it simpler and even beneficial to employ a service to provide information on a specific topic or for a specific project.

Other findings from the study which seem to support this recommendation included frustrations in the use of information: time involved in searching (66 percent), lack of physical access to resources (44 percent), and lack of familiarity with electronic databases (40 percent).

Further reinforcement for the strategy comes from Florence Skelly's paper on library patron expectations in the 21st century, "Expect increasing use by small business. Small business and at-home businesses will become part of the library patron network."[16] Skelly is the President of Telematics, a U.S. West Company. Preservationists, working as independent contractors, may well be considered small business.

10. Establish clearinghouses to solicit, index, abstract, and disseminate the vast interdisciplinary information critical to the field.

Much indexing and abstracting of preservation literature is being accomplished; nevertheless, there is much more to be done. In 1989 Constance C. Gould and Mark Handler prepared *Information Needs in the Social Sciences: An Assessment* for the Research Libraries Group. Their report included deficiencies for anthropology, one of the disciplines of preservation, at that time: (1) development of a machine-readable index to the holdings of Harvard's Tozzer Museum Library and the Museum of Mankind Library in London; (2) documentation of and access to the ephemeral ("gray") literature of the field, including government environmental reports, archeological site reports produced under contract, and a national site register; (3) production of machine-readable linguistic databases including standardized vocabulary lists; and (4) provision of databases such as a national union catalog of museum holdings, a comprehensive fossil data base, and a work-in-progress data base.[17]

Some of these projects are now underway. Nevertheless, a national effort, with regional centers to cover specific aspects of the problem, may be justified.

CONCLUSION

The recommendations were developed according to Don R. Swanson's application of Karl Popper's model of knowledge to library problems. Popper's theory, fully discussed in his *The Poverty of Historicism*, prefers a problem-oriented approach to the development of knowledge over one of subject or discipline.[18]

Popper, himself, acknowledged Kant's influence on the development of his philosophy:

To yield to every whim of curiosity, and to allow our passion for inquiry to be restrained by nothing but the limits of our ability, this shows an eagerness of mind not unbecoming to scholarship. But it is wisdom that has the merit of selecting from among the innumerable problems which present themselves, those whose solution is important to mankind.[19]

Scholarship has been employed by two individuals to compile these recommendations, but the wisdom of many will be necessary to discriminate among them. Some may be implemented by the National Center; others may be activated by Watson Library. Historic preservation cannot be dealt with on a discipline-oriented basis, for far too many fields are involved. In reference to anthropology, Gould and Handler stated, "The interests of anthropologists lead them not only beyond the bounds of their own discipline, but outside those of the social sciences as well. Archeology, in its

methods for dating and determining the effects of the environment on artifacts, draws on physics, chemistry, geology and climatology."[20] And archeology and anthropology are only two of the areas of historic preservation.

Both librarians and historic conservationists are faced with maintaining the positive aspects of our heritage while charting a course for an unknown future. Continuity and transformation are vital elements of both professions; the promise of our confluence or partnership raises expectations like an incoming tide.

NOTES

1. H. Ward Jandl, "Preservation Technology and Training Symposium," *The National Center for Preservation Technology and Training at Northwestern State University of Louisiana*, no.1 (July 1994): 4.

2. National Center for Preservation Technology and Training, "Concept Paper," (National Park Service, Department of the Interior, 1993).

3. U.S. Congress, Office of Technology Assessment, *Technologies for Prehistoric and Historic Preservation* (Washington, DC: U.S. Government Printing Office, 1986), 107.

4. Ada D. Jarred and Martha V. Henderson, "Communication Patterns of Historic Preservationists," in *Knowledge Organization and Quality Management*, vol. 4 of *Advances in Knowledge Organization* (Frankfurt: INDEKS Verlag, 1994), 272-279.

5. Peter Stott and Arlene Fleming, "Considerations on the Information Management Component of the National Center for Preservation Technology and Training," National Park Service, Natchitoches, Louisiana, May 1994.

6. Noriko Wood, *Computer Use in State Historic Preservation Offices* (Washington, DC: National Park Service, 1990); Betsy Chittenden, "When Cultures Collide: Computer Technology and the Cultural Resources Professional," *The Public Historian: A Journal of Public History* 13, no.3 (Summer 1991): 55-73.

7. Donald O. Case, "The Collection and Use of Information by Some American Historians: A Study of Motives and Methods," *Library Quarterly* 61, no.1 (January 1991): 61-82; Bella Weinberg, "Why Indexing Fails the Researcher," *Proceed-*

ings of the 50th ASIS Annual Meeting 24 (October 1987): 241-244; Helen Tibbo, "Abstracts, Online Searching, and the Humanities: An Analysis of the Structure and Content of Abstracts of Historical Discourse" (Ph.D. diss., University of Maryland, College Park, 1989); Lisbeth Björklund, "The Potential of Using Knowledge Organizing Tools in Collaborative System Development," in *Knowledge Organization and Quality Management*, vol. 4 of *Advances in Knowledge Organization* (Frankfurt: INDEKS Verlag, 1994), 264-271.

8. John J. Jax and Van Houlson, "A Current Awareness Service for Faculty and Staff: The Stout Experience," *College & Research Libraries* 49 (November 1988): 514-522; John T. Butler, "A Current Awareness Service Using Microcomputer Databases and Electronic Mail," *College & Research Libraries* 54 (March 1993): 115-123; Robert Stueart, "The Liberal Arts College Library: Paradox or Panacea," *College & Research Libraries* 51 (November 1990): 524-529.

9. Ronald Leach and Judith Tribble, "Electronic Document Delivery: New Options for Libraries," *Journal of Academic Librarianship* 18, no.6 (January 1993): 364.

10. Kathleen Kurosman and Barbara Ammerman Durniak, "Document Delivery: A Comparison of Commercial Document Suppliers and Interlibrary Loan Services," *College & Research Libraries* 55 (March 1994): 138.

11. W. David Penniman, "Presentation to the FEDLINK Spring Membership Meeting, May 11, 1992. Reference to the "Strategic Vision for Professional Librarians" statement developed by the "Strategic Visions Steering Committee" (draft) in December 1991 and distributed via listserver. Supported by the Council on Library Resources.

12. Susan K. Martin, "Strategic Vision for the Library Profession" in *Federal Librarians in the 21st Century: Changing Roles in the Electronic Age* (Washington, DC: Library of Congress, September 15, 1993): 3.

13. Julie Bichteler and Dederick Ward, "Information-Seeking Behavior of Geoscientists," *Special Libraries* 180, no.3 (Summer 1989): 172.

14. Stott and Fleming, *Considerations on the Information Management*, Appendix I, 1-17.

15. Case, "The Collection and Use of Information," 80.

16. Florence Skelly, "Patron Expectations in the 21st Century," in David Kohl, ed. *12 Years Till 2000: Preparing for Reference in the 21st Century* (Chicago: Reference & Adult Services Division, American Library Association, 1990), 14.

17. Constance Gould and Mark Handler, *Information Needs in the Social Sciences: An Assessment* (Mountain View, CA: Research Libraries Group, 1989), 41-48.

18. Don R. Swanson, "Librarians and the Growth of Knowledge," *Library Quarterly* 49 (January 1979): 3-25; Karl J. Weintraub, "The Humanistic Scholar and the Library," *Library Quarterly* 50, no.1 (January 1980): 29.

19. Popper, Karl R., *The Poverty of Historicism* (Boston: The Beacon Press, 1957), 56.

20. Gould and Handler, *Information Needs*, 43.

The University Library as Information Provider and Communication Facilitator:

A Faculty Research Database

Judith R. J. Johnson and Anne E. Hedrich

ABSTRACT

The current "information explosion," coupled with rapid electronic developments and pervasive economic constraints, is forcing academic communities and their libraries to refine and rethink their policies and services in order to increase efficient dissemination of information. This requires close monitoring of and quicker response to the changing needs of their own user communities. This collaborative project addresses these issues by collecting and correlating information obtained directly from university faculty and research units, tracking elements such as research interests, projects, patents, funding sources, publications, and courses taught. Preliminary findings and the significance of providing wide electronic access to the results are discussed.

INTRODUCTION

The Faculty Research Interests database project grew out of a desire to more carefully hone collection development at Merrill Library to meet the information needs of Utah State University. The library's collection development has historically been based primarily on curricular information. Anticipation of new demands concurrent with static or even reduced acquisitions budget alloca-

tions prompted the search for a means to delineate and track active research areas as well.

We determined that the most reasonable approach to this problem was to obtain the information through direct contact with faculty members and research adjuncts of the University. A programmed series of specific questions directed to each researcher would provide the information which we could then organize for our use. Storing

Judith R. J. Johnson and Anne E. Hedrich are Reference Librarians at Merrill Library, Utah State University, Logan, Utah.

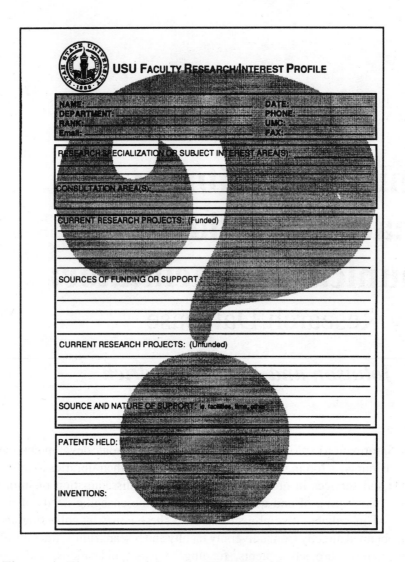

Figure 1: First page of Faculty Research/Interest questionnaire

this information in an electronic relational database would allow flexibility in both anticipated and potential uses. Information would be easily accessible, could be updated annually, and would be available for electronic dissemination.

APPROACH

It is difficult to gather information from university faculty, because such individuals are both perpetually overloaded with work and frequently the target of surveys from a variety of agencies. Because ever-rising costs and the proliferation of journal titles have captured the attention of university faculty and researchers, this awareness was our hook for eliciting the cooperation of our user community.

In order to include all 1000+ faculty members and researchers in the survey, it was necessary to address all academic departments as well as research units and other university affiliates. Sheer numbers dictated the use of a printed survey questionnaire. Drawing heavily on the work of Don Dillman* and other social scientists, a four-page questionnaire was designed and tested which visually delineated various groups of questions by subject. A large shadow-toned question mark was used as a watermark on the first page of the survey, and the university seal was depicted on two of the four pages to reinforce the official nature of the survey (Figure 1).

```
PROFILE GUIDE                        Plants, Soils and Biometeorology

                              SB   Plant culture

                                                             Level: _____

     LC CLASS          SUBJECT DESCRIPTION           COMMENTS AND RELATED LC CLASSES

_____  SB 107-109   Economic botany          _____  SB 91     World crops
_____  110-112      Methods for special areas
                       Including dry-land and tropical agriculture,    _____  QK 757-924.5  Remote sensing. Plant canopies
                       and irrigation farming        _____  QC 581-999   Meteorology. Climatology
_____  113.2-118.45 Seeds. Propagation. Nurseries.                     Atmospheric conditions. Aeronomy
_____  183-317      Field crops. Forage crops. Crop physiology
_____  317.5-450.87 Horticulture             _____  QE 500-625   Dynamic and structural geology
_____  320-353.5       Vegetables            _____  QE 581+      Erosion
_____  354-402         Fruit culture and orchard care   _____  QH 75+    Nature conservation. Landscape protection
_____  403-450.87      Flowers. Ornamental plants  _____  QH 84       Soil biology
_____  415          Greenhouses. Greenhouse management   _____  QR 111   Soil microbiology
_____  435          Arboriculture            _____  SD 390-426   Forest soils. Forest reserves
_____  450.9-467    Gardens and gardening
_____  454.6           Garden center retail management   _____  TA 705+  Soil mechanics
_____  469-476.4       Landscape architecture   _____  TC 801+    Irrigation engineering
_____  481-485      Parks and public reservations   _____  TD 388   Water conservation
_____  599-990.5    Diseases and pests       _____  TD 878     Soil pollution
                       Including treatment and control
_____  992-998      Economic zoology. Agricultural pests

                              S   Agriculture

_____  S 494.5      Biotechnology            _____  S 604.8-621.5  Reclamation and irrigation of
_____  583-589.6    Agricultural chemistry and physics                farmland. Organic farming.
_____  590-599.9    Soils                    _____  622-627      Soil conservation
_____  592             Soil chemistry. Soil physics   _____  631-667   Fertilizers. Soil improvement
_____  600-604      Meteorology. Crop systems   _____  900-954    Conservation of natural resources
                                             _____  950-954      Land conservation

                    Other (please specifiy): _____

  Please indicate your area(s) of research interest by putting a check on the line in front of the most appropriate subject heading(s).
                    Sub-headings may be circled if appropriate, or specifics can be added.
```

Figure 2: Page 4 of the Faculty Research/Interest questionnaire

The questionnaire was constructed to define research interests by free text description and the researcher's own choice of the Library of Congress (LC) subject headings that best describe their interests (Figure 2). There is space for five journal titles considered primary in the faculty member's discipline, and five journal titles essential for his/her particular research. The respondent is asked to indicate which of the journals in each category he/she personally subscribes to, and list reasons for the subscription, such as membership in a professional association, personal convenience, and/or absence from the library's collection (Figure 3).

Data on research conducted at Utah State University will aid in collection development, and may provide crucial information for decisions being made in an era of reduced budgets and endangered serials collections. Based upon the questionnaire, Merrill Library can identify specific journals needed for research by university faculty. Although it is impossible to purchase every journal needed by every researcher, previously undetected trends in titles needed may be uncovered. Since the information will be updated annually, these trends may be tracked over time. One of the greatest benefits of the project will be data delineating long term patterns and sudden shifts in research emphases at the University.

List five (5) JOURNALS considered primary in your field:

☐ _____
☐ _____
☐ _____
☐ _____
☐ _____

● Check if you hold a personal subscription. Please indicate why you subscribe (eg. Library doesn't have it, comes with association membership, through grant, personal convenience, etc.).

List five (5) JOURNALS most essential to your work: (may include titles from above)

☐ _____
☐ _____
☐ _____
☐ _____
☐ _____

● Check if you hold a personal subscription. Please indicate why you subscribe (eg. Library doesn't have it, comes with association membership, through grant, personal convenience, etc.).

Please list any electronic journals that you subscribe to and their cost to you:

_____
_____
_____
_____

List JOURNALS, TRANSACTIONS or PROCEEDINGS in which you have published:

_____
_____
_____
_____
_____

FOREIGN LANGUAGES READ:

_____
_____

Please attach a complete **BIBLIOGRAPHY OF YOUR PUBLICATIONS** for the USU Faculty Publications Bibliography database. (Include the following information):

Book/Journal Title: Chapter/Article Name:
Publisher: Author/Co-authors:
Publication Year: Vol/Ed:
Issue: Pages:

Figure 3: Page 2 of Faculty Research/Interest questionnaire

Selected LC classification ranges can be used to refine or reconfigure book approval profiles currently in use, and analyze journal holdings and needs.

The questions developed to characterize journal use patterns suggested other access issues critical to academic libraries at the present time. Increasing use of Interlibrary Services to obtain articles or copies of articles, and the appearance of new document delivery vehicles and vendors, inspired a series of questions regarding individual use of Interlibrary Services, in terms of both frequency and quantity. Additional questions were aimed at assessing the use of a new electronic ordering and notification service our ILS depart-

ment had recently developed, as well as exploring the feasibility of using commercial document delivery services (Figure 4). Would faculty be willing to pay for enhanced document delivery services, and if so, how much?

Campus interest in the questionnaire grew and the original vision of the database expanded to include research and teaching personnel, with added questions about courses taught, consultation areas, and foreign language expertise to supplement identifying information such as department and email addresses. In the future, photographic images and other biographical materials may be added. These enhancements will offer prospective faculty and graduate students the opportunity

INTERLIBRARY SERVICES - DOCUMENT DELIVERY

Approximate number of photocopy requests you make in a year? _____

Approximate number of book/thesis requests you make in a year? _____

Do you send ILL requests and receive notification electronically (VAX)? ☐ Yes ☐ No
Did you know you could? ☐ Yes   ☐ No

What would you consider a reasonable turn-around time from date of request to ILL until you are notified of arrival? _____

What would you consider to be a reasonable flat fee cost for 24 - 48 hour document delivery to you for an article? _____

Would you be willing to pay part or all of the expense of 24 - 48 hour document delivery service for materials obtained off campus? _____% _____ all _____ none

Would you be willing to pay for delivery from the Library to your office? ☐ Yes ☐ No

LIST COURSES YOU TEACH:
Course #   Course Title:

_____ _____
_____ _____
_____ _____
_____ _____
_____ _____

What materials or services would you find most useful as additions to the new Science and Technology Library (eg. book or journals titles, CD-ROM, databases...)?

Additional Comments about the Library/Research interface:

MERRILL LIBRARY

We appreciate your cooperation in completing this form. This information will foster more productive collaboration between the Research Community and the Library. For clarification or information call: Judith R. J. Johnson x 3331 or Anne E. Hedrich x 2165.

Figure 4: Page 3 of Faculty Research/Interest questionnaire

to investigate campus research areas and expands the services provided at the Reference Desk. Patrons with specialized information or service needs can locate local experts through the database.

The University Research Office expressed interest and suggested that more specific information on research projects, such as sources and nature of support for both funded and unfunded research, be added to the database.

COLLABORATION

Working with other units and agencies both on and off campus to make information electronically available and to improve services represents a new collaborative aspect of library activity. The University Research Council indicated interest in the tracking of research specialties, grant funding and faculty publications, and the Research Office subsequently provided funding to underwrite the expenses of software, programming and student help. The University's Research Park affirmed their own interest and suggested tracking of inventions and patents as well. A database coordinating these varied aspects of the research scene could have numerous uses outside the library, in such areas as research and consultation team building, fund raising, recruitment of new faculty and graduate students, and assessment of new directions in research emphasis.

Yankee Book Peddler, a library vendor, provided a copy of their basic outline of Library of Congress subject headings and call number ranges which they use to develop customized Approval Profiles (APs). We adapted their outline in order to test some aspects of user profiling against the current APs in use at this library. Comparison could be made between the call numbers of the journal titles respondents indicated they considered important to own and read with the call number ranges and allied subject headings that they specified as areas they considered descriptive of their work interests. This information could then be compared to existing collection APs for the library, as well as to our holdings in both book and journal titles. We could then modify APs where necessary and also provide Yankee Book Peddler with a different way to test their own subject area configuration matrix.

Merrill Library's part in this collaborative effort consisted of project development and management. Support was also provided in the form of staff hours, electronic hardware, office space, and supplies.

ELECTRONIC STORAGE AND ACCESS

The primary criterion applied in selecting the software used for the databases was easy availability to any library or unit interested in using or emulating the project. Research focused on commercially-produced programs. Microsoft's *FoxPro* relational database software was selected for its flexibility and ease of use. *Papyrus* bibliographic software by Research Software Design was chosen to organize the faculty publications database. The faculty bibliography will be available independently from the rest of the information as well as in an integrated format.

Networking capability was another important consideration in the choice of software.

Electronic availability campus-wide and, potentially, via the Internet is critical to the usefulness of the instrument being developed. Electronic access makes it available to many more people than the information would be in print.

Electronic storage makes the information readily available for any number of different uses and also allows easy updating.

PRELIMINARY RESULTS

Data input is under way with the information that has been amassed, using input screens designed for this purpose by a programmer utilizing existing *FoxPro* features (Figure 5). Information provided in response to those questions which were open-ended has been tabulated, and some trends are beginning to appear. On the one hand, appreciation for library services in place is frequently expressed; there are requests for some new services and resources which we are already in the process of making available. On the other hand, some requests are for currently existing services or holdings, indicating either inadequate promotion by the library or a lack of diligent library use on the faculty member's part.

Journal titles listed by respondents in the essential to their work and primary in their field categories are being compared to current journal holdings in Merrill Library. It is too early to draw significant conclusions; however, the trend in College of Science departments to this point seems to indicate a surprisingly high degree of correlation, approximately 80% in each area, considering the ongoing pressure by departments to obtain new titles. This apparent trend may falter as analysis extends to non-science disciplines.

CONCLUSION

Collecting local information on researchers and educators is a familiar undertaking. Processing, storing and making it electronically available to the university community is a new aspect of information provision for Merrill Library. This role becomes more valuable as competition for qualified faculty and students, and research and development dollars increases. Librarians, as experts on the local university community, can take on an expanding role as information organizers and providers. Detailed knowledge of specific research areas aids in the provision of services with the least cost.

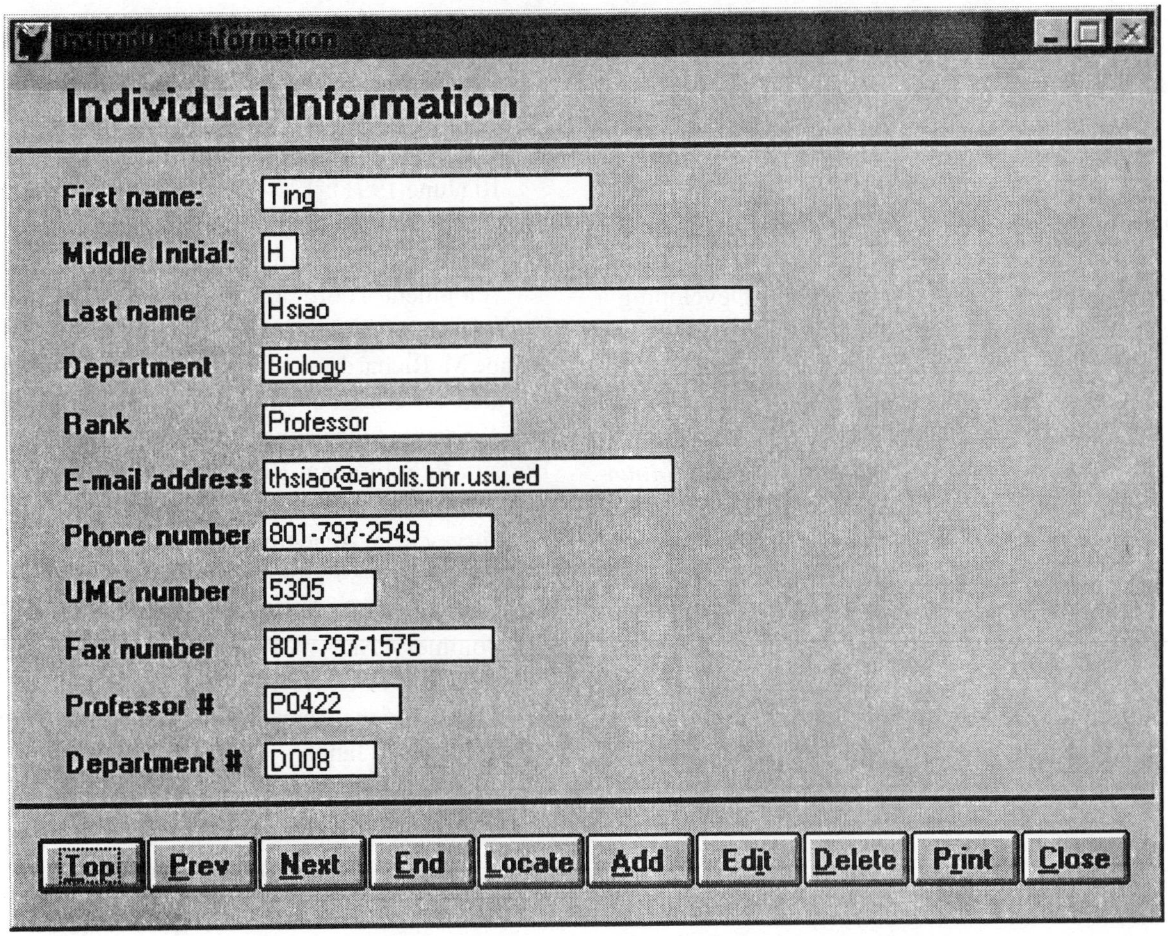

Individual Information

First name:	Ting
Middle Initial:	H
Last name	Hsiao
Department	Biology
Rank	Professor
E-mail address	thsiao@anolis.bnr.usu.ed
Phone number	801-797-2549
UMC number	5305
Fax number	801-797-1575
Professor #	P0422
Department #	D008

Top | Prev | Next | End | Locate | Add | Edit | Delete | Print | Close

Figure 5: Example of data input screen developed in *FoxPro*

There are some reservations about the project. The survey methods we have implemented have yielded what is in survey terms a highly successful return; however, complete information has been gathered from only 69% overall of university faculty/researchers at this point. To be able to make informed and balanced journal collection development decisions, information from all researchers is the ideal goal. We expect to receive greater participation as we conduct annual updates and the resulting databases are seen to have practical application. For libraries considering a similar undertaking, the costs in time and labor for a project of this magnitude need to be carefully weighed.

Although we are still in the process of building our databases and processing our data, one of the most significant results of this project may well have already manifested itself. We have discovered an upsurge in interest in the library and its' activities as the university community has become aware of the nature and goals of our undertaking. The library is being seen as an active, even proactive, force on campus rather than the passive body many formerly perceived it to be. This provides us with an excellent opportunity to build stronger liaison relationships in the various educational roles the modern academic library is prepared to perform. If the services already being provided receive greater exposure across campus and positive changes are seen to come from our project, the improved access and services the library will be providing should continue to build greater participation and support in the community of users we are committed to serve.

SELECTED BIBLIOGRAPHY

Mike Brennan and Janet Hoek, "The Behavior of Respondents, Nonrespondents, and Refusers Across Mail Surveys," *Public Opinion Quarterly* 56 (Winter 1992): 530-535.

*Don A. Dillman, *Mail and Telephone Surveys: The Total Design Method* (New York: Wiley, 1978).

Joan G. Hubbard and Kathryn Payne, "Developing a Research Level Journal Collection in Applied Mathematics: A Collaboration Between Librarians and Mathematicians," in *Window to the World: The Challenge of Change: Proceedings of the Research Forum, Academic Library Section, Mountain Plains Library Association, MPLA/WLA Joint Conference Held in Cheyenne, Wyoming September 30 - October 3, 1992*, ed. Mary C. Bushing (Emporia, Kansas: Emporia State University Press, 1992): 73-91.

Harry Llull, "Meeting the Academic and Research Information Needs of Scientists and Engineers in the University Environment," *Science and Technology Libraries* 11 (Spring 1991): 83-90.

Lyn MacCorkle, "Communications: Publishing an Annual Faculty Bibliography at the University of Miami," *Information Technology and Libraries* 10 (June 1991): 121-127.

Catherine E. Pasterczyk, "A Microcomputer-based Faculty Research Interest File: A Collection Development Tool," *Microcomputers for Information Management* 2 (December 1985): 265-276.

Jeanne M. Richardson, "Faculty Research Profile Created for Use in a University Library," *Journal of Academic Librarianship* 16 (July 1990): 154-157.

Barbara F. Schloman, Roy S. Lilly, and Wendy Hu, "Targeting Liaison Activities: Use of a Faculty Survey in an Academic Research Library," *RQ* 29 (Summer 1989): 496-505.

Ernst J. Schuegraf, Liam T. Keliher, and Martin F. van Bommel, "An Analysis of Personal Journal Subscriptions of University Faculty. Part 1. Science," *Journal of the American Society for Information Science* 43 (January 1992): 28-33.

Distance Learning and the Academic Library

Carolyn A. Snyder and Jay Starratt

ABSTRACT

Technology-based distance learning programs are proliferating on college campuses and are forecast to be an important and significant aspect of the total university teaching effort in the near future. This paper examines aspects of the academic library organization and the needs of distance learning programs, and suggests that the match between the libraries capabilities and experience and the requirements of distance learning make the library an ideal home for the program.

Academic libraries have the opportunity to broaden their role as the central campus learning support organization by assuming a leadership role in the establishment and growth of distance learning programs within the university. The library is strongly positioned and uniquely able to provide the broad spectrum of support required for a successful distance learning program. Expertise and experience in program coordination, technical and organizational networking, facility management, and course development and support services, provide the credentials necessary to excel in leading a distance learning initiative. By convincing campus administrators that the library can and should assume a primary responsibility in distance learning, and by remaining active and central in the technological changes taking place in the campus learning environment, the library can continue to enhance all its services and secure its role as the primary academic support organization. This position is supported by the experiences of the library at Southern Illinois University at Carbondale, where the library dean and other library faculty and staff have assumed these responsibilities.

Described in its simplest form, distance learning is the delivery of formal courses and other continuing education opportunities to remote sites. New initiatives deliver these courses through interactive video and telecommunications. These offerings can be received in any appropriately equipped and wired classroom in an interactive mode with the instructor and students in two or

Carolyn A. Snyder is Dean of Library Affairs and Jay Starratt is Director of Technical and Automation Services at Southern Illinois University at Carbondale.

more classrooms, and at one or many sites. With access to satellites and to other rapidly transforming technologies, distance education opportunities today are evolving quickly and promise to develop into an important part of the university's effort. Substantial amounts of funding for technologically delivered teaching will expand learning opportunities bringing them closer to students' homes, indeed, to the students' home. Universities and libraries must be leaders in this movement if they are to remain viable.

These programs are evolving at a time when academic libraries are at a critical juncture in their development and are actively redefining their place in campus information technology, telecommunications, networking, and continuing education activities. It is our position that academic libraries must actively and creatively define the scope of their organizations to include the full range of information services, including distance learning. As campuses and libraries refine the vision for the "Library of the Future" (or the "Virtual Library"), strategic planning for the library should include distance learning by taking a broader view of the library's service role, and the important relationship these services have to academic matters. If that role includes distance learning coordination and support, the library's chances of remaining the most central and vital academic support unit on campus are greatly enhanced.

As information sources have become more easily available through a variety of sources, effective libraries have strengthened their positions as the key academic service unit by providing expert library faculty and other specialists to assist users in finding the information and documents they need in the ever expanding mass of information available, and by developing the campus library as a true center for learning on campus, in both the physical library building and through the library services delivered through campus networks. The addition of distance learning classrooms and multi-media course development support to the library's charges is a natural companion to these efforts. As distance learning becomes

more a part of the fabric of the university cloth, and often comes with no added resources for the departments expected to deliver courses, there is every reason for the university to turn to the central, most reliable, and successful support group on campus to provide the infrastructure of services that make for a successful distance learning program.

On most campuses, the library earned its role as the key, universal campus support organization for research and for learning by providing many more services and facilities than shelves and a catalog. Classroom space, media services, informed and expert training, formal courses for all majors and disciplines, and many other services and resources have fed into the ability of the library to claim a role larger and broader than any other unit in the full activities of the campus. The library's obligations range from orienting the entering undecided freshman, to assisting the research of internationally known scholars and to all points in between. The diverse and plentiful qualities required of current academic libraries and librarians in order to meet the many demands and expectations arising from the university reassure us that libraries can move easily and effectively into distance learning. The list below describes some of the most important of these points.

- No other support organization on campus has the knowledge and long-term experience in working with all the colleges, departments, and campus academic programs. Libraries should never underestimate the importance of their understanding of the academic missions of the university's departments, or the value of their integration into the activities of individual faculty and students. This understanding and familiarity are more important to our future success in technological endeavors than are our burgeoning technical skills.
- No other support unit on campus has consistently demonstrated its effectiveness in supporting the learning process. Reserve book and media rooms, bibliographic instruction

programs and individualized teaching at the reference desk are only three examples of the broad and well-received services the library offers in support of the curriculum.

- Library deans, directors and other key administrators usually have demonstrated their leadership and management ability in organizing technology-based learning services.

- Over the past decades, and especially in the past few years, many libraries have become involved at a primary level in network and other technological developments on campus. They have shown a facility for developing new expertise on a continual basis, and demonstrated a talent for tying traditional faculty efforts (and traditional faculty) to new technology developments. We are so deeply entrenched in campus technology planning and provision that we forget that many of our skills were built in great haste not too long ago. We can develop skills for distance learning in the same manner. The knowledge and skills required to support Geographic Information Systems, to support and develop multimedia collections, and to support the provision of networked information are the same skills, abilities, organizational know-how, and adaptability needed for distance learning.

- Another critical area that is often solely within the province of the library's experience is the ability to cooperate with other schools or agencies. Multi-type library networks, cooperative borrowing agreements, all and sundry networks, consortia and other cooperative endeavors that require a large part of a library's time and attention are not always familiar to other university entities. Libraries cooperate as institutions and such cooperation is enormously important in distance learning enterprises.

- Libraries are also becoming more and more familiar with bringing in people with different expertise and making them productive in a large but focused umbrella organization.

Southern Illinois University at Carbondale provides an example where distance learning coordination has become the responsibility of the library. Although this leadership role was formalized just recently, in May 1994, the information services expertise and instructional technology leadership of the library was acknowledged during the university's two year planning process for distance learning. The recognition of this expertise was confirmed with the appointment, more than two years ago, of the library dean as the university representative to a state higher education board telecommunications committee. The committee developed a plan and funding proposal for distance learning state-wide, which was strongly supported by the state higher education board, the community college board, and the governor's office. The legislature allocated $15M in 1993-94 to equip and wire 125 classrooms throughout the state.

The Library Dean and staff work closely with state, regional and campus constituents to coordinate the university's distance learning program. The Dean is the University's academic representative to the two regional consortiums which have distance learning classrooms on campus. Equipping and renovating these classrooms is the work of library staff as is the development of faculty training programs and the integration of other technology-based teaching tools. The library staff charged with these duties include librarians, instructional developers, video production staff and systems personnel. The library is also, of course, responsible for developing an infrastructure to deliver course-related information resources to our remote students. Such resource sharing in Illinois is a long and vibrant tradition and contributes to our ability to work in the larger arena of cooperation necessitated by the interlocking complexities of consortia teaching.

Although other groups on campus do have some of the experience, expertise, resources and abilities required for coordinating distance learning, there is no organization on campus that is as committed to support and service for the total academic mission as is a good library. There is often no organization on campus that combines the dedication to serve all users (departments and individuals) with the thorough knowledge of the particular programs and faculty that comprise those programs, and the technical skills to meet new technological challenges. Also, there is often no other unit as successful at marshaling the campuses pockets of expertise into united efforts. It is logical and beneficial, for the university and the library, for the distance learning infrastructure to reside in the library.

Libraries/Academic Computing Centers Collaboration:

Linking Faculty with Instructional Software and Multimedia

Carol Wright

ABSTRACT

Instructional software and multimedia packages can significantly enhance student learning. However, individually authoring and designing programs for local applications can be prohibitively labor intensive, expensive, and intimidating for faculty. Faculty need the option to identify existing software and multimedia packages to meet their instructional objectives. At Penn State, collaboration between the Libraries and the Center for Academic Computing helps faculty locate existing software and helps them meet instructional goals via emerging technologies.

The advantages of using instructional technologies for higher education applications are clear. Instructional software, courseware, and multimedia packages can significantly enhance student learning. Software can simulate phenomena which are difficult to replicate in real time, or in a hazard-free environment. All disciplines and subjects are suitable candidates for technological applications. Students can interactively participate in their learning through simulation and interaction with the scientific principles involved in aerodynamics, geologic processes, or chemistry experiments. Students can tour art galleries, requesting to learn more about an individual artist or artistic period, or can choose to listen to music or narration related to a particular work. They can choose to examine portions of an art work in minute detail. Or, students can study anatomy and physiology, simulating laser surgery, and analyzing anatomical cross sections not otherwise possible. Also, computers can link text, graphs, sound, and animation to create total learning packages in a manner which mirrors the manner in which humans process information.[1] Instruc-

Carol Wright is a Reference Librarian at Pattee Library, Pennsylvania State University, University Park, Pennsylvania.

tional technologies can help conceptualize very abstract principles, so that learners can apply those principles rather than learn the principles as an end in itself. It allows students to control the learning environment, such as speed of delivery, and the repetition required to reinforce difficult concepts. Advances in technologies and networking are the basis for the growth of distance education as a viable alternative to traditional methods of instruction.

Many faculty are convinced of the benefits of instructional technologies, courseware and multimedia, and are anxious to incorporate it into their instruction. But they are discouraged by the perception that successful integration of technology requires that they author their own courseware, software, and multimedia packages. Insufficient time, lack of technical expertise, and other academic demands seriously hinder faculty creation of courseware and multimedia for local applications. Faculty are often unaware of the existing sources of instructional software at their disposal. Faculty need assistance and administrative support to learn about the varieties of technological resources available, and to incorporate technology into the teaching/learning process.[2]

Several factors have recently converged to encourage and enable faculty to investigate the use of preexisting software:

- First, commercially available packages are becoming more widely available for higher education applications, and can often be purchased at quite reasonable costs.
- Second, services on the Internet such as World Wide Web and Gopher have simplified the process of identifying and previewing software files, so that programs and packages prepared by academic colleagues can easily be shared.
- Third, instructional networking initiatives as alternatives to in-class instruction will incorporate alternative media and technologies in the new delivery systems.

- Finally, this current generation of students have grown up with sophisticated visual and interactive communications as part of their educational and recreational experience. These students consider the interactive, hypermedia environment a natural and expected dimension of learning.

The trend to investigate the availability of preexisting software is reinforced by a 1993 survey conducted by the James Irvine Center for Scholarly Technology at the University of Southern California, which found that directors of academic computing at 981 two-year and four-year colleges say that finding off-the-shelf software for faculty is more important than assisting professors in creating their own courseware.[3] Resources simply do not exist to support the duplication of courseware which may already be available to meet instructional goals.

LIBRARY - COMPUTER INFORMATION SYSTEMS PARTNERSHIP

At Penn State University, the Libraries have had a long and successful history of collaboration with the Computer and Information Systems Division, Center for Academic Computing. One division within the Center for Academic Computing is Educational Technology Services, a faculty support group charged with the mission of empowering faculty in the use of interactive technologies in teaching and learning. ETS consults with faculty members on matching technology to specific instructional needs, consults in the use and integration of existing instructional resources, provides training in the design and use of technology resources for instruction, and develops new instructional resources in cooperation with the faculty.

ETS annually sponsors a Faculty Technology Initiative Program. This program reviews and selects faculty proposals for projects which implement interactive teaching and learning technologies. Project awards are made on a competitive basis, with usually about 40% of the project proposals accepted. An integral part of the Proposal

Review is the identification of existing software which may meet the faculty's instructional goals. The University Libraries are a natural partner to assist in the effort. While ETS maintains a collection of vendor catalogs, the Libraries already has multiple resources, including online databases, directories, and journals to augment and target the software search effort. For this audience, the libraries consider the information coordination and outreach another extension of reference and instructional services. In addition to the proposal review, collaboration occurs at many levels:

- The Libraries and ETS jointly prepared a guide for faculty to use during a software search.
- ETS refers software search requests to the Libraries, and shares new information about resources so that they may be included in the search guide.
- The Libraries and ETS co-sponsor workshops to promote understanding of access to pre-existing software.

SOFTWARE SEARCH STRATEGIES

The goal of the Libraries' search service is to allow faculty to become self-reliant to independently search less complex resources, and to provide more direct, personalized assistance for more sophisticated online databases and internet services such as Gopher and World Wide Web. To that end, the guide to software/courseware search strategies ranges from in-house directories and review sources, to internet archives of software files which can be downloaded for preview. Those previewed programs which are suitable follow the author's directions for compensation and distribution.

An integral part of the Libraries' search strategy is to identify not only specific software packages, but also to identify appropriate readings and supportive material which describe the process of integrating courseware into the curriculum, which highlight differences among the disciplines in software applications, and which identify individuals and institutions with experience in incor-

porating them in higher education. Resources used to identify this supplemental material and courseware include the Internet, online databases, journal literature, software directories, vendor catalogs, and professional associations.

INTERNET RESOURCES
Listservs

Faculty are encouraged to subscribe to listservs in their own disciplines, and also to lists discussing educational technology. They learn to scan assorted lists on Netnews. They may post a question regarding specific content or hardware, or general queries about instructional technologies.

Gopher

Gopher can lead to a wide range of resources, from discussion groups, to descriptions of available software, to archive sites of existing software. The EDUCOM gopher, IKE [IBM Kiosk for Education, formerly ISSAC], the Apple Computer Higher Education Gopher Server, MAC Courseware Archives, the University of Michigan Software Archives, Washington University Archives, and the Purdue University Archives are examples of useful sites. Other discipline specific sites, such as the Clearinghouse for Subject-Oriented Guides [University of Michigan] also often contain menus which include software files. A Veronica search can target more specific queries.

World Wide Web

The Libraries are in the process of creating a Mosaic 'Home Page' for instructional software, courseware and multimedia. This service will enhance the ability to retrieve and preview sophisticated programs.

ONLINE DATABASES
ERIC

Produced by the U.S. Office of Education, ERIC is the comprehensive database for literature in education and related areas, including instructional technologies. A search may be limited to software programs, or a broader search can identify individuals and institutions engaged in software development and implementation. ERIC is one of the databases loaded onto LIAS, the Penn State Libraries Online Catalog, and is therefore accessible from remote locations by members of the Penn State community. Faculty may also choose to use ERIC on compact disc in the reference room.

WORLDCAT/FirstSearch

FirstSearch allows a search to be limited to "publication type," including computer datafiles and software. Then, a subject search may use any keywords desired. A free public terminal is available for patron use in the Reference Room.

[TOC] Table of Contents Database

Also loaded onto LIAS and available to the Penn State community at remote locations is our TOC, the Table of Contents Database. A table of contents database expands searching power by scanning a predetermined set of journal titles to review the contents of new issues. Faculty are encouraged to scan educational technology titles as well as discipline-specific ones. Other libraries may provide access to a table of contents database search as Uncover.

DIRECTORIES

Collections of software directories, catalogs and reviews are available throughout the library collections. Faculty are given a list of selected titles, and also encouraged to use the online catalog. They are provided with suggestions for doing a boolean search with LCSH subject heading terms and their discipline keywords.

VENDOR CATALOGS

The Libraries maintain a collection of vendor catalogs of software and multimedia, from both commercial sources and software dissemination consortiums. Many vendors specialize in a nar-row range of subject disciplines. The file is continuously updated, and materials may circulate from the reference room. Several vendors such as Intellimation, now offer their catalog on compact disc, which allows searching by student level and discipline, and which supports previewing and a simplified ordering system.

PROFESSIONAL ASSOCIATIONS

Professional associations are an excellent source of recent developments in technology. In addition to faculty's own association contacts, the search guide includes a selected list of educational technology associations, and ideas for search terms in the Encyclopedia of Associations.

PUBLICITY AND PROMOTIONAL EFFORTS

Once each semester, the Libraries and ETS co-sponsor a workshop on identifying and evaluating pre-existing software. Particularly successful is the Libraries' participation in week-long ETS workshops during semester break to faculty from campuses outside of University Park to introduce them to new technologies. The Search Strategies guide is available at library kiosks, and is promoted through campus newsletters and traditional news release channels.

WHAT REMAINS TO BE DONE?

Neither the Libraries nor ETS presently have satisfactory previewing facilities, nor support for learning to navigate new systems and practice using the software. This kind of support is needed to provide the critical link to boost faculty into the exploding world of instructional technology. The Michigan State University Libraries Instructional Software Collection, which provide demonstration software and a software demonstration/preview facility, is a model worthy of emulation in future planning.[4] Continued collaboration between ETS and the Libraries will ensure optimum use of University human and technological resources.

THE FUTURE

Headlines in the April 27, 1994 Chronicle of Higher Education proclaim that a new wave, a "Coming Revolution" of Information Technology will transform academe as never before. Networking and instructional technology initiatives are causing the most significant reassessments of technology's role in higher education since the advent of personal computers in the 1980's.[5] Libraries have the opportunity to develop an evolving set of services in the emerging technological environment, which will promote their leadership role central to the instructional mission of the University. Libraries need to position themselves to lead their campuses and faculty into new instructional solutions with technology. Partnership and collaboration with the campus computer center is an excellent vehicle for that leadership role.

NOTES

1. Diane Oblinger, "Introduction to Multimedia in Instruction. An IAT Technology Primer," University of North Carolina at Chapel Hill, Institute for Academic Technology (Bethesda, Md: ERIC Document Reproduction Service No. ED 358 856, 1992).

2. E. Michael Staman, "An Action Plan for Infusing Technology into the Teaching/Learning Process," *Cause/Effect* 13 (Summer 1990): 34-40.

3. Thomas J. DeLoughry, "Academic-Computing Directors Give Low Priority to Developing Instructional Software," *The Chronicle of Higher Education* 40 (October 23, 1993) A26-27.

4. Nancy A. Lucas and Kathy D. Stuut, "Cooperative Instructional Computing Resource Centers," *EDUCOM Review* 27 (November-December, 1992) 32-37.

5. Robert L. Jacobson, "The Coming Revolution," *The Chronicle of Higher Education* (April 27, 1994) 40 A26-29.

Heading Toward the Virtual Library:
Examples & Issues

Nancy H. Dewald

ABSTRACT

Librarians and futurists are predicting a time when the "library without walls," or the virtual library, will essentially replace libraries as we know them. What is this vision of the virtual library? How far along are we on the way to this vision? What issues must we face as this vision is becoming reality? This paper shows examples from the Pennsylvania State University Libraries, the Columbia University Libraries, and a parallel to the virtual library model in the business world, then looks at issues of copyright, economics, control, and access, which will need to be resolved as the virtual library emerges.

Imagine sitting down with a computer less than an inch thick and about the size of a book, with which you connect to a remote location and begin to search a database. You find several articles that will be helpful for a report you must write for work, and you electronically transfer the full text of the articles, including graphs, charts and images, to your computer. In another database, you discover a video, and you select relevant segments from it, including both sound and moving images, to transfer electronically to your computer. You are unsure if there is more to be searched, so you contact the librarian, who suggests more databases for you to try, as well as some the librarian can search for you. Later, the results of the librarian's search, including the full text and images from the articles, are found in your electronic mail.

You call up one of the articles onto your computer screen, and begin to read. If at any point you need a question answered, you can electronically connect to a reference source (such as a specialized encyclopedia) to find the information you need, then return to reading your document.

Later in the day you search another database, this time to find some recreational reading. You are able to scan the front and back covers and tables of contents of recent best-selling novels that interest you, and upon selecting a title, have it transferred to your computer, from which you read it.

This is one version of what is called the "virtual library." You have never left your desk.

Nancy H. Dewald is Reference Librarian at the Thun Library, Pennsylvania State University, Berks Campus, Reading, Pennsylvania.

As long ago as 1980, (though 1980 seems like yesterday to some of us, in the computer world it was an eon ago!) A.J. Harley of the British Library said that some day the library "might be seen as a machine with many simultaneous users, each of whom perceives that he has the whole collection to himself, and further, through connections to other libraries,...access to much greater resources than are physically present." He added that "In the ultimate virtual library, [the user] has access to universal knowledge without delay, at his desk."[1]

Many elements of the virtual library are already here. An on-line catalog such as Penn State's Library Information Access System, or LIAS, can be accessed from remote locations, and the holdings of the university and its campuses throughout Pennsylvania are available. Indexes, abstracts, and table of contents databases in a wide variety of disciplines are accessible on LIAS, and access to the holdings of other research libraries is also available. With the Z39.50 protocol, most of these databases can be searched using the same command language and interface as is used for LIAS. In addition, a variety of electronic journals are also located on LIAS. Uncover, a database of journal articles in many fields, is accessible, with the option of document delivery available to the user as well. And access through LIAS to the Internet, the vast network of computer networks, opens up additional on-line library catalogs, campus information systems, and other sources from around the entire world. Plans for the future include adding linkage to full-image materials via LIAS, adding more databases, and providing bibliographic access to the variety of collections in different formats throughout the university.[2] This system is an outstanding example of the virtual library as it exists in the mid-1990s.

A parallel to education's virtual library exists in the business world right now. I know an engineer in business who uses the tools of the virtual library every day. From his lap-top personal computer, he has access to CD-ROMs and online databases, and connections to his company's information in offices throughout the world. He and others in the company add to these databases and search through them with tools such as Lotus Notes, a workgroup applications software which can provide flexible database access and distribution. This software can also "integrate[e] graphics, text, images, sound, video and other multimedia formats that will become more commonplace in the future."[3] Students and faculty who will be working in universities and businesses this year and in the future will need to be familiar with the possibilities that the virtual library holds for them.

Further progress toward the virtual library will come with technological advances in the next years and decades. Raymond Kurzweil, writing in Library Journal, expects that by the turn of the century electronic books will be as comfortable to read as paper and ink.[4] He also predicts that, with a combination of fiber optics and wireless communications, people will be able "to meet with anyone at any time with high-resolution video conferencing."[5]

Progress toward the virtual library is also being made at Columbia University, where the Digital Library Project JANUS began in 1990. JANUS was first a project of the Columbia Law School Library, working in collaboration with Thinking Machines Corporation and Future InfoSystems, Inc., in response to a critical need for additional library space. The project "utilizes the power of a massively parallel supercomputer to provide users with access to texts, images, sound and video from remote and local workstations."[6] Project JANUS will make available in digital format rare and archival materials as well as the latest electronic journals, with plans for powerful search capabilities including similarity searching and Boolean searching of full text.[7]

Amid all these exciting developments, there are fears. Any "brave new world" is not without its risks and negative aspects. We will have to be bold enough to recognize and wrestle with them. Some of the issues that are being debated as the virtual library emerges include copyright, economics, control, and access, all of which are interrelated.

COPYRIGHT ISSUES

For example, copyright issues will have to be resolved when electronic books, journals, audio, or video can be transferred easily to anyone's computer. Publishers, producers, and librarians will have to grapple with the dilemmas posed by the need, on the one hand, for information access and the need, on the other hand, to pay creators and distributors for their work. Currently there is no way to provide sufficient control of electronic distribution to ease publishers' fears,[8] and lack of protection for copyright undoubtedly discourages many authors and publishers from making their works available over the Internet. Various cost models being debated for libraries include payment per use, a flat-fee structure based on user population, purchasing blocks of use, or end-user payment (such as by credit card).[9] J. D. Gilbert writes that payment for services provided will probably be the best basis for solving the copyright issue for libraries.[10] However, according to a federal panel charged with developing policies for the National Information Infrastructure, the vision of the virtual library being able to provide universal information access at no charge to users will not be possible; new cost structures must be developed for the copyright issue to be resolved.[11] M.E.L. Jacob writes that "Networks must be able to offer both free services and commercial services and must provide adequate protection and recompense to each."[12]

At this writing, copyright issues as they affect the academic community are being debated. The American Library Association replied to the initial draft report, "Intellectual Property and the National Information Infrastructure," which was issued by the Working Group on Intellectual Property Rights of the White House Information Infrastructure Task Force. In response to the report's call for an extension of owners' rights in electronic transmission, the ALA comments recommended that any expansion of copyright holders' rights be balanced by "limitations on those rights in areas such as fair use, classroom use, and library use."[13]

Publishers feel that the 1976 copyright law is "workable in a digital environment," but they are concerned about ease of electronic redistribution leading to increased copyright infringement.[14] Laura N. Gasaway points out that the 1976 law was written to be "technologically neutral" and is still relevant today. She states, "There is nothing in either the [copyright] law or the legislative history to indicate that Congress intended fair use to be available only in the print environment."[15] She explains that the act may need revision, however, to include new methods of distribution via new technologies. But the fair use and education provisions must be retained to maintain the rights of students, researchers and the public to use materials in digital format.[16]

The Association of Research Libraries (ARL) membership has adopted a statement of principles concerning copyright and the research library community. It states that loss of the fair use and library exemptions "would greatly harm scholarship, teaching, and the operations of a free society," and that replacement of publicly available information in libraries with commercial information vendors would lead to "information haves and have-nots." Other principles adopted by ARL include:

- provision must be made for the archival preservation of information by libraries by any technological means that is appropriate.
- licensing agreements may be developed which can offer a variety of payment methods for copyrighted works, but these agreements "should not be allowed to abrogate the fair use and library provisions authorized in the copyright statute."
- U.S. government information should not be copyrighted, but should remain in the public domain.
- librarians and educators must encourage copyright compliance.
- authors and copyright owners must continue to receive fair compensation for their works in the digital environment.[17]

Colleges and universities could not teach effectively today without the fair use provisions of the 1976 copyright laws. The future viability of virtual libraries in academia depend on academic librarians continuing to be active members of this debate. Judging from the initial draft report from the Working Group on Intellectual Property Rights, publishers have very effectively expressed their concerns. We in the Association of College and Research Libraries should support the Association of Research Libraries and the American Library Association statements of library concerns and responsibilities so that librarians' voices are effectively heard in Washington.

ECONOMIC ISSUES

Economic issues include both database costs and infrastructure costs. Database costs involve both the costs of getting materials into digital format, and the costs to libraries to access those materials. Infrastructure costs include both the costs of making the national (and global) connections necessary to link users to each other and to sources of information, as well as the costs for libraries of providing ever more sophisticated workstations to access information.

The prospects for getting materials in digital format via electronic publishing will depend not only on solving the copyright problems but also the economic issues. Potential pricing models for electronic publishing are complex, and Greg Anderson writes that "at the moment when it becomes possible to generate revenues from electronic publications, the commercial publishers will be very active participants."[18] Much is now being done by volunteers to put classic texts into digital form; for example the Gutenberg Project headed by Michael Hart has been going on since 1971.[19] It remains to be seen how university presses will enter into electronic publishing and whether these ventures will help bring down the costs of academic journals.[20] But until it is economically feasible for publishers to provide new publications in digital format, and until libraries can afford to support this format, we will remain in the expensive times

of needing to provide access to both print and digitized materials. To paraphrase Mark Twain, reports of the imminent death of the physical library are greatly exaggerated.

The other half of the economic issue is infrastructure costs. For individual libraries, that means funding the hardware, the software, the needed outside connections to link with the global network, and the costs of training staff to work with the new technology. As technology improves, hardware and software will need to be upgraded, and staff will need further training. The difficulty of trying to find money in tight budgets to continue buying the printed resources that libraries are still expected to hold, while at the same time trying to prepare for the library of the future, is a dilemma most college and university libraries are now facing. Cooperative projects among institutions can help finance the creation of the virtual library: both the costs of accessing databases and the costs of financing the infrastructure could be shared among groups of cooperating libraries.[21] In the future, colleges and universities will be restructuring the way they offer education. Their plans will very likely include more distance learning alongside traditional classroom learning. With virtual libraries, students at remote locations will be able to connect to the same electronic resources as students on the campus. We will need to make our administrators understand that the virtual library will be a vital part of the university mission to reach its students where they are located, and it should be funded accordingly.

One significant cost to academia is access to the Internet. As of January 1, 1995, Australian universities are to be charged for Internet access by the megabyte.[22] Whether metered pricing of network access will find its way into the United States remains to be seen, but privatization of portions of the networks could threaten access, as cost recovery brings information retrieval out of reach of poorer academic institutions. This would be an ironic turn, since the historic antecedents of the Internet were created to facilitate communication between universities and government agencies.

The larger network infrastructure costs must be handled nationally, with an eye on the global connections. Vice President Albert Gore has been working to convince the nation that a combination of federal seed money and private investment is needed to fund the necessary network development. He wants legislative and regulatory action to begin the process, and the private and non-profit sector to continue the work of creating the National Information Infrastructure (or NII), with the goal being a network "to connect all of our classrooms, all of our libraries, and all of our hospitals and clinics by the year 2000."[23]

Federal seed money is already being used to further the process of digitizing materials so they are accessible via computer networks. Over the next four years, $24 million is to be given to six universities by the National Science Foundation, the National Aeronautics and Space Administration, and the Advanced Research Projects Agency of the Defense Department, to support demonstration projects in storing various types of materials in digital format, "including text, numerical data, symbols, sounds, spoken words, and video clips."[24] This exciting development involves not only the six universities receiving the grant money, but other universities, public agencies, and private companies with which they will be working. The projects will not only deal with the technical issues of digitization, but also how to help library users retrieve the information as easily as possible, and how to charge for information. All libraries will gain from what is learned from these projects.[25]

CONTROL ISSUES

Michael Gorman, Dean of Library Services at California State University at Fresno, warns that futuristic scenarios which depict the end of books and libraries will ultimately result in the end of intellectual freedom. The economics of converting from a print-based to an electronic system will require massive amounts of capital coming from an alliance of government and industry. He writes,

"Those who invest billions in the new digitized world will have control over every aspect of it. The potential for censorship, control of access to knowledge and information, and limitation of intellectual freedom is boundless."[26] Vice President Gore has done his homework, and he is well aware of these fears. His plan is based on principles which include not only the necessary private investment to build the information infrastructure, but also the encouragement of fair competition among service providers. These two guides in the development of the "information superhighway" will, one hopes, balance each other and help ensure that users' needs for access are met.[27] As long as there are a multitude of information sources, and a choice of service providers, the specter of censorship will be kept at bay. Librarians will have to watch the development of Mr. Gore's agenda to see that it plays out as he envisions it and that there will be healthy competition among service providers.

The second type of control we must be aware of is the technical standards used to develop the National Information Infrastructure. The Committee on Applications and Technology of the National Institute of Standards and Technology outlined policies for development of the national network. Among other issues, the panel noted that whatever standards are used to develop the system in the United States must also be available to other nations, in order to ensure that the networks can communicate with each other.[28] This type of control is a vital step in improving global information exchange.

ACCESS ISSUES

Closely related to the issue of who will control the "information superhighway" are issues of access. Amid all the scenarios for the virtual library, the image of the individual user who has access to his or her own high-tech computer at home causes fears that there will be an ever widening gap between the information haves vs. have-nots. Wealthy colleges or school districts will be able to provide access for their students and faculty, while poorer colleges or school districts may not; larger metropolitan areas may have the infrastructure to supply access, while rural areas may not. Vice President Gore[29] and the Committee on Applications and Technology[30] both note that these fears must be addressed. Gore sees the issue as one of (eventual) access to essential services, and he feels the government therefore has a stake in ensuring universal service.[31]

Toni Carbo Bearman, Dean of the University of Pittsburgh School of Library & Information Science, is the only member of the library community selected to serve on the NII Advisory Council. She plans to help the Council focus on "'individuals and how they can get the information they need,'" because she says "'there is a tendency to focus on the technology instead of the user.'"[32] She said she was heartened that Secretary of Commerce Ron Brown has also focused on the access issue. Nancy Kranich, a member of ALA's Telecommunications Subcommittee, expressed concern that Bearman will be only a single voice on the Council representing the "'public interest and the principles of public access that have been embraced by librarians and educators.'"[33] The Council contains many members from the private sector, and Bearman will also need to make the Council aware of the need to keep adequate room on the networks for non-profit uses as well as commercial uses.

Jean Armour Polly writes that universal access is a wonderful idea, but it still assumes everyone has a computer and modem. She asks, "What good is a superhighway if all you've got is a tricycle?"[34] For those individuals who do not have the personal resources to connect to the virtual library, Polly suggests that the public libraries "could act as an electronic information access center, providing public modems and telecommunications alongside the books and videos."[35] I would add that colleges and universities that increasingly teach adults in their communities could provide access to and training on the networks as a contribution to lifelong learning.

Access to a virtual library also implies the ability to find information in that library effec-

tively. A traditional library is not the same as a warehouse of books, and a virtual library must be more than space on networked computers. When we return to the scenarios that depict the individual user accessing virtual libraries from his or her home or office, a fear of librarians is "Will we be wanted any more?" When people no longer have to enter our physical library space, will they forget that we can offer them guideposts to information and advice on how to access particular information most effectively and efficiently? We may know that we are needed, but will the user? Many college freshmen who have used Readers' Guide and their high school's online catalog think they know everything about libraries. Many semi-experienced Internet users think they know how to navigate cyberspace to find all they need.

Academic librarians will need to address this aspect of the access issue in several ways. We will need to continue library instruction programs, updating them to reflect the changing nature of the library, and adding instruction in the use of the virtual libraries our students can access. Instruction will benefit our students and faculty in their future use of virtual libraries (in academia, in business, or in their private work) no matter how libraries change, because any familiarity with electronic media makes the next encounter with it a bit easier.

We will also need to continue to encourage the creation and use of more user-friendly search systems, including natural language searching capabilities; use of common search interfaces such as the Z39.50 protocol; careful indexing of electronic materials; search instruments such as Veronica and the various Web browsers; and subject-arranged Gophers and World Wide Web servers (or whatever the next generation of organizing and searching software will be). Our expertise includes understanding user search patterns, and we should be advocates for systems that help the user of the virtual library.

We should also actively "market" ourselves as information consultants to our faculty, our administrators, and our students. Perhaps one additional item on our Gopher and Web menus could one day be "Consult a Librarian," and either an email connection or even a telephone connection to a real, live person could be made.

CONCLUSION

As we head toward the virtual library, issues will need to be resolved on the national and local levels. In the area of copyright, librarians will need to fight for the continuation of the principles of fair use in the electronic environment, in order that our colleges and universities can effectively continue their educational mission.

In the area of economics, we will need to obtain commitments from our administrators for sufficient funding to build, maintain, support, and staff the virtual library. On the issue of control, librarians can let our legislators know that we feel there should be healthy competition among service providers to ensure that no single entity controls all information available through virtual library gateways. We can also speak in favor of technical standards that are global, not just national.

On the issues of access, librarians and educators will need to continue to support the principle of public access to information, so that we can avoid creating a nation of information haves and have-nots. Reference and instruction librarians will need to address the access issue in terms of patrons effectively and efficiently finding the information they need. There are so many options for students searching the virtual library, it will be a challenge for librarians to encourage the development of better search engines and to guide users in effective search methods.

I cannot predict, with precision, what the information technology of the future will be. Search methods will be different, the hardware and the software will be different, but the librarian's goal of helping people find the information they need will remain. As the public and private sectors work out the issues of copyright, economics, control, and access, it will be important for librarians to voice their opinions. We have the significant perspective of the user's needs to add to the discussions. Librarians need to be the leading proponents on our campuses of the importance of providing access to information in whatever format it may come. Users who have experienced some of the vast sea of information available through the library gateway will be helped most by our working toward equitable solutions in the continuing evolution of the virtual library.

NOTES

1. A. J. Harley, "Towards the Virtual Library," The Nationwide Provision and User of Information: ASLIB/IIS/LA Joint Conference Proceedings (London: Library Association, 1980), 163-166, quoted in Laverna M. Saunders, "The Virtual Library Revisited," *Computers in Libraries* 12 (November 1992): 51.

2. Nancy M. Cline, "The University Libraries Strategic Plan Update, January 1994" (Pennsylvania State University Libraries, photocopy), 47-49.

3. Kristen Liberman and Jane L. Rich, "Lotus Notes Databases: the Foundation of a Virtual Library," *Database* 16 (June 1993): 35.

4. Raymond Kurzweil, "The Future of Libraries Part 2: The End of Books," *Library Journal* 117 (15 February 1992): 141.

5. Raymond Kurzweil, "The Virtual Library," *Library Journal* 118 (15 March 1993): 55.

6. Willem Scholten (17 March 1994). "Project JANUS." [e-mail to Nancy Dewald], [Online]. Available e-mail: NHD@PSULIAS.PSU.EDU

7. Ibid.

8. Brett Butler, "Electronic Editions of Serials: The Virtual Library Model," *Serials Review* 18 (Spring-Summer 1992): 105.

9. Barbara von Wahlde and Nancy Schiller, "Creating the Virtual Library: Strategic Issues," in *The Virtual Library: Visions and Realities*, ed. Laverna M. Saunders (Westport: Meckler, 1992), 33.

10. J.D. Gilbert, "Are We Ready for the Virtual Library? Technology Push, Market Pull and Organisational Response," *Information Services & Use* 13 (1993): 14.

11. David L. Wilson, "Panel Outlines Uses of Data Highway in Education and Libraries," *Chronicle of Higher Education,* 11 May 1994, p. A18.

12. M.E.L. Jacob, "Networking Applications for Re-

search Libraries," in *Networks, Open Access, and Virtual Libraries: Implications for the Research Library*, ed. Brett Sutton and Charles H. Davis. ([Urbana-Champaign], Graduate School of Library and Information Science, University of Illinois at Urbana-Champaign, c1992), 100.

13. Carol C. Henderson, "Washington Hotline: Intellectual Property and the NII," *College & Research Libraries News* 55 (October 1994): 597.

14. Carol A. Risher and Laura N. Gasaway, "The Great Copyright Debate, Two Experts Face Off," *Library Journal* 119 (15 September 1994): 34.

15. Risher and Gasaway, 34-36.

16. Risher and Gasaway, 36.

17. "Affirming the Rights and Responsibilities of the Research Library Community in the Area of Copyright," *ARL* 175 (July 1994): 1-3.

18. Greg Anderson, "Virtual Qualities for Electronic Publishing," in *The Virtual Library: Visions and Realities,* ed. Laverna M. Saunders (Westport: Meckler, 1992), 92.

19. Michael S. Hart (6 October 1993). "Project Gutenberg Blurb." *Gutnberg Discussion List* [Online]. Available e-mail: GUTNBERG@ UIUCVMD.BITNET

20. Eric Bryant and Amy Boaz Nugent, "University Presses Show Commitment to Electronic Future," *Library Journal* 119 (August 1994): p.12-13.

21. von Wahlde and Schiller, 32.

22. Geoffrey Maslen, "Internet Users in Australia Will Be Charged for Each Megabyte of Data They Send or Receive," *Chronicle of Higher Education*, 5 October 1994, p. A23.

23. Albert Gore, "The National Information Infrastructure: Information Conduits, Providers, Appliances and Consumers," *Vital Speeches of the Day* 60 (1 February 1994): 230.

24. Thomas J. DeLoughry, "Government Provides $24-Million for 'Virtual Libraries' Projects," *Chronicle of Higher Education*, 5 October 1994, p. A26.

25. Ibid.

26. Michael Gorman, "The Treason of the Learned: The Real Agenda of Those Who Would Destroy Libraries and Books," *Library Journal* 119 (15 February 1994): 130-131.

27. Gore, p.231.

28. Wilson, p. A18.

29. Gore, p.232.

30. Wilson, p. A18.

31. Gore, p.232.

32. "Clinton Selects Librarian to Serve on NII Advisory Council," *Library Journal* 119 (1 February 1994): 16.

33. Ibid.

34. Jean Armour Polly, "NREN for ALL: Insurmountable Opportunity," *Library Journal* 119 (1 February 1993): 38.

35. Ibid.

Characterizing the Modern Library Experience:
Rationality or Fantasia?

Gary P. Radford

ABSTRACT

The increasing adoption of information technology is transforming the nature of the modern library experience for both librarian and user. In addressing these changes, Library and Information Science has taken a model of knowledge derived from the positivistic social sciences. However, recent scholarship suggests that this model may be obsolete when applied to the library setting. An account of the library developed by Foucault foregrounds these rationalist assumptions and provides the basis of an alternative characterization which may better inform the practices of librarians and users in a rapidly changing technological library environment.

The concept of the traditional library is changing. The advent of new and sophisticated information storage, processing, and retrieval technologies is transforming the nature of the modern library experience for both the librarian and user. Also changing are the relationships between the librarian, user, and the texts the library houses or has access to elsewhere. The field of library and information science has taken, both explicitly and implicitly, a model of knowledge developed by the positivist social sciences as the basis for describing the nature of the library and these changes. However, recent scholarship in the philosophy of science has suggested that this traditional model of knowledge may be as obsolete as the model of the traditional library. The positivist model of knowledge, far from providing useful accounts of change, may be contributing to a lack of understanding of the modern library experience. In other words, it becomes part of the problem to be addressed by library scholars.

This paper considers the relationship between models of knowledge and the modern library experience. A model derived from Michel Foucault's[1] *The Fantasia of the Library,* a work of literary criticism, is considered as a basis for conceptualizing the modern library experience. By considering the library experience from the perspective of

Gary P. Radford is an Assistant Professor of Communication at The William Paterson College of New Jersey, Wayne, New Jersey.

literature, the rationalistic assumptions of a positivist epistemology can be foregrounded and critiqued along with the conception of the library it supports. It is argued that the modern library experience is grounded in a concept of totalizing rationality that excludes the subjectivities and ambiguities of the individual user. This view is inappropriate for the modern library in which a user has much more power in terms of direct access to and control of texts. Using Foucault's notion of "fantasia" as a foundation, it is argued that the rationality (or irrationality) of individual users, i.e., the manner in which they choose to order texts, is central to the understanding of the modern library experience.

RATIONALITY

Traditional images of the library and positivist notions of knowledge are historically and philosophically related. This can be seen in the western literary tradition where the library has long been taken as a metaphor for order and rationality.[2,3] It represents, in institutional form, the ultimate realization of a place where each item within it has a fixed place and stands in an a priori relationship with every other item. As the library imposes a completely consistent system upon a collection of unique texts, so positivist science seeks the system by which unique observations derived from nature can be ordered and classified according to a set of general principles. Jeffrey Garrett has argued that there exists a "collective belief, unchallenged until recently, in the existence of a scientifically derived and classifiable body of knowledge" and that the library is "one of the most visible and important temples that society has erected to this belief".[3, p. 382]

The association of library with order underlies many common stereotypes of librarians. The representation of the librarian as stern and forbidding is common.[4,5,6] These stereotypes may, at first glance, seem trivial and unimportant but library practitioners seem to be at a loss as to how to change them[7] Such images serve to reinforce a particular network of power relations that connect the librarian, the user, and the text. In this network, the librarian's domain is that of the creation and maintenance of order and the library user represents a threat to that order. The raised finger to the librarian's lips reinforces these roles and foregrounds the polarization of order and disorder. The librarian is responsible for a system where every text has its proper place. This system demands the investment of much time, effort, and care. The image of the perfect library, the end result of the librarian's efforts, is that of a place where all is ultimately accounted for, of "closed and dusty" volumes in "the hushed library, with its columns of books, with its titles aligned on shelves to form a tight enclosure."[1, p. 90] The ideal library, in this view, is one that is never used or disrupted. Order becomes the end in itself.

This image is graphically portrayed in Umberto Eco's[8] *The Name of the Rose*. The abbey library plays a central role in the novel, both as a physical location in which much of the action takes place, and, more importantly, as a metaphor for the nature and power of knowledge. Eco's library is a fortress containing a labyrinth, with secret passages, booby-trapped rooms, and a system of organization that is known only to a single librarian. The abbot describes the library as follows:

> The library was laid out on a plan which has remained obscure to all over the centuries, and which none of the monks is called upon to know. Only the librarian has received the secret, from the librarian who preceded him, and he communicates it, while still alive, to the assistant librarian, so that death will not take him by surprise and rob the community of that knowledge. And the secret seals the lips of both men. Only the librarian has, in addition to that knowledge, the right to move through the labyrinth of books, he alone knows where to find them, and where to replace them, he alone is responsible for their safekeeping.[8, pp. 35-36]

Eco's fortress library is a place which both orders and protects texts. The librarians role is to keep the texts, and the knowledge they contain, safe from harm as well as making them available to library users.

In contrast to the librarian, the library user is a person who disrupts and ultimately prevents the ideal of the complete library. There is a tension between the goals of order and completeness with the goal of providing the user with service, since allowing texts to circulate introduces disorder. The images of the stereotypical librarian are formed from the perception of this tension that is felt by both librarians and users.

Such tensions structure the experience of the modern library environment for both librarian and user. It is common for the user to be overawed by the library, not by the sheer volume of texts the library contains, but by the overpowering sense of order and the rules and procedures that need to be learned in order to use it successfully.[9,10,11] It is claimed by their creators that such systems are designed with the goal of facilitating access to texts. However, in the context of the tension created by the contrast of order with disorder, it may also be the case that such systems are perceived as barriers that serve to deny that same access.[5] A user will usually feel confident the needed text or information is there. It is the tortuous path one has to traverse in order to locate it which evokes fear and uncertainty. Jorge Borges[12], in the short story *The Library of Babel*, expresses this contrast:

> When it was proclaimed that the Library contained all books, the first impression was one of extravagant happiness. All men felt themselves to be masters of an intact and secret treasure. There was no personal or world problem whose eloquent solution did not exist in some hexagon. The universe was justified, the universe suddenly usurped the unlimited dimensions of hope.[12, pp. 54-55]

However, the means by which any particular piece of knowledge could be located was perplexing and, ultimately, impossible. In Borges tale, to

have knowledge of the order was tantamount to having the status of a god:

> On some shelf in some hexagon (men reasoned) there must exist a book which is the formula and perfect compendium of <u>all the rest</u>: some librarian has gone through it and he is analogous to a god....Many wandered in search of Him. For a century they exhausted in vain the most varied areas. How could one locate the venerated and secret hexagon which housed Him? Someone proposed a regressive method: To locate book A, consult first a book B which indicates A's position; to locate book B, consult first a book C, and so on to infinity...[12, p. 56]

Borges tale is allegorical, but it represents in a literary fashion some of the undercurrents that structure the user's interaction with the library. The user is confronted with the "librarian-god," the guardian of rationality and knowledge, whose domain of order the user dares to violate, and who has the power to render discipline and punishment. Is it any wonder that some library users have claimed that they will seek the help of the librarian only as a desperate and last resort.[6]

FANTASIA

The library's embodiment of order and rationality stands in direct contrast to the notion of fantasia. Fantasia is a work in which an author's fancy roves unrestricted by such codes or conventions. Fantasy is a free play of imagination, not bound by the tenets of order, but made possible by the lack of them. Foucault's[1] *The Fantasia of the Library* develops a concept of knowledge in which the apparant opposites of "library" and "fantasia" are conjoined to form a new notion of each.

Foucault's essay is an appreciation of Gustave Flaubert's[13] *The Temptation of Saint Anthony* which draws upon the "library" and the "fantasia" as hitherto polarized terms. The heart of Foucault's appreciation is the claim that Flaubert's work represents a new space of knowledge in which the realms of the library and the fantastic, the rational and the imaginative, can no longer be kept apart. Foucault writes that "the domain of phantasms is no longer the night, the sleep of reason, or the uncertain void that stands before desire, but, on the contrary, wakefulness, untiring attention, zealous erudition, and constant vigilance."[1, p. 90] He continues: "the imaginary now resides between the book and the lamp. The fantastic is no longer a property of the heart, nor is it found among the incongruities of nature; it evolves from the accuracy of knowledge, and its treasures lie dormant in documents."[1, p. 90] Finally, Foucault writes that:

> Dreams are no longer summoned with closed eyes, but in reading; and a true image is now a product of learning; it derives from words spoken in the past, exact recensions, the amassing of minute facts, monuments reduced to infinitesimal fragments, and the reproductions of reproductions. In the modern experience, these elements contain the power of the impossible.[1, pp. 90-91]

The production of a fantasia from a domain previously given to reason, rationality, and order is what Foucault has called the "modern experience"[1, p. 91], "a literary space wholly dependent on the network formed by books of the past."[1, p. 91] The library is not a backdrop to this work as a separate realm, but is an integral part of it. The library has become a component of a text it previously stood outside of. Flaubert's book "dreams other books...books that are taken up, fragmented, displaced, combined, lost, set at an unapproachable distance by dreams, but also brought closer to the imaginary and sparkling realization of dreams."[1, p. 92]

The dissolution of the library/fantasia dichotomy produces new conceptions of both, and it is the conception of the library that is of interest here. As the library becomes integral to the experience of Flaubert's fantasia, so *The Temptation* has taken on the characteristics of the library. For Foucault, *The Temptation* "may appear as merely another new book to be shelved alongside all the others, but it serves, in actuality, to extend the space that existing books can occupy. It recovers other books; it hides and displays them and, in a single movement, it causes them to glitter and disappear."[1, p. 91-92] Flaubert's text is itself a catalog which places and orders other texts. *The Temptation* is a library, but the rationality which derives its order is of a different kind. As Foucault graphically states, in *The Temptation*, "the library is on fire."[1, p. 92]

THE FANTASIA OF THE LIBRARY AND THE MODERN LIBRARY EXPERIENCE

Foucault's fantasia of the library is far different from the vision of the library informed by a positivist view of knowledge. It is a conception that deserves serious consideration as the positivist model and the practices of actual librarians and users begin to lose touch with each other. Brenda Dervin and Michael Nilan[14] have argued that a "major tension"[(p. 5)] exists between primarily positivist conceptions and the behaviors that users and systems display in practice. This tension is seen in the stereotypical images of librarians discussed earlier, and how they come to be seen as natural aspects of the librarian/user relationship. This paper has attempted to demonstrate that such characterizations follow from a positivist world view in which the library and the user are placed in specific relationship with one another; a relationship in which the library determines order and the relevancy of information for specific needs, as represented by the fortress library of Eco's[8] *The Name of the Rose*. Library and user are separate domains; the library is the domain of order and the user the domain of ambiguity. In the librarian/user interaction, order is given to the user to alleviate disorder through the provision of texts. However, the flow of influence is essentially one-way, lest madness enter the rationality of the library.

These characterizations of the librarian as an information giver providing specific information found in specific texts for the alleviation of specific problems, are simply not appropriate for describing the practice of actual library searches.[15],[16] With the development of increasingly sophisticated information technologies, the location of specific texts or facts is simply not the issue in most library searches, and the role of the librarian as a fact provider is becoming increasingly difficult to maintain. Susan Anthes[17] has argued that "because of high technology any library can have vast amounts of information, much more than any student or faculty would want, need, or use. The librarian's job now becomes more one of interpretation, filtering, and evaluation."[17, p. 57] What is being "interpreted, filtered, and evaluated" is not which specific text is required to meet a specific need, but rather which collection of texts and the explanation of a criteria which relates them as a coherent set. It is that which <u>relates texts</u> which becomes the information that is valuable rather than the specific information contained within a specific text. Where the information within a text is fixed, the relationships between texts are open and created anew each time a modern library search is carried out. Garrett makes this point as follows:

> Modern library searches do not lead from point A (the catalog, the reference desk) to point B (the book, the answer, the truth), but instead invite their computer-literate users to explore on their own the many recesses of a multicursal maze, placing them again and again in decision situations, at forks or nodes where multiple paths lead down through the hierarchies of subject headings, on their way to what may or may not be a useful or even existing document.[3, p. 381]

The librarian's role becomes that of a guide, not only to the pre-existing order of the library that comprises its catalogs and indexes, but to the <u>creation of new orders</u> made possible by the capabilities of computer searching. The experience of the multicursal maze does not lead to a particular answer located in a specific text but rather the creation of new rationalities which define the

usefulness or worthlessness of any specific text. As Garrett explains, "the library user creates with every search his or her own ad hoc library of five, fifty, or five thousand book and journal citations, cut out from that great "virtual" library that is the universe of all accessible books, all stored information."[3, p. 381] And from this "ad hoc library" the user must create the unique catalog which orders and unites them. In this act, every modern library user becomes Flaubert writing *The Temptation*.

In the interface between the user and library system, the fantasia becomes an integral part of the library experience, and not a domain to be suppressed and marginalized to a separate domain of irrationality. Foucault writes that:

> **the imaginary is not formed in opposition to reality as its denial or compensation**; it grows among signs, from book to book, in the interstice of repetitions and commentaries; it is born and takes shape in the interval between books. **It is a phenomenon of the library**.[1, p. 91, (emphasis mine)]

In the fantasia of the library, there is no longer a canon to turn to and master. Everything is potentially valuable or worthless, depending on its position in the temporary contexts that are created in individual library searches. This notion is entirely foreign to a positivist outlook where library and fantasia are separated. The positivist framework cannot conceive of a library where collections are temporary rather then universal, subjective rather than objective, and follows individual structures of rationality. Yet in the continuing evolution of the modern library, temporary collections of texts located and ordered directly by users will become the norm.[18]

In the direct interaction of user with library, the notion of an absolute order mediated by the "librarian-god" is circumvented. Flaubert's *The Temptation* becomes the symbol of the modern library experience. Foucault's analysis of *The Temptation* represents the experience of a modern library search; the uniting of texts through the creation of rationalities that are not the province of a universal order. Unlike the positivist model of the library, the ambiguity of the user, previously considered a source of irrationality to be excluded from the library experience, becomes the creative source of fantasia. Foucault's "fantasia of the library" is a construct that represents an alternative to traditional models of the library which are rapidly becoming obsolete in the modern library environment, and one that deserves more widespread attention in the library community.

REFERENCES

1. Foucault, Michel. "Fantasia of the Library." Translated by Donald F. Bouchard and Sherry Simon. In *Language, Counter-Memory, Practice: Selected Essays and Interviews by Michel Foucault*, edited by Donald F. Bouchard. Ithaca, NY: Cornell University Press, 1977.

2. Castillo, Debra A. *The Translated world: A Postmodern Tour of Libraries in Literature*. Tallahassee, FL: Florida State University Press, 1984.

3. Garrett, Jeffrey. "Missing Eco: Reading `The Name of the Rose' as Library Criticism." *Library Quarterly*, 61 (October 1991): 373-388.

4. Mount, Ellis. "Communication Barriers and the Reference Question." *Special Libraries*, 57 (1966): 575-578.

5. Radford, Marie L. "Relational Aspects of Reference Interactions: A Qualitative Investigation of the Perceptions of Users and Librarians in the Academic Library." Ph. D dissertation, Rutgers-The State University of New Jersey, 1993.

6. Swope, Mary Jane, and Katzer, Jeffrey. "The Silent Majority: Why Don't They Ask Questions?" *RQ*, 12 (1972): 161-166.

7. Black, Sandra M. "Personality - Librarians as Communicators." *Canadian Library Journal*, 38 (1981): 65-71.

8. Eco, Umberto. *The Name of the Rose*. Translated by William Weaver. New York, NY: Warner, 1983.

9. Kuhlthau, Carol C. "Developing a Model of the Library Search Process: Cognitive and Affective Aspects." *RQ*, 28 (1988): 232-242.

10. Kuhlthau, Carol C. "Perceptions of the Information Search Process in Libraries: A study of Changes from High School Through College. *Information Processing and Management,* 24 (1988): 419-427.

11. Kuhlthau, Carol C. "The Information Search Process: From Theory to Practice." *Journal of Education for Library and Information Science*, 31 (1990): 72-75.

12. Borges, Jorge Luis. "The Library of Babel." Translated by James E. Irby. In *Labyrinths: Selected Stories and Other Writings*, edited by Donald A. Yates and James E. Irby. Norfolk, CT: New Directions Books, 1962.

13. Flaubert, Gustave (1926). *The temptation of Saint Antony*. London, England: Privately Printed. (Original work published 1874).

14. Dervin, Brenda, and Nilan, Michael. "Information Needs and Uses." In *Annual review of information science and technology* (Vol. 21), edited by Martha E. Williams. White Plains, NY: Knowledge Industry Publications, 1986.

15. Belkin, Nicholas J. "Anomalous States of Knowledge as a Basis for Information Retrieval. *Canadian Journal of Information Science*, 5 (1980): 133-143.

16. Taylor, Robert S. "Question Negotiation and Information Seeking in Libraries." *College and Research Libraries*, 29 (1968): 178-194.

17. Anthes, Susan H. "High Tech/High Touch: Academic Libraries Respond to Change in the Behavioral Sciences." *Behavioral and Social Sciences Librarian*, 5 (1985): 53-65.

18. Epstein, Hank. "Libraries in the 21st Century." *Media and Methods*, 26 (1989): 63-64.

Melvil Dewey, CD-ROMs, and the Future of Librarianship

Robert L. Bolin

ABSTRACT

The spirit of Dewey and the other founders of modern librarianship can guide librarians today. As a case study, this paper will use the integration of CD-ROMs into the University of Idaho Library. Is shows that the notion of self-service which grew out of the revolution led by Dewey and his associates can be applied to CD-ROMs and other electronic resources.

Before Melvil Dewey and others founded modern librarianship in America there were few libraries of any consequence and librarianship was highly personal. The fascinating report on *Public Libraries in the United States of America*[1] from 1876 shows that libraries of more than a few hundred books were rare. Since there was no formal library education, librarians were amateurs and dilettantes. Because there were no standards, libraries were arranged idiosyncratically and many had very limited hours and restrictive policies. To use a library effectively, a person had to get both the help and permission of the librarian. If the librarian had a good memory or a good catalog, the user was in luck.

THE REVOLUTION

Dewey and his colleagues changed everything. Whether they intended to or not, they invented the "self-service" library. They did that by making a critical intellectual breakthrough as well as by promoting standardization and professionalization.

Relative Arrangement

The notion of relative arrangement was the basis for a profound revolution in librarianship. Dewey's decimal classification provided an effective means of arranging books by subject and relative arrangement allowed new books to be interfiled. Relative arrangement of books by classification made libraries vastly more simple to

Robert L. Bolin is the Electronic Resources Librarian at the University of Idaho, Moscow, Idaho.

understand and use. That also made libraries much more easy to administer since the shelving can be moved and rearranged as long as the books are kept in the proper relative arrangement.

Application of relative arrangement to the catalog resulted in the card catalog.

A card catalog was truly revolutionary information technology for its day. It was much more flexible and easy to use than the printed or hand-written lists that had been used as catalogs. The catalog provided easy intellectual access to library material as shelving by classification provided easy physical access.

Librarians cannot take credit for it, but the application of relative arrangement to printing made cumulative indexes profitable. The notion of a periodical index is simple. In the last century, a number of indexing projects were undertaken. Most failed because of economics. There was a relatively small market and printing costs were high. As new material was indexed, cumulative editions were needed. However, resetting type to produce cumulative editions was prohibitively expensive. In the 1890's, Halsey W. Wilson solved the problem. He realized that newly set linotype slugs — a single line of type — could be interfiled with slugs set previously to create cumulative publications.[2]

He perfected this technique to produce the *Cumulative Book Index* and later used it to produce *Reader's Guide* and the other indexes of the H.W. Wilson Company.

Relative arrangement had a revolutionary impact in areas outside libraries. JoAnne Yates discusses the introduction of vertical filing — the application of relative arrangement to filing business records and correspondence — in a very interesting article, "From Press Book and Pigeonhole to Vertical Filing: the Revolution in Storage and Access Systems for Correspondence."[3] In her award winning book, *Control Through Communication: The Rise of System in American Management*,[4] Yates argues that vertical filing was one of a number of technological innovations which made modern, large-scale businesses possible.

Dewey himself was a leader of the information technological revolution of his day. He founded the Library Bureau and considered that to be one of his major contributions to librarianship. The Library Bureau became an important manufacturer of equipment and supplies for businesses and government as well as libraries. The Bureau was a leading vendor promoting the use of vertical filing and card files and filing systems to serve many information needs. In the library sphere, the Bureau helped implement the library revolution by supplying card catalog cases and improved library shelving systems.

Putting the "Science" in Library Science

By "library science," the founders of modern librarianship actually meant a standardized, systematic approach. Take the case of a critical invention, the card catalog. The Library Bureau standardized card size and supplied card catalog cabinets. Cutter supplied rules for descriptive cataloging. Dewey provided a classification system to link the catalog cards with the books. The result was not a "scientific" accomplishment in the way that word is used in the hard sciences, but it was a good example of the fruits of library science. For its day, it was an impressive intellectual achievement which provided a powerful tool that made it possible to organize and manage larger libraries. It gave the average library user a way to find books without asking the librarian for help.

Professionalization

Professionalization is closely related to standardization. Dewey himself was present at the founding of the American Library Association, the first library school, and the Library Journal. All of those are educational instruments to promote new approaches to librarianship, standard technology to allow implementation of new approaches, and a sense of professional identity. A common understanding of problems and solutions, in turn, has led to standardization of libraries all over the country.

THE MEANING OF THE LIBRARY REVOLUTION

The library revolution of the last century was a profound social and educational revolution. The meaning of those social changes and the intentions of the leaders of the library revolution have been the subject of scholarship and controversy for years. These propositions are beyond dispute:

1. *Librarianship is no longer personal.* Now, most library users rely on mechanical or electronic catalogs and indexes to find material and ask the librarian for help if that fails.
2. *Libraries are much easier to use.* "Self-service" libraries are now the norm. Because of standardization in cataloging and classification, the introduction of the card catalog, and relative arrangement of books by classification, even children can master most libraries.

WHAT DEWEY HAD TO SAY TO ME

When I became CD-ROM librarian at the University of Idaho Library, the CD-ROM collection manifested the characteristics of a pre-Dewey library. The library was in the process of changing from a divisional arrangement to a centralized organization. CD-ROMs had been handled differently in each division. Some were cataloged and some were not. That didn't matter much since CD-ROMs were not "shelved" in the conventional sense. They were locked in drawers and cabinets, stacked on desks, permanently mounted in dedicated workstations, and so on. All a cataloging record told the user was that a disc was available in the building and, maybe, where to start asking for it. Similarly, the CD-ROM workstations had various types of user interfaces and required varying degrees of librarian intervention. In many cases, a person wanting to use a CD-ROM database had to ask a librarian for help, and if a librarian were not on duty, the CD-ROM was not available. Documentation for CD-ROMs was also scattered around the library.

My understanding of library history led me to believe that self-service access should be provided for the CD-ROMs. The CD-ROMs should be organized so that users can identify, locate, and use them easily. Happily, the solution that I came up with proved to be a low-tech solution we could afford. I proposed to integrate CD-ROMs into the library collection by:

1. Cataloging all CD-ROMs;
2. Shelving them together in an accessible location;
3. Making the search software for all of them available on workstations with a standard user interface; and
4. Making documentation available by bundling it with the discs or by catalog it separately.

Cataloging the CD-ROMs

All CD-ROM publications we own are cataloged. At the University of Idaho Library, call number prefixes are used to show special locations. We chose to use the prefix "CD-ROM" for the material in our CD-ROM collection. A large part of our collection is discs received through the Federal Depository Documents Program. All government document CD-ROMs which we consider "active" are cataloged. Superseded depository discs, which are being held simply because permission has not been received to destroy them, are not listed in the catalog.

Because they are all cataloged and clearly identified with the prefix "CD-ROM" on their call numbers, the library catalog is the main tool for finding CD-ROMs just as it for finding books, maps, and other material.

Shelving CD-ROMs

Nearly all the CD-ROMs are "shelved" together at the Reserve Desk. A handful are permanently mounted in stand-alone workstations. CD-ROMs containing primarily data — such as the Census statistical and TIGER/Line file discs — are allowed to circulate for several days and they may be taken out of the library. There are several computer labs on campus where users can find statistical and cartographic software to use with those discs.

General Purpose CD-ROM Workstations

Search software is provided with many CD-ROM publications. As a matter of policy, we determined to make all of the search software for **all** of the disks available in the library. In order to do that, I invented the general-purpose CD-ROM workstation.

The conceptual breakthrough that made it possible to load large numbers of software packages on a single PC was that subdirectories can be organized by call number. For example, the *Statistical Abstract of the United States* on CD-ROM is filed under Superintendent of Documents Number C3.134/7, and the software related to that disk is stored in a subdirectory on the hard drive. Here is the full path to that subdirectory:

C:\SUDOC\C3\134\7

All of the software related to government document CD-ROMs is stored under the "SUDOC" subdirectory and all related to the Census Bureau under "SUDOC\C3." Because the software is organized using a system that corresponds to the call numbers used for the discs, it is easy to find a particular software package if it is necessary to modify or delete it. Given a large enough hard drive, the search software for a couple of hundred separate CD-ROM publications can be loaded on a single PC.

The CD-ROM workstations are located directly in front of the Reserve Desk where the CD-ROMs are stored. Those workstations have two menus to provide access to the search software. One is arranged in call number order, and the other by title.

No database, spreadsheet, wordprocessing, cartographic, or graphics software is available on the general purpose CD-ROM workstations. Users may display, print, or download the results of their searches, but they must go elsewhere to use the data obtained. *The library provides data, but not analytical software.* Of course, library users are free to take many of the discs to computer labs where analytical software is readily available.

Documentation

Access to documentation for CD-ROMs is provided in two ways. In some cases the documentation is bundled with the discs. For example, the disc may be stored in a pocket in the binder containing the documentation. In other cases, the documentation is cataloged separately for the reference collection. Of course, documentation which is cataloged separately may be located using the library catalog. Also, an introductory screen appears when each search software package is started. The introductory screen contains a brief description of the CD-ROM publication and points users to useful information such as documentation or parallel paper editions of the publication.

THE LESSON

CD-ROMs can be made easily accessible to library users. We have made approximately 500 CD-ROM discs available at the University of Idaho Library. Access to CD-ROMs is self-service without any librarian intervention. Users can look up the CD-ROM they want in the catalog, check it out from Reserve, and run it on a general purpose CD-ROM workstation any time the library is open.

In the spirit of Dewey and the other pioneers of library science, I am obliged to make my discoveries available to others in the profession. In addition to this presentation, I have written articles describing in detail our CD-ROM workstations [5] and the approach to organizing CD-ROMs which we developed.[6]

THE FUTURE

Two further challenges are apparent. One is that users have to come to the library to use our CD-ROM resources. The other is that CD-ROMs are only one type of electronic resource which we want to make available to our users.

I believe that the answer is to provide mount-on-demand remote access to the CD-ROMs and then to provide direct access to remote databases — CD-ROMs and others — from within our OPAC. What we intend to do is to use our present general purpose CD-ROM workstation as a proto-type remote access server. We will install software to allow remote users to telnet to the workstation and select a CD-ROM disk to use. The operator on duty at the reserve desk will be notified and will load the appropriate CD-ROM. Although there a few technical problems to be overcome, I do not anticipate much difficulty.

Since we use CARL system software for our OPAC, it will be more difficult to provide direct access to electronic resources from within the OPAC. We will work with CARL Systems on this. We want to be able to catalog electronic resources. When a user encounters an electronic resource in the catalog, he or she will have the option of choosing to access that resource immediately. The resource could be a CD-ROM disc available at the Reserve desk or a remote database accessible through the Internet. One feature we want to incorporate is automatic notification if an attempt to access a database fails. That will allow us to weed obsolete references.

Within five years I expect that library users will be able to access various types of electronic resources — including CD-ROM discs — directly from our library catalog. That service will be available to users in the building and to remote users. I believe that will be in the spirit of the library revolution begun by Dewey and others over a hundred years ago.

NOTES

1. *Public Libraries in the United States of America: Their History, Condition, and Management* (Washington, D.C.: Government Printing Office, 1876).
2. John Lawler, *The H.W. Wilson Company* (Minneapolis: University of Minnesota Press, 1950), pp. 25-26.
3. *Journal of Business Communications*, 19(Summer 1982):5-26.
4. (Baltimore: Johns Hopkins University Press, 1989).
5. Robert L. Bolin, "Setting Up General Purpose CD-ROM Workstations" *Library Hi Tech*, 9(1991):53-62.
6. Robert L. Bolin, "A Model CD-ROM Library" (submitted).

Pushing the Envelope:
Maximizing the User Experience through a Statewide Information System

Barbara F. Schloman and Phyllis O'Connor

ABSTRACT

OhioLINK is a multi-dimensional, statewide information system with increasing demonstrated impact on the information activities of its users. The Central Catalog and catalogs of thirty-five member libraries use the same integrated library system and are updated in real-time. An online borrowing feature, coupled with a ground delivery system, offer timely access to available books held statewide. Centrally mounted databases also use the same search system and provide a link to library holdings. Electronic delivery of image full-text is available for selected articles. Additionally, a gopher provides access to Internet services. This paper discusses the impact that such a statewide system can have on the information needs of users, beyond what an individual academic library can support.

INTRODUCTION

In light of ever-changing developments in information technology, academic librarians continue to relook and rethink what services can be offered to their clientele to take advantage of new possibilities and significantly impact existing information-seeking behavior. We experienced this with the advent of CD-ROM tools and more recently with the burgeoning development of Internet resources. Many of us are also experimenting with other vendors, such as commercial document delivery suppliers, in order to get information into the hands of our users more quickly than has traditionally been possible.

In Ohio, the impact on the users' information experience has begun to be dramatically influenced by the development of OhioLINK, a statewide information system. OhioLINK is now more fully developed than reported earlier in the literature.[1,2,3,4] This paper will share how such a large system, operating in a networked environment, serves the user in a more complete and immediate way than has typically been possible or even expected before.

Barbara F. Schloman is Chair, OhioLINK User Services Committee and Head of Reference and Information Services at Kent State University Libraries, Kent, Ohio. Phyllis O'Connor is Chair, OhioLINK Inter-Campus Services Committee and Assistant Dean of University Libraries, University of Akron, Akron, Ohio.

Public Universities

Bowling Green University   Shawnee State University
Central State University   University of Akron
Cleveland State University   University of Cincinnati
Kent State University   University of Toledo
Miami University   Wright State University
Ohio State University   Youngstown State University
Ohio University

Private Universities

Case Western Reserve University
University of Dayton

Medical Colleges

Medical College of Ohio
Northeastern Ohio Universities College of Medicine

State Library of Ohio

Two-Year Colleges

Belmont Technical College   Lorain County Community College
Cincinnati Technical College   Northwest Technical College
Clark State Community College   Owens Technical College
Columbus Community College   Rio Grande Community College
Cuyahoga Community College   Sinclair Community College
Edison State Community College   Southern State Community College
Hocking College   Terra Technical College
Jefferson Technical College   Washington State Community College
Lakeland Community College

Figure 1: OhioLINK Member Institutions

OhioLINK was created in 1988 as the result of a study initiated by the Ohio Board of Regents to investigate how the use of statewide library resources might be maximized. Specifically, there was concern that the ever-growing requests for capital funds to build new library facilities would quickly outstrip available state funding. Therefore, alternatives to new construction were studied. Two major initiatives within the State are the results of this study. One, the creation of four high-density, regional storage facilities, addresses the physical space requirements of the libraries. The second, and the one we want to tell you about today, is the commitment to use developing information technology and networks to share available resources within all the publicly-assisted academic libraries in the State and to deal more effectively with the growing amount of information. From the beginning, funding for OhioLINK has been through the State's higher education budget.

DESCRIPTION

Here is a thumbnail sketch that describes some of the key components of the project. OhioLINK is comprised of fifteen four-year universities (two of which are private institutions), two public medical colleges, the State Library, and seventeen two-year colleges (Figure 1). It serves a potential user group of 340,000+ FTE students and 32,000 FTE faculty.

OhioLINK offers a variety of resources through the central site: a Central Catalog, centrally-mounted databases, and a gopher to Internet resources. Local libraries and the central site are linked via OARnet, the state's Internet provider (Figure 2). The OhioLINK network supports 3,400 simultaneous users.

For its library system, OhioLINK uses Innovative Interfaces' software. Innovative is implemented locally at each site, with installations being phased in over three years. The Central Catalog is the centerpiece of the system. It also runs on Innovative software and represents the holdings of all member libraries, updated in real time with

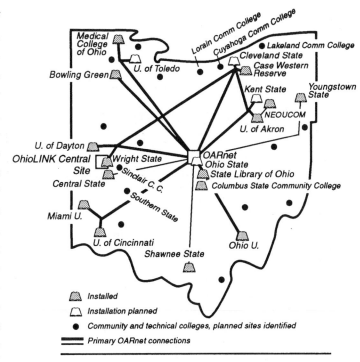

Figure 2: OhioLINK Network via OARnet

cataloging and circulation data. The Central Catalog will have over fifteen million holdings, representing seven to eight million unique titles, after all sites are implemented. The Central Catalog has been enriched by the addition of over 33,000 table of content records from Blackwell North America and by the Center for Research Libraries' records.

A user can search a local catalog, and, not finding what is needed, "transparently" pass the search to the Central Catalog to determine what is held statewide. If the item is available, the user can initiate a borrowing request online. This is processed by the lending library and delivered to the user's home library within 48 hours.

The reference databases cover the range of disciplinary interests. At present, twenty-six databases are offered (Figure 3). Fifteen of these run under the Innovative Interfaces' software. The others are from three other vendors. For selected references in ABI/Inform and Periodical Abstracts, full-text of the articles is available from UMI's PowerPages. This service allows a user to request an image copy of the full-text of an article to be delivered to a local laser printer or fax machine.

Innovative Interfaces

ABI/INFORM   Dissertation Abstracts
Applied Science & Technology   Education Index
Art Index   Essay & General Literature Index
Biography Index   Index to Legal Periodicals
Biological & Agricultural Index   Library Literature
Book Review Digest   Newspaper Abstracts

CD-Plus

AIDSLine
CancerLit
Health Planning
MEDLINE
Nursing & Allied Health
PsychInfo

OCLC

WorldCat

Research Libraries Group

Anthropological Literature
Avery Index to Architectural Periodicals
Handbook of Latin American Studies
Hispanic American Periodicals Index
History of Science & Technology

Figure 3: OhioLINK Reference Databases by Vendor Search Interface

OhioLINK is also pursuing the development of workstation software to enable users to retrieve, evaluate and use information from a variety of resources for personal applications. The intention is to provide users with an integrated interface of necessary software tools to maximize the effective use of information. This client software will be designed to run in a variety of hardware and software environments.

CHANGING THE USER EXPERIENCE
How has OhioLINK changed the user experience?

1. The overall array and <u>richness of resources</u> is more than any user has access to on any campus. To date, the duplication rate in the Central Catalog is about forty percent—that is, sixty percent of the titles are held by a single institution only. The Catalog includes research quality collections in numerous areas, ranging from polymer and liquid crystal research to popular culture collections. It is further enriched by the addition of table of contents records, catalog records for major microform sets, government documents records, and the holdings of the Center for Research Libraries. The availability of the myriad of reference databases supports basic information needs of users in a range of disciplines. The Internet gopher provides organized access to Internet resources, which is especially significant to those campuses without local gopher or Web servers.

2. The dynamic linkage between the local OPACs and Central Catalog provides <u>real-time currency</u> of the information available. Order records, new catalog records or holdings added to a local system immediately update the Central Catalog as well. In addition to providing valuable information to collection development staff, this currency allows users to access the most up-to-date information available. Also, the circulation status of materials is given in real time so that users know when they can expect their request to be filled and can track the progress of each of their requests.

3. Providing <u>networked services</u> extends the availability of these resources to all valid users with access to their campus network. The number of simultaneous users that can be supported exceeds what most institutions can do locally. Time of day no longer restricts access to information resources.

4. Use of the <u>same search interface</u> for the local and Central catalogs and for a majority of the reference databases allows users to develop greater familiarity with one system and move easily from one resource to another without extensive training.

5. With a single key stroke, a user can "transparently" <u>pass a search</u> from the local system to the Central Catalog where the query is immediately processed. This allows the user to identify materials beyond the local collection with great ease and efficiency.

6. Through the <u>online borrowing</u> feature in the Central Catalog, users have more than just bibliographic access to books. They can easily request a copy from anywhere within the state without library mediation and with immediate confirmation that their request has been accepted (Figure 4).

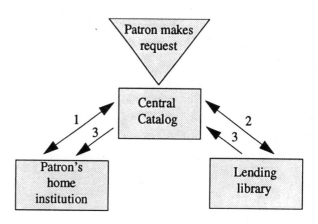

Figure 4: OhioLINK Borrowing Process

7. OhioLINK policy provides the <u>same level of access and service</u> to all types of valid users: students (graduate and undergraduate), faculty, staff, and even courtesy card holders. Specifically, online borrowing privileges and document delivery services are the same for all users. And, although there are no charges at this time, future charges will be assessed equally to all users.

8. Users can expect a book requested through online borrowing to be <u>delivered within 48 hours</u> to their home library. This is accomplished through a ground courier service that presently has 101 primary delivery sites (Figure 5). OhioLINK libraries are committed to meeting the 48-hour turnaround time as a shared objective. This feature, which ensures that information needs that cannot be met locally will nevertheless be met quickly and easily, meaningfully extends the collection available to users beyond that of their own library.

9. Through statewide implementation of UMI's PowerPages, a user can request an <u>image copy of the full-text</u> of an article to be delivered to a local laser printer or fax machine. This first step toward providing electronic full-text of periodical articles gives a user a convenient and economical option for securing a document from any of nearly 1,000 heavily used periodical titles. Additionally, OhioLINK will be providing access to two Chadwyck-Healey full-text databases: *English Poetry* and *English Verse Drama*.

10. Meaningful sharing of materials is made possible by the design of the system and by OhioLINK policies which ensure the accessibility of each institution's library collections. This opens the opportunity for member libraries to coordinate their collection development and <u>increase the extent and depth of resources</u> held statewide and available to each valid user.

11. The size of the OhioLINK project has given participating libraries the opportunity to advocate for needed <u>vendor development</u> to improve system performance for users. OhioLINK's common user interface, its online borrowing feature, and the UMI PowerPages project are evidence of successful development agendas to date.

MEASURING THE IMPACT ON USERS

Statistics demonstrate the growing use of the bibliographic resources <u>and</u> of the online borrowing feature. Central Catalog usage increased significantly through 1994 (Table 1). Reference databases for which there is data for both 1993 and 1994 also showed a more marked increase, patterning activity with the academic calendar (Table 2). The online borrowing feature began in January 1994, and use shows a dramatic increase (Table 3). The peak week had over 2,600 requests, and this was only with one-third of the libraries implemented and capable of offering this function to users. Interestingly, undergraduate use has been

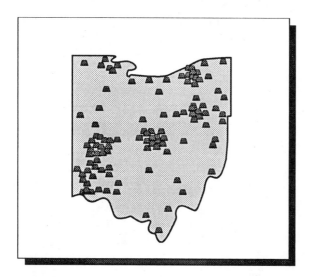

Figure 5: OhioLINK Ground Delivery Sites

very high. Graduate student use is higher than that of faculty (Table 4).

CONCLUSION

Even without statistics, comments from users on our campuses tell us OhioLINK is making a quantum change in their use of information. Undergraduates welcome the ready availability and convenience. Faculty appreciate the richness of the resources available. This statewide information system is changing the way we do business and serve our users.

Acknowledgments

The authors acknowledge the OhioLINK staff, committee members, and librarians of member institutions whose work this paper represents.

NOTES

1. Crowe, W. J., & Sanders, N. P. (1991). Collection development in the cooperative environment. *Journal of Library Administration,* 15(3-4), 37-48.
2. Hawks, C. P. (1992). The integrated library system of the 1990s: The OhioLINK experience. *Library Resources and Technical Services*, 36(1), 61-77.
3. Kohl, D. F. (1993). OhioLINK: Plugging into progress. *Library Journal,* 118(16), 42-46.
4. Sessions, J. (1992). OhioLINK: Technology and teamwork transforming Ohio libraries. *Wilson Library Bulletin*, 66(10), 43-45.

TABLE 1: Comparison of Total Number of Searches of the OhioLINK Central Catalog, 1993 & 1994

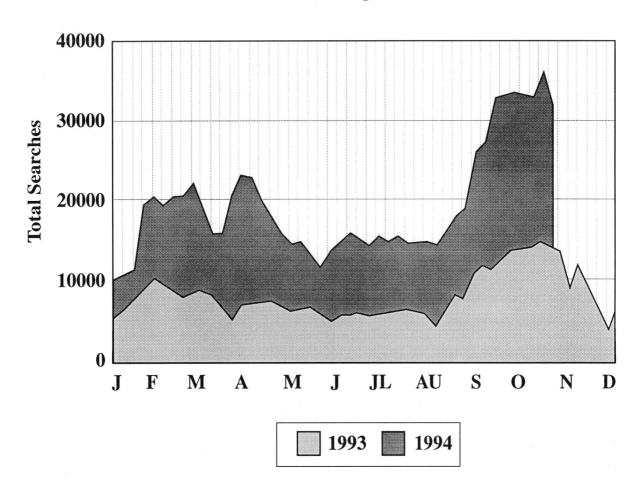

**TABLE 2: Comparison of Total Number of Searches of
OhioLINK Reference Databases, 1993 & 1994**

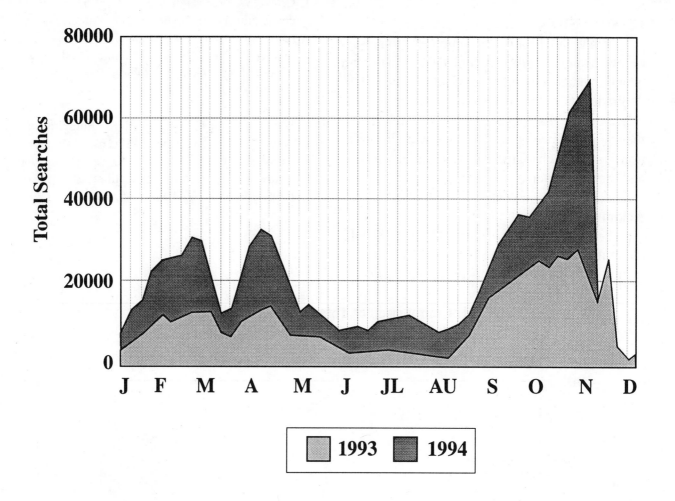

**TABLE 3: Number of Online Borrowing Requests through the
OhioLINK Central Catalog, January - June, 1994**

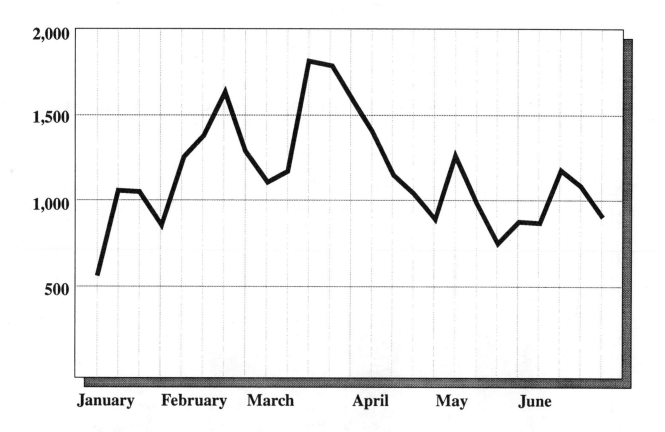

TABLE 4: Number of Online Borrowing Requests by User Type, January - June, 1994

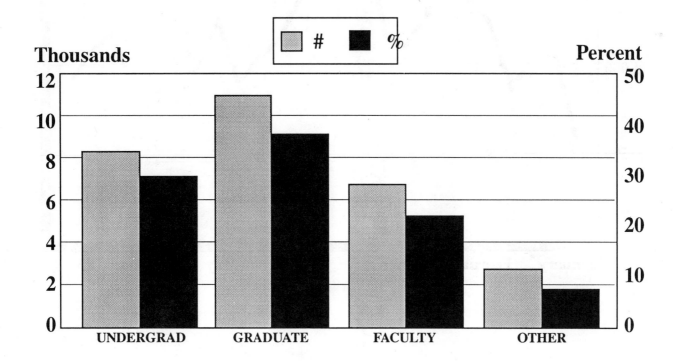

You Want it When?

Document Delivery in the 1990s

Lorraine J. Haricombe and T.J. Lusher

ABSTRACT

As the population of remote users of electronic resources explodes, libraries are faced with the challenge to move from their traditional role as information gatekeepers to potential gateways to global information networks. One traditional service which is experiencing this gateway evolution is interlibrary loan. As individuals change their information gathering habits, interlibrary loan departments are challenged to identify new ways to respond to users' requests. This paper will focus on the impact this evolution has on traditional library document delivery services, including funding, service policies, local collection development, and the expectations of users of this service.

Interlibrary loan departments are representative of the general trend in academic libraries that relies on electronic communication technology to satisfy the increasing demand by patrons for more access to information. The use of electronic communication technology by interlibrary loan departments has changed the very nature of journal article delivery. The impact of this trend has changed the traditional sharing of resources between libraries to the use of alternative, often commercially-based, resources to fill the patrons' request for materials. While libraries will continue some traditional modes of resource sharing, it is the availability of full-text journal articles which has created new alternative modes of delivery.

DEFINITIONS

When uncontrolled growth or change occurs in an area such as interlibrary loan, the vocabulary and its definitions often become individualized. The definitions below are how the authors define and label the activities involved in this area.

Interlibrary loan

For the purpose of this paper interlibrary loan will be defined as the borrowing of material and the loaning of material through cooperative agreements among all types of libraries. This paper will focus on interlibrary loan departments in academic libraries.

Lorraine J. Haricombe is Head of the Circulation Department and T. J. Lusher is a Reference Librarian at Northern Illinois University, Dekalb, Illinois.

Document delivery

The authors use the 1983 ALA definition of document delivery. This definition has two parts. 1) An information retrieval system, the provision of documents, published or unpublished, in hard copy or microform, at an established cost upon request. 2) The delivery of requested documents from the library collection to the office or residence of library users.[1]

Remote users

This is a popular term and in general refers to library users who are some distance from the main library. The authors believe that in the future a remote user will come to be identified as anyone who uses the library's resources through the Internet. Thus, a remote user may be on the same campus or in a different geographical location as the library from which they are requesting service.

In this paper the present activity of delivering information in any format will be called interlibrary loan. For discussion purposes, document delivery services will refer to the interlibrary loan departments of the future. Remote users will be more common in the document delivery services model than they are under the current model.

INTERLIBRARY LOAN TODAY

Theoretically speaking, the library successfully "delivers the document" whenever patrons 1) locate the item(s) in the catalog and 2) finds the item(s) in the library. When the library fails to deliver an item for a patron other collections are tapped to satisfy the patron's request for information. The basic elements of interlibrary loan services are a requestor, a lender, and the means to deliver the item that is requested. Historically, the library has assumed the role of requestor or intermediary in searching, locating, and requesting material from outside suppliers for the patron. Interlibrary loan departments have relied on other libraries to provide access to those materials not available in the local collection. Through reciprocal agreements and working through consortiums such as OCLC or RLIN to identify document suppliers, libraries have been able to meet most of

the needs of their patrons.[2] The emerging computer technologies have allowed more libraries to offer rapid access to other libraries' OPACs, CD-ROM databases, and to commercially-based information vendors. Accessibility to these electronic databases allows patrons to do more extensive searching for information in less time than using the traditional print resources.

The result of this extensive searching for information is the unearthing of articles, papers and/or books in sources that are not available in the local collection due to limited library material budgets. During the 1980s and 1990s libraries have been stretching budgets with less purchasing power. To cope with this reality, libraries are having to redefine their collection development profiles, thereby reducing the number of standing serial subscriptions and monographs ordered during a given year.[3]

These two forces, easier access to electronic databases, and the increased demand for material not in the local collection, have impacted directly on the volume of interlibrary loan requests for items that have been identified but are not available locally. For example, in 1982-83 ARL libraries loaned 2.8 million items and borrowed 781,409 items. By 1992-93 the number of items loaned rose to 4.3 million items with 1.5 million items being borrowed.[4]

This increase in demand does not translate into increased staffing of interlibrary loan departments. While statistics on staffing in interlibrary loan departments are not kept with regularity, general staffing trends can help give a snapshot of library wide patterns. In ARL libraries in 1982-83, the total number of professional staff was 11,504; support staff totalled 20,708; student assistants totalled 6,951. In 1992-93 in those same libraries professional staff increased by 3.7 percent to 11,951 employees, while support staff experienced an increase of 4.3 percent to 21,617 employees. The number of student assistants also increased. One might assume from this information that interlibrary loan departments experienced the same type of staffing pattern. If this assumption is correct, then fewer professional librarians and more support staff members have managed the increased demand for interlibrary loan services during this time period.[5]

In addition, interlibrary loan departments faces a new type of patron. This new patron, defined as a 'remote user', uses computer technology to gain access to the library's sources without setting foot in the library. The remote user also has different expectations and needs.

REMOTE USERS CHARACTERISTICS AND EXPECTATIONS

According to Sally Kalin, "remote users do not fit into tidy categories. They can be anybody and everybody; their individual characteristics and backgrounds are unknown." Despite this claim, some characteristics and expectations of remote users have been defined in the literature. [6]

Remote users expect the library to fill their information needs without having to come to the library, propelling the library to look for alternative and effective ways of meeting those needs. For them, rapid access to information sources will not be enough; quick delivery of the material will need to follow suit.[7]

Fueled by the media hype touting the benefits of computer technology, remote users are led to believe that anything is possible once they get onto the "Internet- the information highway." This assumption produces a user population with high expectations, without an understanding of the technical limitations of various applications, costs, or contractual agreements between the library and the vendors providing the access. Remote users are not only persistent; they demand increasingly more of the available technology and of the libraries they use. They view information databases as products and expect them to perform well. If the product performs well they expect to pay for it. If the product fails to perform well, the users are likely to blame the library without recognizing the intellectual effort and technological sophistication of the librarians who made the service possible.[8]

ACCESS versus DELIVERY

Realizing the availability and convenience of rapid bibliographic access, remote users also expect speedy document delivery of the information they need. Interlibrary loan departments' delivery of requested material, however, has lagged behind, pointing to the inverse relationship between access to information and availability of information. CD-Rom products and Internet access to OPACs offer immediate bibliographic access to global possibilities but do not offer immediate physical access to items not available locally. Only the book catalog and card catalog, which focus on the local collection offer both immediate access to the information and immediate availability.[9]

Historically, interlibrary loan departments have relied on these modes of delivery to provide for the transfer of information from the lender to the requestor:

- The use of the postal service
- Teletype facilities
- Facsimile copies
- Commercial parcel carriers
- Courier services

These traditional systems were efficient and patrons were satisfied with the results, until the norm for waiting periods shrunk from days to hours. Remote users who have access to telefacsimile machines, electronic mail, and the Internet are not only changing waiting period expectations but are also forcing interlibrary loan services to broaden the scope of their information suppliers. Today interlibrary loan services include resource sharing between libraries and the delivery of information from commercially-based vendors in their group of information suppliers. These vendors, such as Carl Uncover or ISI Genuine Article promise to send the full text of an article within a certain time frame. Use of these delivery systems, though, adds to the cost of each transaction.

Technology has been employed to update the traditional methods of document delivery. In the early eighties, telefacsimiles were considered to be a futuristic feature, but interlibrary loan departments are now using these machines routinely to meet the new expectations of document delivery periods. Some libraries, in an attempt to meet or exceed remote users expectations, are now using Ariel, a system which allows the transfer of information in digital form, to further increase speed of document delivery.[10]

RETHINKING DOCUMENT DELIVERY

It is not surprising that the disparity between bibliographic access and physical access has caused libraries to review their document delivery operations. In doing so, libraries have to consider the expectations of an expanding clientele of remote users. There are alternative models to the traditional interlibrary loan departments available in the library world today.

One such model of service is the fee-based document delivery system which provides document delivery on demand. Some academic libraries offer these services in addition to their traditional interlibrary loan services. These services are available to patrons who need someone to conduct a search for them or when a document is needed immediately. In her 1993 article, *Fee-Based Services and Document Delivery*, Lee Ann George noted that fee-based information services have existed since the late 1960s. These services are now experiencing tremendous growth in popularity because they are equipped to fulfill the demand that interlibrary loan departments fail to meet, namely, rapid document delivery. The clients are willing to pay for this document delivery service.[11]   Libraries, though, have one characteristic not shared by these fee-based information services; libraries pride themselves on providing their services free or for a small minimal fee. By blending the commitment of rapid document delivery of the fee-based information services and interlibrary loan's commitment to free or minimal cost services, the library offers one

possible model for addressing the needs of remote users of the future. Blending and adopting practices from each of the systems will have a ripple effect on staffing patterns, funding and service policies. It will also require libraries to venture into the area of marketing their services to remote users.

THE IMPACT OF LIBRARIES AS GATEWAYS TO INFORMATION NETWORKS
Marketing

Remote access to commercially-based vendors that combine quick access with fast document delivery to fill patrons' information needs creates a new challenge for libraries to provide services that can compete with the many potential suppliers of information. Any new service will be as good as that which libraries are able to deliver, requiring careful planning and continuous assessment of the service once implemented.

Remote users are difficult to identify thus making it even more difficult for libraries to mount an effective marketing campaign. Libraries can no longer rely solely on a printed handout to advertise remote access. They will have to become actively involved in the continuous marketing of the library's services to a wider clientele.

Brochures are readily accessible to patrons who come to the library or who call for assistance, but they fail to reach the remote user who may never come to the library. Kalin is of the opinion that a built-in feature in the OPAC may be the easiest method to update patrons of new services or system changes. Many libraries advertise sign-up sessions for instruction in the library, campus bulletins, and campus newspapers. This publicity could be expanded to include the local newspaper and local news media. One library held a press conference when remote access became operational![12]

Tapping the computer dealers in the community has proven to be mutually beneficial to the library and to the dealer. Informing local computer dealers about remote access not only prepares them to answer prospective customers' technical questions, but doing so also promotes this library service. Increasingly, libraries and computer services collaborate to present on-campus workshops. Computing staff handle questions related to the technical aspects of computer applications, while librarians provide support in acquiring the skills necessary to do searches. The collaborative efforts between these two units contribute to promoting a "futuristic" image for the library. Using the Internet/gopher to promote the library's services and updates on system changes has the potential to reach a large proportion of computer users who rely on the Internet for new information.

Service policies

The implementation of new services and technology impacts on existing procedures and policies. Remote access to online computers has a direct impact on interlibrary loan activities. The effect of the new service goes beyond an increase in interlibrary loan activity, it also necessitates a review of circulation policies, procedures, and distribution of workload, all of which underscore the fundamental philosophy of service and convenience to the user. One pilot document delivery service resulted in new policies and procedures with regard to number of items that patrons could request, work flow to process the requests expeditiously, and methods to notify patrons.

Libraries need to consider what type of support services they will provide to remote users who are not associated with the institution. Will the remote users enjoy the same access privileges as the traditional user categories? If so, how will the library offset the cost of providing free access and document delivery to all remote users when library budgets are shrinking? Notwithstanding the ALA's policy of free access to information, Galvin claims that many libraries have already responded to this demand by charging a service fee for online searching.[13]

Staffing

Unless there is a change in the funding level of academic libraries, future increases in staffing is unlikely. Perhaps additional staffing will not be necessary as interlibrary loan departments become more of a gateway or direct connection for the remote users and information suppliers. Bluh, in her article on document delivery in 2000 notes, ". . . the nature of the staff-patron relationship is changing as more and more document delivery services require less and less staff intervention." Thus, librarians will be reassigned and the support staff remaining in document delivery services will, working with reference/research librarians, serve as consultants in assisting patrons to select an appropriate information supplier. Interlibrary loan will only intervene directly when the information supplier is another library.[14]

It is in this role as reference/research consultant that the librarians currently involved with interlibrary loan will maintain their ties to the future service. Reference/research librarians will assist both internal and remote users to identify appropriate electronic and print sources. They will guide the patron to the suppliers of information, whether it is the local collection or an outside source. Indeed in the future, librarians, who work in acquisitions, collection development, reference, and interlibrary loan today, may work even closer in bringing patrons and information together. As a team, these librarians will set policy, develop procedures, and plan the future direction of the service.[15]

Funding

Libraries will have to reallocate monies from acquisitions and collection development to designated funds to pay for access to electronic databases and, for the forseeable future, document delivery service. Some savings of money may be realized through the continuing cancellation of print indexes and those journals available through the Internet in full-text format. Cooperative collection development efforts may also release money from monographic acquisition budgets.

The reallocated monies should be used to improve the research/document delivery services as well as paying for access to more electronic databases held both locally and those available through the Internet. Money should be funnelled

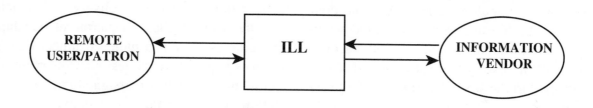

FIGURE 1: Traditional Interlibrary Loan

towards buying computers, telefacsimile machines, and any other future communication equipment needed by the document delivery staff to provide quality service. Finally, a fund to pay for the charges incurred in acquiring the information should be established. This fund would allow libraries to continue to offer free service to patrons both local and remote.

New sources of monies could be raised through remote user fees for Internet access privileges and document delivery services. Remote users could be charged fees on a graduated level. Basic fees would give remote users access to passwords for a selected group of remote databases. Premium fees would allow remote users access to passwords for all of the databases the library subscribes to. The cost of document delivery to the remote user's address would be included in the fee.

Another source of funding would require the creation of a new budget line from the University to the library for electronic library services. This new budget line would draw from the campus-wide computer fees, renamed the electronic resources fee. This fee will provide students, faculty, and staff passwords to search Internet-based databases using university accounts. Money in the new budget line would fund free document delivery services for the campus community. The money would also pay for the library's subscriptions to Internet-based databases.

THE RESULTING DOCUMENT DELIVERY MODEL

The future of document delivery service will rest on Internet participation by database producers/vendors. Internet access will provide patrons with direct access to OPACs, CD-ROM databases, and commercially-based information vendors. Traditional delivery services will continue for some formats. However, new models of document delivery for journal articles will occur in phases, beginning with the interlibrary loan services acting as intermediary between the patron and the information vendor, to the patron contacting the information vendor after consulting with a librarian, and, finally, to direct interaction between patron and the information vendor.

In the first phase, which is now occurring, the patron requests that the library locates and retrieves the required journal articles (Fig. 1). The articles are faxed or electronically transmitted from another library or a commercially-based information vendor to the borrowing library. The home library notifies the patron to pick up the articles or sends it to a campus address.

In the second phase, the patron interacts with a reference/research librarian to select appropriate Internet databases for the patron to search (Fig. 2). Once the patron retrieves the appropriate articles, he/she checks the local library for holdings of the needed item. If the articles cannot be located in the

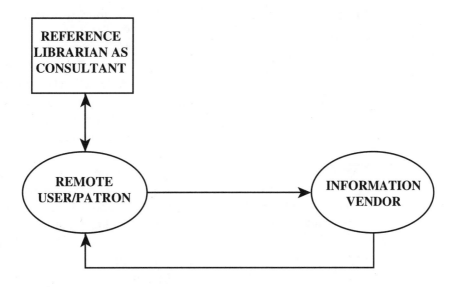

FIGURE 2: Library as Consultant

FIGURE 3: Remote User as Independent Searcher

local library, the patron returns to consult with the reference/research librarian to locate an information vendor to provide the articles. The patron transmits the citation that was downloaded from the Internet database to the vendor's electronic ordering division for direct delivery to the patron's e-mail, street, or office address.

In the third and final phase, the remote user selects and searches the Internet database and information vendors without consulting a reference/research librarian. The library and information vendors form a partnership in providing ac-

cess to different types of materials (Fig.3). The library provides direct access for the remote user to its holdings, while information vendors provide direct access to and direct delivery of journal articles not held in the local library. The remote user accesses both information databases as a part of his/her Internet searching.

The true impact of remote access and remote users have yet to be analyzed. The telecommunication hardware and software of the future may very well be develop in ways we cannot foresee. Future funding levels and spending priorities will decide what-technology is adopted and how monies will be reallocated. While these are all unknowns, simply waiting for the future to happen is unwise also. Careful planning, discussion, experimentation, and evaluation of the new services will help libraries today prepare the library of tomorrow be a gateway to the "global information village."

NOTES

1. Heartstill Young, ed., The *ALA Glossary of Library and Information Science* (Chicago: American Library Association, 1983), 77.
2. Frederick W. Lancaster, *If you want to evaluate your library....* (Champaign, IL: University of Illinois, 1988), 104.
3. While the authors used the *ARL Statistics for 1992-93*, the reader could use any of the annual compilations put out by the Association of Research Libraries. For this paper budget figures for monographs and current serial subscriptions are listed in *ARL Statistics, 1992-93*, Nicola Daval and Patricia Brennan, comps. *ARL Statistics, 1992-93* (Washington, D.C.: Association of Research Libraries, 1994), 32.
4. These statistics were taken from the annual compilation of ARL statistics. To see the complete tables refer to Carol A. Mandel and Alexander Lichtenstein, comps. *ARL Statistics 1982-83* (Washington, D.C.: Association of Research Libraries, 1984), 20 and Nicola Daval and Patricia Brennan, comps. *ARL Statistics 1992-93* (Washington, D.C.:Association of Research Libraries, 1994), 39. The numbers were rounded off by the authors. The survey compilation by Marilyn M. Roche *ARL/RLG Interlibrary Loan Cost Study* (Washington, D.C.: Association of Research Libraries and Washington,D.C.: Research Libraries Group, 1993),1.
5. See Carol A. Mandel and Alexander Lichtenstein, comps. *ARL Statistics 1982/83*, (Washington,D.C.: Association for Research Libraries, 1984), 21 and the *ARL Statistics 1992/93*, (Washington,D.C.: Association for Research Libraries, 1994),39.
6. Sally W.Kalin, "Support Services for Remote Users of Online Public Access Catalogs," *RQ* 31, no.2 (Winter,1991): 199. Pat Molholt, "Libraries and Campus Information: Redrawing the Boundaries," *Academic Computing* 42 (February 1990): 43. Elizabeth H. Dow, "The Impact of Home and Office Workstations Use On an Academic Library" (Ph.D diss., University of Pittsburgh Graduate School of Library and Information Science, 1988), 63.
7. Mary E. Jackson, "Resource Sharing and Document Delivery in the 1990s," *Wilson Library Bulletin* 67, no.6 (February,1993): 36. Brian Aveney, "Online Catalogs: the Transformation Continues," *Wilson Library Bulletin* 58, no.6 (February, 1984): 406.
8. Pat Molholt, "Libraries and Campus Information: Redrawing the Boundaries," *Academic Computing* 42 (February, 1990): 43.
9. Sally W. Kalin, "Support Services for Remote Users of Online Public Access Catalogs," *RQ* 31, no.2 (Winter, 1991): 200.
10. Cheryl LaGuardia and Connie V.Dowell, "The Structure of Resource Sharing in Academic Research Libraries," *RQ* 30, no.3 (Spring,1991): 373.
11. Lee Anne George, "Fee-Based Information Services and Document Delivery," *Wilson Library Bulletin* 67, no.6(February, 1993): 41-42.
12. Sally W. Kalin, "Support Services for Remote Users of Online Public Access Catalogs," *RQ* 31, no.2 (Winter, 1991): 204, and Sally W. Kalin, "The Invisible Users of Online Catalogs: A Public Services Perspective," *Library Trends* 35, no.4 (Spring, 1987): 592.
13. Thomas J. Galvin, "From Document Delivery to Information Access: Convergence at the National Level," *The Reference Librarian* no.34 (1991): 135.
14. Pamela Bluh, "Document Delivery 2000: Will it Change the Nature of Librarianship?" *Wilson Library Bulletin* 67, no.6 (February, 1993): 49 and Mary E. Jackson, "Resource Sharing and Document Delivery in the 1990s," *Wilson Library Bulletin* 67, no.6 (February, 1993): 36, 110.
15. Mary E. Jackson, "Resource Sharing and Document Delivery in the 1990s," *Wilson Library Bulletin* 67, no.6 (February, 1993): 110.

Interlibrary Loan and Customer Satisfaction:

How Important is Delivery Speed?

Wilbur Stolt, Pat Weaver-Meyers, and Molly Murphy

ABSTRACT

Analysis of a recent user satisfaction survey completed at the University of Oklahoma suggests that customers' perception of timeliness and customer satisfaction with interlibrary loan services may be more dependent on interactions with staff than on speed of delivery. This paper takes the position that a disproportionate emphasis has been placed on delivery speed. Academic librarians, by focusing on delivery speed as the most emphasized measure of quality interlibrary loan service, may be under serving a more important customer need and may be attaching more value to document delivery providers than they deserve.

The rise of quality management activities in the private and public sectors of society has created an increased interest in customer (user) satisfaction surveys. Satisfaction research is one of the fastest growing areas of research in marketing field and it has been used by librarians as a means of gathering information.[1] The University of Oklahoma Libraries has employed user satisfaction surveys to examine its programs and services. This paper reports on a survey of interlibrary loan (ILL) services, and how some unexpected results raise questions about our assumptions of user needs and what academics value in document delivery services.

In recent years, ILL has transformed from a supplementary service to a high-visibility service. The dramatic reduction in serial titles in academic libraries and the trend toward "just in time" versus "just in case" collection development strategies have created interest in the role and abilities of ILL to provide alternate information access for the academic user. Some of this current interest in ILL operations can be seen in recent Association of Research Libraries and Research Libraries Group studies about ILL costs and growth in activity.[2]

Concomitant with this interest in ILL, is the explosion in the number of commercial document delivery vendors in the information market. Reductions in journal subscriptions, advances in elec-

Wilbur Stolt is Director of Library Public Services, Pat Weaver-Meyers is Head of Access Services, and Molly Murphy is a Library Technician in the Interlibrary Loan Office at the University of Oklahoma Libraries, Norman, Oklahoma.

tronic full-text information, a reevaluation of ownership versus access among library managers, demand for convenient services, reductions in library staff, and steady increases in ILL have created multiple opportunities for vendors. Document delivery providers are capitalizing on the situation and are vigorously marketing delivery speed and convenience. Increasing use of vendor services suggest that these providers are filling a an unmet need, but are the values promoted by vendors the key to user satisfaction?

THE SURVEY

User surveys have been employed by libraries since the 1960s, but opinions about their usefulness is mixed according to F. W. Lancaster.[3] More recently, Total Quality Management (TQM) strategies have been introduced in libraries. Paula Warnken and others have used in-depth marketing research which combined focus group interviews and user surveys to identify academic customer values and needs.[4] Peter Hernon and Charles McClure emphasize in a discussion of performance measures that "just because an activity has high quality and excellent measures of effectiveness and/or efficiency, it is not the same as saying that activity has 'value.'"[5] Determining what customers value is a necessary component of a thorough evaluation.

The University of Oklahoma Libraries ILL Department developed a survey to measure user satisfaction and to gather information about customer values. The survey included some of the factors identified by Higginbotham and Bowdoin as essential to a complete evaluation of borrowing services. According to Higginbotham and Bowdoin, all the following factors may be helpful in formulating an analysis of effective borrowing services: location finders, number of requests submitted, growth in service, fill rate, speed of delivery, document quality, flexibility and ease of use, reader satisfaction (including a measure of potential demand), balance and fairness (supplier's perspective), and costs.[6]

Higginbotham and Bowdoin's criteria are also helpful in placing the University of Oklahoma's ILL services in perspective with other ILL operations. The majority of customers are graduate students, 55 percent, while 33 percent are faculty and 8 percent are undergraduates. The fill rate for borrowing requests the previous fiscal year was 82 percent filled, 8 percent owned and 10 percent canceled. Total number of requests received was 17,336. The most recent rankings among ARL libraries (including law and medical libraries) place the University of Oklahoma sixth in number of items borrowed.[7] Growth in borrowing shows an increase of 79 percent since 1988/89. An internal cost study revealed borrowing costs were comparable with other Big 8 libraries: $14.72/request compared to $14.88/request (mean for Big 8 libraries in ARL/RLG study).[8] The criteria indicate the University of Oklahoma is comparable to other mid-size universities.

The University of Oklahoma Libraries's survey evaluates selected Bowdoin and Higginbotham criteria: speed of delivery, timeliness and usefulness of the item provided, perceived convenience or ease of use, and level of satisfaction with the particular transaction. Other questions were included to find out how interested patrons were in new services (See Appendix).

A draft of the survey was reviewed by faculty members and revisions were made to insure validity. Two hundred forms were distributed randomly with the mailing or pickup of completed ILL requests. Therefore, the survey does not include non-users (latent demand) or users whose requests were canceled. A total of 75 surveys were returned.

RESULTS

Our basic hypothesis assumed user's estimation of timeliness and their satisfaction with the service would correlate directly with speed of delivery. Response frequencies and means were used to determine satisfaction levels and identify areas of concern among the users. Correlations were run to identify what characteristics of the

TABLE 1

Significant Correlations P<.05

Question x question	Corr.	Prob.
Satisfaction with transaction x		
1. Length of time btw notification & pickup or receipt of item.	.3307	.02
2. Item received in a timely manner	.7089	.0001
3. Satisfied with telephone interactions with staff	.4617	.0010
4. Receipt of item took so long, it was no longer useful	-.3542	.0135
5. I will use ILL in the future	.4671	.0008
6. Item received was correct	.5603	.0001
7. Willing to pay $10 for 48 hr. service	-.4325	.0021
8. Convenient to pickup requests	.4855	.0005

service most affected satisfaction and timeliness, thereby pinpointing where limited resources might be directed.

The survey reveals a mean for "satisfaction with the transaction" of 1.25 with a standard deviation of .48 (1=strongly agree they are satisfied). Many respondents use the service frequently. The mean number of requests ordered/patron on ILL equals 43. The mean turnaround is 10.47 days.

Many of the correlations are confirmation of common sense deductions. For example, the responses for "it took so long to receive this item it was no longer useful" and "I received this item in a timely manner" negatively correlated. Correlations with timeliness and satisfaction, though, are surprising in two areas. We expected that timeliness and satisfaction would be strongly correlated with speed of delivery. However, there is no significant correlation between these variables.

Secondly, we are not surprised to see a correlation between "satisfaction with the transaction" and "satisfaction with telephone interactions with staff". We are surprised, though, to see a significant correlation between perceived timeliness and "satisfaction with telephone interactions". Further, we note a significant correlation with perceived timeliness and "availability of staff to answer questions"

In analyzing the reason for these results, consider that the number of days required to receive an item did not correlate with timeliness, but "receipt of item took so long, it was no longer useful" did negatively correlate. This relationship appears to support the assertion that speed affects perceptions of timeliness only when the patron's definition of usefulness is exceeded. When delivery falls within a "useful period", satisfaction with the service rests more on staff interactions. It is interesting to note that F. W. Lancaster empha-

TABLE 2

Significant Correlations P<.05

Question x question	Corr.	Prob.
Timeliness　　　x		
1. Satisfied with telephone interactions with staff	.3858	.0068
2. Receipt of item took so long, it was no longer useful	-.5554	.0001
3. I will use ILL in the future	.6071	.0001
4. Item received was correct	.3846	.0069
5. Willing to pay $10 for 48hr service	-.3802	.0077
6. ILL staff is readily available to answer questions	.3425	.0172
7. Convenient to pickup requests	.6257	.0001

sized the importance of usefulness as early as 1977.[9]

IMPLICATIONS

Herbert White has suggested that we have trained users to be passive about their need for rapid delivery.[10] The growth of vendor services appears to support the claim that there is an unmet need to deliver documents more rapidly and conveniently. Rapid delivery, however, may be getting a disproportionate amount of attention because of vendors' marketing emphasis and librarians' assumptions, and because it is easy to measure. Furthermore, recent research on vendor effectiveness, costs and future capacities raise questions about the speed and convenience achieved by vendors.[11]

Mounir Khalil points out that resistance to paying for documents has limited use of commercial vendors by some academics.[12] In our survey, only 24 percent of the users would have been willing to pay a $10 fee for 48 hour delivery. This compares to the findings of a 1983 study of commercial document delivery users in which there was 12 percent demand for rapid delivery at a cost of $14.[13] While a comparison of the surveys suggest there are now more users willing to pay for fast delivery, the total is still less than 25 percent.

CONCLUSIONS

Although this survey is not adequate to draw definitive conclusions nor is the paper intended to be a rigorous research report, some of the results suggest a need to reexamine our assumptions about document delivery speed and service quality. If faster delivery is not always essential to patron satisfaction, then how do librarians determine when to spend resources on faster delivery and when to invest in the staff necessary to achieve "satisfying" services for customers whose criteria for satisfaction rests on more qualitative factors?

Few, if any, academic ILL customers would argue that the sooner they get a needed item the better. Most librarians would also prefer faster turnaround for requests. But, our survey suggests that a high percentage of users do not have tight time constraints on their research needs. For them, perceptions about effectiveness of service may not always be dependent upon quick delivery. Developing relationships with users may help staff interpret time constraints based on past experiences with customers and their research habits. Good communications also may determine whether rapid delivery or customized personal service is more critical to user satisfaction. Establishing a quality relationship may be the key to achieving the most satisfying customer service at the most cost effective level.

Librarians should understand vendor marketing strategies and question their own assumptions about customer needs. Technology in libraries has not proven to be a replacement for staff or a means to save funds. The modern document delivery service, like technology, is becoming important in meeting the needs of today's researcher. However, these survey results suggest that it does not replace the role of library staff in providing a high-quality service to the academic community - at least not yet. Customizing or personalizing a service through staff interaction may contribute as much to user satisfaction as decreasing delivery time.

As ILL is transformed by the influences of document delivery vendors and full-text availability of information, the goal for librarians will be to refocus regularly on the question of what satisfies the customer. Soliciting user reactions to the transformation of information provision is an important role for librarians. Only then can librarians redirect that transformation by customizing programs to meet individual user needs, insuring effective, efficient, and <u>valuable</u> services.

NOTES

1. Laura Loro, "Customer is Always Right, Satisfaction Research Booms." *Advertising Age* 63 (Feb. 10, 1992): 25; Arlene Farber Sirkin,"Customer Service: Another Side of TQM", *Journal of Library Administration* 18 (1/2 1993):
71-83.

2. Association of Research Libraries, *ARL Statistics 1990-91.* (Washington, D. C.: Association of Research Libraries, 1992); Marilyn M. Roche, *ARL/RLG Interlibrary Loan Cost Study: A Joint Effort by the Association of Research Libraries and the Research Libraries Group* (Washington, D. C.: Association of Research Libraries, 1993), 4.

3. F. W. Lancaster, *The Measurement and Evaluation of Library Services* (Washington, D. C.: Information Resources Press, 1977), 308.

4. Paula Warnken, Vicki Young, and Bob Ahuja, "Beyond the Survey: Using Market Research Techniques to Improve Library Services and Collections." Paper presented at the Association of College and Research Libraries Sixth National Conference, Salt Lake City, April 12-15, 1992.

5. Peter Hernon and Charles McClure, *Evaluation and Library Decision Making* (Norwood, N. J.: Ablex, 1990), 34.

6. Barbara Buckner Higginbotham and Sally Bowdoin, *Access Versus Assets: A Comprehensive Guide to Resource Sharing for Academic Libraries* (Chicago: American Library Association, 1994), 275-280.

7. Association of Research Libraries, *ARL Statistics 1992-93.* (Washington, D. C.: Association of Research Libraries, 1994), 65.

8. Marilyn M. Roche, *ARL/RLG Interlibrary Loan Cost Study,* 5.

9. F. W. Lancaster, *The Measurement and Evaluation of Library Services,* 235.

10. Herbert White, "Interlibrary Loan: An Old Idea in a New Setting." *Library Journal* 112 (July 1987): 53-54.

11. Kathleen Kurosman and Barbara Ammerman Durniak, "Document Delivery: A Comparison of Commercial Document Suppliers and Interlibrary Loan Services." *College and Research Libraries* 55 (March 1994): 129-139; Keith Glavash, "Full-text Retrieval for Document Delivery - A Viable Option?" *Online* 18 (May 1994): 81-84.

12. Mounir Khalil, "Document Delivery: A Better Option?" *Library Journal* 118 (Feb. 1993): 43-47.

13. Richard Boss, *Document Delivery in the United States: A Report to the Council on Library Resources.* (Washington, D. C.: Council on Library Resources, 1983), 56.

APPENDIX

University of Oklahoma Libraries
Interlibrary Loan Services (ILL) - Survey 1993

The item attached is the result of a request you made for an interlibrary loan. We are interested in you opinion of the quality of this service. Please take a few moments and respond to the questions below. Your input will help the OU Libraries improve. If you have already completed this form for another item, please complete this form AGAIN! Your opinion of each transaction is an important part of our study. When you are done, fold the completed form in half, staple closed and return in campus mail. All responses are anonymous.

Thank you.

1) When did you receive the attached interlibrary loan item? __/__/__.

2) In the past year, about how many books or articles have you requested from ILL?
_____.

Please answer the following by selecting the rating which most represents your opinion of the statement and write that rating in the space provided.

1 = strongly agree   2 = agree   3 = neutral   4 = disagree   5 = strongly disagree

a) _____   I received this item in a timely manner.

b) _____   I am satisfied with telephone interactions I have had with
                 interlibrary loan staff.

c) _____   Based on this transaction, I am satisfied with interlibrary loan service.

d) _____   Because it took so long to receive this item, it was no longer useful to me.

e) _____   I will be using interlibrary loan service in the future.

f) _____   The item I received is the item I requested.

g) _____   If I could be guaranteed 48 hour delivery, I would be willing to pay a fee of
                 $10 to get this item faster.

h) _____   I found it convenient and easy to place a request.

i) _____   I would use email to place a request if it were possible to do so.

j) _____   The interlibrary loan staff are readily available to answer my questions.

k) _____ It is convenient for me to pick up books I receive on interlibrary loan at the main library.

l) _____ I currently order some materials I need directly from commercial vendors on the Internet (CARL, FirstSearch).

Comments?_____

_____

_____

Office Use Only

Item requested via: ___OCLC _____RLIN _____Mail _____Fax _____ARIEL
Article transmitted via: _____mail _____courier _____ARIEL _____Fax
Date Requested: _____ Date Received: _____
Type of notification: _____phone _____mail   Date notified: __/__/__

Electronic Networks
The Role of the Librarian/Information Specialist: Views from an LIS Classroom

Vicki L. Gregory

ABSTRACT

A case study of Library and Information Science students, as the future professionals in the library and information field, was undertaken in a Library Networks and Systems course at the University of South Florida in order to examine students' initial beliefs and changing views, as they became more familiar and comfortable using the Internet, concerning (a) types of networked information that should be available for patrons and staff in various library settings, (b) how such information should be made available, and (c) the library's and librarians' roles in providing networked information. The project also assessed perceived abilities of students to use networks and student perceptions of patrons' abilities to make use of them. This paper examines these student opinions, discusses librarians' problems related to the Internet, and emphasizes aspects of library education affecting the provision of information services in networked environments.

INTRODUCTION

The rapidly changing information environment in academic and research libraries is resulting in the addition to the academic librarian's already heavy workload of many new resources in various media and multiple ways of accessing those resources. The problem presented is the classic overabundance of riches. As Pamela McLaughlin states: "All [of these new resources and services] continue to co-exist to some degree and librarians have been faced with the challenge of coping with the explosion, learning how the pieces all fit together, offering a coherent group of resources and services, and continually discovering, evaluating and updating."[1]

In a paper entitled "Networked Information: A Revolution in Progress,"[2] Clifford Lynch, in a discussion of the new roles being played by libraries in the world of networked information, points out that "Libraries can play a vital role through evaluation and selection: They can choose infor-

Vicki L. Gregory is an Associate Professor at the School of Library and Information Science, University of South Florida, Tampa, Florida.

mation refiners, or they can themselves be information refiners."[3] In a similar vein, Michael Malinconico noted in *American Libraries* that:

> Until now... librarians have only been 'passive participants in the information-transfer process;' when information is delivered their role is over. However, modern technology makes it possible to refine, synthesize, and transfer information into the most useful form to users. This will transform librarians from 'passive catalysts to publishers who create information on demand.'[4]

I believe this posited transformation in the librarian's role to be accurate not only as a theoretical matter but also reflective of an emerging critical aspect of librarianship generally. Unfortunately, this proactive, creative function is one that both many present librarians, and a significant portion of the librarians/information specialists of the future (i.e., those persons who are currently enrolled in Library and Information Science [LIS] programs), find themselves uncomfortable in attempting.

Since the views of the current crop of LIS students, who will very shortly be active professionals in all the various types of libraries and information centers, will doubtless shape the future of their libraries as they become more involved in dealing with the issues of networked information, I undertook a case study of LIS students in an experimental course in Library Networks and Systems offered during Fall Semester 1993 at the Tampa main campus of the University of South Florida (USF). The purpose of the study was to examine LIS students' initial beliefs and (hopefully) changing views concerning (a) the types of networked information that should be available for patron and staff use in various types of library settings, (b) how these resources should be made available, and (c) the proper role of the library and the librarian toward the provision and servicing of networked information.

Another important aspect of this project, in addition to perceptions of the emerging role changes of librarians and information specialists, was an assessment of the perceived ability of LIS students to use electronic networks efficiently and effectively and their perceptions of patrons' abilities to make use of these same networked sources in the ordinary library context. Because of the rapidly growing and changing nature of information networks, those in the profession who have used the Internet and other networks for a number of years, and have therefore become at least comparatively sophisticated users of the new technology, should not lose sight of the perceptions of new student/ professional users, who begin their contact with information networks at about the same level of proficiency as general end-users of networked information. Thus, LIS student perceptions of the tools and interfaces needed by end-users should be of significant value to those information professionals who are involved in designing, implementing, and making accessible networks in various settings.

METHODOLOGY

This study was qualitative in nature, using several data-gathering techniques. Perceptions of 24 graduate LIS students enrolled in a USF course entitled "Library Networks and Systems" were studied in relation to use of the Internet in a library setting for both staff and patrons. To gain baseline information about these students' respective levels of experience with the Internet, a questionnaire was administered during the first class session in order that responses from both new and more experienced users could be analyzed separately. Each student also received a secret number to use for identification on the questionnaire and on subsequent "freewrites." Analysis of the questionnaire results indicated that out the 24 students, 16 were currently employed in some capacity in a library; eight worked in a university library, one in a community college library, four in public libraries, and three in special libraries (one medical and two law). The overwhelming majority of the class members were essentially new users of the Internet; 16 students had never used the Internet and five indicated that they had very limited experience, with only two students claiming extensive Internet experience. Nineteen of the students reported access to a personal computer at home and 12 had access to a modem at home. All but one student had access to a personal computer and modem at either their home or their place of work.

As part of the Library Networks and Systems course work, students were able to experience various approaches to organizing networked information through the use of the LUIS system. At the time of the class, the Florida Center for Library Automation had recently revamped the LUIS system into much more than an online catalog, including a menu interface allowing access to numerous library catalogs and other resources available on the Internet. In addition, students had access to the Florida Information and Resources Network (FIRN), which also allows access to the Internet with access at the time to a limited number of Internet resources as menu items, and a BITNET/Internet account on the IBM mainframe of the Central Florida Data Center. As students progressed through the course and obtained experience in using Listservs, Telnet, FTP, Gophers, Archie, Veronica, WAIS, etc., their opinions as to the "best" uses of these resources in a library setting and the role of the librarian in making all or some of these resources available for patron use were collected through a series of "freewrites."

Freewriting is a method used by composition theorists and instructors to aid professional and beginning writers in organizing their thoughts, knowledge, interests, and conclusions about their current work and has become an accepted instructional technique in many high schools and colleges. Users of this methodology are expected to compose their thoughts on paper (or the computer screen) much as they would talk to themselves with no concern for their audience, rules of grammar, spelling, etc. The purpose of freewriting is to get students to express on paper what they are thinking and feeling about a subject, thus making

it an appropriate methodology for this type of qualitative study.[5]

In the freewrites, students were asked to provide their opinions anonymously and to express any feelings they might have respecting the systems available to them, including hesitations about the network resources, as well as problems encountered in accessing and using the Internet. A content analysis of these freewrites was performed in the following way: First all the essays were read and important words or ideas were highlighted. Then the data was categorized into concepts and recorded in such a way so as to allow the grouping of the results relative to particular points in time in the course.

In addition, throughout the semester, the students were required to compile a diary of their usage of networked information (a) showing the sources they had actually used, as well as which sources they had tried but had failed to be able to use, and (b) setting forth some discussion as to their successes, failures, and general comments on the use of networked information by library professionals and end-users. This data was used to supplement and verify information gathered through the freewrite essays and to pinpoint particularly troublesome features and aspects that the students experienced in using the various networks and software tools.

CONTENT ANALYSIS OF FREEWRITES
Electronic Mail

The first freewrite, which was performed at the sixth class session, consisted of student responses to a request to provide their reactions to, and to comment upon the usefulness for librarians and patrons of, electronic mail and electronic discussion groups. The majority of the students who had not previously used e-mail found both the FIRNMAIL and IBM VM commands difficult to master at first. Most felt that e-mail would be useful for library staff to use in communicating within and outside the library, but would be too difficult for general patron use. One student commented that "Anything that makes an OPAC look like the ultimate in ergonomic design needs some work." Another stated that "The thought of offering e-mail service to library patrons seems like a nightmare to me."

One of the students who had had previous experience using e-mail and the Internet pointed out that "The major problems are that mainframe-based e-mail systems are clumsy to use and differ widely from each other. There can be a steep learning curve for non-technical people. It's amazing when novice users can pick them up at all. I have strong reactions against non-intuitive systems."

However, another student who had not had any previous experience using e-mail was of the view that an entire library system could be based around e-mail and a bulletin board system. The student provided drafts of potential patron menus which included (in addition to traditional menus for an online catalog) message screens for various departments so that a patron could send messages to various library departments in general or to specific individuals in the library.

Experience and confidence in using e-mail was growing by the time of the second freewrite in the ninth week of the semester. Several more students now indicated that e-mail could be useful in allowing patrons to ask questions of a library's reference staff. Especially noteworthy, they felt, was the asynchronous nature of e-mail, which could allow reference staff to answer questions during "quiet" periods at the reference desk; this was seen as a great advantage by these students. For example, one new user of e-mail wrote: "I think that e-mail is a quick, fun, and less intrusive means of communication for librarians. I would much rather receive e-mail messages that I can read at my leisure rather than phone calls that interrupt my day at busy moments."

From a strictly student perspective, several students, who were commuting to Tampa from locations one to three hours drive time away and thus on campus only one day a week, found that e-mail was an excellent means of communication both with the instructor and classmates concern-

ing homework, papers, and other assignments. Obviously, as more and more colleges and universities come to engage in distance education, the provision of electronic communication facilitated by a local library may help to remove some of the disadvantages and feelings of isolation for these students.

Electronic Discussion Groups (LISTSERVS)

Most students were initially very enthusiastic and eager to join many of the various types of electronic discussion groups, both library-related ones and those that reflected personal interests and hobbies. The following Table shows the listservs most commonly joined by the students in the class.

Most Commonly Joined Electronic Discussion Groups

Library-Related	Hobbies or Personal Interest
PACS-L	STREK-D
STUMPERS-L	BEER-L
LIBREF-L	CATHOLIC-L
KIDLIT-L	MEDIEV-L
JESSE	ANSAXNET
COLLDV-L	

By the time of the second freewrite, many students had, however, become severely disenchanted with the electronic discussion groups, generally because of the sheer number of messages they typically found awaiting them each time they signed onto the system, resulting in the consequent necessity to wade through a lot of "junk" mail in order to find those messages that did contain something of interest. The instructor attempted to convince the students to try a number of groups, find the ones that most interested them, and "unsubscribe" to the rest. One student commented that, after three weeks of subscribing to several listservs, he or she had determined some of the lists were so very time consuming that it was critical for the librarian to weigh carefully the benefits of subscribing.

However, a few students' enthusiasm for listservs continued to grow throughout the semester. For example, one student new to the use of the Internet wrote:

My initial enthusiasm has not waned a bit (despite my difficulties unsubscribing to some pesky listservs). The amount of information available from this single (though diversified) source is staggering. The listservs are a great forum for subject focused thought. . . . The library's role as information provider to its community requires that it allow user access to any of the reference resources available to the librarians. If this dictates terminals dedicated for this [Internet access] in the stacks, then fine. If this demands that the files and gophers be available through modems to the community, then better.

Local area Free-nets were mentioned by two students as one solution to public access to listservs and other Internet resources. Other students felt that before any of the sources of information would be useful to patrons, access would have to be made much easier. Of course, new developments in interface software (that were not available to these students) are working to do just that. For instance, the relatively new graphical interfaces such as WinGopher and Mosaic are geared to make access easier.

A few students experienced electronic storage problems; these students apparently had a difficult time psychologically discarding messages. In class, they frequently expressed the feeling that they might want to refer to most, if not all of their messages again in the future. Attempts to show them how to retrieve archived messages from the host computer did not always solve this "pack rat" tendency. [The inclinations of the monkish guardians of the libraries of medieval times to save all materials, no matter how seemingly insignificant, apparently remains endemic in the library profession, even in the electronic age! The problem, though, is a serious one. How <u>do</u> we decide what

to keep and what to discard in regards to the electronic information available over the Internet? Also just keeping messages in a reader does not solve the retrieval problem. How should librarians organize electronic resources as to be able to retrieve them when needed? At the very least, greater levels of libraries concerning information databases are going to be needed in the future.]

By the third freewrite in week eleven of the semester, students had become interested in electronic journals. Many now felt that libraries should routinely make electronic journals available to patrons. At this point, most were aware of a few library-oriented electronic serials that had been introduced to them in class. However, some of the students who were subscribing to several listservs had been made aware of the numbers of titles available in many subject areas, and had begun to realize that this itself was not an easy issue. For instance, should the library archive copies or expect patrons to retrieve issues from electronic archives? If the library archives them, it will necessitate considerable computer storage space, but if the library expects the patrons to be able to retrieve needed issues over the Internet, much staff time would be taken up in explaining and working with the patron in the use of the necessary File Transfer Protocol (FTP) in order to retrieve the needed files. [Based on the students' diaries, FTP seemed to be the most difficult activity for most of them to handle successfully, and thus was viewed as a major problem and time-consumer for reference librarians in dealing with patrons.] Also, students were hesitant about librarian-selection of electronic titles and nearly all thought that selection should be through patron survey. Of course, this approach leads to the problem that there may exist electronic serials on the Internet that would be useful and used if patrons only knew to request them.

At week eleven. many of the students also remained hesitant about offering e-mail and listserv access to library patrons. They generally felt that the interfaces were too difficult and would result in too much time staff time being expended on instruction, trouble-shooting, and maintenance. About a fourth of the class, however, felt that e-mail would be a good way to let patrons communicate needs, problems, etc. to the library staff. Three students were most enthusiastic and felt that e-mail would be a great way to handle many reference questions. On the other hand, one of the students most experienced with use of the Internet expressed the feeling that its use will ultimately enable the smallest college/community college to compete more effectively with the institutions enjoying much larger university libraries.

Internet Tools: — Gopher, Veronica, Archie, etc.

By the time of the third freewrite, use of Telnet had been quickly followed by Gopher and other Internet tools. Students found the ability to Telnet to other library catalogs highly relevant to their needs and thought this service would be useful to patrons, particularly if a link could be made to interlibrary loan or some other method of document delivery. The use of Gophers, both at USF and at other locations, was seen to make this process relatively simple.

Because officers of the USF student-affiliate of ALA (acronym ALIS for Association of Library and Information Science Students) were in the class, they became interested in creating their own ALIS Gopher with information about the chapter, the USF library school, placement information and job advertisements, and other information deemed useful to LIS students. The ALIS Gopher was soon complemented by a listserv discussion group intended primarily for USF LIS students. (It is not set up as a closed list, so others may join if they so desire [ALIS@nosferatu.cas.usf.edu]).

As evidenced by their diaries, many students, even at the end of the semester, were not comfortable using FTP, Veronica, Archie, or Jughead. Several thought that Gopher administrators should be able to solve some of the problems by adding more and better terms in the Gopher menus and providing a more menu-drive FTP, so that these

more difficult tools would be unnecessary for successful Internet navigation.

The Changing Role of Librarians

In the second freewrite a student volunteered the following assessment:

The network systems obviously are changing the job of librarians for themselves and for patrons. The librarian must be the first kid on the block to master this technology because he/she is at the center of the community. The library traditionally is the place where one turns for research, reference, and study. It is only logical that it should become the place for electronic information access. Generally, when there is question that a person cannot answer, the direction is "ask at the library." Requests for Internet services and information will happen more and more as people become aware of the Internet.

Another student commented that: "In the near future electronic sources will cause librarians to create a serious [Internet] marketing strategy for the library. People need to know what is available, how it can be accessed, and especially why they need the Internet."

At the time of the fourth freewrite in week 13 of the semester, all students were specifically asked to comment upon the role of the librarian as libraries become more and more attuned to the idea of the electronic "virtual" library, particularly considering facilitation of access to the Internet, maintenance and selection of items for library Gophers, Free-nets, etc. By this time, most students appeared to feel overwhelmed by the vast number of resources available over the Internet and had begun to question whether librarians would even be able, given the vastness and seemingly geometric expansion of the resources coupled with the limited time likely to be available for working librarians to devote to the Internet, to guide patrons adequately through the quality versus quantity issues. In other words, information overload and a throw-up-one's-hands attitude was beginning to creep in. Unfortunately for these frustrated budding librarians, it appears that, once the student, staff, and faculty populations have achieved basic skills in accessing the Internet, as they will surely do over time, the sorting and organizing of access to the "best" electronic materials will almost inevitably become a rather basic requirement for the librarian of the future, just as such skills have always been critical with respect to the selection of print or other "hard copy" media.

One student suggested that either the government or some new type of bibliographic utility would be required to perform this organization of electronic resources. However, as another student commented: "Simply throwing patrons to the Internet and leaving them to feast or famine doesn't do anything to further the premise that libraries aren't expendable."

Along the same lines, a perceptive student wrote:

> Throughout time librarians have been around to acquire, organize, and retrieve information. This is only a change of format — the information still needs to be preserved and retrieved. The ever increasing volume of information available on the Internet only accents the need for us to provide access. When people couldn't afford books, libraries provided them by means of local collections or through resource sharing — today many patrons will only have access to the Internet and other electronic services if provided by their library.

CONCLUSION

The public at large in only the last year or so has been made aware through articles in general newspapers and magazines about the "wonders" of the Internet, and many individuals have become intrigued by its potential. The current college-age generation is generally much more computer literate than some who are currently employed in libraries (and some library school students for that matter). And yet, as the views of LIS students in the case study described in this paper bear out, the promise of the Internet remains just that for too many of those who will soon be the persons in our colleges and society most directly charged with the responsibility of guiding the general public in respect of these new sources of information. Viewed from that angle, simplification and standardization of methods of accessing the new electronic resources would seem to be a critical goal. Few would argue with that conclusion, but at the same time, we must not let the hesitancy of those not so comfortable with computers and electronic media dictate the networked resources to be made available to the patrons of our libraries. If the general current level of staffing makes provision of Internet resources difficult, use of student assistants from computer, engineering, or business MIS programs might be a solution. Although these kinds of students may not have been attracted to work in the library in a print environment, the introduction of Internet services might just be the drawing card necessary to interest them in working in the library, and not just as undergraduates; such exposure might also influence them to enroll in a graduate program of library and information science and thus become a library and information science professional, salting the profession with people possessed of new ways of looking at things, non-traditional skills and aptitudes and an assurance that they will not be left hitchhiking at some dead-end exit ramp along the information superhighway.

NOTES

1. Pamela Whiteley McLaughlin, "Embracing the Internet: The Changing Role of Library Staff," *Bulletin of the American Society for Information Science* 20 (February/March 1994), p.16.
2. Clifford A. Lynch, "Networked Information: A Revolution in Progress" in *Networks, Open Access, and Virtual Libraries: Implications for the Research Library*, edited by Brett Sutton and Charles H. Davis (Urbana: Graduate School of Library and Information Science, University of Illinois at Urbana-Champaign, 1991), p. 12-39.
3. Ibid., p. 35.

4. "ALA's 112th Annual Conference: Upbeat and Hopeful in New Orleans," *American Libraries* 24 (July/August 1993), p. 614-615.

5. Constance Ann Mellon, *Naturalistic Inquiry for Library Science: Methods and Applications for Research, Evaluation, and Teaching* (New York: Greenwood Press, 1990), p. 62-63.

Measuring the Library Research Skills of Education Doctoral Students

Claudia J. Morner

ABSTRACT

The development of a reliable and valid test of library research skills for doctoral students in education, and the results of an administration of this instrument to a random sample of students, are the focus of this paper. Test and survey data gathered confirmed reports in library literature that education doctoral students have wide-ranging knowledge of library research, and many educational doctoral students neither avail themselves of instruction nor are equipped to conduct doctoral level library research. Librarians could improve instruction to doctoral students in education by utilizing this test to measure a student's ability and to prepare appropriate training.

INTRODUCTION

Recent literature on library use suggests that doctoral students may be unprepared for conducting the literature review portion of their dissertations. However, there has been no up-to-date and effective tool to measure the library research abilities of this population. This study was initiated to fill this measurement gap by developing a valid and reliable instrument for the use of librarians who work with doctoral students. This instrument will allow librarians to measure what currently are only impressions about the quality of library research done by students at the doctoral level.

BACKGROUND

The education and library science literature on library use overwhelmingly suggest that graduate students are unprepared for the work expected of them, especially the dissertation literature review. Dreifuss[1] found that 91 percent of faculty believe graduate students should already know how to use the library and that faculty make assignments assuming graduate students have the requisite skills; however only 14 percent of graduate students surveyed, from the same institution, reported that they knew basic resources and services offered by the university library. In a national survey of education doctoral students more than one-half of 898 graduate students felt that their library research skills were deficient.[2] Because this study relied on students' self-appraisal of their library skills, the research design was weakened by the lack of an instrument to measure the skills of these doctoral students.

Claudia J. Morner is Associate University Librarian for Access Services, Boston College, Chestnut Hill, Massachusetts.

Librarians in Colorado,[3] who surveyed primarily undergraduate library users, found self-assessment was an unreliable method for judging students' library research capabilities. During the first year of a state-mandated assessment program, library users were asked to rate their library skills. In the second year of the program, the library staff developed a library skills test and found that, when measured with such a test, library users' scores were dramatically lower than the previous year. Fields[4] also called for the development of a test instrument to measure library competency of graduate students.

Although there is a wealth of literature on instructional programs designed for undergraduates, there is much less information on how graduate students find information in the library. Furthermore, the past fifteen years have seen a dramatic increase in the volume of published material and technologies available to libraries. The explosion of information and advances in library automation make using academic libraries today a far more complicated task than in the past.

Also, given the economic environment of higher education in the 1990s and the rising costs of library automation and materials, academic libraries need to target their efforts to utilize shrinking resources better. Librarians give extensive instruction to graduate students, but do not have an effective way to assess students' library progress. If a good test of library skills existed, librarians could use the instrument to measure students' abilities before offering instruction. This same instrument could also measure the effectiveness of the teaching effort of library staff when used as a post-test.

The idea of assessing students' needs before instruction is likely to be especially appropriate for graduate students who are adult learners. Research shows that adults learn differently than younger students do and are much more likely to seek out independently what they need to learn.[5] Other research in adult learning also confirms that adult learners are busy people with numerous responsibilities and roles;[6] therefore a test such as

the proposed instrument would be well suited to the needs of this student population, because the test would give graduate students a quick indication of their library research abilities. Once tested, these students, with help of a librarian, could proceed to learn and develop needed skills in library use.

Education doctoral students were chosen for a number of reasons, but the primary reason was need. Unlike students in other disciplines, doctoral students in education come to their programs with previous degrees from a variety of disciplines. Because they have such varied backgrounds, they need a wide array of library services and they may not be familiar with standard and important education and related literature. The literature also suggests that many doctoral students in education do not have the requisite library research skills for doctoral-level work.[7]

A more practical reason for limiting the test to doctoral students in education was to find a balance between the need to cover appropriate content areas and the need to have an instrument of reasonable length so that it could be effectively administered. Since a significant percentage of doctorates are awarded in the field of education, a reliable, valid, and up-to-date test of library abilities would be useful to a potentially large number of doctoral students and librarians working with that population.

PRELIMINARY QUALITATIVE STUDY

This investigation began with a preliminary qualitative study to learn more about education doctoral students' attitudes and use of academic libraries. Ten students, at various stages of their doctoral programs, were interviewed about their patterns of library use, knowledge of specific library resources, and attitudes about the library. Students were asked to describe their last visit to the library, to tell what they liked and disliked about the library, and to rate their own library abilities on a scale of 1-5. Data collected from this pilot study confirmed information found in a review of library science literature that most students did not fully grasp important techniques of library research and that they felt inadequate to the task of conducting a dissertation literature review. Nearly all students described initial or continuing feelings of fear or intimidation caused by the size and complexity of the library. This preliminary study confirmed the need for a test of library research skills and it helped to define important issues and concerns for this student group. These data were valuable in the next phase of the research, the development of the test content.

TEST DEVELOPMENT

The fundamental question about test content was: "What do doctoral students in education need to know to conduct library research effectively?" A number of steps were taken to develop the content of the test. Published and unpublished tests, library handouts, books, and articles on library education resources were reviewed. Ultimately, the basis for the test content was the document, "Information Retrieval and Evaluation Skills for Education Students"[8] published by the Bibliographic Instruction for Educators Committee of the EBSS Section of ACRL. This document describes library knowledge areas for both graduate and undergraduate students of education. The document was used as the basis for defining content clusters which represent basic areas of knowledge required for successful library research in the field of education. These content clusters include: how literature is generated and communicated, intellectual access, knowing the parts of a citation, physical access, and evaluating information sources.

Once the test content was established, a multiple-choice format was determined to be the best and most efficient method to measure the library research knowledge and skills of a large number of students in a short period of time. Since a key aspect of the research design was using a cluster random sample, and involved testing students in required classes, the testing time needed to be short enough that faculty members would be willing to give up class time for the testing sessions. A multiple choice format was chosen for two reasons. This type of test can measure higher order thinking and, given time constraints, would be likely to be more reliable than a test in which students write the answers. However, writing good multiple-choice test items is challenging, time consuming, and requires a good deal of creativity.

The actual item construction process underwent numerous iterations. Writing clear, unambiguous test items with equally plausible alternative answers is a real challenge. As items were developed, several of criteria were used to evaluate individual items, including:

- the avoidance of the use of "all of the above" or "none of the above;"
- removal of word clues, such as same word in stem and alternative;
- negative stems were avoided and if used, negative words were underlined;
- the length of alternatives was made consistent, brief and clear;
- items were rewritten to improve clarity;
- grammar and punctuation were made consistent;
- as a method to randomize the order of correct answers, alternatives for each item were placed in alphabetic order.

This process of writing took many drafts, each reviewed for comments and reactions by colleagues. Additional demographic and attitude questions were developed which were thought to be useful in helping evaluate the test results. Demographic and attitude questions covered variables such as gender, attitudes about or experience with computers, year last academic degree was completed, international or USA nationality, and full- or part-time status.

When the researcher was satisfied that the test items represented a fair test of library research skills for education doctoral students, the test was ready for piloting. Pilot testing is a very important step in this kind of research, a free home trial of how students from the population will interpret the test questions.

PILOT TESTING

Pilot testing was conducted on a volunteer sample of fifteen education doctoral students from Boston College. Students were instructed individually by the researcher and given the test to complete at home. After students had returned the test answer sheets, ten were given follow-up interviews. They were asked if any questions were unfair, ambiguous, or unclear. Overall the students responded that they felt the test was fair and clear, and some gave specific examples of difficulty, such as the use of acronyms. A consistent and surprising response was that the test made then "feel stupid" or "like an idiot." This strong reaction was helpful in developing an introduction to the test to future test takers.

Item analysis data including difficulty, discrimination, and percent choosing was produced and reviewed. Difficulty tells how many students answered a given item correctly. Discrimination is a statistical measure that indicates an item may be confusing. It looks at how high-scoring and low-scoring students answer the question. If high-scoring students tend to answer incorrectly and low-scoring students answer correctly, then the item has a negative discrimination value; this indicates that the question probably needs revision. Percent choosing simply shows how often each of the alternatives was chosen. Ideally, all alternatives should be chosen by some of the test takers. After reviewing this item analysis data, and the qualitative information provided by students, the test was revised and improved.

CONTENT VALIDITY

The next step was to submit the test to outside experts for content validity. Three highly qualified education librarians with advanced degrees in education, were selected to provide this review. The experts were sent a copy of the test and a copy of the list of content clusters, and were instructed to perform two tasks. First, the judges were asked to evaluate the individual test items for clarity of expression and for meaningfulness as a library research skill, on a scale from 0 to 3. Next, they were asked to assign one of the content clusters to each of the test items. The results of this evaluation are shown in table 1 and table 2. Table one shows that on the placement of content clusters, two out of three experts agreed with the researcher for 95 percent of the items.

For the item rating part, the results were also high: for 93 percent of the items, two out of three experts assigned the score of 2 or higher out of a possible range of 0 to 3.

The mean score for all three experts was two or better for 81 percent of the items. The five items which got an average score below 2 were revised or rewritten. With these results, the content was judged valid by these experts.

TEST ADMINISTRATION

After a final revision, the test was administered during class time to a cluster random sample of education doctoral students from Boston College, Boston University, and Fordham University who were enrolled in required doctoral level classes. Because all students in a given doctoral program take required courses such as dissertation seminar, statistics, or research design, a random sample would be expected by testing students in these classes during a given semester. The sample would be considered random because all students in the program would have an equal chance of being selected. The decision to choose the three universities was made for two reasons: access provided to the researcher and the similarity of library resources available to students attending these universities. This consistency was an important aspect of the research design; otherwise variations in available library resources might have skewed the test results. Ultimately the sample consisted of 149 students of near equal proportion from the three universities. Overall response rate was 75 percent.

TABLE 1: Assignment of Items to Content Clusters by Three Experts

ITEM	1	2	3	4	5	6	7	8	9	10
EXPERT # 1	G	G	G	F	F	F	F	H	H	H
EXPERT # 2	G	G	G	F	F	F	F	H	H	H
EXPERT # 3	G	G	G	F	F	F	F	H	H	H
RESEARCHER	G	G	G	F	F	F	F	H	H	H

ITEM	11	12	13	14	15	16	17	18	19	20
EXPERT # 1	H	B	C	D	D	C	G	G	H	H
EXPERT # 2	H	B	A	D	D	C	G	G	H	C
EXPERT # 3	H	B	C	D	D	C	D		H	H
RESEARCHER	H	B	C	D	D	C	G	G	H	H

ITEM	21	22	23	24	25	26	27	28	29	30
EXPERT # 1	A	A	B	C	B	C	D	C	A	E
EXPERT # 2	A	A	B	C	B	D	A	C	A	E
EXPERT # 3	A	A	D	C	B	C	D	C	A	E
RESEARCHER	A	A	B	C	B	C	D	C	A	E

ITEM	31	32	33	34	35	36	37	38	39	40
EXPERT # 1	B	B	D	D	A	E	E	B	A	B
EXPERT # 2	E	E	D	D	A	E	E	B	A	B
EXPERT # 3	B	B/E		B	D	E	E	B	A	B
RESEARCHER	E	E	D	E	A	E	E	B	A	B

ITEM	41	42	43
EXPERT # 1	C	E	G
EXPERT # 2		E	G
EXPERT # 3	C	E	G
RESEARCHER	D	E	G

Table 2: Item Rating by Three Experts

ITEM	1	2	3	4	5	6	7	8	9	10
EXPERT # 1	3	0	0	3	2	3	3	3	3	3
EXPERT # 2	3	3	1	3	3	3	3	3	3	2
EXPERT # 3	3	3	2	3	3	3	3	3	2	3
MEAN	3	2	1	3	2.6	3	3	3	2.6	2.6

ITEM	11	12	13	14	15	16	17	18	19	20
EXPERT # 1	3	3	2	3	3	3	1	2	3	2
EXPERT # 2	3	3	3	3	2	3	3	3	3	3
EXPERT # 3	2	2	0	3	3	1	3	0	2	1
MEAN	2.6	2.6	1.6	3	2.6	2.3	2.3	1.6	2.6	2

ITEM	21	22	23	24	25	26	27	28	29	30
EXPERT # 1	3	3	3	3	2	3	3	3	3	3
EXPERT # 2	3	3	3	3	2	3	3	3	3	1
EXPERT # 3	3	2	2	3	2	3	3	3	3	3
MEAN	3	2.6	2.6	3	2	3	3	3	3	2.3

ITEM	31	32	33	34	35	36	37	38	39	40
EXPERT # 1	3	3	0	3	2	3	3	2	2	1
EXPERT # 2	3	3	1	1	1	2	3	3	3	2
EXPERT # 3	3	3	0	0	3	2	3	0	3	0
MEAN	3	3	0.3	1.3	2	2.3	3	1.6	2.6	1

ITEM	41	42	43
EXPERT # 1	3	1	1
EXPERT # 2	3	1	3
EXPERT # 3	3	3	3
MEAN	3	1.6	2.3

FIGURE 1: Frequency Distribution of Test Scores

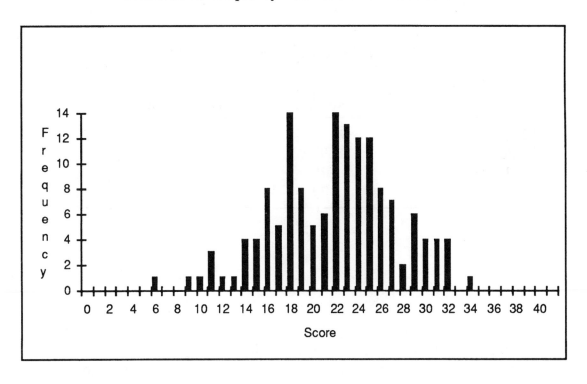

THE RESULTS

A number of statistical procedures were performed to analyze the test data. Descriptive statistics, (see table 3), show that with a mean score of almost 22, the average student got only 50 percent of the answers right, and that a Kuder Richardson reliability score of .72 is adequate for an instrument with only 41 items.

Mean	21.95
Standard Deviation	5.35
KR Reliability	.724
Standard Error of Measurement	2.809
n=149	

TABLE 3 - Descriptive Statistics

Descriptive statistics also showed the data to be fairly normally distributed, with a broad range of scores, from 14.6 percent to 82.9 percent correct (see figure 1).

These results were consistent across the three sites. No item in the test had a negative discrimination, and the item difficulty ranged from the easiest question, where 91.3 percent of the students correctly answered the item, to the most difficult item answered correctly by only 8.1 percent.

RELIABILITY AND VALIDITY

In order to judge test stability, a form of reliability, the test was administered to a class of ten students twice with a two-week interval between testing. Results of this test-retest indicated general stability of scores over time.

To measure criterion-related validity, a second test, a library performance test, was developed. This consisted of twenty-two items that were designed to measure the same information or skill as twenty-two of the forty-one items in the multiple choice test. The library performance test was administered individually to ten students who had scored either in the top or bottom 20 percent on

TABLE 4: Mean Score by Gender and Student Status

Category	Number	Percent	Mean Score
Male	52	34.9%	22.1
Female	97	65.1%	21.8
Full time	70	47%	21.93
Part time	79	53%	21.96

the multiple choice test. Students were asked to perform actual tasks in the library corresponding to test items. The performance of each student on the two tests was compared for stability, change, and direction of change. A large percentage of test items, 72 percent, remained unchanged from the multiple-choice test to the library performance test. These data suggest that, although there is not a one-to-one correspondence between the multiple-choice test and performance in the library, the multiple-choice test was based on real library performance and not other factors such as test taking ability.

INTERPRETATION—WHAT THESE RESULTS SAY ABOUT THE STUDENTS

Because the 149 students had a wide range of scores, from 14.6 percent to 82.9 percent, the test clearly confirms reports in the literature that doctoral students have a wide range of library abilities.[9] Since students begin doctoral studies in education with varying backgrounds and a variety of library research skills, it would be surprising to find a large number of doctoral students who would achieve near perfect scores on this instrument. But the results do indicate that librarians should assess doctoral level students and provide

varied instruction depending on their needs and abilities.

Another strength of the test of library research skills is that the test is apparently equivalent for different kinds of students (see table 4). Because test results did not differ significantly for men versus women, or for groups such as part-time versus full-time, the test should not need revision for different settings.

Data gathered for this study on whether students had participated in library instructional programs confirm previous studies[10] that a large proportion of students do not avail themselves of opportunities to learn more about library research (see table 5).

In this study, 41.7 percent of the respondents had participated in no form of library instruction and another 18 percent had only taken a physical tour of the library. Combining these two groups showed that nearly 60 percent of the students who took this test had not participated in any classes, workshops, or in-depth one-on-one instruction in library use. The data also show a trend of increasing test scores for students who had participated in more extensive instruction programs, but the differences in scores are not large enough with this limited sample to draw any conclusions about

TABLE 5: Mean Score of Students with Varying Levels of Instruction

Level of Instruction	Mean Score	Number	Percent	Valid Percent
No Instruction	22.28	58	38.9%	41.7%
Minimal	20.60	25	16.8%	18.0%
Moderate	22.23	52	34.9%	37.4%
High	24.25	4	2.7%	2.9%
Missing		10	6.7%	missing

Note. N=139, 10 missing cases

the overall effectiveness of instruction to doctoral students in education.

A final consideration relates to the attitudes of students who participated in this investigation. There was a high degree of enthusiasm for the project at all stages of test development at all three sites. Students were very willing to be interviewed and to participate in the pilot test. The pilot test takers discussed their opinions of the test and made many useful recommendations for improving it. Many test takers from all three schools thanked the researcher for testing them. The ten students who participated in the library performance test were most willing to answer all questions and all ten found the test and follow-up explanation a useful learning experience. Faculty, even those not known to the researcher, expressed a high degree of interest in the project. They were willing to give up thirty minutes of class time for testing, and in many instances invited the researcher back to class at a later date to discuss the test or aspects of her research. This level of interest suggests that students want to assess their abilities to conduct library research and that the test should have broad appeal and usefulness.

Based on the above interpretation, the test can be used for a number of purposes: screening students for varying kinds of library instruction, conducting pretest-posttest studies to measure what students learned in library instruction, assessing the overall library research capabilities of beginning doctoral students in education, and for confirming or refuting the many impressions about library use of doctoral students that have been reported in the literature.

Doctoral students in education have gained knowledge of libraries from a variety of experiences, and may have an uneven, nonsystematic knowledge of how to find information in a library. The best purpose of the test for individual doctoral students would be to give beginning doctoral students an indication of how much they know, relative to other doctoral students, and to motivate them to seek out further instruction. It is the researcher's experience that when doctoral students see test scores in the 50 percent range, they are motivated to seek out further instruction.

SUGGESTIONS FOR FUTURE RESEARCH

Future research might include extending the testing to students at dissimilar institutions, including those in other parts of the country, and at public colleges and universities. The test could be administered at schools with fewer or more library resources available to doctoral students to see if size of library or access to computerized resources affects students' scores.

The test could also be modified for masters-level graduate students, many of whom are required to write a thesis.

A byproduct of this study was a clear indication that many doctoral students in education fear libraries and dread the literature review. Research on the undergraduate level on library anxiety [11] should be replicated for graduate students, who do not appear to be immune from this disorder.

CONCLUSION

In summary, a test of library research skills was developed in response to a need expressed in the literature. The forty-one item multiple choice test evolved during a process of writing, piloting, and reviewing by experts. The test was administered to a cluster random sample of 149 education doctoral students. Item analysis and reliability and validity investigations were performed. These showed that the test, as a whole, adequately measured doctoral students' library performance, and corroborated previous findings that many education doctoral students are unequipped for the doctoral-level library research necessary for conducting the dissertation literature review.

NOTES

1. Richard A. Dreifuss, "Library Instruction and Graduate Students: More Work for George," *RQ* 21, 2 (Winter 1981): 121-123.
2. Camila A. Alire, "A Nationwide Survey of Education Doctoral Students' Abilities Regarding the Importance of the Library and the Need for Bibliographic Instruction," (Unpublished dissertation, University of Northern Colorado, 1984).
3. Arlene Greer, Lee Weston, and Mary Alm, "Assessment of Learning Outcomes: a Measure of Progress in Library Literacy," *College and Research Libraries* 52, 6 (1991): 549-557.
4. Carolyn B. Fields, "Using Results of a Pre-test to Determine Lecture Content: A Case Study," *Research Strategies* 5, 1(Winter 1987): 29-35.
5. Malcolm Knowles, *The Adult Learner: A Neglected Species*, 3rd. ed. (Houston TX: Gulf Publishing House, 1984).
6. A. Q. Lynch and Arthur W. Chickening, "Comprehensive Counseling and Support for Adult Learners: Challenges to Higher Education," in *New Perspectives on Counseling Adult Learners*, eds. H. B. Gelatt, Garry R. Walz, and Libby Benjamin (Ann Arbor MI: ERIC/CAPS, 1985).
7. Mary L. Compton, *A Study of the Information Resources and Library Services Used by Doctoral Students in Science Education at the University of Georgia* (Available from ERIC Document Research Service, No. ED 313 041, 1989); M. Farid, "A Study of Information Seeking Behavior of Ph.D. Students in Selected Disciplines" (Unpublished dissertation, Syracuse University, 1984); Nelda Hernandez, *The Fourth, Composite "R" for Graduate Students: Research* (Available from ERIC Documentation Research Service No. ED 276 671, 1985); Patricia Libutti, "Library Support for Graduate Education Research and Teaching" (Available from ERIC Documentation Research Service, No. ED 349 007, 1991); Betsy Park, Information Needs: Implications for the Academic Library (Available from ERIC Documentation Research Service, No. ED 288 525, 1986); David R. Watkins, "The Role of Instruction in the Academic Library," *LACUNY Journal* 2 (1973): 8-10.
8. ACRL-EBSS-BIE (Association of College and Research Libraries—Education and Behavioral Sciences Section—Bibliographic Instruction for Educators Committee), "Information Retrieval and Evaluation Skills for Education Students," *College and Research Libraries News* 53, (1992): 583-588.
9. Peyton Hurt, "The Need of College and University Instruction in the Use of the Library," *The Library Quarterly* IV, 3 (1934): 436-448; Alire, op. cit.; Denise Madland, "Library Instruction for Graduate Students," *College Teaching* 33, 4 (Fall 1985): 163-164.
10. Watkins, op. cit.; Alire, op. cit.; Lyn Thaxton, "Dissemination and Use of Information by Psychology Faculty and Graduate Students: Implications for Bibliographic Instruction," *Research Strategies* 3, 3 (Summer 1985): 116-124; Greer, op. cit.

11. Constance A. Mellon, "Library Anxiety: A Grounded Theory and Its Development, *College and Research Libraries* 47, (1986): 160-165.

Contributed Papers

Multiculturalism and Internationalism

Reference Services in a Multicultural University Library

Maria de Jesus Ayala-Schueneman and Roberta Pitts

ABSTRACT

This paper will focus on ways library reference services at an academic library are being developed to meet the needs of a multicultural university. This university is one of the few institutions of higher education in the United States that is majority Hispanic. As such our experiences may be useful toothers. Staffing and collections as they relate to information services and issues of diversity will also be explained. Additionally this paper will address cultural awareness andbriefly review how universities in similar settings are addressing these issues.

The fact that academic institutions in the U. S. are becoming increasingly multicultural in nature is a widely acknowledged phenomena. The literature abounds with demographics and population statistics that predict a multiethnic future. But for many academic libraries, the futureis not all that distant. Institutions with large minority populations and high international student enrollment are already grappling with issues of cultural awareness and diversity. Hardly a professional journal exists that has not touched upon the subject of a diverse workforce and the library's role in a multicultural world. One significant role of libraries is to prepare individuals for meaningful participation in economic and social responsibilities in a multicultural environment. Such preparation is not possible if libraries themselves are not prepared.[1] As we move toward the predictions of the future, libraries continue to be challenged to change old practices and develop new ones to ensure that diversity is incorporated into information services. Such changes include not only diverse collections and new approaches to services, but attitudes as well. The key to such change often rests at the initial point of contact for most students —reference services. This paper will focus on ways reference services at Texas A&M University-Kingsville are being developed to meet the needs of a multicultural university. TAMUK is one of the few institutions of higher education in the U.S.

Maria de Jesus Ayala-Schueneman is Coordinator of Reference Services and Roberta Pitts is Director of the James C. Jernigan Library at Texas A&M University-Kingsville in Kingsville Texas.

that is majority Hispanic specifically Mexican-American. As such our experiences may be useful for others. Indeed all those institutions where diversity is highly evident serve as pathfinders for the remainder who are searching for ways to incorporate cultural awareness and a multicultural perspective. Staffing and collections as they relate to information services and issues of diversity will also be explored. Additionally the paper will address cultural awareness and briefly review how universities in similar settings are addressing these issues.

Texas A&M University-Kingsville, located in South Texas, is a multicultural campus with an enrollment of approximately 6,500 students from 31 states and 50 foreign countries. The Hispanic student population is about 62 percent and the total minority population is approximately 65 percent. In 1992 TAMUK had 318 international students (5%) of which 211 were graduate students.[2] Of the 368 faculty members, Hispanic faculty members represented approximately 14 per cent of that number. Black faculty members represented just under three percent.

The emphasis at Texas A&M-Kingsville (TAMUK) is on providing an intellectually challenging education while retaining a selectively open admission policy. The University is dedicated to serving an ethnically and culturally diverse population.[3] A primary mission of the University is to create a middle class in South Texas. TAMUK provides 70 percent of the bilingual teachers in Texas. It consistently ranks among the country's top ten producers of Hispanic engineers.

Census Bureau projections report that the Hispanic population in the U.S. may double in the next thirty years. California and Texas will continue to have the largest Hispanic populations followed by New York, Florida, and Illinois. In Texas the number of Hispanics is projected to increase from 4.9 million to 10.3 million by the year 2020.[4] With such dramatic population shifts, the term "minority" is being replaced by the term "emerging majorities."[5]

Nationally only 53 percent of Hispanics were high school graduates compared to 70 percent of blacks and 78 percent of whites. However, from 1974 to 1993 the number of Hispanics with a high school education increased from 36.5 percent to 53 percent.[6] The number of Hispanics who have completed college is low. In Texas only 8 percent of Hispanics have college degrees. Retention rates for Hispanic student populations indicate that as many as 80 percent leave their undergraduate institution without receiving a degree.[7] "High minority teen birthrates, financial pressures, poor academic preparation, lack of family or other role models, and other social circumstances contribute to low college progression and low graduation rates among minority youth."[8]

At Texas A&M-Kingsville, the College I program was developed to increase retention of minority students. A variety of activities implemented within College I include an Academic Rescue Program, a mentoring program pairing freshmen with upper-division students, faculty or staff; and a Student-to-Student Development program. Developmental courses in reading, writing, and math are available.

Study skills and library research skills are also offered through a College I Success course required of all freshmen. Before 1994, university faculty assigned to teach the College I course also taught the library skills section that included a tour of the library. Beginning with the 1994-95 academic year, reference librarians volunteered to take on that portion of the course aimed at research skills. This was done to insure that all students received the same level of instruction and to provide the most practical level of library use. We wanted students to feel successful about their library experience and build lifelong learning patterns. Downing, McAdam and Nichols agree that librarians need to take matters into their own hands.

College and university libraries affect students at all levels and across all academic disciplines. Sooner or later most students pass through the library's doors. The library is in a singular position to have an impact on a large segment of the campus population. Here is an opportunity for librarians to take a proactive stance and to help set the pace, not only for other libraries, but also for the larger institutions they serve. [9]

Research has shown that often students feel better about approaching another minority person for help in the library. Within the team that offers reference services the Library was able to assign two Hispanic librarians, three Hispanic staff members, and two Hispanic graduate students to the ReferenceDesk. The Reference team echoes Davidow's belief that "customers judge service by the quality of their interactions with the people who provide it. The more contact employees have with customers, the more critical employee behavior is to perception of service quality."[10] We have attempted to blend into the Reference Desk a variety of individuals with different experiences, traditions, cultures and backgrounds. The common bond is a desire to serve library patrons. We strive to be aware of culture and ethnicity of our patrons along with a healthy respect for their individuality. Some aspects of a more diversified reference services are obvious. Language readily stands out. It is not possible to have library staff who know all the languages a reference librarian might encounter but it is possible to have reference librarians with basic skills in a predominant language. This is especially important in areas like South Texas where Spanish is spoken by a significant majority of the population. Certainly most transactions are in English but the need for Spanish does arise. Our Reference staff has conducted tours in Spanish for students from Mexico and Chile. The Agriculture Department has been asked to consult at a University in Saltillo and they have asked our librarians to help them with library matters. Obviously such international cooperation would not be possible without the key of language.

It is not always possible to know a patron's native tongue but the Reference Librarian can show sensitivity toward the patron's culture. Sometimes this can be as easy as knowing a little history

and keeping up with current events. International students are very impressed when one displays a knowledge of their country and can carry on a conversation about the politics of their country. These are minor things but they can help create an atmosphere of trust and of course one can not forget simple kindness.

Our majority Mexican-American students are proud of their heritage and we encourage that pride through regular displays and special events. A current display case prepared by a graduate student highlights Latino literature in the United States. When we celebrated National Library theme our banners carried the double theme, "Libraries Change Lives - Bibliotecas Cambian Vidas!"

Staffing continues to be a challenge as libraries attempt to recruit minorities. In a 1992 article Otis Chadley noted that minorities are still underrepresented in library science graduate school. Hispanic librarians represented only 2 percent of the total library work force, and among 10 percent of ACRL librarians that are minorities, only 15 percent are Hispanic.[11] One of the authors of this paper who is both a librarian and an Hispanic was one of the few minority students who attended the masters program in Library Science at San Jose State University in the late seventies. ALA was already concerned with minority enrollment (or rather the lack of minority enrollment), and during an accreditation visit minority recruitment was an issue brought forward by ALA. The author was recruited by the Library Science Department to make a video demonstrating that while not numerous, minorities did benefit from and value the library science program at San Jose State. The point here is that lack of minority enrollment was seen as a crisis in the late seventies and it has hardly gotten better in the years since. Chadley cites low pay and previous experience requirements as some of the barriers minorities face in entering the library science field. But it may be inaccurate to identify problems that apply to all library science graduates as being special problems for Hispanics or other minorities — and low salaries certainly are a problem that all library professionals face. Another identified barrier is the seeming reluctance of minority professionals to relocate.

As minorities are recruited care should be taken within the library staff itself to avoid stereotyping. For example, many Hispanics would hate to be solely identified with mariachi music. How many librarians are aware of the strong classical music tradition in Mexico? No one would consider identifying country music as the only expression of U.S. music, but often in cultural matters of food, music, and literature non-hispanic whites see only a narrow or preconceived view of the Mexican-American. Generalizations should be avoided; there is more complexity to the Mexican-American portrait than most non-hispanic whites see. We must ensure that Hispanics and other minorities are not stereotyped into certain positions. It is easy to assume that Hispanic librarians, for example, would be ideal for positions requiring Spanish language materials or a knowledge of Tejano music. Certainly it may be the case, but equally it might not. A better effort to recruit minorities must be made on the basis of how a diverse library staff can enrich the entire mission of the library.

The staffing problem is partly one of the recruitment into the library school in the first place. As Margaret Myers says, we must use "our vision for the future to promote our profession actively and strategically."[12] Minorities must be attracted to the idea of serving in the information industry. One way to do this is to emphasize the power of information. Not only are many minority neighborhoods and third word countries materially poor, they are also information poor. One of the author's experience with the Benjamin Franklin Library (USIS) in Mexico City was the determining factor in her decision to seek a career in the library world. Partly this was because the power of information was amply demonstrated. We must energize minorities - and all those we seek to recruit into the profession - with the vision that the librarian will be a "power job" in the 21st century.[13]

Another aspect of the staffing equation is to sensitize that staff to different cultures. At TAMUK we have been fortunate to participate in a program that seeks to familiarize faculty and staff in the Mexican-American culture. The librarians who serve at the Reference Desk are encouraged to participate in a transculturation project. Though aimed at the Mexican-American culture, developing an appreciation and value for one culture spills over into other areas, broadening one's entire multicultural perspective. The Transculturation Project at TAMUK began in 1989 through a three-year grant from the Fund of the Improvement of Postsecondary Education (FIPSE) under the U. S. Department of Education. A total of about 90 faculty have been transculturated over the last five years. Led by Dr. Rosario Torres Raines from the Department of Sociology and Psychology and Dr. Ward S. Albro from the Department of History, the one semester course includes a weekly three-hour seminar with nationally recognized Hispanic scholars and culminates at the end of the semester with a two-week stay in Cuernavaca, Mexico with intensive Spanish language instruction. The transculturation experience helps participating faculty and staff to understand and recognize the Hispanic's biculturalism and bilingualism, and by doing so, include these dimensions in teaching and interacting with the majority of the students at TAMUK. These transcultural experiences are designed to produce changes in attitudes, values and beliefs about a culture other than one's own. The objective is better performance, higher retention rates and recruitment levels for both students and faculty within the university.[14] Almost 60 percent of the library faculty have participated in the program. Another benefit of the program is a greater sensitivity to all cultures public service librarians come into contact with (specifically at the Reference Desk). The experience of living in a foreign land, with languages and cultures not well understood, mirrors the experience of many international students. Sometimes at the Reference Desk, one faces language and cultural problems. Language problems are easily dealt with.

Cultural problems are sometimes harder to face. In some cultures it is not usual for women to work and therefore it is difficult for some international students to relate to women. It is also difficult for some non-Hispanics to relate to Hispanic librarians just as it is difficult for some male Hispanics to relate to women librarians.

The sensitivity gained from the FIPSE program helps librarians understand that cultures even though different if approached with respect, understanding and knowledge can be a valued asset in dealing with others and with one's own culture.

Academic libraries across the U.S. are developing equally innovative ways to meet the needs of their diverse student populations. At the University of Michigan, PIC, a Peer Information Counseling Program, was developed as a minority student support program. The program uses trained student volunteers who help other minority students with term paper research or general instruction in use of the library. A welcome letter with an explanation of services available is sent to all under-graduate first-year minority students. Newsletters and testimonials from students who have used the program are part of a well-developed publications package.[15]

The University of California at Santa Cruz opted to call a halt to a search for a business reference specialist and changed the position to a Multicultural Services Librarian. The decision came after library faculty attended a minority student group meeting and faced the realization that they were not serving a large portion of their student body as well as they might. The new Multicultural Services Librarian takes the library message into dorms and other campus areas. The library was heavily involved in the university's Summer Bridge Program which helps incoming students who need special tutoring.[16]

Yoshi Hendricks at the University of Nevada, Reno, realized some cultural awareness was necessary when students from their Japanese campus in Tokyo began arriving in Reno. Language was obviously a major obstacle in bibliographic instruction, but just as important was an understanding of culture. One example she uses is the fact that a Japanese student might nod while listening indicating to an American that the student understood when in fact it is simply a part of listening behavior in Japanese society. Her discussion of culture-bound assumptions are useful in helping staff become alert to cultural differences.[17]

Reference materials are another area of concern. It is certainly gratifying to see many more published reference sources concerning minorities. One immediately thinks of the various special works that Gale has published concerning the literature of Blacks and Hispanics. These areas were often neglected in the past, and it is important to rectify any imbalances that may exist.

It is essential to subscribe and collect "popular" materials for minority groups as well. This is especially the case if (as is the case at TAMUK) the minority actually comprises a majority of the student body. We have tried to meet these needs by subscribing to popular magazines like Hispanic, as well as political opinion journals from Mexico like Proceso and Este Pais and newspapers like El Norte (published in Mexico). Sometimes there are specific journals in academic areas that deal especially with minority concerns. Latin American Music Review and The Hispanic Journal of Behavioral Sciences are two examples of such journals. It is not the case that such materials are out-of-the-way sorts of things. El Norte, besides supporting Hispanic culture generally, is very specifically used by the Political Science Department. Other departments, including Business and Language & Literature, have expressed a need for multicultural materials. The popular and multicultural is usually just as academic as any other class of materials, and does not need special pleading. Monographs are also included in the equation. Our Library has undertaken the task of collecting most Latino fiction. We have tried to identify certain publishers (like Arte Publico) and authors (like Rolando Hinojosa) and to obtain nearly everything they publish. Access to the material must be insured through indexes and bibliographies such as the Chicano Index, HAPI,

Handbook of Latin American Studies, and Fichero Bibliografico Hispanoamericano. In addition, the Library has a Bilingual Collection whose mission is to collect materials dealing with bilingual and bicultural education, Spanish juvenile books, and similar materials. Money has been tight in recent years, but a renewed effort is now under way to upgrade the Bilingual Collection materials.

Deborah Curry has identified four general goals that Reference Departments should strive to accomplish. These include the hiring of more non-white librarians, innovative use made of non-white student workers, the creation of a task force to evaluate the services offered by the Library, and the development of a reference collection that supports the concept of multiculturalism.[18] TAMUK has striven to fulfill these goals. But more than fulfilling goals or buying specific materials, multiculturalism must first of all represent a way of looking at the world. The Library, and especially reference services, must view the new cultural demands of our increasingly heterogeneous society as a challenge to be met and not as another dreary fad. Libraries have always been multicultural to some extent; now we are called upon to go the extra mile and fulfill our destiny as the repository of knowledge and a place of "humanness." By humanness we mean all that pertains to human life and we envision a library environment that is supportive of human differences.[19] Surely there could be no higher mission than to gather together all the many streams of humanity in a place of knowledge. Within the limits of time and place, we can become such repositories. Texas A&M University-Kingsville has made a start on the road to humanness. Through TAMUK's diverse students, staff, and collections, an attempt has been made to see the human face in all its many facets.

The success of multiculturalism is a "continuum rather that a constant state."[20] Success is a process which needs to be nourished, expanded, and diversified to be realized"[21] and reference services whether they are provided to one or to several must always be nourished, expanded and diversified.

NOTES

1. Carla J. Stoffle and Patricia A. Tarin, "No Place for Neutrality: the Case for Multiculturalism," *Library Journal* 19 (July 1994): 46-49.

2. *Statistical Report, fiscal year 1993 September 1, 1992 - August 31, 1993.* (Texas Higher Education Coordinating Board):299.

3. Texas A&M University-Kingsville, *1994-1995 Catalog* (Kingsville, TX: University Publications, 1993): 3.

4. Paul R. Campbell, *Population Projections for States, by Age, Sex, Race, and Hispanic Origin: 1993 to 2020*, (U.S. Bureau of the Census, Current Population Reports, P25-1111, U.S. Government Printing Office, Washington, D.C. (1994): xvii.

5. Shelley Quezada, "Mainstreaming Library Services to Multicultural Population: the Evolving Tapestry," *Wilson Library Bulletin* 66(1992): 28-29.

6. Jeff Claassen, "Study Finds Hispanics Miss out on Education," *Corpus Christi Caller-Times* (July 25, 1994): A20.

7. V. Scott Solberg, Jesse Valdez, and Pete Villarreal, "Social Support, Stress and Hispanic College Adjustments: Test of a Diathesis-Stress Model," *Hispanic Journal of Behavioral Science* 16 (August 1994): 230-239.

8. Karen E. Downing, Barbara McAdam, and Darlene P. Nichols, *Reaching a Multicultural Student Community; A Handbook for Academic Librarians* (Wesport, CT: Greenwood Press, 1993): 14.

9. Ibid., 15.

10. William H. Davidow, *Total Customer Service: The Ultimate Weapon* (New York: Harper, 1989): 133.

11. Otis A. Chadley, "Addressing Cultural Diversity in Academic and Research Libraries," *College & Research Libraries* (May 1992): 207.

12. Kathleen de la Pena McCook and Paula Geist, "Diversity Deferred: Where are the Minority Librarians," *Library Journal* 118 (November 1, 1993): 38.

13. Vicki Anders, Colleen Cook and Roberta Pitts, "A Glimpse into a Crystal Ball: Academic Libraries in the Year 2000," *Wilson Library Bulletin* 67 (October 1992): 39.

14. Texas A&M University-Kingsville, *Transculturation Seminar 8 Syllabus and Calendar* (Kingsville, TX: Department of Sociology, 1994): 2.

15. Downing, McAdams and Nichols, *Reaching a Multicultural Student Community: A Handbook for Academic Librarians*, : 210.

16. Allan J. Dyson, "Reaching for Outreach," *American Libraries* 20 (November 1989): 952-954.

17. Yoshi Hendricks, "The Japanese as Library Patrons," *College & Research Libraries News* 52 (April 1991): 221-225.

18. Curry, Deborah, "Assessing and Evaluating Diversity in the Reference Department," *The Reference Librarian* 38 (1992): 119.

19. James Fish, "Responding to Cultural Diversity: A Library in Transition," *Wilson Library Bulletin* 66(1992): 34-37.

20. Irene Hoadley, "Guest Editorial: Defining Success," *College & Research Libraries*, 55(1994): 99-100.

21. Ibid., 100.

Information Literacy for ESL Students:

Retooling Instructional Models to Accommodate Diversity

Barbara J. Bowley and Lynn Whitnall Meng

ABSTRACT

Because of the tremendous diversity within the English as a Second Language (ESL) population, these students pose unique challenges for those of us who design information literacy programs. To accommodate the variety in information-skill levels, intellectual backgrounds, language abilities, etc., that ESL students exhibit, it is essential to use a sophisticated, yet flexible instructional design model. In developing such a model, the authors used a number of concepts from the Bibliographic Instructional Design (BID) approach of Jakobovits and Nahl-Jakobovits and retooled the BID paradigm to meet the specific needs of a multicultural ESL population. The result is a powerful, yet responsive model for promoting information literacy among a multicultural user group.

In recent years the concept of information literacy has become more sophisticated, and with it the task of designing library instruction programs has become increasingly challenging. The challenge continues to grow as our student populations become more diverse. A class of English as a Second Language (ESL) students, for example, will have a history of experience with libraries that directly reflects the diversity of their cultures. But even as we have become more aware that the backgrounds of multicultural students intimately affect their information-seeking behavior in libraries, we have not always adapted our library instruction programs to accommodate their diversity.

Barbara J. Bowley is Head of Information Services and Lynn Whitnall Meng is an Associate Professor of English at Union County College in Cranford, New Jersey.

I. Physical Access of Materials

	Level 1 - Orientation	Level 2 - Interaction
AFFECTIVE	Show interest in obtaining a book	Demonstrate willingness to check book out at circulation desk
COGNITIVE	Understand concept of call number system Recognize location of ESL section Use call number "cheat sheet" to locate topics of interest	Recognize purpose of library card Understand basic rules of borrowing
SENSORIMOTOR	Select book	Check out book

Figure 1. Access Skill Matrix for Beginning-Level ESL Students

Essentially, any library instruction paradigm that assumes a level playing field for students will fail to address the diversity in information skills among ESL and other multicultural student populations. We have found with our own information literacy program for ESL students, the best way to accommodate diversity is with a flexible, user-oriented model of instruction. But this flexibility must also be grounded in a framework that insures overall information literacy objectives are identical for all students, regardless of the diversity of their backgrounds. We began with the *ACRL Model Statement of Objectives for Academic Bibliographic Instruction*[1] as our general paradigm and looked for an approach that would be compatible with the *Model Statement*.

We have found one of the most promising models is the "integrated-matrix" approach to curriculum design proposed by Leon Jakobovits and Diane Nahl-Jakobovits.[2] Their matrix begins with general information-literacy curriculum ob-

jectives such as those found in the *Model Statement* and then breaks out specific components of the general learning objectives. The components are then categorized as belonging to one of the three traditional domains of learning: cognitive, affective, or sensorimotor. Finally, each cognitive, affective, or sensorimotor component is then identified as constituting a basic level of information skill (called orientation), or greater skills ("interaction" and finally, "actualization"). This approach produces a matrix that enables a course developer to cover all three domains of learning in each learning objective, as well as assuring that different levels of student skill can be accommodated within each objective. Carol Wright has applied this model to a basic information skills program at Penn State University[3], and Figure 1 depicts how we have used the matrix at the earliest skill level of an ESL information literacy program. We have found the integrated-matrix model allows us to be exceptionally responsive to the varied skill levels of our ESL students, in both designing and delivering an information literacy course.

The advantages of the model are particularly clear when we examine some of the possible ranges in information skills in any ESL class. For example, an ESL student with a university degree from a country outside the U.S. may have had prior experience with cognitive information skills such as evaluating research material, but could be hampered in U.S. libraries by affective factors such as a hesitancy to ask for help. Furthermore, this student might also be held back by unfamiliarity with library automation or with the pathways of an open stack system. This in turn directly affects the student's ability to develop the necessary sensorimotor abilities for full information proficiency, such as expertise in using information technology or locating a desired book on the shelf.

By contrast, an ESL student from a U.S. high school might have had prior exposure to the American library system and may report no affective problems (e.g. feelings of being hesitant or overwhelmed) vis-a-vis libraries, but might need assistance in developing cognitive competencies such as information evaluation that are needed for full information literacy. Alternatively, this person may have experience with information technology, but they might require a number of successful library research experiences to develop the affective states that allow them to value information competency as a tool for lifelong learning.

The importance of being especially aware of such affective barriers to information literacy has been discussed by Jakobovits and Nahl-Jakobovits.[4]

Their perspective is supported by a number of researchers who have documented the difficulty some multicultural students have in overcoming affective barriers toward library use. [5,6]

To overcome such barriers to information literacy Jakobovits and Nahl-Jakobovits recommend user-based Bibliographic Instructional Design (BID), which combines the integrated matrix with an instructional design that employs frequent user feedback to ensure that information instruction is truly responsive to user needs. For those designing ESL information literacy curricula, the BID method could begin with obtaining information about a student's previous library experience, and then determining what skills to introduce in each of the affective cognitive, and sensorimotor domains during instruction. Intermittent feedback from assignments can assure instructional objectives are being met throughout the course of a semester.

Because it has the power to address the many variables critical to designing an ESL information literacy curriculum, we have used the Jakobovits and Nahl-Jakobovits integrated-matrix BID approach as our intellectual anchor. However, we have also found that several issues should be considered in order to adapt the model most effectively to an ESL student population.

1. Collaboration Between Librarians and ESL Faculty.

The need for cooperation between these two groups in designing information literacy instruction is more than an issue of collegiality. Librarians may not always be aware of how to best handle the levels of language ability among ESL students. ESL faculty members may not know how to effectively approach the notion of information literacy for their students — nor that such a program can, and should, begin at the earliest levels of ESL instruction in order to build the scaffolding for information literacy.

2. Focused Evaluation Methods.

Most traditional-style library orientation sessions fall flat for ESL students because they do not address the three domains of the integrated-matrix model. A first step to remedying this is to distribute an information literacy needs-assessment survey before the first library instruction session. The survey should address all three domains of learning. A post-instructional survey distributed at the end of the semester is important as well, and especially beneficial for assessing affective outcomes of instruction (See Appendix).

Even more effective than post-instructional surveys is the analysis of student assignments. In particular, an assignment segmented over the course of a semester provides multiple opportunities to gauge student progress, particularly in the cognitive and sensorimotor domains. A research paper, oral presentation, scrapbook or journal assignment, for example, can be broken into smaller assignments tied to specific instructional objectives. Students can first obtain citations, then abstracts, then choose relevant articles, etc., until the final draft is submitted. In this way, each step of the learning process can be easily evaluated, enabling faculty and librarians to monitor students' progress in their use of library resources. This feedback for students and faculty is especially important among a population as diverse as in many ESL classes.

3. Targeting Instruction Across the ESL Curriculum.

One of the advantages of developing an information literacy curriculum for an ESL population is that many ESL students progress from beginning to advanced levels in their own English curriculum. This progression fits the dynamic of the integrated-matrix model. A series of skill-based modules, beginning with basic skills at the earliest ESL levels, and moving toward internalization of literacy objectives, can create a truly comprehensive information literacy program for these students.

Ultimately, we chose the integrated-matrix model for the flexibility and power it provided us in curriculum design, but its most rewarding aspect has been the regular feedback it gives us from our students. Many of our ESL students report their library instruction has been useful in building their success as students, has empowered them personally, and sometimes, touchingly, has provided them with their most fulfilling academic experience. As we have come to see how important information skills are to them, we also see the importance of developing instructional models that meet their specific needs — in all their diversity.

NOTES

1. Carolyn Dusenbury, et al., ed. *Read This First: An Owner's Guide to the New Model Statement of Objectives for Academic Bibliographic Instruction* (Chicago:ACRL/ALA, 1991).
2. Jakobovits, Leon A. and Diane Nahl-Jakobovits, "Learning the Library: Taxonomy of Skills and Errors." *College & Research Libraries* 48(May 1987):203-214.
3. Wright, Carol A., "Application of the Model Statement to a Basic Information Access Skills Program at Penn State University," in Carolyn Dusenbury, et al., ed. *Read This First: An Owner's Guide Bibliographic Instruction* (Chicago:ACRL/ALA, 1991):22-23.
4. Nahl-Jakobovits, Diane and Leon A. Jakobovits, "Bibliographic Instructional Design for Information Literacy: Integrating Affective and Cognitive Objectives," *Research Strategies* 11(Spring 1993):73-88.
5. Sever, Irene, "Electronic Information Retrieval as Culture Shock: an Anthropological Exploration," *RQ* 33(Spring 1994):336-341.
6. Liu, Ziming, "Difficulties and Characteristics of Students from Developing Countries in Using American Libraries," *College & Research Libraries* 54(January 1993):25-31.

APPENDIX

UCC Libraries   Evaluating Your Library Instruction

Course No. : _____

Professor's Name : _____

Your Name :_____

1. Could you describe the assignment or project you worked on and the major sources you used?

_____

_____

_____

2. Say a bit about the quality of the library instruction you had. Was it helpful? If you had designed the library instruction session yourself what would you have done differently?

_____

_____

_____

3. Do you feel differently about yourself as a researcher now that you have had library instruction?

_____

_____

_____

4. Describe skills that you acquired during library instruction sessions that will help you with your future research.

_____

_____

_____

Invisible Collections Within Women's Studies:

Practical Suggestions for Access and Assessment

Cindy Faries and Patricia A. Scott

ABSTRACT

This paper will present practical ideas which can be used by library staff to help patrons access materials, and to help librarians assess invisible collections within women's studies. The authors define 'invisible' collections as those dealing with non-mainstream populations of women such as lesbians, disabled women, or elderly women. By using lesbians as our model of an 'invisible' population, we will provide useful suggestions on accessing information and on assessing the collection about this group. These suggestions came to us from research and experience, but we feel they are valuable and can be applied by other library staff working with 'invisible' or hidden collections in other interdisciplinary fields.

INTRODUCTION

Access to women's studies materials and assessment of women's studies collections in academic libraries can provide many challenges for librarians working with these materials. We all know about the problems encountered when working with interdisciplinary collections. And, if library staff recognize the difficulties involved with these collections just imagine what barriers our patrons may encounter as they use these materials.

The title of this paper comes from a conference I attended at my university in February 1994 entitled *Feminist Symposium, The Third Wave:*

(In)Visible Women. As I heard papers on lesbians, elderly women, and physically challenged women among others, I began to think about collections of materials in my library relating to these populations. As the women's studies librarian, I was naturally very concerned that perhaps I was not doing enough to assure that the right types of materials were being purchased for these 'invisible' populations within women's studies.

Later that spring, my co-author, Pat, came to me with concerns about access to our collection especially relating to lesbians. She had been helping a patron and found it somewhat difficult to

---

Cindy Faries is Reference and Women's Studies Librarian and Patricia A. Scott is Maps Specialist at Penn State University in University Park, Pennsylvania.

retrieve citations. How can we provide better access to our collection, was her concern? Finally, I heard two provocative papers at the conference *Women, Information and the Future* held at Radcliffe College in June 1994 which further sparked my excitement on this topic. First, Professor Hope Olson of the University of Alberta talked about the problems of subject headings and patriarchal language in our library classification systems; and second, Professors Elizabeth Futas of the University of Rhode Island and Shelia Intner of Simmons College, talked about their experiences in doing assessments of women's studies collections.

Thus, the germ of this paper grew, and as Pat and I discussed it, we decided we wanted to present a paper of practical ideas and suggestions, something I wish I would have had as a beginning women's studies librarian six years ago. By choosing one specific population, lesbians, as our model, we hope to outline some of the special problems regarding access and assessment, but more importantly, we hope to provide you with practical ideas and solutions to use in your own libraries. Pat will begin by discussing access issues.

ACCESS ISSUES
Accessing Lesbian Literature

In *Another Mother Tongue: Gay Words, Gay Worlds,* Judy Grahn describes her frustrating attempt to access lesbian literature in a less tolerant era:

> In 1961, when I was twenty-one, I went to a library in Washington, D.C., to read about homosexuals and Lesbians, to investigate, explore, compare opinions, learn who I might be, what others thought of me, who my peers were and had been. The books on such a subject, I was told by indignant terrified librarians unable to say the word homosexual, were locked away. Only professors, doctors, psychiatrists and lawyers for the criminally insane could see them, check them out, hold them in their hands. The books I wanted to check out were by "experts" on the subject of homosexuality as it was understood at the time. The severe reaction of the women librarians, who by all rights

should have been my allies, plus the censorship of the official, professional written material of which my own person was the subject, constituted some of the serious jolts I experienced in my early twenties concerning the position of Gay people in American society.[1]

Libraries and librarians have changed dramatically since Grahn's experience. We no longer lock books in cages, yet much lesbian literature remains hidden. One obstacle to access is that users who would find such material valuable are often unaware of its existence. Those users who are aware of lesbian literature are confused by the complexities of its subject cataloging and often need help in mapping a route through the vast array of sources.

Library staff who want to make lesbian literature accessible to patrons must know who uses the material, understand the vocabulary of search terms necessary for successful catalog searches and provide users with guides that will enable them to access key sources independently.

Outreach

Identifying the users of lesbian collections is imperative if we are committed to linking people with information. Since academic libraries support the curricula of the institions they serve, the librarian must know which courses and faculty members use, and are likely to use, the collection. Close contacts with faculty will reveal course needs as well as individual faculty research interests.

Womens studies courses and courses aimed at diversity enhancement are the most obvious choices for faculty contacts, but it is important to consider that lesbian literature, like womens studies in general, overlaps the areas of history, political science, psychology, theology and many other disciplines.

Bibliographic instruction sessions conducted in a classroom setting are an excellent way to introduce the structure of lesbian literature, to show how past bias determined subject headings and call numbers and to explain how to navigate around these difficulties to find needed information. The classroom environment gives students the opportunity to see librarians as teachers and encourages questions and discussion that might not occur across the reference desk. "Librarians in general, and especially Bibliographic Instructors, have the opportunity to not only demonstrate the use of appropriate sources of information, but ... also have the opportunity to shatter myths and stereotypes which otherwise inhibit the transmission of information."[2]

Students and faculty may be the primary users of lesbian literature in academic libraries, but they are not the only users. Staff members and local residents may rely on the library to satisfy personal information needs and to supply recreational reading. Lesbians who are in the process of coming out to themselves or to others often rely heavily on books to help deal with the problems of transition.[3]

Establishing contacts with the local women's resources center, campus and local gay/lesbian/bisexual groups, and feminist bookstores will help library workers to understand the concerns and information needs of the lesbian community. Such contacts also enable the staff to make referrals to hotlines, support groups and local and regional organizations.

Historically, community outreach has not been a concern of academic libraries, despite the fact that local residents often rely on the local college library to satisfy information needs not met by the public library.

As an advocate of intellectual freedom and a proponent of diversity, the librarian is a logical choice to address groups on these issues as they affect information access. While few librarians would volunteer to become sex educators or to address openly hostile groups, those committed to making lesbian literature accessible must be willing to educate others by reaching out beyond the reference desk. Volunteering to speak to campus or community organizations, to compile bibliographies for workshops, and to become an informa-

tion resource contact for campus and community groups can do much to build a sense of community for all involved.

Displays and exhibits are forms of outreach that can inform, educate and raise consciousness about lesbian issues. Womens History Month (March) and the anniversary of the Stonewall Riots (June 27, 1969) are two opportunities to showcase lesbian literature.

The Closet Catalog

Perhaps the biggest challenge users face in locating lesbian literature is the lack of easy subject access. Users who do subject searches under only the terms **lesbians** or **lesbianism** will find only a fraction of the relevant sources. **Feminism, gays, homosexuality, women,** and **women's rights** are a few of the subject terms that include information on lesbians. Subject headings may also include terms that denote race, age, or occupation: **Afro-American lesbians, middle aged lesbians, lesbian nuns**. In searching for information about lesbians in the context of a larger subject, such as psychology, it is necessary to use the term lesbian as a subdivision.

Since the average user has neither the time nor the inclination to master the intricacies of Library of Congress subject headings, library staff must do so. To avoid the difficultues of subject searching users often rely on poorly constructed keyword searches that result in a discouraging overabundance of hits. Staff knowledge of proper search strategies will save time and frustraton for everyone. A helpful source is *Women in LC's Terms, A Thesaurus of Library of Congress Subject Headings Relating to Women.*[4]

Remember that access to information about lesbians is not limited to the library's catalog. Explore the Internet to find sources such as *The Queer Resource Directory* and pertinent electronic journals.

Info to Go

User aides or pathfinders are a good way to offer a concise explanation of subject searching and to provide the user with some terms with which to start. Since fiction dealing with lesbian themes was not always subject cataloged as such, it is difficult for users to locate. This renders invisible even a landmark work such as Radclyffe Hall's *The Well of Loneliness*. A user aide can address this problem by providing the titles of bibliographies of lesbian fiction and by listing the names of famous or popular authors. You may also want to include instructions for accessing lesbian information via the Internet.

Written guides empower users with "info to go" in the form of search strategies and key sources, while enabling users who so desire to conduct research without the help of library staff.

ASSESSMENT ISSUES

As Pat has shared with you, providing access to materials about lesbians can be a real challenge for any library staff member at a public service desk. My job now is to share some of my ideas about assessment of these collections.

The literature on collection evaluation or assessment is large, and several good articles and monographs can be cited which give an excellent overview of this topic. I have provided a handout which lists several titles on collection assessment. [Reviewers, see last page.] Almost all of these works talk about the time, energy and committment involved in doing any kind of collection assessment, and all of them stress that any assessment must take into account the goals, objectives, and mission of the library.

These articles also outline the traditional or standard methods for doing collection assessments, all of which are usually tied to one of two approaches: collection-centered or user-centered. It is not my purpose to give an overview of all of these methods today (you can read about them from the sources I have provided you), but I would like to briefly mention some of the more common methods under each approach.

Under collection-centered approaches, the following techniques are most often cited:
1. Checking Lists or Bibliographies
2. Using Statistics such as Gross Size of the Collection; Volumes Added per Year; Number of Periodicals; or Expenditures
3. Using Forumlas (for example the one worked out by Clapp and Jordan whose article is on your reading list),
4. Doing Shelflist or Title Counts Based on Dewey Decimal or Library of Congress Classification Systems
5. Using Experts to Examine the Collection
6. Using Established Standards
7. Doing Citation Studies

Under user-centered approaches, the following methods are most often cited:
1. Doing User Surveys
2. Looking at Circulation Records
3. Looking at Interlibrary Loan Requests
4. Doing Studies of Materials Used In-House

I could elaborate on the advantages and disadvantages of all of these methods, but again, that is not my purpose today. Suffice it to say that while problems exist with all types of collection evaluation methods, these problems are compounded when you are trying to assess any type of interdisciplinary collection, be it women's studies, African American studies, or area studies.

The suggestions which follow are not earth-shattering by any means. I have come to them through experience in doing an assessment of the women's studies collection at my library; reading and reserch about collection assessment for interdisciplinary fields; listening and talking to other librarians; and working with the faculty, staff and students at Penn State.

1. Check Bibliographies and Lists

Of all the traditional methods mentioned above, this one does have value especially now that many important bibliographies have appeared on the subject of lesbians. Some of the titles I would suggest for list checking include:

> *Feminist Collections: A Quarterly of Women's Studies Resources.* (This is an excellent current source which always has articles on special topics, such as the Winter 1994 issue which featured an article on finding lesbians in popular culture.)
> *Gay and Lesbian Library Service*
> *Lesbianism: An Annotated Bibliography and Guide to the Literature, 1976-1991*
> *Out On the Shelves: Lesbian Books Into Libraries*
> (Please note that the full citations for these sources are on the reading list.)

Of course, bibliographies are appearing for many other special populations, so depending on the area you want to evaluate in your collection, there should be some current useful bibliographies.

2. Meet with Faculty

By my attendance at monthly faculty meetings of the women's studies program, I have heard of journals to add to the collection such as *Lesbian Ethics*; learned about research projects students are working on; and learned that a faculty member at one of the Penn State campuses was doing research on gays and lesbians. I can also take the time to talk to faculty about what they are teaching, and request copies of their syllabi so I have their reading lists. I would not have this knowledge without attending these meetings. If regular faculty meetings do not occur, call up your faculty and go visit them.

3. Use the Internet

The Internet can provide a vast wealth of information. The service Women's Studies Resources from the University of Maryland provides among other things conference listings; bibliographies; reference sources; and course syllabi from faculty all over the country. Additionally, I have discovered many new titles, especially fictional

works about lesbians, through my subscription to WMST-L. There are many, many listservs that one can subscribe to for various populations which can provide valuable information for collection development and evaluation. Finally, you can use the Internet to compare your holdings against the holdings of other libraries.

4. Check Status Inquiries on Your Catalog

I can't tell you the number of times I have found materials on lesbians as "reported missing" on Penn State's OPAC. I have often come across these missing items while checking a source such as *Feminist Collections*. I mention this as a method for assessment, because missing items indicate to me a very real interest in these materials, and tells me that perhaps I should be ordering second copies of some titles.

5. Talk to Other Subject Selectors in Your Library

I use the knowledge, expertise, and experience of all of my colleagues doing collection development and reference work in other areas especially Sociology, Literature, Contemporary Topics, History, and Health. After a question came to our Health Sciences Librarian about lesbians and menopause, the two of us looked at the collection and began to add materials (few as they are) relating to health issues of lesbians.

6. Make Connections with Non-Library Offices or Groups on Your Campus or in Your Community

I work closely with people in the Women's Studies Program office and the Center for Women Students on my campus. Both offices have small libraries and I have discovered materials to purchase for our library. Other groups to work with include the health center on campus, any women's resource centers in you community, or groups working with AIDS awareness and education.

7. Attend Meetings of Student or Faculty/Staff Groups on Your Campus

Penn State has a Lesbian, Gay, and Bisexual Student Alliance for undergraduates; a special committee within the Graduate Student Association for lesbian, gay, and bisexual students; and a formal Committee on Gay, Lesbian, and Bisexual Equity composed of faculty, staff, technical service workers, administrators and students which reports to the President of the University. I have had formal and informal contact with all of these groups, and I often hear about what the library needs from these people.

8. Attend Conferences

The conference I mentioned at the beginning of this paper was a feminist conference on my own campus, but the Feminist Task Force of the Social Responsibilites Roundtable; the Women's Studies Section of ACRL; and the Women's Materials and Women Library Users Discussion Group of RASD all within the American Library Association have provided excellent programs, handouts, newletters, etc. which have benefitted me as women's studies selector. Keep your eyes open for conferences which you could attend to increase your knowledge and awareness of new resources for your library.

CONCLUSION

Women's studies and other interdisplinary collections can often seem invisible to our users, but those parts of these collections which may deal with special populations or sensitive topics perhaps are so hidden that they may seem (to borrow a phrase from a talented undergrad at my university) "invisible within invisibility." Thus, for library staff providing access to these collections, and for those librarians wishing to assess an interdisciplinary collection or even part of one, there are definite challenges; challenges, because the traditional methods of access and assessment often do not work. However, when dealing with nontraditional collections, new ideas and approaches must be tried. We hope we have provided you with some useful and practical ideas, and that we have stimulated your thinking to provide us with further suggestions.

Thank you.

NOTES

1. Judy Grahn, *Another Mother Tongue: Gay Words, Gay Worlds* (Boston: Beacon Press, 1984), xi.
2. See Janet A Creelman and Roma M. Harris, "Coming Out: The Information Needs of Lesbians," *Collection Building* 10(1119): 37.
3. Gary M. Klein, "Helping Students Find Sensitive Materials: A Guide to the Literature on Homosexuality for Librarians and Faculty," 1986, ERIC, ED 359990.
4. Ruth Dickstein, Victoria A. Mills and Ellen J. Waite, eds., *Women in LC's Terms, A Thesaurus of Subject Headings Relating to Women* (Phoenix: Oryx Press, 1978).

READING LIST ON COLLECTION ASSESSMENT

American Library Association. *Guide to the Evaluation of Library Collections*. Edited by Barbara Lockett. Collection Management and Development Guides, No. 2. Chicago: American Libary Association, 1989. (This guide has a lengthy bibliography.)

Baker, Sharon L., and F. Wilfrid Lancaster. *The Measurement of Library Services*. 2nd ed. Arlington, Va.: Information Resources Press, 1991.

Bonn, George S. "Evaluation of the Collection." *Library Trends* 22(January 1974): 265-304.

Clapp, Vernon W., and Robert T. Jordan. "Quantitative Criteria for Adequacy of Academic Library Collections." *College & Research Libraries* 26(1965):371-80.

Creelman, Janet A.E., and Roma M. Harris. "Coming Out: The Information Needs of Lesbians." *Collection Building* 10(1990): 37-41.

Faigel, Martin. "Methods and Issues in Collection Evaluation Today." *Library Acquisitions: Practice and Theory* 9(1985): 21-35.

Hall, Blaine H. *Collection Assessment Manual for College and University Libraries*. Phoenix: Oryx Press, 1985.

Mosher, Paul. "Evaluation in Research Libraries: The Search for Quality, Consistency, and System in Collection Development." *Library Resources & Technical Services* 23(Winter 1979): 16-23.

Mosher, Paul H. "Collection Evaluation or Analysis: Matching Library Acquistions to Library Needs." In *Collection Development in Libraries: A Treatise*, edited by Robert D. Stueart and George B. Miller, Jr., 527-45. Foundations in Library and Information Science, v. 10. Greenwich, Conn.: JAI Press, 1980.

Mosher, Paul H. "Quality and Library Collections: New Directions in Research and Practice in Collection Evaluation." *Advances in Librarianship* 13(1984): 211-38.

SELECTED TITLES FOR LIST CHECKING FOR LESBIAN LITERATURE

Allen, Jane, comp., and others. *Out On the Shelves: Lesbian Books Into Libraries*. Newcastle-under-Lyme: Association of Assistant Librarians, 1989.

Cough, Cal, and Ellen Greenblatt, eds. *Gay and Lesbian Library Service*. Jefferson, N.C.: McFarland, 1990.

Feminist Collections: A Quarterly of Women's Studies Resources. Madison, Wis.: Women's Studies Librarian, University of Wisconsin System, 1980-.

Maggiore, Dolores J. *Lesbianism: An Annotated Bibliography and Guide to the Literature, 1976-1991*. Metucher, N.J.:Scarecrow Press, 1992.

Making the Interdisciplinary Multicultural:

Collection Building for the New Millennium

G. Margaret Porter

ABSTRACT

Collection development and subject librarians in academic libraries are increasingly aware of the need for building diversity into all areas of library collections. In order to do so effectively there needs to be an understanding of the tools and methodology that enables us to do that. Collection building in interdisciplinary areas such as woman's studies, gender studies, African-American studies, and other ethnic studies areas can provide us with some of the tools for building diversity into more narrowly defined subjects. Collection development policies which define levels of diversity, internationalism, and multiculturalism are discussed. Sources used for collection development and material selection for interdisciplinary areas are identified and can be used to build multicultural components into all subject areas and materials. Collection assessment procedures used for interdisciplinary topics can be used to evaluate how well multiculturalism and diversity are integrated into specific subject collects. In addition, strategies need to be developed for providing bibliographic access to material and resources that are dispersed throughout the collection and that often lack appropriate bibliographic control and subject headings.

In the Point of View section of the *Chronicle of Higher Education* for July 13, 1994, bell hooks, professor of English at the City College of the City University of New York, writes: "Separatism of any kind promotes marginalization of those unwilling to grapple with the whole body of knowledge and creative works available to others. This is true of black students who do not want to read works by white writers, of female students of any race who do not want to read books written by men, and of white students who only want to ready works of white thinkers. When the issue is learning, racial separatism of any kind reinforces the dangerous notion that it is acceptable for one group to distort ideas to perpetuate its own specific interests and biases. The dangers are apparent

G. Margaret Porter is Coordinator for Database and Reference Support Service at the Univeristy of Notre Dame in Notre Dame, Indiana.

when we remember that it has taken years to undo the racist and sexist scientific scholarship that once held that women were biologically inferior to men and blacks were inferior to whites."[0] As librarians involved in higher education it is imperative that we reinforce the notion that inclusiveness needs to be at the core of the educational process, that we build collections that reflect the multicultural and international aspects of our institutions, as well as society at large, that we develop methods of assessing our collections with these aspects in mind, and that we provide our users with effective strategies for accessing the resources we provide.

How do we work towards accomplishing these three goals? What methods and strategies can we use? I suggest that we start by looking at how collection development, assessment, and bibliographic access are accomplished in interdisciplinary areas such as women's or gender studies, African American studies, and other ethnic area studies. Many institutions have academic programs and library collections supporting interdisciplinary areas, but it is still important that multicultural and international concerns are addressed within particular subject areas. As gender, sexual orientation, race, and ethnicity become embedded in courses in all subject areas, it is even more important that librarians working with collection development and access are inclusive in their efforts.

The foundations we build our collections on should be reflected in our collection development policies. As noted by Bernice Lacks in her introduction to *Women's Studies Collection Development Policies,* published by ACRL's Women's Studies Section, acquiring interdisciplinary works is often the responsibility of the selector for women's studies, or other area studies as the case may be, but the materials reach into every traditional discipline.[1] When collection development responsibilities and budget allocations are split between a specific subject and an interdisciplinary area guidelines as to who collects what should be reflected in the policies. For example, a collection

development policy for Native American studies should outline what is collected within the scope of that area and what is collected within the scope of American history. Does feminist literary theory fall within the scope of women's studies or literature? How is French feminist theory differentiated from English? An explicit collection development policy is equally important when there are no separate interdisciplinary studies, but when the selection of materials that reflect diversity and internationalism is included in the collection development for specific subjects or disciplines. For example, the inclusion of economic conditions as they relate to women, minority groups, and geographic areas outside Western industrialized countries probably should be spelled out, even if, or maybe especially, if there are no specific course offerings covering these areas. The selection of fiction, poetry, and short stories by writers other than white, Western, male heterosexuals should be a given in an ideal world, but for now specifying diversity as a conscious goal certainly is not be out of place. Well written, frequently reviewed and updated policies minimize the possibility of materials "falling between the cracks" in the selection process. Before I leave the discussion of collection development policies a *caveat:* detailed collection development policies do not substitute for cooperation and sharing of resources among librarians. I have found, in my work as a subject librarian for several interdisciplinary areas, that I depend on my colleagues a great deal, both for their suggestions of material, but also for them to order material that my budget allocations either cannot or should not handle. For example, the budget for theology is a great deal larger than for African American studies, therefore I prevail upon the theology librarian to purchase materials dealing with African American churches and preaching, even though these materials support research and courses in the African American studies program.

When building inclusive collections it is helpful to look at the methods used for collection development in interdisciplinary areas. If your institution uses an academic approval plan look at the profile for the library. Is it as inclusive as it ought to be? When was it last revised or altered? Academic publishing has become more inclusive and much is published in areas that would have been considered marginal a few years ago. Examples include women and gender, gay and lesbian studies and theories, global issues such as eco-feminism, women in world-wide development, and anthologies of literature that are both gender and ethnic specific. Much of the material purchased for interdisciplinary studies come from small presses which tend to focus more on diversity and multiculturalism in their publishing output. However, elusiveness can be problematic where small press publishing is concerned, as can the "here today, gone tomorrow" phenomenon. An approval plan for small presses is a possible solution, but both the profile and the included publishers have to be reviewed and revised in order to fit the sometimes changing needs of the institution and its constituents. Being on the mailing list of small presses and alternative publishers is one of the best ways to stay abreast of what is available. A couple of tools, primarily directed towards writers, but that can be used to locate and select small presses of interest are *Words to the Wise: a Writer's Guide to Feminist and Lesbian Periodicals and Publishers*.[2] This is a slim volume that can easily be looked through in its entirety and which describes the focus of the presses and journals listed. In the case of presses it lists titles published. Another, more substantial and less specialized title is *The International Directory of Little Magazines and Small Presses*,[3] too large to browse through, but with a subject index, so one can select for example Native Americans, Chicano/a and then pursue only the listings under these headings. There are two companion publications that are useful when pursuing small press material: *Small Press Record of Books in Print*,[4] which has a reasonably well developed subject index, and the review journal *Small Press Review*, which since June 1994 also includes *Small Magazine Review*.[5]

In 1977 Elizabeth Futas reported that in the response to a survey question regarding major selection tools *Choice* ranked as #1 in 105 of 136 libraries.[6] In the 1984 survey the major selection tool had shifted to *Library Journal*.[7] While both of these journals are premier tools for libraries, their division by discipline make them less useful for interdisciplinary studies. More useful, but also more time consuming, since it is not a one-stop-shopping approach, is the systematic use of specialized reviewing journals such as *Women's Review of Books*,[8] which reviews titles on women and gender in all disciplines. Another approach is to regularly go through the book review sections of specialized journals. *African American Review*[9] with its focus on the literature and art of African Americans provides book reviews for the humanities selectors; one journal even uses its multi-disciplinary content in its subscription ads: "Question: what do you get when you cross an anthropologist, a historian, and a literary critic? Answer: 4 issues/year of AIQ", that is the *American Indian Quarterly*.[10] And yes, the book reviews reflect this multidisciplinary approach. The book review section of the *Journal of Homosexuality*[11] covers homosexuality from different perspectives such as sociology, medicine, literature. An excellent source both for its reviews and articles is the journal *Multicultural Review*.[12] The library and information science journal *Collection Building*,[13] in addition to having as its primary focus all aspects of collection development and management, has regular columns dealing with small presses as well as alternative publishing. These columns often contain bibliographies that are useful for collection development and evaluation. Bibliographies published in a variety of sources, both print and electronic, are valuable tools. The specialized listservs for many interdisciplinary areas are invaluable, both in terms of the lists of titles that often appear in response to queries, but also because one can get informed opinions from scholars in a variety of fields. Many also have archives that can be searched for specific information.

The activities associated with developing multicultural and interdisciplinary collections are time consuming and labor intensive. However, Otis Chadley, in the article "Addressing Cultural Diversity in Academic and Research Libraries" makes the point that research libraries, like higher education in general, have to provide quality services to all clientele and access to collections which reflect the lives and experiences of all Americans. In regards to the use of material on racial and ethnic minorities 74% of libraries that responded to a questionnaire, reported that this material was in demand.[14]

Collection assessment is a very labor intensive undertaking and in most cases an imprecise endeavor, but it is even more so when one is working with multi-disciplinary collections. A standard measuring tool for research libraries, the National Shelflist Count, with its broad LC classifications is of little help. For example, it does not allow for measuring within PR 8309-9899: English Literature: Provincial, Colonial what is Nigerian, Indian, or South African, much less the strength of one's collection of, for example, African women writers. HQ: Family, Marriage, Woman, Sexual Life does not allow for measuring the finer points of gender based materials. Scanning the shelves can be a component in collection analysis, but at best it provides only a sketchy picture of distinct subject areas. It is even less useful when titles are scattered all through the collection.

If there is no subject librarian for an interdisciplinary area, then the librarians responsible for individual subjects are the ones to assess the strengths of the multicultural components within their collections. In some subjects this is easier to accomplish than others. LC classification schedules and subject headings can be helpful in separating out various components in history, sociology, economics, but not so in literature. What we are left with is using bibliographies as tools for measuring our collections. Reference tools such as *Alternative Press Index*[15] under the heading "Bibliographies" supplies references to any number of useful items, as does the *Bibliographic*

Index,[16] when one checks under a variety of headings pertaining to any given group, subject or area.

The Conspectus approach to collection evaluation has been used in many research libraries, but it is a difficult, if not impossible approach to use for assessing multidisciplinary collections or the multicultural components of a particular subject collection. Sara Pritchard developed an RLG Conspectus for Women's Studies, the only interdisciplinary Conspectus at this time.[17] It can serve as a model for other multi-disciplinary areas. It is important to note that when values are assigned to note collection strength rating is done on the portion that deals with women (or Asian Americans, or gays and lesbians) not on the larger subject area, such as history, literature or sociology. I have not found at this time any reports on using a Conspectus as a tool for evaluating interdisciplinary or multicultural collections. In fact, Jim Coleman points out in "The RLG Conspectus: A History of Its Development and Influence and a Prognosis for its Future" that one of the notable disadvantages of this tool is that "it did not recognize nor allow for the modern trend towards interdisciplinary studies."[18] I should add that I have not found much reported on collection evaluation of interdisciplinary or multicultural studies in general.

One of the most vexing problems is to devise a yardstick against which one's own holdings can be measured. It is one thing to check a number of bibliographies, or actually be able to count items in a specific area, but it is quite another to know exactly what it all means. Measuring your collection against bibliographies is only useful if there are established guidelines for the level of collecting. The levels for multicultural or area studies materials will vary according to the individual institutions, but one would hope that an institution that collects at the highest levels in American literature would be highly inclusive in collecting literature dealing with gender and American ethnic and racial groups. Ideally, levels of collecting are established in the collection development policies. In today's electronic environment it is also possible to measure your collections against those of other institutions, either on a title-by-title basis, or by numbers of titles within certain preselected call number ranges or subject areas. Most of us have a number of so-called peer institutions (and these often vary based on what you are comparing) whose library holdings we can use for comparison. The use of peer institutions is the basis for the Amigos/OCLC CD-Rom product which lets a library compare its holdings and collection development activity against pre-selected groups of peer institutions. However, this product also uses the LC subject divisions, which again do not adequately measure interdisciplinary subjects.

Many of us are working very hard towards creating collections that are responsive to the needs and demands of all our constituents, collections that contain materials of all formats, that are inclusive and international in scope. However, we also know that we have to work equally hard towards making sure that there is at least adequate access to the materials. As in the case of methods for collection assessment, we are working, for the most part, with a less than perfect system, the Library of Congress Subject Headings and classification scheme. Also, libraries in addition to using controlled vocabularies like LCSH have to depend on the quality of the cataloging copy contributed through shared resources.[19]

Interdisciplinary, multicultural and international materials typically combine at least two approaches, one usually a traditional discipline and the other gender, racial, ethnic, or geographic. As Hope Olson points out in "Subject Access to Women's Studies Materials" this problem can sometimes be overcome by using keywords and Boolean searching. As I get more and more involved with providing access and bibliographic instruction for multicultural programs and classes, the less I can imagine functioning well in these capacities without the existence of an online catalog with sophisticated search capabilities and, I might add, "see" and "see also" references displayed online. Even so, bibliographic instruction has taken on a new dimension, as I pile term upon

term to describe an ethnic group, or try to cover all possibilities for sexual preference. The term "inclusive" has truly acquired meaning. By the third or fourth term the eyes of the average undergraduate become glazed. The most disturbing aspect of this is that very little is likely to change in the near future. Hope Olson also points out that many of the Library of Congress subject heading policies are based on the practical difficulty of changing headings. Those of us who are involved with the subject headings at the other end, know of the "practical difficulty" in using them. Changing the structure of the headings should not be done in the name of "political correctness", but in the interest of ease of access.

In her essay "Changing Users: Bibliographic Instruction for Whom"[20] Lizabeth Wilson discussed the impact of an increasingly multicultural student body and global interdependence on higher education. Bibliographic instruction can no longer be "designed with the generic student in mind". Teaching styles have to be selected with sensitivity in order to be suitable for multicultural, multiethnic students. However, an equally compelling reason to be as inclusive as we can, is that all of us need to develop a greater understanding and tolerance. I would like to finish the same way I started, with a quote from the same article by bell hooks: "We are rarely able to interact only with folks like ourselves, who think as we do. No matter how much some of us deny this reality and long for the safety and familiarity of sameness, inclusive ways of knowing and living offer us the only true way to emancipate ourselves from the divisions that limit our minds and imaginations.[21]

NOTES

1. bell hooks, "Black Students Who Reject Feminism," *Chronicle of Higher Education,* 13 July 1994, p. A.44.
2. Bernice Lacks, "Introduction" in *Women's Studies Collection Development Policies,* (Chicago: ACRL, 1992).
3. Andrea Fleck Clardy, *Words to the Wise: A Writers Guide to Feminist and Lesbian Periodicals and*

Publishers, rev. 2d. ed. (Ithaca: Firebrand Books, 1987).

4. Len Fulton, ed., *The International Directory of Little Magazines and Small Presses,* 29th ed. (Paradise, CA: Dustbooks, 1994).

5. *Small Press Record of Books in Print* (Paradise, CA: Dustbooks).

6. *Small Press Review* (Paradise, CA: Dustbooks).

7. Elizabeth Futas, *Library Acquisitions Policies and Procedures* (Phoenix: Oryx Press, 1977).

8. Elizabeth Futas, *Library Acquisitions Policies and Procedures* (Phoenix: Oryx Press, 1984).

9. *Women's Review of Books* (Wellesley: Wellesley College Center for Research on Women).

10. *African American Review* (Terre Haute: Department of English, Indiana State University).

11. *American Indian Quarterly* (Lincoln: University of Nebraska Press).

12. *Journal of Homosexuality* (New York: Haworth Press).

13. *Multicultural Review* (Westport, CT: Greenwoood Publishing Group).

14. *Collection Building* (New York: Neal-Schuman Publishers).

15. Otis A. Chadley, "Addressing Cultural Diversity in Academic and Research Libraries," *College and Research Libraries* 53, no.3 (1992): 206-214.

16. *Alternative Press Index* (College Park: Alternative Press Centre).

17. *Bibliographic Index* (New York: H.W. Wilson Co).

18. Sarah Pritchard, "RLC Conspectus: Women's Studies," in *Women's Studies Collection Development Policies* (Chicago: ACRL, 1992), C1-C32.

19. Jim Coleman, "The RLG Conspectus: A History of Its Development and Influence and a Prognosis for Its Future," in *Collection Assessment: A Look at the RLG Conspectus,* eds. Richard J. Wood and Katina Strauch (New York: Haworth Press, 1992), 35-43.

20. Hope Olson, "Subject Access to Women's Studies Materials," in *Cataloging Heresy: Challenging the Standard Bibliographic Product,* ed. Bella Hass Weinberg (Medford, NJ: Learned Information, Inc., 1992), 159-169.

21. Lizabeth A. Wilson, "Changing Users: Bibliographic Instruction for Whom,: in *The Evolving Educational Mission of the Library,* eds. Betsy Baker and Mary Ellen Litzinger (Chicago: ACRL, 1992): 20-53.

22. bell hooks, "Black Students Who Reject Feminism," *Chronicle of Higher Education,* 13 July 1994, p. A44.

The Academic Librarian:
The Student's Link to a Multicultural World

Elizabeth Burns

ABSTRACT

Multiculturalism is the politically correct catchword of the day. There are committees on multiculturalism and cultural diversity on college and university campuses across the United States. New courses have been designed around the concept of multiculturalism. In order for students to live and work in this multicultural world, they must understand cultural diversity. Academic librarians provide the student's link to knowledge about this multicultural world. This paper demonstrates the need for a multicultural collection, suggests methods of collection development, and provides the steps to ensure collection utilization by the students.

Multiculturalism is too important to be just a politically correct catchword. Committees on multiculturalism and cultural diversity are on college and university campuses all across the United States. New courses have been designed around the concept of multiculturalism. The term appears in speeches, news interviews, and class presentations. Courses in every discipline contain materials on multiculturalism and cultural diversity.

Multi means many and culture, according to Sir E. B. Tylor, "is that complex whole which includes knowledge, belief, art, morals, law, custom, and any other capabilities and habits acquired by man as a member of society."[1] World-wide,

culturally diverse groups are demanding the recognition of their cultural identities in addition to the citizenship of their countries. If college and university students are to succeed in today's world, they need to learn about these cultural differences.[2]

Academic librarians are the student's link to this multicultural world.[3] We provide them with the resources to climb the barriers of cultural differences. As we build collections, we address the issues of minority authors, third world literature, nonverbal communication, and cultural diversity in education and the workplace. This paper demonstrates the need for a multicultural collec-

Elizabeth Burns is an Instructor/Reference Librarian at Ohio State University at Mansfield in Mansfield, Ohio.

tion, suggests the resources for collection development, and provides the steps to ensure collection utilization by the students.

There are several reasons why colleges and universities need multicultural collections in their libraries. One, students want to know more about their own ethnic heritage. As their knowledge of history and literature expands, they want to learn where they fit into the picture. These students begin to question: what caused their ancestors to leave their homes; how did they adjust to the changes they found here; and what did they contribute to their new country?[4]

A second reason for multicultural collections in college and universities libraries is for the literary value of the collection. Joyce Carol Oates said that "reading is the sole means by which we slip, involuntarily, often helplessly, into another's skin, another's voice, another's soul."[5] Students need to read and analyze literature written by multicultural writers in this country and other countries. High school English literature textbooks do not cover many of the lesser known ethnic authors; academic libraries should fill this gape in their education.

These collections need to be developed for a third reason. Many students do not know much about cultures other than their own. They have spent their lives in communities where the ethnic background is European. My students, the students of North Central Technical College and the Ohio State University at Mansfield, represent these students.

A seven county area in north-central Ohio provides the students for the shared campus of The Ohio State University at Mansfield and the North Central Technical College. Statistically, the ethnic percentages for this area are:

White, including Hispanic	97.84%
African American (Black)	1.68%
American Indian, Eskimo, or Aleut	.14%
Asian or Pacific Islander	.34%[6]

These students attend a college and university where the majority of the faculty and student body is of the same ethnic background. Some of these students will return to their home communities and spend their entire lives there. However, they still need to understand cultural diversity.

If they major in education and become elementary and secondary school teachers, one of two things happens. They return home but they teach students that do not remain in the community. What they teach these students about multiculturalism may have a bearing on how well they succeed in life. Or the teachers may leave their ethnically-restricted geographic area and teach in schools where the majority of their students are from an ethnic minority group.[7] These students may have different learning styles due to their cultural background. Either way the teachers need to understand the cultures of many societies before they can in turn teach their students about cultural differences.[8]

College and university students that major in law, business, or medicine, just to name a few fields, will need to understand other cultures, no matter where they practice their professions. Hospitals, physicians, nurses, and social workers have found that meeting patients' cultural needs are as necessary as medicine, for their return to good health. Business professionals need to understand the concept of time and personal space in reference to the cultural identity of the individuals with whom they are conducting business.[9]

Diplomats, journalists, missionaries, and scholars should understand the cultural idiosyncrasies of the people that they are serving or studying. For example, recently a journalist for my local newspaper reported on a court case involving a member of the Amish society. As I read these articles which contained quotes of the ruling judge and lawyers, it was apparent to me, an Amish scholar, that neither the reporting journalist nor the officials understood many of the cultural aspects of the Amish society, although this settlement has been located in our community for forty years.

Becoming aware of the need for multicultural knowledge is the first step. However, before a person can find out about his cultural heritage or other cultural backgrounds, he must locate the necessary materials. Before professors can require students to conduct research and write papers dealing with multiculturalism, there must be resources available in the library. Before students can read and study literature about and by multiethnic authors, here and abroad, the literary works must be available in the library. Academic librarians provide the link from students and professors to these multicultural materials.[10]

Having created the need for a multicultural collection, the second area of discussion in this paper is the development of this collection. Collection development is one of the most rewarding, yet frustrating jobs that a librarian has. In a large university library, collection development may be the work of several librarians, each with a special area of development, such as a Black Studies Librarian, or an Asian-American Studies librarian whose collection is either a library in itself or part of the larger library.

In a small library, such as the development of collection in a branch or regional library of a larger university, collection development is the responsibility of one person. It covers every multiethnic group and encompasses every course that is taught on campus. Therefore the academic librarian has to have a general knowledge of every field of study. This is the type of library that I am referring to in the rest of this paper.

When the librarian starts the job of developing a multicultural collection for the library, funding of the collection needs to be considered. Since budgets are restricted at this time, the librarian first checks for grants that might fund this collection. Also, there may be an individual or group in the local community that would like to donate funds for materials supporting their ethnic group. If there is a Friends of the Library group, a multicultural collection development proposal should be discussed with the group.

At the same time, the search for collection materials begins. A literature review of existing materials revealed that although there was much material for the development of elementary and middle school collections, there were very few lists and bibliographies available for the academic collection development librarian.

This librarian has to create her own lists. There are several ways to do this: (1) read reviews in magazines and periodicals, for example, *Choice*, the periodical which reviews materials for academic librarians, *The Library Journal*, and specialty journals such as *The Ethnic Forum*; (2) read the catalogs of the presses, particularly the small presses;[11] (3) collect bibliographies from all sources, books, articles, newspapers, and conferences; (4) network with other librarians; and most importantly, (5) read.

I keep a card file that consists of books that I want to read at a later date, reference materials and annotated bibliographies from other libraries, that I need to locate and browse through. I also keep a reader's advisory journal of the books that I have read. Were they interesting and authentic in their portrayal of the ethnic group? Would I recommend this book or author to others? These two items help me when I start ordering for my collection. As a collection development librarian, you make the decisions yourself, as to the value of an item to be added to your collection.[12] However, to assist you, take advantage of any networking that is available to you.

Read the newsletters and attend the roundtable meetings of the American Library Association. Attend conferences like the Association of College and Research Libraries conference where other collection development librarians will be gathered. Talk with other librarians at meetings, workshops, conferences, and on listserves and e-mail. Readers among your faculty and the community-at-large can also help you locate books that you might want in your multicultural collection. By building this collection, the academic librarian provides the link between the publisher and the student.

March 29 - April 1, 1995, Pittsburgh, Pennsylvania

Once a multicultural collection is in place in the library, the job of the academic librarian is just beginning. No collection is of any value unless it is utilized by the professors and students. There are three main ways that the librarian can publicize the collection. This is through the library, through the professors, and through the university.

Alert the professors; send out new acquisitions list to the entire faculty. Send out personal notes to individual faculty members, relating how a new book will lend itself to either an area of personal research of that faculty member or the content of a course that the professor is teaching.[13] Good collection development librarians know the areas of study that their professors are currently researching.

Get yourself placed on committees for cultural diversity, lecture series, or student/faculty discussion groups. Create browsing or new acquisitions areas in your library. Create bulletin boards and arrange exhibits in display cases in the library and around the campus that explore various ethnic and cultural heritages. Write book reviews for the student newspaper.

When creating bibliographic instruction materials, you can have the students look up books about different cultures and by ethnic authors. You can get to know the students on a one-on-one basis and build up a working rapport. If a student requests help with an idea for a research paper, suggest a multicultural idea, then help the student locate the proper materials for their research. Academic librarians provide the link between the multicultural collection and student.

College and university students need to understand the many cultures in the world. To help faculty and students in this endeavor, academic librarians create and maintain multicultural collections. They ensure that these collections are utilized by the methods listed in this paper.

NOTES

1. Tylor, Edward Burnett, "Primitive Culture." In *High Points in Anthropology*, 2nd ed., edited by Paul Bohannan and Mark Glazer, (New York: McGraw-Hill, 1988), 64.
2. Sylva Simsova, "Multicultural Populations: Their Nature and Needs. "In *Multicultural Librarianship: An International Handbook*, edited by Marie F. Zielinska with Francis T. Kirkwood, (Munchen: Saur, 1992), 18.
3. Claudia J. Gollop, "Selection and Acquisition of Multicultural Materials at the Libraries of the City University of New York," *Urban Academic Librarian* 8 (Winter 1991): 22.
4. Simsova, 13.
5. Johnson, 31.
6. U.S. Bureau of Census. *1990 Census of Population: General Population Characteristics; Ohio.* Washington D.C., 1992
7. Brenda Mitchell-Powell, "Why Multiculturalism? Why Now?" *Urban Academic Librarian*, 9 (Winter 1994): 18.
8. Johnson, 19.
9. Simsova, 1992.
10. Kay F. Jones, "Multicultural Diversity and the Academic Library," *Urban Academic Librarian* 8 (Winter 1990): 18.
11. Kay Ann Cassell, "Small Presses: Multicultural Anthologies," *Collection Building* 11 (1993): 47.
12. Lauri Johnson and Sally Smith, *Dealing with Diversity Through Multicultural Fiction: Library Classroom Partnerships*, (Chicago: American Library Association, 1993), 46-57.
13. Lois Buttlar and Lubomyr R. Wynar, "Cultural Pluralism and Ethnic Diversity: Authors as Information Users in the Field of Ethnic Studies," *Collection Management*, 16 (1992): 15.

The International Poster Collection:

A Window to the World

Holley R. Lange and Chris Nelson

ABSTRACT

As current demographic trends are increasingly reflected in universities and colleges across the country, academic libraries must seek and provide additional multicultural and multinational resources. Colorado State University's International Poster Collection provides a window to the world that only a visual medium such as posters can give. The collection, representing approximately forty countries, offers a striking alternative to more traditional multicultural print resources. This paper introduces the collection, addresses some of the challenges in providing access to it, and discusses its potential as a multicultural and multinational resource.

Our university and college campuses increasingly reflect current demographic trends and the reality of our national multicultural mosaic. In addition to this national mosaic, academic institutions reflect an internationalism apparent in a broadly multinational student body. But beyond these more local campus realities, lies a complex, interactive, and ever changing world that calls for an informed understanding of other peoples and cultures. To serve the varied needs of students, faculty, and the future requires an expanded perspective, and libraries are seeking to meet these demands through resources that reflect this multicultural and multinational view. As Heitor Gurgulino de Souza, rector of the United Nations University points out: "Without tolerance and respect for different cultures we know that there will inevitably be misconceptions and conflicts rather than understanding and enrichment through cultural exchange. . . . Multiculturalism implies . . . respect for different cultures and the enhancement of universal human values, without effacing the diversities of cultures or attempting to create 'the human culture.'"[1] We need to value our own culture, heritage, language, and people, but also learn about others in order to understand and appreciate our similarities and differences.

Librarians must take action to meet these varied needs. Indicative of this is the growing professional literature addressing such topics as developing multicultural collections, serving a diverse student body, or having a library staff that more nearly reflects the cultural or ethnic background of the student body it serves. At present, librarians

Holley R. Lange is a Catalog Librarian and Chris Nelson is an Assistant Professor of Art History at Colorado State University in Fort Collins, Colorado.

in academic institutions tend to mirror the traditionally predominant culture, and even the most diverse staff cannot possibly reflect the wide diversity of the world around them. However, librarians can develop an informed understanding of others and provide their students and faculty with appropriate resources. We must seek new resources, or, particularly in today's world of decreasing budgets and rising costs, look at existing resources with imagination and creativity to see how they might serve new needs.

Although the printed word is a powerful force, predominating virtually all fields of knowledge, other media can provide important and complementary alternatives. An image can speak instantly and intensively, transcending words. One specific medium, the poster, visually and cognitively reflects the time, place, and concerns in effect at its creation.

At Colorado State University a recently acquired resource, the International Poster Collection, provides a window to the world as only a visual medium can. While clearly valuable in the study of art history or graphic design, its international scope expands its value for it also can serve to complement or augment more traditional printed multinational and multicultural resources. This presentation will briefly introduce our poster collection, note some opportunities and challenges in accessing such a collection, discuss its place as a resource in today's academic library, and share the potential of some images in the collection.

While not sought as a specialized multicultural or multinational resource, the International Poster Collection serves this purpose ably as it spans nearly all the continents, representing almost forty countries as widespread as Mexico, Hungary, Japan, Zimbabwe, and the United States. Our collection of approximately 500 contemporary posters evolved out of the biennial Colorado International Invitational Poster Exhibition, an exhibition begun in 1979 and hosted by the Department of Art. Unique in the United States, the exhibition attracts entries by distinguished poster artists from around the world. In 1992 posters from the 1991

exhibition were transferred to the library with the agreement that those from subsequent shows would follow. The 1993 exhibition posters are now part of our collection as well.

Although this collection is unique, it may serve as an example to others seeking out new or additional multicultural or multinational resources. The focus here is the use of existing resources in new ways, for the poster collection, received from and considered primarily as a resource for the Department of Art, has potential to serve other audiences. The exhibition and the posters collected for it are part of an ongoing effort which will result in a collection that regularly captures worldwide issues and concerns as seen through the unique view of graphic designers.

Along with the positive benefits the collection brings, we are facing some challenges as well. Certainly such a collection is of little value if it cannot be used, but we must serve a dual role of promotor and protector, and devise appropriate means to access this oversized and sometimes fragile visual medium. In order to be used the posters must be accessible in a relatively indestructible format. We are in the process of making the images and their descriptions available through Kodak Photo-CD, with on-going experiments in providing access through the Internet via the World Wide Web and Mosaic, with on-campus access limitations. If these are to be active resources rather than archived materials they must be used, not just warehoused.

Once the posters are easily and dependably available we can encourage our students and faculty to broaden their traditionally print-based focus by using these materials as part of their teaching and learning. As Bunting notes, scholars in many disciplines are seeking to bring together "a variety of material and desire to see this material treated as integral parts of the culture or society which has produced it."[2] Certainly poster art can serve this purpose ably. We are creating descriptive records, which have their base in traditional cataloging, but will go further and eventually will be expanded to provide information on the artist, time period, background to the event, work, or person that is the subject of the poster, as well as a digital representation of the poster itself. The image, visually powerful, will be all the more strengthened with the addition of this information.

Posters from the collection speak from and to a variety of cultural and national views, and in this way can serve as an appropriate resource in examining or exemplifying multicultural or multinational issues. These contemporary posters from around the world focus on global concerns such as poverty, AIDS, human rights, the environment and world peace. Distinct national characteristics persist and the posters reflect their country of origin, representing as well a multitude of ethnic, political and religious backgrounds. The collection includes a variety of images that may provide social or political commentary, announce a film, opera, or exhibition, or promote a product or an artist, providing a global perspective on today's events or concerns. Our posters could serve to spark discussions on multicultural issues, demonstrate a broad range of national interests, or foster an understanding of differences and similarities. While all posters do not deal with dramatic or controversial subjects, they do lend a powerful and alternative visual statement, as the following examples will illustrate.

Four posters in the 1993 Poster Exhibition were created by graphic designers from France, Germany and the United States for the quincentennial of Columbus' voyage across the Atlantic in 1492. These challenge more traditional views of the voyage and the man. A photographic image of a Native American, defaced by a marker to make the face appear skull-like, includes the text "Celebrate Columbus, 1492-1992."[3] In another, an Aztec armed with both machine gun and traditional shield, is accompanied by the text "500 Years of Indian, Black and Popular Resistance."[4] A third poster incorporates only the letterforms of the "Coca-Cola" trademark, spelling instead "Christopher-Columbus," with the full text "For 500 Years Christopher Columbus has Enjoyed America!"[5] The last "Columbus" poster

consists of the image of a potato peel, titled "Tartufolo Bianco," perhaps deriding the Spanish identification of the potato as a "tartufo bianco" or "white truffle."[6] Any one of these posters, or all taken together might spark contrasting reactions in different people, whether Native American, Mexican, North American, Spanish or Portuguese, but all could serve to initiate a discussion that might foster an understanding of alternative views of history. Further discussion might examine the posters for their perspective of an "across the world view" of these events, as perceived by one German and two French designers.

A particularly gripping poster depicts the sharp and menacing edge of racial prejudice through the word itself, for the only image is the word "racism" scrawled out in graffiti-like letters, the "C" forming an open red mouth with bared, sharp teeth.[7] Another poster, forcefully commenting on the issue of human rights, depicts a pig, with the words "human rights" emanating from its nether end, on which a world map is drawn, and where, most appropriately, a hole has been made in the poster[8]

The International Poster Collection documents political events worldwide, from the posters created by a Japanese artist addressing the nuclear accident at Chernobyl;[9] to one commenting on the Israeli occupation of Palestine;[10] to those that serve as visual manifestations of events in Eastern Europe and the former Soviet Union: a poster from Hungary titled "Tovarishchi Konets!" (Comrades, It's Over) shows the back of a man's head, a man in uniform;[11] a Russian poster with only a hammer and sickle bears the title "Rekviem" (Requiem);[12] and a rat trap with red-star bait from Hungary, is simply "'56.10.23."[13] A poster echoing fear, entitled "Pravda Pomnit' Avgust 19, 1991" (Pravda. Remember August 19,1991), the date of the coup against Gorbachev, shows Stalin's face and juxtaposed skeletons.[14]

Even film or music posters serve to foster recognition and understanding of differences and similarities. The international appeal of jazz is clear in the numerous posters dealing with festivals or performances. Jazz posters from Portugal, the Czech Republic, Poland, Switzerland, Mexico and the United States could be examined to look for common threads, or differences in imagery and style. Film festivals are another popular topic, from a promotional for the film "Stalin's Funeral,"[15] to festivals in Mexico, Zimbabwe, and Spain.

The International Poster Collection does not perfectly meet multicultural needs, and only a few of the many of the diverse populations that make up our national mosaic are included. The collection is, however, broadly international in scope and in topic. It demonstrates how existing materials acquired for other purposes could be put to new uses and how visual formats might augment traditional print formats in meeting the demands for multicultural and multinational resources. In our constantly changing world we must seek to understand both the familiar and the new. Appropriate resources, regardless of media, can reflect the cultural makeup of a student body, a nation, or the world, while demonstrating differences, and fostering discussion and understanding. This very visual medium, the poster, adds dimension to the learning experience, reflecting culture and understanding through the power of imagery. The International Poster Collection meets the challenge of providing additional multicultural and multinational resources as we seek to utilize and promote existing resources in new ways.

NOTES

1. Heitor Gurgulino de Souza. "Multiculturalism and the New World Order," *National Geographic Research & Exploration* 8:261 (Summer 1992).
2. Christine Bunting "Questioning Representation: When Art History Becomes Visual Culture," *Visual Resources,* 10:63 (1993).
3. Poster by James Victore, New York City, N.Y., 1992.
4. Poster by Fanch LeHanaff, Brittany, France, 1992.
5. Poster by T. A. Lewandowski, France, 1992.
6. W. G. Burton. *The Potato.* 3rd. ed. Harlow, Essex, England: Longman Scientific & Technical, 1989. p. 15; Poster by Gunter Rambow, Germany, 1992.
7. Poster by James Victore, New York City, N.Y., [1992?]
8. Poster by Helmut Feliks Buttner, Germany, 1993.
9. Poster by Yoshiteru Asai, Japan, *Never Leave Tragic Chernobyl*, [1992?]
10. Poster by David Tartakover, Israel, *Danger-Frontie[r A]head-No Passage*, 1992.
11. Poster by Istvan Orosz, Hungary, [1990?]
12. Poster by Valeria Kourigina, Russia, 1990.
13. Poster by Peter Pocs, Hungary, 1989.
14. Poster by James Thorpe, College Park, MD, [1991?]
15. Poster by Yuri Bokser, Russia, 1991.

Contributed Papers

Society, Economics, and Politics

Winning the War:
A Framework for Selecting Electronic Sources of Government Information and Making Them Available

Debora Cheney

ABSTRACT

Charles Seavey has argued that libraries are not prepared to provide access to non-bibliographic information available in electronic formats. It is true that many libraries have been less than successful in providing access to electronic formats of government information. This paper puts this failure into a historical perspective and suggests that, if libraries are to be successful making these sources available, they must create a vision for making these sources available in their library. Using the Seven Rules of Access as a guide, libraries can avoid many of the pitfalls inherent in trying to collect and provide access to electronic sources of government information while also trying to create a vision that is appropriate for each library and its users. Finally, libraries must be prepared to evaluate each electronic source within a recommended Evaluation Framework before adding the source to its collections or providing access in order to ensure that the library's vision for these sources is achieved.

Recently in an article in *American Libraries*, Charles Seavey (Associate Professor, University of Arizona Graduate Library School in Tucson) argued that libraries are not prepared to provide access to non-bibliographic information available in electronic formats. In general, Seavey assails libraries for not providing access to the wide range of government information distributed via the Depository Library Program (DLP) on CD-ROM, in particular the *1990 Census of Population and Housing*.[1] It is true that many libraries have been less than successful in providing access to the *1990 Census on CD-ROM*.[2] However it is necessary to put this into historical perspective and to move on from there to provide an Evaluation Framework for libraries to use so they can win the war against electronic government information.

Debora Cheney is the Head of the Documents/Maps Section of the Pattee Library at The Pennsylvania State University in University Park, Pennsylvania.

HISTORY REPEATS ITSELF

History has begun to repeat itself. The growth in the number of government information sources in electronic formats is the latest step in a growing progression away from paper documents and toward non-print formats in documents collections. This continues a trend, begun in 1978, when microfiche were first distributed to depository libraries. In the case of microfiche, libraries were very concerned about this change in format, and many libraries, at that time were simply unprepared to provide adequate access to these materials. However, over time libraries were able to adjust to microfiche and are now able to make a bad situation bear less heavily on library users by reexamining many of their service priorities and preconceived ideas about this format.

Depository libraries are required to treat depository microfiche just as they treat paper publications they must: catalog, process, and provide access (either by circulating or providing a wide variety of viewing and duplicating equipment) for these materials.[3] Despite the initial need to play catch-up, libraries are now more prepared than are users to handle and use microfiche. Generally, users have never fully accepted microfiche, and studies show that most users will avoid microfiche entirely.[4] Yet, most depository libraries can truly be credited with making the best of a very difficult situation. In short, depository libraries have not themselves become a barrier to the government information contained in microfiche format.

In 1988, just as depository libraries and library users had settled into "status quo," the first electronic formats arrived via the DLP. As before, the growth in the number and variety of electronic formats has taken librarians and users by surprise. Yet, the concerns and need to grapple with these new formats remains the same: print, and now, microfiche, publications are being replaced by electronic formats. While many government agencies view electronic sources as a more effective way to make information available to the public or a way to reduce paperwork, libraries and librarians are sadly aware that, in fact, these formats often

present significant barriers to the information, particularly in this transition period. Until every home is connected to the Internet or until other locations, such as post offices, provide access to the Internet, libraries may be the only avenue of access for many Americans.[5] Yet, in some cases, the sources are so useful to many library users that it has become increasingly more imperative that all libraries, just as Seavey points out, be able to provide access to these materials. As they did previously with microfiche, libraries will need to set aside institutional problems and preconceived ideas about these materials or they, too, may become an additional barrier to information available in electronic format. Libraries must be aware that the role of many libraries within their community or academic institution may not be completely fulfilled without providing access at some level to electronic information. For these reasons, the costs and the stakes are even higher with these new formats.

Higher Costs—Higher Stakes

Electronic formats "contain the very seeds of destruction for the old order of public information distribution embodied in the scheme of depository libraries."[6]

As the DLP evaluates its role and how it will function in an information infrastructure that is increasingly electronic-based, the costs of providing access to electronic information and each library's stake in this change are increasing. The stakes are higher because the move toward electronic formats has transferred much of the cost of making government information available to the public onto the library, and, in some cases, to the user, to a degree not previously experienced. It is said that libraries spend ten dollars for every federal dollar spent on the DLP.[7] Electronic formats have surely raised that figure another notch; libraries still must process, house, and provide reference service to these sources, but there are additional costs to libraries as well:

- to provide equipment (including computers and printers) and supplies (such as paper and ribbons for users to convert the information back into a paper format) to access these sources;

- to provide telecommunication connections to online sources (either direct dial-up access or via the Internet, the World Wide Web (WWW), or Gophers);
- to provide professional staff experienced enough and knowledgeable enough to deal with these formats (this may be librarians and/or technical support staff);
- to provide training for staff and for library users;
- to provide labor intensive user support at reference desks;
- to identify, evaluate, plan, and prepare access to these sources;
- to publicize these new sources.

Libraries find themselves in the awkward position of trying to ameliorate the costs user's are experiencing while grappling with the increased costs to themselves and doing so within an environment of ever fewer resources.

The stakes are also higher because traditional avenues of distribution, such as the DLP, can not be relied upon to provide copies of (in the case of CD-ROMs and floppy disks) or access to (in the case of electronic bulletin boards (EBBs), or gopher or WWW sites) many electronic sources. In his article in *American Libraries*, Seavey focuses on government information on CD-ROM available via the DLP. However, these sources are "a drop in the bucket" of the total number and variety of sources libraries should consider making accessible in their libraries. Today, most electronic sources are only available directly from government agencies, not via the DLP. For example, look at two publication lists: the *CD-ROMs & Optical Discs Available from NTIS* and the *SIGCAT CD-ROM Compendium*. Most of the titles listed are not distributed via the DLP. In 1991 government agencies offered more than 60 EBBs[8] alone and only two had been made available via the DLP—the Department of Commerce's *EBB* and the Gov-

ernment Printing Office's *Federal Bulletin Board*. The growth of the Internet and use of gophers and the WWW to provide access to online sources, since the beginning of 1993 alone, has raised this number dramatically and presented a new challenge for libraries and for users. Title 44 limits GPO's role to largely receiving sources (largely paper and microfiche) that agencies choose to distribute via the DLP. GPO has few enforcement powers to force agencies to include "fugitive" sources. More important, however, is the fact that a great deal of disagreement exists over whether electronic sources even fall under the purview of Title 44 at all. In short, GPO cannot be expected to make electronic sources available in the 1,400 depository libraries, let alone in the many non-depository libraries that could make use of these sources.

The stakes are also higher because a growing number of print and, now, microfiche publications are being replaced by electronic equivalents (for example, *Current Industrial Reports* and the data tables from *Business Statistics*). Other titles are heading in this direction: the *Congressional Record*, the *Federal Register*, the *U.S. Code* are now being made available in electronic formats in accordance with the GPO Access legislation.[9]

The stakes are also higher because libraries are faced with providing access to a wider:

- variety of electronic formats (including floppy disks, CD-ROMs, and EBBs);
- range of information types (including numeric, microdata, bibliographic, a mix of bibliographic and numeric, full text, graphic, and multi-media);
- range of software interfaces (including menu-driven and command-driven).

Because of the variety of formats libraries are waging the "access" battle on several fronts. Take, for example, the *1990 Census of Population and Housing*, libraries must now consider whether gopher (including access from home and/or library), the WWW, CD-ROM, or print access is most effective or useful for our library users. In fact, we may need a variety of these avenues of access in order to serve the diverse needs of our user populations. Yet, each presents unique challenges.

In short, providing access to government information in electronic formats is a significant challenge for even the most well-funded, well-staffed, and highly-automated library. For those libraries with significantly less funding, automation, and staff the challenge can seem insurmountable. (In hindsight, it makes microfiche seem downright simple.)

Many libraries were not and still are not prepared, as Seavey points out, to provide access to electronic-formatted sources. However, the speed with which this development has come upon libraries <u>and</u> the magnitude of the problem means that libraries may now be playing "catch up" just as they did in 1978 with microfiche. However, if libraries are to win the war against electronic government information sources, the first step is to find ways to meet the challenge these sources present.

HOW TO WIN THE WAR

... the "silvery disk symbolizes a new and startling age of 'usefulness' for public information"[10]

In general, government information and publications have always possessed an aura of "being different." Even the most seasoned reference librarian blanches at the thought of working at the government documents reference desk. Government publications are perceived as different, difficult, overwhelming, yet necessary (particularly in some disciplines), and sanctified because they are public records—because they are, in some sense, a symbol of the principle of freedom of information that lies at the heart of our Constitution and political system. (Many librarians would characterize them as necessary evils). If computer technology (another societal "sacred cow") is added

into this mix, government information in electronic format can seem to be overwhelmingly powerful, necessary, and useful.

Yet, not all information is equally useful to all users and this is particularly true of government information in electronic format. Libraries must evaluate each electronic source on its own merits. Only then can the need for the information (based on user needs); the ability to support that information source (based on staff, availability of equipment, administrative support); and its accessibility (based on the user interface, information format) be evaluated in each library on its own merits, not simply on the aura of its appearance (shiny), format (electronic), and origin (the government). in order to effectively evaluate electronic sources, each library must create a vision for making these sources available that is appropriate for that library.

CREATE A VISION: THE SEVEN RULES OF ACCESS

Perhaps the single most important step in making electronic formats of government information available in any library is a vision of how these sources can be made accessible. The following rules provide some guidance in developing that vision. They also provide libraries with approaches that can be used to avoid the pitfalls inherent in electronic sources of government information: the poor (or nonexistent) software interfaces, the lack of user support, the lack of documentation, and the wide range of database types. Each of these pitfalls can present significant challenges for libraries and major stumbling blocks in creating a vision. Yet, despite the challenges they present, electronic sources also offer some advantages. For example, they save space, they allow libraries to provide access to sources they may not previously have been able to provide, they provide libraries and librarians with a new and exciting role, and they can provide faster access to information.

Rule 1. Collect for your users

The population each library serves has specific characteristics. Keep the following in mind when selecting electronic sources:

- what your users need and want;
- the skill level of your users;
- the type of users you serve (students, elderly, children, business people, etc.);
- role of the library within its "community."

Academic libraries operate within an educational framework. For this reason, they may implement sources because faculty would like their students exposed to particular sources. Public libraries operate within a service environment. Sources such as the *HCFA CD-ROM* (Health Care Finance Administration) that might be implemented in an academic library might not be appropriate for users who are unfamiliar with reading laws and regulations and would be more comfortable with a phone number to a regional office to answer a personal question.

Rule 2. Implement selectively

Many librarians are overwhelmed by the great number of government electronic sources. However, just as libraries must collect print sources within the confines of their budget and collection development statements, so too, should electronic sources be collected. To do so, begin by selecting and implementing a few sources before expanding to include a greater number.[11] Also first implement those that are easiest to use and support and will be used by the greatest number of users. Consider the following:

- depth of the collection in specified subject areas;
- the curriculum (if an academic institution);
- computing resources available;[12]
- where the library would like to expand and develop its electronic resources (CD-ROMs, gopher access, WWW access);

- available non-computing resources—staff and budgets (not just in collections, but also those that support equipment and staff).

Every collection has strengths and electronic sources can complement and enhance a library's collection. Don't expect to collect every source or subscribe to every *EBB*, if you rarely need these sources or have the information available in other sources. Use your collection development policy to highlight those areas where electronic sources can make the biggest contribution.

Consider also where the library would like to expand and develop its electronic resources. Which electronic formats is it best able to support—CD-ROMs, online database, floppy disks? Can the library's catalog serve as a gateway to other systems? Can the library provide telnet, gopher, or WWW access? Seavey is right: many more libraries should be providing access to the electronic forms of the *1990 Census of Population and Housing*. However, there are many ways to do so. Each library should evaluate which is most effective for its users.

Rule 3. Circulate, Circulate, Circulate

Circulating electronic formats allows you to provide access to these sources without having to provide the technical support, hardware, and software needed to use the information. In addition, some electronic sources simply cannot and should not be installed on a public workstation, yet they may be a valuable addition to your collection. For example, the Energy Department's floppy disk files.

Create policies and procedures for circulating these materials. The goodwill created by making these materials available to users is an extremely positive role for libraries—users appreciate it. If electronic sources are circulated exactly as print sources are, your circulation policies for replacement of lost, damaged, or late materials can be used.

Rule 4. Train, Train, Train

Your staff's support for these new sources will be a direct corollary of your ability to help them understand the sources you select and make available. Nothing frustrates and makes staff feel more helpless than not being able to answer a user's basic questions about a source. Training takes a lot of time, but the workload can be distributed among your staff using some creative approaches. Empower your staff by:

- creating an "information sheet" for each source selected with basic information (title, call number, location, whether it circulates, its content, software interface, availability of documentation, print equivalents) about each source;[13]
- making them "owners" of specific titles—have them learn how to use, prepare user aids, and train other staff to use this title; be sure to give them credit for this work by including their names on the user aids and mentioning it in their annual evaluations;
- providing them with a way out when users need more information than they can provide by making your business cards available at the reference desk so they can give these to users who need or want more information than they can provide;
- holding regular "shop talk" sessions that focus on a single sources; schedule these during department meetings or during quiet times during the year.

If your staff are well-trained or at least have a positive attitude toward these formats, it will be much easeir to "train" your library users.

Rule 5. Develop simple procedures for making documentation and user aids available

Every electronic format should have some form of documentation to provide information about the information supplied, its structure, the user interface, and how to install the source. Government sources are notoriously lax in providing this documentation in a print format with the source itself. However, the documentation is often available in EBB text files (.txt), in CD-ROM and floppy disk readme.bat files, and from the agencies themselves. Libraries will need to develop simple approaches for providing themselves and their users with this information.

- purchase documentation, if available, rather than printing it from the source (especially, if you do not have access to a laser printer or good word processing capabilities). For example, the *Monthly Products Announcements* frequently list documentation that can be purchased for Census Bureau sources.
- don't reinvent the wheel. If user aides are available from other libraries or commercial vendors or on the source itself, use these sources or modify them to your own library's needs. The Government Documents Roundtable (GODORT) Handout Exchange is an excellent source of sample user aides for electronic sources of government information.[14]
- focus your efforts on the sources you will be making available on public workstations in the library. For example, don't spend a lot of time printing out the read.me file for every floppy disk and CD-ROM source, if these sources are only going to circulate. Note the presence of the files on the "Information sheet" you prepare for each title and be prepared to help the user read them, **if** a user needs your help.
- learn some basic DOS commands to make it possible to determine which of the above approaches is appropriate for each source.

Clearly, providing documentation for these sources is a significant challenge for most libraries, however, there are ways to approach this problem to make it more manageable.

Rule 6. Create Partnerships

Electronic sources present unique opportunities to develop partnerships with other areas of the library and the organization. Electronic government information crosses into every discipline.

This is an opportunity to provide the Business Library or the Health Sciences Library with sources they may be willing to implement with their users in mind. Similarly, electronic sources present new opportunities to develop relationships with computing services on campus or other libraries. You may be able to gain support from others simply by implementing the *1990 Census of Population and Housing* on CD-ROM using the Census Bureau's user-friendly GO software interface. This interface essentially provides a page turner approach to all Census Summary Tape Files (STF) CD-ROMs. If users can select their town and the data they need from lists, they can use the GO software. For some users it is easier to use than the printed volumes and certainly takes less space, if the hardware is available. The GO software allows users to download and print data and it is easy to install (type GO at the DOS prompt). At universities, computing service offices are frequently overwhelmed with requests to access Census STF data on computer tape. However, these requests are frequently backed up because this requires programming to pull specific data from computer tapes for researchers and students. These requests may also receive lower priority for a vareity of reasons (amount of data needed; the status of the requestor; familiarity with the STF tapes; etc.). Also many computer programmers don't necessarily understand Census data, and users may be requesting data that may not be appropriate for their research question. Libraries can provide this support role and the data itself with the CD-ROM. The CD-ROM equivalents of the STFs give researchers more control over the data and the ability to download that data themselves. The GO software allows users who want only a few data items to retreive that data quickly and easily. Users will be happier and so will computing services staff. And you will be providing a much needed service. For users with more complex Census data needs, it may be necessary to provide more flexible downloading access. Again, libraries have many options: to implement *Extract* software; to purchase a product such as Wessex's *Pro/Filer* software and data;

to provide access to *DBase*; to circulate the CD-ROM; to send users to computing services; or to send them to another library better equipped to handle such questions (having established that partnership first, of course).

Rule 7. Take on a New Role

Electronic sources of government information create a new role for libraries and librarians. The library is a key gateway to these sources that many users simply cannot access on their own. However, be aware that you cannot be an expert on every government source. You can be an advisor and educator about this information. Frequently users do not need or want information in electronic formats; they do not need the raw data but rather a summary or analysis of that data; they do not understand the limits of the data they are using. Each of these situations presents an opportunity for libraries to advise and help users with the information they are seeking. For example, catalog records for electronic sources in your library's catalog will result in requests for these sources. Don't panic. Frequently users simply want a single statistic contained in the print equivalent of the electronic source. For this reason, take care to note print equivalents in your Information Sheet for each title.

Once a vision has been created for making electronic formats of government information available, it will be necessary to ensure that the unique needs of these sources are considered and provided for, including the different needs of different formats, the physical surroundings, service demands (staffing levels, education, location), and access needs (cataloging and processing) evaluate each source to determine its suitability for each library.[15] Finally, a framework for evaluating sources is also needed.

USE THE EVALUATION FRAMEWORK

Because of the institutional environment, making electronic source available in any library presents unique challenges beyond those an individual may experience if implementing the same source on their home or office computer. Libraries will want to ask several basic questions about each electronic sources in order to have the information necessary to enact the Seven Rules of Access for their particular library. These questions are:

- What information does this source provide?
- Who was the information originally intended for?
- How easy is this source to use and support?
- What kind of equipment is needed to make this source available?
- Is this information available in other formats?
- What does my library and its user's lose or gain by making this source available?

What information does this source provide?

As we know, electronic formats of government information are just as likely to provide numeric data, images, full-text, bibliographic, or a mix of any of these types on a single source (dubbed: "electronic file drawers").[16] For this reason the type of information provided by a given electronic source should be carefully evaluated before a library commits to a particular electronic format. Of the wide variety of sources available, probably the electronic file drawer sources, such as the *NTDB CD-ROM* (National Trade Databank) *NESE DB* CD-ROM (National Economic, Social, and Environmental Data Bank), are the most versatile and useful to libraries simply because they contain a wide variety of sources and data types.

For example, the *NESE DB* includes the full-text of 90 sources, including the *Health Security Act* and the *Toxic Release Inventory*, and selected data tables from the *Statistical Abstract* and the *1990 Census* (sources that are also available in print and in other electronic formats). The main advantages of electronic file drawer sources are that they provide users with the text of a number of different sources related to common subject or theme (economic, social, and the environment, in this case); they provide a single user interface for all of these sources that allows cross-source search-

ing; they can more easily be added to local area networks; they provide downloading and printing capabilities; user aids and documentation are more readily accessible (since most of these sources have been designed with the public in mind); and they provide CD-ROM access to sources that are also available on gophers and electronic bulletin boards—formats that may be less accessible to some libraries and users. In libraries that do not have extensive collections and limited staff resources, electronic file drawer sources are good choices for making a lot of government information available in an electronic format. Electronic file drawer sources can be viewed as "back-ups" to print sources; they are also a way to begin familiarizing users and staf with electronic sources.[17]

Who was the information intended for?

"... government information products are produced and designed for very specific, or narrow purposes:.... Very rarely are they thought of, designed, tested, refined, and distributed with the general public specifically in mind."[18]

More frequently these sources are intended to "streamline (or reduce) an agency's paper work"; "take advantage of technologies or administrative environments"; or respond to the "limited needs of a special interest group or economic interest with direct ties to the agency's program."[19] The agency's intended audience for each source influences the interface supplied with the source, the structure of the database, and its content. All of this may have an impact on whether the users in your library will be able to make use of a particular source. The intended audience also influences a source's ease of use and the level of staff support it will require.

How easy is this source to use and support?

John Shuler has provided readers with a way of categorizing CD-ROM interfaces that can be extended to all electronic formats. According to Shuler, interfaces can be:
- **basic** (intended audience: the computer literate and self sufficient)

Sources in this category include a wide range of, largely, raw data in ASCII (or other data type) format that is intended for users who will want to use the data for further analysis, but are most likely to use their own statistical analysis package (SAS, LOTUS, DBASE, etc.).

- **limited: "electronic page turners"** (intended audience: the general public)

Sources in this category include a number of electronic equivalents of the same information in paper of microfiche format. The interface is easy to use and limited in its ability to download and display data. The GO software offered by the Census Bureau is an excellent example of software that allows users to electronically turn the pages of census data.

- **enhanced** (intended audience: agency staff, subject specialists)

Sources in this category include a number of electronic sources (CD-ROMs, in particular) that were developed to address staff needs within agencies or for specialized user groups. The interface is typically "relatively sophisticated" (usually the agency has contracted with a company to create a interface to be used with the source), and thus, may also be very useful in some libraries. These sources can allow libraries to make accessible a wide variety of specialized materials. However, libraries will need to selectively implement these sources based on their own library users. A medical library, for example, would make dramatically different choices from this category than a public library or academic library.[20]

Libraries should carefully evaluate the user interface. However, do not be dismayed or discouraged by interfaces in the "enhanced" category. Users are notoriously forgiving of computer interfaces and librarians (and staff) are extremely good at developing user aids to make sense of these sources.

Is this information available in other formats?

The most overlooked factor for evaluating electronic sources of government information is probably the availability of the same information in another format, including paper, microfiche, and other electronic formats. Take, for example, the *Federal Register*. The *Federal Register* is available in the following formats from government and commercial sources:

- paper
- microfilm and microfiche
- CD-ROM (Counterpoint)
- computer file
- online database (LEXIS, S W A I S / W A I S server Legi-Slate, WESTLAW)

The *Federal Register* can be accessed via a gopher, telnet, WAIS, FTP, and e-mail; it can be received abstracted, extracted, as full-text, and indexed. It is the ultimate example of government information available in every possible way and format.

Because government information is copyright free, commercial vendors are able to purchase the "raw" information and resell that information, often in a different format or with value-added interface, but not always.[21] Value-added information may include a user friendly interface, legal annotations, faster updates, more reliable receipt, statistical analysis, and multiple titles in one location with a single interface. However, commercial sources can also be less than the government sources (particularly where paper sources are involved, for example, the *Treasury Bulletin* on LEXIS does not include the tables that are an integral part of this source).

Of course, not all government information is as widely available as the *Federal Register*, but neither are all libraries as aware as they should be of the fact that same government information can often be found in a variety of sources, including paper sources. Publishers of business sources frequently repackage government data. For example, many people want Census data by zip code. This information is available on the STF 3B CD-ROM and can be displayed with the GO software. However, many commercial sources present this information much more effectively in print and electronic format. Nothing is necessarily gained by a library having the Census Bureau STF3B CD-ROM, if a commercial source serves the needs of your library's users. Libraries may be wise to avoid the costs of implementing the government source when a better-designed commercial equivalent is available. The hidden costs (usually in staff time and equipment) of making a government source available must be compared with the more visible costs of using the commercial version and weighed against your users needs.

What does my library and its users gain or lose by making this source available?

When GPO first began converting paper documents to microfiche there was, and still is, a great deal of concern about the use of this medium to supply materials that were entirely inappropriate for microfiche format (for example, loose-leaf volumes, numerical tables, maps).[22] Similarly, much information is being converted to electronic formats that is simply inappropriate for this format or where the user interface is inadequate to make effective use of the information. Probably the best example of this was the GPO Pilot Project for the *Congressional Record on CD-ROM*. By itself, the software interface provided with this important source was so difficult to use that it threatened to make this key source almost entirely inaccessible.

Libraries also should take care to ensure that the electronic version of a government information source is appropriate for the information itself and that the user interface provides the necessary searching capabilities to make use of the information. In some cases, print, or even microfiche equivalents, may actually provide greater access to the information or be more appropriate for certain users.

For example, libraries that are providing access to LEXIS, WESTLAW or Legi-Slate or who have print copies of the *U.S. Code* may want to consider carefully whether they want to implement the *U.S. Code on CD-ROM* in their library. It duplicates information already available in other formats and it does not provide as much information, as, for example, the *United States Code Service* (USCS) (Lawyer's Co-operative) or the *United States Code Annotated* (USCA) (West Publishing Company). However, a library that has not been able to afford USCA, USCS, LEXIS, WESTLAW, or Legi-Slate, but would like to provide access to the *U.S. Code* to its users, should carefully consider the *U.S. Code on CD-ROM*—the price is right ($34) and the interface is fairly straightforward (however, it does require *Windows*) keeping in mind that it is not being updated on a regular schedule despite GPO's best intentions.

In a complex world, decisions are always based on many factors. In addition, each library will weight the questions in the Evaluation Framework differently. For example, the need to provide a user-friendly interface may far outweigh the content of an electronic source in some libraries. Regardless of how individual items within the Evaluation Framework are weighted, it can be combined with the Seven Rules of Access in each library to help libraries evaluate electronic sources of government information and make decisions about how they will make those sources available in their libraries.

CONCLUSION

There are many good reasons for ensuring that electronic formats of government information are available in libraries, including: many print sources are disappearing and information is only available in electronic format; electronic formats provide additional access and flexibility (for example, keyword searching and more frequent updating); they can save space, they can make it possible to make previously unavailable sources accessible in your library, and, perhaps most importantly, libraries have a commitment to providing government information to the people. Yet libraries can fulfil this commitment at different levels based on the needs of their users and collections and the capabilities of their staff and budgets by beginning to evaluate these sources carefully withing the Evaluation Framework and Seven Rules of Access. Libraries should treat electronic sources just as they did paper and microfiche formats before them. Electronic sources should be cataloged, processed, and circulated just as all other library materials are. Libraries have always selected from a wide variety of sources. Now we must also select from a wide variety of formats—its all part of the job, if we are to win the war.

NOTES

1. Charles Seavey, Jr., "A Failure of Vision: Librarians are Losing the War for Electronic Professional Turf," *American Libraries* 24(November 1993):943-44.

2. Based on a recent survey, depository libraries have made the transition from print to electronic sources. According to GPO, "Depository libraries have made enormous progress in positioning themselves to serve the public with eletronic government information." See J.D. Young, "Report on the Electronic Capabilities Survey," *Administrative Notes* 15(November 25, 1994):8-16.

3. The summary of the 1989 *Biennial Survey* (the most recent summary available) shows that libraries in nearly every category are providing fiche readers. Many libraries also provide reader/printers and a few provide fiche duplicators. See, "Statistical Profile of Depository Libraries Based on the 1989 *Biennial Survey*," *Administrative Notes* 11(August 31, 1990): 15-23. See also the *Federal Depository Library Manual* (Washington, D.C.: Government Printing Office, 1993) and the *Instructions to Depository Libraries* (Washington, D.C.: Government Printing Office, 1992).

4. Patricia Reeling, Mary Fetzer, and Daniel O'Connor, "Use of Government Publications in an Academic Setting," *Government Publications Review* 18(September/October 1991): 489-515.

5. Depository libraries are extremely well-positioned to play this role, "80-90% of all depository libraries have PC's, CD-ROM, and access to the Internet." See Young, "Report on the Electronic Capabilities Survey (1994)," 10.

6. John A. Shuler, "Democracy on a Disc," *CD-ROM Librarian* 7(November 1992):27.

7. U.S. Office of Technology Assessment. *Informing the Nation: Federal Information Dissemination in the Electronic Age*. Washington, D C: Government Printing Office, 1988.

8. For a list of EBBs, see Florence Olsen, "Bulletin Boards Give Users the Line on Federal Info," *Administrative Notes* 12(June 30, 1991):20-23.

9. "Government Printing Office Electronic Information Access Enhancement Act of 1993," (PL 103-40, 8 June 1993), 107 *United States Statutes at Large*, pp. 112-114.

10. Shuler, "Democracy on a Disk (1992)," 27.

11. Robert E. Dugan and Anthony Cipriano, "Making it Happin in a Depository Library: Those Pesky CD-ROMs," *Government Information Quarterly* 10(number 3): 341-355.

12. Elizabeth Stephenson, "Public Service for Numeric Data Files: Issues for Depository Librarians," Paper presented at the *Public Service for Numeric Datafiles: Issues for Depository Librarians*. Preconference sponsored by the International Association for Social Science Information Service & Technology (IASSIST), February 3, 1994, Los Angeles, CA.

13. Debora Cheney, "Information Sheet" in "Electronic Corner: Readers Exchange," *Administrative Notes: Newsletter of the Federal Depository Library Program* 14(February 15, 1993): 7-8.

14. Larry Romans, "GODORT Education Committee Handout Exchange," *DTTP* (Documents to the People) 22(September 1994):170-72.

15. See the "Checklist for Providing Access to Electronic Formats," in Debora Cheney, "Technology in Document Collections." Diane Smith, ed., *Management of Government Information Resources in Libraries* (Englewood, CO: Libraries Unlimited, 1993), 123.

16. John Shuler, "Democracy on a Disc," *CD-ROM World* 8(January 1993):66.

17. Dugan and Cipriano, 346-47.

18. Shuler, "Democracy on a Disk (1992)," 28.

19. Ibid., 28.

20. Ibid., 28-29.

21. For a discussion and examples of how commercial vendors resell government information, see Daniel Gross, "Byting the Hand That Feeds Them: Information Vendors Are Robbing the Government Blind," *Washington Monthly* 23 (November 1991):37-41.

22. Herbert B. Landau, "Microform vs. CD-ROM: Is There a Difference," *Library Journal* 115 (October 1, 1990): 59.

Outsourcing Library Production:
The Leader's Role

Carroll H. Varner

ABSTRACT

An opportunity for leadership is present now through outsourcing of technical services activities. Creative management of the academic library's technical services subculture is needed. Outsourcing offers advantages in cost and efficiency, but it is the possibilities for structural change which will greatly affect technical services personnel. There are strong cultural taboos against radical changes such as outsourcing within the library. Careful analysis to identify productive change processes is a role for librarians motivated to choose more fulfilling future activities for themselves and for staff. A new shared vision and mental model is then possible. The key to the process is staff development.

For librarians, outsourcing the production functions in technical services is, to use a Yogi Berra phrase, an "insurmountable opportunity." The opportunity for progress is present, but an indefinable something holds us back. That something is the web of common understandings and values which make up the academic library culture.

Technical services librarians are seeing very rapid developments at OCLC and among vendors which may soon create the opportunity for a non-technical services librarian to order books directly from the vendor using a personal computer. All the necessary fund accounting will occur automatically when the book is ordered. If it is already in the collection or on order, the librarian will be told to give a specific override command. When the book is shipped to the library, the OCLC catalog record will go into the library's online public access catalog as "on order" and when it is received at the library, both funding and cataloging records will be updated automatically. The librarian and the faculty member who requested the book will be notified by the system that the book is available once a barcode, shelving label, and ownership stamps are applied.

While this process seems simple to achieve given the new technology, there are very powerful cultural taboos within the organization which ex-

Carroll H. Varner is Associate University Librarian for Administrative and Technical Services at Illinois State University in Normal, Illinois.

plain why the new materials production paradigm will be resisted. The current method of acquiring, cataloging, and delivering books and journals is the domain of specialists within our libraries. In analyzing the subculture of technical services within the larger academic library culture, the basic assumption for these specialists is that their roles are valuable and should be preserved. They have come to identify their roles in the process, not the product of their labor, as the important part of the activity. Their artifacts, assumptions, and values are based on believing that their role is an important and integral part of the organization's mission and their subculture will resist any indication otherwise. This is a natural part of institutional growth and development. Meddling with a system which to the minds of the technical services personnel isn't broken is not advisable.

The case that will be made when outsourcing is proposed is that the current system is familiar, productive, and performs the service adequately. A challenge to this basic assumption releases extreme anxiety and defensiveness. Woodsworth and Williams state in their book on outsourcing,

> The tension in this work that results from differing values systems and beliefs are deeply rooted. For that reason we anticipate that portions of this book may engender strong reaction and counter-arguments from those who disagree with the models we have proposed and would argue to be the future for successful information resource managers. We welcome this debate.

However, if librarians consider it a "debate" or a "tension", the individuals within the departments consider it more a threat to their self worth, their value in the organization, and ultimately, to their very livelihood. How then, do academic library leaders assist the transition from ownership processes into outsourcing contracts and then into new access roles for librarians?

THEORY

The culture of any organization acts as a primary resistance to change. Individuals do not want to give up the stability of their daily lives. Analyzing the technical services subculture reveals that all the motivation and control systems, as well as the deeper values of organizational stability, are based upon the materials ownership and production processes. Changes which challenge these processes result in culture shock!

A number of theoretical descriptions of organizational structures have been described which shed light on the academic library culture and offer new ways to accomplish the organizational goals. Among them are the clan , the organized anarchy, and the loosely coupled structure in addition to the traditional professional hierarchy. In each, the library culture has positive ways to accomplish tasks as well as control mechanisms for keeping its members focused on the existing processes - the status quo. Newer structures seek to find ways to assist innovation such as outsourcing and to release control of the processes from the technical services librarians and staff.

Librarians faced with outsourcing, or contracting out, or exporting of production functions, react against the hierarchical control mechanisms of the academic library. They usurp the control of the organization's resources through a process called "ritualization of procedures." Ritualization, or continuation of familiar procedures in spite of good reasons to the contrary, makes the technical services staff secure in their work, prevents retraining, and maintains their expert status. The library production function becomes inefficient and loses its effectiveness in meeting faculty collection development needs.

The organization becomes ill. In 1986, David Lewis described a new way of operating dependent on outsourcing to cure this illness. He said,

"By exporting much of the production part of what academic libraries do, there will be less conflict between the parts of the organization that must be structured for production and the parts of the organization that are structured to provide information services to the members of the academic community. The export of production functions will make academic library organizations less schizophrenic."

The malaise still threatens many academic libraries. The question then for the leader is, "How can roles, structures, and leadership be altered to take advantage of the opportunities outsourcing presents while reducing the stress to the technical services subculture?"

RESEARCH

Many studies of library structures and library leadership have been completed in the last decade. They provide the research framework in

which to analyze and understand the production functions in a particular library technical services subculture. A thorough understanding of the meaning of the processes allows one to evaluate how and why the subculture's efforts run counter to the library's interests or, more importantly, where they have common ground. It is the common ground, the information products, whether print or electronic, that must be emphasized over the process.

The analyses of library processes are ongoing with OCLC as the focus. The work of Glen Holt, is an example of analysis which seeks out the common ground. Whether providing books or access, the technical services role will continue to be important. He posits a new and positive role for librarians as "access managers" for libraries and patrons.

PRACTICE

The transformation of the technical services function and the technical services staff in academic libraries is an opportunity and challenge for today's academic library leaders. The production function utilizes a huge amount of organizational resources, both human and financial. The leader must first want to get involved with seeking better alternatives to the present system. The leader must

then create the organizational conditions which will mobilize the staff in technical services to begin applying new methods. Leaders must impress upon the technical services staff the imperative for each person to choose to build the new future. It cannot be a passive desire, but rather it is an active process of organizational change which results in a transformed system.

STAFF DEVELOPMENT

In the Power of Vision, Joel Barker explains that everyone needs to visualize a positive future for themselves. Communication of a positive future for the staff in the midst of extreme changes is part of the new role of administration. In fact, the new work of librarians in technical services may well be to analyze their operations and design new and better organizations.

They are responsible for building organizations where people continually expand their capabilities to understand complexity, clarify vision, and improve shared mental models - that is, they are responsible for learning.
Peter Senge

A new term for this process of focusing the staff on providing products and services, rather than on their own role in the process, is "informate," which sounds like "automate" but is subtly different. While "automate" means more efficiency through performing tasks with machines, îinformateî means to increase the value of our services by bringing the best information, and thus the most current, efficient processes to bear on our tasks to make them effective. It is the individual doing the task, and not the administrator, who must bring their best skill and knowledge to bear.

Cynthia Gozzi puts this need into clear perspective as a limiting factor, a hurdle, in the pursuit of a new processing environment. She says, "While there are many transferable skills, new information management and automation skill sets will need to be developed. This equates to a considerable need for training and staff development.î In his forthright article on re-engineering technical services, Arnold Hirshon projects for technical services librarians the role of "case workers responsible for identifying networked information resources, and providing customer training and outreach."

To overcome these barriers and arrive at a positive future, more attention should be given to the technical services subculture's development by academic library leadership. Greater efficiency may give rise to greater effectiveness, but it should also lead to a more participative academic library culture. Transformational leadership encourages individual leadership through staff development that creates new futures in the minds of the participants.

NOTES

1. For a complete discussion of the cultural analysis process, see Edgar H. Schein, *Organizational Culture and Leadership*, 2nd edition (San Francisco: Jossey-Bass, 1992).

2. Anne Woodsworth and James F. Williams, II, *Managing the Economics of Owning, Leasing and Contracting Out Information Services* (Brookfield, VT: Ashgate Pub., 1993):xiii.

3. See William G. Ouchi and Raymond L. Price, "Hierarchies, Clans, and Theory Z: A New Perspective on Organizational Development," *Organizational Dynamics* 7:35 (August, 1978).

4. See Michael D. Cohen and James G. March, *Leadership and Ambiguity* (Boston: Harvard Business School Press, 1974).

5. See Karl E. Weick, "Educational organizations as Loosely Coupled Systems," *Administrative Science Quarterly* 21 (March, 1976): 1-19.

6. Selwyn W. Becker and Duncan Neuhauser, *The Efficient Organization* (New York: Elsevier North-Holland, 1975).

7. David W. Lewis, "An organizational Paradigm for Effective Academic Libraries," *College and Research Libraries* 47 (July, 1986): 337-353.

8. See, for example, Helen A. Howard, "Organizational Structure and Innovation in Academic Libraries," *College and Research Libraries* 42 (Sept., 1981): 425-434.

9. Glen Holt, "Public Library Cataloging and Technical Services: Changing Work Because of Computers and Networks," in *The Future is Now: The Changing Face of Technical Services* (Dublin, OH: OCLC Online Computer Library Center, 1994): 21-27.

10. Michael Gorman, "A Good Heart and an Organized Mind: Leadership in Technical Services," in Donald E. Riggs, *Library Leadership: Visualizing the Future* (Phoenix, AZ: Oryx Press, 1982): 73-94.

11. Joel Barker, *The Power of Vision* (videorecording) (Burnsville, MN: Charthouse, 1990).

12. Peter M. Senge, *The Fifth Discipline: The Art & Practice of the Learning Organization* (New York: Doubleday, 1990): 340.

13. Shoshana Zuboff, *In the Age of the Smart Machine: The Future of Work and Power* (New York: Basic Books, 1984).

14. Cynthia I. Gozzi, "Technical Processing, Today and Tomorrow: A Scenario for One Large Research Library," in *The Future is Now: The Changing Face of Technical Services* (Dublin, OH: OCLC Online Computer Library Center, 1994): 28-32.

15. Arnold Hirshon, "The Lobster Quadrille: The Future of Technical Services in a Re-engineering World," in *The Future is Now: The Changing Face of Technical Services* (Dublin, OH: OCLC Online Computer Library Center, 1994): 14-20.

Panel Sessions

Panel Sessions
Knowledge Workers and Their Organizations

BENCHMARKING QUALITY LIBRARY SERVICE

Patricia M. Kelley, Eastern Washington University; Dona Hotopp, GOAL/QPC (Growth Opportunity Alliance of Lawrence/Quality, Productivity, Competitiveness); Sarah Pritchard, Smith College; Janet Fore, University of Arizona

As concern about quality and productivity of higher education sweeps the country, libraries recognize the need to measure and assess the quality of service to students and faculty. More accustomed to measuring our resources than our results, we struggle to identify key indicators of quality and ways to measure them. As we identify useful measures that can be understood by our own staff and will be acceptable to university administrators, governing boards and accrediting bodies, we still ask ourselves, How good is good enough? One way to address that question is benchmarking. Beginning with a consultant in benchmarking, we will address the why, what and how of benchmarking. The next speaker will discuss benchmarking in the context of academic libraries. The final speaker will propose benchmarking processes for key measures of quality in library services. Through active audience participation facilitated by ACRL Statistics Committee members, we will generate discussion and feedback to clarify issues so that we begin to form a consensus about key measures and their benchmarks.
Sponsored by the ACRL Statistics Committee

BEHAVIORAL STYLES OF LIBRARIANS: IMPLICATIONS FOR THE LIBRARY AS AN ORGANIZATION AND FOR RECRUITMENT AND RETENTION TO THE PROFESSION

Anne K. Beaubien, University of Michigan; Susan Jurow, Association of Research Libraries; Mary Jane Scherdin, Edgewood College

In this hands-on, interactive session, participants will complete a self-scoring Myers Briggs Type Indicator (MBTI) profile; get an immediate interpretation of their scores; learn how their own behavioral styles relate to their work as librarians; and explore organizational implications of the MBTI findings. Panelists will report new findings from analyses of MBTI, SII (Strong Interest Inventory), and demographic data done since the 1992 program at the ALA annual conference. This is data gathered from a study of 2000 librarians conducted by the ACRL Vocational Interest Inventories Task Force in 1992, and funded by ACRL, the ALA Office of Library Personnel Resources, and Consulting Psychologists Press. Panelists will address questions such as "What are the common traits of persons new to the profession?" "How do these differ from the defining behaviors of those long established in their careers?" "How do librarians compare to the general population or to other professionals on these points?" Participants will focus on how behavioral styles come into play when issues of recruitment and retention are being considered. They will also be challenged to consider how we, as academic librarians, with all of our varied styles, add value to higher education and the world of information.

CULTURAL DIVERSITY AND SYNERGY: COLLABORATION BETWEEN LIBRARIANS AND ACADEMIC COMPUTER CENTER STAFF

Tara Lynn Fulton, Ann de Klerk, Bucknell University; Bryce Allen, University of Illinois at Champaign-Urbana; Larry Hardesty, Eckerd College; Kevin Long, Rice University

Computer centers and libraries have been collaborating on projects for several decades, but only recently has the pervasiveness of information technology and resources on college campuses led to such a blurring of lines of responsibilities. Long-term joint ventures and even mergers are evolving. The two professional groups acknowledge what appears to be fundamental differences in problem solving tactics, work styles, service priorities, and planning mechanisms. At first, such cultural differences led to an "us/them" mentality and manifested itself in stand-offs on many campuses. Such isolationist views can no longer be tolerated if higher education institutions are to move forward with sophisticated Internet access, multimedia development, and coordinated networking. Now the question is: how do we maximize the possibilities that interaction between these groups has to offer? We must learn one another's unique languages and come to value the strengths that each group can bring to our service initiatives. Each of these panelists has moved beyond the stereotypic characterization of the "other" and found unique ways to evolve genuine appreciation of diversity among staffs in both "camps." They will share their own insights gained from positive experiences, and will provide some advise on how to harness the potential synergy created when diverse and divergent professional cultures learn to work together for their own and their clients' benefit.

Ann de Klerk will address the role of management in both libraries and computer centers in facilitating the work of professionals and in creating a synergy for planning new initiatives. The computer center at Bucknell has recently undergone a major reorganization into teams and a change in leadership; the co-directors of the center worked closely with the library on several projects, and Ann will describe how the collaboration resulted in significant advancements in service. Kevin Long will talk about team dynamics and communication styles, and the process by which professionals from two different "cultures" learn to speak one another's language and appreciate one another's unique perspectives and strengths. He will describe Rice University's innovative merger of the computer center help desk and the library reference desk, and other initiatives that have involved a direct melding of the two cultures to improve services. Both of these panelists will speak from a practitioner's perspective about the ongoing challenges involved in such efforts.

The other two panelists will share research results which inform our efforts to successfully bridge the traditional schism between computer center and library staff. Bryce Allen will look at the research base on personality traits and individual differences as it relates to academic professionals, and will speculate on what we can conclude from the literature on cognitive styles and psychological types about effective collaboration efforts. Larry Hardesty recently toured the country interviewing college computer center and library directors. He will share with us some of the joys and frustrations expressed to him, as well as some ideas gleaned about the perspectives and structures that best facilitate successful collaboration.

THE USER-CENTERED LIBRARY AND LIBRARY COMMUNITY ANALYSIS: MAKING IT HAPPEN

Betsy Wilson, Steve Hiller, Nancy Huling, Carla Rickerson, University of Washington

To achieve the strategic goal of being user-centered, libraries need to review who they users are, assess user needs, define services, and measure user satisfaction. An active, ongoing community analysis program allows libraries to position themselves to make judicious use of resources, to select the best from a growing array of options, to market services realistically, and to get feedback from the growing numbers of invisible users. "The User-Centered Library and Community Analysis" uses the University of Washington Libraries as a case study for developing and implementing community analysis, needs assessment, and user studies. The panel presentation will engage the audience in demonstrating how to move beyond a traditional, segmented, reactive mechanism for user feedback to an active, integrative program of community assessment. Specific assessment tools and implementation strategies will be outlined. The panel will share models showing how user information can be used to assist decision making in such areas as strategic planning, library services, facilities and budgeting and suggest ways to "operationalize" measurement and evaluation activities so that they become an essential part of the organization.

ACADEMIC LIBRARIES AND STUDENT RETENTION

Deborah C. Masters, Cheryl Beil, Stephen Loflin, George Washington University

Colleges and universities operate in an increasingly competitive environment, investing significant resources in marketing, recruitment and financial aid in order to attract and admit their desired student population. Once students are enrolled, it is the responsibility of all campus units to contribute to the retention of those who meet the academic requirements. Studies of retention at George Washington show that students need to feel connected and integrated, with personal connections to faculty, that they decide in their first six weeks at the University whether to stay or go, and that the highest proportion leave in their freshman or sophomore years. Both academic and social strategies can contribute to the first year freshman experience, both in and out of the classroom. Student interaction with others in the academic community, and in particular faculty involvement with students, can serve to encourage diversity and enhance student success, as well as serve to contribute to graduate student retention. The academic library can and should play an active and proactive role by contributing to academic and social strategies by other campus units, and by initiating its own strategies consistent with these objectives.

The panel members will discuss the potential and actual contribution of the academic library to retention, with [particular examples from Gelman Library and GW. The panel discussion will include a characterization of GW as an institution, what we know about student retention, and the integration of the academic and social side in fostering retention. Examples of the library role in the academic side will include user education, term paper assistance, and the Student Liaison program. It will also include discussion of the mission of student activities on campus, the scope and nature of the activities offered by GW's Campus Activities office, and the library's role and integration in those activities through participation in such programs as Colonial Inauguration, student orientation, and Cafe Gelman.

GOING ABOUT OUR BUSINESS . . . PARTNERING, STRATEGIC PLANNING AND TQM: MANAGEMENT OPTIONS FOR THE 90S

Karen Kinney, Don Bosseau, San Diego State University; Karyle S. Butcher, Oregon State University; Barton Lessin, Wayne State University

Today, many academic libraries find themselves involved with a situation which evokes memories of a condition experienced by businesses in this country in the 1970s. With falling revenues, rising costs, and an ever-growing need to accomplish more with less, academic libraries are seeking methods to improve quality and the effective use of human, material and financial resources. At the same time, library managers are also grappling with the challenge of defining, creating and sustaining breakthrough service. Supporting the diverse needs of our diverse constituencies requires meeting these challenges head-on. Nothing more. Nothing less. Redirecting resources is central not only to our survival as institutions in these times, but also to our successful growth. Today, a number of management techniques are available to library managers, including partnering, strategic planning and Total Quality Management (TQM). This panel presentation will detail the experience of academic libraries located at several institutions of higher education with these management techniques. What are the key concepts of partnering? Of strategic planning? Of TQM? What does the "process" of each of these techniques really look like? Can these techniques be implemented in a manner which reflects a specific organization and its vision, goals and objectives? Do any of these techniques really have a significant impact on the way a library goes about the business of providing its services and supporting its constituency?

WHO'S WHO OR WHO'S ON FIRST: DEFINING THE ROLES OF SUPPORT STAFF AND LIBRARIANS

Jeniece Guy, American Library Association; Larry Oberg, Willamette University; Judy Orahood, Ohio Wesleyan University

Recent studies indicate that the work assigned to support staff in academic libraries is changing. They are taking on more duties formerly assigned to the librarians. What issues are arising from this trend? What are the implications for academic libraries and for librarians?

Larry Oberg, University Librarian at Willamette University will present "Who's Who in Academic Libraries?" Oberg's research has shown that distinctions between professional and support staff work are blurring. Oberg will explore how this change is likely to affect libraries and librarians.

Judy Orahood, support staff member at Ohio Wesleyan University will present "What Do Support Staff Want?" Based on a study conducted by the ALA Office for Library Personnel Resources and sponsored by the *World Book Encyclopedia*, Orahood will discuss terminology, role definition, librarian and support staff communication, and continuing education for support staff.

Jeniece Guy, Assistant Director of the ALA Office for Library Personnel Resources will present, "Using the Fair Labor Standards Act and the Experience of others as a Guide." The U.S. Department of Labor uses specific criteria to determine whether work is at the professional level. The penalties for misclassifying an employee can be substantial. Does the blurring of professional and support staff roles signal danger for academic libraries in this regard? Guy will also discuss the evolution of the concept of paraprofessional work in other professions, and discuss the parallels between paraprofessional work in librarianship and in other fields.

Panel Sessions
Technology and the Service-Centered Library

TECHNOLOGICAL INNOVATION AND LIBRARY INSTRUCTION
Bill Orme, Kenneth E. Hay, Indiana University Purdue University Indianapolis; Ann Bevilacqua, President, Upper Broadway Bodega Software

Computerized databases, networking capabilities, and navigational resources have expanded the world of information resources beyond our most hopeful predictions. Library instruction, the education of library patrons concerning the use and understanding of those resources, will be the next beneficiary of technological advance. Many fear that technology and education are inimical. This program brings theory and practice together to illustrate how technology may be used to enhance libraries' instructional efforts.

Kenneth E. Hay, Assistant Professor of Instructional Systems Technology with the School of Education at Indiana University-Purdue University Indianapolis, will address issues of pedagogy as the relate to technology.

Bill Orme, Bibliographic Instruction Coordinator at Indiana University Purdue University Indianapolis, will showcase L140 "Information Resources and Student Research", a one-credit course offered via cable television to the Indianapolis community. Orme will tell how perceived limitations of the "one-shot" presentation influenced the development of L140 and how the technologies used for this course may spin off to other library instruction efforts.

Ann Bevilacqua, developer of Research Assistant and formerly library instruction coordinator at New York University, will showcase "Research Assistant", a toolbook program intended to help novice undergraduate researchers become acclimated to an academic library environment. Bevilacqua will focus upon the development of "Research Assistant" and the role of computer-assisted instruction in a library's overall bibliographic instruction effort.

THE POTENTIAL OF ATM TECHNOLOGY FOR SHARING LIBRARY RESOURCES AND BROADENING ACCESS TO INFORMATION
Ilene Rockman, California Polytechnic University; Joan Berman, Humboldt State University; Linda S. Dobb, San Francisco State University

The technology offered by Asynchronous Transfer Mode (ATM) is touted to be superior to other technologies (such as ethernet and FDDI) for the transmission of varied information formats (computer data, multimedia, interactive video, images, etc.) over high speed networks. Cooperative projects between libraries, and among librarians and computer professionals, show great potential for using the technology.

This panel presentation will describe cooperative project objectives from the California State

University system for establishing statewide degree-granting program in library science, and innovative curriculum development efforts incorporating multimedia and distance learning, using ATM to overcome obstacles of limited bandwidth and barriers between LANS and WANS.

BEAM ME IN, SCOTTIE: TRANSFORMING REMOTE USERS INTO PRIMARY USERS

Sally Kalin, Pennsylvania State University; Tom Peters, Northern Illinois University; Pam Snelson, Drew University

Telecommunications, personal computers, international networks and online information systems combine to make the concept of "libraries without walls" a reality. With this new reality comes a new group of library users which has been labeled "remote users." Rather than simply including this group of users in current library programs, library and information professionals have a unique opportunity to rethink the existing paradigm of library services. In the world of "libraries without walls," it is the LIBRARY that is remote—not the individual seeking information. Academic librarians need to question the adequacy of traditional service models as remote users become a large community of information system users. Little is known about their searching behaviors or information needs; yet this growing remote user community has important implications for systems design and support. This panel presentation features academic librarians known for their research on remote users and online catalogs. Topics to be covered include the definition and scope of remote users, access issues such as authentication and economics, searching behaviors as identified by research studies, unfulfilled research needs, support service challenges and strategies, and an exploration of the future of remote library services.

THE INTEGRATED LIBRARY: DESIGNING LEARNING SPACES TO UTILIZE ADVANCED TECHNOLOGY AND NETWORKED INFORMATION

David W. Lewis, Donna Burrow, Indiana University-Purdue University Indianapolis; Susan Barnes, Cornell University; Philip Tompkins, Estrella Mountain Community College Center; Charlene Hurt, George Mason University

The panel will present the experiences of three of the nation's most technologically advanced libraries in the design of spaces to utilize advanced technology and networked information. It will consider the differing assumptions and philosophies that institutions bring to the design process, and will explore how the resulting spaces and technological infrastructures actually worked. Two of the facilities to be discussed are completed and occupied. The remaining facility is in the design phase.

The case studies will focus on the architecture of the integrated library, both the technical infrastructure and the design of the physical spaces. Particular attention will be paid to the philosophies that guided design and the effect these philosophies had on design decisions. These expectations will be compared with the experience the institutions had when the spaces and systems became real. Issues of system and user support, and staffing will be addressed. The libraries with completed facilities will provide video tape and/or slides to document their presentations.

The Albert A. Mann Library at Cornell University, winner of the 1993 ALA/Meckler Library of the Future Award, is widely recognized for its work in providing access to electronic information and for the excellence of its print collection. Mann is the largest academic agricultural library in the United States, with over 600,000 volumes in its printed collections. Mann presently provides access to over 200 bibliographic, textual, and numeric databases in its electronic library, The Mann Gateway. The library is about to undergo a $40 million addition and renovation project. The goal of the project is to build an integrated facility in which electronic and print information is archived and preserved and in which instruction in information management is conducted.

The University Library at Indiana University Purdue University Indianapolis opened in the fall of 1993. The 260,000 square foot building contains over 1,700 connections with a full compliment of single mode fiber, multi-mode fiber, shielded and unshielded twisted pair. Over 100 scholars workstations located in the library's stacks. In addition, the library will circulate laptop computers and offer network connectivity to laptops from over 650 study carrels. The scholars workstations and laptops will have access to the "Information System", a multi-platform graphical-user interface to electronic formats including full motion video (VHS/S-VHS), satellite downlink, CDI, videodisc, CD-ROM, Betacam SP, Hi-8, U-Matic SP, and the Internet. The scholars workstations will combine access to information sources with a wide variety of productivity tools including word processing, spreadsheets, bibliographic reference management packages, object-oriented databases, animation, graphics, and FAX. The information system also provides storage of source information from a variety of formats into an "electronic book bag".

Two community college facilities will be featured: Estrella Mountain and Mesa Community College. Estrella Mountain has completed and occupied Phase I of an Integrated Library/High Technology facility of 54,000 square feet, to be enlarged in Phase II to 100,000 square feet. Mesa has completed planning for a 175,000 square foot Integrated Library/High Technology facility to be constructed upon the successful passage of an anticipated 1994 bond issue in the greater Phoenix metropolitan area. These facilities represent a smaller and a larger integrated facility attached to institutions devoted exclusively to teaching and learning. Information access across the curricu-

lum is a major planning assumption for both facilities together with the independent lifelong learner as the center of the planning effort. Regardless of size, the major functional areas of these two buildings will be emphasized as necessary to allow new learning communities to develop in collaboratively managed facilities. The integration of heretofore separate functions implies integration of heretofore separate staffs.

Attendees will learn how advanced technology has been deployed in several technologically sophisticated new library buildings; the problems and advantages of presented by this use of advanced technology; and the effect of the use of sophisticated technology on teaching, learning, and research.

MOVING INTO THE FUTURE THROUGH A GATEWAY LIBRARY

Caroline M. Kent, Lawrence Dowler, Laura Farwell, Joseph Bourneuf, Harvard College

All academic libraries are facing the problems of integrating local automated systems and access to networked resources into organizations with shrinking budgets. Older academic libraries with huge, historic paper-based collections have particular difficulties with these problems. In many of these organizations, services to users have at best shared the library's primary focus with collection-building; at worst, services have taken a back seat to collections. Harvard College Library classically illustrates the latter situation.

Automation and networked resources demand greater commitment to direct services. Many users continue to want to depend on library organizations for being the primary supplier of their materials, but also need greater assistance in locating and accessing much of what they need. But altering or adapting old, well-established library organizations' fundamental philosophies and value structures is extremely difficult. At the Harvard College Library, we had initially discussed the development of a "gateway library" in our 1992 strategic planning. In 1993, we entered a new phase of strategic planning for public services under the umbrella of developing a "gateway library."

The themes emerging from this planning effort were the following:

- The Gateway Library as a paradigm for strategic planning or agenda setting in public services
- The university-wide politics and controversies associated with developing a "gateway" library
- Physical architecture versus network architecture
- Role of collection-centered research libraries in the networked environment

TWO CASE STUDIES OF ACCESS TO RESEARCH RESOURCES VIA THE INTERNET: *MEDLINE* AND THE *ENCYCLOPEDIA BRITANNICA*

Sharon A. Hogan, Marilyn Borgendale, Karen Graves, Thomas Jevec, Elaine Martin, University of Illinois at Chicago

Until quite recently, academic libraries delivered information to their users almost exclusively via the medium of paper. The paper itself, for the most part, was from the onsite collection of the library. For a cost, always in time and sometimes also in money, the library also provides access to offsite paper materials via interlibrary loan. As academic libraries contracted for offsite access to electronic information from database vendors such as Dialog and BRS, they passed on the access costs to the users. This was the case primarily out of fear that free and open access would cost more than the library could afford.

Internet resource servers offer the ease of use and lower cost of CD-ROMs and the ubiquity of mainframe databases. Individual users access the remote server via the Internet using a special client on their desktop microcomputer. This form of access brings its own set of challenges. Challenges include the hardware and networking require-

ments; the training and support of remote users; the integration of these services into the existing suite of information services on campus; and making the users aware of the existence and usefulness of a resource.

The University of Illinois at Chicago (UIC) has addressed these challenges in its implementation of campus-wide access to two Internet servers. UIC is the first large public university to participate in the National Library of Medicine's fixed fee Grateful Med via the Internet project. The University was also a beta-test site for the Encyclopedia Britannica's Britannica Online project.

The presenters will discuss how UIC has addressed these challenges in its implementation of campus-wide access to two Internet servers. The presenters will not only describe the various approaches to training, publicity, documentation and technical support but will also report on how successful each approach was. Among the specific issues to be explored are: the extent to which library public service staff needs to be involved in hardware, software and networking issues; the computer literacy issues to be addressed; how to provide training, documentation, and support to offsite users; and how to diagnose and resolve problems.

THE NEXT GENERATION: LIBRARY SERVICES OF THE FUTURE HAVE ARRIVED!

Nancy L. Gaynor, Illinois Institute of Technology; Rick J. Bean, DePaul University; Jack Fritts, Carol Moulden, National-Louis University; Jerilyn Marshall, Northwestern University; Maria Otero-Boisvert, Loyola University, Mallinckrodt Campus

Extended campus libraries can serve as a microcosm of all the issues facing libraries today and in the future. Panelists will discuss such issues as technology, reference services, collection development, bibliographic instruction, document delivery, and patron segmentation (e.g. adult learners).

The speakers work for a variety of academic institutions, with programs ranging from engineering to business to engineering. How do they address the needs of students at a distance from the "main campus" and the "main library"? How is instruction delivered? How is information delivered and using what technologies? How is instruction and library use different when a majority of the students are adult, working professionals?

These are just a few of the topics the panelists will cover. There will also be time for a question and answer period.

ROADSIGNS ON THE ELECTRONIC HIGHWAY: TEACHING ACCESS TO COMPUTERIZED INFORMATION
Cheryl LaGuardia, Harvard University; Stella Bentley, Andrea Duda, Christine Oka, University of California, Santa Barbara

Many students and faculty are starting down the information superhighway without benefit of map or compass. Teaching informed access to materials available over electronic networks has emerged as an essential component of working in an academic library setting of the 1990's. At the University of California at Santa Barbara Library, a combination of techniques are being used to reach and teach potential academic online users in the mysteries and wonders of the Internet.

This panel discusses the variety of techniques used at the UCSB Library for networked online instruction, which includes: credit-bearing and subject-specialized interactive group instruction in a state-of-the-art library electronic classroom; an in-house-developed gopher-based library skills online tutorial; library guides and instructional publications available via the library gopher; and one-on-one electronic instruction from librarian to user. The four members of this panel developed the facilities and systems described.

POWER UP: GETTING FACULTY AND STUDENTS PLUGGED IN
Cristina Yu, Ellen Knott, Rhoda Channing, Wake Forest University

PowerUp! was first offered as a pilot project to introduce incoming freshmen to information technologies available at Wake Forest University. The three day workshop was developed as one of the pre-college programs on campus. Because of its success and popularity, it was then extended to faculty and staff. Topics covered range from campus computing, Internet, word processing, graphics, and multimedia. PowerUp! was a collaborative effort among the staff in the Library, Computer Center, and Student Life and several faculty with the Library Director as the chair of the planning committee.

DELIVERING TEXT AND DOCUMENTS FOR THE VIRTUAL LIBRARY
Carol Tenopir, University of Tennessee; Mimi Drake, Georgia Institute of Technology; Patrick J. Mullin, University of North Carolina at Chapel Hill; Tom Sanville, Ohio Library and Information Network (OhioLINK); Sean Devine, Information Access Company

How can academic and research libraries use technology's latest developments to provide a greater number of patrons with more information? This is the central question which this panel will discuss during this program.

In recent years, academic and research libraries have made great strides in modernizing their resources to reach the demands of their patrons. However, the availability of certain systems has sparked a desire for even more advancements, such as instant access to databases, broader journal coverage, and the ability to retrieve and print articles complete with text and graphics.

Database licensing programs represent one possible solution to the library's need for distributing more information across a broader patron base. By making resources available over a wide network, database licensing programs maximize the use of existing investments, thereby improving patron access and reducing the cost of citation access and article delivery. Additionally, these programs allow libraries to share information with other libraries, thereby conserving and consolidating library resources.

Despite the established benefits, questions about database licensing programs and other options for the virtual library persist. How do libraries determine the level of need for modernization? How can we choose the best delivery means for our patrons? What resources should remain in CD-ROM or print format? What timing and budget issues should be determined before implementation?

This panel program will include four speakers who hold significant decision-making roles on these issues at their own institutions. They will discuss the factors and approaches used to answer some of the questions listed above, and will comment on what they would do differently if they could start again from scratch. Finally, the panelists will examine how the choices they made today on these issues will affect their budgets, patron needs, and information capabilities in the future.

COLLABORATIVE PROFESSIONAL DEVELOPMENT: INFORUM AND ITS IMPACT

Charlotte Hess, Kris Brancolini, Phyllis Davidson, Howard Rosenbaum, Indiana University

INforum is a creative and successful collaborative professional development series developed by Indiana University librarians and technologists in 1993. This panel, presented by designers of and participants in INforum, will offer some highlights and varying perspectives on this innovative venture. Media Librarian, Kristine Brancolini will give a brief history of INforum, a summary of its programs and introduce the panel speakers. Phyllis Davidson from the University Computing Services will present an information technologist's perspective on the benefits of efforts to unite the professions and the benefits derived from better understanding with the academic library profession. She will also discuss interviews she conducted with other technologists about the INforum venture. Howard Rosenbaum, a faculty member of the School of Library and Information Science, will focus on the perspective of Information Science Education. He will discuss the need for library students to be exposed to the world of information technology, the ways in which this is being done at Indiana University, and the growing convergence of the information professions. Librarian Charlotte Hess will concentrate on the development and possibilities of grassroots professional development initiatives. In focus will be two collaborative outgrowths of INforum: the Internet Librarian Conference, which took place at Indiana University in May 1994 and a teleconference sponsored by the Indiana University Libraries and Computing Services with speakers Clifford Lynch, Michael Roberts, Paul Evan Peters, and Jim O'Donnell, scheduled for October 28, 1994. The presentations will be followed by a question/answer session with the audience.

THE ADULT LEARNER AND THE NEW TECHNOLOGY

Kathryn M. Crowe, Amy J. McKee, University of North Carolina at Greensboro

College and university libraries have changed significantly, even in the last five years. At the same time, the pool of traditional-aged students has shrunk and institutions are increasingly trying to attract and retain diverse groups of students. In 1991, 38.4% of college students were aged twenty-five or older. The technological innovations in libraries require adult learners to rethink how they do research, seek information and use libraries. As a result, instruction librarians also have to revise their approach when they teach the new technology to this audience. Library instruction "isn't just for kids anymore."

Another group of adults that need instruction in electronic resources is faculty. The new technology requires them to update their library skills and revise some of their research processes. Even our most experienced researchers seek training in using new databases and remote access technology.

The University of North Carolina at Greensboro (UNCG) is a doctoral-granting university with approximately 12,000 students and 600 faculty. As librarians at UNCG have worked with these adult learners, we have identified certain commonalities among faculty and adult students. Most are highly competent professionals who either have little library experience or are unfamiliar with the new library resources. They represent educated individuals who are eager to update their library skills but may be intimidated by the new technology or even by computers in general. This group of users presents a different set of challenges to the instruction librarian than the traditional (18 to 24 year-old) student.

This panel presentation will identify the unique needs of adult learners using the new technology and offer techniques for teaching them.

1. Reassurance about using computers in general.
2. Explanation of the content and structure of the appropriate systems or databases. This explanation should not include jargon or highly technical details.
3. Designing a search strategy:
   a. Choosing a database
   b. Identifying major concept groups
   c. Choosing keywords or descriptors
   d. Using a thesaurus
   e. Boolean logic
   f. Commands and mechanics of the database
4. Hands-on practice
5. Providing clear and concise handouts that users may consult on their own.

DIGITAL LIBRARIES: A MECHANISM FOR RESOURCE SHARING

Kimberly K. Kertis, Jose-Marie Griffiths, University of Tennessee; Mark Needleman, University of California, Berkeley; Rowena Chester, Martin Marietta Energy Systems

The National Information Infrastructure emphasizes the federal, public and private interest in expanding availability of computing resources and information. In response, several agencies are building Digital Libraries to place in the NII, and information and computer scientists are investigating limitations of existing networks. These limitations include capacities, addressing conventions and locator services, as well as concerns with compatibility, standards and performance of new and legacy systems. Beyond the technical aspects of networking, there are the issues of information access and management. In this context, the access issues range from logical to physical. Who will be participants, as users and as providers? What standards are needed to support transparency in navigation? How will collections, directories and services be managed and controlled? As the network expands, the need increases for various information identification and location tools for effective information retrieval. This panel will explore issues and current developments of digital libraries such as metadata standards, metadata access and retrieval mechanisms, information tracing and validation techniques.

Panel Sessions
Multiculturalism and Internationalism

DIGITIZING AFRICAN AMERICAN RESOURCES FOR ELECTRONIC ACCESS

Birdie O. Weir, Alabama Agricultural and Mechanical University; Gladys Smiley Bell, Kent State University; Sylvia Y. Curtis, University of California, Santa Barbara; William Welburn, University of Iowa; Itibari M. Zulu, University of California, Los Angeles

This session will be a panel discussion focusing on the republication of significant reference works and the creation of more bibliographic electronic resources in the area of African American Studies. Program participants will address the problems associated with republication of these materials as well as the creation of African American resources in electronic formats. Of importance in the discussion will be the political, social and economic issues surrounding the publication of African American resources in electronic formats and the problems associated with access to African American resources republished in this form. These issues will be addressed so that libraries and scholars engaged in research can be more effective and efficient in their study of African American issues now and into the future.

LIBRARY SCHOOLS AND ACADEMIC LIBRARIES: PARTNERING FOR DIVERSITY IN THE GLOBAL SOCIETY

Marianne Cooper, Shoshana Kaufmann, Queens College

The authors will explore current and future individual and cooperative activities and plans of academic libraries and graduate library/information studies programs regarding multicultural concerns within the same academic institution. Issues examined will include the following:

1. the extent of ethnic and linguistic diversity of students, faculty and staff in the parent institution, the graduate library/information studies program and the library;
2. methods that academic libraries and graduate library/information studies programs have introduced to transform and expand their activities and services to address the needs of culturally, ethnically and linguistically diverse student and faculty populations;
3. the extent to which technology modifies the impacts of cultural andlinguistic differences in academic libraries and graduate library/ information studies programs.

Although Queens College will be used as a case study, it will be placed in a broader context by surveying similar activities of academic libraries and graduate library/information studies programs in other selected institutions.

THE INTERNET AS A BRIDGE TO GLOBAL LIBRARIANSHIP

Martin Kesselman, Rutgers University; Diane Kovacs, Kent State University; David Thomas, Brunel University;Nelson P. Valdes, Latin American Institute, University of New Mexico

Without boundaries of geography or time, the Internet provides a wealth of information resources and has become a conduit for the sharing of information and experiences among librarians. As we enter a new era of global librarianship, it no longer matters where in the world the information is housed or where the librarian or user is physically situated. In the global networked environment, unique databases and other information resources can be made available to the scholarly community worldwide. These resources include full-text information, electronic journals, alerting services, specialized bulletin boards, electronic conferences, statistical and other reference information, and access to commercial and government-sponsored database services.

The networked environment lends itself to cooperation and the sharing of ideas and solutions to problems common to academic libraries no matter where they are located. Emerging technologies, such as low-orbiting satellites, allow for the first time for libraries in developing countries to tap into the expanding pool of networked information and human resources, which beforehand were inaccessible. The panel presentation is organized and moderated by Martin Kesselman, of Rutgers University Libraries, on behalf of the ACRL International Relations Committee.

This session will focus on how the Internet minimizes the geographic distance between libraries and provides opportunities for librarians around the world to share ideas, discuss issues and solve problems that are common to academic libraries everywhere; how the Internet provides pathways and access to unique information resources around the world of interest to academic institutions; and, on the problems of libraries in developing countries in getting access to the Internet and the potential of low orbiting satellites as a technology for making connections to the Internet possible around the world.

Diane Kovacs, of Kent State University Libraries, discusses how reference librarians from more than fifty countries participate in discussions on the LIBREF-L (Library Issues in Reference Service) listserv and what these librarians gain from their participation both professionally and institutionally. Kovacs will also discuss how an editorial board consisting of librarians throughout the world collaborate in producing LIBRES: Library and Information Science Research, a peer-reviewed electronic journal. David Thomas, of Brunel University Library in the United Kingdom, discusses the wealth of information available worldwide via the Internet and highlight resources available via JANET, the Joint Academic Network, in the UK such as BUBL, the Bulletin Board for Librarians and NISS, National Information on Software and Services, both of which provide access to various specialized databases, software, directories, and news groups. Thomas will also review other networked resources available from Europe such as those from ECHO, the Economic Community Host Organization. Nelson Valdes, of the Latin American Institute at the University of New Mexico, reviews the problems of developing countries in getting connected and as a case study, will discuss his experiences in providing training to Cuban librarians on the Internet. Valdes will also discuss the promise of low-orbiting satellites as a technology for bringing Internet access to libraries in developing countries.

MULTICULTURAL EDUCATION FOR ACADEMIC LIBRARIANSHIP: DEVELOPING A COMPREHENSIVE MODEL

Rosie L. Albritton, Sallie H. Ellison, Judith J. Field, Manuel R. Mazon, Deborah J. Tucker, Wayne State University

The University Library System at Wayne State University, including the Libraries and the Library and Information Science Program, has been actively fostering concepts of "multiculturalism" and "diversity" through the development and implementation of a Comprehensive Model of Multiculturalism, for faculty/staff professional development and the curriculum of the MLIS program. This approach to multicultural education focuses on practical library issues grounded in theoretical concepts of culture, racio-ethnicity, and diversity awareness, and has resulted in the development of a new course offered to MLIS students: "Multicultural Information Services and Resources." Representatives from the Libraries, the Library and Information Science Program, and the College of Education (bicultural/multilingual program) will speak on the model from both practical and theoretical perspectives of multiculturalism/diversity for professional development, curriculum planning, specialized services and collection building. The presentations will provide instruction for: 1) understanding the nature of multiculturalism as a "social force" and the significance of accepting a broad definition of "culture;" 2) translating multicultural concerns into "services" that reflect the "needs" of individual populations; and 3) identifying "resources" for building different cultural "collections."

WORKING TOWARDS CREATING A DIVERSE WORK FORCE: THE PENN STATE EXPERIENCE.

Katie Clark, Jenae Williams, Pennsylvania State University

Increasing the diversity of our work force is a challenge facing all academic libraries. The first step in achieving this goal is developing a strategic plan with specific goals and objectives. In order to meet these goals, the Pennsylvania State University libraries acknowledged that we must actively recruit new staff who normally might not consider a career in librarianship. As a result, a two-year minority internship position was established for a Penn State graduate to work in the Life Sciences library. The intern participates in reference service, bibliographic instruction, library wide diversity issues, and outreach activities. Although ultimately the intern may not chose to pursue a MLS degree, the program has been an unqualified success. The creation of this position required a significant financial and time commitment, but the Libraries benefitted tremendously. This panel will discuss development and implementation of a diversity strategic plan from three points of view. The first panelist will discuss minority recruitment and the design of the internship position. An administrator will talk about the strategic planning process and goals for the future. Of note here is that the Libraries have participated in the University's Professional Entry Program for interns. Finally one of the interns will describe her experience working in the Libraries.

Panel Sessions
Society, Economics, and Politics

MATERIALS BUDGET ALLOCATION IN THE ELECTRONIC LIBRARY

Frank R. Allen, Virginia Commonwealth University; Gay N. Dannelley, Ohio State University; Nancy H. Marshall, College of William and Mary; Ray Metz, Case Western Reserve University; Merrily E. Taylor, Brown University

The transformation of the academic library from that of a primarily print based environment to a multi-media environment is accelerating. One aspect of this transformation which is surfacing is the impact this has on budgeting, particularly materials budgeting. Libraries which have traditionally treated the materials budget as a discrete, distinguishable line item are facing a host of expenditures which, though not materials per se, provide access to materials. Examples are: computer software, computer hardware, file storage costs, software and hardware maintenance, pre-processing and servicing, and licensing fees. Additionally, libraries are bearing ever growing costs associated with document delivery. These developments are posing a financial dilemma to the library community. Do we fund these non-traditional expenses from our materials budget, or do we include them in operating funds or some other budget? Neither option seems particularly desirable. The traditionalists will object that the materials budget is being squeezed and compro-

mised. Others may object to using the operating budget because this would crowd out essential operating needs. If the library is not able to find the funding internally, then it faces the task of convincing campus or outside agencies for additional funds to support these unfunded needs. In an era of higher education downsizing this can be a challenge. Furthermore, campus budget offices and outside agencies do not always comprehend this library transformation and resulting shift in funding requirements.

POLITICAL CORRECTNESS MEETS NETIQUETTE: NEW FRONTIERS FOR INTELLECTUAL FREEDOM IN THE ACADEMIC SETTING

Candace Morgan, ALA Intellectual Freedom Committee; Barbara Jones, ACRL Intellectual Freedom Committee; Judith F. Krug, ALA Office for Intellectual Freedom

Increasingly, academic libraries are experiencing intellectual freedom controversies. From an anonymous academic library user's open announcement that he had stolen, with no intent to return, materials with which he disagreed, to demands that accessibility of particular USENET news groups be restricted or removed, academic and research libraries have become a more frequent battleground for intellectual freedom issues.

Judith F. Krug, director of the American Library Association's Office for Intellectual Freedom, will recap recent academic library intellectual freedom controversies and discuss how academic libraries can continue to foster an atmosphere of free inquiry and access to information from all points of view despite increasing censorship pressures. She will address some recent, and unfortunate, policy pratfalls which have occurred in the area of access to electronic resources, and controversies over such things as hate speech, revisionism, sexism, and homophobia.

LIBRARY PUBLISHING IN THE 90'S: FUTURE GENERATIONS WILL ASK...

James Neal, Indiana University; John N. Berry III, Library Journal and Library Hotline; GraceAnne A. DeCandido, Wilson Library Bulletin; Larry Oberg, "Research Notes," College & Research Libraries; Gloriana St. Clair, College & Research Libraries; Patricia Glass Schuman, Neal Schuman Publishers

A provocative discussion starts by taking the temperature of the current state of library publishing. These editors will reflect on what is healthy about the current state of library publishing, on what missing from the library literature, what trends they see in library publishing, and what practicing librarians can do to contribute to the literature of their profession. The presentations will both frame the issues from a philosophical point of view and offer practical advice. Topics explored will include what the editors of library journals think of the current state of library publishing and what these editors think the future of library publishing will be. Attendees will learn how they can contribute to the library literature.

STATEWIDE VIRTUAL LIBRARY PLANNING IN VIRGINIA: CORNERSTONES AND COMPONENTS

Sarah Watstein, Barbara J. Ford, Virginia Commonwealth University; Wendell Barbour, Christopher Newport University; Buddy Litchfield, Virginia Tech; Virginia S. O'Herron, Old Dominion University; Nancy Marshall, College of William and Mary; Carol Pfeiffer, University of Virginia

Come to Virginia . . . where librarians are in the process of visualizing their future and planning the evolution of their libraries into virtual libraries. Come to Virginia . . . where the merger of libraries, computer technology, and telecommunications is transforming the access and distribution of information. Come to Virginia . . . where coordinated planning for a statewide virtual library has the potential of insuring that the Virginia Virtual Library will retain the great characteristics of a good library while maximizing the use of new technologies.

A statewide "virtual library" will become reality in Virginia with a $5.2 million allocation from the General Assembly to the academic libraries. The funding initiative will lay the foundation during the 1994-96 biennium for electronic networking of library resources by the 51 libraries at the state's public universities, colleges and community colleges and can be expanded to reach all the people of Virginia. Key goals of the Virginia Virtual Library project are to increase overall access to information throughout the Commonwealth by enhancing resource sharing, reducing unnecessary duplication of holdings, and increasing service to students and faculty.

Panel members will discuss both the components of the planning process designed to bring this vision of the library of the 21st century to reality, and discuss the cornerstones of the emerging virtual library. The essential elements or features of the emerging virtual library encompass electronic document delivery, electronic journals, full text databases, end-user searching and training, network access, OPAC enhancements, cooperative development of databases and hardware. Equally essential to the success of the virtual library are planning, policies, services and strategies that emphasize access over ownership.

Specifically, panelists will explore how one state has defined the essential elements and features of the emerging virtual library. Of particular interest will be the challenge of designing and implementing a planning process for the virtual library that is based on an incremental approach to ensure both the successful introduction of new systems and services, and the successful integration of new services with those of the traditional print library. Panelists will also review the development and implementation of policies, services or reallocations that emphasize access over ownership, and that apply to libraries at public universities, colleges and community colleges.

CRITICAL HISTORICAL PERSPECTIVES ON LIBRARIANSHIP AND TECHNOLOGY

John Buschman, Rider University; John Budd, University of Missouri-Columbia; Stan Hannah, University of Kentucky; Roma Harris, University of Western Ontario

Librarianship historically has done very little critical questioning of its assumptions concerning the new information technologies. Given the enormous changes to the profession which have already taken place, as well as the ones contemplated for our future, the time is long since past for a critical balance to our discussions of technology.

Our literature is replete with descriptions of the exciting possibilities of information technologies, as well as shot through with the assumption that technological change is a juggernaut we must join. One of the best ways to balance the profession's assessment of new technology is to give some historical perspective on the questions of technologically-driven change. The three panelists are all scholars who have addressed sizable portions of this challenge in their written work. They have come together on this panel to focus on the topic by updating and presenting their scholarship. Dr. Stan Hannah discussed his work with co-author Dr. Michael Harris in their book *Into the Future*. Hannah describes the role of post-industrial social theory and its relationship to librarianship's reaction to, and planning for, the "paperless" or "virtual" library. In so doing, Hannah explores the historical basis of a number of our assumptions concerning the social effects and benefits of technology - and how these will affect libraries. Dr. Roma Harris discusses librarianship in the context of other historically feminized professions. By looking at the historical similarities and dissimilarities between librarianship, nursing, social work, and teaching, Harris formulates a general explanation of the profession's response to new information technologies. As an alternative, Harris draws on her historical analysis to offer a service-centered model as a positive counter to the dominance of technology over traditionally feminized professions.

Dr. John Budd discusses the long-term historical aims and values of the profession to give historical perspective on the current debate over the future of the profession. By looking at the shifting social priorities of librarianship over time, Budd highlights the historical contingency of some of our professional goals and values. This historical perspective sheds some light on our current technology-driven reexamination of our institutions, associations, and profession.

HOW RESEARCH LIBRARIES CAN HELP THEIR CHANGING UNIVERSITIES

Peter S. Graham, Rutgers University; Toni Carbo Bearman, University of Pittsburgh; Stanley Chodorow, University of Pennsylvania; Paula Kaufman, University of Tennessee; Martin Runkle, University of Chicago Library

Universities are going through self-examinations, reprogramming, resizing, and redefinitions. Recent issues of *Daedalus* and of *Teachers College Record* were each devoted to "The Future of the Research University". In them, university leaders presented widely varying goals, and serious questions about how to reach these goals. Libraries seldom have explicit roles in these discussions, yet can offer assistance in ways that may need more emphasis than university administrators have yet received. The panel will allow thoughtful senior librarians and a university administrator to address how research libraries can assist their parent institutions as their universities grapple with the changes required in this period. The intent is to show how our libraries can be initiators rather than simply reactors as our universities grapple with problems of demographics, electronic and intellectual property, downsizing, diversity, research/teaching, reprogramming, faculty productivity, values, liberal arts and professionalism, and the horizontal university. To take libraries seriously is to assert the importance of what we do for the university. Our contribution areas include scholarly communication, service to constituencies, information technology, external relations, and models for programmatic cooperation. The audience includes present and potential leaders at university research libraries and at the many colleges where significant research is conducted.

Index

S

T

U